3450 3358

HYUNDAI
COUPES/SEDANS
1994-98 REPAIR MANUAL

CHILTON'S

Covers all U.S. and Canadian models of Hyundai Accent, Elantra, Excel, Scoupe, Sonata and Tiburon

by James R. Marotta, A.S.E.

CHILTON Automotive Books

PUBLISHED BY HAYNES NORTH AMERICA, Inc.

AUTOMOTIVE PARTS & ACCESSORIES ASSOCIATION MEMBER

Manufactured in USA
© 1997 Haynes North America, Inc.
ISBN 0-8019-8953-1
Library of Congress Catalog Card No. 97-77323
7890123456 9876543210

Haynes Publishing Group
Sparkford Nr Yeovil
Somerset BA22 7JJ England

Haynes North America, Inc
861 Lawrence Drive
Newbury Park
California 91320 USA

ABCDE
FGHI

1F1

WITHDRAWN

Contents

Contents

SAFETY NOTICE

Proper service and repair procedures are vital to the safe, reliable operation of all motor vehicles, as well as the personal safety of those performing repairs. This manual outlines procedures for servicing and repairing vehicles using safe, effective methods. The procedures contain many NOTES, CAUTIONS and WARNINGS which should be followed, along with standard procedures to eliminate the possibility of personal injury or improper service which could damage the vehicle or compromise its safety.

It is important to note that repair procedures and techniques, tools and parts for servicing motor vehicles, as well as the skill and experience of the individual performing the work vary widely. It is not possible to anticipate all of the conceivable ways or conditions under which vehicles may be serviced, or to provide cautions as to all possible hazards that may result. Standard and accepted safety precautions and equipment should be used when handling toxic or flammable fluids, and safety goggles or other protection should be used during cutting, grinding, chiseling, prying, or any other process that can cause material removal or projectiles.

Some procedures require the use of tools specially designed for a specific purpose. Before substituting another tool or procedure, you must be completely satisfied that neither your personal safety, nor the performance of the vehicle will be endangered.

Although information in this manual is based on industry sources and is complete as possible at the time of publication, the possibility exists that some car manufacturers made later changes which could not be included here. While striving for total accuracy, the authors or publishers cannot assume responsibility for any errors, changes or omissions that may occur in the compilation of this data.

PART NUMBERS

Part numbers listed in this reference are not recommendations by Haynes North America, Inc. for any product brand name. They are references that can be used with interchange manuals and aftermarket supplier catalogs to locate each brand supplier's discrete part number.

SPECIAL TOOLS

Special tools are recommended by the vehicle manufacturer to perform their specific job. Use has been kept to a minimum, but where absolutely necessary, they are referred to in the text by the part number of the tool manufacturer. These tools can be purchased, under the appropriate part number, from your local dealer or regional distributor, or an equivalent tool can be purchased locally from a tool supplier or parts outlet. Before substituting any tool for the one recommended, read the SAFETY NOTICE at the top of this page.

ACKNOWLEDGMENTS

The publisher expresses appreciation to Hyundai Motor Company for their generous assistance.

1

GENERAL INFORMATION AND MAINTENANCE

HOW TO USE THIS BOOK

Chilton's Total Car Care manual for the 1994–98 Hyundai is intended to help you learn more about the inner workings of your vehicle while saving you money on its upkeep and operation.

The beginning of the book will likely be referred to the most, since that is where you will find information for maintenance and tune-up. The other sections deal with the more complex systems of your vehicle. Operating systems from engine through brakes are covered to the extent that the average do-it-yourselfer becomes mechanically involved. This book will not explain such things as rebuilding a differential for the simple reason that the expertise required and the investment in special tools make this task uneconomical. It will, however, give you detailed instructions to help you change your own brake pads and shoes, replace spark plugs, and perform many more jobs that can save you money, give you personal satisfaction and help you avoid expensive problems.

A secondary purpose of this book is a reference for owners who want to understand their vehicle and/or their mechanics better. In this case, no tools at all are required.

Where to Begin

Before removing any bolts, read through the entire procedure. This will give you the overall view of what tools and supplies will be required. There is nothing more frustrating than having to walk to the bus stop on Monday morning because you were short one bolt on Sunday afternoon. So read ahead and plan ahead. Each operation should be approached logically and all procedures thoroughly understood before attempting any work.

All sections contain adjustments, maintenance, removal and installation procedures, and in some cases, repair or overhaul procedures. When repair is not considered practical, we tell you how to remove the part and then how to install the new or rebuilt replacement. In this way, you at least save the labor costs. Backyard repair of some components is just not practical.

Avoiding Trouble

Many procedures in this book require you to "label and disconnect . . . " a group of lines, hoses or wires. Don't be lulled into thinking you can remember where everything goes—you won't. If you hook up vacuum or fuel lines incorrectly, the vehicle will run poorly, if at all. If you hook up electrical wiring incorrectly, you may instantly learn a very expensive lesson.

You don't need to know the official or engineering name for each hose or line. A piece of masking tape on the hose and a piece on its fitting will allow you to assign your own label such as the letter A or a short name. As long as you remember your own code, the lines can be reconnected by matching similar letters or names. Do remember that tape will dissolve in gasoline or other fluids; if a component is to be washed or cleaned, use another method of identification. A permanent felt-tipped marker can be very handy for marking metal parts. Remove any tape or paper labels after assembly.

Maintenance or Repair?

It's necessary to mention the difference between maintenance and repair. Maintenance includes routine inspections, adjustments, and replacement of parts which show signs of normal wear. Maintenance compensates for wear or deterioration. Repair implies that something has broken or is not working. A need for repair is often caused by lack of maintenance. Example: draining and refilling the automatic transmission fluid is maintenance recommended by the manufacturer at specific mileage intervals. Failure to do this can ruin the transmission/transaxle, requiring very expensive repairs. While no maintenance program can prevent items from breaking or wearing out, a general rule can be stated: MAINTENANCE IS CHEAPER THAN REPAIR.

Two basic mechanic's rules should be mentioned here. First, whenever the left side of the vehicle or engine is referred to, it is meant to specify the driver's side. Conversely, the right side of the vehicle means the passenger's side. Second, most screws and bolts are removed by turning counterclockwise, and tightened by turning clockwise.

Safety is always the most important rule. Constantly be aware of the dangers involved in working on an automobile and take the proper precautions. See the information in this section regarding SERVICING YOUR VEHICLE SAFELY and the SAFETY NOTICE on the acknowledgment page.

Avoiding the Most Common Mistakes

Pay attention to the instructions provided. There are 3 common mistakes in mechanical work:

1. Incorrect order of assembly, disassembly or adjustment. When taking something apart or putting it together, performing steps in the wrong order usually just costs you extra time; however, it CAN break something. Read the entire procedure before beginning disassembly. Perform everything in the order in which the instructions say you should, even if you can't immediately see a reason for it. When you're taking apart something that is very intricate, you might want to draw a picture of how it looks when assembled at one point in order to make sure you get everything back in its proper position. We will supply exploded views whenever possible. When making adjustments, perform them in the proper order; often, one adjustment affects another, and you cannot expect even satisfactory results unless each adjustment is made only when it cannot be changed by any other.

2. Overtorquing (or undertorquing). While it is more common for overtorquing to cause damage, undertorquing may allow a fastener to vibrate loose causing serious damage. Especially when dealing with aluminum parts, pay attention to torque specifications and utilize a torque wrench in assembly. If a torque figure is not available, remember that if you are using the right tool to perform the job, you will probably not have to strain yourself to get a fastener tight enough. The pitch of most threads is so slight that the tension you put on the wrench will be multiplied many times in actual force on what you are tightening. A good example of how critical torque is can be seen in the case of spark plug installation, especially where you are putting the plug into an aluminum cylinder head. Too little torque can fail to crush the gasket, causing leakage of combustion gases and consequent overheating of the plug and engine parts. Too much torque can damage the threads or distort the plug, changing the spark gap.

There are many commercial products available for ensuring that fasteners won't come loose, even if they are not torqued just right (a very common brand is Loctite®). If you're worried about getting something together tight enough to hold, but loose enough to avoid mechanical damage during assembly, one of these products might offer substantial insurance. Before choosing a threadlocking compound, read the label on the package and make sure the product is compatible with the materials, fluids, etc. involved.

3. Crossthreading. This occurs when a part such as a bolt is screwed into a nut or casting at the wrong angle and forced. Crossthreading is more likely to occur if access is difficult. It helps to clean and lubricate fasteners, then to start threading with the part to be installed positioned straight in. Then, start the bolt, spark plug, etc. with your fingers. If you encounter resistance, unscrew the part and start over again at a different angle until it can be inserted and turned several times without much effort. Keep in mind that many parts, especially spark plugs, have tapered threads, so that gentle turning will automatically bring the part you're threading to the proper angle, but only if you don't force it or resist a change in angle. Don't put a wrench on the part until it's been tightened a couple of turns by hand. If you suddenly encounter resistance, and the part has not seated fully, don't force it. Pull it back out to make sure it's clean and threading properly.

Always take your time and be patient; once you have some experience, working on your vehicle may well become an enjoyable hobby.

TOOLS AND EQUIPMENT

♦ **See Figures 1 thru 17 (p. 3–6)**

Naturally, without the proper tools and equipment it is impossible to properly service your vehicle. It would also be virtually impossible to catalog every tool that you would need to perform all of the operations in this book. Of course, It would be unwise for the amateur to rush out and buy an expensive set of tools on the theory that he/she may need one or more of them at some time.

The best approach is to proceed slowly, gathering a good quality set of those tools that are used most frequently. Don't be misled by the low cost of bargain tools. It is far better to spend a little more for better quality. Forged wrenches, 6 or 12-point sockets and fine tooth ratchets are by far preferable to their less expensive counterparts. As any good mechanic can tell you, there are few worse experiences than trying to work on a vehicle with bad tools. Your monetary savings will be far outweighed by frustration and mangled knuckles.

Begin accumulating those tools that are used most frequently: those associated with routine maintenance and tune-up. In addition to the normal assortment of screwdrivers and pliers, you should have the following tools:

Fig. 3 A hydraulic floor jack and a set of jackstands are essential for lifting and supporting the vehicle

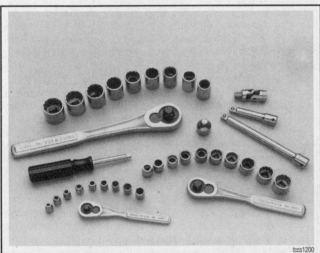

Fig. 1 All but the most basic procedures will require an assortment of ratchets and sockets

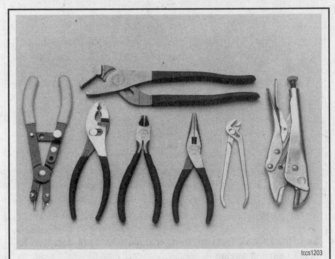

Fig. 4 An assortment of pliers, grippers and cutters will be handy for old rusted parts and stripped bolt heads

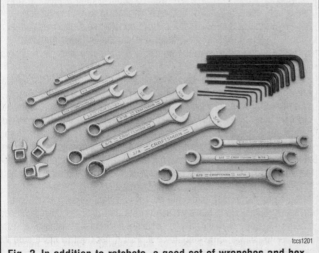

Fig. 2 In addition to ratchets, a good set of wrenches and hex keys will be necessary

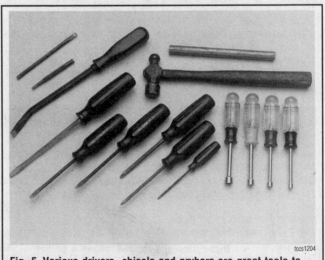

Fig. 5 Various drivers, chisels and prybars are great tools to have in your toolbox

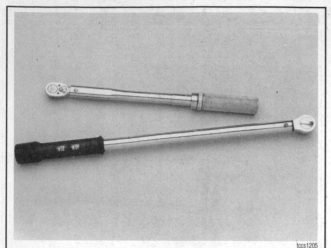

Fig. 6 Many repairs will require the use of a torque wrench to assure the components are properly fastened

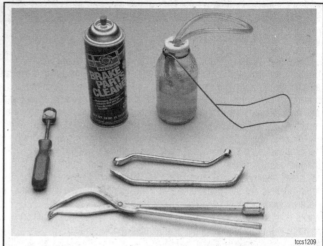

Fig. 9 Although not always necessary, using specialized brake tools will save time

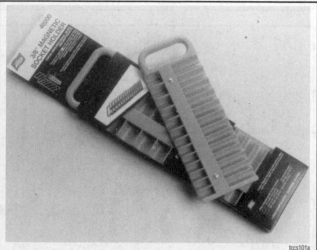

See Fig. 7 Tools from specialty manufacturers are designed to make your job easier . . .

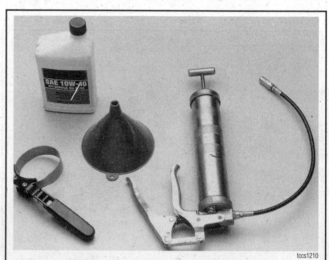

Fig. 10 A few inexpensive lubrication tools will make maintenance easier

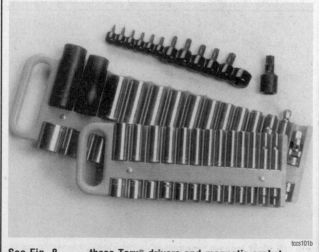
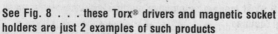

See Fig. 8 . . . these Torx® drivers and magnetic socket holders are just 2 examples of such products

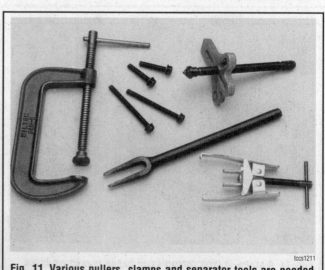

Fig. 11 Various pullers, clamps and separator tools are needed for many larger, more complicated repairs

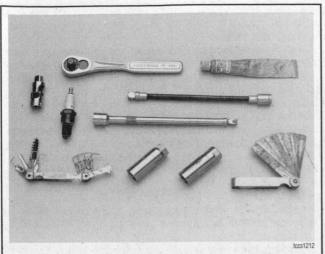

Fig. 12 A variety of tools and gauges should be used for spark plug gapping and installation

Fig. 15 A vacuum/pressure tester is necessary for many testing procedures

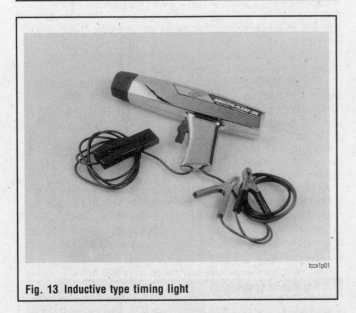

Fig. 13 Inductive type timing light

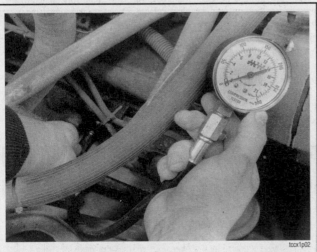

Fig. 14 A screw-in type compression gauge is recommended for compression testing

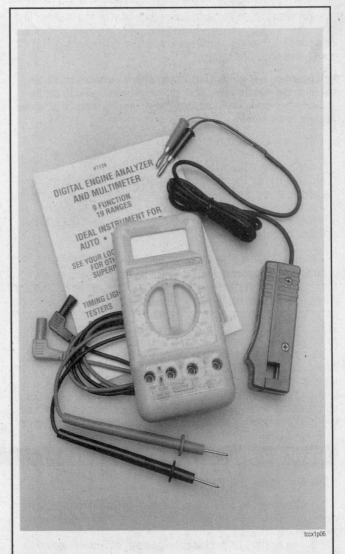

Fig. 16 Most modern automotive multimeters incorporate many helpful features

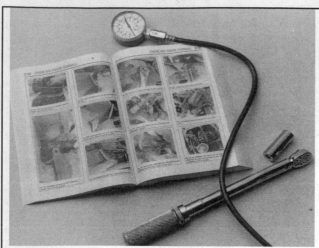

Fig. 17 Proper information is vital, so always have a Chilton Total Car Care manual handy

• Wrenches/sockets and combination open end/box end wrenches in sizes from ⅛–¾ in. or 3mm–19mm (depending on whether your vehicle uses standard or metric fasteners) and a 13⁄16 in. or ⅝ in. spark plug socket (depending on plug type).

➡**If possible, buy various length socket drive extensions. Universal-joint and wobble extensions can be extremely useful, but be careful when using them, as they can change the amount of torque applied to the socket.**

• Jackstands for support.
• Oil filter wrench.
• Spout or funnel for pouring fluids.
• Grease gun for chassis lubrication (unless your vehicle is not equipped with any grease fittings—for details, please refer to information on Fluids and Lubricants found later in this section).
• Hydrometer for checking the battery (unless equipped with a sealed, maintenance-free battery).
• A container for draining oil and other fluids.
• Rags for wiping up the inevitable mess.

In addition to the above items there are several others that are not absolutely necessary, but handy to have around. These include Oil Dry® (or an equivalent oil absorbent gravel—such as cat litter) and the usual supply of lubricants, antifreeze and fluids, although these can be purchased as needed. This is a basic list for routine maintenance, but only your personal needs and desire can accurately determine your list of tools.

After performing a few projects on the vehicle, you'll be amazed at the other tools and non-tools on your workbench. Some useful household items are: a large turkey baster or siphon, empty coffee cans and ice trays (to store parts), ball of twine, electrical tape for wiring, small rolls of colored tape for tagging lines or hoses, markers and pens, a note pad, golf tees (for plugging vacuum lines), metal coat hangers or a roll of me-

chanics's wire (to hold things out of the way), dental pick or similar long, pointed probe, a strong magnet, and a small mirror (to see into recesses and under manifolds).

A more advanced set of tools, suitable for tune-up work, can be drawn up easily. While the tools are slightly more sophisticated, they need not be outrageously expensive. There are several inexpensive tach/dwell meters on the market that are every bit as good for the average mechanic as a professional model. Just be sure that it goes to a least 1200–1500 rpm on the tach scale and that it works on 4, 6 and 8-cylinder engines. (If you have one or more vehicles with a diesel engine, a special tachometer is required since diesels don't use spark plug ignition systems). The key to these purchases is to make them with an eye towards adaptability and wide range. A basic list of tune-up tools could include:

• Tach/dwell meter.
• Spark plug wrench and gapping tool.
• Feeler gauges for valve or point adjustment. (Even if your vehicle does not use points or require valve adjustments, a feeler gauge is helpful for many repair/overhaul procedures).

A tachometer/dwell meter will ensure accurate tune-up work on vehicles without electronic ignition. The choice of a timing light should be made carefully. A light which works on the DC current supplied by the vehicle's battery is the best choice; it should have a xenon tube for brightness. On any vehicle with an electronic ignition system, a timing light with an inductive pickup that clamps around the No. 1 spark plug cable is preferred.

In addition to these basic tools, there are several other tools and gauges you may find useful. These include:

• Compression gauge. The screw-in type is slower to use, but eliminates the possibility of a faulty reading due to escaping pressure.
• Manifold vacuum gauge.
• 12V test light.
• A combination volt/ohmmeter
• Induction Ammeter. This is used for determining whether or not there is current in a wire. These are handy for use if a wire is broken somewhere in a wiring harness.

As a final note, you will probably find a torque wrench necessary for all but the most basic work. The beam type models are perfectly adequate, although the newer click types (breakaway) are easier to use. The click type torque wrenches tend to be more expensive. Also keep in mind that all types of torque wrenches should be periodically checked and/or recalibrated. You will have to decide for yourself which better fits your purpose.

Special Tools

Normally, the use of special factory tools is avoided for repair procedures, since these are not readily available for the do-it-yourself mechanic. When it is possible to perform the job with more commonly available tools, it will be pointed out, but occasionally, a special tool was designed to perform a specific function and should be used. Before substituting another tool, you should be convinced that neither your safety nor the performance of the vehicle will be compromised.

Special tools can usually be purchased from an automotive parts store or from your dealer. In some cases special tools may be available directly from the tool manufacturer.

SERVICING YOUR VEHICLE SAFELY

♦ **See Figures 18, 19, 20 and 21**

It is virtually impossible to anticipate all of the hazards involved with automotive maintenance and service, but care and common sense will prevent most accidents.

The rules of safety for mechanics range from "don't smoke around gasoline," to "use the proper tool(s) for the job." The trick to avoiding injuries is to develop safe work habits and to take every possible precaution.

Do's

• Do keep a fire extinguisher and first aid kit handy.
• Do wear safety glasses or goggles when cutting, drilling, grinding or prying, even if you have 20–20 vision. If you wear glasses for the sake of vision, wear safety goggles over your regular glasses.
• Do shield your eyes whenever you work around the battery. Batteries contain sulfuric acid. In case of contact with the eyes or skin, flush the area with water or a mixture of water and baking soda, then seek immediate medical attention.

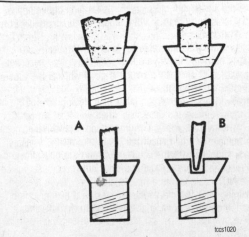

Fig. 18 Screwdrivers should be kept in good condition to prevent injury or damage which could result if the blade slips from the screw

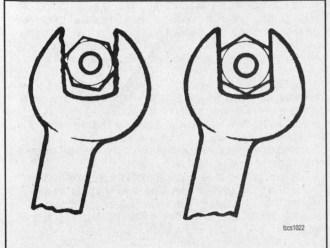

Fig. 20 Using the correct size wrench will help prevent the possibility of rounding off a nut

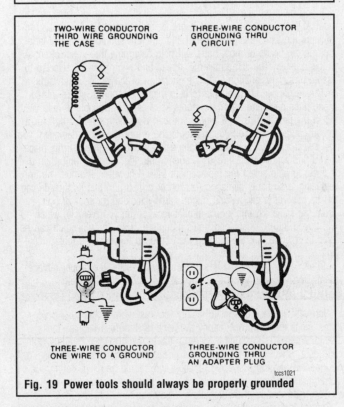

Fig. 19 Power tools should always be properly grounded

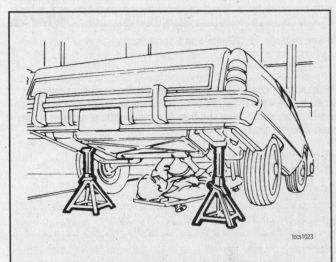

Fig. 21 NEVER work under a vehicle unless it is supported using safety stands (jackstands)

• Do use safety stands (jackstands) for any undervehicle service. Jacks are for raising vehicles; jackstands are for making sure the vehicle stays raised until you want it to come down. Whenever the vehicle is raised, block the wheels remaining on the ground and set the parking brake.

• Do use adequate ventilation when working with any chemicals or hazardous materials. Like carbon monoxide, the asbestos dust resulting from some brake lining wear can be hazardous in sufficient quantities.

• Do disconnect the negative battery cable when working on the electrical system. The secondary ignition system contains EXTREMELY HIGH VOLTAGE. In some cases it can even exceed 50,000 volts.

• Do follow manufacturer's directions whenever working with potentially hazardous materials. Most chemicals and fluids are poisonous if taken internally.

• Do properly maintain your tools. Loose hammerheads, mushroomed punches and chisels, frayed or poorly grounded electrical cords, excessively worn screwdrivers, spread wrenches (open end), cracked sockets, slipping ratchets, or faulty droplight sockets can cause accidents.

• Likewise, keep your tools clean; a greasy wrench can slip off a bolt head, ruining the bolt and often harming your knuckles in the process.

• Do use the proper size and type of tool for the job at hand. Do select a wrench or socket that fits the nut or bolt. The wrench or socket should sit straight, not cocked.

• Do, when possible, pull on a wrench handle rather than push on it, and adjust your stance to prevent a fall.

• Do be sure that adjustable wrenches are tightly closed on the nut or bolt and pulled so that the force is on the side of the fixed jaw.

• Do strike squarely with a hammer; avoid glancing blows.

• Do set the parking brake and block the drive wheels if the work requires a running engine.

Don'ts

• Don't run the engine in a garage or anywhere else without proper ventilation—EVER! Carbon monoxide is poisonous; it takes a long time to leave the human body and you can build up a deadly supply of it in your system by simply breathing in a little every day. You may not realize you are slowly poisoning yourself. Always use power vents, windows, fans and/or open the garage door.

• Don't work around moving parts while wearing loose clothing. Short sleeves are much safer than long, loose sleeves. Hard-toed shoes with neoprene soles protect your toes and give a better grip on slippery surfaces. Jewelry such as watches, fancy belt buckles, beads or body adornment of any kind is not safe working around a vehicle. Long hair should be tied back under a hat or cap.

• Don't use pockets for toolboxes. A fall or bump can drive a screwdriver deep into your body. Even a rag hanging from your back pocket can wrap around a spinning shaft or fan.

• Don't smoke when working around gasoline, cleaning solvent or other flammable material.

• Don't smoke when working around the battery. When the battery is being charged, it gives off explosive hydrogen gas.

• Don't use gasoline to wash your hands; there are excellent soaps available. Gasoline contains dangerous additives which can enter the body through a cut or through your pores. Gasoline also removes all the natural oils from the skin so that bone dry hands will suck up oil and grease.

• Don't service the air conditioning system unless you are equipped with the necessary tools and training. When liquid or compressed gas refrigerant is released to atmospheric pressure it will absorb heat from whatever it contacts. This will chill or freeze anything it touches. Although refrigerant is normally non-toxic, R-12 becomes a deadly poisonous gas in the presence of an open flame. One good whiff of the vapors from burning refrigerant can be fatal.

• Don't use screwdrivers for anything other than driving screws! A screwdriver used as an prying tool can snap when you least expect it, causing injuries. At the very least, you'll ruin a good screwdriver.

• Don't use a bumper or emergency jack (that little ratchet, scissors, or pantograph jack supplied with the vehicle) for anything other than changing a flat! These jacks are only intended for emergency use out on the road; they are NOT designed as a maintenance tool. If you are serious about maintaining your vehicle yourself, invest in a hydraulic floor jack of at least a 1½ton capacity, and at least two sturdy jackstands.

FASTENERS, MEASUREMENTS AND CONVERSIONS

Bolts, Nuts and Other Threaded Retainers

◆ **See Figures 22, 23, 24 and 25**

Although there are a great variety of fasteners found in the modern car or truck, the most commonly used retainer is the threaded fastener (nuts, bolts, screws, studs, etc). Most threaded retainers may be reused, provided that they are not damaged in use or during the repair. Some retainers (such as stretch bolts or torque prevailing nuts) are designed to deform when tightened or in use and should not be reinstalled.

Whenever possible, we will note any special retainers which should be replaced during a procedure. But you should always inspect the condition of a retainer when it is removed and replace any that show signs of damage. Check all threads for rust or corrosion which can increase the torque necessary to achieve the desired clamp load for which that fastener was originally selected. Additionally, be sure that the driver surface of the fastener has not been compromised by rounding or other damage. In some cases a driver surface may become only partially rounded, allowing the driver to catch in only one direction. In many of these occurrences, a fastener may be installed and tightened, but the driver would not be able to grip and loosen the fastener again. (This could lead to frustration down the line should that component ever need to be disassembled again).

If you must replace a fastener, whether due to design or damage, you must ALWAYS be sure to use the proper replacement. In all cases, a retainer of the same design, material and strength should be used. Markings on the heads of most bolts will help determine the proper strength of the fastener. The same material, thread and pitch must be selected to assure proper installation and safe operation of the vehicle afterwards.

Thread gauges are available to help measure a bolt or stud's thread. Most automotive and hardware stores keep gauges available to help you select the proper size. In a pinch, you can use another nut or bolt for a thread gauge. If the bolt you are replacing is not too badly damaged, you can select a match by finding another bolt which will thread in its place. If you find a nut which threads properly onto the damaged bolt, then use that nut to help select the replacement bolt. If however, the bolt you are replacing is so badly damaged (broken or drilled out) that its threads cannot be used as a gauge, you might start by looking for another bolt (from the same assembly or a similar location on your vehicle) which will thread into the damaged bolt's mounting. If so, the other bolt can be used to select a nut; the nut can then be used to select the replacement bolt.

In all cases, be absolutely sure you have selected the proper replacement. Don't be shy, you can always ask the store clerk for help.

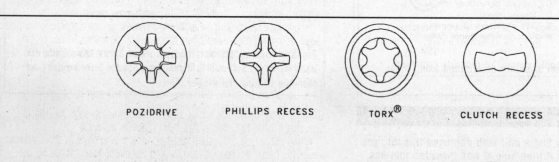

POZIDRIVE   PHILLIPS RECESS   TORX®   CLUTCH RECESS

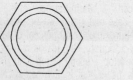

INDENTED HEXAGON   HEXAGON TRIMMED   HEXAGON WASHER HEAD

Fig. 22 Here are a few of the most common screw/bolt driver styles

tccs1037

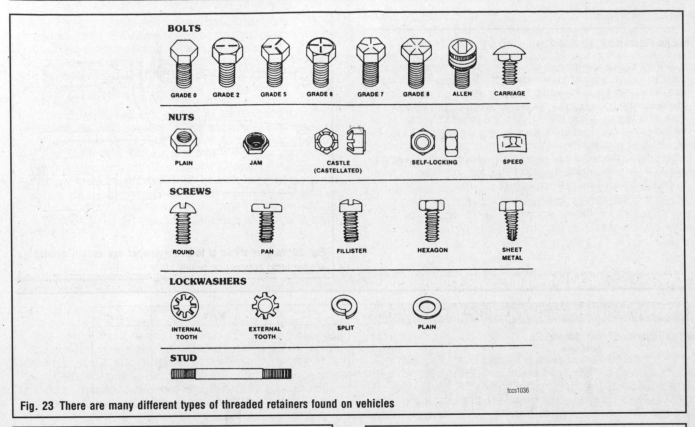

Fig. 23 There are many different types of threaded retainers found on vehicles

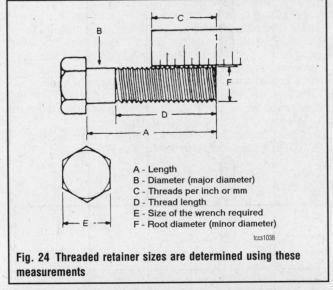

A - Length
B - Diameter (major diameter)
C - Threads per inch or mm
D - Thread length
E - Size of the wrench required
F - Root diameter (minor diameter)

tccs1038

Fig. 24 Threaded retainer sizes are determined using these measurements

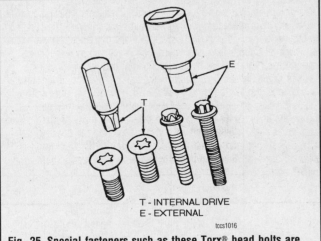

T - INTERNAL DRIVE
E - EXTERNAL

tccs1016

Fig. 25 Special fasteners such as these Torx® head bolts are used by manufacturers to discourage people from working on vehicles without the proper tools

✳✳ WARNING

Be aware that when you find a bolt with damaged threads, you may also find the nut or drilled hole it was threaded into has also been damaged. If this is the case, you may have to drill and tap the hole, replace the nut or otherwise repair the threads. NEVER try to force a replacement bolt to fit into the damaged threads.

Torque

Torque is defined as the measurement of resistance to turning or rotating. It tends to twist a body about an axis of rotation. A common example of this would be tightening a threaded retainer such as a nut, bolt or screw. Measuring torque is one of the most common ways to help assure that a threaded retainer has been properly fastened.

When tightening a threaded fastener, torque is applied in three distinct areas, the head, the bearing surface and the clamp load. About 50 percent of the measured torque is used in overcoming bearing friction. This is the friction between the bearing surface of the bolt head, screw head or nut face and the base material or washer (the surface on which the fastener is rotating). Approximately 40 percent of the applied torque is used in overcoming thread friction. This leaves only about 10 percent of the applied torque to develop a useful clamp load (the force which holds a joint together). This means that friction can account for as much as 90 percent of the applied torque on a fastener.

TORQUE WRENCHES

♦ See Figures 26, 27 and 28

In most applications, a torque wrench can be used to assure proper installation of a fastener. Torque wrenches come in various designs and most automotive supply stores will carry a variety to suit your needs. A torque wrench should be used any time we supply a specific torque value for a fastener. A torque wrench can also be used if you are following the general guidelines in the accompanying charts. Keep in mind that because there is no worldwide standardization of fasteners, the charts are a general guideline and should be used with caution. Again, the general rule of "if you are using the right tool for the job, you should not have to strain to tighten a fastener" applies here.

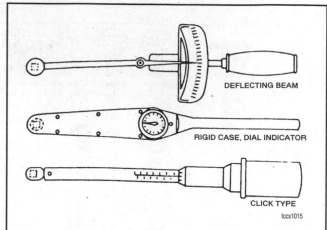

DEFLECTING BEAM

RIGID CASE, DIAL INDICATOR

CLICK TYPE

tccs1015

Fig. 26 Various styles of torque wrenches are usually available at your local automotive supply store

	Mark	Class		Mark	Class
Hexagon head bolt	Bolt head No. 4 — 5 — 6 — 7 — 8 — 9 — 10 — 11 —	4T 5T 6T 7T 8T 9T 10T 11T	Stud bolt	No mark	4T
	No mark	4T			
Hexagon flange bolt w/ washer hexagon bolt	No mark	4T		Grooved	6T
Hexagon head bolt	Two protruding lines	5T			
Hexagon flange bolt w/ washer hexagon bolt	Two protruding lines	6T	Welded bolt		4T
Hexagon head bolt	Three protruding lines	7T			
Hexagon head bolt	Four protruding lines	8T			

tccs1240

Fig. 27 Determining bolt strength of metric fasteners—NOTE: this is a typical bolt marking system, but there is not a worldwide standard

Class	Diameter mm	Pitch mm	Specified torque					
			Hexagon head bolt			Hexagon flange bolt		
			N·m	kgf·cm	ft·lbf	N·m	kgf·cm	ft·lbf
4T	6	1	5	55	48 in.·lbf	6	60	52 in.·lbf
	8	1.25	12.5	130	9	14	145	10
	10	1.25	26	260	19	29	290	21
	12	1.25	47	480	35	53	540	39
	14	1.5	74	760	55	84	850	61
	16	1.5	115	1,150	83	—	—	—
5T	6	1	6.5	65	56 in.·lbf	7.5	75	65 in.·lbf
	8	1.25	15.5	160	12	17.5	175	13
	10	1.25	32	330	24	36	360	26
	12	1.25	59	600	43	65	670	48
	14	1.5	91	930	67	100	1,050	76
	16	1.5	140	1,400	101	—	—	—
6T	6	1	8	80	69 in.·lbf	9	90	78 in.·lbf
	8	1.25	19	195	14	21	210	15
	10	1.25	39	400	29	44	440	32
	12	1.25	71	730	53	80	810	59
	14	1.5	110	1,100	80	125	1,250	90
	16	1.5	170	1,750	127	—	—	—
7T	6	1	10.5	110	8	12	120	9
	8	1.25	25	260	19	28	290	21
	10	1.25	52	530	38	58	590	43
	12	1.25	95	970	70	105	1,050	76
	14	1.5	145	1,500	108	165	1,700	123
	16	1.5	230	2,300	166	—	—	—
8T	8	1.25	29	300	22	33	330	24
	10	1.25	61	620	45	68	690	50
	12	1.25	110	1,100	80	120	1,250	90
9T	8	1.25	34	340	25	37	380	27
	10	1.25	70	710	51	78	790	57
	12	1.25	125	1,300	94	140	1,450	105
10T	8	1.25	38	390	28	42	430	31
	10	1.25	78	800	58	88	890	64
	12	1.25	140	1,450	105	155	1,600	116
11T	8	1.25	42	430	31	47	480	35
	10	1.25	87	890	64	97	990	72
	12	1.25	155	1,600	116	175	1,800	130

tccs1241

Fig. 28 Typical bolt torques for metric fasteners—WARNING: use only as a guide

Beam Type

♦ **See Figure 29**

The beam type torque wrench is one of the most popular types. It consists of a pointer attached to the head that runs the length of the flexible beam (shaft) to a scale located near the handle. As the wrench is pulled, the beam bends and the pointer indicates the torque using the scale.

Click (Breakaway) Type

♦ **See Figure 30**

Another popular design of torque wrench is the click type. To use the click type wrench you pre-adjust it to a torque setting. Once the torque is reached, the wrench has a reflex signaling feature that causes a momentary breakaway of the torque wrench body, sending an impulse to the operator's hand.

Pivot Head Type

♦ **See Figure 31**

Some torque wrenches (usually of the click type) may be equipped with a pivot head which can allow it to be used in areas of limited access. BUT, it must be used properly. To hold a pivot head wrench, grasp the handle lightly, and as you pull on the handle, it should be floated on the pivot point. If the handle comes in contact with the yoke extension during the process of pulling, there is a very good chance the torque readings will be inaccurate because this could alter the wrench loading point. The design of the handle is usually such as to make it inconvenient to deliberately misuse the wrench.

➡ It should be mentioned that the use of any U-joint, wobble or extension will have an effect on the torque readings, no matter what type of wrench you are using. For the most accurate readings, install the socket directly on the wrench driver. If necessary, straight extensions (which hold a socket directly under the wrench driver) will have the least effect on the torque reading. Avoid any extension that alters the length of the wrench from the handle to the head/driving point (such as a crow's foot). U-joint or Wobble extensions can greatly affect the readings; avoid their use at all times.

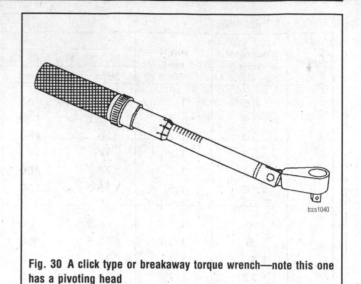

Fig. 30 A click type or breakaway torque wrench—note this one has a pivoting head

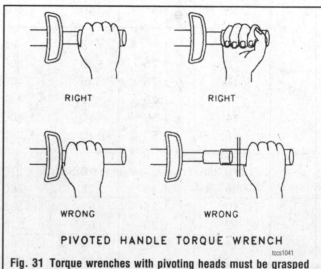

RIGHT   RIGHT

WRONG   WRONG

PIVOTED HANDLE TORQUE WRENCH

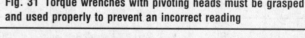

Fig. 31 Torque wrenches with pivoting heads must be grasped and used properly to prevent an incorrect reading

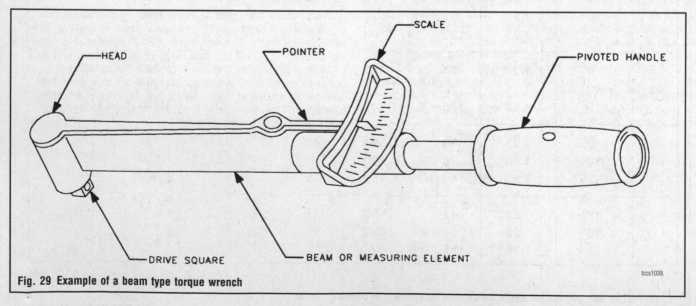

SCALE

POINTER

HEAD

PIVOTED HANDLE

DRIVE SQUARE

BEAM OR MEASURING ELEMENT

Fig. 29 Example of a beam type torque wrench

Rigid Case (Direct Reading)

▶ See Figure 32

A rigid case or direct reading torque wrench is equipped with a dial indicator to show torque values. One advantage of these wrenches is that they can be held at any position on the wrench without affecting accuracy. These wrenches are often preferred because they tend to be compact, easy to read and have a great degree of accuracy.

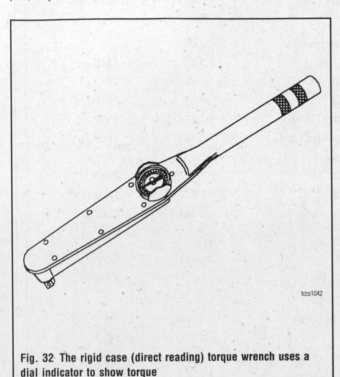

tccs1042

Fig. 32 The rigid case (direct reading) torque wrench uses a dial indicator to show torque

TORQUE ANGLE METERS

▶ See Figure 33

Because the frictional characteristics of each fastener or threaded hole will vary, clamp loads which are based strictly on torque will vary as well. In most applications, this variance is not significant enough to cause worry. But, in certain applications, a manufacturer's engineers may determine that more precise clamp loads are necessary (such is the case with many aluminum cylinder heads). In these cases, a torque angle method of installation would be specified. When installing fasteners which are torque angle tightened, a predetermined seating torque and standard torque wrench are usually used first to remove any compliance from the joint. The fastener is then tightened the specified additional portion of a turn measured in degrees. A torque angle gauge (mechanical protractor) is used for these applications.

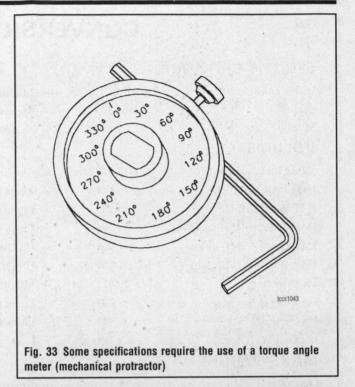

tccs1043

Fig. 33 Some specifications require the use of a torque angle meter (mechanical protractor)

Standard and Metric Measurements

▶ See Figure 34

Throughout this manual, specifications are given to help you determine the condition of various components on your vehicle, or to assist you in their installation. Some of the most common measurements include length (in. or cm/mm), torque (ft. lbs., inch lbs. or Nm) and pressure (psi, in. Hg, kPa or mm Hg). In most cases, we strive to provide the proper measurement as determined by the manufacturer's engineers.

Though, in some cases, that value may not be conveniently measured with what is available in your toolbox. Luckily, many of the measuring devices which are available today will have two scales so the Standard or Metric measurements may easily be taken. If any of the various measuring tools which are available to you do not contain the same scale as listed in the specifications, use the accompanying conversion factors to determine the proper value.

The conversion factor chart is used by taking the given specification and multiplying it by the necessary conversion factor. For instance, looking at the first line, if you have a measurement in inches such as "free-play should be 2 in." but your ruler reads only in millimeters, multiply 2 in. by the conversion factor of 25.4 to get the metric equivalent of 50.8mm. Likewise, if the specification was given only in a Metric measurement, for example in Newton Meters (Nm), then look at the center column first. If the measurement is 100 Nm, multiply it by the conversion factor of 0.738 to get 73.8 ft. lbs.

CONVERSION FACTORS

LENGTH–DISTANCE

Inches (in.)	x 25.4	= Millimeters (mm)	x .0394	= Inches
Feet (ft.)	x .305	= Meters (m)	x 3.281	= Feet
Miles	x 1.609	= Kilometers (km)	x .0621	= Miles

VOLUME

Cubic Inches (in3)	x 16.387	= Cubic Centimeters	x .061	= in3
IMP Pints (IMP pt.)	x .568	= Liters (L)	x 1.76	= IMP pt.
IMP Quarts (IMP qt.)	x 1.137	= Liters (L)	x .88	= IMP qt.
IMP Gallons (IMP gal.)	x 4.546	= Liters (L)	x .22	= IMP gal.
IMP Quarts (IMP qt.)	x 1.201	= US Quarts (US qt.)	x .833	= IMP qt.
IMP Gallons (IMP gal.)	x 1.201	= US Gallons (US gal.)	x .833	= IMP gal.
Fl. Ounces	x 29.573	= Milliliters	x .034	= Ounces
US Pints (US pt.)	x .473	= Liters (L)	x 2.113	= Pints
US Quarts (US qt.)	x .946	= Liters (L)	x 1.057	= Quarts
US Gallons (US gal.)	x 3.785	= Liters (L)	x .264	= Gallons

MASS–WEIGHT

Ounces (oz.)	x 28.35	= Grams (g)	x .035	= Ounces
Pounds (lb.)	x .454	= Kilograms (kg)	x 2.205	= Pounds

PRESSURE

Pounds Per Sq. In. (psi)	x 6.895	= Kilopascals (kPa)	x .145	= psi
Inches of Mercury (Hg)	x .4912	= psi	x 2.036	= Hg
Inches of Mercury (Hg)	x 3.377	= Kilopascals (kPa)	x .2961	= Hg
Inches of Water (H_2O)	x .07355	= Inches of Mercury	x 13.783	= H_2O
Inches of Water (H_2O)	x .03613	= psi	x 27.684	= H_2O
Inches of Water (H_2O)	x .248	= Kilopascals (kPa)	x 4.026	= H_2O

TORQUE

Pounds–Force Inches (in–lb)	x .113	= Newton Meters (N·m)	x 8.85	= in–lb
Pounds–Force Feet (ft–lb)	x 1.356	= Newton Meters (N·m)	x .738	= ft–lb

VELOCITY

Miles Per Hour (MPH)	x 1.609	= Kilometers Per Hour (KPH)	x .621	= MPH

POWER

Horsepower (Hp)	x .745	= Kilowatts	x 1.34	= Horsepower

FUEL CONSUMPTION*

Miles Per Gallon IMP (MPG)	x .354	= Kilometers Per Liter (Km/L)
Kilometers Per Liter (Km/L)	x 2.352	= IMP MPG
Miles Per Gallon US (MPG)	x .425	= Kilometers Per Liter (Km/L)
Kilometers Per Liter (Km/L)	x 2.352	= US MPG

*It is common to covert from miles per gallon (mpg) to liters/100 kilometers (1/100 km), where mpg (IMP) x 1/100 km = 282 and mpg (US) x 1/100 km = 235.

TEMPERATURE

Degree Fahrenheit (°F)	= (°C x 1.8) + 32
Degree Celsius (°C)	= (°F – 32) x .56

Fig. 34 Standard gend metric conversion factors chart

tccs1044

SERIAL NUMBER IDENTIFICATION

Vehicle

▶ See Figure 35

The Vehicle Identification Number (VIN) is located at three positions on the vehicle. The first is at the top left side of the dashboard, viewable through the windshield.

The second location is at the top of the firewall in the engine compartment. Some VIN numbers are stamped into the firewall, while others are stamped into a vehicle identification tag that is secured to the firewall.

The third location is at the door jamb, below the tire inflation pressure label.

The seventeen-digit vehicle number is composed of an identification number and a five or six-digit serial number.

The two most important digits are the sixth and eighth. The sixth digit identifies the engine type. This will be used later in the book to identify the engines in the specification charts. The eighth digit identifies the model year.

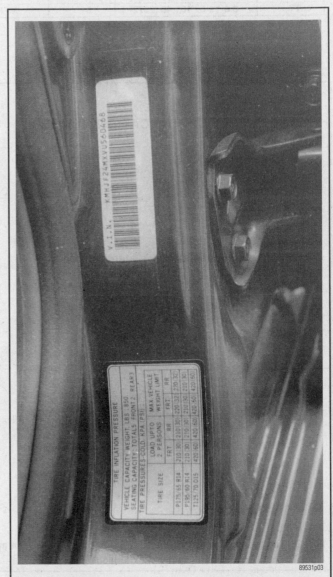

The VIN is also located at the driver's door jamb, above the tire inflation pressure label

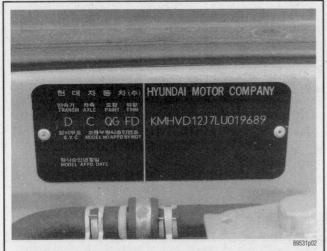

The Vehicle Identification Number (VIN), at the top left of the dashboard, is visible through the windshield

The VIN is either stamped into a plate at the top of the firewall or directly into the firewall itself

VEHICLE IDENTIFICATION CHART

Code	Liters	Cu. In. (cc)	Cyl.	Fuel Sys.	Eng. Mfg.
J	1.5	89.60 (1468)	4	MFI	Hyundai
E	1.5	91.17 (1495)	4	MFI	Hyundai
E	1.5	91.17 (1495)	4	MFI-T	Hyundai
K	1.5	91.17 (1495)	4	MFI	Hyundai
R	1.6	97.29 (1595)	4	MFI	Hyundai
M	1.8	109.54 (1795)	4	MFI	Hyundai
M	1.8	112.04 (1836)	4	MFI	Hyundai
F	2.0	120.52 (1975)	4	MFI	Hyundai
P	2.0	121.90 (1997)	4	MFI	Hyundai
T	3.0	181.40 (2972)	6	MFI	Hyundai

Engine Code

Model Year	
Code	Year
94	R
95	S
96	T
97	V
98	W

MFI : Multi-Port Fuel Injection
MFI-T: Multi-Port Fuel Injection Turbocharged

89531c01

VEHICLE IDENTIFICATION NUMBER

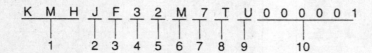

K M H J F 3 2 M 7 T U 0 0 0 0 0 1

1   2 3 4 5 6 7 8 9   10

1. World manufacturer's identifier code

2. Line and drive type

3. Body Type

4. Series (Body style and version)

5. Restraint system (Front seat)

6. Engine type

7. Check digit

8. Product year

9. Plant code

10. Vehicle production sequence number

89531g02

Fig. 35 The two most important digits of the vehicle identification number are the sixth and eighth. The sixth digit identifies the engine type. This will be used later in the book to identify the engines in the specification charts. The eighth digit identifies the model year

Engine

♦ **See Figures 36 thru 41 (p. 17–18)**

The engine identification number is stamped on a pad at the top edge of the cylinder block. The pad is located as follows:
• Accent and Scoupe—on the front of the engine, below the water outlet.
• Excel—on the right side of the engine, near the water pump.
• Sonata 4-cyl. and 1994–95 Elantra—on the front of the engine, behind the alternator.

• Sonata 6-cyl.—on the rear of the engine, near the transaxle.
• 1996–98 Elantra and Tiburon—on the rear of the engine, above the transaxle bell housing.

The eleven-digit engine number is composed of an identification number and a six-digit production sequence number. The two most important digits are the fourth and fifth. The fourth digit identifies the engine type. This will be used later in the book to identify the engine in specification charts. The fifth digit identifies the model year.

ENGINE IDENTIFICATION

Year	Model	Engine Displacement Liters (cc)	Engine Series (ID/VIN)	Fuel System	No. of Cylinders	Engine Type
1994	Excel	1.5 (1468)	J	MFI	4	SOHC
	Scoupe	1.5 (1495)	E	MFI	4	SOHC
	Scoupe	1.5 (1495)	E	MFI-T	4	SOHC
	Elantra	1.6 (1595)	R	MFI	4	DOHC
	Elantra	1.8 (1836)	M	MFI	4	DOHC
	Sonata	2.0 (1997)	P	MFI	4	DOHC
	Sonata	3.0 (2972)	T	MFI	6	SOHC
1995	Scoupe	1.5 (1495)	E	MFI	4	SOHC
	Scoupe	1.5 (1495)	E	MFI-T	4	SOHC
	Accent	1.5 (1495)	K	MFI	4	SOHC
	Elantra	1.6 (1595)	R	MFI	4	DOHC
	Elantra	1.8 (1836)	M	MFI	4	DOHC
	Sonata	2.0 (1997)	P	MFI	4	DOHC
	Sonata	3.0 (2972)	T	MFI	6	SOHC
1996	Accent	1.5 (1495)	K	MFI	4	SOHC
	Accent	1.5 (1495)	K	MFI	4	DOHC
	Elantra	1.8 (1795)	M	MFI	4	DOHC
	Sonata	2.0 (1997)	P	MFI	4	DOHC
	Sonata	3.0 (2972)	T	MFI	6	SOHC
1997	Accent	1.5 (1495)	K	MFI	4	SOHC
	Accent	1.5 (1495)	K	MFI	4	DOHC
	Elantra	1.8 (1795)	M	MFI	4	DOHC
	Tiburon	1.8 (1795)	M	MFI	4	DOHC
	Tiburon	2.0 (1975)	F	MFI	4	DOHC
	Sonata	2.0 (1997)	P	MFI	4	DOHC
	Sonata	3.0 (2972)	T	MFI	6	SOHC
1998	Accent	1.5 (1495)	K	MFI	4	SOHC
	Accent	1.5 (1495)	K	MFI	4	DOHC
	Elantra	1.8 (1795)	M	MFI	4	DOHC
	Tiburon	1.8 (1795)	M	MFI	4	DOHC
	Tiburon	2.0 (1975)	F	MFI	4	DOHC
	Sonata	2.0 (1997)	P	MFI	4	DOHC
	Sonata	3.0 (2972)	T	MFI	6	SOHC

MFI : Multi-Port Fuel Injection
MFI-T : Multi-Port Fuel Injection Turbocharged
SOHC: Single Overhead Camshaft
DOHC: Dual Overhead Camshaft

89531c02

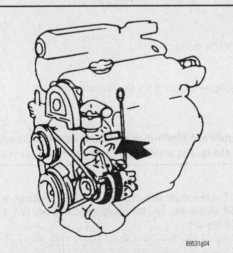

Fig. 36 The engine identification number is located on the front of the engine, below the water outlet—Accent and Scoupe

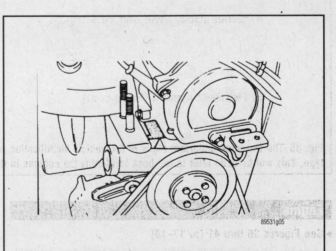

Fig. 37 The engine identification number is located on the right side of the engine near the water pump—Excel

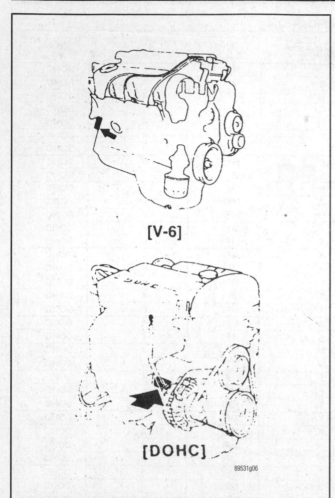

[V-6]

[DOHC]

Fig. 38 The engine identification number is located on the front of the engine behind the alternator (4-cyl.), or at the rear of the engine near the transaxle (6-cyl.)—Sonata

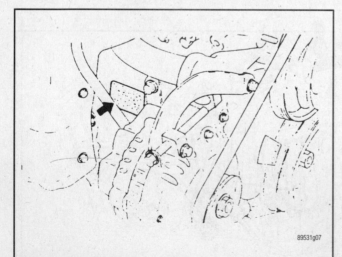

Fig. 39 The engine identification number is located on the front of the engine behind the alternator—1994–95 Elantra

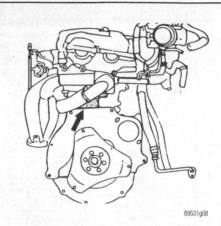

Fig. 40 The engine identification number is located on the rear of the engine, above the transaxle bell housing—1996–98 Elantra and Tiburon

ENGINE IDENTIFICATION NUMBER

1. Engine fuel

2. Engine range

3. Engine development order

4. Engine capacity

5. Product year

6. Engine production sequence number

Fig. 41 The two most important digits of the engine identification number are the fourth and fifth. The fourth digit identifies the engine type. This will be used later in the book to identify the engine in specification charts. The fifth digit identifies the model year

Transaxle

◆ **See Figures 42, 43 and 44**

The transaxle identification number is located on the top of the bell housing (all vehicles except Excel), or at the top of the transaxle, adjacent to the transaxle mount (Excel).

The twelve-digit transaxle number is composed of an identification number and a six-digit production sequence number. The two most important digits are the first and second. The first digit identifies the transaxle model. The second digit identifies the production year.

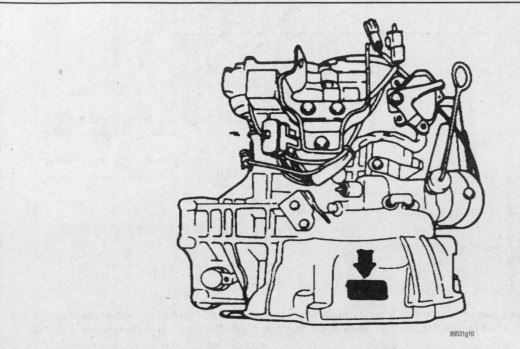

89531g10

Fig. 42 The transaxle identification number is located at the top of the bell housing—except Excel

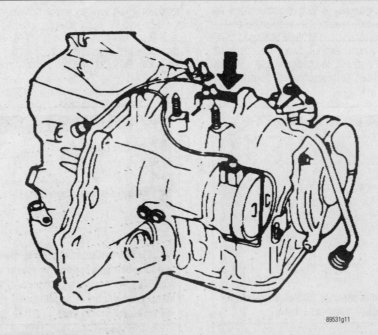

89531g11

Fig. 43 The transaxle identification number is located on top of the transaxle, adjacent to the transaxle mount—Excel

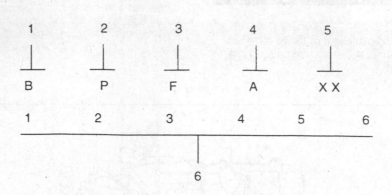

1. Model

2. Product year

3. Final gear ratio

4. Classification of detail

89531g12

Fig. 44 The twelve-digit transaxle number is composed of an identification number and a six-digit production sequence number. The two most important digits are the first and second. The first digit identifies the transaxle model. The second digit identifies the production year

ROUTINE MAINTENANCE AND TUNE-UP

Proper maintenance and tune-up is the key to long and trouble-free vehicle life, and the work can yield its own rewards. Studies have shown that a properly tuned and maintained vehicle can achieve better gas mileage than an out-of-tune vehicle. As a conscientious owner and driver, set aside a Saturday morning, say once a month, to check or replace items which could cause major problems later. Keep your own personal log to jot down which services you performed, how much the parts cost you, the date, and the exact odometer reading at the time. Keep all receipts for such items as engine oil and filters, so that they may be referred to in case of related problems or to determine operating expenses. As a do-it-yourselfer, these receipts are the only proof you have that the required

The VECI label, located on the underside of the hood, contains pertinent tune-up information

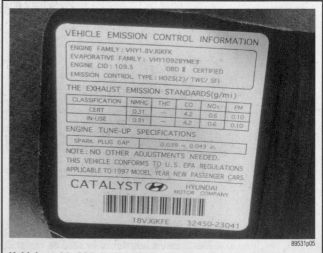

Vehicles with OBD II compliant engines will be identified on the VECI label

UNDERHOOD COMPONENT LOCATIONS—EARLY MODEL

1. Air Cleaner
2. Brake Booster
3. Brake Fluid Reservoir
4. Fuel Filter
5. Clutch Fluid Reservoir
6. Distributor
7. Engine Oil Level Dipstick
8. Positive Crankcase Ventilation (PCV) Valve
9. Underhood Fuse and Relay Box
10. Windshield Washer Fluid Reservoir
11. Spark Plugs
12. Radiator Cap
13. Battery
14. Coolant Reservoir
15. Engine Oil Filler Cap
16. Vehicle Identification Number (VIN) Plate
17. Spark Plug Wires

89531p06

UNDERHOOD COMPONENT LOCATIONS—LATE MODEL

1. Vehicle Identification Number (VIN) Plate
2. Brake Booster
3. Brake Fluid Reservoir
4. Underhood Fuse and Relay Box
5. Battery
6. Transmission Fluid Level Dipstick
7. Air Cleaner
8. Ignition Coil Pack
9. Spark Plugs (under cover)
10. Engine Oil Filler Cap
11. Radiator Cap
12. Windshield Washer Fluid Reservoir
13. Power Steering Fluid Reservoir
14. Coolant Reservoir
15. Positive Crankcase Ventilation (PCV) Valve
16. Engine Oil Level Dipstick

89531p07

maintenance was performed. In the event of a warranty problem, these receipts will be invaluable.

The literature provided with your vehicle when it was originally delivered includes the factory recommended maintenance schedule. If you no longer have this literature, replacement copies are usually available from the dealer. A maintenance schedule is provided later in this section, in case you do not have the factory literature.

Air Cleaner

The air cleaner contains a dry paper element that keeps most dirt and dust from entering the engine. The paper cartridge should be replaced every 30,000 miles (48,000 km).

➡**Check the air filter cartridge more frequently if the vehicle is operated under severe conditions or in a dusty environment.**

REMOVAL & INSTALLATION

Excel, Scoupe and 1994–95 Elantra

1. Remove the air intake hose air duct.
2. Disengage the air flow sensor connector from the air cleaner filter cover.

The air flow sensor uses a weatherproof connector. Inspect the seal for damage and replace as necessary

Unscrew the clamp that attaches the air hose duct to the air filter assembly

Take care when removing the air hose duct. The air flow sensor inside the air filter is easily damaged

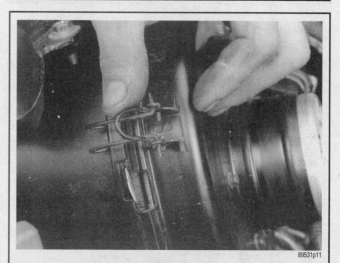

Unfasten the air filter cover clips by unlatching them as shown—Excel, Scoupe and 1994–95 Elantra

Carefully remove the air filter cover. The air flow sensor (arrow) is at the center of the cover

The round air filter element is made of paper and cannot be cleaned. When dirty, it must be replaced

The air filter element is a flat paper design. Inspect it carefully and replace it when dirty or damaged

3. Unfasten the air cleaner filter cover clips and remove the cover.
4. Remove the old filter element.

➡The air cleaner filter cover should be removed carefully because on most models, it contains the air flow sensor.

5. Clean the air box with a dry rag and insert a new filter element.
6. Install the air cleaner filter cover and fasten the clips.
7. Connect the air flow sensor connector.
8. Install the air intake hose air duct.

Tiburon and 1996–98 Elantra

1. Remove the air intake hose air duct.
2. Disengage the air flow sensor connector from the air cleaner filter cover.
3. Disengage the intake air temperature sensor connector.
4. Unfasten the air cleaner filter cover clips and remove the cover.
5. Remove the old filter element.

➡The air cleaner filter cover should be removed carefully because on most models, it contains the air flow sensor.

6. Clean the air box with a dry rag and insert a new filter element.
7. Install the air cleaner filter cover and fasten the clips.
8. Connect the air flow sensor connector.
9. Connect the intake air temperature sensor connector.
10. Install the air intake hose air duct.

Accent and Sonata

▶ See Figure 45

1. Remove the air intake cover attaching bolts.
2. Remove the air intake cover.
3. Remove the old filter element.
4. Clean the air box with a dry rag and insert a new filter element.
5. Install the air cleaner filter cover and fasten securely with attaching bolts.

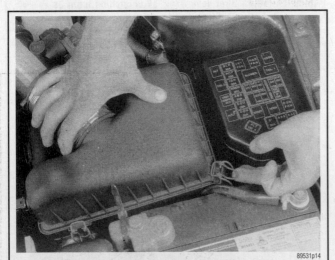

Unfasten the air cleaner filter cover clips by unlatching them as shown—Tiburon and 1996–98 Elantra

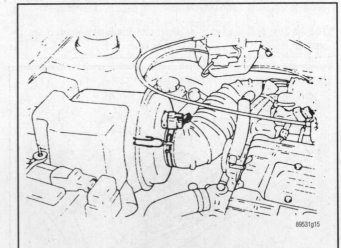

Fig. 45 The Accent and Sonata air cleaner assemblies, which contain no sensors, are secured by latches

Fuel Filter

The fuel filter is an inline canister type. It should be replaced every 52,000 miles (84,000 km). On all vehicles except Sonata, the fuel filter is located on the firewall, adjacent to the master cylinder. On Sonata, the fuel filter is located at the rear of the vehicle, mounted to the floor pan in front of the fuel tank.

Firewall mounted fuel filter location. Use a wrench and socket to remove the banjo bolt securing the fuel line

89531p16

FUEL PRESSURE RELIEF

The fuel injection system is under constant pressure even when the engine is not running. This residual pressure must be relieved from the fuel system before servicing.

Accent, Elantra, Sonata and Tiburon
▶ See Figure 46

The fuel pump connector is located at the fuel tank sending unit on top of the fuel tank. The connector is accessible through a door located under the rear seat.
1. Remove the rear seat cushion.
2. Disengage the fuel pump harness connector at the fuel tank sending unit.

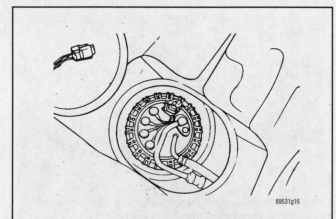

Fig. 46 The fuel pump connector is located at the fuel tank sending unit on top of the fuel tank. The connector is accessible through a door located under the rear seat—except Excel and Scoupe

89531g16

3. Start the engine and allow it to run until it stalls.
4. Turn the ignition switch to the **OFF** position.
5. Disconnect the negative battery cable.
6. Reconnect the fuel pump harness connector.

Excel and Scoupe
▶ See Figure 47

The fuel pump connector is located to the right of the fuel tank.
1. Disengage the fuel pump harness connector at the rear of the fuel tank.
2. Start the engine and allow it to run until it stalls.
3. Turn the ignition switch to the **OFF** position.
4. Disconnect the negative battery cable.
5. Reconnect the fuel pump harness connector.

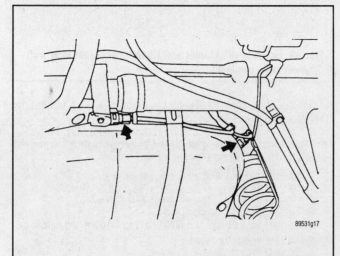

Fig. 47 The fuel pump connector is located to the right of the fuel tank—Excel and Scoupe

89531g17

REMOVAL & INSTALLATION

Except Sonata
▶ See Figures 48 and 49

1. Properly relieve fuel system pressure.
2. Disconnect the negative battery cable.

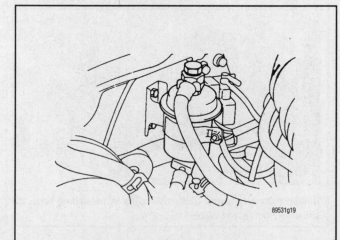

Fig. 48 On all vehicles except Sonata, the fuel filter is located on the firewall, adjacent to the master cylinder

89531g19

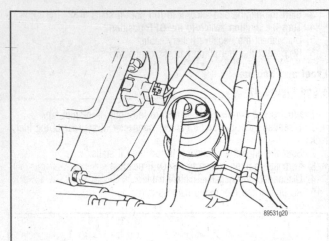

Fig. 49 The 1996–98 Elantra and Tiburon use a fuel filter with different style connectors

3. Place a rag under the fuel filter to catch any residual fuel that may leak out when the filter is removed.

4. Remove the inlet and outlet connections while holding the fuel lines stationary. Inspect the gaskets for damage and replace them as necessary.

5. Loosen the fuel filter clamp bolt.

6. Remove the filter.

7. Place the new fuel filter into the mounting bracket.

8. Tighten the fuel filter clamp bolt.

9. Connect the fuel inlet and outlet lines to the filter and tighten the banjo bolts securely.

10. Connect the negative battery cable.

11. Start the engine and check the filter connections for leaks by running the tip of your finger around each banjo bolt connection.

Sonata

▶ See Figure 50

1. Properly relieve fuel system pressure.

2. Disconnect the negative battery cable.

3. Raise and support vehicle safely.

4. Place a rag under the fuel filter to catch any residual fuel that may leak out when the filter is removed.

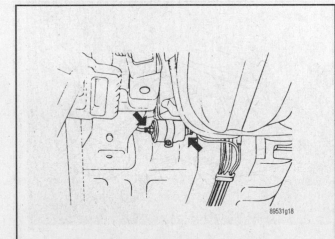

Fig. 50 On Sonata, the fuel filter is located at the rear of the vehicle, mounted to the floor pan in front of the fuel tank

5. Loosen the inlet and outlet fittings while holding the fuel lines stationary.

6. Loosen the fuel filter clamp bolt.

7. Remove the filter.

8. Place the new fuel filter into the mounting bracket.

9. Tighten the fuel filter clamp bolt.

10. Connect the fuel inlet and outlet lines to the filter and tighten the fittings to 22–29 ft. lbs. (30–34 Nm).

11. Lower the vehicle.

12. Connect the negative battery cable.

13. Start the engine and check the filter connections for leaks by running the tip of your finger around each connection.

PCV Valve

A positive crankcase ventilation (PCV) system is used to prevent pollutants (blow-by gasses) from being released into the atmosphere. The PCV system supplies fresh air to the crankcase through the air cleaner. The fresh air mixes with the gases and is passed through the PCV valve to the intake manifold. the gasses are then reburned in the combustion process. The PCV system should be inspected every 52,000 miles (84,000 km).

When removing the PCV hose, check it for obstructions by blowing through the hose

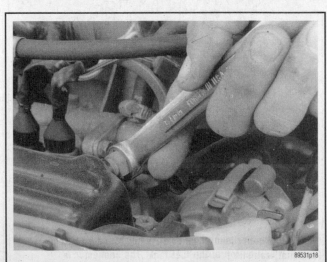

Carefully loosen the PCV valve with a wrench and remove it from the rocker cover

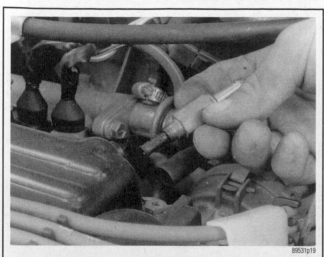

When removed, shake the PCV valve. If a rattle is heard, the valve is operational

➥For more information on the Positive Crankcase Ventilation (PCV) system, please refer to Section 4 of this manual.

REMOVAL & INSTALLATION

1. Disconnect the ventilation hose from the PCV valve.
2. Remove the valve from the rocker cover.
3. Thread the new valve into the rocker cover and tighten to 6–9 ft. lbs. (8–12 Nm).
4. Connect the ventilation hose to the valve.

Evaporative Emission Canister

◗ **See Figure 51**

The evaporative emission system stores gasoline vapors which rise from the sealed fuel tank. The system prevents these unburned hydrocarbons from polluting the atmosphere. It consists of a charcoal vapor stor-

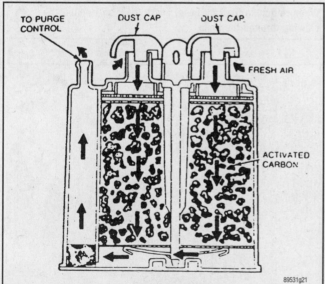

Fig. 51 Cross-sectional view of a typical activated carbon (charcoal) canister

age canister, check or purge valves and interconnecting lines. The system should be inspected every 52,000 miles (84,000 km).

➥For more information on the evaporative emission system, please refer to Section 4 of this manual.

SERVICING

Visually inspect the fuel vapor lines for loose connections, sharp bends, distortion, cracks or fuel leakage. Inspect the canister for cracks or damage. Replace components as necessary.

Battery

PRECAUTIONS

Always use caution when working on or near the battery. Never allow a tool to bridge the gap between the negative and positive battery terminals. Also, be careful not to allow a tool to provide a ground between the positive cable/terminal and any metal component on the vehicle. Either of these conditions will cause a short circuit, leading to sparks and possible personal injury.

Do not smoke, have an open flame or create sparks near a battery; the gases contained in the battery are very explosive and, if ignited, could cause severe injury or death.

All batteries, regardless of type, should be carefully secured by a battery hold-down device. If this is not done, the battery terminals or casing may crack from stress applied to the battery during vehicle operation. A battery which is not secured may allow acid to leak out, making it discharge faster; such leaking corrosive acid can also eat away at components under the hood.

Always visually inspect the battery case for cracks, leakage and corrosion. A white corrosive substance on the battery case or on nearby components would indicate a leaking or cracked battery. If the battery is cracked, it should be replaced immediately.

REMOVAL & INSTALLATION

1. Disconnect the negative and then the positive battery cables.
2. Loosen the hold-down clamp or strap retainers.
3. Remove the battery hold-down device.
4. Remove the battery from the vehicle.

Loosen the battery hold-down device retainer . . .

. . . then remove the battery hold-down device

Brush on a solution of baking soda and water to clean the tray

Remove the battery from the vehicle

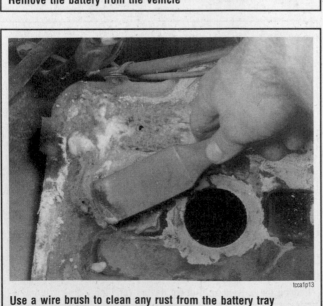
Use a wire brush to clean any rust from the battery tray

After cleaning the tray thoroughly, wash it off with some water

While the battery is removed, it is a good idea and opportunity to check the condition of the battery tray. Clear it of any debris, and check it for soundness (the battery tray can be cleaned with a baking soda and water solution). Rust should be wire brushed away, and the metal given a couple coats of anti-rust paint.

To install:

5. Install the battery and tighten the hold-down clamp or strap securely. Do not overtighten, as this can crack the battery case.

6. Connect the positive and then the negative battery cables.

GENERAL MAINTENANCE

♦ **See Figure 52**

A battery that is not sealed must be checked periodically for electrolyte level. You cannot add water to a sealed maintenance-free battery (though not all maintenance-free batteries are sealed); however, a sealed battery must also be checked for proper electrolyte level, as indicated by the color of the built-in hydrometer "eye."

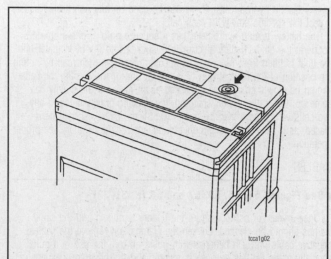

tcca1g02

Fig. 52 A typical location for the built-in hydrometer on maintenance-free batteries

Always keep the battery cables and terminals free of corrosion. Check these components about once a year. Refer to the removal, installation and cleaning procedures outlined in this section.

Keep the top of the battery clean, as a film of dirt can help completely discharge a battery that is not used for long periods. A solution of baking soda and water may be used for cleaning, but be careful to flush this off with clear water. DO NOT let any of the solution into the filler holes. Baking soda neutralizes battery acid and will de-activate a battery cell.

Batteries in vehicles which are not operated on a regular basis can fall victim to parasitic loads (small current drains which are constantly drawing current from the battery). Normal parasitic loads may drain a battery on a vehicle that is in storage and not used for 6–8 weeks. Vehicles that have additional accessories such as a cellular phone, an alarm system or other devices that increase parasitic load may discharge a battery sooner. If the vehicle is to be stored for 6–8 weeks in a secure area and the alarm system, if present, is not necessary, the negative battery cable should be disconnected at the onset of storage to protect the battery charge.

Remember that constantly discharging and recharging will shorten battery life. Take care not to allow a battery to be needlessly discharged.

BATTERY FLUID

Check the battery electrolyte level at least once a month, or more often in hot weather or during periods of extended vehicle operation. On non-sealed batteries, the level can be checked either through the case on translucent batteries or by removing the cell caps on opaque-cased types. The electrolyte level in each cell should be kept filled to the split ring inside each cell, or the line marked on the outside of the case.

If the level is low, add only distilled water through the opening until the level is correct. Each cell is separate from the others, so each must be checked and filled individually. Distilled water should be used, because the chemicals and minerals found in most drinking water are harmful to the battery and could significantly shorten its life.

If water is added in freezing weather, the vehicle should be driven several miles to allow the water to mix with the electrolyte. Otherwise, the battery could freeze.

Although some maintenance-free batteries have removable cell caps for access to the electrolyte, the electrolyte condition and level on all sealed maintenance-free batteries must be checked using the built-in hydrometer "eye." The exact type of eye varies between battery manufacturers, but most apply a sticker to the battery itself explaining the possible readings. When in doubt, refer to the battery manufacturer's instructions to interpret battery condition using the built-in hydrometer.

➡**Although the readings from built-in hydrometers found in sealed batteries may vary, a green eye usually indicates a properly charged battery with sufficient fluid level. A dark eye is normally an indicator of a battery with sufficient fluid, but one which may be low in charge. And a light or yellow eye is usually an indication that electrolyte supply has dropped below the necessary level for battery (and hydrometer) operation. In this last case, sealed batteries with an insufficient electrolyte level must usually be discarded.**

Checking the Specific Gravity

♦ See Figure 53 (p. 31)

A hydrometer is required to check the specific gravity on all batteries that are not maintenance-free. On batteries that are maintenance-free, the specific gravity is checked by observing the built-in hydrometer "eye" on the top of the battery case. Check with your battery's manufacturer for proper interpretation of its built-in hydrometer readings.

tcca1p07

On non-maintenance-free batteries, the fluid level can be checked through the case on translucent models; the cell caps must be removed on other models

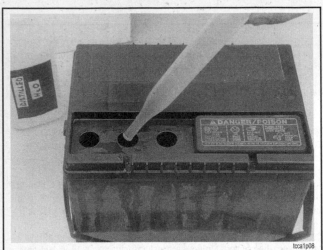

If the fluid level is low, add only distilled water through the opening until the level is correct

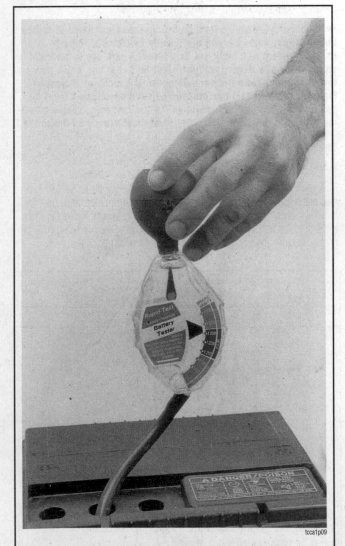

Check the specific gravity of the battery's electrolyte with a hydrometer

✳✳ CAUTION

Battery electrolyte contains sulfuric acid. If you should splash any on your skin or in your eyes, flush the affected area with plenty of clear water. If it lands in your eyes, get medical help immediately.

The fluid (sulfuric acid solution) contained in the battery cells will tell you many things about the condition of the battery. Because the cell plates must be kept submerged below the fluid level in order to operate, maintaining the fluid level is extremely important. And, because the specific gravity of the acid is an indication of electrical charge, testing the fluid can be an aid in determining if the battery must be replaced. A battery in a vehicle with a properly operating charging system should require little maintenance, but careful, periodic inspection should reveal problems before they leave you stranded.

As stated earlier, the specific gravity of a battery's electrolyte level can be used as an indication of battery charge. At least once a year, check the specific gravity of the battery. It should be between 1.20 and 1.26 on the gravity scale. Most auto supply stores carry a variety of inexpensive battery testing hydrometers. These can be used on any non-sealed battery to test the specific gravity in each cell.

The battery testing hydrometer has a squeeze bulb at one end and a nozzle at the other. Battery electrolyte is sucked into the hydrometer until the float is lifted from its seat. The specific gravity is then read by noting the position of the float. If gravity is low in one or more cells, the battery should be slowly charged and checked again to see if the gravity has come up. Generally, if after charging, the specific gravity between any two cells varies more than 50 points (0.50), the battery should be replaced, as it can no longer produce sufficient voltage to guarantee proper operation.

CABLES

▶ See Figures 54, 55, 56, 57 and 58 (p. 31–32)

Once a year (or as necessary), the battery terminals and the cable clamps should be cleaned. Loosen the clamps and remove the cables, negative cable first. On batteries with posts on top, the use of a puller specially made for this purpose is recommended. These are inexpensive and available in most auto parts stores. Side terminal battery cables are secured with a small bolt.

Clean the cable clamps and the battery terminal with a wire brush, until all corrosion, grease, etc., is removed and the metal is shiny. It is especially important to clean the inside of the clamp thoroughly (an old knife is useful here), since a small deposit of foreign material or oxidation there will prevent a sound electrical connection and inhibit either starting or charging. Special tools are available for cleaning these parts, one type for conventional top post batteries and another type for side terminal batteries. It is also a good idea to apply some dielectric grease to the terminal, as this will aid in the prevention of corrosion.

After the clamps and terminals are clean, reinstall the cables, negative cable last; DO NOT hammer the clamps onto battery posts. Tighten the clamps securely, but do not distort them. Give the clamps and terminals a thin external coating of grease after installation, to retard corrosion.

Check the cables at the same time that the terminals are cleaned. If the cable insulation is cracked or broken, or if the ends are frayed, the cable should be replaced with a new cable of the same length and gauge.

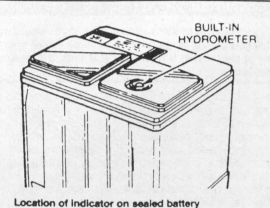

BUILT-IN HYDROMETER

Location of indicator on sealed battery

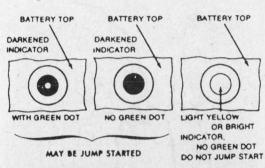

BATTERY TOP — DARKENED INDICATOR — WITH GREEN DOT

BATTERY TOP — DARKENED INDICATOR — NO GREEN DOT

MAY BE JUMP STARTED

BATTERY TOP — LIGHT YELLOW OR BRIGHT INDICATOR, NO GREEN DOT — DO NOT JUMP START

Check the appearance of the charge indicator on top of the battery before attempting a jump start; if it's not green or dark, do not jump start the car

Fig. 53 A typical sealed (maintenance-free) battery with a built-in hydrometer—NOTE that the hydrometer eye may vary between battery manufacturers; always refer to the battery's label

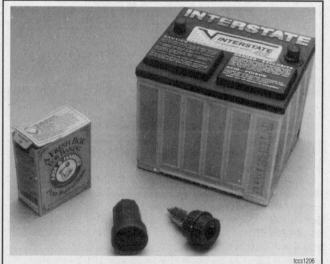

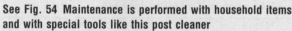

See Fig. 54 Maintenance is performed with household items and with special tools like this post cleaner

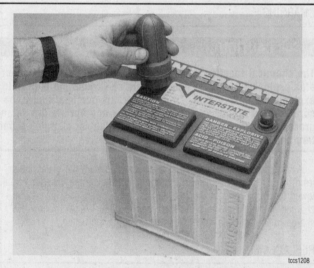

Fig. 56 Place the tool over the battery posts and twist to clean until the metal is shiny

See Fig. 55 The underside of this special battery tool has a wire brush to clean post terminals

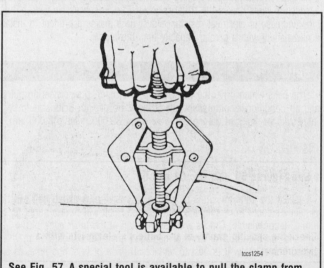

See Fig. 57 A special tool is available to pull the clamp from the post

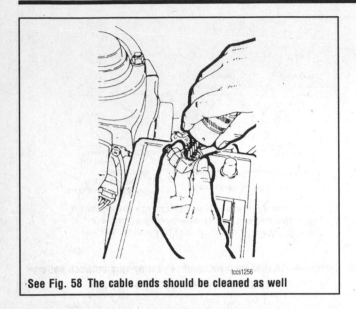

See Fig. 58 The cable ends should be cleaned as well

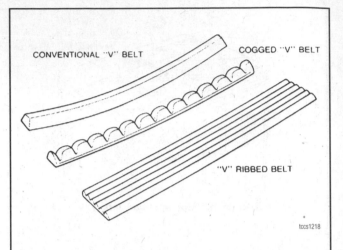

Fig. 59 There are typically 3 types of accessory drive belts found on vehicles today

CHARGING

✳✳ CAUTION

The chemical reaction which takes place in all batteries generates explosive hydrogen gas. A spark can cause the battery to explode and splash acid. To avoid serious personal injury, be sure there is proper ventilation and take appropriate fire safety precautions when connecting, disconnecting, or charging a battery and when using jumper cables.

A battery should be charged at a slow rate to keep the plates inside from getting too hot. However, if some maintenance-free batteries are allowed to discharge until they are almost "dead," they may have to be charged at a high rate to bring them back to "life." Always follow the charger manufacturer's instructions on charging the battery.

REPLACEMENT

When it becomes necessary to replace the battery, select one with an amperage rating equal to or greater than the battery originally installed. Deterioration and just plain aging of the battery cables, starter motor, and associated wires makes the battery's job harder in successive years. The slow increase in electrical resistance over time makes it prudent to install a new battery with a greater capacity than the old.

Belts

The belts which drive the water pump, alternator, power steering pump and air conditioner compressor are of the V-rib design. Belts should be inspected for signs of damage or wear every 30,000 miles (48,000 km).

INSPECTION

▶ See Figures 59, 60, 61, 62 and 63

Inspect the belts for signs of glazing or cracking. A glazed belt will be perfectly smooth from slippage, while a good belt will have a slight texture of fabric visible. Cracks will usually start at the inner edge of the belt and run outward. All worn or damaged drive belts should be replaced immediately. It is best to replace all drive belts at one time, as a preventive maintenance measure, during this service operation.

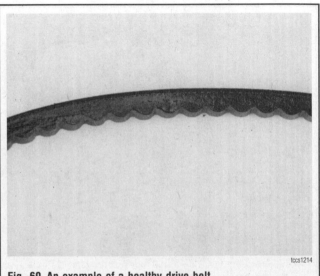

Fig. 60 An example of a healthy drive belt

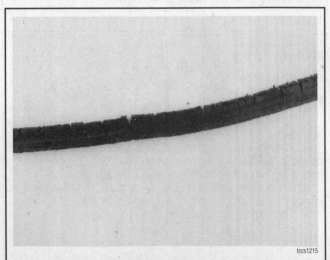

Fig. 61 Deep cracks in this belt will cause flex, building up heat that will eventually lead to belt failure

Fig. 62 The cover of this belt is worn, exposing the critical reinforcing cords to excessive wear

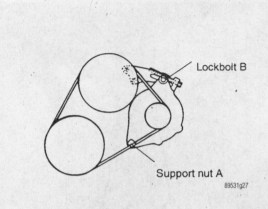

Fig. 64 Alternator support nut "A" and tension adjuster lockbolt "B" location—except Sonata

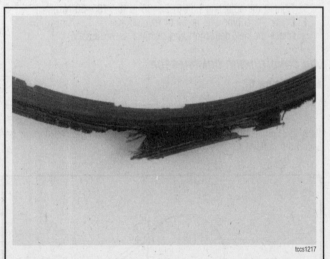

Fig. 63 Installing too wide a belt can result in serious belt wear and/or breakage

Alternator tension adjuster bolt nut "B" runs through the adjusting mechanism into the alternator case

ADJUSTING

Alternator

EXCEPT SONATA V6

▶ See Figure 64

1. Loosen the alternator support nut "A" and the tension adjuster lock-bolt "B".
2. Using the tension adjuster bolt, adjust the belt tension so the belt deflects 0.35–41 inches (9–11mm) when 77–110 lbs (350–500 N) of force is exerted on the belt midway between the pulleys.
3. Tighten the adjuster lockbolt "B" 9–11 ft. lbs. (12–15 Nm) and the alternator support bolt "A" to 14–18 ft. lbs. (20–25 Nm).
4. Check the belt deflection and readjust as necessary.

The alternator tension adjuster bolt is used to hold the tension on the alternator belt

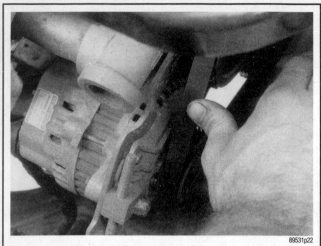

Using a finger, check the deflection on the belt. If too loose or too tight, adjust tension with the adjuster bolt

SONATA V6

♦ See Figure 65

➡A single procedure adjusts both the alternator and power steering pump belt tension on Sonata.

1. Loosen the tension pulley bolt "A".
2. Using the tension adjuster bolt, adjust the belt tension so the belt deflects 0.15–0.19 inches (4–5mm) when the belt is pressed midway between the pulleys.

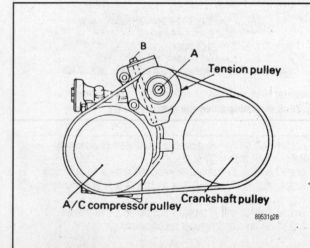

Fig. 65 Power steering pump pulley bolt "A" and tension adjuster "B" location—Sonata

3. Tighten the tension pulley bolt "A" to 28–43 ft. lbs. (30–60 Nm).
4. Check the belt deflection and readjust as necessary.

POWER STEERING PUMP

♦ See Figure 66

1. Loosen the power steering pump adjuster bolt.
2. Move the power steering pump to adjust belt tension so the belt deflects 0.24–0.35 inches (6–9mm) when pressed midway between the pulleys.

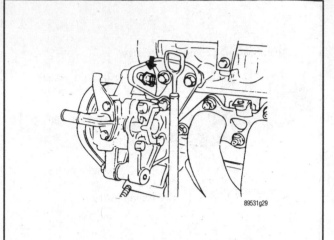

Fig. 66 Power steering pump adjuster bolt location—except Sonata V6

3. Tighten the adjusting bolt to 25–36 ft. lbs. (35–50 Nm).
4. Crank the engine one or more revolutions.
5. Check the belt deflection and readjust as necessary.

AIR CONDITIONING COMPRESSOR

♦ See Figure 67

1. Loosen the tension pulley adjusting bolt "A".
2. Adjust the belt deflection with adjustment bolt "B" so the belt deflects 0.31 inches (8mm) when pressure is exerted on the belt midway between the pulleys.

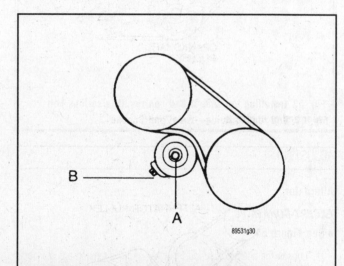

Fig. 67 Air conditioning compressor tension pulley adjusting bolt "A" and adjustment bolt "B" location

3. Tighten the tension pulley adjusting bolt "A" to 15–22 ft. lbs. (20–30 Nm).
4. Crank the engine one or more revolutions.
5. Check the belt deflection and readjust as necessary.

REMOVAL & INSTALLATION

♦ See Figures 68, 69, 70, 71 and 72

It may be necessary to remove more than one belt in order to access the desired belt. Always note belt routing for reference upon installation.

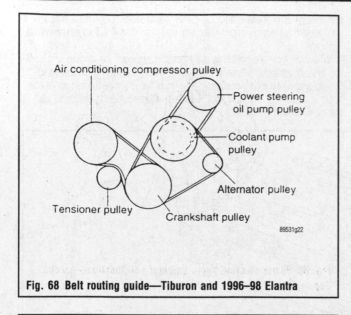

Fig. 68 Belt routing guide—Tiburon and 1996–98 Elantra

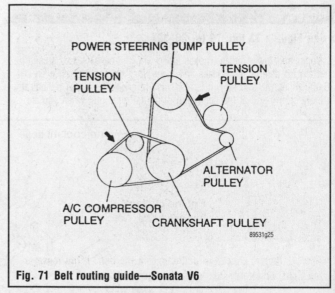

Fig. 71 Belt routing guide—Sonata V6

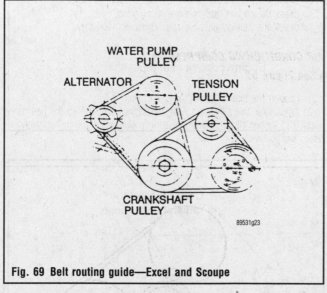

Fig. 69 Belt routing guide—Excel and Scoupe

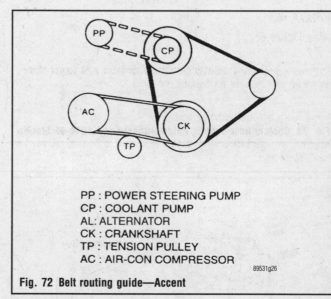

PP : POWER STEERING PUMP
CP : COOLANT PUMP
AL: ALTERNATOR
CK : CRANKSHAFT
TP : TENSION PULLEY
AC : AIR-CON COMPRESSOR

Fig. 72 Belt routing guide—Accent

1. Loosen belt tension as described in adjustment procedure.
2. Remove belt from engine.
3. Inspect pulleys for damage or wear and replace as necessary.
4. Install belt, routing as noted or as specified in belt routing illustration.
5. Ensure that the belt is properly positioned on all pulleys.
6. Adjust belt tension to proper specification.

Timing Belt

✳✳ WARNING

Timing belt maintenance is extremely important. All Hyundai models use interference-type non-freewheeling engines. Should the timing belt break in these engines, the valves in the cylinder head may come in contact with the pistons, causing potentially serious engine damage. The recommended replacement interval for timing belts is 60,000 miles (96,600 km). Refer to Section 3 for information on servicing the timing belt.

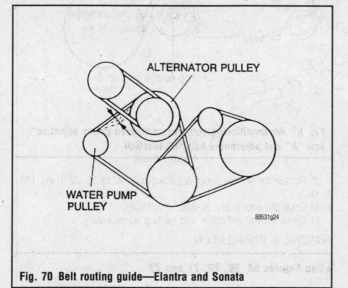

Fig. 70 Belt routing guide—Elantra and Sonata

Hoses

◆ **See Figures 73 thru 79 (p. 36–39)**

Upper and lower radiator hoses along with the heater hoses should be checked for deterioration, leaks and loose hose clamps at least every 30,000 miles (48,000 km). It is also wise to check the hoses periodically in early spring and at the beginning of the fall or winter when you are

performing other maintenance. A quick visual inspection could discover a weakened hose which might have left you stranded if it had remained unrepaired.

Whenever you are checking the hoses, make sure the engine and cooling system are cold. Visually inspect for cracking, rotting or collapsed hoses, and replace as necessary. Run your hand along the length of the hose. If a weak or swollen spot is noted when squeezing the hose wall, the hose should be replaced.

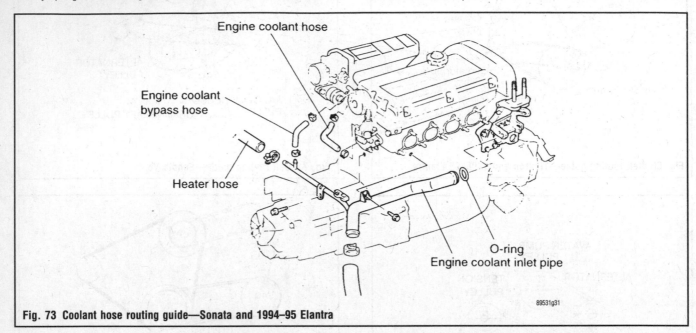

Fig. 73 Coolant hose routing guide—Sonata and 1994–95 Elantra

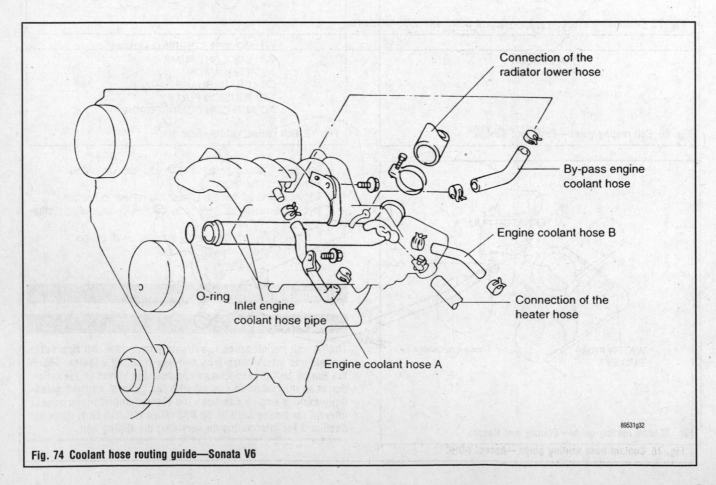

Fig. 74 Coolant hose routing guide—Sonata V6

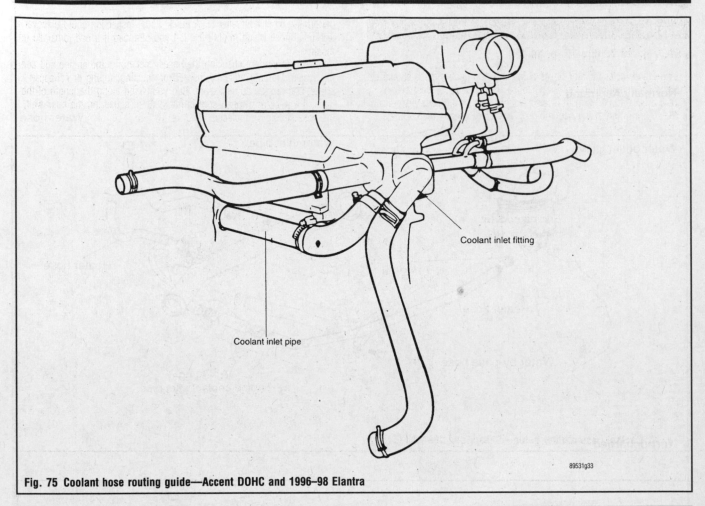

Coolant inlet fitting

Coolant inlet pipe

89531g33

Fig. 75 Coolant hose routing guide—Accent DOHC and 1996–98 Elantra

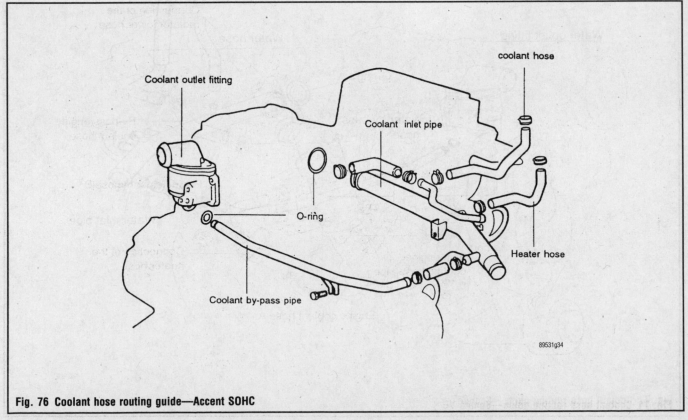

Coolant outlet fitting

coolant hose

Coolant inlet pipe

O-ring

Heater hose

Coolant by-pass pipe

89531g34

Fig. 76 Coolant hose routing guide—Accent SOHC

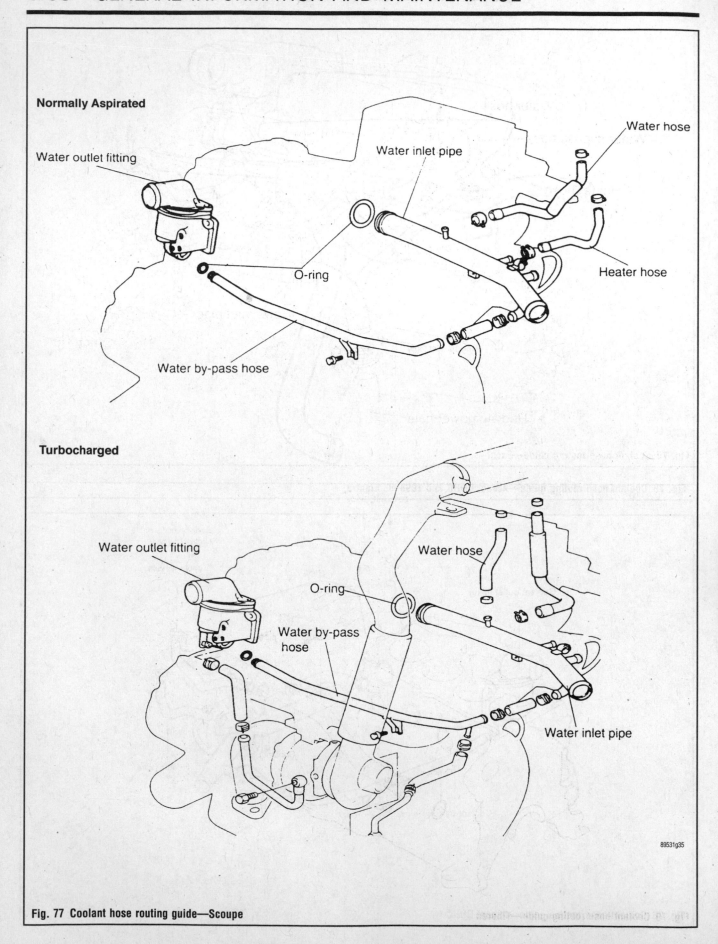

Normally Aspirated

Water outlet fitting

Water inlet pipe

Water hose

O-ring

Heater hose

Water by-pass hose

Turbocharged

Water outlet fitting

O-ring

Water hose

Water by-pass hose

Water inlet pipe

89531g35

Fig. 77 Coolant hose routing guide—Scoupe

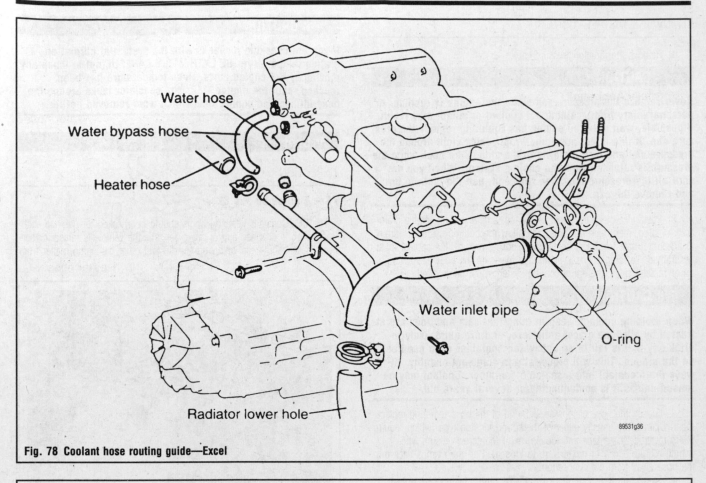

Water hose

Water bypass hose

Heater hose

Water inlet pipe

O-ring

Radiator lower hole

89531g36

Fig. 78 Coolant hose routing guide—Excel

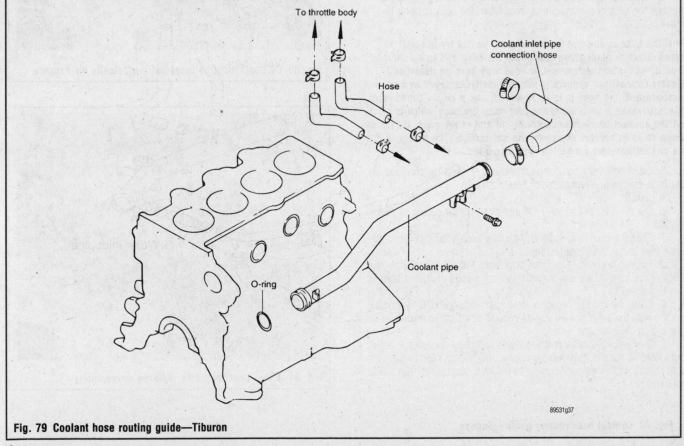

To throttle body

Coolant inlet pipe connection hose

Hose

Coolant pipe

O-ring

89531g37

Fig. 79 Coolant hose routing guide—Tiburon

REMOVAL & INSTALLATION

1. Remove the radiator pressure cap.

❋❋ CAUTION

Never remove the pressure cap while the engine is running, or personal injury from scalding hot coolant or steam may result. If possible, wait until the engine has cooled to remove the pressure cap. If this is not possible, wrap a thick cloth around the pressure cap and turn it slowly to the stop. Step back while the pressure is released from the cooling system. When you are sure all the pressure has been released, use the cloth to turn and remove the cap.

2. Position a clean container under the radiator and/or engine drain-cock or plug, then open the drain and allow the cooling system to drain to an appropriate level. For some upper hoses, only a little coolant must be drained. To remove hoses positioned lower on the engine, such as a lower radiator hose, the entire cooling system must be emptied.

❋❋ CAUTION

When draining coolant, keep in mind that cats and dogs are attracted by ethylene glycol antifreeze, and are quite likely to drink any that is left in an uncovered container or in puddles on the ground. This will prove fatal in sufficient quantity. Always drain coolant into a sealable container. Coolant may be reused unless it is contaminated or several years old.

3. Loosen the hose clamps at each end of the hose requiring replacement. Clamps are usually either of the spring tension type (which require pliers to squeeze the tabs and loosen) or of the screw tension type (which require screw or hex drivers to loosen). Pull the clamps back on the hose away from the connection.

4. Twist, pull and slide the hose off the fitting, taking care not to damage the neck of the component from which the hose is being removed.

➡If the hose is stuck at the connection, do not try to insert a screwdriver or other sharp tool under the hose end in an effort to free it, as the connection and/or hose may become damaged. Heater connections especially may be easily damaged by such a procedure. If the hose is to be replaced, use a single-edged razor blade to make a slice along the portion of the hose which is stuck on the connection, perpendicular to the end of the hose. Do not cut deep so as to prevent damaging the connection. The hose can then be peeled from the connection and discarded.

5. Clean both hose mounting connections. Inspect the condition of the hose clamps and replace them, if necessary.

To install:

6. Dip the ends of the new hose into clean engine coolant to ease installation.

7. Slide the clamps over the replacement hose, then slide the hose ends over the connections into position.

8. Position and secure the clamps at least ¼in. (6.35mm) from the ends of the hose. Make sure they are located beyond the raised bead of the connector.

9. Close the radiator or engine drains and properly refill the cooling system with the clean drained engine coolant or a suitable mixture of ethylene glycol coolant and water.

10. If available, install a pressure tester and check for leaks. If a pressure tester is not available, run the engine until normal operating temperature is reached (allowing the system to naturally pressurize), then check for leaks.

❋❋ CAUTION

If you are checking for leaks with the system at normal operating temperature, BE EXTREMELY CAREFUL not to touch any moving or hot engine parts. Once temperature has been reached, shut the engine OFF, and check for leaks around the hose fittings and connections which were removed earlier.

CV-Boots

INSPECTION

◆ **See Figures 80 and 81**

The CV (Constant Velocity) boots should be checked for damage each time the oil is changed and/or any other time the vehicle is raised for service. These boots keep water, grime, dirt and other damaging matter from

Fig. 80 CV-boots must be inspected periodically for damage

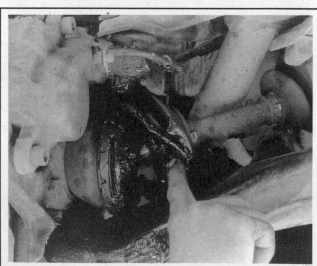

Fig. 81 A torn boot should be replaced immediately

entering the CV-joints. Any contamination could cause early CV-joint failure which can be expensive to repair. Heavy grease thrown around the inside of the front wheel(s) and on the brake caliper/drum can be an indication of a torn boot. Thoroughly check the boots for missing clamps and tears. If the boot is damaged, it should be replaced immediately. For more information on CV-Boots, please refer to Section 7 of this manual.

Spark Plugs

♦ See Figure 82

A typical spark plug consists of a metal shell surrounding a ceramic insulator. A metal electrode extends downward through the center of the insulator and protrudes a small distance. Located at the end of the plug and attached to the side of the outer metal shell is the side electrode. The side electrode bends in at a 90° angle so that its tip is just past and parallel to the tip of the center electrode. The distance between these two electrodes (measured in thousandths of an inch or hundredths of a millimeter) is called the spark plug gap.

The spark plug does not produce a spark but instead provides a gap across which the current can arc. The coil produces anywhere from 20,000 to 50,000 volts (depending on the type and application) which travels through the wires to the spark plugs. The current passes along the center electrode and jumps the gap to the side electrode, and in doing so, ignites the air/fuel mixture in the combustion chamber.

SPARK PLUG HEAT RANGE

♦ See Figure 83

Spark plug heat range is the ability of the plug to dissipate heat. The longer the insulator (or the farther it extends into the engine), the hotter the plug will operate; the shorter the insulator (the closer the electrode is to the block's cooling passages) the cooler it will operate. A plug that absorbs little heat and remains too cool will quickly accumulate deposits of oil and carbon since it is not hot enough to burn them off. This leads to plug fouling and consequently to misfiring. A plug that absorbs too much heat will have no deposits but, due to the excessive heat, the electrodes will burn away quickly and might possibly lead to preignition or other ignition problems. Preignition takes place when plug tips get so hot that they glow sufficiently to ignite the air/fuel mixture before the actual spark occurs. This early ignition will usually cause a pinging during low speeds and heavy loads.

The general rule of thumb for choosing the correct heat range when picking a spark plug is: if most of your driving is long distance, high speed travel, use a colder plug; if most of your driving is stop and go,

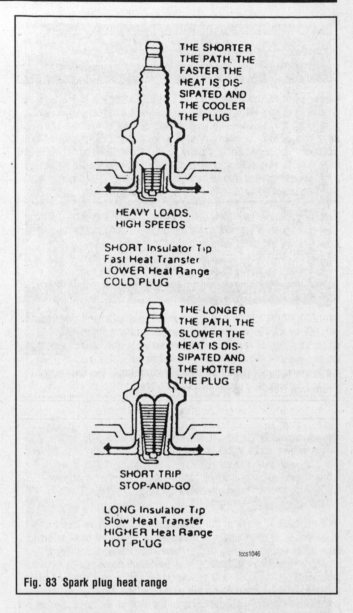

Fig. 83 Spark plug heat range

use a hotter plug. Original equipment plugs are generally a good compromise between the 2 styles and most people never have the need to change their plugs from the factory-recommended heat range.

REMOVAL & INSTALLATION

Hyundai recommends that spark plugs be replaced every 24,000 miles (40,000 km). In normal operation plug gap increases about 0.001 in. (0.025mm) for every 2500 miles (4000 km). As the gap increases, the plug's voltage requirement also increases. It requires a greater voltage to jump the wider gap and about two to three times as much voltage to fire the plug at high speeds than at idle. The improved air/fuel ratio control of modern fuel injection combined with the higher voltage output of modern ignition systems will often allow an engine to run significantly longer on a set of standard spark plugs, but keep in mind that efficiency will drop as the gap widens (along with fuel economy and power).

When you're removing spark plugs, work on one at a time. Don't start by removing the plug wires all at once, because, unless you number them, they may become mixed up. Take a minute before you begin and number the wires with tape.

1. Disconnect the negative battery cable, and if the vehicle has been run recently, allow the engine to thoroughly cool.

2. Carefully twist the spark plug wire boot to loosen it, then pull up-

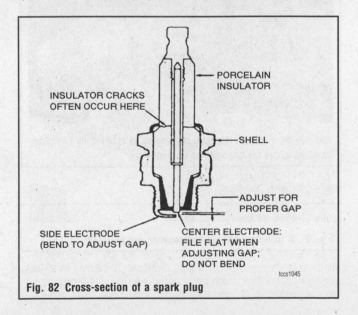

Fig. 82 Cross-section of a spark plug

A slight twist on the spark plug boot will allow the wire to be removed from the spark plug more easily

Using a spark plug socket equipped with a rubber insert, carefully remove the spark plug from the engine

ward and remove the boot from the plug. Be sure to pull on the boot and not on the wire, otherwise the connector located inside the boot may become separated.

3. Using compressed air, blow any water or debris from the spark plug well to assure that no harmful contaminants are allowed to enter the combustion chamber when the spark plug is removed. If compressed air is not available, use a rag or a brush to clean the area.

➡ Remove the spark plugs when the engine is cold, if possible, to prevent damage to the threads. If removal of the plugs is difficult, apply a few drops of penetrating oil or silicone spray to the area around the base of the plug, and allow it a few minutes to work.

4. Using a spark plug socket that is equipped with a rubber insert to properly hold the plug, turn the spark plug counterclockwise to loosen and remove the spark plug from the bore.

⁂ WARNING

Be sure not to use a flexible extension on the socket. Use of a flexible extension may allow a shear force to be applied to the plug. A shear force could break the plug off in the cylinder head, leading to costly and frustrating repairs.

To install:

5. Inspect the spark plug boot for tears or damage. If a damaged boot is found, the spark plug wire must be replaced.

6. Using a spark plug gapping tool, check and adjust the spark plug gap. When using the tool, the proper size should pass between the electrodes with a slight drag. The next larger size should not be able to pass while the next smaller size should pass freely.

7. Lubricate the threads of the spark plug with oil (cast iron cylinder head) or anti-seize compound (aluminum cylinder head). Carefully thread the plug into the bore by hand. If resistance is felt before the plug is almost completely threaded, back the plug out and begin threading again. In small, hard to reach areas, an old spark plug wire and boot could be used as a threading tool. The boot will hold the plug while you twist the end of the wire and the wire is supple enough to twist before it would allow the plug to crossthread.

⁂ WARNING

Do not use the spark plug socket to thread the plugs. Always carefully thread the plug by hand or using an old plug wire to prevent the possibility of crossthreading and damaging the cylinder head bore.

8. Carefully tighten the spark plug to 15–21 ft. lbs. (20–30 Nm).

9. Apply a small amount of silicone dielectric compound to the end of the spark plug lead or inside the spark plug boot to prevent sticking, then install the boot to the spark plug and push until it clicks into place. The click may be felt or heard, then gently pull back on the boot to assure proper contact.

You can gain insight into how an engine is running by checking its spark plugs for deposits or damage

INSPECTION & GAPPING

◆ See Figures 84 thru 92 (p. 43–46)

Check the plugs for deposits and wear. If they are not going to be replaced, clean the plugs thoroughly. Remember that any kind of deposit will decrease the efficiency of the plug. Plugs can be cleaned on a spark plug cleaning machine, which can sometimes be found in service stations, or you can do an acceptable job of cleaning with a stiff brush. If

TCCS2135

Fig. 84 A normally worn spark plug should have light tan or gray deposits on the firing tip

TCCS2136

Fig. 85 A carbon fouled plug, identified by soft, sooty, black deposits, may indicate an improperly tuned vehicle. Check the air cleaner, ignition components and engine control system

the plugs are cleaned, the electrodes must be filed flat. Use an ignition points file, not an emery board or the like, which will leave deposits. The electrodes must be filed perfectly flat with sharp edges; rounded edges reduce the spark plug voltage by as much as 50%.

Check spark plug gap before installation. The ground electrode (the L-shaped one connected to the body of the plug) must be parallel to the center electrode and the specified size wire gauge (please refer to the Tune-Up Specifications chart for details) must pass between the electrodes with a slight drag.

➡**NEVER adjust the gap on a used platinum type spark plug.**

Always check the gap on new plugs as they are not always set correctly at the factory. Do not use a flat feeler gauge when measuring the gap on a used plug, because the reading may be inaccurate. A round-wire type gapping tool is the best way to check the gap. The correct gauge should pass through the electrode gap with a slight drag. If you're in doubt, try one size smaller and one larger. The smaller gauge should go through easily, while the larger one shouldn't go through at all. Wire gapping tools usually have a bending tool attached. Use that to adjust the side electrode until the proper distance is obtained. Absolutely never attempt to bend the center electrode. Also, be careful not to bend the side electrode too far or too often as it may weaken and break off within the engine, requiring removal of the cylinder head to retrieve it.

TCCS2137

Fig. 86 A physically damaged spark plug may be evidence of severe detonation in that cylinder. Watch that cylinder carefully between services, as a continued detonation will not only damage the plug, but could also damage the engine

TCCS2138

Fig. 87 An oil fouled spark plug indicates an engine with worn piston rings and/or bad valve seals allowing excessive oil to enter the chamber

Spark Plug Wires

♦ See Figure 93 (p. 46)

REMOVAL & INSTALLATION

1. Label each spark plug wire and make a note of its routing.

➡ Don't rely on wiring diagrams or sketches for spark plug wire routing. Improper arrangement of spark plug wires will induce voltage between wires, causing misfiring and surging. Be careful to arrange spark plug wires properly.

2. Starting with the longest wire, disconnect the spark plug wire from the spark plug and then from the distributor or coil pack.

To install:

3. If replacing the spark plug wires, match the old wire with an appropriately sized wire in the new set.

4. Lubricate the boots and terminals with dielectric grease and install the wire on the distributor or coil pack. Make sure the wire snaps into place.

5. Route the wire in the exact path as the original and connect the wire to the spark plug.

6. Repeat the process for each remaining wire, working from the longest wire to the shortest.

Fig. 88 This spark plug has been left in the engine too long, as evidenced by the extreme gap—Plugs with such an extreme gap can cause misfiring and stumbling accompanied by a noticeable lack of power

Fig. 89 A bridged or almost bridged spark plug, identified by a build-up between the electrodes caused by excessive carbon or oil build-up on the plug

TESTING

◆ See Figures 94 and 95 (p. 47)

Spark plug wires should be inspected at every tune-up/safety inspection. Visually check the spark plug wires for burns, cuts or breaks in the insulation. Check the boots and the nipples on the distributor cap and/or coil pack. Replace any damaged wiring.

Every 30,000 miles (48,000 km) or 30 months, the resistance of the wires should be checked with an ohmmeter. Wires with excessive resistance will cause misfiring, and may make the engine difficult to start in damp weather.

To check resistance on distributor equipped engines, disconnect the distributor cap from the distributor and disconnect the spark plug wire from spark plug. Using a digital ohmmeter, measure the resistance between the terminal inside the distributor cap and the terminal at the spark plug end of the wire. Resistance should be LESS than 10,000 ohms per foot of wire. If resistance is not within specification, replace the wire.

➡️**If one spark plug wire is found to be out of specification, it is a good idea to replace the entire set.**

To check resistance on distributorless ignition engines, disconnect the spark plug wire from both the coil pack and the spark plug. Using a digi-

Fig. 90 A variety of tools and gauges should be used for spark plug gapping and installation

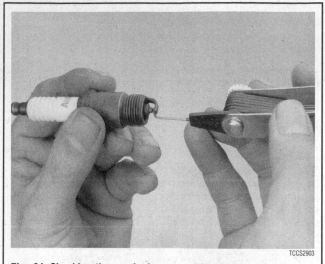

Fig. 91 Checking the spark plug gap with a feeler gauge

Spark plug wires should be routed so that they do not touch or cross each other at less than a 45 degree angle

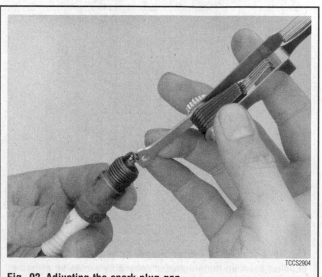

Fig. 92 Adjusting the spark plug gap

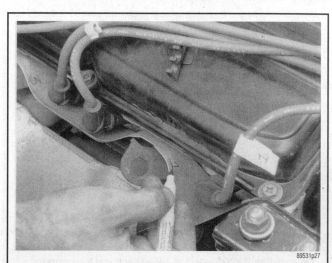

Label each spark plug wire with its corresponding cylinder number . . .

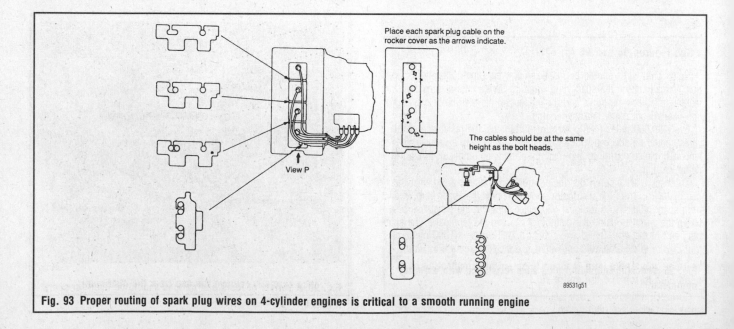

Fig. 93 Proper routing of spark plug wires on 4-cylinder engines is critical to a smooth running engine

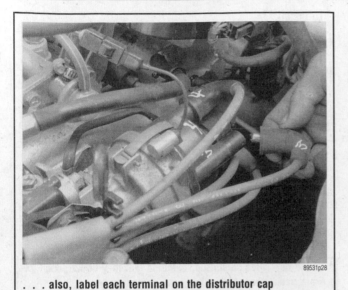

. . . also, label each terminal on the distributor cap

tal ohmmeter, measure the resistance between the coil end terminal and the spark plug end terminal. Resistance should be LESS than 10,000 ohms per foot of wire. If resistance is not within specification, replace the wire.

Distributor Cap and Rotor

REMOVAL & INSTALLATION

1. Disconnect the negative battery cable.
2. Label and disconnect the spark plug wires from the distributor cap.

➡**Depending on the reason for removing the distributor cap, it may make more sense to leave the spark plug wires attached. This is handy if you are testing spark plug wires or if removal was necessary to access other components and wire play allows you to reposition the cap out of the way.**

3. Disengage the two spring clips or remove the two attaching screws attaching the cap to the distributor.
4. Remove the cap and rotor from the distributor.

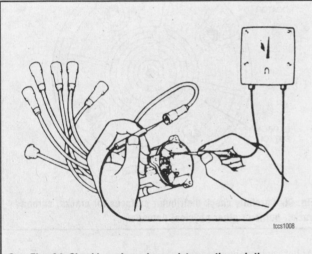

See Fig. 94 Checking plug wire resistance through the distributor cap with an ohmmeter

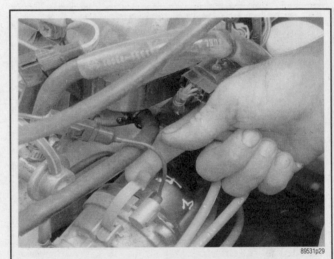

To remove the distributor cap, disengage the clips on the side of the cap . . .

Fig. 95 Checking individual plug wire resistance with a digital ohmmeter

. . . then carefully remove the cap from the distributor

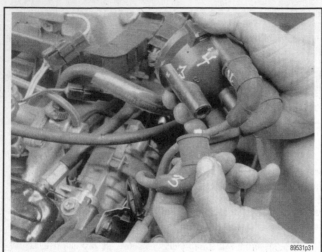

As necessary, remove the wires from the distributor cap. A small twist makes wire removal easier

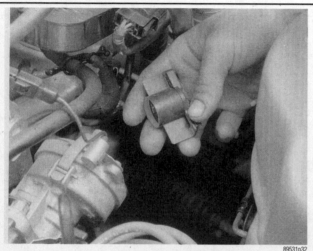

The distributor rotor is removed by simply pulling it straight off the shaft

To install:

5. Align the rotor on the distributor shaft and install by pressing into place.

6. Align the distributor cap on the distributor and attach using the spring clips.

7. Connect the spark plug wires to their proper terminals.

8. Connect the negative battery cable.

INSPECTION

♦ **See Figures 96 and 97**

Clean the distributor cap and rotor. Carefully check all surfaces for cracks, carbon tracks, burns or other physical damage. Make sure the carbon button is free of damage. Check the cap terminals for dirt or corrosion. Check the rotor blade for and spring closely for damage. Replace components as necessary.

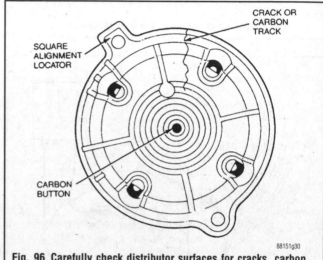

Fig. 96 Carefully check distributor surfaces for cracks, carbon tracks, burns or other physical damage

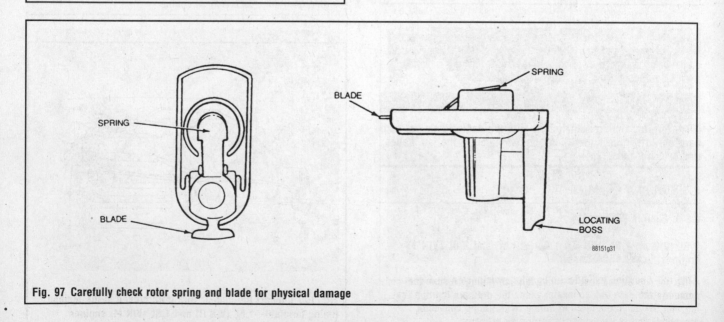

Fig. 97 Carefully check rotor spring and blade for physical damage

Ignition Timing

GENERAL INFORMATION

➡No periodic adjustment of the ignition timing is necessary for any of the vehicles covered by this manual. However, the ignition system used on the 1.5L (VIN J), 1.6L (VIN R), 1.8L (VIN M) AND 3.0L (VIN T) engines does allow for adjustment, should the distributor be removed or otherwise disturbed.

Ignition timing is the measurement, in degrees of crankshaft rotation, of the point at which the spark plugs fire in each of the cylinders. It is measured in degrees before or after Top Dead Center (TDC) of the compression stroke.

Ideally, the air/fuel mixture in the cylinder will be ignited by the spark plug just as the piston passes TDC of the compression stroke. If this happens, the piston will be at the beginning the power stroke just as the compressed and ignited air/fuel mixture forces the piston down and turns the crankshaft. Because it takes a fraction of a second for the spark plug to ignite the mixture in the cylinder, the spark plug must fire a little before the piston reaches TDC. Otherwise, the mixture will not be completely ignited as the piston passes TDC and the full power of the explosion will not be used by the engine.

The timing measurement is given in degrees of crankshaft rotation before the piston reaches TDC (BTDC). If the setting for the ignition timing is 5 BTDC, each spark plug must fire 5 degrees before each piston reaches TDC. This only holds true, however, when the engine is at idle speed.

As the engine speed increases, the pistons go faster. The spark plugs have to ignite the fuel even sooner if it is to be completely ignited when the piston reaches TDC. On all engines covered in this manual, spark timing changes are accomplished electronically by the Electronic Control Module (ECM) based on input from engine sensors.

If the ignition is set too far advanced (BTDC), the ignition and expansion of the fuel in the cylinder will occur too soon and tend to force the piston down while it is still traveling up. This causes engine ping. If the ignition spark is set too far retarded after TDC (ATDC), the piston will have already started on its way down when the fuel is ignited. The piston will be forced down for only a portion of its travel, resulting in poor engine performance and lack of power.

Timing marks or scales can be found on the rim of the crankshaft pulley and the timing cover. The marks on the pulley correspond to the position of the piston in the No. 1 cylinder. A stoboscopic (dynamic) timing light is hooked onto the No. 1 cylinder spark plug wire. Every time the spark plug fires, the timing light flashes. By aiming the light at the timing marks while the engine is running, the exact position of the piston within the cylinder can be easily read (the flash of light makes the mark on the pulley appear to be standing still). Proper timing is indicated when the mark and scale are in specified alignment.

✳✳ CAUTION

When making timing adjustments with the engine running, take care not to get the timing light wires tangled in the fan blades and/or drive belts.

INSPECTION & ADJUSTMENT

◆ See Figures 98 thru 104

1.5L (VIN J), 1.6L (VIN R), 1.8L (VIN M) and 3.0L (VIN T) Engines

➡Do not use a scan tool to check ignition timing. A scan tool connected to the data link connector reads the ordinary ignition timing, not the basic the ignition timing (with timing connector grounded) that is necessary to set timing properly.

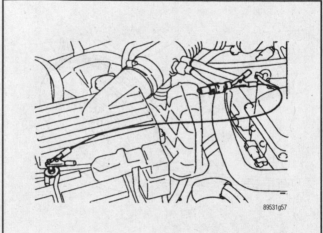

Fig. 98 Connect the jumper wire from ground to the ignition timing terminal—1.5L (VIN J) engine

Fig. 99 Connect the jumper wire from ground to the ignition timing terminal—3.0L (VIN R) engine

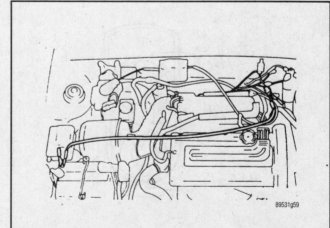

Fig. 100 Connect the jumper wire from ground to the ignition timing terminal—1.6L (VIN R) and 1.8L (VIN M) engines

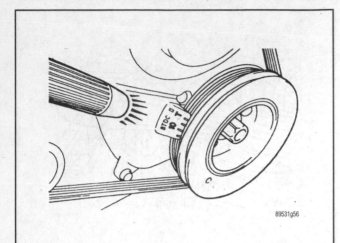

Fig. 101 Aim the timing light at the timing marks or scale, found on the rim of the crankshaft pulley and timing cover

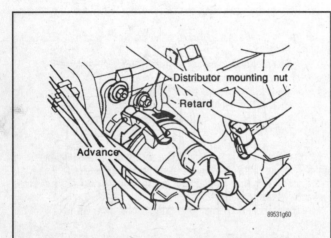

Fig. 102 Loosen the distributor hold-down nut and turn the distributor clockwise to retard or counterclockwise to advance the timing—1.5L (VIN J) engine

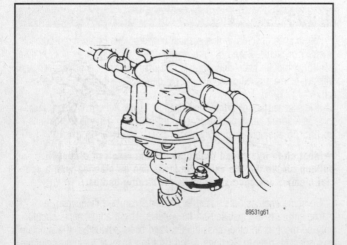

Fig. 103 Loosen the distributor hold-down nut and turn the distributor to adjust the timing—3.0L (VIN R) engine

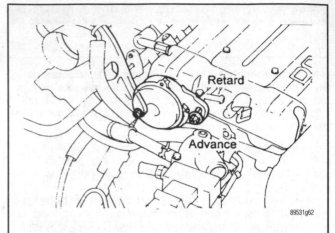

Fig. 104 Loosen the crankshaft position sensor hold-down nut and turn the sensor counterclockwise to retard or clockwise to advance the timing —1.6L (VIN R) and 1.8L (VIN M) engines

1. Place the vehicle in **P** or **N** with the emergency brake applied and the drive wheels blocked.

2. Start the engine and let it reach normal operating temperature. Make sure all accessories are off.

3. Connect a suitable tachometer and timing light to the engine, as per the manufacturers' instructions.

4. On 1.6L (VIN R) and 1.8L (VIN M) engines, increase engine speed to 2,000–3,000 rpm for 5 seconds, then allow engine to idle for 2 minutes

5. Check that the idle speed is within the specified rpm range and adjust as necessary.

6. Stop the engine and connect a jumper wire from the ignition timing adjustment connector (located at the rear of the engine compartment) to ground.

7. Start engine and allow it to idle.

8. Following the manufacturer's instructions, aim the timing light and check the basic ignition timing. As the light flashes, note the position of the mark on the crankshaft pulley against the scale on the timing cover. Basic timing (with the connector grounded) should be 3–7 degrees BTDC.

9. If timing is not within specification, loosen the distributor hold-down nut and turn the distributor as needed to obtain a proper basic timing.

10. Tighten the distributor hold-down nut to 7–9 ft. lbs. (10–13 Nm).

11. Recheck the basic timing and readjust as necessary.

12. Stop the engine and remove the jumper wire. Be sure to remove the tachometer and timing light.

Valve Lash

All engines covered in this manual, except the 1.5L (VIN J) and 1.5L (VIN E), use hydraulic valve lash adjusters. No periodic valve lash adjustments are necessary or possible on these engines. If the engine is determined to have a valve tap, a complete inspection of the valve train must be made to determine the faulty components.

The 1.5L (VIN J) and 1.5L (VIN E) engines use manual valve lifters which require periodic adjustment.

Valve adjustment determines how far the valves enter the cylinder and how long they stay open and closed. If the valve clearance is too loose (large), part of the lift of the camshaft will be used in removing the excessive clearance. Consequently, the valve will not be opening as far as it should. If the valve clearance is too tight (small), the intake valve and the exhaust valves will open too far and they will not fully seat on the cylinder head when they close.

Improper valve adjustment can have several effects on engine performance. If valve adjustment is too loose, the valve train components will emit a tapping sound as they take up the excessive clearance. Engine performance will be poor because the valves are not opening fully and allowing the proper amount of gases to flow into and out of the engine.

If valve adjustment is too tight, the valves may not seat against the cylinder head. The engine will run poorly because of the gases escaping from the combustion chamber and damage to valve train components may result due to overheating.

ADJUSTMENT

♦ See Figure 105

1.5L (VIN J) and 1.5L (VIN E) Engines

1. Run the engine until it reaches normal operating temperature and then turn it OFF.
2. Remove the spark plug wires from their clips on the rocker cover.
3. Remove the rocker cover bolts and carefully lift the rocker cover off the cylinder head.
4. Using a torque wrench, ensure all cylinder head bolts are all tightened to specification.

On this engine, intake valves are at the top, near the intake manifold, and exhaust valves at the bottom

Adjust the valve lash by unlocking the nut, turning the screw and testing with a feeler gauge

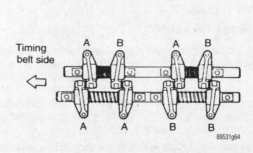

Fig. 105 Adjust the valves marked "A" when the No. 1 cylinder is at TDC. Adjust the valves marked "B" when the No. 4 cylinder is at TDC

5. Remove the spark plugs to make it easier to turn the engine manually.
6. Turn the crankshaft pulley to bring the No. 1 piston to TDC of the compression stroke.
7. Adjust the valves marked "A" in the illustration, using a feeler gauge.
8. Valve clearance should be as follows:
   a. 1.5L (VIN J) engine—0.006 in. (0.15mm) Intake, 0.010 in. (0.25mm) Exhaust
   b. 1.5L (VIN E) engine—0.010 in. (0.25mm) Intake, 0.012 in. (0.30mm) Exhaust
9. A feeler gauge of the proper size should fit between the rocker arm and the tip of the valve with a slight drag. If the clearance is not correct, loosen the locknut and turn the adjusting screw to obtain the proper clearance. Tighten the lock nut securely.
10. Turn the crankshaft pulley to bring the No. 4 piston to TDC of the compression stroke.
11. Adjust the valves marked "B" in the illustration, using a feeler gauge.
12. Using a new gasket and the proper adhesive, install the rocker cover and tighten bolts to 48–60 inch lbs. (5.4–6.8 Nm)
13. Start the engine and check idle speed. Readjust as necessary.

Idle Speed and Mixture Adjustments

All engines covered in this manual utilize sophisticated multi-port fuel injection systems. Based on information from various sensors, an engine control computer constantly adjusts and maintains proper idle speed and mixture to meet driving conditions. No periodic adjustments are necessary.

If idle speed is not within specification, check the spark plugs, injectors, idle speed control actuator, compression and general engine tune-up prior to attempting adjustments.

➡Most often idle speed problems are the result of a deposit buildup on the throttle valve. Deposits can be cleaned with a special cleaner designed specifically for throttle bodies.

On some engines, idle speed adjustments can be made when replacement parts are installed on the vehicle. These adjustments should only be made if all other possibilities have been exhausted. If a problem is suspected, refer to Sections 4 and 5 of this manual for more information.

ADJUSTMENT

1.5L (VIN J) Engine

▶ See Figures 106 and 107

1. Warm the engine to operating temperature. Ensure the lights, electric cooling fan and accessories are off. The transaxle should be in **P** or **N.** The steering wheel should be in the straight ahead position for vehicles with power steering.

2. Install a tachometer by disconnecting the noise filter connector and installing a special tool (SST 09273-24000), or equivalent, between them. Connect the tachometer to the special tool.

➡**A scan tool may be connected to the diagnostic connector in the fuse box to read engine rpm if a tachometer and special tool are not available.**

3. Start the engine and allow it to idle.

4. Run the engine for 5 seconds or more at 2,000–3,000 rpm. Then allow the engine to idle for 2 minutes.

5. Check and note the engine idle speed.

6. If idle speed is not within specification, first check for proper ignition timing. If ignition timing is within specification, proceed as follows.

7. Loosen the accelerator cable.

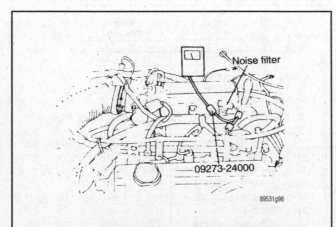

Fig. 106 Install a tachometer by detaching the noise filter connector and installing a special tool (SST 09273-24000), or equivalent, between them. Connect the tachometer to the special tool

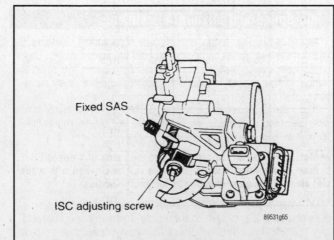

Fig. 107 Fixed Speed Adjusting Screw (SAS) and Idle Speed Control (ISC) adjusting screw locations—1.5L (VIN J) engine

8. Turn the ignition switch **ON** but do not start the engine. Leave the key in this position for at least 15 seconds. Check to see that the Idle Speed Control (ISC) servo is fully retracted to the curb idle position.

➡**When the ignition switch is turned to the ON position, the ISC plunger extends to the fast idle position opening. After 15 seconds, it retracts to the fully closed (curb idle) position.**

9. Turn the ignition switch **OFF.**

10. Disconnect the ISC motor connector.

11. In order to prevent the throttle valve from sticking, open it 2 or 3 times, then allow it to click shut. Loosen the fixed Speed Adjusting Screw (SAS) sufficiently.

12. Start the engine and allow it to run at idle speed. Turn the ISC adjusting screw to obtain proper idle speed.

13. Tighten the fixed SAS until the engine speed starts to increase. Then, loosen the screw until the engine speed ceases to drop (touch point) and loosen an additional ½ turn.

14. Turn the ignition switch **OFF.**

15. Turn the ignition switch **ON** but do not start the engine.

16. Check Throttle Position Sensor (TPS) output voltage. If voltage is not within specification, adjust TPS.

17. Turn the ignition switch **OFF** and adjust the accelerator cable.

18. Connect the ISC motor connector.

19. Start the engine and check to be sure that the idle speed is correct.

20. Turn the ignition switch **OFF,** disconnect the negative battery cable for 15 seconds and re-connect. This will erase the data stored in memory during ISC adjustment.

1.6L (VIN R) and 1.8L (VIN M) Engines

▶ See Figures 108 and 109

1. Warm the engine to operating temperature. Ensure that the lights, electric cooling fan and accessories are off. The transaxle should be in **P** or **N.** The steering wheel should be in the straight ahead position for vehicles with power steering.

2. Install a tachometer by disconnecting the noise filter connector and installing a special tool (SST 09273-24000), or equivalent, between them. Connect the tachometer to the special tool.

➡**A scan tool may be connected to the diagnostic connector in the fuse box to read engine rpm if a tachometer and special tool are not available.**

3. Start the engine and allow it to idle.

4. Check and adjust basic ignition timing to specification. Leave the ignition timing adjustment terminal grounded.

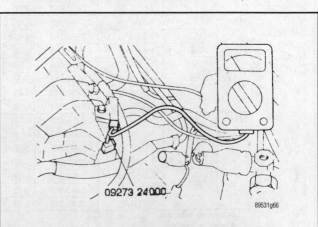

Fig. 108 Install a tachometer by detaching the noise filter connector and installing a special tool (SST 09273-24000), or equivalent, between them. Connect the tachometer to the special tool

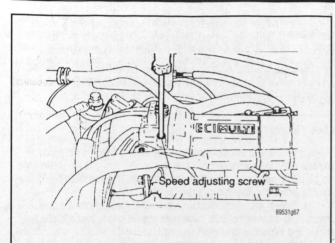

Fig. 109 Turn the Speed Adjusting Screw (SAS) until proper idle speed is obtained—1.6L (VIN R), 1.8L (VIN M) and 2.0L (VIN P) engines

5. Check and note basic idle speed.

6. If idle speed is not within specification, loosen the accelerator cable.

7. Run the engine for 5 seconds or more at 2,000–3,000 rpm and them allow it to idle for 2 minutes.

8. Check and note the engine idle speed.

➡️**If the engine stalls or engine speed is low, check for deposits on the throttle valve area. Clean deposits with throttle body cleaner.**

9. If idle speed is not within specification, adjust the Speed Adjusting Screw (SAS) until proper idle speed is obtained.

➡️**If idle speed is higher than specification, even with the SAS fully closed, check whether the idle switch has been previously adjusted. If the switch has been moved, re-adjust the idle switch to proper specification.**

10. Turn the ignition switch **OFF**.

11. Disconnect the scan tool or tachometer. Unground the data link connector and ignition timing connector, as necessary.

12. Start the engine and allow it to idle for 10 minutes or more. Check for proper idle.

GASOLINE ENGINE TUNE-UP SPECIFICATIONS

Year	Engine ID/VIN		Engine Displacement Liters (cc)	Spark Plugs Gap (in.)	Ignition Timing (deg.) MT	AT	Fuel Pump (psi)	Idle Speed (rpm) MT	AT	Valve Clearance In. ⑨	Ex. ⑨
1994	J		1.5 (1468)	0.039-0.043	3-7B	3-7B	48	600-800	600-800	0.006	0.010
	E		1.5 (1495)	0.039-0.043	4-14B	4-14B	43	700-900	700-900	0.010	0.012
	E		1.5 (1495)	0.039-0.043	4-14B	4-14B	43	700-900	700-900	0.010	0.012
	R		1.6 (1595)	0.039-0.043	3-7B	3-7B	48	650-850	650-850	HYD	HYD
	M		1.8 (1836)	0.039-0.043	3-7B	3-7B	48	600-800	600-800	HYD	HYD
	P		2.0 (1997)	0.039-0.043	3-7B	3-7B	48	650-850	650-850	HYD	HYD
	T		3.0 (2972)	0.039-0.043	3-7B	3-7B	48	600-800	600-800	HYD	HYD
1995	E		1.5 (1495)	0.039-0.043	4-14B	4-14B	43	700-900	700-900	0.010	0.012
	E		1.5 (1495)	0.039-0.043	4-14B	4-14B	43	700-900	700-900	0.010	0.012
	K		1.5 (1495)	0.039-0.043	6-16B	6-16B	43	700-900	700-900	HYD	HYD
	R		1.6 (1595)	0.039-0.043	3-7B	3-7B	48	650-850	650-850	HYD	HYD
	M		1.8 (1836)	0.039-0.043	3-7B	3-7B	48	600-800	600-800	HYD	HYD
	P		2.0 (1997)	0.039-0.043	3-7B	3-7B	48	650-850	650-850	HYD	HYD
	T		3.0 (2972)	0.039-0.043	3-7B	3-7B	48	600-800	600-800	HYD	HYD
1996	K	①	1.5 (1495)	0.039-0.043	6-16B	6-16B	43	700-900	700-900	HYD	HYD
	K	②	1.5 (1495)	0.039-0.043	4-14B	4-14B	43	700-900	700-900	HYD	HYD
	M		1.8 (1795)	0.039-0.043	3-7B	3-7B	48	650-850	650-850	HYD	HYD
	P		2.0 (1997)	0.039-0.043	3-7B	3-7B	48	650-850	650-850	HYD	HYD
	T		3.0 (2972)	0.039-0.043	3-7B	3-7B	48	600-800	600-800	HYD	HYD
1997	K	①	1.5 (1495)	0.039-0.043	6-16B	6-16B	43	700-900	700-900	HYD	HYD
	K	②	1.5 (1495)	0.039-0.043	4-14B	4-14B	43	700-900	700-900	HYD	HYD
	M	④	1.8 (1795)	0.039-0.043	3-7B	3-7B	48	650-850	650-850	HYD	HYD
	M	⑤	1.8 (1795)	0.039-0.043	5-15B	5-15B	43	700-900	700-900	HYD	HYD
	F		2.0 (1975)	0.039-0.043	5-15B	5-15B	43	700-900	700-900	HYD	HYD
	P		2.0 (1997)	0.039-0.043	3-7B	3-7B	48	650-850	650-850	HYD	HYD
	T		3.0 (2972)	0.039-0.043	3-7B	3-7B	48	600-800	600-800	HYD	HYD
1998	K	①	1.5 (1495)	0.039-0.043	6-16B	6-16B	43	700-900	700-900	HYD	HYD
	K	②	1.5 (1495)	0.039-0.043	4-14B	4-14B	43	700-900	700-900	HYD	HYD
	M	④	1.8 (1795)	0.039-0.043	3-7B	3-7B	48	650-850	650-850	HYD	HYD
	M	⑤	1.8 (1795)	0.039-0.043	5-15B	5-15B	43	700-900	700-900	HYD	HYD
	F		2.0 (1975)	0.039-0.043	5-15B	5-15B	43	700-900	700-900	HYD	HYD
	P		2.0 (1997)	0.039-0.043	3-7B	3-7B	48	650-850	650-850	HYD	HYD
	T		3.0 (2972)	0.039-0.043	3-7B	3-7B	48	600-800	600-800	HYD	HYD

HYD: Hydraulic Valve Lifters
B: Before Top Dead Center

① SOHC
② DOHC
③ Valve clearance is checked with engine hot
④ Elantra
⑤ Tiburon

89531c03

2.0L (VIN P) Engine

◆ **See Figure 109 (p. 53)**

1. Warm the engine to operating temperature. Ensure that the lights, electric cooling fan and accessories are off. The transaxle should be in **P** or **N**. The steering wheel should be in the straight ahead position for vehicles with power steering.

2. Connect a scan tool to the data link connector in the fuse box.

3. If a scan tool is not available, connect a tachometer to the engine and ground the diagnostic link connector.

4. Ground the ignition timing adjustment terminal.

5. Run the engine for 5 seconds or more at 2,000–3,000 rpm and them allow it to idle for 2 minutes.

6. Check and note the engine idle speed.

➡**If idle speed is higher than specification, even with the SAS fully closed, check whether the idle switch has been previously adjusted. If the switch has been moved, re-adjust the idle switch to proper specification.**

7. If idle speed is not within specification, adjust the Speed Adjusting Screw (SAS) until proper idle speed is obtained.

8. Turn the ignition switch **OFF**.

9. Disconnect the scan tool or tachometer. Unground the data link connector and ignition timing connector, as necessary.

10. Start the engine and allow it to idle for 10 minutes or more. Check for proper idle.

Air Conditioning System

SYSTEM SERVICE & REPAIR

➡**It is recommended that the A/C system be serviced by an EPA Section 609 certified automotive technician utilizing a refrigerant recovery/recycling machine.**

The do-it-yourselfer should not service his/her own vehicle's A/C system for many reasons, including legal concerns, personal injury, environmental damage and cost. The following are some of the reasons why you may decide not to service your own vehicle's A/C system.

According to the U.S. Clean Air Act, it is a federal crime to service or repair (involving the refrigerant) a Motor Vehicle Air Conditioning (MVAC) system for money without being EPA certified. It is also illegal to vent R-134a refrigerant into the atmosphere.

State and/or local laws may be more strict than the federal regulations, so be sure to check with your state and/or local authorities for further information. For further federal information on the legality of servicing your A/C system, call the EPA Stratospheric Ozone Hotline.

➡**Federal law dictates that a fine of up to $25,000 may be levelled on people convicted of venting refrigerant into the atmosphere. Additionally, the EPA may pay up to $10,000 for information or services leading to a criminal conviction of the violation of these laws.**

When servicing an A/C system you run the risk of handling or coming in contact with refrigerant, which may result in skin or eye irritation or frostbite. Although low in toxicity (due to chemical stability), inhalation of concentrated refrigerant fumes is dangerous and can result in death; cases of fatal cardiac arrhythmia have been reported in people accidentally subjected to high levels of refrigerant. Some early symptoms include loss of concentration and drowsiness.

Also, refrigerants can decompose at high temperatures (near gas heaters or open flame), which may result in hydrofluoric acid, hydrochloric acid and phosgene (a fatal nerve gas).

R-134a refrigerant is a greenhouse gas which, if allowed to vent into the atmosphere, will contribute to global warming (the Greenhouse Effect).

It is usually more economically feasible to have a certified MVAC automotive technician perform A/C system service to your vehicle. While it is illegal to service an A/C system without the proper equipment, the home mechanic would have to purchase an expensive refrigerant recovery/recycling machine to service his/her own vehicle.

PREVENTIVE MAINTENANCE

◆ **See Figures 110 and 111**

Although the A/C system should not be serviced by the do-it-yourselfer, preventive maintenance can be practiced and A/C system inspections can be performed to help maintain the efficiency of the vehicle's A/C system. For preventive maintenance, perform the following:

• The easiest and most important preventive maintenance for your A/C system is to be sure that it is used on a regular basis. Running the system for five minutes each month (no matter what the season) will help ensure that the seals and all internal components remain lubricated.

➡**Some newer vehicles automatically operate the A/C system compressor whenever the windshield defroster is activated. When running, the compressor lubricates the A/C system components; therefore, the A/C system would not need to be operated each month.**

tccs1233

Fig. 110 A coolant tester can be used to determine the freezing and boiling levels of the coolant in your vehicle

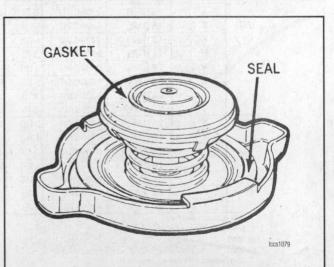

GASKET

SEAL

tccs1079

See Fig. 111 To ensure efficient cooling system operation, inspect the radiator cap gasket and seal

• In order to prevent heater core freeze-up during A/C operation, it is necessary to maintain a proper antifreeze protection. Use a hand-held coolant tester (hydrometer) to periodically check the condition of the antifreeze in your engine's cooling system.

➡️**Antifreeze should not be used longer than the manufacturer specifies.**

• For efficient operation of an air conditioned vehicle's cooling system, the radiator cap should have a holding pressure which meets manufacturer's specifications. A cap which fails to hold these pressures should be replaced.

• Any obstruction of or damage to the condenser configuration will restrict air flow which is essential to its efficient operation. It is, therefore, a good rule to keep this unit clean and in proper physical shape.

➡️**Bug screens which are mounted in front of the condenser (unless they are original equipment) are regarded as obstructions.**

• The condensation drain tube expels any water, which accumulates on the bottom of the evaporator housing, into the engine compartment. If this tube is obstructed, the air conditioning performance can be restricted and condensation buildup can spill over onto the vehicle's floor.

SYSTEM INSPECTION

◆ See Figure 112

Although the A/C system should not be serviced by the do-it-yourselfer, preventive maintenance can be practiced and A/C system inspections can be performed to help maintain the efficiency of the vehicle's A/C system. For A/C system inspection, perform the following:

The easiest and often most important check for the air conditioning system consists of a visual inspection of the system components. Visually inspect the air conditioning system for refrigerant leaks, damaged compressor clutch, abnormal compressor drive belt tension and/or condition, plugged evaporator drain tube, blocked condenser fins, disconnected or broken wires, blown fuses, corroded connections and poor insulation.

A refrigerant leak will usually appear as an oily residue at the leakage point in the system. The oily residue soon picks up dust or dirt particles from the surrounding air and appears greasy. Through time, this will build up and appear to be a heavy dirt impregnated grease.

For a thorough visual and operational inspection, check the following:
• Check the surface of the radiator and condenser for dirt, leaves or other material which might block air flow.
• Check for kinks in hoses and lines. Check the system for leaks.

• Make sure the drive belt is properly tensioned. When the air conditioning is operating, make sure the drive belt is free of noise or slippage.
• Make sure the blower motor operates at all appropriate positions, then check for distribution of the air from all outlets with the blower on **HIGH** or **MAX**.

➡️**Keep in mind that under conditions of high humidity, air discharged from the A/C vents may not feel as cold as expected, even if the system is working properly. This is because vaporized moisture in humid air retains heat more effectively than dry air, thereby making humid air more difficult to cool.**

• Make sure the air passage selection lever is operating correctly. Start the engine and warm it to normal operating temperature, then make sure the temperature selection lever is operating correctly.

Windshield Wiper (Elements)

ELEMENT (REFILL) CARE AND REPLACEMENT

◆ See Figures 113 thru 122 (p. 55–57)

For maximum effectiveness and longest element life, the windshield and wiper blades should be kept clean. Dirt, tree sap, road tar and so on will cause streaking, smearing and blade deterioration if left on the glass. It is advisable to wash the windshield carefully with a commercial glass cleaner at least once a month. Wipe off the rubber blades with the wet rag afterwards. Do not attempt to move wipers across the windshield by hand; damage to the motor and drive mechanism will result.

To inspect and/or replace the wiper blade elements, place the wiper switch in the **LOW** speed position and the ignition switch in the **ACC** position. When the wiper blades are approximately vertical on the windshield, turn the ignition switch to **OFF**.

Examine the wiper blade elements. If they are found to be cracked, broken or torn, they should be replaced immediately. Replacement intervals will vary with usage, although ozone deterioration usually limits element life to about one year. If the wiper pattern is smeared or streaked, or if the blade chatters across the glass, the elements should be replaced. It is easiest and most sensible to replace the elements in pairs.

If your vehicle is equipped with aftermarket blades, there are several different types of refills and your vehicle might have any kind. Aftermarket blades and arms rarely use the exact same type blade or refill as the original equipment. Here are some typical aftermarket blades; not all may be available for your vehicle:

The Anco® type uses a release button that is pushed down to allow

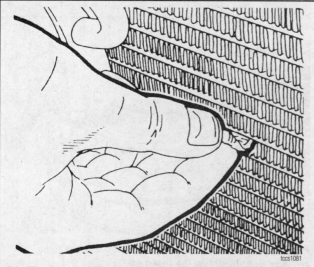

See Fig. 112 Periodically remove any debris from the condenser and radiator fins

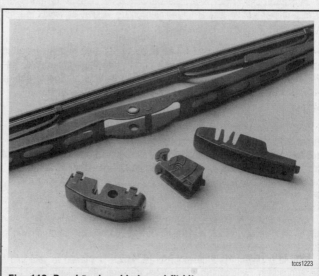

Fig. 113 Bosch® wiper blade and fit kit

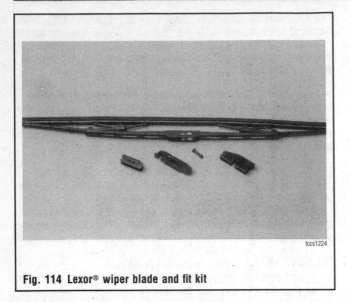

Fig. 114 Lexor® wiper blade and fit kit

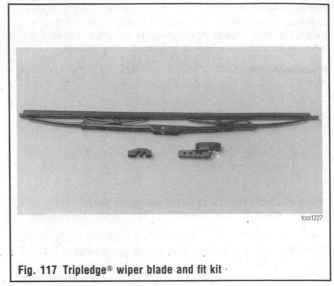

Fig. 117 Tripledge® wiper blade and fit kit

Fig. 115 Pylon® wiper blade and adaptor

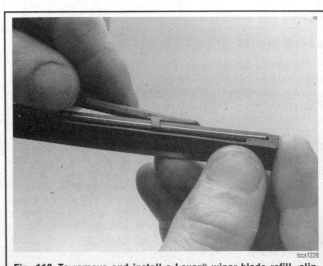

Fig. 118 To remove and install a Lexor® wiper blade refill, slip out the old insert and slide in a new one

Fig. 116 Trico® wiper blade and fit kit

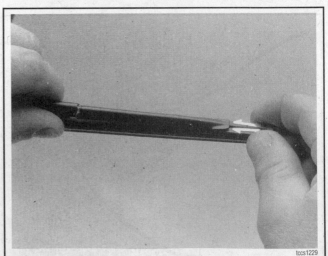

Fig. 119 On Pylon® inserts, the clip at the end has to be removed prior to sliding the insert off

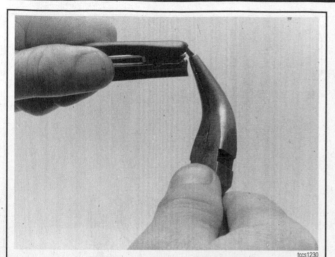

tccs1230

Fig. 120 On Trico® wiper blades, the tab at the end of the blade must be turned up . . .

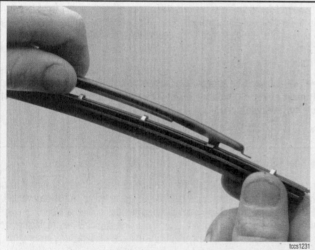

tccs1231

Fig. 121 . . . then the insert can be removed. After installing the replacement insert, bend the tab back

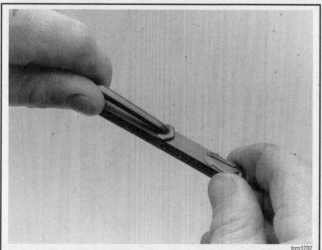

tccs1232

Fig. 122 The Tripledge® wiper blade insert is removed and installed using a securing clip

the refill to slide out of the yoke jaws. The new refill slides back into the frame and locks in place.

Some Trico® refills are removed by locating where the metal backing strip or the refill is wider. Insert a small screwdriver blade between the frame and metal backing strip. Press down to release the refill from the retaining tab.

Other types of Trico® refills have two metal tabs which are unlocked by squeezing them together. The rubber filler can then be withdrawn from the frame jaws. A new refill is installed by inserting the refill into the front frame jaws and sliding it rearward to engage the remaining frame jaws. There are usually four jaws; be certain when installing that the refill is engaged in all of them. At the end of its travel, the tabs will lock into place on the front jaws of the wiper blade frame.

Another type of refill is made from polycarbonate. The refill has a simple locking device at one end which flexes downward out of the groove into which the jaws of the holder fit, allowing easy release. By sliding the new refill through all the jaws and pushing through the slight resistance when it reaches the end of its travel, the refill will lock into position.

To replace the Tridon® refill, it is necessary to remove the wiper blade. This refill has a plastic backing strip with a notch about 1 in. (25mm) from the end. Hold the blade (frame) on a hard surface so that the frame is tightly bowed. Grip the tip of the backing strip and pull up while twisting counterclockwise. The backing strip will snap out of the retaining tab. Do this for the remaining tabs until the refill is free of the blade. The length of these refills is molded into the end and they should be replaced with identical types.

Regardless of the type of refill used, be sure to follow the part manufacturer's instructions closely. Make sure that all of the frame jaws are engaged as the refill is pushed into place and locked. If the metal blade holder and frame are allowed to touch the glass during wiper operation, the glass will be scratched.

Tires and Wheels

Common sense and good driving habits will afford maximum tire life. Fast starts, sudden stops and hard cornering are hard on tires and will shorten their useful life span. Make sure that you don't overload the vehicle or run with incorrect pressure in the tires. Both of these practices will increase tread wear.

➡**For optimum tire life, keep the tires properly inflated, rotate them often and have the wheel alignment checked periodically.**

Inspect your tires frequently. Be especially careful to watch for bubbles in the tread or sidewall, deep cuts or underinflation. Replace any tires with bubbles in the sidewall. If cuts are so deep that they penetrate to the cords, discard the tire. Any cut in the sidewall of a radial tire renders it unsafe. Also look for uneven tread wear patterns that may indicate the front end is out of alignment or that the tires are out of balance.

TIRE ROTATION

◆ **See Figures 123, 124 and 125**

Tires must be rotated periodically to equalize wear patterns that vary with a tire's position on the vehicle. Tires will also wear in an uneven way as the front steering/suspension system wears to the point where the alignment should be reset.

Rotating the tires will ensure maximum life for the tires as a set, so you will not have to discard a tire early due to wear on only part of the tread. Regular rotation is required to equalize wear.

When rotating "unidirectional tires," make sure that they always roll in the same direction. This means that a tire used on the left side of the vehicle must not be switched to the right side and vice-versa. Such tires should only be rotated front-to-rear or rear-to-front, while always remaining on the same side of the vehicle. These tires are marked on the sidewall as to the direction of rotation; observe the marks when reinstalling the tire(s).

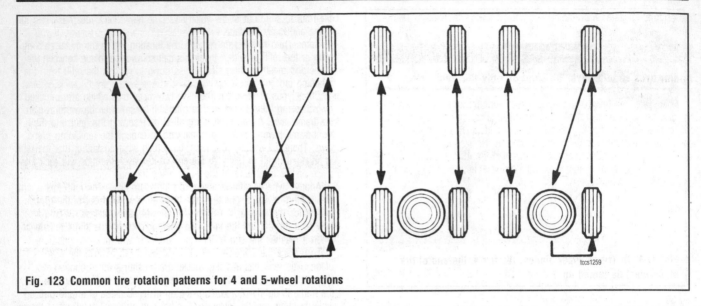

Fig. 123 Common tire rotation patterns for 4 and 5-wheel rotations

Fig. 124 Compact spare tires must NEVER be used in the rotation pattern

(FOR NON-DIRECTIONAL TIRES AND WHEELS) (FOR DIRECTIONAL TIRES AND WHEELS)

Fig. 125 Unidirectional tires are identifiable by sidewall arrows and/or the word "rotation"

Some styled or "mag" wheels may have different offsets front to rear. In these cases, the rear wheels must not be used up front and vice-versa. Furthermore, if these wheels are equipped with unidirectional tires, they cannot be rotated unless the tire is remounted for the proper direction of rotation.

➡ The compact or space-saver spare is strictly for emergency use. It must never be included in the tire rotation or placed on the vehicle for everyday use.

TIRE DESIGN

◆ See Figure 126

For maximum satisfaction, tires should be used in sets of four. Mixing of different types (radial, bias-belted, fiberglass belted) must be avoided. In most cases, the vehicle manufacturer has designated a type of tire on which the vehicle will perform best. Your first choice when replacing tires should be to use the same type of tire that the manufacturer recommends.

When radial tires are used, tire sizes and wheel diameters should be selected to maintain ground clearance and tire load capacity equivalent to

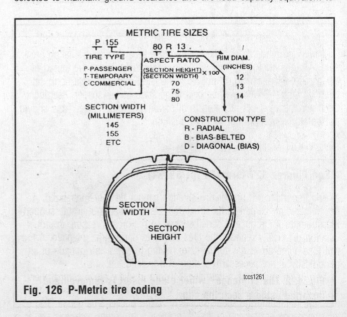

Fig. 126 P-Metric tire coding

the original specified tire. Radial tires should always be used in sets of four.

Radial tires should never be used on only the front axle.

When selecting tires, pay attention to the original size as marked on the tire. Most tires are described using an industry size code sometimes referred to as P-Metric. This allows the exact identification of the tire specifications, regardless of the manufacturer. If selecting a different tire size or brand, remember to check the installed tire for any sign of interference with the body or suspension while the vehicle is stopping, turning sharply or heavily loaded.

Snow Tires

Good radial tires can produce a big advantage in slippery weather, but in snow, a street radial tire does not have sufficient tread to provide traction and control. The small grooves of a street tire quickly pack with snow and the tire behaves like a billiard ball on a marble floor. The more open, chunky tread of a snow tire will self-clean as the tire turns, providing much better grip on snowy surfaces.

To satisfy municipalities requiring snow tires during weather emergencies, most snow tires carry either an M + S designation after the tire size stamped on the sidewall, or the designation "all-season." In general, no change in tire size is necessary when buying snow tires.

Most manufacturers strongly recommend the use of 4 snow tires on their vehicles for reasons of stability. If snow tires are fitted only to the drive wheels, the opposite end of the vehicle may become very unstable when braking or turning on slippery surfaces. This instability can lead to unpleasant endings if the driver can't counteract the slide in time.

Note that snow tires, whether 2 or 4, will affect vehicle handling in all non-snow situations. The stiffer, heavier snow tires will noticeably change the turning and braking characteristics of the vehicle. Once the snow tires are installed, you must re-learn the behavior of the vehicle and drive accordingly.

➡**Consider buying extra wheels on which to mount the snow tires. Once done, the "snow wheels" can be installed and removed as needed. This eliminates the potential damage to tires or wheels from seasonal removal and installation. Even if your vehicle has styled wheels, see if inexpensive steel wheels are available. Although the look of the vehicle will change, the expensive wheels will be protected from salt, curb hits and pothole damage.**

TIRE STORAGE

If they are mounted on wheels, store the tires at proper inflation pressure. All tires should be kept in a cool, dry place. If they are stored in the garage or basement, do not let them stand on a concrete floor; set them on strips of wood, a mat or a large stack of newspaper. Keeping them away from direct moisture is of paramount importance. Tires should not be stored upright, but in a flat position.

INFLATION & INSPECTION

◆ **See Figures 127 thru 134 (p. 59–61)**

The importance of proper tire inflation cannot be overemphasized. A tire employs air as part of its structure. It is designed around the supporting strength of the air at a specified pressure. For this reason, improper inflation drastically reduces the tires ability to perform as intended. A tire will lose some air in day-to-day use; having to add a few pounds of air periodically is not necessarily a sign of a leaking tire.

Two items should be a permanent fixture in every glove compartment: an accurate tire pressure gauge and a tread depth gauge. Check the tire pressure (including the spare) regularly with a pocket type gauge. Too often, the gauge on the end of the air hose at your corner garage is not ac-

curate because it suffers too much abuse. Always check tire pressure when the tires are cold, as pressure increases with temperature. If you must move the vehicle to check the tire inflation, do not drive more than a mile before checking. A cold tire is generally one that has not been driven for more than three hours.

A plate or sticker is normally provided somewhere in the vehicle (door post, hood, tailgate or trunk lid)

which shows the proper pressure for the tires. Never counteract excessive pressure build-up by bleeding off air pressure (letting some air out). This will cause the tire to run hotter and wear quicker.

Never exceed the maximum tire pressure embossed on the tire! This is the pressure to be used when the tire is at maximum loading, but it is rarely the correct pressure for everyday driving. Consult the owner's manual or the tire pressure sticker for the correct tire pressure.

Once you've maintained the correct tire pressures for several weeks, you'll be familiar with the vehicle's braking and handling personality. Slight adjustments in tire pressures can fine-tune these characteristics,

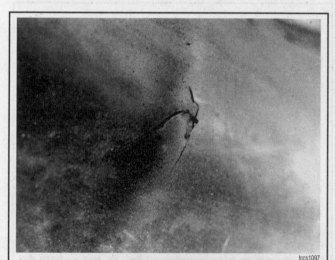

tccs1097

Fig. 127 Tires should be checked frequently for any sign of puncture or damage

tccs1095

Fig. 128 Tires with deep cuts, or cuts which show bulging should be replaced immediately

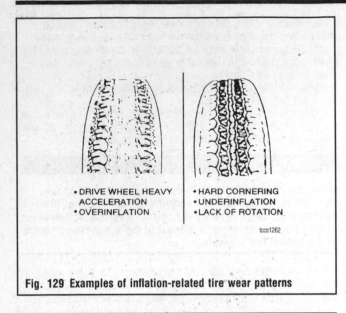

- DRIVE WHEEL HEAVY ACCELERATION
- OVERINFLATION

- HARD CORNERING
- UNDERINFLATION
- LACK OF ROTATION

tccs1262

Fig. 129 Examples of inflation-related tire wear patterns

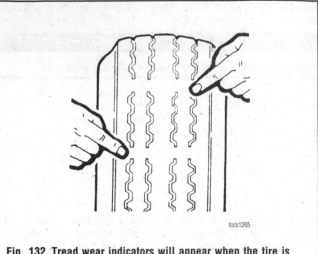

tccs1265

Fig. 132 Tread wear indicators will appear when the tire is worn

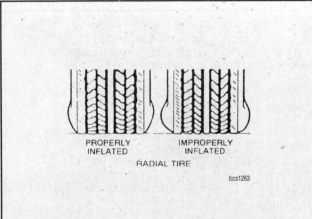

PROPERLY INFLATED   IMPROPERLY INFLATED

RADIAL TIRE

tccs1263

Fig. 130 Radial tires have a characteristic sidewall bulge; don't try to measure pressure by looking at the tire. Use a quality air pressure gauge

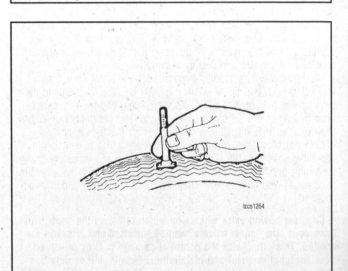

tccs1264

Fig. 133 Accurate tread depth indicators are inexpensive and handy

CONDITION	RAPID WEAR AT SHOULDERS	RAPID WEAR AT CENTER	CRACKED TREADS	WEAR ON ONE SIDE	FEATHERED EDGE	BALD SPOTS	SCALLOPED WEAR
EFFECT							
CAUSE	UNDER-INFLATION OR LACK OF ROTATION	OVER-INFLATION OR LACK OF ROTATION	UNDER-INFLATION OR EXCESSIVE SPEED*	EXCESSIVE CAMBER	INCORRECT TOE	UNBALANCED WHEEL / OR TIRE DEFECT *	LACK OF ROTATION OF TIRES OR WORN OR OUT-OF-ALIGNMENT SUSPENSION.
CORRECTION	ADJUST PRESSURE TO SPECIFICATIONS WHEN TIRES ARE COOL ROTATE TIRES			ADJUST CAMBER TO SPECIFICATIONS	ADJUST TOE-IN TO SPECIFICATIONS	DYNAMIC OR STATIC BALANCE WHEELS	ROTATE TIRES AND INSPECT SUSPENSION

*HAVE TIRE INSPECTED FOR FURTHER USE.

tccs1267

Fig. 131 Common tire wear patterns and causes

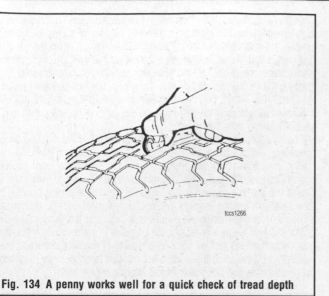

Fig. 134 A penny works well for a quick check of tread depth

using a Lincoln head penny. Slip the Lincoln penny (with Lincoln's head upside-down) into several tread grooves. If you can see the top of Lincoln's head in 2 adjacent grooves, the tire has less than ¹⁄₁₆in. (1.5mm) tread left and should be replaced. You can measure snow tires in the same manner by using the "tails" side of the Lincoln penny. If you can see the top of the Lincoln memorial, it's time to replace the snow tire(s).

CARE OF SPECIAL WHEELS

If you have invested money in magnesium, aluminum alloy or sport wheels, special precautions should be taken to make sure your investment is not wasted and that your special wheels look good for the life of the vehicle.

Special wheels are easily damaged and/or scratched. Occasionally check the rims for cracking, impact damage or air leaks. If any of these are found, replace the wheel. But in order to prevent this type of damage and the costly replacement of a special wheel, observe the following precautions:

• Use extra care not to damage the wheels during removal, installation, balancing, etc. After removal of the wheels from the vehicle, place them on a mat or other protective surface. If they are to be stored for any length of time, support them on strips of wood. Never store tires and wheels upright; the tread may develop flat spots.

• When driving, watch for hazards; it doesn't take much to crack a wheel.

• When washing, use a mild soap or non-abrasive dish detergent (keeping in mind that detergent tends to remove wax). Avoid cleansers with abrasives or the use of hard brushes. There are many cleaners and polishes for special wheels.

• If possible, remove the wheels during the winter. Salt and sand used for snow removal can severely damage the finish of a wheel.

• Make certain the recommended lug nut torque is never exceeded or the wheel may crack. Never use snow chains on special wheels; severe scratching will occur.

but never change the cold pressure specification by more than 2 psi. A slightly softer tire pressure will give a softer ride but also yield lower fuel mileage. A slightly harder tire will give crisper dry road handling but can cause skidding on wet surfaces. Unless you're fully attuned to the vehicle, stick to the recommended inflation pressures.

All tires made since 1968 have built-in tread wear indicator bars that show up as ½in. (13mm) wide smooth bands across the tire when ¹⁄₁₆in. (1.5mm) of tread remains. The appearance of tread wear indicators means that the tires should be replaced. In fact, many states have laws prohibiting the use of tires with less than this amount of tread.

You can check your own tread depth with an inexpensive gauge or by

FLUIDS AND LUBRICANTS

Fluid Disposal

Used fluids such as engine oil, transaxle fluid, antifreeze and brake fluid are hazardous wastes and must be disposed of properly. Before draining any fluids, consult with your local authorities; in many areas waste oil, etc. is being accepted as a part of recycling programs. A number of service stations and auto parts stores are also accepting waste fluids for recycling.

Be sure of the recycling center's policies before draining any fluids, as many will not accept different fluids that have been mixed together.

Fuel and Engine Oil Recommendations

FUEL

➡**Some fuel additives contain chemicals that can damage the catalytic converter and/or oxygen sensor. Read all of the labels carefully before using any additive in the engine or fuel system.**

All vehicles covered by this manual are designed to run on unleaded fuel. The use of a leaded fuel in a vehicle requiring unleaded fuel will plug the catalytic converter and render it inoperative. It will also increase exhaust backpressure to the point where engine output will be severely reduced. Obviously, use of leaded fuel should not be a problem, since most companies have stopped selling it for quite some time.

For all Hyundai models, the minimum octane rating of the unleaded fuel being used must be at least 86 (as listed on the pumps), which usually means regular unleaded. Some areas may have even lower octanes available, which would make 86 a midgrade fuel. In these cases a minimum fuel octane of 86 should STILL be used.

Fuel should be selected for the brand and octane which performs best with your engine. Judge a gasoline by its ability to prevent pinging, its engine starting capabilities (cold and hot) and general all weather performance. The use of a fuel too low in octane (a measurement of anti-knock quality) will result in spark knock. Since many factors such as altitude, terrain, air temperature and humidity affect operating efficiency, knocking may result even though the recommended fuel is being used. If persistent knocking occurs, it may be necessary to switch to a different brand or grade of fuel. Continuous or heavy knocking may result in engine damage.

➡**Your engine's fuel requirement can change with time, mainly due to carbon buildup, which will in turn change the compression ratio. If your engine pings or knocks switch to a higher grade of fuel. Sometimes just changing brands will cure the problem.**

The other most important quality you should look for in a fuel is that it contains detergents designed to keep fuel injection systems clean. Many of the major fuel companies will display information right at the xxpumps telling you that their fuels contain these detergents. The use of a high-quality fuel which contains detergents will help assure trouble-free operation of your car's fuel system.

OIL

♦ **See Figure 135**

The recommended oil viscosities for sustained temperatures ranging from below -20° (-30°C) to above 100°F (40°C) are listed in the section. The only oil type shown is multi-viscosity. Multi-viscosity oils are recommended because of their wider range of acceptable temperatures and driving conditions.

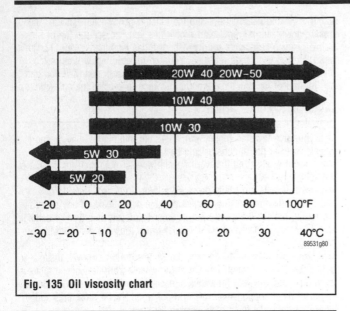

Fig. 135 Oil viscosity chart

Look for the API oil identification label when choosing your engine oil

When adding oil to the crankcase or changing the oil and filter, it is important that oil of an equal quality to original equipment be used in your car. The use of inferior oils may void the warranty, damage your engine, or both.

The Society of Automotive Engineers (SAE) grade number of the oil indicates the viscosity of the oil—its ability to lubricate at a given temperature. The lower the SAE number, the lighter the oil; the lower the viscosity, the easier it is to crank the engine in cold weather, but the less the oil will lubricate and protect the engine at high temperatures. This number is marked on every oil container.

When using engine oil, there are two types of ratings with which you should be familiar: viscosity and service (quality). There are several service ratings, resulting from tests established by the American Petroleum Institute. The most current rating, SG, is recommended by Hyundai for use in all engines. No other service ratings are acceptable.

Oil viscosities should be chosen from those oils recommended for the lowest anticipated temperatures during the oil change interval. Due to the need for an oil that embodies both good lubrication at high temperature and easy cranking in cold weather, multigrade oils have been developed.

Basically, a multigrade oil is thinner at low temperatures and thicker at high temperatures. For example, a 10W–40 oil (the W stands for winter) exhibits the characteristics of a 10-weight (SAE 10) oil when the car is first started and the oil is cold. Its lighter weight allows it to travel to the lubricating surfaces quicker and offer less resistance to starter motor cranking than a heavier oil. But after the engine reaches operating temperature, the 10W–40 oil begins acting like straight 40-weight (SAE 40) oil. It behaves as a heavier oil, providing greater lubrication and protection against foaming than lighter oils.

The American Petroleum Institute (API) designations, also found on oil containers, indicate the classification of engine oil used for given operating conditions. Only oils designated Service SG (or the latest superceding designation) heavy-duty detergent should be used in your car. Oils of the SG-type perform many functions inside the engine besides their basic lubrication. Through a balanced system of metallic detergents and polymeric dispersants, the oil prevents high and low temperature deposits and also keeps sludge and dirt particles in suspension. Acids, particularly sulfuric, as well as other by-products of engine combustion are neutralized by the oil. If these acids are allowed to concentrate, they can cause corrosion and rapid wear of the internal engine parts.

Engine

OIL LEVEL CHECK

1. Park the car on a level surface.
2. The engine may be either hot or cold when checking oil level. However, if it is hot, wait a few minutes after the engine has been shut off to allow the oil to drain back into the crankcase. If the engine is cold, do not start it before checking the oil level.
3. Open the hood and locate the dipstick, at the front of the engine. Pull the dipstick from its tube, wipe it clean, and reinsert it.
4. Pull the dipstick from its tube again holding it horizontally, read the oil level. The oil should be between the MIN and MAX mark. If the oil is below the MIN mark, add oil of the proper viscosity through the capped opening of the rocker cover.
5. Replace the dipstick, and check the level again after adding any oil. Be careful not to overfill the crankcase. Approximately one quart of oil will raise the level from the low mark to the high mark. Excess oil will generally be consumed at an accelerated rate even if no damage to the engine seals occurs.

The engine oil dipstick is located at the front of the engine compartment, either on the passenger's side . . .

. . . or on the driver's side

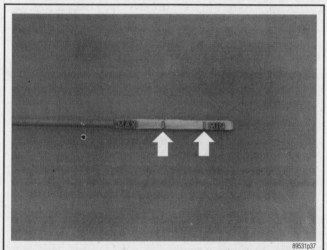

The oil level should be between the MIN and MAX marks on the dipstick

OIL & FILTER CHANGE

❋❋ CAUTION

Prolonged and repeated skin contact with used engine oil, may be harmful.

➡ **The engine oil and oil filter should be changed at the recommended intervals on the Maintenance Chart. Though some manufacturer's have at times recommended changing the filter only at every other oil change, we recommend that you always change the filter with the oil. The benefit of fresh oil is quickly lost if the old filter is clogged and unable to do its job. Also, leaving the old filter in place leaves a significant amount of dirty oil in the system.**

The oil should be changed more frequently if the vehicle is being operated in a very dusty area. Before draining the oil, make sure that the engine is at operating temperature. Hot oil will hold more impurities in suspension and will flow better, allowing the removal of more oil and dirt.

It is a good idea to warm the engine oil first so it will flow better. This can be accomplished by 15–20 miles of highway driving. Fluid which is warmed to normal operating temperature will flow faster, drain more completely and remove more contaminants from the engine.

1. Raise and support the vehicle safely on jackstands. Make sure the oil drain plug is at the lowest point on the oil pan. If not, you may have to raise the vehicle slightly higher on one jackstand (side) than the other.

2. Before you crawl under the car, take a look at where you will be working and gather all the necessary tools: such as a few wrenches or a strip of sockets, the drain pan, a clean rag, and, if the oil filter is more accessible from underneath the vehicle, you will also want to grab a bottle of oil, the new filter and a filter wrench at this time.

3. Position the drain pan beneath the oil pan drain plug. Keep in mind that the fast flowing oil, which will spill out as you pull the plug from the pan, will flow with enough force that it could miss the pan. Position the drain pan accordingly and be ready to move the pan more directly beneath the plug as the oil flow lessens to a trickle.

4. Loosen the drain plug with a wrench (or socket and driver), then carefully unscrew the plug with your fingers. Use a rag to shield your fingers from the heat. Push in on the plug as you unscrew it so you can feel when all of the screw threads are out of the hole (and so you will keep the oil from seeping past the threads until you are ready to remove the plug). You can then remove the plug quickly to avoid having hot oil run down your arm. This will also help assure that have the plug in your hand, not in the bottom of a pan of hot oil.

The engine oil drain plug is located at the bottom of the oil pan, directly below the engine

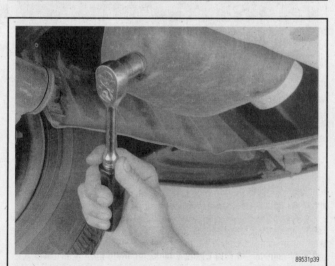

Using the proper size wrench, loosen, but do not remove the oil drain plug

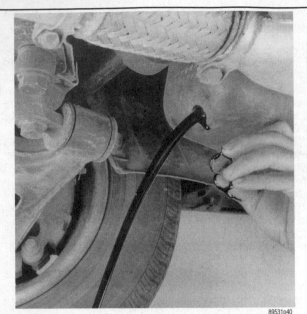

Carefully unscrew the drain plug with your fingers, keeping pressure on the plug to prevent spills

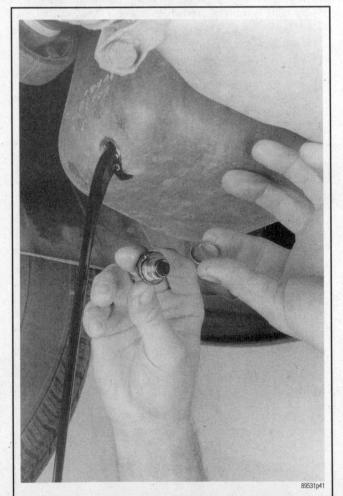

Always check the drain plug gasket for damage and replace it as necessary

The oil filter is located beneath the engine, near the oil pan rail, and can be easily unscrewed with a wrench

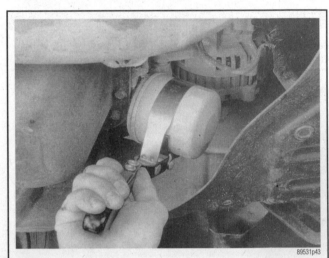

Be sure to slide the oil filter wrench as far up on the filter as possible, to avoid crushing it during removal

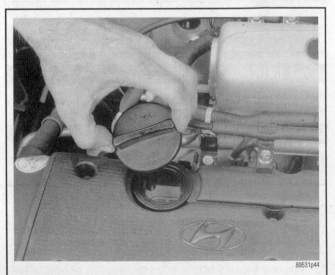

Twist and remove the oil filler cap . . .

. . . then pour new oil into the engine. Always use the proper grade of oil for your driving conditions

✳✳ CAUTION

Be careful of the oil; when at operating temperature, it is hot enough to cause a severe burn.

5. Allow the oil to drain until nothing but a few drops come out of the drain hole. Check the drain plug to make sure the threads and sealing surface are not damaged. Carefully thread the plug into position and tighten it with a torque wrench to 25–33 ft. lbs. (34–44 Nm). If a torque wrench is not available, snug the drain plug and give a slight additional turn. You don't want the plug to fall out (as you would quickly become stranded), but the pan threads are EASILY stripped from overtighening (and this can be time consuming and/or costly to fix).

6. To remove the filter, you may need an oil filter wrench since the filter may have been fitted too tightly and/or the heat from the engine may have made it even tighter. A filter wrench can be obtained at any auto parts store and is well-worth the investment. Loosen the filter with the filter wrench. With a rag wrapped around the filter, unscrew the filter from the boss on the side of the engine. Be careful of hot oil that will run down the side of the filter. Make sure that your drain pan is under the filter before you start to remove it from the engine; should some of the hot oil happen to get on you, there will be a place to dump the filter in a hurry and the filter will usually spill a good bit of dirty oil as it is removed.

7. Wipe the base of the mounting boss with a clean, dry cloth. When you install the new filter, smear a small amount of fresh oil on the gasket with your finger, just enough to coat the entire contact surface. When you tighten the filter, rotate it about a half-turn after it contacts the mounting boss (or follow any instructions which are provided on the filter or parts box).

✳✳ WARNING

Never operate the engine without engine oil, otherwise SEVERE engine damage will be the result.

8. Remove the jackstands and carefully lower the vehicle, then IMMEDIATELY refill the engine crankcase with the proper amount of oil. DO NOT WAIT TO DO THIS because if you forget and someone tries to start the car severe engine damage will occur.

9. Refill the engine crankcase slowly, checking the level often. You may notice that it usually takes less than the amount of oil listed in the capacity chart to refill the crankcase. But, that is only until the engine is run and the oil filter is filled with oil. To make sure the proper level is obtained, run the engine to normal operating temperature, shut the en-

gine **OFF,** allow the oil to drain back into the oil pan, and recheck the level. Top off the oil at this time to the fill mark.

➡**If the vehicle is not resting on level ground, the oil level reading on the dipstick may be slightly off. Be sure to check the level only when the car is sitting level.**

10. Drain your used oil in a suitable container for recycling and clean-up your tools, as you will be needing them again in a couple of thousand more miles (kilometers?).

Manual Transaxle

FLUID RECOMMENDATIONS

Hyundai recommends the use of SAE 75-85W or 85W-90 GL-4/GL-5 gear oil.

LEVEL CHECK

◆ **See Figures 136, 137 and 138**

1. Park the vehicle on a level surface, turn the engine **OFF,** FIRMLY apply the parking brake and block the drive wheels.

➡**Ground clearance may make access to the transaxle filler plug impossible without raising and supporting the vehicle, BUT, if this is done, the car MUST be supported at four corners and level. If only the front or rear is supported, an improper fluid level will be indicated.**

2. Remove the filler plug from the side of the transaxle. The fluid level should be even with the bottom of the filler hole.
3. If additional fluid is necessary, add it through the filler hole using a siphon pump or squeeze bottle.
4. When you are finished, carefully install the filler plug and tighten to 22–25 ft. lbs. (30–35 Nm).

➡**DO NOT overtighten the filler plug, as this can damage the transaxle.**

DRAIN & REFILL

◆ **See Figures 136 thru 141**

It is a good idea to warm the transmission fluid first so it will flow better. This can be accomplished by 15–20 miles of highway driving. Fluid which is warmed to normal operating temperature will flow faster, drain more completely, and remove more contaminants from the housing.

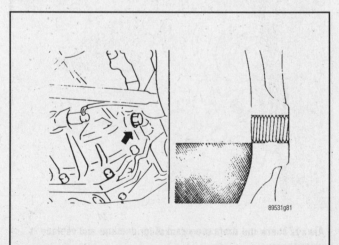

Fig. 136 Manual transaxle fluid filler plug location—Excel and Scoupe

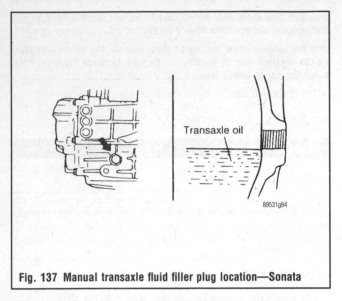

Fig. 137 Manual transaxle fluid filler plug location—Sonata

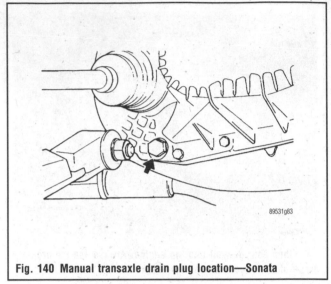

Fig. 140 Manual transaxle drain plug location—Sonata

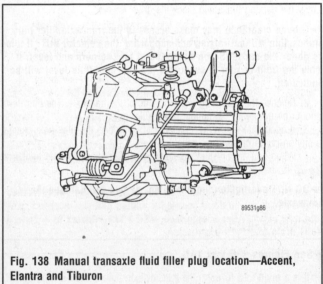

Fig. 138 Manual transaxle fluid filler plug location—Accent, Elantra and Tiburon

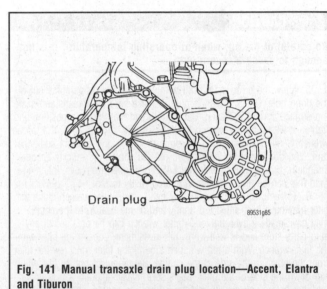

Fig. 141 Manual transaxle drain plug location—Accent, Elantra and Tiburon

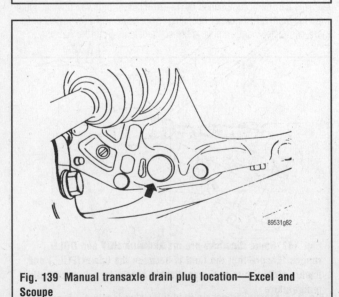

Fig. 139 Manual transaxle drain plug location—Excel and Scoupe

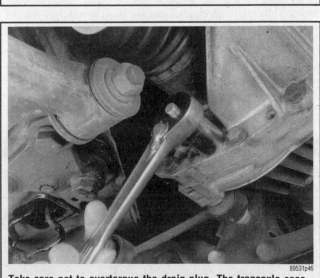

Take care not to overtorque the drain plug. The transaxle case is aluminum and is easily damaged

Manual transmission fluid should be translucent. If it is dark brown or black, suspect transaxle problems

1. Raise and support the vehicle securely on jackstands. Remember that the vehicle must be supported level (usually at four points) so the proper amount of fluid can be added.

2. Place a drain pan under the transaxle housing, below the drain plug. Remember that the fluid will likely flow with some force at first (arcing outward from the transaxle), and will not just drip straight downward into the pan. Position the drain pan accordingly and move it more directly beneath the drain plug as the flow slows to a trickle.

3. Remove the filler plug from the transaxle.

4. Remove the drain plug and allow the transmission fluid to drain out.

5. Once the transaxle has drained sufficiently, install the the drain plug and tighten to 22–25 ft. lbs. (30–35 Nm).

6. Fill the transaxle to the proper level with the required fluid through the filler hole.

7. Reinstall the filler plug and tighten to 22–25 ft. lbs. (30–35 Nm).

8. Remove the jackstands and carefully lower the vehicle.

Automatic Transaxle

FLUID RECOMMENDATIONS

Hyundai recommends the use of Mopar ATF Plus Type 7176 automatic transmission fluid, or equivalent.

➥It is highly recommended to search out this specific fluid, as performance problems have been noted when using Dexron® type fluids.

LEVEL CHECK

◆ See Figure 142

It is very important to maintain the proper fluid level in an automatic transaxle. If the level is either too high or too low, poor shifting operation and internal damage are likely to occur. For this reason, a regular check of the fluid level is essential.

1. Drive the vehicle for 15–20 minutes, allowing the transaxle to reach operating temperature.

➥If the car is driven at extended highway speeds, is driven in city traffic in hot weather or is being used to pull a trailer, fluid temperatures will likely exceed normal operating and checking ranges. In these circumstances, give the fluid time to cool (about 30 minutes) before checking the level.

2. Park the car on a level surface, apply the parking brake and leave the engine idling. Make sure the parking brake is FIRMLY ENGAGED. Shift the transaxle and engage each gear, then place the selector in P (PARK).

3. Open the hood and locate the transaxle dipstick. Wipe away any dirt in the area of the dipstick to prevent it from falling into the filler tube. Withdraw the dipstick, wipe it with a clean, lint-free rag and reinsert it until it fully seats.

4. Withdraw the dipstick and hold it horizontally while noting the fluid level. It should be between the upper (FULL) and the lower (ADD) marks.

5. If the level is below the lower mark, use a funnel and add fluid in small quantities through the dipstick filler neck. Keep the engine running while adding fluid and check the level after each small amount. DO NOT overfill as this could lead to foaming and transmission damage or seal leaks.

➥Since the transmission fluid is added through the dipstick tube, if you check the fluid too soon after adding fluid an incorrect reading may occur. After adding fluid, wait a few minutes to allow it to fully drain into the transmission.

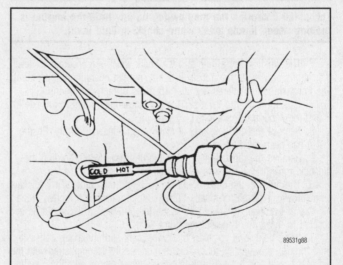

Fig. 142 Some dipsticks are marked with HOT and COLD ranges. Ensure that the fluid is between the upper (FULL) and lower (ADD) limits of the applicable range, based on operating temperature

On some models, the automatic transaxle dipstick is located on the driver's side of the engine compartment

✳✳ CAUTION

The electric cooling fan may switch on any time the engine is running. Keep hands away when checking fluid level.

6. The dipstick has a high and low mark which are accurate for level indications only when the transaxle is hot (normal operating temperature). The transaxle is considered hot after 15 miles of highway driving.

7. Park the car on a level surface with the engine idling, transaxle in **P** and the parking brake applied.

8. Remove the dipstick, wipe it clean, then reinsert it firmly. Ensure that it has been inserted fully.

9. Remove the dipstick and check the fluid level while holding the dipstick horizontally. The level should be between the two marks.

10. The fluid on the dipstick should be bright red color. If it is discolored (brown or black), or smells burnt, serious transaxle troubles, probably due to overheating, should be suspected. The transaxle should be inspected to locate the cause of the burnt fluid.

11. If the fluid level is below the lower mark add automatic transaxle fluid through the dipstick tube. This is more easily accomplished with the aid of a funnel and hose. Check the level often between additions, being careful not to overfill the transaxle.

➡Overfilling the will cause slippage, seal damage, and overheating. Approximately one pint of fluid will raise the level from the low mark on the dipstick to the high mark.

DRAIN & REFILL

The preferred Hyundai automatic transaxle service procedure requires the inspection and/or replacement of the transaxle filter at every fluid change. Refer to Pan and Filter Service for the complete procedure.

PAN & FILTER SERVICE

◆ **See Figures 143 and 144**

1. Raise the front of the vehicle and support it safely.

2. Remove the drain plug from the bottom of the transaxle and allow the fluid to drain.

3. Position a large drain pan under the transaxle pan and have plenty of rags on hand.

4. Slightly loosen all the pan bolts. Tap one corner of the pan with a soft hammer to break the seal.

5. Once the pan is broken loose, support it, remove all the bolts, and then tilt it to one side to drain the remaining fluid.

6. Check the oil filter for clogging and damage and replace as necessary.

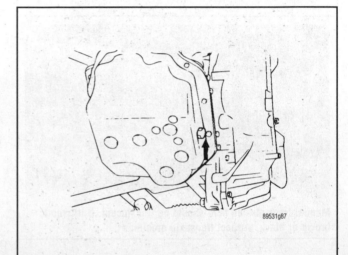

Fig. 143 On most models, the automatic transaxle drain plug is located on the side of the fluid pan

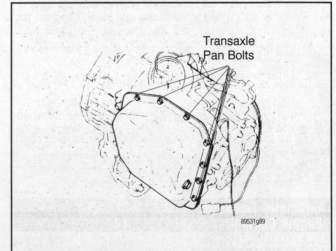

Fig. 144 To remove the transaxle pan, carefully loosen the pan bolts. Keep the pan horizontal to prevent bending the pan rail

Some models have the drain plug (arrow) located in the transaxle case

The automatic transaxle is filled through the dipstick tube. A funnel is a must to prevent spills

LEVEL CHECK

Any time you have the hood open, glance at the coolant reserve tank to make sure it is properly filled. Top off the cooling system using the recovery tank and its LOW and FULL markings as a guideline. If you top off the system, make a note to check it again soon.

➡**Never overfill the reserve tank.**

A coolant level that consistently drops is usually a sign of a small, hard to detect leak, although in the worst case it could be a sign of an internal engine leak (blown head gasket/cracked block? . . . check the engine oil for coolant contamination). In most cases, you will be able to trace the leak to a loose fitting or damaged hose.

Evaporating ethylene glycol antifreeze will leave small, white (salt-like) deposits, which can be helpful in tracing a leak.

NEVER remove the radiator cap when the engine is HOT

7. Clean all the gasket surfaces and the inside of the pan thoroughly. Then, raise the pan and gasket in position with the bolt holes lined up.

8. Support the pan and replace the bolts, tightening them only very gently with your fingers.

9. Tighten the pan bolts diagonally in several stages to 7.5–8.5 ft. lbs. (10–12 Nm).

10. Install the drain plug and torque to 22–25 ft. lbs. (30–35 Nm).

11. Refill the transaxle carefully through the dipstick tube. Add small quantities of fluid and check the fluid level several times until it reaches the lower mark on the dipstick.

12. Start the engine and allow it to idle for about two minutes so that the fluid has a chance to warm to normal operating temperature.

13. Check the fluid level and add fluid as necessary.

Engine Coolant

FLUID RECOMMENDATIONS

Hyundai recommends the use of a good quality ethylene glycol based or other aluminum compatible antifreeze. It is best to add a 50/50 mix of antifreeze and water to avoid diluting the coolant in the system.

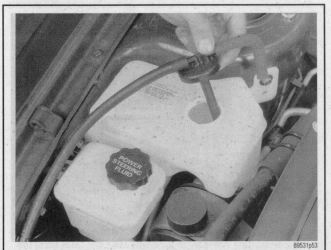

The reserve tank fills with coolant when the engine is hot and returns it to the engine as it cools

Add antifreeze and water to the reserve tank to keep the system full. Do not exceed the FULL mark

89531p54

Fill the radiator to the filler neck seat with a 50/50 mixture of antifreeze and water

89531p52

DRAIN, FLUSH & REFILL

✳✳ CAUTION

When draining coolant, keep in mind that cats and dogs are attracted to ethylene glycol antifreeze, and are likely to drink any that is left in an uncovered container or in puddles on the ground. This will prove fatal in sufficient quantity. Always drain coolant into a sealable container. Coolant may be reused unless it is contaminated or several years old.

Ensure that the engine is completely cool prior to starting this service.

1. Remove the radiator and reserve tank caps.
2. Place a drain pan of sufficient capacity under the radiator and open the petcock (drain).

➡**The petcock is plastic and easily binds. Before opening the radiator petcock, spray it with some penetrating lubricant.**

3. When the system is completely drained, close the petcock and fill the system with a radiator cleaning fluid (clean water may also be used, but is not as efficient).

The petcock is located at the bottom corner of the radiator

89531p55

4. Idle the engine until the upper radiator hose gets hot.
5. Allow the engine to cool and drain the system again.
6. Repeat this process until the drained water is clear and free of scale.
7. Flush the reserve tank with water and leave empty.
8. Determine the capacity of the coolant system, then properly refill the cooling system with a 50/50 mixture of fresh coolant and water, as follows:

   a. Fill the radiator with coolant until it reaches the radiator filler neck seat.

   b. Start the engine and allow it to idle until the thermostat opens (the upper radiator hose will become hot).

   c. Turn the engine **OFF** and refill the radiator until the coolant level is at the filler neck seat.

   d. Fill the engine coolant overflow tank with coolant to the FULL mark, then install the radiator cap.

9. If available, install a pressure tester and check for leaks. If a pressure tester is not available, run the engine until normal operating temperature is reached (allowing the system to naturally pressurize), then check for leaks.

10. Check the level of protection with an antifreeze/coolant hydrometer.

Brake Master Cylinder

FLUID RECOMMENDATION

Hyundai recommends the use of only fresh, uncontaminated brake fluid meeting or exceeding DOT 3 standards.

LEVEL CHECK

1. Check the level of brake fluid in the brake fluid reservoir. The fluid should be maintained between the MIN and MAX lines on the reservoir.

➡**Any sudden decrease in fluid level indicates a probable leak in the system and should be inspected immediately.**

2. Clean around the reservoir cap with a shop rag to prevent contaminating the fluid with dirt.

3. Remove the cap and add the required amount of fluid to the system.

➡**When making additions of fluid, use only fresh, uncontaminated brake fluid meeting or exceeding DOT 3 standards. Be careful not**

Brake fluid level should never be above the MAX line or below the MIN line

Use only fresh, uncontaminated brake fluid when filling the system

to spill any brake fluid on painted surfaces, because it will damage the paint. Do not allow the fluid container or brake fluid reservoir to remain open any longer than necessary; brake fluid absorbs moisture from the air, reducing its effectiveness and causing brake line corrosion.

4. Install the reservoir cap.

Clutch Master Cylinder

FLUID RECOMMENDATIONS

Hyundai recommends the use of only fresh, uncontaminated brake fluid meeting or exceeding DOT 3 standards.

LEVEL CHECK

1. Check the level of brake fluid in the clutch reservoir. The fluid should be maintained between the MIN and MAX lines on the reservoir.

➡ Any sudden decrease in fluid level indicates a probable leak in the system and should be inspected immediately.

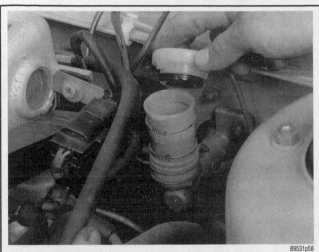

The clutch fluid reservoir is located on the firewall and is filled with brake fluid meeting DOT 3 specifications

2. Clean around the reservoir cap with a shop rag to prevent contaminating the fluid with dirt.

3. Remove the cap and add the required amount of fluid to the system.

➡ When making additions of fluid, use only fresh, uncontaminated brake fluid meeting or exceeding DOT 3 standards. Be careful not to spill any brake fluid on painted surfaces, because it will damage the paint. Do not allow the fluid container or clutch reservoir to remain open any longer than necessary; brake fluid absorbs moisture from the air, reducing its effectiveness and causing brake line corrosion.

4. Install the reservoir cap.

Power Steering Pump

FLUID RECOMMENDATIONS

Hyundai recommends the use of DEXRON®II automatic transmission fluid.

LEVEL CHECK

Remote Reservoir

1. Park the car on a level surface.
2. Start the engine and turn the steering wheel all the way to the left and right several times. This will raise the fluid temperature to approximately 122°F (50°C).
3. With the engine idling, check the level of brake fluid in the power steering reservoir. The fluid should be maintained at the MAX line with the engine idling and at the MIN line with the engine off.
4. If the system requires fluid, clean around the reservoir cap with a shop rag to prevent contaminating the fluid with dirt.
5. Remove the cap and add the required amount of fluid to the system.

➡ When making additions of fluid, use only fresh, uncontaminated brake fluid meeting or exceeding DOT 3 standards. Be careful not to spill any brake fluid on painted surfaces, because it will damage the paint. Do not allow the fluid container or clutch reservoir to remain open any longer than necessary; brake fluid absorbs moisture from the air, reducing its effectiveness and causing brake line corrosion.

6. Install the reservoir cap.

The remote power steering fluid reservoir is located on the inner fender, near the coolant reserve tank

Fill the reservoir carefully. Overfilling could cause the fluid to foam and damage the pump

Pump Mounted Reservoir

1. Park the car on a level surface.
2. Start the engine and turn the steering wheel all the way to the left and right several times. This will raise the fluid temperature to approximately 122°F (50°C).
3. Turn the engine **OFF.**
4. Remove the dipstick from the reservoir. The level should be between the "MIN" and "MAX" marks on the dipstick.
5. If the system requires fluid, clean around the reservoir cap with a shop rag to prevent contaminating the fluid with dirt.
6. Remove the cap and add the required amount of fluid to the system.
7. Compare the levels in the power steering pump reservoir with and without the engine running. If the level varies 0.2 in. (5mm) or more, there is air in the system. If the fluid level rises suddenly after stopping the engine, this is also an indication that air is trapped in the system.

➡**If checking the level in extremely cold weather, a grinding noise may be heard from the power steering pump as soon as the engine is started and you begin to turn the steering wheel. This is normal and is due to the flow characteristics of the power steering fluid in cold temperatures.**

Chassis Greasing

BALL JOINT & STEERING LINKAGE SEALS, STEERING & DRIVESHAFT BOOTS

Ball joint and steering linkage seals and steering and driveshaft boots are permanently lubricated at the factory. They require no periodic lubrication. Inspect the seals and boots for damage and signs of leakage. Replace damaged boots and seals as necessary.

Body Lubrication

LOCK CYLINDERS

Apply graphite lubricant sparingly through the key slot. Insert the key and operate the lock several times to be sure that the lubricant is worked into the lock cylinder.

DOOR HINGES

Spray a silicone lubricant or white lithium grease on the hinge pivot points to eliminate any binding conditions. Open and close the door several times to be sure that the lubricant is evenly and thoroughly distributed.

HATCH

Spray a silicone lubricant or white lithium grease on all of the pivot and friction surfaces to eliminate any squeaks or binds. Work the tailgate to distribute the lubricant.

Rear Wheel Bearings

REPACKING

➡**Sodium based grease is not compatible with lithium based grease. Read the package labels and be careful not to mix the two types. If there is any doubt as to the type of grease used, completely clean the old grease from the bearing and hub before replacing.**

Before handling the bearings, there are a few things that you should remember to do and not to do.
DO the following:
• Remove all outside dirt from the housing before exposing the bearing.
• Treat a used bearing as gently as you would a new one.
• Work with clean tools in clean surroundings.
• Use clean, dry canvas gloves, or at least clean, dry hands.
• Clean solvents and flushing fluids are a must.
• Use clean paper when laying out the bearings to dry.
• Protect disassembled bearings from rust and dirt. Cover them up.
• Use clean rags to wipe bearings.
• Keep the bearings in oil-proof paper when they are to be stored or are not in use.
• Clean the inside of the housing before replacing the bearing.
Do NOT do the following:
• Don't work in dirty surroundings.
• Don't use dirty, chipped or damaged tools.
• Try not to work on wooden work benches or use wooden mallets.
• Don't handle bearings with dirty or moist hands.
• Do not use gasoline for cleaning. Use a safe solvent.
• Do not spin dry bearings with compressed air. They will be damaged.
• Avoid using cotton waste or dirty cloths to wipe bearings.
• Try not to scratch or nick bearing surfaces.

• Do not allow the bearing to come in contact with dirt or rust at any time.

Only the rear wheel bearings require periodic maintenance. A premium high melting point grease meeting such as NLGI No. 2 or equivalent must be used. Long fiber type greases must not be used. This service is recommended any time the rear brake drum is removed.

1. Raise and support the vehicle safely.
2. Remove the wheel bearings.
3. Clean all parts in a non-flammable solvent and let them air dry.

➡Only use lit free rags to dry the bearings. Never spin-dry a bearing with compressed air, as this will damage the rollers!

4. Check for excessive wear and damage. Replace the bearing as necessary.

5. Packing wheel bearings with grease is best accomplished by using a wheel bearing packer (available at most automotive stores). If one is not available they may be packed by hand.

6. Place a healthy glob of grease in the palm of one hand and force the edge of the bearing into it so that the grease fills the space between the rollers and the bearing cage. Do this until the whole bearing is packed.

7. Place the packed bearing on a clean sheet of paper until time for installation.

8. Install the wheel bearing.

Refer to Section 8 of this manual for information on servicing wheel bearings.

TRAILER TOWING

General Recommendations

Your vehicle was primarily designed to carry passengers and cargo. It is important to remember that towing a trailer will place additional loads on your vehicles engine, drivetrain, steering, braking and other systems. However, if you decide to tow a trailer, using the prior equipment is a must.

Local laws may require specific equipment such as trailer brakes or fender mounted mirrors. Check your local laws.

Trailer Weight

The weight of the trailer is the most important factor. A good weight-to-horsepower ratio is about 35:1, 35 lbs. of Gross Combined Weight (GCW) for every horsepower your engine develops. Multiply the engine's rated horsepower by 35 and subtract the weight of the vehicle passengers and luggage. The number remaining is the approximate ideal maximum weight you should tow, although a numerically higher axle ratio can help compensate for heavier weight.

Hitch (Tongue) Weight

◆ See Figure 145

Calculate the hitch weight in order to select a proper hitch. The weight of the hitch is usually 9–11% of the trailer gross weight and should be measured with the trailer loaded. Hitches fall into various categories:

those that mount on the frame and rear bumper, the bolt-on type, or the weld-on distribution type used for larger trailers. Axle mounted or clamp-on bumper hitches should never be used.

Check the gross weight rating of your trailer. Tongue weight is usually figured as 10% of gross trailer weight. Therefore, a trailer with a maximum gross weight of 2000 lbs. will have a maximum tongue weight of 200 lbs. Class I trailers fall into this category. Class II trailers are those with a gross weight rating of 2000–3000 lbs., while Class III trailers fall into the 3500–6000 lbs. category. Class IV trailers are those over 6000 lbs. and are for use with fifth wheel trucks, only.

When you've determined the hitch that you'll need, follow the manufacturer's installation instructions, exactly, especially when it comes to fastener torques. The hitch will subjected to a lot of stress and good hitches come with hardened bolts. Never substitute an inferior bolt for a hardened bolt.

Cooling

ENGINE

Overflow Tank

One of the most common, if not THE most common, problems associated with trailer towing is engine overheating. If you have a cooling system without an expansion tank, you'll definitely need to get an aftermarket expansion tank kit, preferably one with at least a 2 quart capacity. These kits are easily installed on the radiator's overflow hose, and come with a pressure cap designed for expansion tanks.

Flex Fan

Another helpful accessory for vehicles using a belt-driven radiator fan is a flex fan. These fans are large diameter units designed to provide more airflow at low speeds, by using fan blades that have deeply cupped surfaces. The blades then flex, or flatten out, at high speed, when less cooling air is needed. These fans are far lighter in weight than stock fans, requiring less horsepower to drive them. Also, they are far quieter than stock fans. If you do decide to replace your stock fan with a flex fan, note that if your vehicle has a fan clutch, a spacer will be needed between the flex fan and water pump hub.

Oil Cooler

Aftermarket engine oil coolers are helpful for prolonging engine oil life and reducing overall engine temperatures. Both of these factors increase engine life. While not absolutely necessary in towing Class I and some Class II trailers, they are recommended for heavier Class II and all Class III towing. Engine oil cooler systems usually consist of an adapter, screwed on in place of the oil filter, a remote filter mounting and a

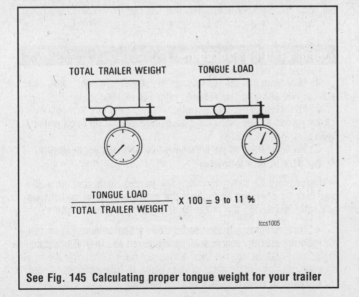

TOTAL TRAILER WEIGHT

TONGUE LOAD

$$\frac{\text{TONGUE LOAD}}{\text{TOTAL TRAILER WEIGHT}} \times 100 = 9 \text{ to } 11 \text{ \%}$$

tccs1005

See Fig. 145 Calculating proper tongue weight for your trailer

multi-tube, finned heat exchanger, which is mounted in front of the radiator or air conditioning condenser.

TRANSAXLE

An automatic transaxle is usually recommended for trailer towing. Modern automatics have proven reliable and, of course, easy to operate, in trailer towing. The increased load of a trailer, however, causes an increase in the temperature of the automatic transmission fluid. Heat is the worst enemy of an automatic transaxle. As the temperature of the fluid increases, the life of the fluid decreases.

It is essential, therefore, that you install an automatic transaxle cooler. The cooler, which consists of a multi-tube, finned heat exchanger, is usually installed in front of the radiator or air conditioning compressor, and hooked in-line with the transaxle cooler tank inlet line. Follow the cooler manufacturer's installation instructions.

Select a cooler of at least adequate capacity, based upon the combined gross weights of the vehicle and trailer.

Cooler manufacturers recommend that you use an aftermarket cooler in addition to, and not instead of, the present cooling tank in your radiator. If you do want to use it in place of the radiator cooling tank, get a cooler at least two sizes larger than normally necessary.

➡**A transaxle cooler can, sometimes, cause slow or harsh shifting in the transaxle during cold weather, until the fluid has a chance to come up to normal operating temperature. Some coolers can be purchased with or retrofitted with a temperature bypass valve which will allow fluid flow through the cooler only when the fluid has reached a certain operating temperature.**

Handling A Trailer

Towing a trailer with ease and safety requires a certain amount of experience. It's a good idea to learn the feel of a trailer by practicing turning, stopping and backing in an open area such as an empty parking lot.

TOWING THE VEHICLE

Preferred Method—Flatbed

For maximum safety to the components of your drive train and chassis, it is most desirable to have your vehicle towed by on a flatbed or whole car trailer. The only way to properly place the vehicle on a flatbed is to have it pulled on from the front.

Alternate Method—T-Hook

If a flatbed is unavailable, your vehicle can be towed using a T-hook wrecker. In this case, it is best to tow from the front, with the front wheels off the ground, as this will prevent wear and tear on the drive train. Tow vehicle speed should not exceed 35 mph (56 km/h) when using this method.

When necessary, you can tow using the T-hook in the rear, with the front wheels on the ground. All of the previous conditions for front towing are applicable AND the total distance towed should NOT EXCEED 50 miles (80 km), otherwise transaxle damage may occur.

Last Chance Method—Dolly

If absolutely necessary, you can tow your vehicle with either the front or rear wheels on a dolly. Again the preferred method would be to leave the rear wheels on the ground and the front on the dolly so the drive train is not turning. All conditions which apply to the T-hook method also apply for the dolly method.

JUMP STARTING A DEAD BATTERY

♦ **See Figure 146**

Whenever a vehicle is jump started, precautions must be followed in order to prevent the possibility of personal injury. Remember that batteries contain a small amount of explosive hydrogen gas which is a by-product of battery charging. Sparks should always be avoided when working around batteries, especially when attaching jumper cables. To minimize the possibility of accidental sparks, follow the procedure carefully.

✳✳ CAUTION

NEVER hook the batteries up in a series circuit or the entire electrical system will go up in smoke, including the starter!

Vehicles equipped with a diesel engine may utilize two 12 volt batteries. If so, the batteries are connected in a parallel circuit (positive terminal to positive terminal, negative terminal to negative terminal). Hooking the batteries up in parallel circuit increases battery cranking power without increasing total battery voltage output. Output remains at 12 volts. On the other hand, hooking two 12 volt batteries up in a series circuit (positive terminal to negative terminal, positive terminal to negative terminal) increases total battery output to 24 volts (12 volts plus 12 volts).

Jump Starting Precautions

• Be sure that both batteries are of the same voltage. Vehicles covered by this manual and most vehicles on the road today utilize a 12 volt charging system.

• Be sure that both batteries are of the same polarity (that is, they have the same terminal grounded—in most cases the NEGATIVE one).
• Be sure that the vehicles are not touching or a short could occur.
• On serviceable batteries, be sure the vent cap holes are not obstructed.
• Do not smoke or allow sparks anywhere near the batteries.
• In cold weather, make sure the battery electrolyte is not frozen. This can occur more readily in a battery that has been in a state of discharge.
• Do not allow electrolyte to contact your skin or clothing.

Jump Starting Procedure

1. Make sure that the voltages of the 2 batteries are the same. Most batteries and charging systems are of the 12 volt variety.
2. Pull the jumping vehicle (with the good battery) into a position so the jumper cables can reach the dead battery and that vehicle's engine. Make sure that the vehicles do NOT touch.
3. Place the transmissions/transaxles of both vehicles in **Neutral** (MT) or **P** (AT), as applicable, then firmly set their parking brakes.

➡**If necessary for safety reasons, the hazard lights on both vehicles may be operated throughout the entire procedure without significantly increasing the difficulty of jumping the dead battery.**

4. Turn all lights and accessories OFF on both vehicles. Make sure the ignition switches on both vehicles are turned to the **OFF** position.
5. Cover the battery cell caps with a rag, but do not cover the terminals.
6. Make sure the terminals on both batteries are clean and free of

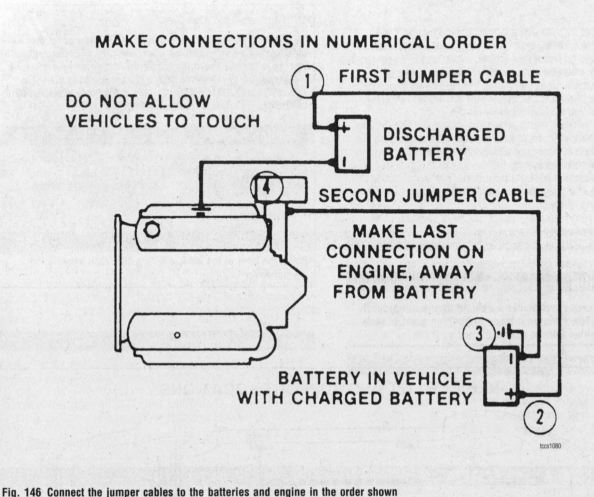

MAKE CONNECTIONS IN NUMERICAL ORDER

(1) **FIRST JUMPER CABLE**

DO NOT ALLOW VEHICLES TO TOUCH

DISCHARGED BATTERY

SECOND JUMPER CABLE

MAKE LAST CONNECTION ON ENGINE, AWAY FROM BATTERY

(3)

(2)

BATTERY IN VEHICLE WITH CHARGED BATTERY

tccs1080

Fig. 146 Connect the jumper cables to the batteries and engine in the order shown

corrosion or proper electrical connection will be impeded. If necessary, clean the battery terminals before proceeding.

7. Identify the positive (+) and negative (-) terminals on both batteries.

8. Connect the first jumper cable to the positive (+) terminal of the dead battery, then connect the other end of that cable to the positive (+) terminal of the booster (good) battery.

9. Connect one end of the other jumper cable to the negative (-) terminal on the booster battery and the final cable clamp to an engine bolt head, alternator bracket or other solid, metallic point on the engine with the dead battery. Try to pick a ground on the engine that is positioned away from the battery in order to minimize the possibility of the 2 clamps touching should one loosen during the procedure. DO NOT connect this clamp to the negative (-) terminal of the bad battery.

✳✳ CAUTION

Be very careful to keep the jumper cables away from moving parts (cooling fan, belts, etc.) on both engines.

10. Check to make sure that the cables are routed away from any moving parts, then start the donor vehicle's engine. Run the engine at moderate speed for several minutes to allow the dead battery a chance to receive some initial charge.

11. With the donor vehicle's engine still running slightly above idle, try to start the vehicle with the dead battery. Crank the engine for no more than 10 seconds at a time and let the starter cool for at least 20 seconds between tries. If the vehicle does not start in 3 tries, it is likely that something else is also wrong or that the battery needs additional time to charge.

12. Once the vehicle is started, allow it to run at idle for a few seconds to make sure that it is operating properly.

13. Turn ON the headlights, heater blower and, if equipped, the rear defroster of both vehicles in order to reduce the severity of voltage spikes and subsequent risk of damage to the vehicles' electrical systems when the cables are disconnected. This step is especially important to any vehicle equipped with computer control modules.

14. Carefully disconnect the cables in the reverse order of connection. Start with the negative cable that is attached to the engine ground, then the negative cable on the donor battery. Disconnect the positive cable from the donor battery and finally, disconnect the positive cable from the formerly dead battery. Be careful when disconnecting the cables from the positive terminals not to allow the alligator clips to touch any metal on either vehicle or a short and sparks will occur.

JACKING

▶ See Figure 147

Your vehicle was supplied with a jack for emergency road repairs. This jack is fine for changing a flat tire or other short term procedures not requiring you to go beneath the vehicle. If it is used in an emergency situation, carefully follow the instructions provided either with the jack or in your owner's manual. Do not attempt to use the jack on any portions of the vehicle other than specified by the vehicle manufacturer. Always block the diagonally opposite wheel when using a jack.

Always raise a vehicle from the approved points on the chassis. Be sure to block the diagonally opposite wheel. Place jackstands under the vehicles at the points mentioned or directly under the frame when you are going to work under the vehicle.

With the exception of a hoist, the most convenient way of raising the vehicle is the use of a garage or floor jack. You may use the floor jack at any of the points illustrated.

Never place the jack under the radiator, engine or transmission components. Severe and expensive damage will result when the jack is raised. Additionally, never jack under the floorpan or bodywork; the metal will deform.

☀ CAUTION

Never work or even reach under a vehicle that is not properly supported. The few minutes it takes to position a set of jackstands are precious little to ask to protect your life.

Raise the front of the vehicle with a floor jack beneath the crossmember . . .

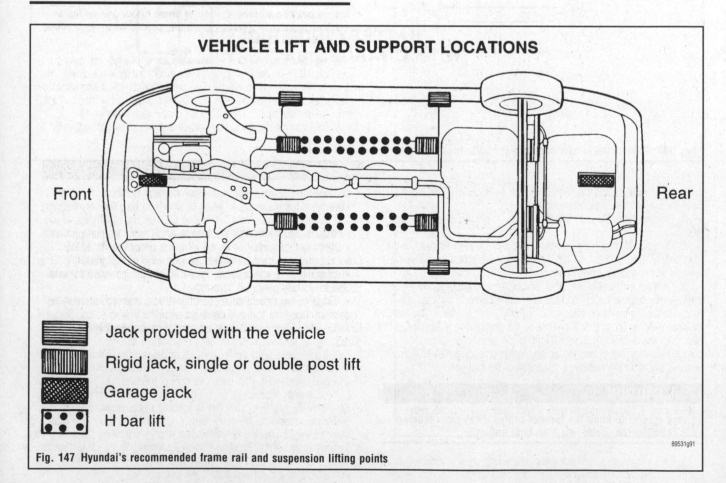

VEHICLE LIFT AND SUPPORT LOCATIONS

Front

Rear

Jack provided with the vehicle

Rigid jack, single or double post lift

Garage jack

H bar lift

Fig. 147 Hyundai's recommended frame rail and suspension lifting points

. . . and secure the vehicle with jackstands beneath the jacking/support points, behind the front wheels

. . . and support it with jackstands positioned under the frame rails

Whenever you plan to work under the vehicle, you must support it on jackstands or ramps. NEVER use cinder blocks or stacks of wood to support the vehicle, even if you're only going to be under it for a few minutes. Never crawl under the vehicle when it is supported only by the tire-changing jack or other floor jack.

➡**Always position a block of wood or small rubber pad on top of the jack or jackstand to protect the lifting point's finish when lifting or supporting the vehicle.**

Small hydraulic, screw, or scissors jacks are satisfactory for raising the vehicle. Drive-on trestles or ramps are also a handy and safe way to both raise and support the vehicle. Be careful though, some ramps may be too steep to drive your vehicle onto without scraping the front bottom panels. Never support the vehicle on any suspension member (unless specifically instructed to do so by a repair manual) or by an underbody panel.

Jacking Precautions

The following safety points cannot be overemphasized:
• Always block the opposite wheel or wheels to keep the vehicle from rolling off the jack.
• When raising the front of the vehicle, firmly apply the parking brake.
• DON'T run the engine while the vehicle is on jackstands, ESPECIALLY if one or more drive wheels are remaining on the ground.
• When the drive wheels are to remain on the ground, leave the vehicle in gear to help prevent it from rolling.
• Always use jackstands to support the vehicle when you are working underneath. Place the stands beneath the vehicle's jacking points. Before climbing underneath, rock the vehicle a bit to make sure it is firmly supported.

Raise the rear of the vehicle with a floor jack beneath the rear frame support . . .

Maintenance Under Normal Usage

NO	DESCRIPTION	MILES X 1000	7.5	15	22.5	30	37.5	45	52.5	60
		KILOMETERS X 1000	12	24	36	48	60	72	84	96
		MONTHS	5	10	20	30	40	50	60	70
	EMISSION CONTROL ITEMS									
1	ENGINE OIL AND FILTER ②		R	R	R	R	R	R	R	R
2	VALVE CLEARANCE ①			I		I		I		I
3	FUEL FILTER								R	
4	FUEL LINES AND CONNECTIONS								I	
5	VACUUM, CRANKCASE VENTILATION HOSES								I	
6	FUEL HOSE, VAPOR HOSE & FUEL FILLER CAP								I	
7	AIR CLEANER FILTER					R				R
8	SPARK PLUGS ③					R				R
9	EVAPORATIVE EMISSION CONTROL SYSTEM								I	

NO	DESCRIPTION	MILES X 1000	7.5	15	22.5	30	37.5	45	52.5	60
		KILOMETERS X 1000	12	24	36	48	60	72	84	96
		MONTHS	5	10	20	30	40	50	60	70
	GENERAL ITEMS									
1	DRIVE BELT (WATER PUMP AND ALTERNATOR)					I				I
2	ENGINE COOLANT				R					R
3	TIMING BELT									R
4	MANUAL TRANSAXLE OIL					I				I
5	AUTOMATIC TRANSAXLE OIL			I		R		I		R
6	BRAKE FLUID					R				R
7	BRAKE HOSES, LINES			I		I		I		I
8	REAR BRAKE DRUMS/LININGS/PARKING BRAKE					I				I
9	BRAKE PADS, CALIPERS, ROTORS			I		I		I		I
10	EXHAUST PIPE CONNECTIONS, MUFFLER & SUSPENSION BOLTS					I				I
11	STEERING GEAR RACK, LINKAGE & BOOTS					I				I
12	WHEEL BEARING GREASE					I				I
13	DRIVESHAFTS & BOOTS			I		I		I		I

R : Replace
I : Inspect, after inspection, clean, adjust, repair or replace if necessary

① Excel/Scoupe only

② On Turbo, replace every 5,000 miles (8,000 km) or every 6 months

③ 3.0L (vint), replace at 60,000 miles (96,000 km) only

89531g92

Maintenance Under Severe Usage

MAINTENANCE ITEM	MAINTENANCE OPERATION	MAINTENANCE INTERVALS	DRIVING CONDITION
ENGINE OIL AND FILTER	R	Every 3,000 miles (4,800 km) or 3 months	A, B, C, F, H
AIR CLEANER FILTER	R	More frequently	C, E
SPARK PLUGS	R	Every 24,000 miles (40,000 km) or 18 months	B, H
BRAKE PADS, CALIPERS, ROTORS	I	More frequently	C, D, G, H
REAR BRAKE DRUMS/ LININGS	I	More frequently	C, D, G, H
STEERING GEAR RACK LINKAGE & BOOTS	I	Every 7,500 miles (12,000 km) or 6 months	C, D, E, F
DRIVESHAFT & BOOTS	I	Every 7,500 miles (12,000 km) or 6 months	C, E, F
AUTOMATIC TRANSAXLE OIL	R	Every 15,000 miles (24,000 km) or 10 months	B, G, F

SEVERE DRIVING CONDITIONS

A = Repeated short distance driving

B = Extensive idling

C = Driving in dusty conditions

D = Driving in areas using salt or other corrosive materials or in very cold weather

E = Driving in sandy areas

F = More than 50% driving in heavy city traffic during hot weather above 90°F (32°C)

G = Driving in mountainous areas

H = Towing a trailer

R : Replace
I : Inspect, after inspection, clean, adjust, repair or replace if necessary

89531g93

CAPACITIES

Year	Model	Engine ID/VIN	Engine Displacement Liters (cc)	Engine Oil with Filter	Transmission (pts.) 4-Spd	5-Spd	Auto.	Transfer Case (pts.)	Drive Axle Front (pts.)	Rear (pts.)	Fuel Tank (gal.)	Cooling System (qts.)
1994	Elantra	R	1.6 (1595)	4.6	—	3.8	12.8	—	—	—	13.8	5.4
	Elantra	M	1.8 (1836)	4.6	—	3.8	12.8	—	—	—	13.8	5.4
	Excel	J	1.5 (1468)	3.6	3.6	3.8	12.2	—	—	—	10.6 ①	5.6
	Scoupe	E	1.5 (1495)	3.4	—	4.4	12.8	—	—	—	11.9	5.6
	Sonata	P	2.0 (1997)	4.0	—	4.0	12.8	—	—	—	17.2	7.7
	Sonata	T	3.0 (2972)	4.0	—	—	12.3	—	—	—	17.0	7.4
1995	Accent	K	1.5 (1495)	3.5	—	4.6	12.8	—	—	—	11.9	5.8
	Elantra	R	1.6 (1595)	4.6	—	3.8	12.8	—	—	—	13.8	5.4
	Elantra	M	1.8 (1836)	4.6	—	3.8	12.8	—	—	—	13.8	5.4
	Scoupe	E	1.5 (1495)	3.4	—	4.4	12.8	—	—	—	11.9	5.6
	Sonata	P	2.0 (1997)	4.0	—	4.0	12.8	—	—	—	17.2	7.7
	Sonata	T	3.0 (2972)	4.0	—	—	12.3	—	—	—	17.0	7.4
1996	Accent	K	1.5 (1495)	3.5	—	4.6	12.8	—	—	—	11.9	5.8
	Elantra	M	1.8 (1795)	4.6	—	3.8	12.8	—	—	—	13.8	5.4
	Sonata	P	2.0 (1997)	4.0	—	4.0	12.8	—	—	—	17.2	7.7
	Sonata	T	3.0 (2972)	4.0	—	—	12.3	—	—	—	17.0	7.4
1997	Accent	K	1.5 (1495)	3.5	—	4.6	12.8	—	—	—	11.9	5.8
	Elantra	M	1.8 (1795)	4.6	—	3.8	12.8	—	—	—	13.8	5.4
	Sonata	P	2.0 (1997)	4.0	—	4.0	12.8	—	—	—	17.2	7.7
	Sonata	T	3.0 (2972)	4.0	—	—	12.3	—	—	—	17.0	7.4
	Tiburon	M	1.8 (1795)	4.2	—	4.6	13.2	—	—	—	NA	6.3
	Tiburon	F	2.0 (1975)	4.2	—	4.6	13.2	—	—	—	NA	6.3
1998	Accent	K	1.5 (1495)	3.5	—	4.6	12.8	—	—	—	11.9	5.8
	Elantra	M	1.8 (1795)	4.6	—	3.8	12.8	—	—	—	13.8	5.4
	Sonata	P	2.0 (1997)	4.0	—	4.0	12.8	—	—	—	17.2	7.7
	Sonata	T	3.0 (2972)	4.0	—	—	12.3	—	—	—	17.0	7.4
	Tiburon	M	1.8 (1795)	4.2	—	4.6	13.2	—	—	—	NA	6.3
	Tiburon	F	2.0 (1975)	4.2	—	4.6	13.2	—	—	—	NA	6.3

① optional 13 gal fuel tank

89531c04

ENGLISH TO METRIC CONVERSION: MASS (WEIGHT)

Current **mass** measurement is expressed in pounds and ounces (lbs. & ozs.). The metric unit of mass (or weight) is the kilogram (kg). Even although this table does not show conversion of masses (weights) larger than 15 lbs, it is easy to calculate larger units by following the data immediately below.

To convert ounces (oz.) to grams (g): multiply th number of ozs. by 28
To convert grams (g) to ounces (oz.): multiply the number of grams by .035

To convert pounds (lbs.) to kilograms (kg): multiply the number of lbs. by .45
To convert kilograms (kg) to pounds (lbs.): multiply the number of kilograms by 2.2

lbs	kg	lbs	kg	oz	kg	oz	kg
0.1	0.04	0.9	0.41	0.1	0.003	0.9	0.024
0.2	0.09	1	0.4	0.2	0.005	1	0.03
0.3	0.14	2	0.9	0.3	0.008	2	0.06
0.4	0.18	3	1.4	0.4	0.011	3	0.08
0.5	0.23	4	1.8	0.5	0.014	4	0.11
0.6	0.27	5	2.3	0.6	0.017	5	0.14
0.7	0.32	10	4.5	0.7	0.020	10	0.28
0.8	0.36	15	6.8	0.8	0.023	15	0.42

ENGLISH TO METRIC CONVERSION: TEMPERATURE

To convert Fahrenheit (°F) to Celsius (°C): take number of °F and subtract 32; multiply result by 5; divide result by 9

To convert Celsius (°C) to Fahrenheit (°F): take number of °C and multiply by 9; divide result by 5; add 32 to total

Fahrenheit (F)		Celsius (C)		Fahrenheit (F)		Celsius (C)		Fahrenheit (F)		Celsius (C)	
°F	°C	°C	°F	°F	°C	°C	°F	°F	°C	°C	°F
−40	−40	−38	−36.4	80	26.7	18	64.4	215	101.7	80	176
−35	−37.2	−36	−32.8	85	29.4	20	68	220	104.4	85	185
−30	−34.4	−34	−29.2	90	32.2	22	71.6	225	107.2	90	194
−25	−31.7	−32	−25.6	95	35.0	24	75.2	230	110.0	95	202
−20	−28.9	−30	−22	100	37.8	26	78.8	235	112.8	100	212
−15	−26.1	−28	−18.4	105	40.6	28	82.4	240	115.6	105	221
−10	−23.3	−26	−14.8	110	43.3	30	86	245	118.3	110	230
−5	−20.6	−24	−11.2	115	46.1	32	89.6	250	121.1	115	239
0	−17.8	−22	−7.6	120	48.9	34	93.2	255	123.9	120	248
1	−17.2	−20	−4	125	51.7	36	96.8	260	126.6	125	257
2	−16.7	−18	−0.4	130	54.4	38	100.4	265	129.4	130	266
3	−16.1	−16	3.2	135	57.2	40	104	270	132.2	135	275
4	−15.6	−14	6.8	140	60.0	42	107.6	275	135.0	140	284
5	−15.0	−12	10.4	145	62.8	44	112.2	280	137.8	145	293
10	−12.2	−10	14	150	65.6	46	114.8	285	140.6	150	302
15	−9.4	−8	17.6	155	68.3	48	118.4	290	143.3	155	311
20	−6.7	−6	21.2	160	71.1	50	122	295	146.1	160	320
25	−3.9	−4	24.8	165	73.9	52	125.6	300	148.9	165	329
30	−1.1	−2	28.4	170	76.7	54	129.2	305	151.7	170	338
35	1.7	0	32	175	79.4	56	132.8	310	154.4	175	347
40	4.4	2	35.6	180	82.2	58	136.4	315	157.2	180	356
45	7.2	4	39.2	185	85.0	60	140	320	160.0	185	365
50	10.0	6	42.8	190	87.8	62	143.6	325	162.8	190	374
55	12.8	8	46.4	195	90.6	64	147.2	330	165.6	195	383
60	15.6	10	50	200	93.3	66	150.8	335	168.3	200	392
65	18.3	12	53.6	205	96.1	68	154.4	340	171.1	205	401
70	21.1	14	57.2	210	98.9	70	158	345	173.9	210	410
75	23.9	16	60.8	212	100.0	75	167	350	176.7	215	414

ENGLISH TO METRIC CONVERSION: LENGTH

To convert inches (ins.) to millimeters (mm): multiply number of inches by 25.4

To convert millimeters (mm) to inches (ins.): multiply number of millimeters by .04

Inches	Decimals	Milli-meters	Inches to millimeters inches	mm
1/64	0.051625	0.3969	0.0001	0.00254
1/32	0.03125	0.7937	0.0002	0.00508
3/64	0.046875	1.1906	0.0003	0.00762
1/16	0.0625	1.5875	0.0004	0.01016
5/64	0.078125	1.9844	0.0005	0.01270
3/32	0.09375	2.3812	0.0006	0.01524
7/64	0.109375	2.7781	0.0007	0.01778
1/8	0.125	3.1750	0.0008	0.02032
9/64	0.140625	3.5719	0.0009	0.02286
5/32	0.15625	3.9687	0.001	0.0254
11/64	0.171875	4.3656	0.002	0.0508
3/16	0.1875	4.7625	0.003	0.0762
13/64	0.203125	5.1594	0.004	0.1016
7/32	0.21875	5.5562	0.005	0.1270
15/64	0.234375	5.9531	0.006	0.1524
1/4	0.25	6.3500	0.007	0.1778
17/64	0.265625	6.7469	0.008	0.2032
9/32	0.28125	7.1437	0.009	0.2286
19/64	0.296875	7.5406	0.01	0.254
5/16	0.3125	7.9375	0.02	0.508
21/64	0.328125	8.3344	0.03	0.762
11/32	0.34375	8.7312	0.04	1.016
23/64	0.359375	9.1281	0.05	1.270
3/8	0.375	9.5250	0.06	1.524
25/64	0.390625	9.9219	0.07	1.778
13/32	0.40625	10.3187	0.08	2.032
27/64	0.421875	10.7156	0.09	2.286
7/16	0.4375	11.1125	0.1	2.54
29/64	0.453125	11.5094	0.2	5.08
15/32	0.46875	11.9062	0.3	7.62
31/64	0.484375	12.3031	0.4	10.16
1/2	0.5	12.7000	0.5	12.70

Inches	Decimals	Milli-meters	Inches to millimeters inches	mm
33/64	0.515625	13.0969	0.6	15.24
17/32	0.53125	13.4937	0.7	17.78
35/64	0.546875	13.8906	0.8	20.32
9/16	0.5625	14.2875	0.9	22.86
37/64	0.578125	14.6844	1	25.4
19/32	0.59375	15.0812	2	50.8
39/64	0.609375	15.4781	3	76.2
5/8	0.625	15.8750	4	101.6
41/64	0.640625	16.2719	5	127.0
21/32	0.65625	16.6687	6	152.4
43/64	0.671875	17.0656	7	177.8
11/16	0.6875	17.4625	8	203.2
45/64	0.703125	17.8594	9	228.6
23/32	0.71875	18.2562	10	254.0
47/64	0.734375	18.6531	11	279.4
3/4	0.75	19.0500	12	304.8
49/64	0.765625	19.4469	13	330.2
25/32	0.78125	19.8437	14	355.6
51/64	0.796875	20.2406	15	381.0
13/16	0.8125	20.6375	16	406.4
53/64	0.828125	21.0344	17	431.8
27/32	0.84375	21.4312	18	457.2
55/64	0.859375	21.8281	19	482.6
7/8	0.875	22.2250	20	508.0
57/64	0.890625	22.6219	21	533.4
29/32	0.90625	23.0187	22	558.8
59/64	0.921875	23.4156	23	584.2
15/16	0.9375	23.8125	24	609.6
61/64	0.953125	24.2094	25	635.0
31/32	0.96875	24.6062	26	660.4
63/64	0.984375	25.0031	27	690.6

ENGLISH TO METRIC CONVERSION: TORQUE

To convert foot-pounds (ft. lbs.) to Newton-meters: multiply the number of ft. lbs. by 1.3

To convert inch-pounds (in. lbs.) to Newton-meters: multiply the number of in. lbs. by .11

in lbs	N-m	in lbs	N-m	in lbs	N-m	in lbs	N-m	in lbs	N-m
0.1	0.01	1	0.11	10	1.13	19	2.15	28	3.16
0.2	0.02	2	0.23	11	1.24	20	2.26	29	3.28
0.3	0.03	3	0.34	12	1.36	21	2.37	30	3.39
0.4	0.04	4	0.45	13	1.47	22	2.49	31	3.50
0.5	0.06	5	0.56	14	1.58	23	2.60	32	3.62
0.6	0.07	6	0.68	15	1.70	24	2.71	33	3.73
0.7	0.08	7	0.78	16	1.81	25	2.82	34	3.84
0.8	0.09	8	0.90	17	1.92	26	2.94	35	3.95
0.9	0.10	9	1.02	18	2.03	27	3.05	36	4.0

tccs1c02

ENGLISH TO METRIC CONVERSION: TORQUE

Torque is now expressed as either foot-pounds (ft./lbs.) or inch-pounds (in./lbs.). The metric measurement unit for torque is the Newton-meter (Nm). This unit—the Nm—will be used for all SI metric torque references, both the present ft./lbs. and in./lbs.

ft lbs	N-m	ft lbs	N-m	ft lbs	N-m	ft lbs	N-m
0.1	0.1	33	44.7	74	100.3	115	155.9
0.2	0.3	34	46.1	75	101.7	116	157.3
0.3	0.4	35	47.4	76	103.0	117	158.6
0.4	0.5	36	48.8	77	104.4	118	160.0
0.5	0.7	37	50.7	78	105.8	119	161.3
0.6	0.8	38	51.5	79	107.1	120	162.7
0.7	1.0	39	52.9	80	108.5	121	164.0
0.8	1.1	40	54.2	81	109.8	122	165.4
0.9	1.2	41	55.6	82	111.2	123	166.8
1	1.3	42	56.9	83	112.5	124	168.1
2	2.7	43	58.3	84	113.9	125	169.5
3	4.1	44	59.7	85	115.2	126	170.8
4	5.4	45	61.0	86	116.6	127	172.2
5	6.8	46	62.4	87	118.0	128	173.5
6	8.1	47	63.7	88	119.3	129	174.9
7	9.5	48	65.1	89	120.7	130	176.2
8	10.8	49	66.4	90	122.0	131	177.6
9	12.2	50	67.8	91	123.4	132	179.0
10	13.6	51	69.2	92	124.7	133	180.3
11	14.9	52	70.5	93	126.1	134	181.7
12	16.3	53	71.9	94	127.4	135	183.0
13	17.6	54	73.2	95	128.8	136	184.4
14	18.9	55	74.6	96	130.2	137	185.7
15	20.3	56	75.9	97	131.5	138	187.1
16	21.7	57	77.3	98	132.9	139	188.5
17	23.0	58	78.6	99	134.2	140	189.8
18	24.4	59	80.0	100	135.6	141	191.2
19	25.8	60	81.4	101	136.9	142	192.5
20	27.1	61	82.7	102	138.3	143	193.9
21	28.5	62	84.1	103	139.6	144	195.2
22	29.8	63	85.4	104	141.0	145	196.6
23	31.2	64	86.8	105	142.4	146	198.0
24	32.5	65	88.1	106	143.7	147	199.3
25	33.9	66	89.5	107	145.1	148	200.7
26	35.2	67	90.8	108	146.4	149	202.0
27	36.6	68	92.2	109	147.8	150	203.4
28	38.0	69	93.6	110	149.1	151	204.7
29	39.3	70	94.9	111	150.5	152	206.1
30	40.7	71	96.3	112	151.8	153	207.4
31	42.0	72	97.6	113	153.2	154	208.8
32	43.4	73	99.0	114	154.6	155	210.2

tccs1c03

ENGLISH TO METRIC CONVERSION: FORCE

Force is presently measured in pounds (lbs.). This type of measurement is used to measure spring pressure, specifically how many pounds it takes to compress a spring. Our present force unit (the pound) will be replaced in SI metric measurements by the Newton (N). This term will eventually see use in specifications for electric motor brush spring pressures, valve spring pressures, etc.

To convert pounds (lbs.) to Newton (N): multiply the number of lbs. by 4.45

lbs	N	lbs	N	lbs	N	oz	N
0.01	0.04	21	93.4	59	262.4	1	0.3
0.02	0.09	22	97.9	60	266.9	2	0.6
0.03	0.13	23	102.3	61	271.3	3	0.8
0.04	0.18	24	106.8	62	275.8	4	1.1
0.05	0.22	25	111.2	63	280.2	5	1.4
0.06	0.27	26	115.6	64	284.6	6	1.7
0.07	0.31	27	120.1	65	289.1	7	2.0
0.08	0.36	28	124.6	66	293.6	8	2.2
0.09	0.40	29	129.0	67	298.0	9	2.5
0.1	0.4	30	133.4	68	302.5	10	2.8
0.2	0.9	31	137.9	69	306.9	11	3.1
0.3	1.3	32	142.3	70	311.4	12	3.3
0.4	1.8	33	146.8	71	315.8	13	3.6
0.5	2.2	34	151.2	72	320.3	14	3.9
0.6	2.7	35	155.7	73	324.7	15	4.2
0.7	3.1	36	160.1	74	329.2	16	4.4
0.8	3.6	37	164.6	75	333.6	17	4.7
0.9	4.0	38	169.0	76	338.1	18	5.0
1	4.4	39	173.5	77	342.5	19	5.3
2	8.9	40	177.9	78	347.0	20	5.6
3	13.4	41	182.4	79	351.4	21	5.8
4	17.8	42	186.8	80	355.9	22	6.1
5	22.2	43	191.3	81	360.3	23	6.4
6	26.7	44	195.7	82	364.8	24	6.7
7	31.1	45	200.2	83	369.2	25	7.0
8	35.6	46	204.6	84	373.6	26	7.2
9	40.0	47	209.1	85	378.1	27	7.5
10	44.5	48	213.5	86	382.6	28	7.8
11	48.9	49	218.0	87	387.0	29	8.1
12	53.4	50	224.4	88	391.4	30	8.3
13	57.8	51	226.9	89	395.9	31	8.6
14	62.3	52	231.3	90	400.3	32	8.9
15	66.7	53	235.8	91	404.8	33	9.2
16	71.2	54	240.2	92	409.2	34	9.4
17	75.6	55	244.6	93	413.7	35	9.7
18	80.1	56	249.1	94	418.1	36	10.0
19	84.5	57	253.6	95	422.6	37	10.3
20	89.0	58	258.0	96	427.0	38	10.6

tccs1c04

ENGLISH TO METRIC CONVERSION: LIQUID CAPACITY

Liquid or fluid capacity is presently expressed as pints, quarts or gallons, or a combination of all of these. In the metric system the liter (l) will become the basic unit. Fractions of a liter would be expressed as deciliters, centiliters, or most frequently (and commonly) as milliliters.

To convert pints (pts.) to liters (l): multiply the number of pints by .47
To convert liters (l) to pints (pts.): multiply the number of liters by 2.1
To convert quarts (qts.) to liters (l): multiply the number of quarts by .95

To convert liters (l) to quarts (qts.): multiply the number of liters by 1.06
To convert gallons (gals.) to liters (l): multiply the number of gallons by 3.8
To convert liters (l) to gallons (gals.): multiply the number of liters by .26

gals	liters	qts	liters	pts	liters
0.1	0.38	0.1	0.10	0.1	0.05
0.2	0.76	0.2	0.19	0.2	0.10
0.3	1.1	0.3	0.28	0.3	0.14
0.4	1.5	0.4	0.38	0.4	0.19
0.5	1.9	0.5	0.47	0.5	0.24
0.6	2.3	0.6	0.57	0.6	0.28
0.7	2.6	0.7	0.66	0.7	0.33
0.8	3.0	0.8	0.76	0.8	0.38
0.9	3.4	0.9	0.85	0.9	0.43
1	3.8	1	1.0	1	0.5
2	7.6	2	1.9	2	1.0
3	11.4	3	2.8	3	1.4
4	15.1	4	3.8	4	1.9
5	18.9	5	4.7	5	2.4
6	22.7	6	5.7	6	2.8
7	26.5	7	6.6	7	3.3
8	30.3	8	7.6	8	3.8
9	34.1	9	8.5	9	4.3
10	37.8	10	9.5	10	4.7
11	41.6	11	10.4	11	5.2
12	45.4	12	11.4	12	5.7
13	49.2	13	12.3	13	6.2
14	53.0	14	13.2	14	6.6
15	56.8	15	14.2	15	7.1
16	60.6	16	15.1	16	7.6
17	64.3	17	16.1	17	8.0
18	68.1	18	17.0	18	8.5
19	71.9	19	18.0	19	9.0
20	75.7	20	18.9	20	9.5
21	79.5	21	19.9	21	9.9
22	83.2	22	20.8	22	10.4
23	87.0	23	21.8	23	10.9
24	90.8	24	22.7	24	11.4
25	94.6	25	23.6	25	11.8
26	98.4	26	24.6	26	12.3
27	102.2	27	25.5	27	12.8
28	106.0	28	26.5	28	13.2
29	110.0	29	27.4	29	13.7
30	113.5	30	28.4	30	14.2

tccs1c05

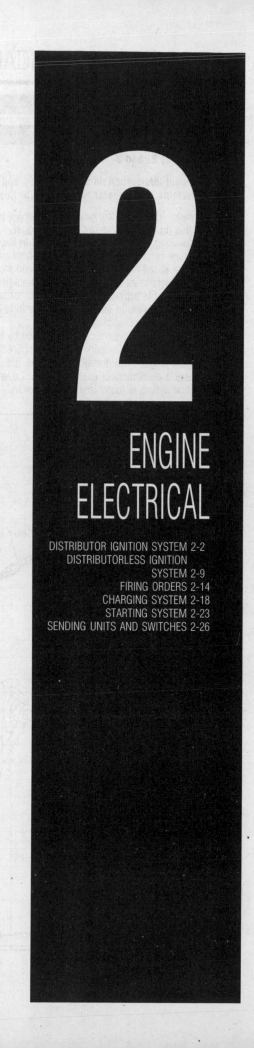

2

ENGINE ELECTRICAL

DISTRIBUTOR IGNITION SYSTEM

General Information

♦ **See Figures 1, 2, and 3**

➡ **For additional information on understanding and troubleshooting electrical systems, please refer to Section 6 of this manual.**

The distributor ignition system has timing controlled by the Electronic Control Module (ECM). The standard reference ignition timing data for the engine operating conditions are programmed in the memory of the ECM. The engine conditions (rpm, load and temperature) are detected by various sensors. Based on these sensor signals and the ignition timing data, a signal is sent to interrupt the primary current at the power transistor. The ignition coil is activated and a spark sent through the distributor, down the spark plug wires to the spark plugs. Ignition timing is controlled by the ECM for optimum performance.

The distributor ignition system can be identified by looking for the presence of a distributor (with spark plug wires connecting the distributor cap to the spark plugs). If no distributor is found, it can be assumed that the engine uses a distributorless ignition system. Coverage of the distributorless ignition system is found later in this section.

Diagnosis and Testing

SECONDARY SPARK TEST

♦ **See Figure 4 (p. 4)**

Hyundai suggests that this procedure can be performed with a standard spark plug. A far better method is to use a spark tester (available at most automotive parts stores). The spark tester resembles a spark plug without the ground electrode. It has a ground clip attached to the metal body and places the proper load on the ignition system during testing. This helps to identify intermittent or hard to find problems.

1. Disconnect a spark plug wire at the spark plug end.
2. Connect the wire to the spark tester and ground to a good ground on the engine.
3. Crank the engine and check for spark at the tester.
4. If spark exists at the tester, the ignition system is functioning properly.
5. If spark does not exist at the spark plug wire, remove the distributor cap and ensure that the rotor is turning when the engine is cranked.

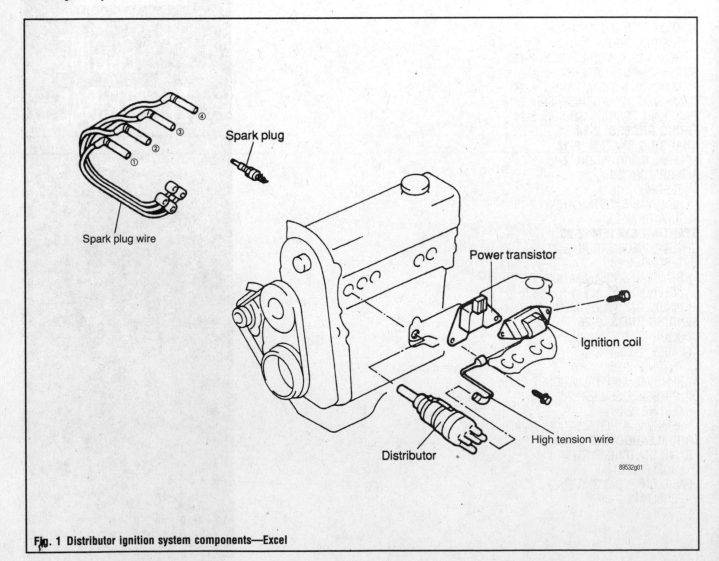

Fig. 1 Distributor ignition system components—Excel

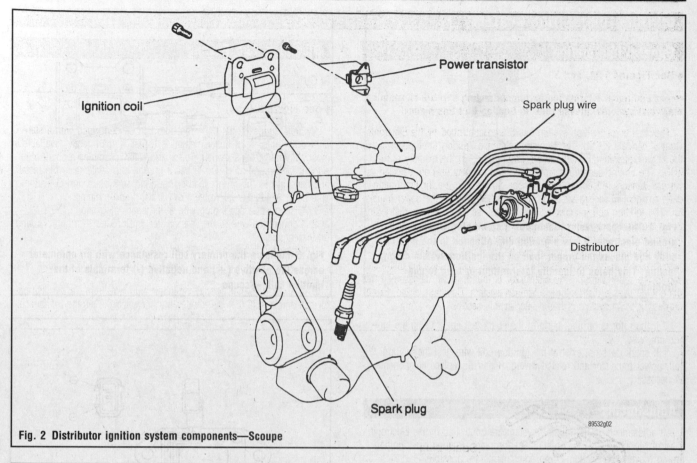

Power transistor

Ignition coil

Spark plug wire

Distributor

Spark plug

89532g02

Fig. 2 Distributor ignition system components—Scoupe

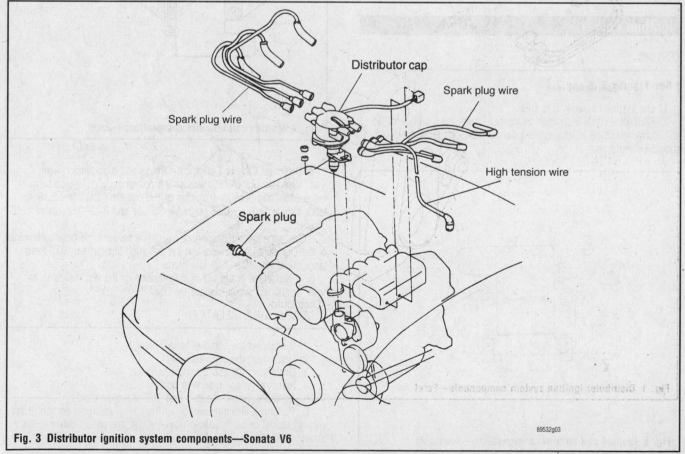

Distributor cap

Spark plug wire

Spark plug wire

High tension wire

Spark plug

89532g03

Fig. 3 Distributor ignition system components—Sonata V6

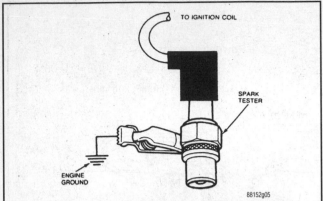

Fig. 4 The spark tester resembles a spark plug without the ground electrode. It has a ground clip attached to the metal body and places the proper load on the ignition system during testing. This helps to identify intermittent or hard to find problems

6. If the rotor is turning, perform the spark test again using the ignition coil wire.

7. If spark does not exist at the ignition coil wire, test the ignition coil, power transistor and related wiring. Repair or replace components as necessary.

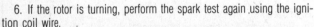

Adjustments

All adjustments in the ignition system are controlled by the Electronic Control Module (ECM) for optimum performance. Beyond base ignition timing (covered in Section 1), no adjustments are possible.

Ignition Coil

TESTING

▶ **See Figures 5, 6 and 7**

1. Ensure that the ignition is **OFF**.
2. Perform a visual inspection of the coil. If the resin portion of the coil is cracked or oil is leaking from the coil, the coil is defective and should be replaced.

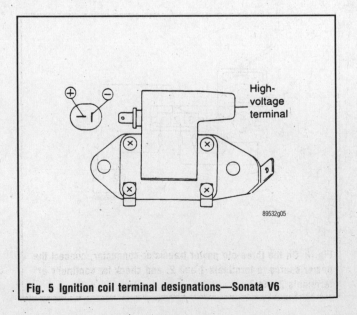

Fig. 5 Ignition coil terminal designations—Sonata V6

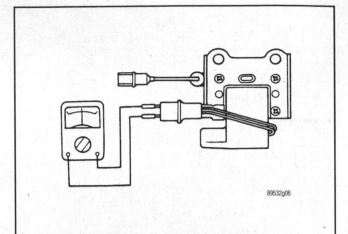

Fig. 6 Measure the primary coil resistance with an ohmmeter across the positive (+) and negative (-) terminals of the ignition coil—Scoupe

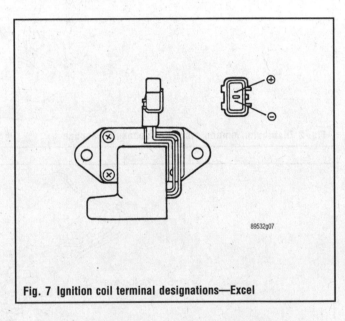

Fig. 7 Ignition coil terminal designations—Excel

3. Disconnect the coil electrical harness and high tension wire.
4. Using an ohmmeter, measure the coil primary resistance between the positive and negative terminals of the coil electrical harness. Resistance should be 0.45–0.55 ohms for Scoupe and 0.72–0.88 ohms for all others.
5. Measure the coil secondary resistance between the positive terminal of the coil electrical harness and the coil high tension terminal. Resistance should be 10.9–13.3 kilo-ohms.
6. If resistance is not within specification or the test results in an open or shorted circuit, replace the coil.

REMOVAL & INSTALLATION

1. Disconnect the negative battery cable.
2. Disconnect the coil wire.
3. Disconnect the coil electrical harness.
4. Remove the coil mounting bolts.
5. Carefully remove the coil from the intake manifold.
6. Perform a visual inspection of the coil. If the resin portion of the coil is cracked or oil is leaking from the coil, the coil is defective and should be replaced.

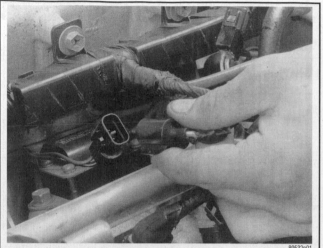

To remove the ignition coil, locate it on the intake manifold and disconnect the electrical harness . . .

Carefully inspect the coil for damage after removal

To install:

7. Position the coil on the intake manifold.
8. Install the mounting bolts and tighten to 9–11 ft. lbs. (12–15 Nm).
9. Connect the coil electrical harness.
10. Connect the coil wire.
11. Connect the negative battery cable.

Power Transistor

TESTING

Three-Pin Connector
▶ See Figure 8

1. Detach the power transistor's electrical connector.
2. Connect the negative terminal of a 3 volt power supply (battery) to terminal 2 of the power transistor.
3. Connect the positive terminals of a 3 volt power supply to terminal 1 of the power transistor.

. . . then remove the mounting bolts . . .

. . . and carefully remove the ignition coil from the intake manifold

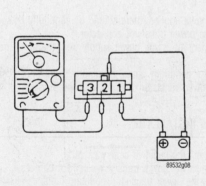

Fig. 8 On the three-pin power transistor connector, connect the power source to terminals 1 and 2, and check for continuity at terminals 2 and 3

4. Connect an ohmmeter across terminals 2 and 3 of the power transistor connector.

5. With 3 volts applied, there should be continuity between terminals 2 and 3 of the power transistor connector.

6. Disconnect the 3 volt power supply from the power transistor connector.

7. Check for continuity again. Continuity should not exist.

8. If the power transistor does not respond as stated, it should be replaced.

Four-Pin Connector

TURBOCHARGED SCOUPE

♦ **See Figure 9**

1. Disconnect the power transistor electrical connector.

2. Connect the negative terminal of a 3 volt power supply (battery) to terminal 1 of the power transistor.

3. Connect the positive terminals of a 3 volt power supply to terminal 4 of the power transistor.

4. Connect an ohmmeter across terminals 1 and 3 of the power transistor connector.

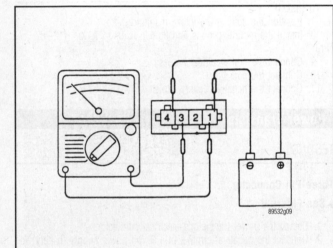

Fig. 9 On the four-pin power transistor connector, connect the power source to terminals 1 and 4, and check for continuity at terminals 1 and 3

5. With 3 volts applied, there should be continuity between terminals 1 and 3 of the power transistor connector.

6. Disconnect the 3 volt power supply from the power transistor connector.

7. Check for continuity again. Continuity should not exist.

8. If the power transistor does not respond as stated, it should be replaced.

REMOVAL & INSTALLATION

1. Disconnect the negative battery cable.
2. Disconnect the power transistor electrical harness.
3. Remove the power transistor mounting bolts.
4. Carefully remove the power transistor from the engine.
To install:
5. Install the power transistor on the engine.
6. Install the mounting bolt and tighten to securely.
7. Connect the power transistor electrical harness.
8. Connect the negative battery cable.

Distributor

REMOVAL & INSTALLATION

♦ **See Figures 10, 11 and 12 (p. 8)**

1. Rotate the engine and bring the No. 1 piston to TDC of its compression stroke.

2. Disconnect the negative battery cable.

3. Label and disconnect the electrical harness from the distributor.

4. Remove the distributor cap and lay it aside with the spark plug wires still attached.

5. Matchmark the rotor to the distributor, and the distributor to the engine.

➡ **Do not rotate the engine after removing the distributor.**

6. Unfasten the distributor mounting nut and remove the distributor assembly.

➡ **If the distributor is hard to remove, the O-rings on the distributor shaft are probably damaged.**

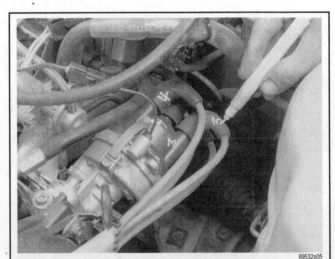

If you must remove the spark plug wires to remove the distributor cap, label them for reassembly

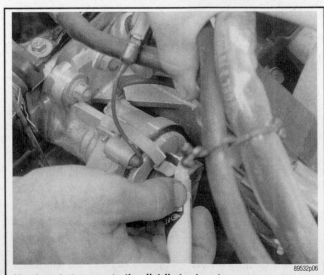

Matchmark the rotor to the distributor housing . . .

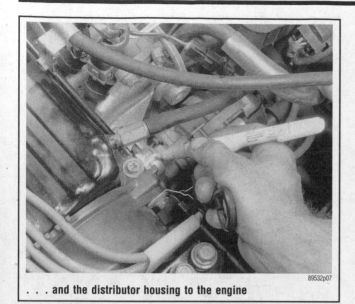

. . . and the distributor housing to the engine

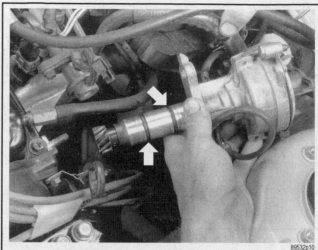

Pull the distributor straight out of the engine. Try not to damage the O-rings (indicated by arrows)

Loosen the distributor hold-down bolt . . .

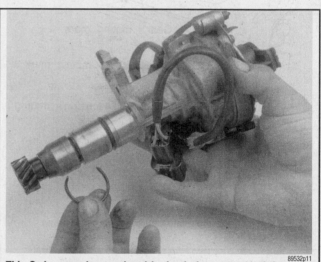

This O-ring was damaged and broke during removal of the distributor. It must be replaced

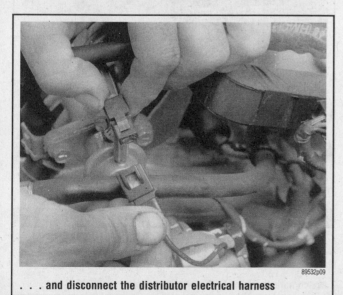

. . . and disconnect the distributor electrical harness

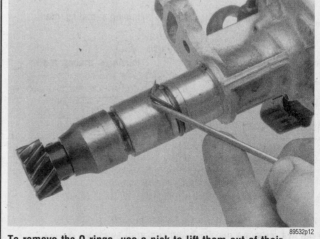

To remove the O-rings, use a pick to lift them out of their grooves and slide them off the distributor shaft

To install:

7. Carefully inspect the O-rings on the distributor shaft and replace as necessary.

➡️**If the engine was disturbed while the distributor was removed, it will be necessary to remove the No. 1 spark plug and rotate the engine clockwise until No. 1 piston is on the compression stroke. Align the timing pointer with TDC on the crankshaft damper.**

8. Align the distributor housing mating mark with the gear mating mark, as illustrated.

9. Lubricate the O-rings on the distributor shaft.

10. Install the distributor into the engine and ensure all matchmarks made during disassembly are aligned.

11. Snug the distributor hold-down nut.

12. Start the engine and adjust the ignition timing.

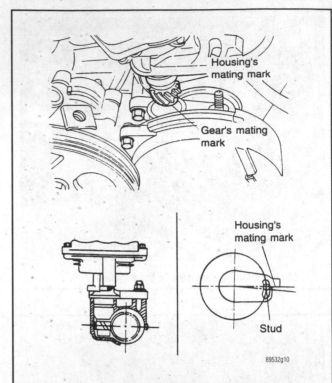

Fig. 12 Aligning the distributor housing and gear mating marks—Sonata V6

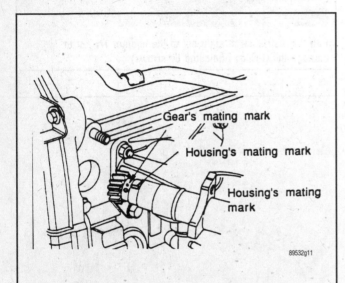

Fig. 10 Aligning the distributor housing and gear mating marks—Excel

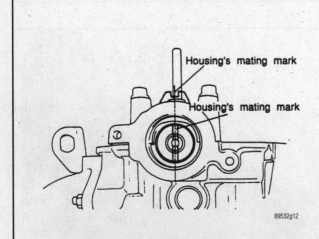

Fig. 11 Aligning the distributor housing and gear mating marks—Scoupe

1. Mating mark on gear   2. Mating mark on housing

Align the mating marks on the distributor housing and gear prior to installing the distributor in the engine

Crankshaft Position Sensor

Refer to Electronic Engine Controls in Section 4 for information on servicing the crankshaft position sensor.

Camshaft Position Sensor

Refer to Electronic Engine Controls in Section 4 for information on servicing the camshaft position sensor.

DISTRIBUTORLESS IGNITION SYSTEM

◆ **See Figures 13, 14, 15 and 16 (p. 9–12)**

The distributorless ignition system has timing controlled by the Electronic Control Module (ECM). The standard reference ignition timing data for the engine operating conditions are programmed in the memory of the ECM. The engine conditions (rpm, load and temperature) are detected by various sensors. Based on these sensor signals and the ignition timing data, a signal is sent to interrupt the primary current at the ignition coil.

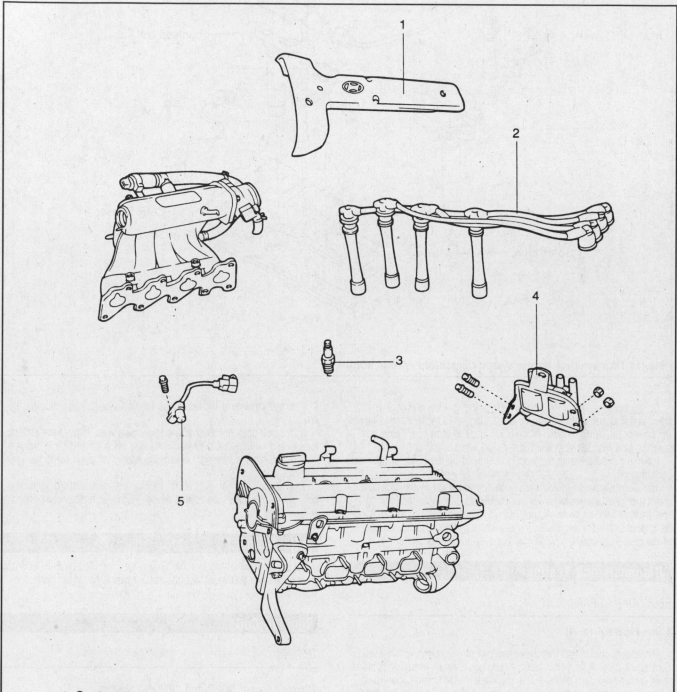

1. Center cover
2. Spark plug wire
3. Spark plug
4. Ignition coil
5. Camshaft position sensor

89532g13

Fig. 13 Distributorless ignition system components—Tiburon and 1996–98 Elantra

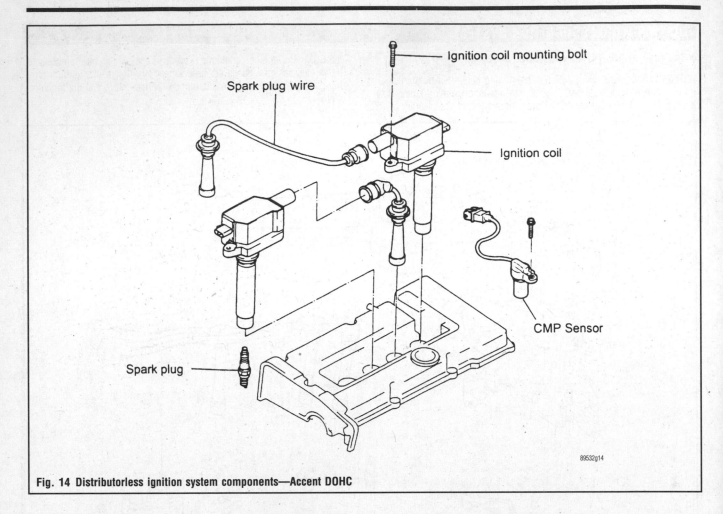

Fig. 14 Distributorless ignition system components—Accent DOHC

On all vehicles except the Accent DOHC, the ignition coil pack is activated and a spark sent through the spark plug wires to the spark plugs. On the Accent DOHC, individual coils are used at each spark plug. The spark is sent through very short spark plug wires to the spark plugs.

Ignition timing for both systems is controlled by the ECM for optimum performance.

The distributorless ignition system can be identified by the lack of a distributor. The spark plug wires are connected directly to the ignition coil pack or ignition coils (Accent DOHC). If a distributor is found, it can be assumed that the engine uses a distributor ignition system. Coverage of the distributor ignition system is found earlier in this section.

Diagnosis and Testing

SECONDARY SPARK TEST

♦ See Figure 4 (p. 4)

Hyundai suggests that this procedure can be performed with a standard spark plug. A far better method is to use a spark tester (available at most automotive parts stores). The spark tester resembles a spark plug without the ground electrode. It has a ground clip attached to the metal body and places the proper load on the ignition system during testing. This helps to identify intermittent or hard to find problems.
1. Disconnect a spark plug wire at the spark plug end.
2. Connect the wire to the spark tester and ground to a good ground on the engine.
3. Crank the engine and check for spark at the tester.

4. If spark exists at the tester, the ignition system is functioning properly.
5. If spark does not exist at the spark plug wire, remove the distributor cap and ensure that the rotor is turning when the engine is cranked.
6. If the rotor is turning, perform the spark test again using the ignition coil wire.
7. If spark does not exist at the ignition coil wire, test the ignition coil, power transistor and related wiring. Repair or replace components as necessary.

Adjustments

All adjustments in the ignition system are controlled by the Electronic Control Module (ECM) for optimum performance. No adjustments are possible.

Ignition Coil

TESTING

Tiburon, Accent SOHC and 1996–98 Elantra
♦ See Figure 17 (p. 12)

1. Ensure that the ignition is **OFF**.
2. Perform a visual inspection of the coil pack. If it is cracked or leaking oil, the coil pack is defective and should be replaced.
3. Disconnect the coil pack electrical harness.

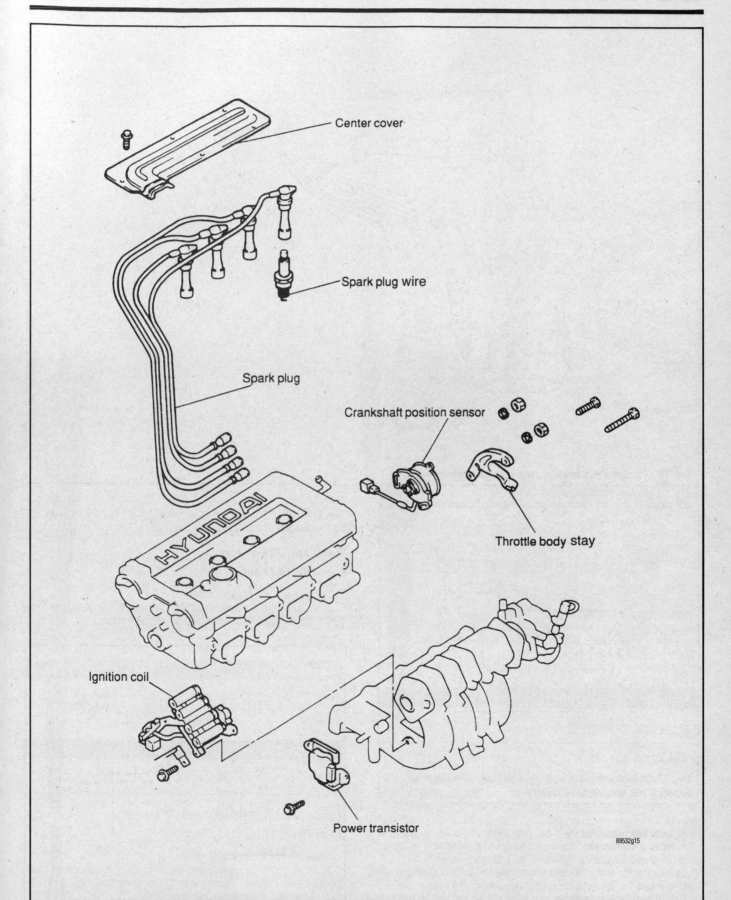

Fig. 15 Distributorless ignition system components—Sonata and 1994–95 Elantra

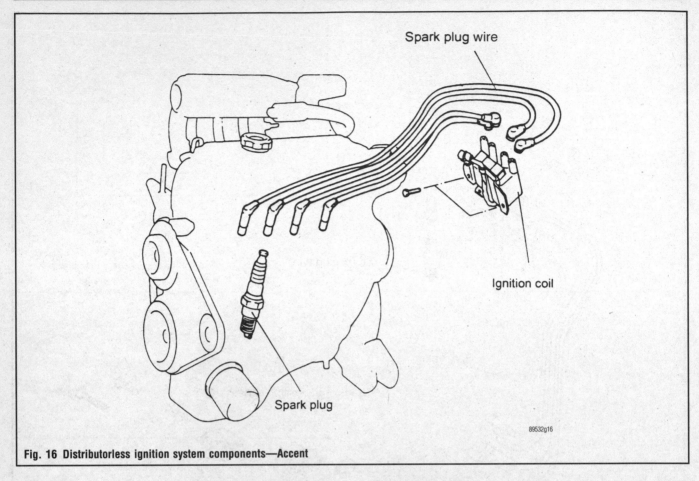

Fig. 16 Distributorless ignition system components—Accent

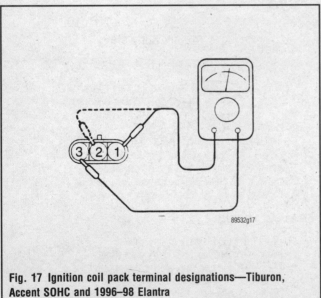

Fig. 17 Ignition coil pack terminal designations—Tiburon, Accent SOHC and 1996–98 Elantra

4. Label and disconnect the spark plug wires.

5. Using an ohmmeter, measure the coil primary resistance between terminals 2 and 3 (coils for cylinders 1 and 4) and terminals 1 and 3 (coils for cylinders 2 and 3). Resistance should be 0.45–0.55 ohms.

6. Measure the coil secondary resistance between the cylinder No. 1 and No. 4 high tension terminals, and also between the cylinder No. 2 and No. 3 high tension terminals. Resistance should be 10.3–13.9 kilo-ohms.

7. If resistance is not within specification, or the test results in an open or shorted circuit, replace the coil pack.

Sonata and 1994–95 Elantra

▶ See Figures 18 and 19

1. Ensure that the ignition is **OFF.**

2. Perform a visual inspection of the coil pack. If it is cracked or leaking oil, the coil pack is defective and should be replaced.

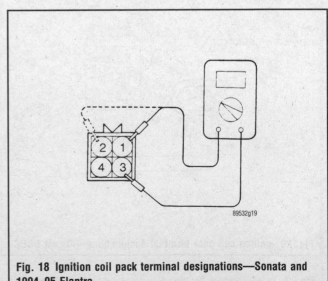

Fig. 18 Ignition coil pack terminal designations—Sonata and 1994–95 Elantra

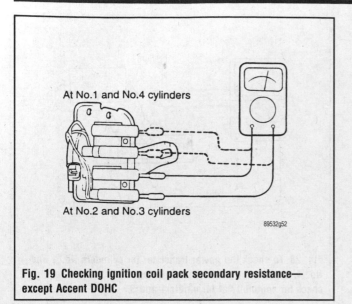

Fig. 19 Checking ignition coil pack secondary resistance—except Accent DOHC

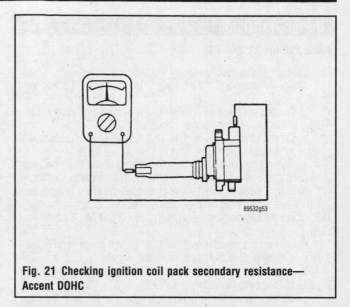

Fig. 21 Checking ignition coil pack secondary resistance—Accent DOHC

3. Disconnect the coil pack electrical harness.

4. Label and disconnect the spark plug wires.

5. Using an ohmmeter, measure the coil primary resistance between terminals 2 and 4 (coils for cylinders 1 and 4) and terminals 1 and 4 (coils for cylinders 2 and 3). Resistance should be 0.77–0.95 ohms.

6. Measure the coil secondary resistance between the cylinder No. 1 and No. 4 high tension terminals and the cylinder No. 2 and No. 3 high tension terminals. Resistance should be 10.3–13.9 kilo-ohms.

7. If resistance is not within specification or the test results in an open or shorted circuit, replace the coil pack.

Accent DOHC

♦ **See Figures 20 and 21**

1. Ensure that the ignition is **OFF**.

2. Perform a visual inspection of the coil pack. If it is cracked or leaking oil, the coil pack is defective and should be replaced.

3. Disconnect the coil pack electrical harness.

4. Label and disconnect the spark plug wires.

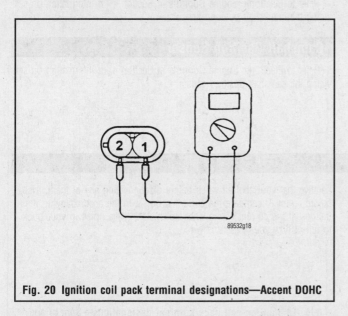

Fig. 20 Ignition coil pack terminal designations—Accent DOHC

5. Using an ohmmeter, measure the coil primary resistance between terminals 1 and 2 of each individual ignition coil. Resistance should be 0.45–0.55 ohms.

6. Measure the coil secondary resistance between the cylinder high tension terminals. Resistance should be 10.3–13.9 kilo-ohms.

7. If resistance is not within specification or the test results in an open or shorted circuit, replace the coil pack.

REMOVAL & INSTALLATION

Accent DOHC

♦ **See Figure 14 (p. 10)**

1. Disconnect the negative battery cable.

2. Disconnect the coil electrical harness.

3. Remove the coil mounting bolt.

4. Disconnect the spark plug wire for the adjoining cylinder from the spark plug.

5. Carefully remove the coil from the spark plug.

6. Perform a visual inspection of the coil. If damaged or leaking, it should be replaced.

To install:

7. Install the coil on the spark plug.

8. Connect the spark plug wire for the adjoining cylinder.

9. Install the mounting bolt and tighten to securely.

10. Connect the coil electrical harness.

11. Connect the negative battery cable.

Except Accent DOHC

1. Disconnect the negative battery cable.

2. Lable and disconnect the spark plug wires.

3. Disconnect the coil pack electrical harness.

4. Remove the coil pack mounting bolts.

5. Carefully remove the coil pack from the intake manifold.

6. Perform a visual inspection of the coil pack and replace if physically damaged or leaking.

To install:

7. Position the coil pack on the engine.

8. Install the mounting bolts and tighten securely.

9. Connect the coil pack electrical harness.

10. Connect the negative battery cable.

Power Transistor

♦ **See Figures 22 and 23**

1. Disconnect the power transistor electrical connector.
2. Check for continuity at the cylinders' No. 1 and No. 4 power transistor.

   a. Connect the negative terminal of a 1.5 volt power supply (battery) to terminal 3 of the power transistor.

   b. Connect the positive terminal of a 1.5 volt power supply to terminal 4 of the power transistor.

   c. Connect an ohmmeter across terminals 3 and 5 (with the negative ohmmeter lead on terminal 5) of the power transistor connector.

   d. With 1.5 volts applied, there should be continuity between terminals 3 and 5 of the power transistor connector.

3. Check for continuity at the cylinders' No. 2 and No. 3 power transistor.

   a. Connect the negative terminal of a 1.5 volt power supply (battery) to terminal 3 of the power transistor.

   b. Connect the positive terminal of a 1.5 volt power supply to terminal 2 of the power transistor.

   c. Connect an ohmmeter across terminals 1 and 3 (with the negative ohmmeter lead on terminal 1) of the power transistor connector.

   d. With 1.5 volts applied, there should be continuity between terminals 1 and 3 of the power transistor connector.

4. Disconnect the 1.5 volt power supply from the power transistor connector.

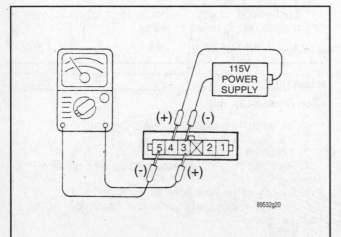

Fig. 22 To check the power transistor for cylinders No. 1 and No. 4, connect the power source to terminals 3 and 4, and check for continuity at terminals 3 and 5

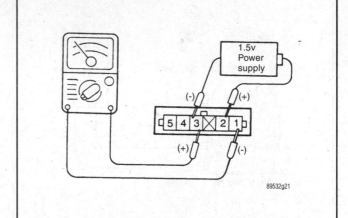

Fig. 23 To check the power transistor for cylinders No. 1 and No. 4, connect the power source to terminals 2 and 3, and check for continuity at terminals 1 and 3

5. Check for continuity again. Continuity should not exist.
6. If the power transistor does not respond as stated, it should be replaced.

REMOVAL & INSTALLATION

1. Disconnect the negative battery cable.
2. Disconnect the power transistor electrical harness.
3. Remove the power transistor mounting bolts.
4. Carefully remove the power transistor from the engine.

To install:

5. Install the power transistor on the engine.
6. Install the mounting bolt and tighten it securely.
7. Connect the power transistor electrical harness.
8. Connect the negative battery cable.

Crankshaft Position Sensor

Refer to Electronic Engine Controls in Section 4 for information on servicing the crankshaft position sensor.

Camshaft Position Sensor

Refer to Electronic Engine Controls in Section 4 for information on servicing the camshaft position sensor.

FIRING ORDERS

♦ **See Figures 24 thru 29**

➡**To avoid confusion, remove and tag the spark plug wires one at a time, for replacement.**

If a distributor is not keyed for installation with only one orientation, it could have been removed previously and rewired. The resultant wiring would hold the correct firing order, but could change the relative placement of the plug towers in relation to the engine. For this reason it is imperative that you label all wires before disconnecting any of them. Also, before removal, compare the current wiring with the accompanying illustrations. If the current wiring does not match, make notes in your book to reflect how your engine is wired.

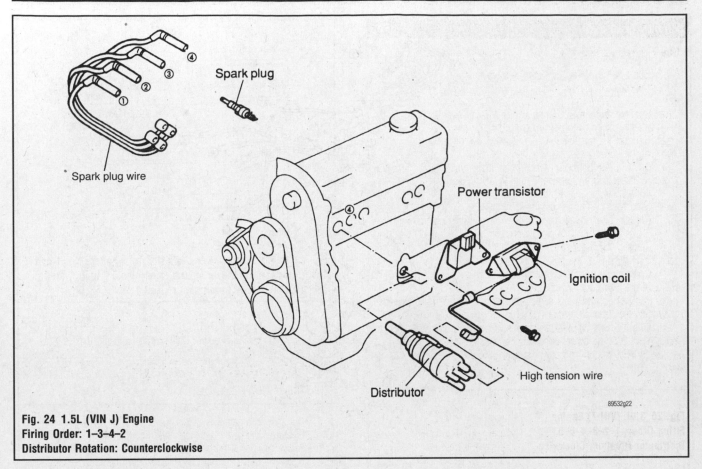

Fig. 24 1.5L (VIN J) Engine
Firing Order: 1–3–4–2
Distributor Rotation: Counterclockwise

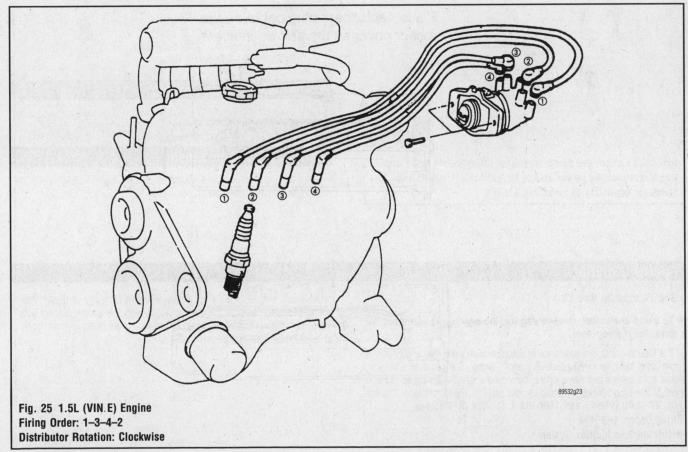

Fig. 25 1.5L (VIN E) Engine
Firing Order: 1–3–4–2
Distributor Rotation: Clockwise

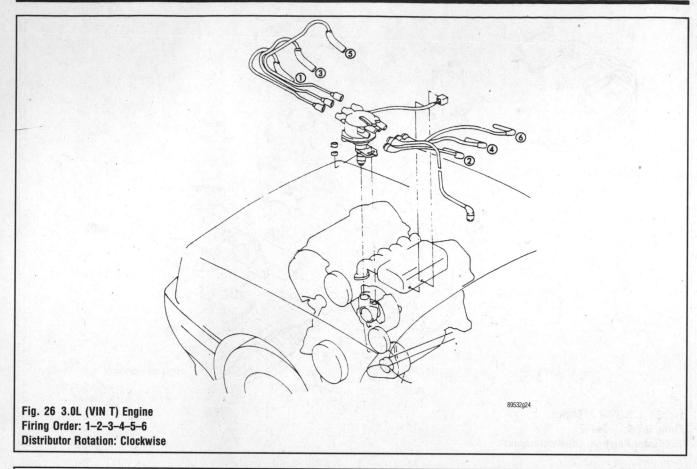

Fig. 26 3.0L (VIN T) Engine
Firing Order: 1–2–3–4–5–6
Distributor Rotation: Clockwise

89532g24

Place each spark plug cable on the
rocker cover as the arrows indicate.

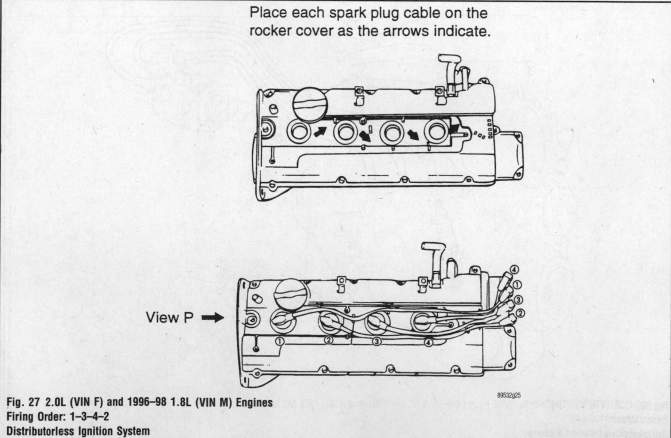

Fig. 27 2.0L (VIN F) and 1996–98 1.8L (VIN M) Engines
Firing Order: 1–3–4–2
Distributorless Ignition System

89532g25

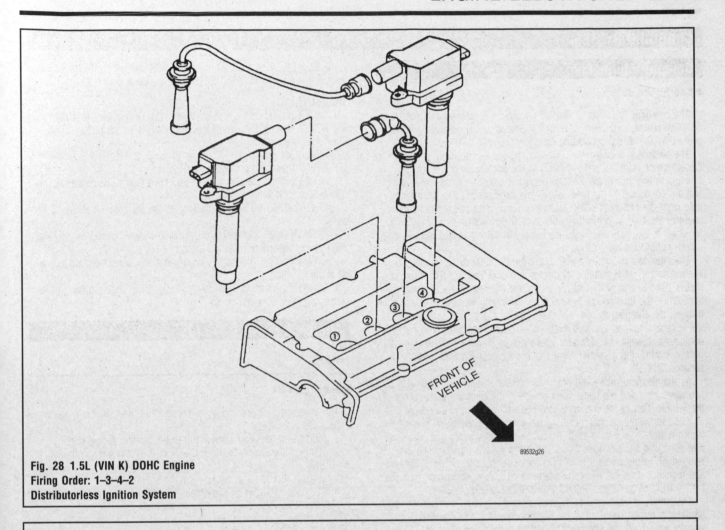

Fig. 28 1.5L (VIN K) DOHC Engine
Firing Order: 1–3–4–2
Distributorless Ignition System

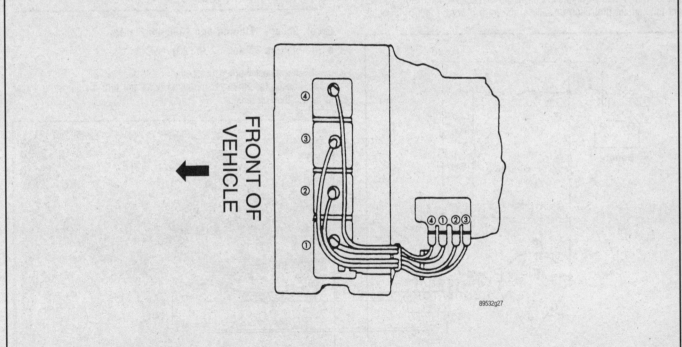

Fig. 29 1.5L (VIN K) SOHC, 2.0L (VIN P), 1994–95 1.6L (VIN R) and 1.8L (VIN M) Engines
Firing Order: 1–3–4–2
Distributorless Ignition System

CHARGING SYSTEM

General Information

♦ **See Figure 30**

The charging system is a negative (-) ground system which consists of an alternator, a regulator, a charge indicator, a storage battery, circuit protection and wiring connecting the components.

The alternator is belt-driven from the engine. Energy is supplied from the alternator (with integral regulator) to the rotating field through two brushes to two slip rings. The slip rings are mounted on the rotor shaft and are connected to the field coil. This energy supplied to the rotating field from the battery is called excitation current and is used to initially energize the field to begin the generation of electricity. Once the alternator starts to generate electricity, the excitation current comes from its own output rather than the battery.

The alternator produces power in the form of alternating current. The alternating current is rectified by diodes into direct current. The direct current is used to charge the battery and power the rest of the electrical system. When the ignition key is turned on, current flows from the battery, through the charging system indicator light on the instrument panel, to the voltage regulator, and to the alternator. Since the alternator is not producing any current, the alternator warning light comes on. When the engine is started, the alternator begins to produce current and turns the alternator light off.

As the alternator turns and produces current, this current is divided in two ways: charging the battery and powering the electrical components of the vehicle. Part of the current is returned to the alternator to enable it to increase its output. In this situation, the alternator is receiving current from the battery and from itself. A voltage regulator is wired into the current supply to the alternator to prevent it from receiving too much current, which would cause it to overproduce current. Conversely, if the voltage regulator does not allow the alternator to receive enough current, the battery will not be fully charged and will eventually go dead.

The battery is connected to the alternator at all times, whether the ignition key is turned on or off. If the battery were shorted to ground, the alternator would also be shorted. This would damage the alternator. To prevent this, circuit protection (usually in the form of a fuse link) is installed in the wiring between the battery and the alternator. If the battery is shorted, the circuit protection will protect the alternator.

PRECAUTIONS

- NEVER ground or short out the alternator or regulator terminals.
- NEVER operate the alternator with any of its or the battery's lead wires disconnected.
- NEVER use a fast battery charger to jump start a dead battery.
- NEVER attempt to polarize an alternator.
- NEVER subject the alternator to excessive heat or dampness (for instance, steam cleaning the engine).
- NEVER use arc welding equipment on the car with the alternator connected.
- ALWAYS observe proper polarity of the battery connections; be especially careful when jump starting the car.
- ALWAYS remove the battery or, at least, disconnect the ground cable while charging.
- ALWAYS disconnect the battery ground cable while repairing or replacing an electrical component.

Alternator

TESTING

♦ **See Figure 31**

The easiest way to test the performance of the alternator is to perform a regulated voltage test.

1. Start the engine and allow it to reach operating temperature.
2. Connect a voltmeter between the positive and negative terminals of the battery.
3. Voltage should be as specified in the chart.
4. If voltage is higher or lower than specification, a problem exists in the alternator or voltage regulator (or in their wiring).

REMOVAL & INSTALLATION

Excel, Scoupe, Tiburon and 1996–98 Elantra

♦ **See Figures 32 and 33 (p. 20)**

1. Disconnect the negative battery cable.
2. Loosen the alternator mounting bolts and turn the adjusting screw to relieve the belt tension.

Fig. 30 The charging system consists of an alternator with integral regulator, a charge indicator, a storage battery, circuit protection and wiring connecting the components

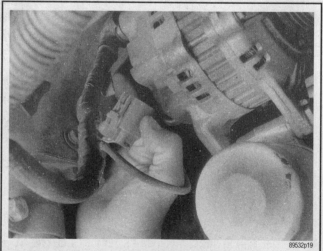

Disconnect the electrical harness from the back of the alternator . . .

Voltage regulator ambient temperature °C(°F)	Regulating voltage V	
	75A generator	90A generator
-20 (-4)	14.2-15.4	14.3-15.2
20 (68)	13.9-14.9	14.1-14.7
60 (140)	13.4-14.6	13.5-14.4
80 (176)	13.4-14.5	13.3-14.3

89532g29

Fig. 31 If regulated voltage is not within specifications, the alternator or regulator is probably faulty

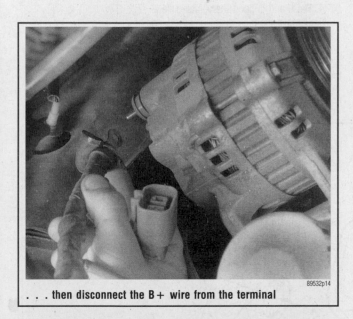

. . . then disconnect the B+ wire from the terminal

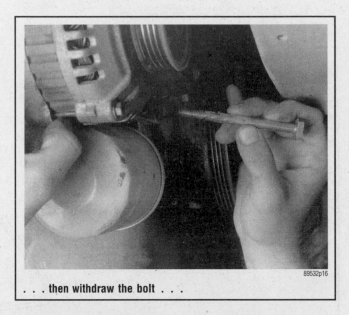

. . . then withdraw the bolt . . .

Loosen the alternator mounting bolt . . .

. . . and remove the alternator from the vehicle

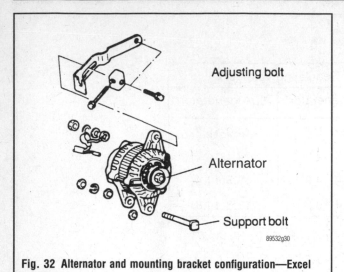

Fig. 32 Alternator and mounting bracket configuration—Excel and Scoupe

To install:

9. Position the alternator and install the mounting bolts.

10. Connect the B+ wire and the electrical harness to the alternator terminal. Make sure the wire nut is tight and the protective cap is firmly placed over the wire connection.

11. Install the left side mud guard.

12. Lower the vehicle.

13. Install and properly tension the drive belt.

14. Tighten the alternator support bolt to 14–18 ft. lbs. (20–25 Nm) and the adjusting lockbolt to 9–11 ft. lbs. (12–15 Nm).

15. Connect the negative battery cable.

16. Start the engine and check the charging system for proper operation.

Sonata DOHC and 1994–95 Elantra

♦ See Figure 34

1. Disconnect the negative battery cable.

2. Remove the radiator attaching bolts.

3. Disconnect the coolant reserve hose and the fan motor electrical harness.

4. Raise and support the vehicle safely.

5. Remove the mud guard under the engine.

6. Disconnect the oil pressure switch electrical harness.

7. Loosen the belt tensioner and remove the accessory drive belt.

8. Disconnect the B+ terminal wire and the electrical harness from the alternator.

9. While lifting up on the radiator, remove the alternator from the vehicle.

3. Remove the drive belt from the alternator pulley.

4. Raise and support the vehicle safely.

5. Remove the mud guard from under the engine.

6. Disconnect the B+ terminal wire and the electrical harness from the alternator.

7. Support the alternator by hand and remove the mounting bolts.

8. Remove the alternator from the engine compartment.

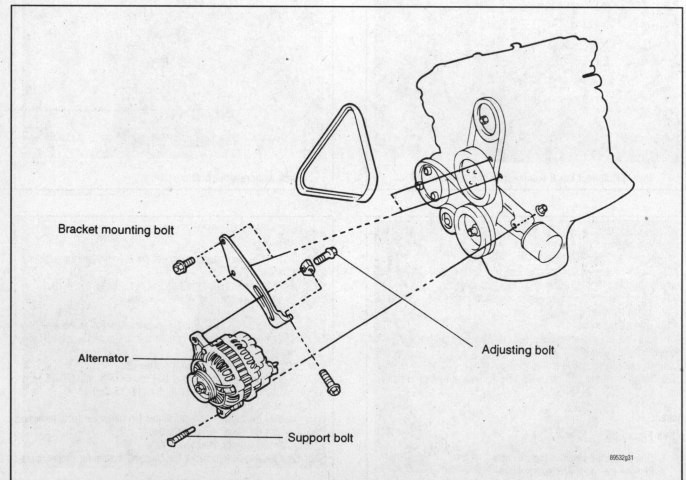

Fig. 33 Alternator and mounting bracket configuration—Tiburon and 1996–98 Elantra

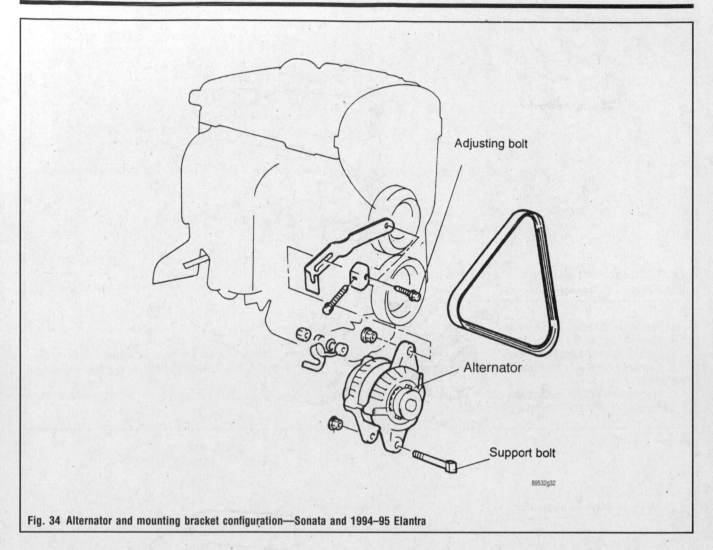

Fig. 34 Alternator and mounting bracket configuration—Sonata and 1994–95 Elantra

To install:

10. While lifting the radiator, position the alternator on the engine mounting fixture.

11. Install the lower mounting bolt and nut. Tighten the nut just enough to allow for movement of the alternator.

12. Lower the radiator.

13. Connect the B+ wire and the electrical harness to the alternator terminal. Make sure the wire nut is tight and the protective cap is firmly placed over the wire connection.

14. Install and properly tension the drive belt.

15. Tighten the alternator support bolt to 14–18 ft. lbs. (20–25 Nm) and the adjusting lockbolt to 9–11 ft. lbs. (12–15 Nm).

16. Connect the oil pressure switch electrical harness.

17. Install the mud guard under the engine.

18. Lower the vehicle.

19. Connect the coolant reserve hose, oil pressure switch and the fan motor electrical harnesses.

20. Connect the negative battery cable.

21. Start the engine and check the charging system for proper operation.

Accent

▶ **See Figure 35**

1. Disconnect the negative battery cable.

2. Remove the radiator attaching bolts.

3. Disconnect the radiator and condenser fan motor electrical harnesses.

4. Loosen the belt tensioner and remove the accessory drive belt.

5. Raise and support the vehicle safely.

6. Disconnect the B+ terminal wire and the electrical harness from the alternator.

7. While lifting up on the radiator, remove the alternator from the vehicle.

To install:

8. While lifting the radiator, position the alternator on the engine mounting fixture.

9. Install the lower mounting bolt and nut. Tighten the nut just enough to allow for movement of the alternator.

10. Lower the radiator.

11. Connect the B+ wire and the electrical harness to the alternator terminal. Make sure the wire nut is tight and the protective cap is firmly placed over the wire connection.

12. Install and properly tension the drive belt.

13. Tighten the alternator support bolt to 14–18 ft. lbs. (20–25 Nm) and the adjusting lockbolt to 9–11 ft. lbs. (12–15 Nm).

14. Lower the vehicle.

15. Connect the radiator and condenser fan motor electrical harnesses.

16. Connect the negative battery cable.

17. Install the radiator attaching bolts.

18. Start the engine and check the charging system for proper operation.

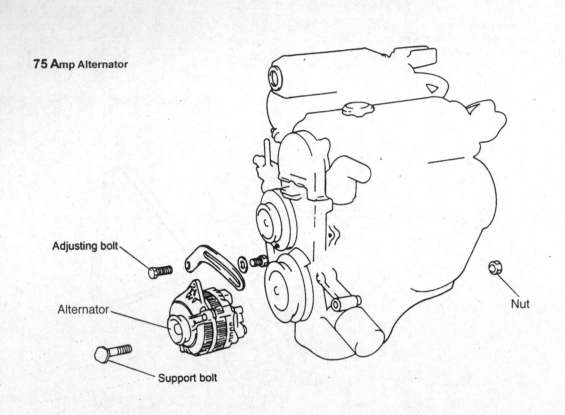

75 Amp Alternator

Adjusting bolt

Alternator

Support bolt

Nut

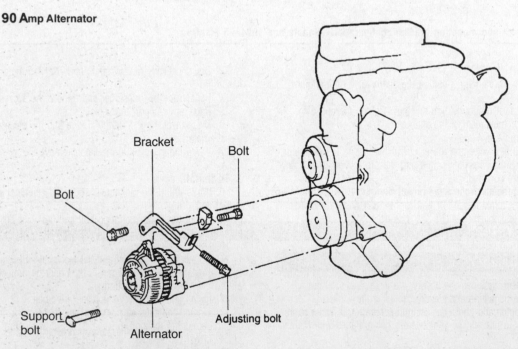

90 Amp Alternator

Bracket

Bolt

Bolt

Support bolt

Alternator

Adjusting bolt

89532g34

Fig. 35 Alternator and mounting bracket configuration—Accent

Sonata V6

▸ **See Figure 36**

1. Disconnect the negative battery cable.
2. Remove the distributor cap and power steering pressure hose nut.
3. Loosen the belt tensioner and remove the accessory drive belt.
4. Remove the timing belt cover cap and timing belt upper cover.
5. Disconnect the B+ terminal wire and the electrical harness from the alternator.
6. Remove the alternator from the engine.

To install:

7. Position the alternator on the engine mounting fixture.
8. Install the lower mounting bolt and nut. Tighten the nut just enough to allow for movement of the alternator.
9. Install and properly tension the drive belt.
10. Tighten the alternator support bolt to 14–18 ft. lbs. (20–25 Nm) and the adjusting lockbolt to 9–11 ft. lbs. (12–15 Nm).

11. Connect the B+ terminal wire and the electrical harness to the alternator.
12. Install the timing belt cover cap and timing belt upper cover.
13. Install the power steering pressure hose nut and distributor cap.
14. Connect the battery cable.
15. Start the engine and check the charging system for proper operation.
16. Check and adjust the power steering fluid level, as necessary.

Regulator

The alternators used on these vehicles contain an internal regulator that is not serviceable separately. If the regulator is determined to be faulty, the alternator must be rebuilt or a replacement alternator must be installed.

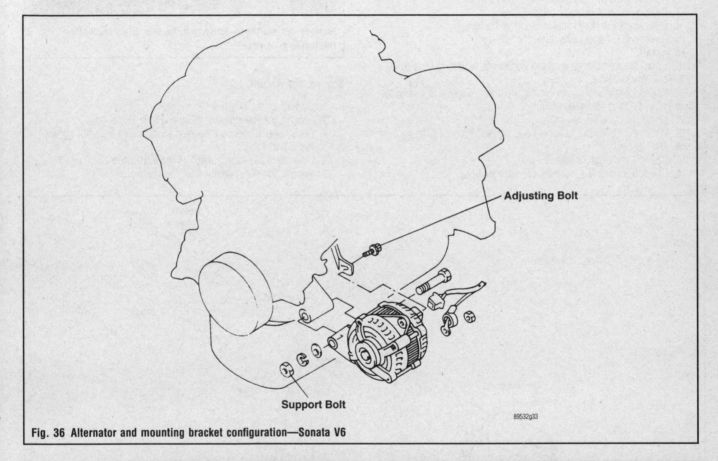

Fig. 36 Alternator and mounting bracket configuration—Sonata V6

Adjusting Bolt

Support Bolt

89532g33

STARTING SYSTEM

General Information

The starting system includes the battery, starter motor, solenoid switch, ignition switch, wiring and battery cables. If the vehicle is equipped with an automatic transaxle, an inhibitor switch is included in the starting system to prevent the vehicle from being started with the car in gear.

When the ignition key is turned to the **START** position, current flows and energizes the starter's solenoid coil. The solenoid plunger and clutch shift lever are activated and the clutch pinion engages the ring gear on the flywheel. The switch contacts close and the starter cranks the engine until it starts.

To prevent damage caused by excessive starter armature rotation when the engine starts, the starter incorporates an over-running clutch in the pinion gear.

TESTING

The easiest way to test the performance of the starter is to perform a voltage drop test.

➡**The battery must be in good condition and fully charged prior to performing this test.**

1. Connect a voltmeter between the positive and negative terminals of the battery.

2. Turn the ignition key to the **START** position and note the voltage drop on the meter.

3. If voltage drops below 11.5 volts, there is high resistance in the starting system.

4. Check for proper connections at the battery and starter.

5. Check the resistance of the battery cables and replace as necessary.

6. If all other components in the system are functional, the starter is faulty.

REMOVAL & INSTALLATION

♦ **See Figure 37**

Excel

1. Disconnect the negative battery cable.
2. Remove the EGR valve assembly, as required.
3. Remove the speedometer cable.
4. Disconnect the starter motor electrical harness.
5. Remove the starter motor from the vehicle.

To install:

6. Install the starter assembly and tighten the mounting bolts to 20–25 ft. lbs. (26–33 Nm).

7. Connect the starter motor electrical harness. Tighten B+ wire terminal nut to 9–11 ft. lbs. (10–16 Nm).

8. Install the speedometer cable.

9. Install the EGR valve assembly and tighten retaining bolts to 7–11 ft. lbs. (10–15 Nm).

10. Connect the negative battery cable.

11. Check the starting system for proper operation.

Remove the starter by loosening the two attaching bolts (indicated by arrows)

Scoupe and Accent

1. Disconnect the negative battery cable.
2. Remove the speedometer cable and shift cable.
3. On Scoupe, disconnect the high tension wire from the ignition coil to the distributor.
4. Disconnect the starter motor electrical harness.
5. Remove the starter motor from the vehicle.

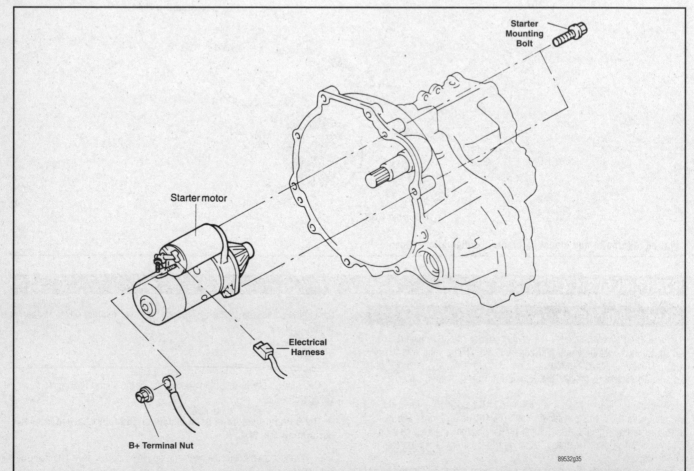

Fig. 37 The starter is mounted to the transaxle bell housing and is easily accessible from the top side of the engine compartment

To install:

6. Install the starter assembly and tighten the mounting bolts to 20–25 ft. lbs. (26–33 Nm).

7. Connect the starter motor electrical harness. Tighten B+ wire terminal nut to 9–11 ft. lbs. (10–16 Nm).

8. Install the speedometer cable and shift cable.

9. Connect the high tension wire from the ignition coil to the distributor, as required.

10. Connect the negative battery cable.

11. Check the starting system for proper operation.

Sonata and 1994–95 Elantra

1. Disconnect the negative battery cable.

2. Disconnect the starter motor electrical harness.

3. Remove the starter motor from the vehicle.

To install:

4. Install the starter assembly and tighten the mounting bolts to 20–25 ft. lbs. (26–33 Nm).

5. Connect the starter motor electrical harness. Tighten B+ wire terminal nut to 7–11 ft. lbs. (10–16 Nm).

6. Connect the negative battery cable

7. Check the starting system for proper operation.

Tiburon and 1996–98 Elantra

1. Disconnect the negative battery cable.

2. Remove the speedometer cable.

3. Remove the air cleaner duct and air cleaner assembly.

4. Disconnect the starter motor electrical harness.

5. Remove the starter motor from the vehicle.

To install:

6. Install the starter assembly and tighten mounting bolts to 20–25 ft. lbs. (26–33 Nm).

7. Connect the starter motor electrical harness. Tighten B+ wire terminal nut to 7–11 ft. lbs. (10–16 Nm).

8. Install the air cleaner duct and air cleaner assembly.

9. Install the speedometer cable.

10. Connect the negative battery cable.

11. Check the starting system for proper operation.

SOLENOID REPLACEMENT

♦ **See Figure 38**

1. Disconnect the negative battery cable.

2. Remove the starter from the vehicle.

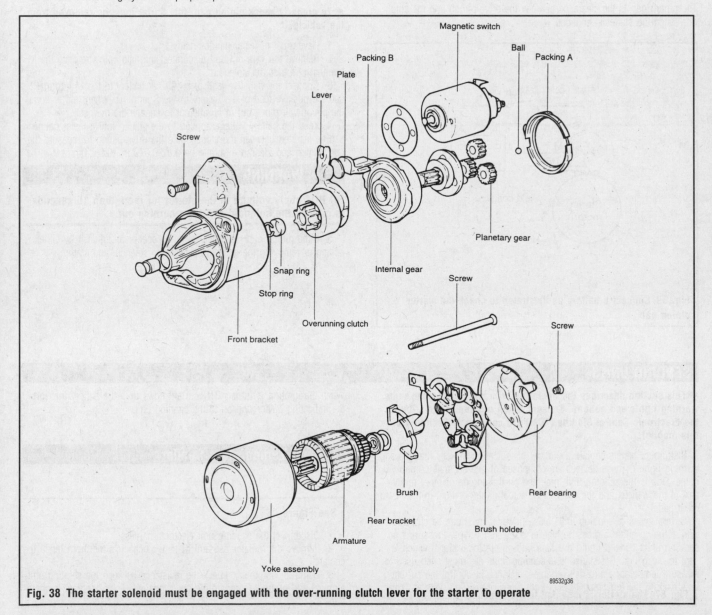

89532g36

Fig. 38 The starter solenoid must be engaged with the over-running clutch lever for the starter to operate

3. Remove the solenoid attaching screws.
4. Disconnect the starter solenoid from the over-running clutch lever.
5. Remove the solenoid from the starter.

➡**Note the amount of shims between the solenoid and starter. These will be used during assembly to adjust the starter pinion gap.**

To install:
6. Install the proper amount of shims between the solenoid and the starter housing.
7. Connect the starter solenoid to the over-running clutch lever.
8. Install the solenoid on the starter.
9. Install the solenoid attaching screws and tighten securely.
10. Check pinion gap and adjust as necessary.
11. Install the starter.
12. Connect the negative battery cable.
13. Check the starting system for proper operation.

PINION GAP ADJUSTMENT

♦ **See Figures 39 and 40**

Pinion gap is the only adjustable specification on the starter motor. The pinion gap is the clearance between the drive pinion and the stop ring when the starter is engaged.

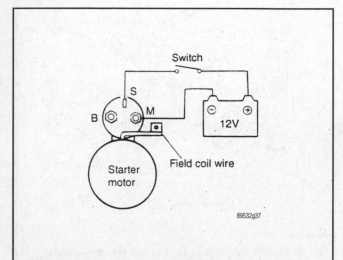

Fig. 39 Connect a battery as illustrated to check the starter pinion gap

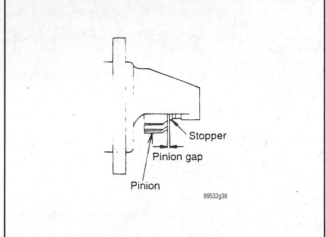

Fig. 40 Using a feeler gauge, check starter pinion gap between the pinion gear and stopper

➡**To properly check pinion gap, the starter must be removed from the vehicle.**

1. Have a set of feeler gauges ready.
2. Remove the wire nut and disconnect the field coil wire from the M terminal of the starter solenoid.
3. Connect the negative lead of a 12V car battery to the M terminal and the positive lead of the battery to the S terminal. When this is done, the pinion will move out in an attempt to engage the flywheel.
4. Keep the battery voltage applied to the starter until a feeler gauge can be inserted between the stopper and the drive pinion to measure the gap. Pinion gap clearance should be 0.02-0.079 in. (0.5-2.0mm).

✳✳ WARNING

DO NOT apply voltage to the starter for more than 10 seconds to prevent the solenoid coil from burning out.

5. If the pinion gap clearance is not as specified, adjust it by either adding or removing the gaskets between the solenoid and starter.

SENDING UNITS

➡**This section describes the operating principles of sending units, warning lights and gauges. Sensors which provide information to the Electronic Control Module (ECM) are covered in Section 4 of this manual.**

Instrument panels contain a number of indicating devices (gauges and warning lights). These devices are composed of two separate components. One is the sending unit, mounted on the engine or other remote part of the vehicle, and the other is the actual gauge or light in the instrument panel.

Several types of sending units exist, however most can be characterized as being either a pressure type or a resistance type. Pressure type sending units convert liquid pressure into an electrical signal which is sent to the gauge. Resistance type sending units are most often used to measure temperature and use variable resistance to control the current flow back to the indicating device. Both types of sending units are connected in series by a wire to the battery (through the ignition switch).

When the ignition is turned **ON,** current flows from the battery through the indicating device and on to the sending unit.

Coolant Temperature Sender

TESTING

♦ **See Figure 41**

1. Disconnect the sending unit electrical harness.
2. Remove the radiator cap and place a mechanic's thermometer in the coolant.
3. Using an ohmmeter, check the resistance between the sending unit terminal and ground. Compare the resistance with actual coolant temperature.

Temperature °C (°F)	50 (112)	60 (140)	70 (158)	115 (239)	120 (248)	122 (252)
Resistance Ω	230	155	104±13.5	23.8±2.5	21	19.5

89532g39

Fig. 41 Coolant temperature-to-resistance specifications

➡**It is best to check resistance with the engine cool, then start the engine and watch the resistance change as the engine warms.**

4. If resistance is not within specification, the sending unit is faulty.

REMOVAL & INSTALLATION

◆ **See Figures 42 thru 48**

1. Locate the coolant temperature sending unit on the engine.
2. Disconnect the sending unit electrical harness.
3. Drain the engine coolant below the level of the switch.
4. Remove the sending unit from the engine.
5. Coat the new sending unit with Teflon® tape or electrically conductive sealer.
6. Install the sending unit and tighten to 11–15 ft. lbs. (15–20 Nm).
7. Attach the sending unit's electrical connector.
8. Fill the engine with coolant.
9. Start the engine, allow it to reach operating temperature and check for leaks.
10. Check for proper sending unit operation.

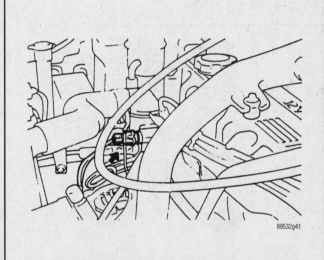

89532g41

Fig. 43 Coolant temperature sending unit location—Scoupe

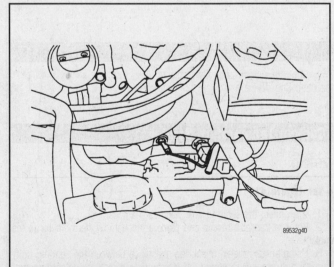

89532g40

Fig. 42 Coolant temperature sending unit location—Excel

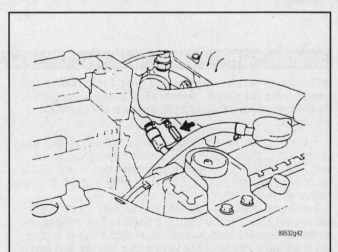

89532g42

Fig. 44 Coolant temperature sending unit location—1994–95 Elantra

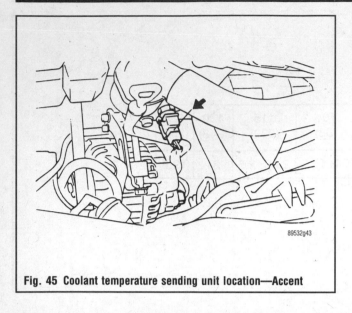

Fig. 45 Coolant temperature sending unit location—Accent

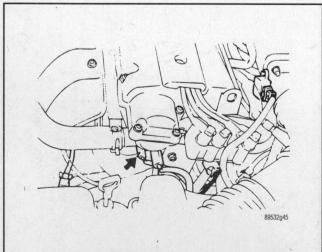

Fig. 46 Coolant temperature sending unit location—Sonata

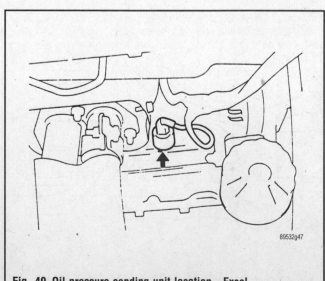

Fig. 47 Coolant temperature sending unit location—1996–98 Elantra

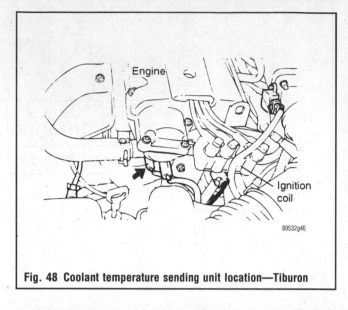

Fig. 48 Coolant temperature sending unit location—Tiburon

Oil Pressure Sender

TESTING

1. Disconnect the sending unit electrical harness.
2. Using an ohmmeter, check continuity between the sending unit terminal and ground.
3. With the engine stopped, continuity should exist.
4. With the engine running, continuity should not exist.
5. If continuity does not exist as stated, the sending unit is faulty.

REMOVAL & INSTALLATION

♦ See Figures 49, 50, 51, 52 and 53

1. Locate the oil pressure sending unit on the engine.
2. Disconnect the sending unit electrical harness.
3. Remove the sending unit from the engine.
4. Coat the new sending unit with Teflon® tape or electrically conductive sealer.

Fig. 49 Oil pressure sending unit location—Excel

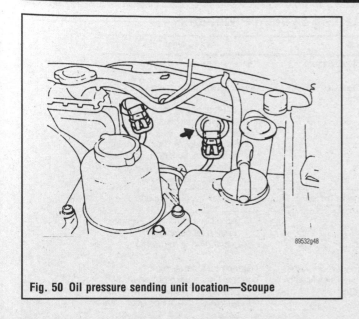

Fig. 50 Oil pressure sending unit location—Scoupe

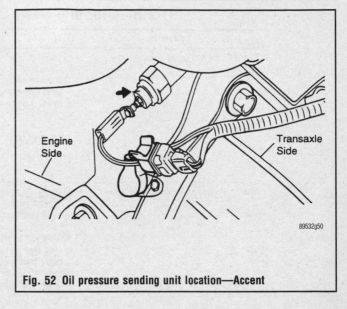

Fig. 52 Oil pressure sending unit location—Accent

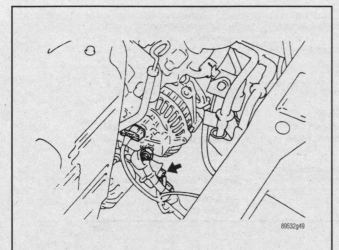

Fig. 51 Oil pressure sending unit location—Sonata and 1994–95 Elantra

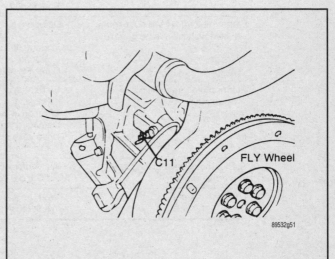

Fig. 53 Oil pressure sending unit location—Tiburon and 1996–98 Elantra

5. Install the sending unit and tighten to 11–15 ft. lbs. (15–20 Nm).
6. Attach the sending unit electrical connector.
7. Start the engine, allow it to reach operating temperature and check for leaks.
8. Check for proper sending unit operation.

Troubleshooting Basic Starting System Problems

Problem	Cause	Solution
Starter motor rotates engine slowly	• Battery charge low or battery defective	• Charge or replace battery
	• Defective circuit between battery and starter motor	• Clean and tighten, or replace cables
	• Low load current	• Bench-test starter motor. Inspect for worn brushes and weak brush springs.
	• High load current	• Bench-test starter motor. Check engine for friction, drag or coolant in cylinders. Check ring gear-to-pinion gear clearance.
Starter motor will not rotate engine	• Battery charge low or battery defective	• Charge or replace battery
	• Faulty solenoid	• Check solenoid ground. Repair or replace as necessary.
	• Damaged drive pinion gear or ring gear	• Replace damaged gear(s)
	• Starter motor engagement weak	• Bench-test starter motor
	• Starter motor rotates slowly with high load current	• Inspect drive yoke pull-down and point gap, check for worn end bushings, check ring gear clearance
	• Engine seized	• Repair engine
Starter motor drive will not engage (solenoid known to be good)	• Defective contact point assembly	• Repair or replace contact point assembly
	• Inadequate contact point assembly ground	• Repair connection at ground screw
	• Defective hold-in coil	• Replace field winding assembly
Starter motor drive will not disengage	• Starter motor loose on flywheel housing	• Tighten mounting bolts
	• Worn drive end busing	• Replace bushing
	• Damaged ring gear teeth	• Replace ring gear or driveplate
	• Drive yoke return spring broken or missing	• Replace spring
Starter motor drive disengages prematurely	• Weak drive assembly thrust spring	• Replace drive mechanism
	• Hold-in coil defective	• Replace field winding assembly
Low load current	• Worn brushes	• Replace brushes
	• Weak brush springs	• Replace springs

tccs2c01

Troubleshooting Basic Charging System Problems

Problem	Cause	Solution
Noisy alternator	• Loose mountings	• Tighten mounting bolts
	• Loose drive pulley	• Tighten pulley
	• Worn bearings	• Replace alternator
	• Brush noise	• Replace alternator
	• Internal circuits shorted (High pitched whine)	• Replace alternator
Squeal when starting engine or accelerating	• Glazed or loose belt	• Replace or adjust belt
Indicator light remains on or ammeter indicates discharge (engine running)	• Broken belt	• Install belt
	• Broken or disconnected wires	• Repair or connect wiring
	• Internal alternator problems	• Replace alternator
	• Defective voltage regulator	• Replace voltage regulator/alternator
Car light bulbs continually burn out—battery needs water continually	• Alternator/regulator overcharging	• Replace voltage regulator/alternator
Car lights flare on acceleration	• Battery low	• Charge or replace battery
	• Internal alternator/regulator problems	• Replace alternator/regulator
Low voltage output (alternator light flickers continually or ammeter needle wanders)	• Loose or worn belt	• Replace or adjust belt
	• Dirty or corroded connections	• Clean or replace connections
	• Internal alternator/regulator problems	• Replace alternator/regulator

tccs2c02

3

ENGINE AND ENGINE OVERHAUL

GENERAL ENGINE SPECIFICATIONS

Year	Engine ID/VIN		Engine Displacement Liters (cc)	Fuel System Type	Net Horsepower @ rpm	Net Torque @ rpm (ft. lbs.)	Bore x Stroke (in.)	Compression Ratio	Oil Pressure @ rpm
1994	J		1.5 (1468)	MFI	81@5500	91@3000	2.97 x 3.23	9.4:1	12@Idle
	E		1.5 (1495)	MFI	92@5500	97@4500	2.97 x 3.29	10.0:1	21@Idle
	E		1.5 (1495)	MFI-T	115@5500	123@4500	2.97 x 3.29	7.5:1	21@Idle
	R		1.6 (1595)	MFI	113@6000	102@5000	3.24 x 2.95	9.2:1	12@Idle
	M		1.8 (1836)	MFI	124@6000	116@5000	3.21 x 3.46	9.2:1	12@Idle
	P		2.0 (1997)	MFI	128@6000	121@5000	3.35 x 3.46	9.0:1	12@Idle
	T		3.0 (2972)	MFI	142@5000	168@2500	3.59 x 2.99	8.9:1	12@Idle
1995	E		1.5 (1495)	MFI	92@5500	97@4500	2.97 x 3.29	10.0:1	21@Idle
	E		1.5 (1495)	MFI-T	115@5500	123@4500	2.97 x 3.29	7.5:1	21@Idle
	K		1.5 (1495)	MFI	92@5500	96@3000	2.97 x 3.29	10.0:1	21@Idle
	R		1.6 (1595)	MFI	113@6000	102@5000	3.24 x 2.95	9.2:1	12@Idle
	M		1.8 (1836)	MFI	124@6000	116@5000	3.21 x 3.46	9.2:1	12@Idle
	P		2.0 (1997)	MFI	137@6000	129@4000	3.35 x 3.46	9.0:1	12@Idle
	T		3.0 (2972)	MFI	142@5000	168@2500	3.59 x 2.99	8.9:1	12@Idle
1996	K	①	1.5 (1495)	MFI	92@5500	97@4000	2.97 x 3.29	10.0:1	21@Idle
	K	②	1.5 (1495)	MFI	105@6000	101@4500	2.97 x 3.29	9.5:1	21@Idle
	M		1.8 (1795)	MFI	124@6000	116@5000	3.23 x 3.35	10.0:1	24@Idle
	P		2.0 (1997)	MFI	137@6000	129@4000	3.35 x 3.46	9.0:1	12@Idle
	T		3.0 (2972)	MFI	142@5000	168@2500	3.59 x 2.99	8.9:1	12@Idle
1997	K	①	1.5 (1495)	MFI	92@5500	97@4000	2.97 x 3.29	10.0:1	21@Idle
	K	②	1.5 (1495)	MFI	105@6000	101@4500	2.97 x 3.29	9.5:1	21@Idle
	M		1.8 (1795)	MFI	124@6000	116@5000	3.23 x 3.35	10.0:1	24@Idle
	F		2.0 (1975)	MFI	140@6000	133@4800	3.23 x 3.68	10.3:1	24@Idle
	P		2.0 (1997)	MFI	137@6000	129@4000	3.35 x 3.46	9.0:1	12@Idle
	T		3.0 (2972)	MFI	142@5000	168@2500	3.59 x 2.99	8.9:1	12@Idle
1998	K	①	1.5 (1495)	MFI	92@5500	97@4000	2.97 x 3.29	10.0:1	21@Idle
	K	②	1.5 (1495)	MFI	105@6000	101@4500	2.97 x 3.29	9.5:1	21@Idle
	M		1.8 (1795)	MFI	124@6000	116@5000	3.23 x 3.35	10.0:1	24@Idle
	F		2.0 (1975)	MFI	140@6000	133@4800	3.23 x 3.68	10.3:1	24@Idle
	P		2.0 (1997)	MFI	137@6000	129@4000	3.35 x 3.46	9.0:1	12@Idle
	T		3.0 (2972)	MFI	142@5000	168@2500	3.59 x 2.99	8.9:1	12@Idle

MFI : Multi-Port Fuel Injection

MFI-T: Multi-Port Fuel Injection Turbocharged

① SOHC

② DOHC

89533c01

VALVE SPECIFICATIONS

Year	Engine ID/VIN		Engine Displacement Liters (cc)	Seat Angle (deg.)	Face Angle (deg.)	Spring Test Pressure (lbs. @ in.)	Spring Installed Height (in.)	Stem-to-Guide Clearance (in.)		Stem Diameter (in.)	
								Intake	Exhaust	Intake	Exhaust
1994	J		1.5 (1468)	45	45	53@1.07	1.420	0.0012-0.0024	0.0020-0.0035	0.2598	0.2598
	E		1.5 (1495)	45	45	44@1.261	1.261	0.0012-0.0024	0.0020-0.0035	0.2364	0.2364
	E	③	1.5 (1495)	45	45	44@1.261	1.261	0.0012-0.0024	0.0020-0.0035	0.2364	0.2364
	R		1.6 (1596)	44-44.5	45-45.5	66@1.575	⑥	0.0008-0.0019	0.0020-0.0033	0.2585-0.2591	0.2571-0.2579
	M		1.8 (1836)	45	45	56@1.458	1.358	0.0008-0.0019	0.0019-0.0033	0.2348-0.2354	0.2334-0.2342
	P		2.0 (1997)	45-45.5	45-45.5	66@1.575	⑥	0.0008-0.0019	0.0020-0.0033	0.2585-0.2891	0.2571-0.2579
	T		3.0 (2972)	44-44.5	45	74@1.591	1.590	0.0012-0.0024	0.0020-0.0035	0.3150	0.3134
1995	E		1.5 (1495)	45	45	44@1.261	1.261	0.0012-0.0024	0.0020-0.0035	0.2364	0.2364
	E	③	1.5 (1495)	45	45	44@1.261	1.261	0.0012-0.0024	0.0020-0.0035	0.2364	0.2364
	K		1.5 (1495)	45	45	54@1.358	1.358	0.0012-0.0024	0.0014-0.0026	0.3920	0.3960
	R		1.6 (1596)	44-44.5	45-45.5	66@1.575	⑥	0.0008-0.0019	0.0020-0.0033	0.2585-0.2591	0.2571-0.2579
	M		1.8 (1836)	45	45	56@1.458	1.358	0.0008-0.0019	0.0019-0.0033	0.2348-0.2354	0.2334-0.2342
	P		2.0 (1997)	45-45.5	45-45.5	66@1.575	⑥	0.0008-0.0019	0.0020-0.0033	0.2585-0.2891	0.2571-0.2579
	T		3.0 (2972)	44-44.5	45	74@1.591	1.590	0.0012-0.0024	0.0020-0.0035	0.3150	0.3134
1996	K	④	1.5 (1495)	45	45	54@1.358	1.358	0.0012-0.0024	0.0014-0.0026	0.3920	0.3960
	K	⑤	1.5 (1495)	45	45	48@1.378	1.378	0.0012-0.0024	0.0020-0.0031	0.2344-0.2350	0.2337-0.2343
	M		1.8 (1836)	45	45	56@1.458	1.358	0.0008-0.0019	0.0019-0.0033	0.2348-0.2354	0.2334-0.2342
	P		2.0 (1997)	45-45.5	45-45.5	66@1.575	⑥	0.0008-0.0019	0.0020-0.0033	0.2585-0.2891	0.2571-0.2579
	T		3.0 (2972)	44-44.5	45	74@1.591	1.590	0.0012-0.0024	0.0020-0.0035	0.3150	0.3134
1997	K	④	1.5 (1495)	45	45	54@1.358	1.358	0.0012-0.0024	0.0014-0.0026	0.3920	0.3960
	K	⑤	1.5 (1495)	45	45	48@1.378	1.378	0.0012-0.0024	0.0020-0.0031	0.2344-0.2350	0.2337-0.2343
	M	①	1.8 (1836)	45	45	56@1.458	1.358	0.0008-0.0019	0.0019-0.0033	0.2348-0.2354	0.2334-0.2342
	M	②	1.8 (1836)	45	45	56@1.457	1.358	0.0008-0.0019	0.0019-0.0033	0.2348-0.2354	0.2334-0.2342
	F		2.0 (1975)	45	45	56@1.457	1.358	0.0008-0.0019	0.0019-0.0033	0.2348-0.2354	0.2334-0.2342
	P		2.0 (1997)	45-45.5	45-45.5	66@1.575	④	0.0008-0.0019	0.0033	0.2585-0.2891	0.2571-0.2579
	T		3.0 (2972)	44-44.5	45	74@1.591	1.590	0.0012-0.0024	0.0020-0.0035	0.3150	0.3134

89533c02

VALVE SPECIFICATIONS

Year	Engine ID/VIN		Engine Displacement Liters (cc)	Seat Angle (deg.)	Face Angle (deg.)	Spring Test Pressure (lbs. @ in.)	Spring Installed Height (In.)	Stem-to-Guide Clearance (in.)		Stem Diameter (in.)	
								Intake	Exhaust	Intake	Exhaust
1998	K	④	1.5 (1495)	45	45	54@1.358	1.358	0.0012-0.0024	0.0014-0.0026	0.3920	0.3960
	K	⑤	1.5 (1495)	45	45	48@1.378	1.378	0.0012-0.0024	0.0020-0.0031	0.2344-0.2350	0.2337-0.2343
	M	①	1.8 (1836)	45	45	56@1.458	1.358	0.0008-0.0019	0.0019-0.0033	0.2348-0.2354	0.2334-0.2342
	M	②	1.8 (1836)	45	45	56@1.457	1.358	0.0008-0.0019	0.0019-0.0033	0.2348-0.2354	0.2334-0.2342
	F		2.0 (1975)	45	45	56@1.457	1.358	0.0008-0.0019	0.0019-0.0033	0.2348-0.2354	0.2334-0.2342
	P		2.0 (1997)	45-45.5	45-45.5	66@1.575	⑥	0.0008-0.0019	0.0020-0.0033	0.2585-0.2891	0.2571-0.2579
	T		3.0 (2972)	44-44.5	45	74@1.591	1.590	0.0012-0.0024	0.0020-0.0035	0.3150	0.3134

① Elantra
② Tiburon
③ Turbo
④ SOHC
⑤ DOHC
⑥ Free Length - 1.902 in.

89533c03

CAMSHAFT SPECIFICATIONS
All measurements given in inches.

Year	Engine ID/VIN		Engine Displacement Liters (cc)	Journal Diameter					Elevation		Bearing Clearance	Camshaft End-Play
				1	2	3	4	5	In.	Ex.		
1994	J		1.5 (1468)	1.336-1.337	1.336-1.337	1.336-1.337	1.336-1.337	—	1.620-1.628	1.620-1.628	0.0020-0.0035	0.0040-0.0080
	E		1.5 (1495)	1.336-1.337	1.336-1.337	1.336-1.337	1.336-1.337	—	1.617	1.625	0.0020-0.0035	0.0040-0.0080
	E	③	1.5 (1495)	1.336-1.337	1.336-1.337	1.336-1.337	1.336-1.337	—	1.625	1.625	0.0020-0.0035	0.0040-0.0080
	R		1.6 (1596)	1.020	1.020	1.020	1.020	1.020	1.386	1.374	0.0020-0.0035	0.0040-0.0080
	M		1.8 (1836)	1.020	1.020	1.020	1.020	1.020	1.397	1.386	0.0020-0.0035	0.0040-0.0080
	P		2.0 (1997)	1.020	1.020	1.020	1.020	1.020	1.397	1.386	0.0020-0.0035	0.0040-0.0080
	T		3.0 (2972)	1.336-1.337	1.336-1.337	1.336-1.337	1.336-1.337	—	1.620-1.628	1.620-1.628	0.0020-0.0035	0.0040-0.0080
1995	E		1.5 (1495)	1.336-1.337	1.336-1.337	1.336-1.337	1.336-1.337	—	1.617	1.625	0.0020-0.0035	0.0040-0.0080
	E	③	1.5 (1495)	1.336-1.337	1.336-1.337	1.336-1.337	1.336-1.337	—	1.625	1.625	0.0020-0.0035	0.0040-0.0080
	K		1.5 (1495)	1.181	1.181	1.181	1.181	1.181	1.687	1.683	0.0020-0.0035	0.0030-0.0110
	R		1.6 (1596)	1.020	1.020	1.020	1.020	1.020	1.386	1.374	0.0020-0.0035	0.0040-0.0080
	M		1.8 (1836)	1.020	1.020	1.020	1.020	1.020	1.397	1.386	0.0020-0.0035	0.0040-0.0080
	P		2.0 (1997)	1.020	1.020	1.020	1.020	1.020	1.397	1.386	0.0020-0.0035	0.0040-0.0080
	T		3.0 (2972)	1.336-1.337	1.336-1.337	1.336-1.337	1.336-1.337	—	1.620-1.628	1.620-1.628	0.0020-0.0035	0.0040-0.0080

89533c04

CAMSHAFT SPECIFICATIONS
All measurements given in inches.

Year	Engine ID/VIN		Engine Displacement Liters (cc)	Journal Diameter					Elevation		Bearing Clearance	Camshaft End-Play
				1	2	3	4	5	In.	Ex.		
1996	K	④	1.5 (1495)	1.181	1.181	1.181	1.181	1.181	1.687	1.683	0.0020-0.0035	0.0030-0.0110
	K	⑤	1.5 (1495)	1.063	1.063	1.063	1.063	1.063	1.703	1.726	0.0014-0.0028	0.0040-0.0080
	M		1.8 (1836)	1.102	1.102	1.102	1.102	1.102	1.750	1.774	0.0008-0.0024	0.0040-0.0080
	P		2.0 (1997)	1.020	1.020	1.020	1.020	1.020	1.397	1.386	0.0020-0.0035	0.0040-0.0080
	T		3.0 (2972)	1.336-1.337	1.336-1.337	1.336-1.337	1.336-1.337	—	1.620-1.628	1.620-1.628	0.0020-0.0035	0.0040-0.0080
1997	K	④	1.5 (1495)	1.181	1.181	1.181	1.181	1.181	1.687	1.683	0.0020-0.0035	0.0030-0.0110
	K	⑤	1.5 (1495)	1.063	1.063	1.063	1.063	1.063	1.703	1.726	0.0014-0.0028	0.0040-0.0080
	M	①	1.8 (1836)	1.102	1.102	1.102	1.102	1.102	1.750	1.774	0.0008-0.0024	0.0040-0.0080
	M	②	1.8 (1836)	1.102	1.102	1.102	1.102	1.102	1.750	1.774	0.0008-0.0024	0.0040-0.0080
	F		2.0 (1975)	1.102	1.102	1.102	1.102	1.102	1.750	1.774	0.0008-0.0024	0.0040-0.0080
	P		2.0 (1997)	1.020	1.020	1.020	1.020	1.020	1.397	1.386	0.0020-0.0035	0.0040-0.0080
	T		3.0 (2972)	1.336-1.337	1.336-1.337	1.336-1.337	1.336-1.337	—	1.620-1.628	1.620-1.628	0.0020-0.0035	0.0040-0.0080
1998	K	④	1.5 (1495)	1.181	1.181	1.181	1.181	1.181	1.687	1.683	0.0020-0.0035	0.0030-0.0110
	K	⑤	1.5 (1495)	1.063	1.063	1.063	1.063	1.063	1.703	1.726	0.0014-0.0028	0.0040-0.0080
	M	①	1.8 (1836)	1.102	1.102	1.102	1.102	1.102	1.750	1.774	0.0008-0.0024	0.0040-0.0080
	M	②	1.8 (1836)	1.102	1.102	1.102	1.102	1.102	1.750	1.774	0.0008-0.0024	0.0040-0.0080
	F		2.0 (1975)	1.102	1.102	1.102	1.102	1.102	1.750	1.774	0.0008-0.0024	0.0040-0.0080
	P		2.0 (1997)	1.020	1.020	1.020	1.020	1.020	1.397	1.386	0.0020-0.0035	0.0040-0.0080
	T		3.0 (2972)	1.336-1.337	1.336-1.337	1.336-1.337	1.336-1.337	—	1.620-1.628	1.620-1.628	0.0020-0.0035	0.0040-0.0080

① Elantra
② Tiburon
③ Scoupe Turbo
④ SOHC
⑤ DOHC

89533c05

CRANKSHAFT AND CONNECTING ROD SPECIFICATIONS

All measurements are given in inches.

Year	Engine ID/VIN		Engine Displacement Liters (cc)	Crankshaft				Connecting Rod		
				Main Brg. Journal Dia.	Main Brg. Oil Clearance	Shaft End-play	Thrust on No.	Journal Diameter	Oil Clearance	Side Clearance
1994	J		1.5 (1468)	1.8898	0.0008-0.0020	0.0020-0.0070	3	1.6535	0.0006-0.0017	0.0040-0.0100
	E		1.5 (1495)	1.9685	0.0013-0.0020	0.0020-0.0070	3	1.6535	0.0013-0.0022	0.0040-0.0100
	E	③	1.5 (1495)	1.9685	0.0013-0.0020	0.0020-0.0070	3	1.6535	0.0013-0.0022	0.0040-0.0100
	R		1.6 (1596)	2.2400	0.0008-0.0020	0.0020-0.0070	3	1.7700	0.0008-0.0020	0.0040-0.0100
	M		1.8 (1836)	2.2400	0.0008-0.0020	0.0020-0.0070	3	1.7700	0.0008-0.0020	0.0040-0.0100
	P		2.0 (1997)	2.2433-2.2439	0.0008-0.0020	0.0020-0.0070	3	1.7709-1.7715	0.0008-0.0020	0.0040-0.0100
	T		3.0 (2972)	2.3614-2.3622	0.0008-0.0020	0.0020-0.0070	3	1.9677-1.9685	0.0006-0.0018	0.0039-0.0098
1995	E		1.5 (1495)	1.9685	0.0013-0.0020	0.0020-0.0070	3	1.6535	0.0013-0.0022	0.0040-0.0100
	E	③	1.5 (1495)	1.9685	0.0013-0.0020	0.0020-0.0070	3	1.6535	0.0013-0.0022	0.0040-0.0100
	K		1.5 (1495)	2.2440	0.0011-0.0018	0.0019-0.0068	3	1.7700	0.0009-0.0016	0.0039-0.0098
	R		1.6 (1596)	2.2400	0.0008-0.0020	0.0020-0.0070	3	1.7700	0.0008-0.0020	0.0040-0.0100
	M		1.8 (1836)	2.2400	0.0008-0.0020	0.0020-0.0070	3	1.7700	0.0008-0.0020	0.0040-0.0100
	P		2.0 (1997)	2.2433-2.2439	0.0008-0.0020	0.0020-0.0070	3	1.7709-1.7715	0.0008-0.0020	0.0040-0.0100
	T		3.0 (2972)	2.3614-2.3622	0.0008-0.0020	0.0020-0.0070	3	1.9677-1.9685	0.0006-0.0018	0.0039-0.0098
1996	K	④	1.5 (1495)	2.2440	0.0011-0.0018	0.0019-0.0068	3	1.7700	0.0009-0.0016	0.0039-0.0098
	K	⑤	1.5 (1495)	2.2440	0.0011-0.0018	0.0019-0.0068	3	1.7700	0.0009-0.0016	0.0039-0.0098
	M		1.8 (1836)	2.2400	0.0008-0.0020	0.0020-0.0070	3	1.7700	0.0008-0.0020	0.0040-0.0100
	P		2.0 (1997)	2.2433-2.2439	0.0008-0.0020	0.0020-0.0070	3	1.7709-1.7715	0.0008-0.0020	0.0040-0.0100
	T		3.0 (2972)	2.3614-2.3622	0.0008-0.0020	0.0020-0.0070	3	1.9677-1.9685	0.0006-0.0018	0.0039-0.0098
1997	K	④	1.5 (1495)	2.2440	0.0011-0.0018	0.0019-0.0068	3	1.7700	0.0009-0.0016	0.0039-0.0098
	K	⑤	1.5 (1495)	2.2440	0.0011-0.0018	0.0019-0.0068	3	1.7700	0.0009-0.0016	0.0039-0.0098
	M	①	1.8 (1836)	2.2440	0.0011-0.0018	0.0023-0.0100	3	1.7700	0.0009-0.0016	0.0039-0.0098
	M	②	1.8 (1836)	2.2440	0.0011-0.0018	0.0023-0.0100	3	1.7700	0.0009-0.0016	0.0039-0.0098
	F		2.0 (1975)	2.2440	0.0011-0.0018	0.0023-0.0100	3	1.7700	0.0009-0.0016	0.0039-0.0098
	P		2.0 (1997)	2.2433-2.2439	0.0008-0.0020	0.0020-0.0070	3	1.7709-1.7715	0.0008-0.0020	0.0040-0.0100
	T		3.0 (2972)	2.3614-2.3622	0.0008-0.0020	0.0020-0.0070	3	1.9677-1.9685	0.0006-0.0018	0.0039-0.0098

89533c06

CRANKSHAFT AND CONNECTING ROD SPECIFICATIONS

All measurements are given in inches.

Year	Engine ID/VIN		Engine Displacement Liters (cc)	Crankshaft				Connecting Rod		
				Main Brg. Journal Dia.	Main Brg. Oil Clearance	Shaft End-play	Thrust on No.	Journal Diameter	Oil Clearance	Side Clearance
1998	K	④	1.5 (1495)	2.2440	0.0011-0.0018	0.0019-0.0068	3	1.7700	0.0009-0.0016	0.0039-0.0098
	K	⑤	1.5 (1495)	2.2440	0.0011-0.0018	0.0019-0.0068	3	1.7700	0.0009-0.0016	0.0039-0.0098
	M	①	1.8 (1836)	2.2440	0.0011-0.0018	0.0023-0.0100	3	1.7700	0.0009-0.0016	0.0039-0.0098
	M	②	1.8 (1836)	2.2440	0.0011-0.0018	0.0023-0.0100	3	1.7700	0.0009-0.0016	0.0039-0.0098
	F		2.0 (1975)	2.2440	0.0011-0.0018	0.0023-0.0100	3	1.7700	0.0009-0.0016	0.0039-0.0098
	P		2.0 (1997)	2.2433-2.2439	0.0008-0.0020	0.0020-0.0070	3	1.7709-1.7715	0.0008-0.0020	0.0040-0.0100
	T		3.0 (2972)	2.3614-2.3622	0.0008-0.0020	0.0020-0.0070	3	1.9677-1.9685	0.0006-0.0018	0.0039-0.0098

① Elantra
② Tiburon
③ Scoupe Turbo
④ SOHC
⑤ DOHC

89533c07

PISTON AND RING SPECIFICATIONS

All measurements are given in inches.

Year	Engine ID/VIN		Engine Displacement Liters (cc)	Piston Clearance	Ring Gap			Ring Side Clearance		
					Top Compression	Bottom Compression	Oil Control	Top Compression	Bottom Compression	Oil Control
1994	J		1.5 (1468)	0.0008-0.0016	0.008-0.014	0.008-0.014	0.008-0.028	0.0012-0.0028	0.0008-0.0024	NA
	P		2.0 (1997)	0.0004-0.0012	0.010-0.018	0.014-0.020	0.008-0.028	0.0012-0.0028	0.0012-0.0028	NA
	T		3.0 (2972)	0.0008-0.0016	0.012-0.018	0.010-0.016	0.008-0.028	0.0012-0.0035	0.0008-0.0024	NA
	E		1.5 (1495)	0.0008-0.0016	0.012-0.020	0.012-0.020	0.010-0.039	0.0016-0.0031	0.0016-0.0031	NA
	E	③	1.5 (1495)	0.0010-0.0018	0.012-0.020	0.012-0.020	0.010-0.039	0.0016-0.0031	0.0016-0.0031	NA
	R		1.6 (1596)	0.0008-0.0016	0.010-0.016	0.014-0.020	0.008-0.028	0.0012-0.0028	0.0012-0.0028	NA
	M		1.8 (1836)	0.0008-0.0016	0.010-0.016	0.018-0.024	0.008-0.028	0.0012-0.0028	0.0012-0.0028	NA
1995	K		1.5 (1495)	0.0008-0.0016	0.008-0.020	0.008-0.020	0.008-0.039	0.0016-0.0033	0.0016-0.0033	NA
	P		2.0 (1997)	0.0004-0.0012	0.010-0.018	0.014-0.020	0.008-0.028	0.0012-0.0028	0.0012-0.0028	NA
	T		3.0 (2972)	0.0008-0.0016	0.012-0.018	0.010-0.016	0.008-0.028	0.0012-0.0035	0.0008-0.0024	NA
	E		1.5 (1495)	0.0008-0.0016	0.012-0.020	0.012-0.020	0.010-0.039	0.0016-0.0031	0.0016-0.0031	NA
	E	③	1.5 (1495)	0.0010-0.0018	0.012-0.020	0.012-0.020	0.010-0.039	0.0016-0.0031	0.0016-0.0031	NA
	R		1.6 (1596)	0.0008-0.0016	0.010-0.016	0.014-0.020	0.008-0.028	0.0012-0.0028	0.0012-0.0028	NA
	M		1.8 (1836)	0.0008-0.0016	0.010-0.016	0.018-0.024	0.008-0.028	0.0012-0.0028	0.0012-0.0028	NA

89533c08

PISTON AND RING SPECIFICATIONS

All measurements are given in inches.

Year	Engine ID/VIN		Engine Displacement Liters (cc)	Piston Clearance	Ring Gap			Ring Side Clearance		
					Top Compression	Bottom Compression	Oil Control	Top Compression	Bottom Compression	Oil Control
1996	K	④	1.5 (1495)	0.0008-0.0016	0.008-0.020	0.008-0.020	0.008-0.039	0.0016-0.0033	0.0016-0.0033	NA
	K	⑤	1.5 (1495)	0.0009-0.0017	0.006-0.012	0.010-0.016	0.008-0.028	0.0015-0.0033	0.0015-0.0033	NA
	P		2.0 (1997)	0.0004-0.0012	0.010-0.018	0.014-0.020	0.008-0.028	0.0012-0.0028	0.0012-0.0028	NA
	T		3.0 (2972)	0.0008-0.0016	0.012-0.018	0.010-0.016	0.008-0.028	0.0012-0.0035	0.0008-0.0024	NA
	M		1.8 (1836)	0.0008-0.0016	0.010-0.016	0.018-0.024	0.008-0.028	0.0012-0.0028	0.0012-0.0028	NA
1997	K	④	1.5 (1495)	0.0008-0.0016	0.008-0.020	0.008-0.020	0.008-0.039	0.0016-0.0033	0.0016-0.0033	NA
	K	⑤	1.5 (1495)	0.0009-0.0017	0.006-0.012	0.010-0.016	0.008-0.028	0.0015-0.0033	0.0015-0.0033	NA
	P		2.0 (1997)	0.0004-0.0012	0.010-0.018	0.014-0.020	0.008-0.028	0.0012-0.0028	0.0012-0.0028	NA
	T		3.0 (2972)	0.0008-0.0016	0.012-0.018	0.010-0.016	0.008-0.028	0.0012-0.0035	0.0008-0.0024	NA
	M	①	1.8 (1836)	0.0008-0.0016	0.010-0.016	0.018-0.024	0.008-0.028	0.0012-0.0028	0.0012-0.0028	NA
	M	②	1.8 (1836)	0.0008-0.0016	0.009-0.015	0.018-0.024	0.008-0.024	0.0015-0.0031	0.0012-0.0027	NA
	F		2.0 (1975)	0.0008-0.0016	0.009-0.015	0.013-0.019	0.008-0.024	0.0015-0.0031	0.0012-0.0027	NA
1998	K	②	1.5 (1495)	0.0008-0.0016	0.008-0.020	0.008-0.020	0.008-0.039	0.0016-0.0033	0.0016-0.0033	NA
	K	⑤	1.5 (1495)	0.0009-0.0017	0.006-0.012	0.010-0.016	0.008-0.028	0.0015-0.0033	0.0015-0.0033	NA
	P		2.0 (1997)	0.0004-0.0012	0.010-0.018	0.014-0.020	0.008-0.028	0.0012-0.0028	0.0012-0.0028	NA
	T		3.0 (2972)	0.0008-0.0016	0.012-0.018	0.010-0.016	0.008-0.028	0.0012-0.0035	0.0008-0.0024	NA
	M	①	1.8 (1836)	0.0008-0.0016	0.010-0.016	0.018-0.024	0.008-0.028	0.0012-0.0028	0.0012-0.0028	NA
	M	②	1.8 (1836)	0.0008-0.0016	0.009-0.015	0.018-0.024	0.008-0.024	0.0015-0.0031	0.0012-0.0027	NA
	F		2.0 (1975)	0.0008-0.0016	0.009-0.015	0.013-0.019	0.008-0.024	0.0015-0.0031	0.0012-0.0027	NA

NA: Not Available

① Elantra
② Tiburon
③ Turbo
④ SOHC
⑤ DOHC

89533c09

TORQUE SPECIFICATIONS

All readings in ft. lbs.

Year	Engine ID/VIN		Engine Displacement Liters (cc)	Cylinder Head Bolts	Main Bearing Bolts	Rod Bearing Bolts	Crankshaft Damper Bolts	Flywheel Bolts	Manifold Intake	Manifold Exhaust	Spark Plugs	Lug Nut
1994	J		1.5 (1468)	①	36-39	23-25	51-72	94-101	12-14	12-14	18	65-80
	E		1.5 (1495)	①	40-43	25-28	140-148	94-101	11-14	11-14	18	65-80
	E	⑩	1.5 (1495)	①	40-43	25-28	140-148	94-101	11-14	18-20	18	65-80
	R		1.6 (1595)	76-83 ④	47-51	36-38	80-94	94-101	18-22	18-22	18	65-80
	M		1.8 (1836)	76-83 ④	47-51	36-38	80-94	94-101	18-22	18-22	18	65-80
	P		2.0 (1997)	76-83 ④	47-51	36-38	80-94	94-101	18-22	18-22	18	65-80
	T		3.0 (2972)	②	55-61	36-38	109-115	65-70	11-14	11-16	18	65-80
1995	E		1.5 (1495)	①	40-43	25-28	140-148	94-101	11-14	11-14	18	65-80
	E	⑩	1.5 (1495)	①	40-43	25-28	140-148	94-101	11-14	18-20	18	65-80
	K		1.5 (1495)	①	40-44	25-28	110-118	94-101	11-14	11-14	18	65-80
	R		1.6 (1595)	76-83 ④	47-51	36-38	80-94	94-101	18-22	18-22	18	65-80
	M		1.8 (1836)	76-83 ④	47-51	36-38	80-94	94-101	18-22	18-22	18	65-80
	P		2.0 (1997)	76-83 ④	47-51	36-38	80-94	94-101	18-22	18-22	18	65-80
	T		3.0 (2972)	②	55-61	36-38	109-115	65-70	11-14	11-16	18	65-80
1996	K	⑥	1.5 (1495)	①	40-44	25-28	110-118	94-101	11-14	11-14	18	65-80
	K	⑦	1.5 (1495)	①	40-43	23-26	103-110	88-96	13-18	22-30	18	65-80
	M		1.8 (1795)	②	⑤	34-39	125-133	88-95	13-18	22-30	18	65-80
	P		2.0 (1997)	76-83 ②	47-51	36-38	80-94	94-101	18-22	18-22	18	65-80
	T		3.0 (2972)	②	55-61	36-38	109-115	65-70	11-14	11-16	18	65-80
1997	K	⑥	1.5 (1495)	①	40-44	25-28	110-118	94-101	11-14	11-14	18	65-80
	K	⑦	1.5 (1495)	①	40-43	23-26	103-110	88-96	13-18	22-30	18	65-80
	M	⑧	1.8 (1795)	③	⑤	34-39	125-133	88-95	13-18	22-30	18	65-80
	M	⑨	1.8 (1795)	③	⑤	34-39	125-133	88-95	11-14	17-22	18	65-80
	F		2.0 (1975)	③	⑤	34-39	125-133	88-95	11-14	17-22	18	65-80
	P		2.0 (1997)	76-83 ④	47-51	36-38	80-94	94-101	18-22	18-22	18	65-80
	T		3.0 (2972)	①	55-61	36-38	109-115	65-70	11-14	11-16	18	65-80
1998	K	⑥	1.5 (1495)	①	40-44	25-28	110-118	94-101	11-14	11-14	18	65-80
	K	⑦	1.5 (1495)	①	40-43	23-26	103-110	88-96	13-18	22-30	18	65-80
	M	⑧	1.8 (1795)	③	⑤	34-39	125-133	88-95	13-18	22-30	18	65-80
	M	⑨	1.8 (1795)	③	⑤	34-39	125-133	88-95	11-14	17-22	18	65-80
	F		2.0 (1975)	③	⑤	34-39	125-133	88-95	11-14	17-22	18	65-80
	P		2.0 (1997)	76-83 ④	47-51	36-38	80-94	94-101	18-22	18-22	18	65-80
	T		3.0 (2972)	②	55-61	36-38	109-115	65-70	11-14	11-16	18	65-80

① Cold: 51-54 ft. lbs.; Warm: 58-61 ft. lbs.
② Cold: 65-72 ft. lbs.; Warm: 72-80 ft. lbs.
③ M10 Bolts - Step 1: 22ft. lbs.; Step 2: Plus 60-65 degrees; Step 3: Plus 60-65 degrees
  M12 Bolts - Step 1: 26 ft. lbs.; Step 2: Plus 60-65 degrees; Step 3: Plus 60-65 degrees
④ Cold
⑤ Step 1: 20-24 ft. lbs.; Step 2: Plus 60-65 degrees
⑥ SOHC
⑦ DOHC
⑧ Elantra
⑨ Tiburon
⑩ Scoupe Turbo

89533c10

ENGINE MECHANICAL

Engine

REMOVAL & INSTALLATION

♦ **See Figures 1 thru 8 (p. 10–15)**

The most important part of engine removal is the labeling of components, wires and hoses to be removed or disconnected from the engine.

In most cases, the engine will be removed one day and installed several days later. This lapse in time makes it very difficult (even for professional mechanics) to remember where each and every connection must be made. A little time spent labeling and taking photographs of the engine compartment will pay big dividends once the engine is ready for installation.

➡**Hyundai recommends that the engine and transaxle be removed as a single unit on all models.**

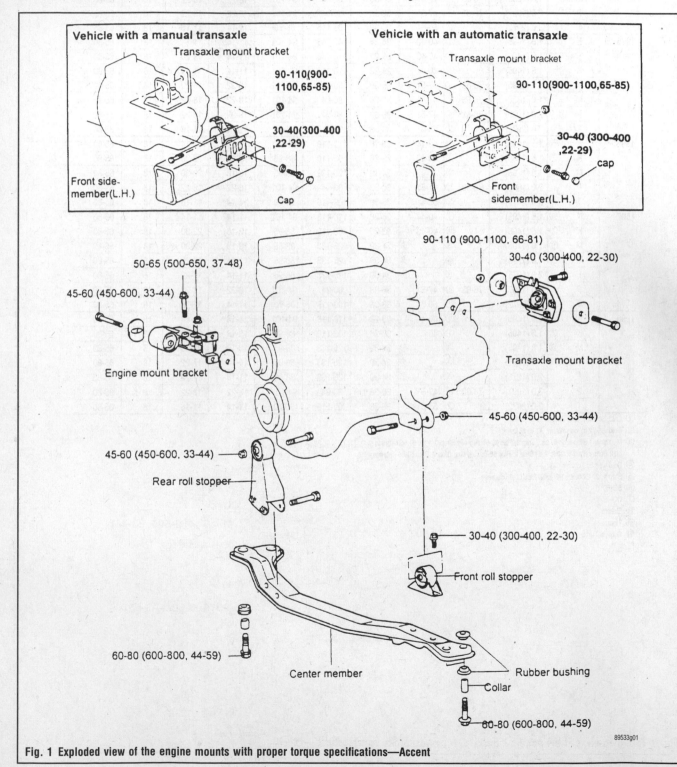

Fig. 1 Exploded view of the engine mounts with proper torque specifications—Accent

89533g01

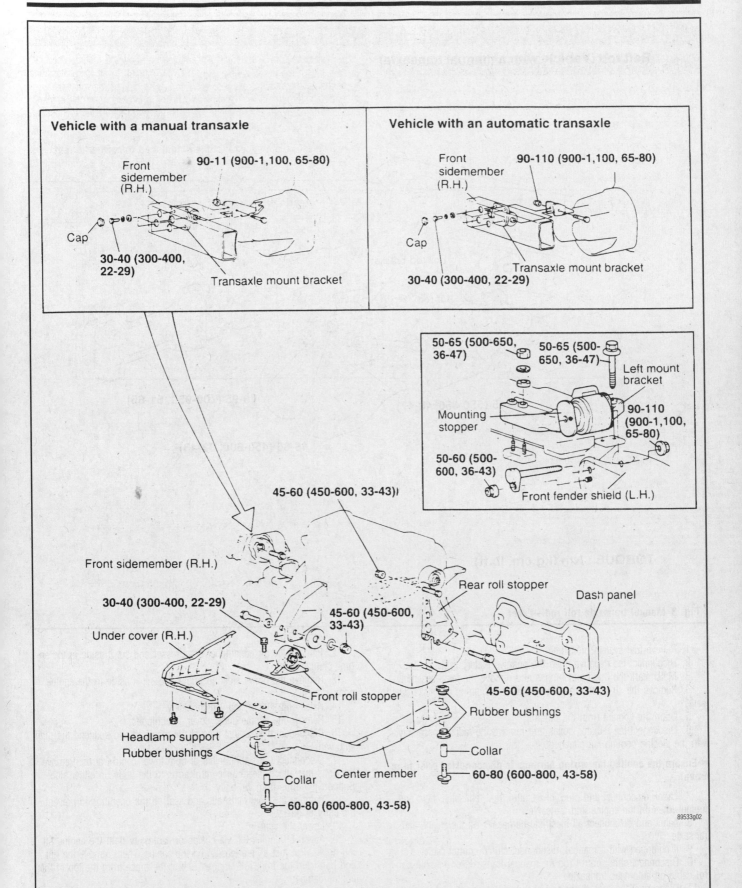

Vehicle with a manual transaxle

90-11 (900-1,100, 65-80)

Front sidemember (R.H.)

Cap

30-40 (300-400, 22-29)

Transaxle mount bracket

Vehicle with an automatic transaxle

90-110 (900-1,100, 65-80)

Front sidemember (R.H.)

Cap

30-40 (300-400, 22-29)

Transaxle mount bracket

50-65 (500-650, 36-47)

50-65 (500-650, 36-47)

Left mount bracket

Mounting stopper

90-110 (900-1,100, 65-80)

50-60 (500-600, 36-43)

Front fender shield (L.H.)

45-60 (450-600, 33-43)

Front sidemember (R.H.)

30-40 (300-400, 22-29)

Under cover (R.H.)

Rear roll stopper

Dash panel

45-60 (450-600, 33-43)

Front roll stopper

45-60 (450-600, 33-43)

Rubber bushings

Collar

60-80 (600-800, 43-58)

Headlamp support
Rubber bushings

Collar

Center member

60-80 (600-800, 43-58)

89533g02

Fig. 2 Exploded view of the engine mounts with proper torque specifications—Excel

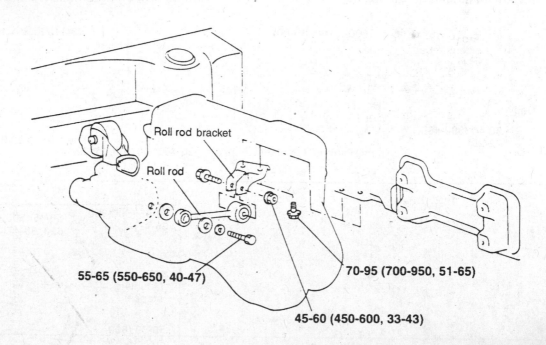

Roll rod (Vehicle with a manual transaxle)

Roll rod bracket

Roll rod

55-65 (550-650, 40-47)

70-95 (700-950, 51-65)

45-60 (450-600, 33-43)

TORQUE : Nm (kg.cm, lb.ft)

89533g03

Fig. 3 Manual transaxle roll rod—Excel

1. Relieve fuel system pressure.
2. Disconnect the negative, then the positive battery cable.
3. Matchmark the hood and hinges and remove the hood assembly.
4. Remove the air cleaner assembly and all adjoining air intake duct work.
5. Drain the coolant from the radiator.
6. Disconnect the radiator hoses and remove the radiator assembly with the electric cooling fan attached.

➡**Ensure the cooling fan wiring harness is disconnected prior to removal.**

7. Label, disconnect and plug all vacuum, fuel, emission, fluid and coolant lines on the engine and transaxle.
8. Label and disconnect all electrical harnesses on the engine and transaxle.
9. If equipped with a manual, disconnect clutch control cable.
10. Disconnect shift control rod on manual transaxle or the shift control cable on automatic transaxle.
11. Disconnect the accelerator and speedometer cables.

12. Remove the air conditioner compressor and set it aside in the engine compartment.
13. Remove the power steering pump and set it aside in the engine compartment.
14. Raise and support the vehicle safely.
15. Remove the engine under cover, if equipped.
16. Disconnect the exhaust pipe at the manifold and suspend the pipe with wire.
17. Disconnect the stabilizer bar at both lower control arms. Remove the bolts that attach the lower control arms to the body on either side. Support the arms from the body.
18. Remove the front halfshafts and seal off the openings to prevent the entry of dirt.
19. Lower the vehicle.
20. Attach an engine lift, via chains or cables, to both the engine lifting hooks. Put just a little tension on the cables. Then, remove the nut and bolt from the front roll stopper; unbolt the brace from the top of the engine damper.
21. Separate the rear roll stopper from the crossmember.

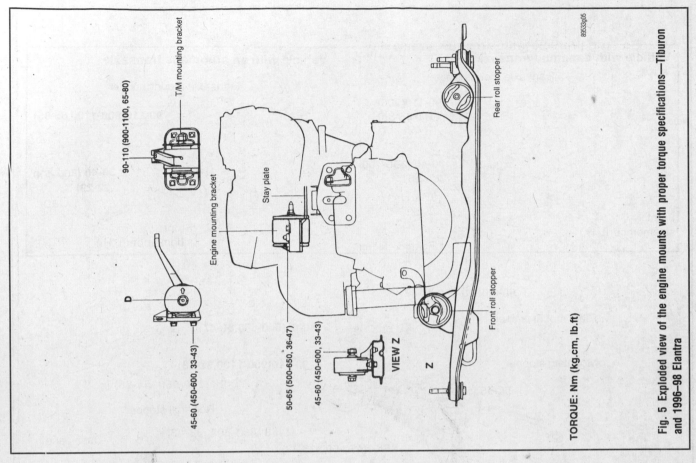

TORQUE: Nm (kg.cm, lb.ft)

Fig. 5 Exploded view of the engine mounts with proper torque specifications—Tiburon and 1996–98 Elantra

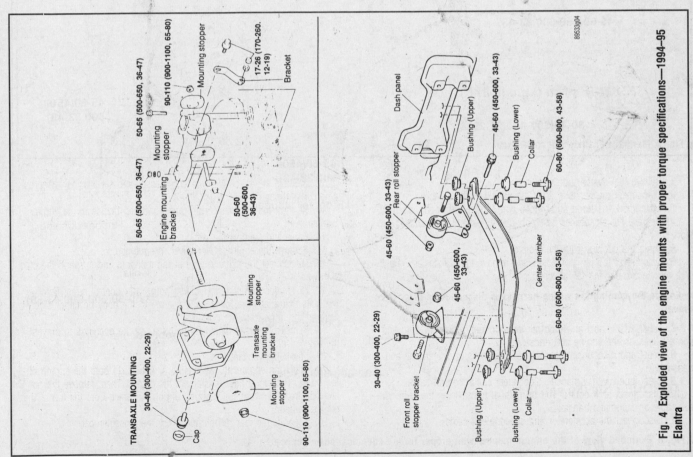

Fig. 4 Exploded view of the engine mounts with proper torque specifications—1994–95 Elantra

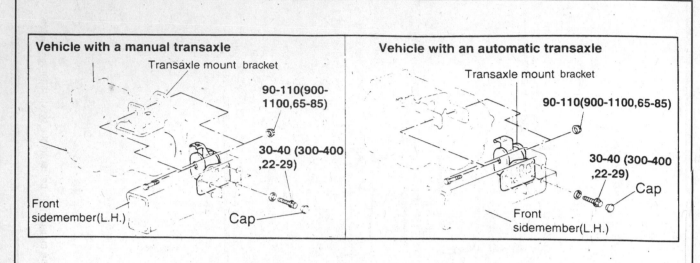

Vehicle with a manual transaxle

Transaxle mount bracket

90-110(900-1100,65-85)

30-40 (300-400,22-29)

Front sidemember(L.H.)

Cap

Vehicle with an automatic transaxle

Transaxle mount bracket

90-110(900-1100,65-85)

30-40 (300-400,22-29)

Cap

Front sidemember(L.H.)

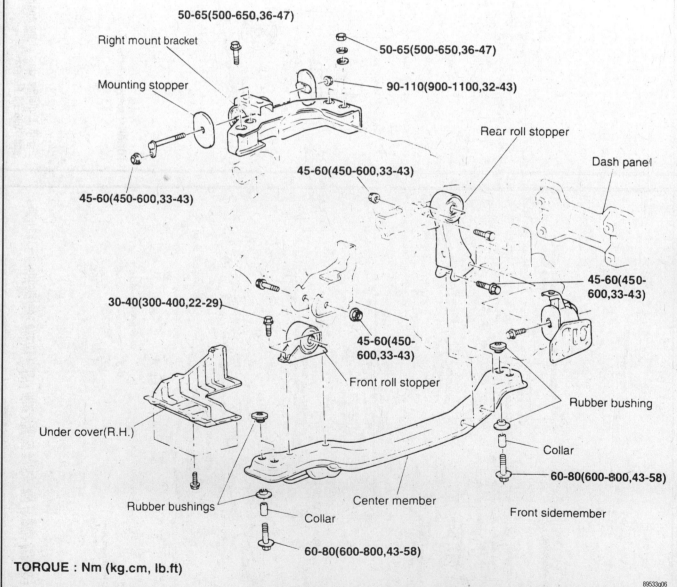

50-65(500-650,36-47)

Right mount bracket

50-65(500-650,36-47)

Mounting stopper

90-110(900-1100,32-43)

Rear roll stopper

Dash panel

45-60(450-600,33-43)

45-60(450-600,33-43)

45-60(450-600,33-43)

30-40(300-400,22-29)

45-60(450-600,33-43)

Front roll stopper

Rubber bushing

Under cover(R.H.)

Collar

60-80(600-800,43-58)

Rubber bushings

Collar

Center member

Front sidemember

60-80(600-800,43-58)

TORQUE : Nm (kg.cm, lb.ft)

89533g06

Fig. 6 Exploded view of the engine mounts with proper torque specifications—Scoupe

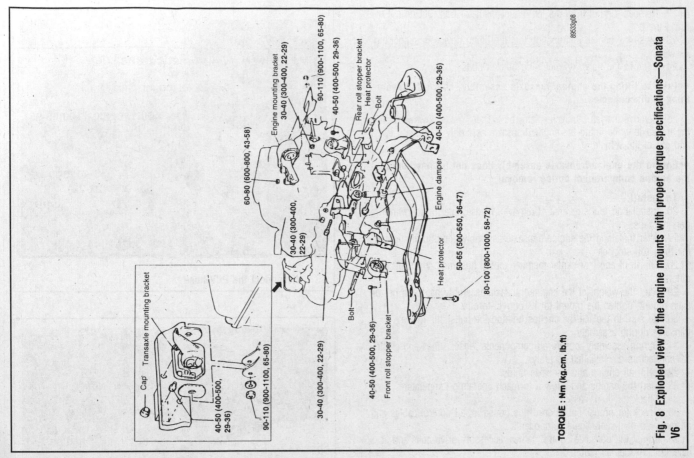

TORQUE : Nm (kg.cm, lb.ft)

Fig. 8 Exploded view of the engine mounts with proper torque specifications—Sonata V6

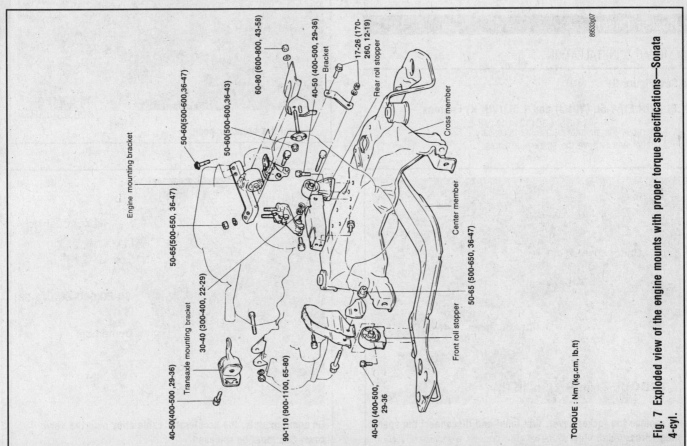

TORQUE : Nm (kg.cm, lb.ft)

Fig. 7 Exploded view of the engine mounts with proper torque specifications—Sonata 4-cyl.

22. Remove the nut from the left mount insulator bolt, but do not remove the bolt.

23. Raise the engine just enough that the lifting device is supporting its weight.

24. Remove the transaxle mounting bracket bolts.

➡️**Prior to lifting the engine/transaxle assembly, check that everything is disconnected.**

25. Remove the left mount insulator bolt. Then, press downward on the transaxle while lifting the engine/transaxle assembly to guide it up and out of the vehicle.

➡️**Ensure the engine/transaxle assembly does not hit anything in the engine compartment during removal.**

To install:

26. Installation is the reverse of removal. Please note the following important steps:

27. After installing the engine/transaxle assembly, temporarily tighten the front roll stopper.

28. The front and rear center member rubber bushings and collar are different.

29. After the weight of the engine/transaxle assembly has been put on each mount, tighten the mount to the correct torque.

30. Be sure to replace the circlips holding the halfshafts in the transaxle during assembly.

31. During assembly, ensure all components, hoses, lines and electrical connectors are installed securely.

32. Refill all engine and transaxle fluids.

33. Start the engine and allow it to reach operating temperature.

34. Check for fluid leaks.

35. Check for proper operation of the transaxle, all control cables and all removed or disconnected components.

36. Adjust the transaxle control cables, accessory drive belts and accelerator linkages as required.

Rocker Cover

REMOVAL & INSTALLATION

▸ **See Figure 9**

1.5L (VIN E), 1.5L (VIN J) and 1.5L (VIN K) Engines

1. Remove the air intake hose, as necessary.
2. Label and remove the spark plug wires.

. . . disconnect the PCV hose . . .

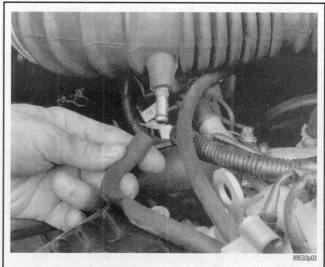

. . . and the breather hose

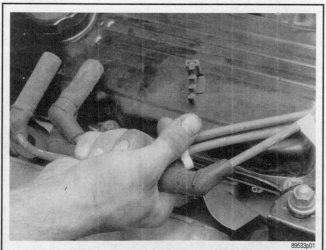

To remove the rocker cover, first label and disconnect the spark plug wires . . .

On some models, the accelerator cable clips onto the valve cover and must be released

Remove the upper timing belt cover . . .

. . . then loosen the attaching bolts and remove the rocker cover

Inspect the rocker cover's rail carefully and straighten as necessary. Always use a new gasket

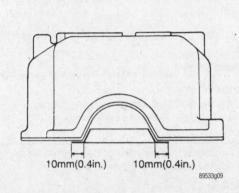

10mm(0.4in.)   10mm(0.4in.)

Fig. 9 Apply a 0.4 in. (10mm) bead of Three Bond No. 1212D or equivalent sealant to each end of the rocker cover as illustrated—1.5L (VIN E), 1.5L (VIN J), 1.5L (VIN K) and 3.0L (VIN T) engines

3. Remove the breather and PCV hoses.
4. Remove the upper timing belt cover.
5. Remove the rocker cover.

To install:

6. Clean all rocker cover gasket mating surfaces.

7. Inspect the breather and PCV ports, camshaft end seal and valve cover end seals. Repair or replace as necessary.

8. Apply a 0.4 in. (10mm) bead of Three Bond No. 1212D or equivalent sealant to the top surface of the cylinder head and camshaft cap. Refer to illustration for specific application points.

9. Install the rocker cover and tighten bolts to 1.0–1.5 ft. lbs. (1.5–2.0 Nm).

→Do not overtighten the valve cover bolts, because warpage of the valve cover and oil leakage could result.

10. Install the upper timing belt cover and tighten bolts to 7–8 ft. lbs. (10–12 Nm).
11. Install the breather and PCV hoses.
12. Install the spark plug wires.
13. Install the air intake hose.
14. Start the engine and allow it to reach operating temperature. Check for leaks.

3.0L (VIN T) Engine

1. Remove the air intake hose, as necessary.
2. Label and remove the spark plug wires.
3. Remove the breather and PCV hoses.
4. Remove the rocker cover.

To install:

5. Clean all rocker cover gasket mating surfaces.

6. Inspect the breather and PCV ports, camshaft end seal and valve cover end seals. Repair or replace as necessary.

7. Apply a 0.4 in. (10mm) bead of Three Bond No. 1212D or equivalent sealant to the top surface of the cylinder head and cam cap. Refer to illustration for specific application points.

8. Install the rocker cover and tighten bolts to 6–7 ft. lbs. (8–10 Nm).

→Do not overtighten the valve cover bolts, because warpage of the valve cover and oil leakage could result.

9. Install the breather and PCV hoses.
10. Install the spark plug wires.
11. Install the air intake hose.

12. Start the engine and allow it to reach operating temperature. Check for leaks.

Except 1.5L (VIN E), 1.5L (VIN J), 1.5L (VIN K) and 3.0L (VIN T) Engines

♦ **See Figures 10 and 11**

1. Remove the air intake hose, as necessary.
2. Remove the rocker arm center cover.
3. Label and remove the spark plug wires.

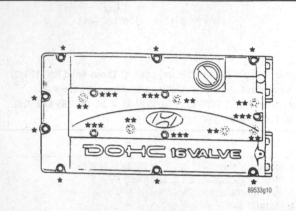

Fig. 10 Rocker cover bolts are of different lengths. Bolts marked as (*) are 25mm long. Bolts marked as (**) are 20mm long. Bolts marked as (***) are 15mm long

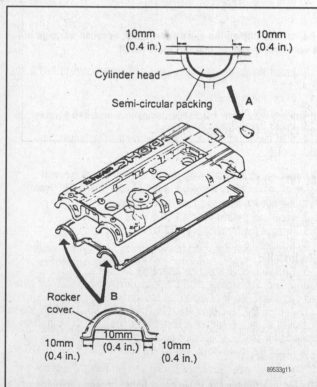

Fig. 11 Apply a 0.4 in. (10mm) bead of Three Bond No. 1212D or equivalent sealant to each end of the rocker cover as illustrated—except 1.5L (VIN E), 1.5L (VIN J), 1.5L (VIN K) and 3.0L (VIN T) engines

4. Remove the breather and PCV hoses.
5. Remove the upper timing belt cover.
6. Remove the rocker cover.

To install:

7. Clean all rocker cover gasket mating surfaces.
8. Inspect the breather and PCV ports, camshaft end seal and valve cover end seals. Repair or replace as necessary.
9. Apply a 0.4 in. (10mm) bead of Three Bond No. 1212D or equivalent sealant to the top surface of the cylinder head and cam cap. Refer to illustration for specific application points.
10. Install the rocker cover and tighten bolts to 2–3 ft. lbs. (3–4 Nm) on 2.0L (VIN P) and 6–7 ft. lbs. (8–10 Nm) on all other engines.

➡ **Do not overtighten the valve cover bolts, because warpage of the valve cover and oil leakage could result.**

11. Install the upper timing belt cover and tighten bolts to 7–8 ft. lbs. (10–12 Nm).
12. Install the breather and PCV hoses.
13. Install the spark plug wires.
14. Install the air intake hose.
15. Install the rocker arm center cover and tighten bolts to 6–7 ft. lbs. (8–10 Nm).
16. Start the engine and allow it to reach operating temperature. Check for leaks.

➡ **Do not overtighten the valve cover bolts, because warpage of the valve cover and oil leakage could result.**

17. Run the engine until normal operating temperature is reached. Shut the engine off and check for oil leaks.

Rocker Arms and Shafts

REMOVAL & INSTALLATION

1.5L (VIN E), 1.5L (VIN J) and 1.5L (VIN K) Engines

♦ **See Figures 12 and 13 (p. 20)**

1. Remove the rocker cover.
2. Loosen the rocker shaft bolts evenly and remove the rocker shaft assembly from the cylinder head with the bolts still in place.
3. Disassemble the rocker shaft by progressively removing each bolt and then the associated springs and rockers, keeping all parts in the exact order of disassembly.

Loosen the rocker shaft bolts evenly to prevent bending the shaft, but do not remove the bolts . . .

. . . then remove the rocker shaft as an assembly

89533p09

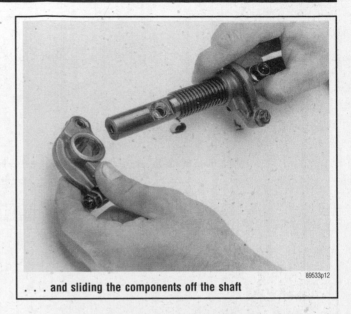

. . . and sliding the components off the shaft

89533p12

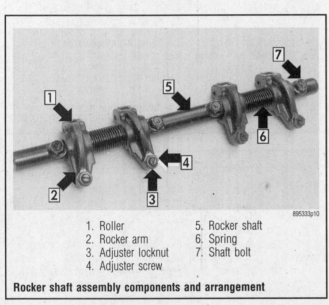

895333p10

1. Roller
2. Rocker arm
3. Adjuster locknut
4. Adjuster screw
5. Rocker shaft
6. Spring
7. Shaft bolt

Rocker shaft assembly components and arrangement

89533p13

Shaft springs may have different tensions and installed heights. Return them to their original positions

89533p11

Disassemble the rocker shaft by removing the shaft bolt . . .

➡It is important to keep all parts in the exact order of removal. Two types of rocker arms are used, and "A" type and a "B" type. Do not mix them up.

To install:

4. Inspect the components as follows:

   a. On engines with roller rockers, inspect the roller on the rocker arm. Replace any rockers where the rollers are dented, damaged or show evidence of seizure. Ensure that the oil hole on the bottom of the rocker arm near the roller is not clogged.

   b. On engines with standard rockers, inspect the rocker face contacting the cam lobe and the adjusting screw that contacts the valve stem for excess wear. If badly worn or damaged, replace the rocker.

   c. Inspect the fit of the rockers on the shaft. Replace rockers or the shaft as necessary.

   d. On engines with hydraulic lash adjusters, inspect the lash adjuster face that contacts the valve stem. Replace the lash adjuster if worn or damaged.

5. Reassemble the rocker shaft making sure all components are installed in their original positions.

6. Install the rocker shaft on the cylinder head and tighten bolts evenly to 14–20 ft. lbs. (20–26 Nm).

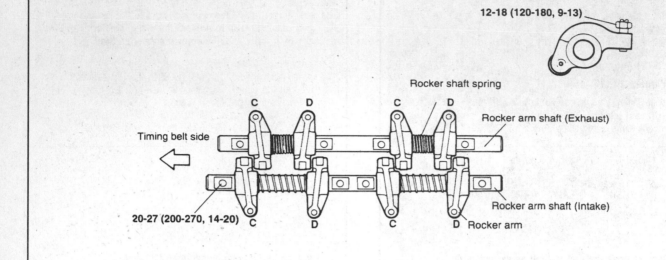

C : Marked 1-3
D : Marked 2-4

TORQUE : Nm (kg.cm, lb.ft)

89533g12

Fig. 12 Rocker assembly components and arrangement. Rockers marked "C" and "D" must be returned to their original positions—1.5L (VIN J) engine

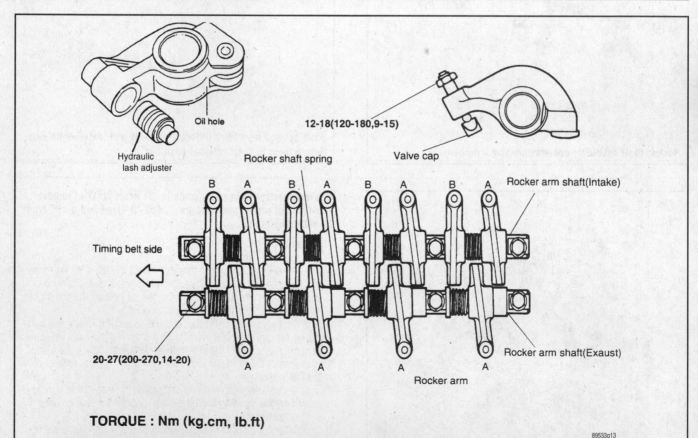

TORQUE : Nm (kg.cm, lb.ft)

89533g13

Fig. 13 Rocker assembly components and arrangement. Rockers marked "A" and "B" must be returned to their original positions—1.5L (VIN E) and 1.5L (VIN K) engines

7. Install the rocker cover using a new gasket.

8. Start the engine and allow it to reach normal operating temperature. Check for leaks.

9. On 1.5L (VIN E) and 1.5L (VIN J) engines, adjust the valve lash.

3.0L (VIN T) Engine

▶ See Figures 14, 15, 16 and 17

➡ The 3.0L (VIN T) engine is equipped with hydraulic lash adjusters. To prevent the lash adjusters from falling out during removal of the rocker arms, special holding clips (PN 09426 32000 or equiv-

alent) are used to hold the adjusters in place. The lash adjuster is filled with diesel fuel. Store the adjusters in the upright position or cover with masking tape to prevent the diesel fuel from spilling out. If the fuel spills out, the adjusters must be bled.

1. Remove the rocker cover.

2. Install special holding clip (PN 09246 3200 or equivalent) on each rocker arm to prevent the hydraulic lash adjusters from falling out during removal (and installation).

3. Loosen the bearing cap bolts evenly and remove the rocker shaft assembly from the cylinder head with the bolts still in place.

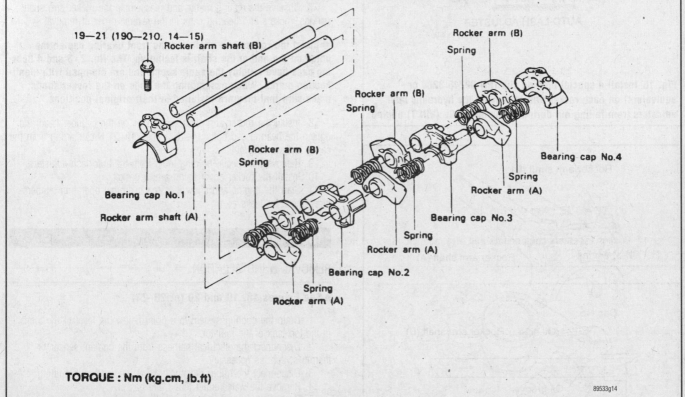

TORQUE : Nm (kg.cm, lb.ft)

89533g14

Fig. 14 Rocker assembly components and arrangement. Rockers marked "A" and "B" must be returned to their original positions— 3.0L (VIN T) engine

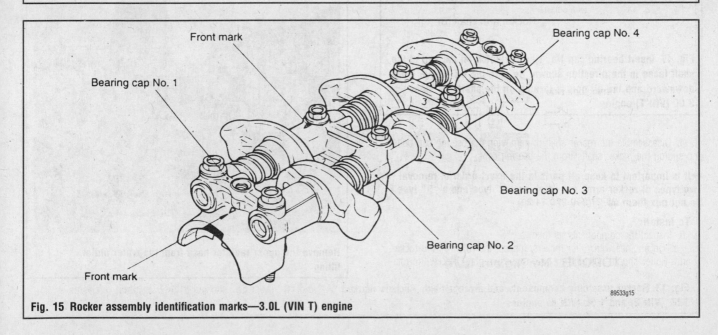

89533g15

Fig. 15 Rocker assembly identification marks—3.0L (VIN T) engine

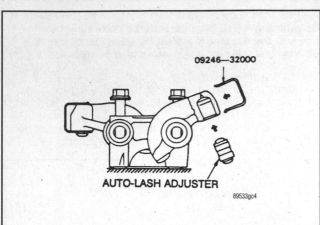

Fig. 16 Install a special holding clip (PN 09246 3200 or equivalent) on each rocker arm to prevent the hydraulic lash adjusters from falling out during servicing—3.0L (VIN T) engine

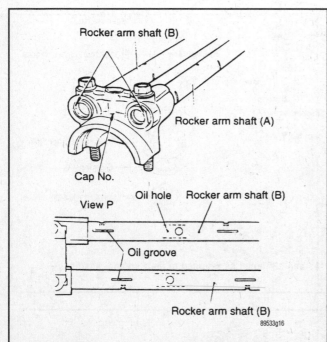

Fig. 17 Insert bearing cap No. 1 so the notch on the end of the shaft faces in the direction shown. Be sure the oil groove faces downward and the oil port is located on the shaft "A" side—3.0L (VIN T) engine

4. Disassemble the rocker shaft by removing the bearing cap bolts and sliding the rocker shafts from the bearing caps.

➡ It is important to keep all parts in the exact order of removal. Two types of rocker arms are used, an "A" type and a "B" type. Do not mix them up.

To install:
5. Inspect the components as follows:
   a. On engines with roller rockers, inspect the roller on the rocker arm. Roller should not bind or have excessive play. If eccentric rota-

tion or backlash is evident, or if rollers are dented, damaged or show evidence of seizure, replace the rocker. Ensure that the oil hole on the bottom of the rocker arm near the roller is not clogged.
   b. On engines with standard rockers, inspect the rocker face contacting the cam lobe and the adjusting screw that contacts the valve stem for excess wear. If badly worn or damaged, replace the rocker.
   c. Inspect the fit of the rockers on the shaft. Replace rockers or the shaft as necessary.
   d. On engines with hydraulic lash adjusters, inspect the lash adjuster face that contacts the valve stem. Replace the lash adjuster if worn or damaged.
6. Lubricate the rocker arm and shafts with clean engine oil.
7. Observe the mating marks and reassemble the rocker arm shafts, springs, rockers and bearing caps in the reverse order of removal.

➡ **Insert the rocker arm shaft into the front bearing cap so the notch on the end of the shaft is facing up. The No. 2, 3 and 4 bearing caps have roughly the same shape and are stamped with identification marks. When assembling the caps on the rocker shafts, make sure that they are installed in their original positions.**

8. Install the rocker arm shaft assemblies on the cylinder head and tighten the bearing cap bolts 14–15 ft. lbs. (19–21 Nm) starting from the center and working out.
9. Remove the special holding tools from the auto lash adjusters.
10. Install the rocker cover using a new gasket.
11. Start the engine and allow it to reach normal operating temperature. Check for leaks.

Thermostat

REMOVAL & INSTALLATION

▶ **See Figures 18, 19 and 20 (p. 23–24)**

1. Drain the cooling system to a point below the level of the tubes in the top tank of the radiator.
2. Disconnect the electrical harness from the coolant sensor or thermo switch, as necessary.
3. Disconnect the upper radiator hose at the water outlet fitting.
4. Remove the water outlet fitting and gasket.
5. Remove the thermostat.

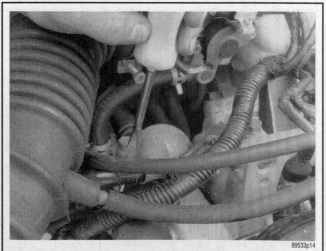

Remove the upper radiator hose from the water outlet fitting . . .

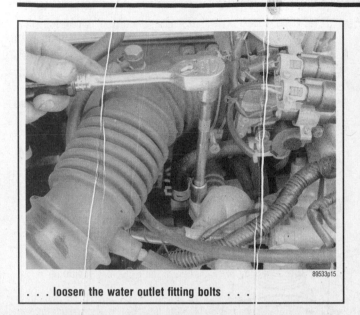

. . . loosen the water outlet fitting bolts . . .

Use a scraper to remove the old gasket material. Take care not to damage the aluminum intake manifold

. . . and remove the water outlet fitting . . .

. . . then remove the thermostat

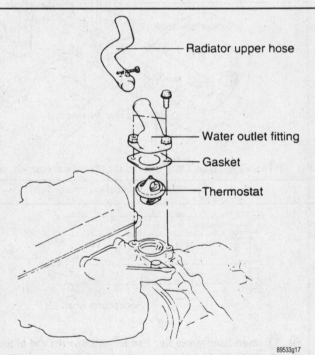

Fig. 18 The water outlet fitting bolts directly to the intake manifold—1.5L (VIN J), 2.0L (VIN P) and 3.0L (VIN T) engines

To install:

6. Clean the mating surfaces of the water outlet fitting and intake manifold thoroughly.

7. Install the thermostat with the spring facing downward.

➡The jiggle valve in the thermostat should be on the manifold side.

8. Install the housing using a new gasket. Tighten the housing bolts to 12–14 ft. lbs. (17–20 Nm).

9. Connect the electrical harness to the coolant sensor or thermo switch.

10. Refill the cooling system.

11. Start the engine and allow it to reach operating temperature. Check for leaks.

12. Once the vehicle has cooled, recheck the coolant level.

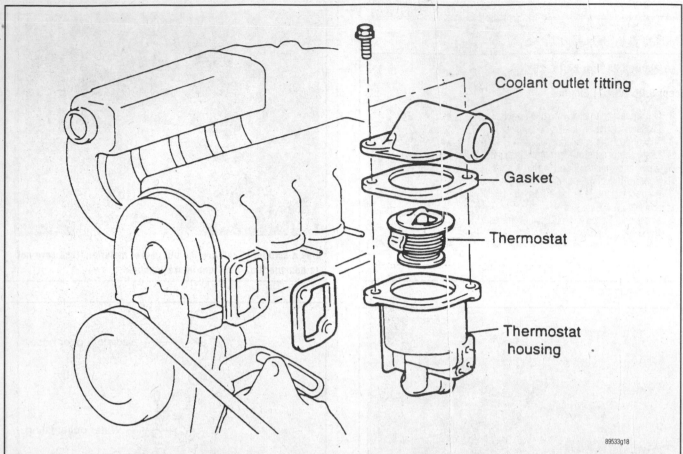

Fig. 19 The water outlet fitting bolts to the thermostat housing, which bolts to the cylinder head—1.5L (VIN E) and 1.5L (VIN K) engines

89533g18

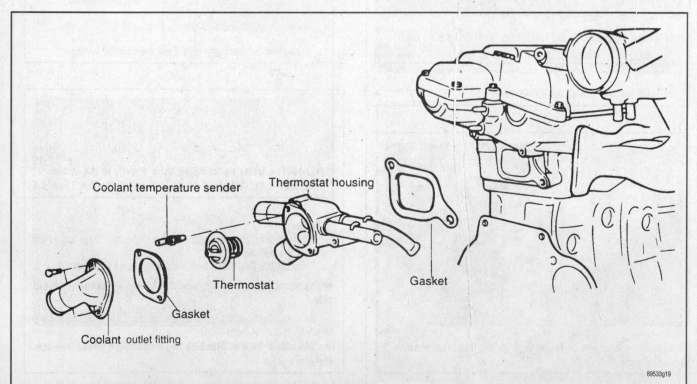

Fig. 20 The water outlet fitting bolts to the thermostat housing, which bolts to the cylinder head.. The heater hoses also connect to the thermostat housing—1.6L (VIN R), 1.8L (VIN M) and 2.0L (VIN F) engines

89533g19

Intake Manifold

REMOVAL & INSTALLATION

▶ See Figures 21 thru 27 (p. 28–31)

Except 3.0L (VIN T) Engine

1. Disconnect the negative battery cable.
2. Disconnect the air intake hose.
3. Disconnect the accelerator cable.
4. Drain the cooling system and disconnect the upper radiator hose.
5. Label and disconnect all wiring harnesses.
6. Remove the throttle body and gasket.
7. Disconnect the PCV hose from the rocker cover and disconnect the brake vacuum hoses.
8. Label and disconnect all vacuum hoses.
9. Relieve the fuel system pressure.

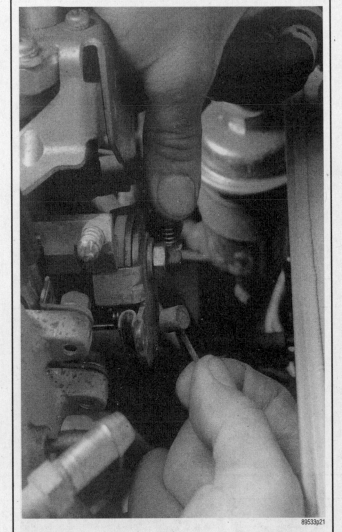

. . . then remove the cable end from the throttle linkage

Many wiring harnesses cross the intake manifold. Label each prior to disconnecting

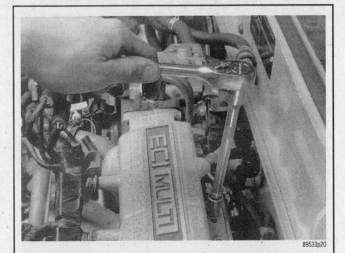

To detach the accelerator cable, first loosen the cable bracket adjusting bolts . . .

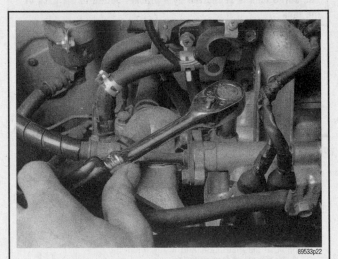

The fuel rail is held in place by two bolts which thread into the intake manifold

The fuel injectors and fuel rail are removed as an assembly. Don't forget to disconnect the fuel line

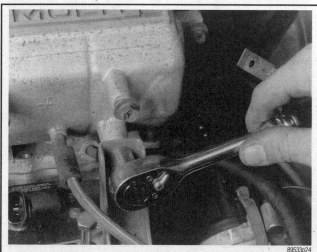

The surge tank is supported by a bracket bolted to the back of the tank . . .

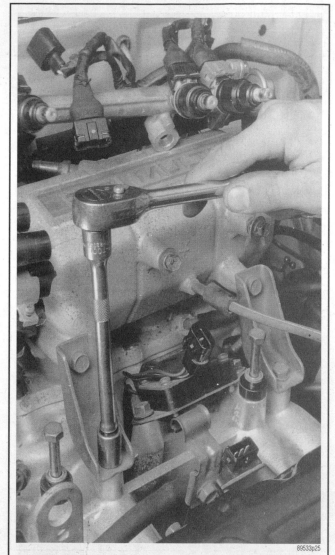

. . . and to the intake manifold. Remove the bolts at the tank and just loosen the bolts at the intake

10. Disconnect the high pressure fuel hose connection from the fuel delivery pipe.

11. Remove the surge tank (and gasket) from the intake manifold.

12. Disconnect the fuel injector harness connectors.

13. Remove the fuel delivery pipe with the pressure regulator attached.

➡Take care not to drop the injectors when removing the delivery pipe.

14. Remove the insulator from the intake manifold and disconnect the heater hose.

15. Disconnect the wiring harness that runs between the water temperature gauge and the water temperature sensor assembly.

16. Remove the water outlet fitting, thermostat and gasket.

17. Label and disconnect the spark plug wires.

18. Remove the distributor and the ignition coil.

19. Remove the intake manifold stay.

20. Remove the intake manifold.

To install:

21. Clean and inspect the intake manifold, cylinder head, surge tank and all other gasket mating surfaces. Inspect the intake manifold and surge tank for cracks. Check the coolant passages for restrictions.

After removing the surge tank mounting nuts, lift the tank from the intake manifold studs

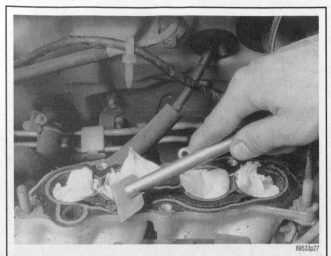

Using a scraper, remove the old surge tank gasket material from the intake manifold

. . . then lift the intake manifold from the cylinder head

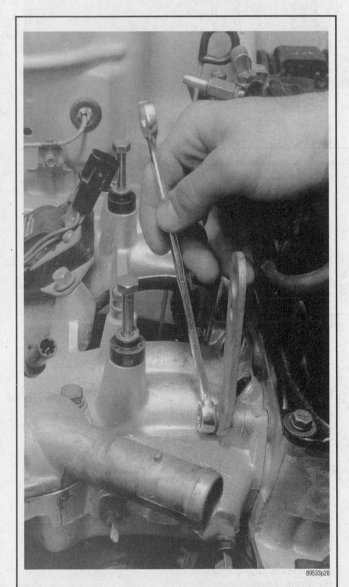

Remove the intake manifold mounting nuts and bolts . . .

Paper towels stuffed in the intake ports keep gasket scrapings from falling into the cylinder head

22. Install the intake manifold using a new gasket. Tighten the intake manifold nuts to 11–14 ft. lbs. (15–20 Nm) starting from the center and working outwards.

23. Install the intake manifold stay and tighten the bolts to 13–18 ft. lbs. (18–25 Nm).

24. Install the ignition coil, distributor, and spark plug wires.

25. Install the thermostat, gasket and water outlet housing. Tighten the bolts to 12–14 ft. lbs. (17–20 Nm).

26. Connect the wiring harness that runs between the temperature sensor and temperature gauge.

27. Install the fuel delivery pipe onto the intake manifold. Torque the retaining bolts to 7–9 ft. lbs. (10–13 Nm).

28. Connect the fuel injector harness connectors.

29. Install the surge tank using a new gasket. Tighten bolts to 11–14 ft. lbs. (15–20 Nm).

30. Connect the high pressure hose to the fuel delivery pipe.

31. Connect the intake manifold, brake and PCV vacuum hoses.

32. Install the throttle body using a new gasket. Tighten bolts to 11–16 ft. lbs. (15–22 Nm).

33. Connect all wiring harnesses.

34. Connect the upper radiator hose to the outlet fitting.

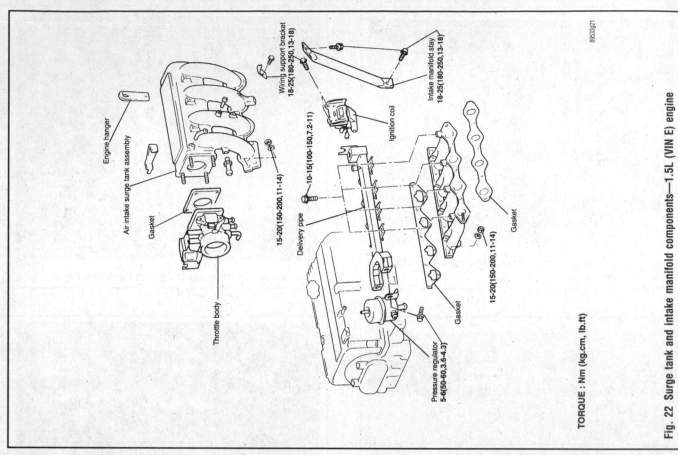

TORQUE : Nm (kg.cm, lb.ft)

Fig. 22 Surge tank and intake manifold components—1.5L (VIN E) engine

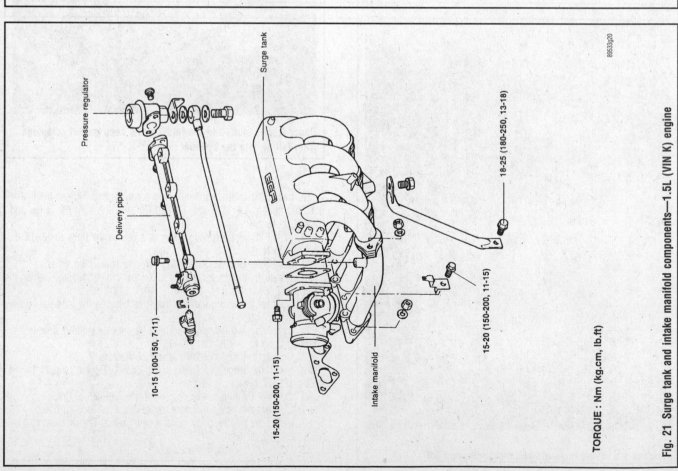

TORQUE : Nm (kg.cm, lb.ft)

Fig. 21 Surge tank and intake manifold components—1.5L (VIN K) engine

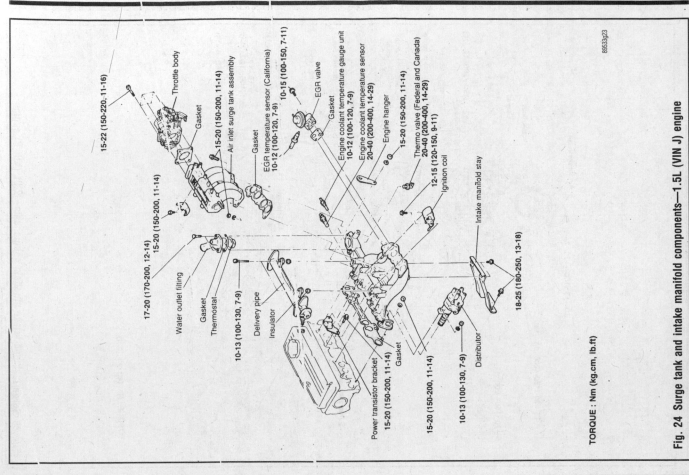

8953g23

15-22 (150-220, 11-16)

Throttle body

Gasket

15-20 (150-200, 11-14)

Air inlet surge tank assembly

15-20 (150-200, 11-14)

15-20 (150-200, 12-14)

17-20 (170-200, 12-14)

Water outlet fitting

Gasket

Thermostat

Delivery pipe

10-13 (100-130, 7-9)

Insulator

Power transistor bracket

15-20 (150-200, 11-14)

Gasket

15-20 (150-200, 11-14)

10-13 (100-130, 7-9)

Gasket

EGR temperature sensor (California)
10-12 (100-120, 7-9)

10-15 (100-150, 7-11)

EGR valve

Gasket

Engine coolant temperature gauge unit
10-12 (100-120, 7-9)

Engine coolant temperature sensor
20-40 (200-400, 14-29)

Engine hanger

15-20 (150-200, 11-14)

Thermo valve (Federal and Canada)
20-40 (200-400, 14-29)

12-15 (120-150, 9-11)

Ignition coil

Intake manifold stay
18-25 (180-250, 13-18)

Distributor

TORQUE : Nm (kg.cm, lb.ft)

Fig. 24 Surge tank and intake manifold components—1.5L (VIN J) engine

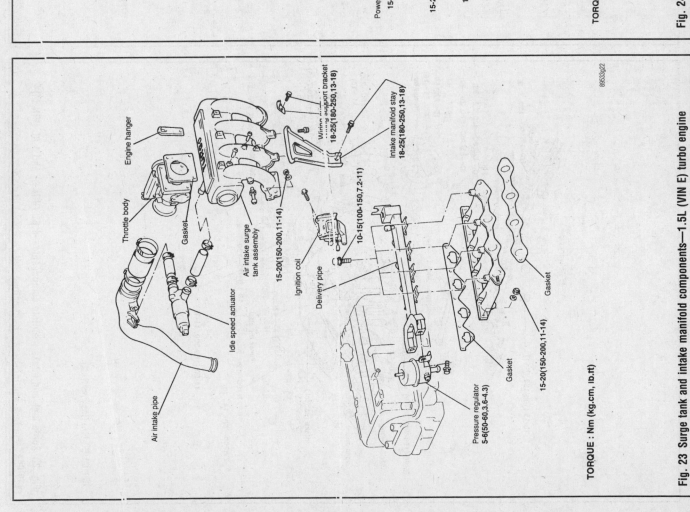

8953g22

Engine hanger

Throttle body

Gasket

Idle speed actuator

Air intake pipe

Air intake surge tank assembly

15-20(150-200, 11-14)

Ignition coil

Delivery pipe

10-15(100-150,7.2-11)

Wiring support bracket
18-25(180-250,13-18)

Intake manifold stay
18-25(180-250,13-18)

Pressure regulator
5-6(50-60,3.6-4.3)

Gasket

Gasket

15-20(150-200,11-14)

TORQUE : Nm (kg.cm, lb.rt)

Fig. 23 Surge tank and intake manifold components—1.5L (VIN E) turbo engine

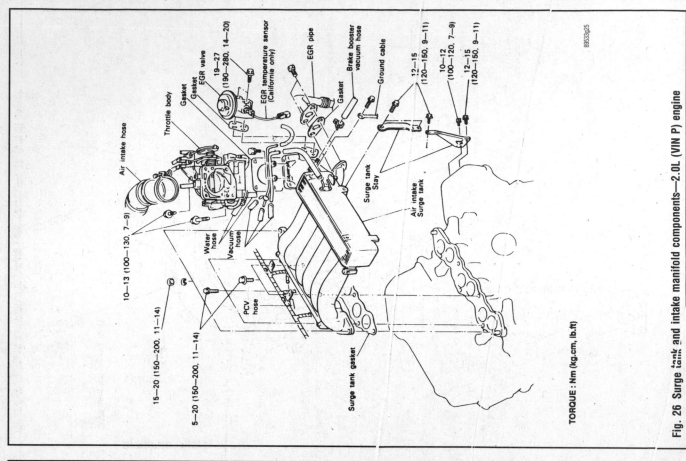

TORQUE : Nm (kg.cm, lb.ft)

Fig. 26 Surge tank and intake manifold components—2.0L (VIN P) engine

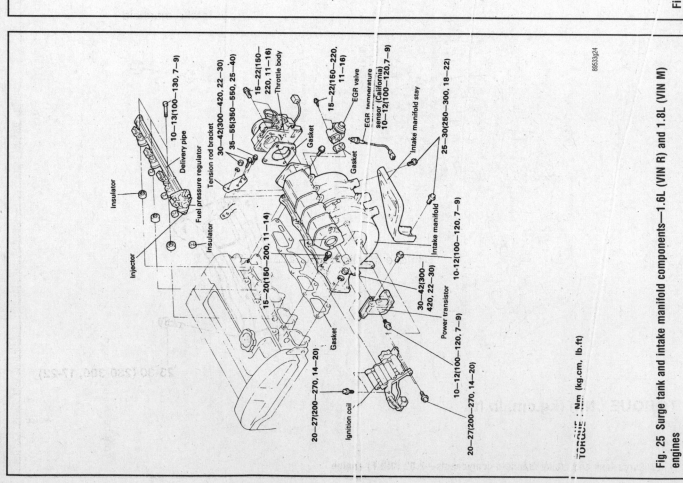

TORQUE : Nm (kg.cm, lb.ft)

Fig. 25 Surge tank and intake manifold components—1.6L (VIN R) and 1.8L (VIN M) engines

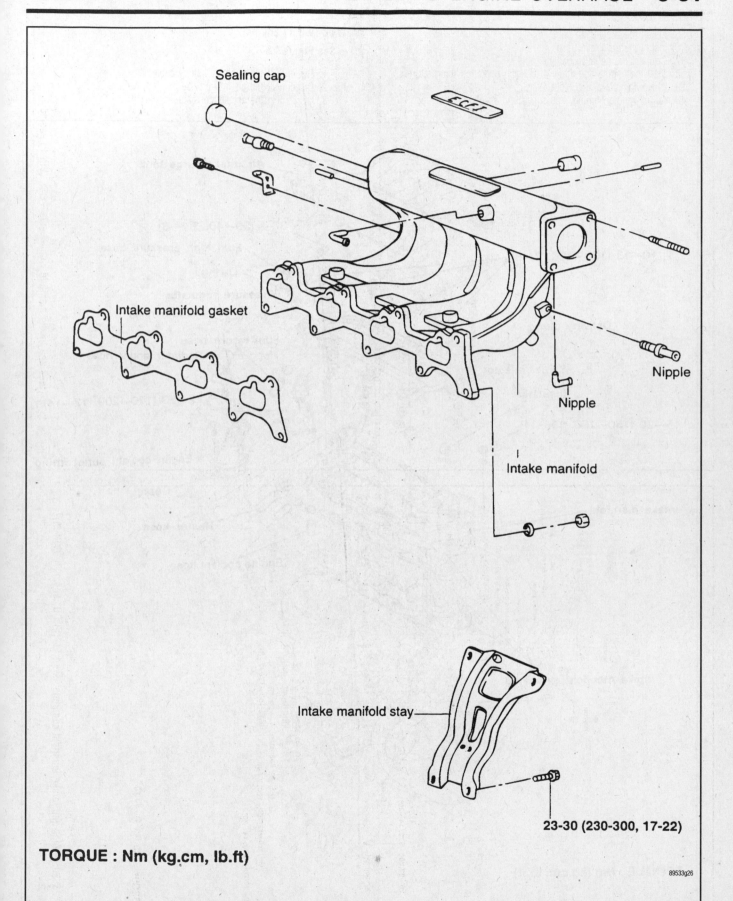

Sealing cap

Intake manifold gasket

Nipple

Nipple

Intake manifold

Intake manifold stay

23-30 (230-300, 17-22)

TORQUE : Nm (kg.cm, lb.ft)

89533g26

Fig. 27 Surge tank and intake manifold components—2.0L (VIN F) engine

35. Install the accelerator cable.
36. Install the air intake hose.
37. Connect the negative battery cable.
38. Start the engine and allow it to reach operating temperature.
39. Check for fuel and coolant leaks.
40. Adjust ignition timing, idle speed and accelerator cable.

3.0L (VIN T) Engine

♦ See Figure 28

1. Disconnect the negative battery cable.
2. Disconnect the air intake hose.
3. Disconnect the accelerator cable.

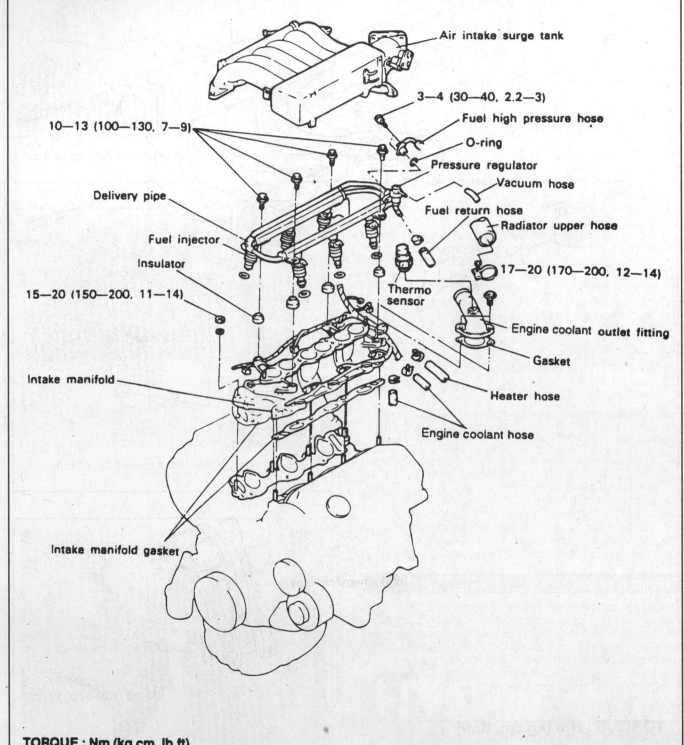

Air intake surge tank

3—4 (30—40, 2.2—3)

Fuel high pressure hose

O-ring

Pressure regulator

Vacuum hose

10—13 (100—130, 7—9)

Delivery pipe

Fuel injector

Insulator

15—20 (150—200, 11—14)

Fuel return hose

Radiator upper hose

17—20 (170—200, 12—14)

Thermo sensor

Engine coolant outlet fitting

Gasket

Intake manifold

Heater hose

Engine coolant hose

Intake manifold gasket

TORQUE : Nm (kg.cm, lb.ft)

89533g27

Fig. 28 Surge tank and intake manifold components—3.0L (VIN T) engine

4. Drain the cooling system and disconnect the upper radiator hose.

5. Label and disconnect all wiring harnesses.

6. Remove the throttle body and gasket.

7. Disconnect the PCV hose from the rocker cover and disconnect the brake vacuum hoses.

8. Label and disconnect all vacuum hoses.

9. Remove the EGR pipe and gasket.

10. Remove the surge tank (and gasket) from the intake manifold.

11. Relieve the fuel system pressure.

12. Disconnect the high pressure fuel hose and return hose connections.

13. Disconnect the fuel injector harness connectors.

14. Remove the fuel delivery pipe with the pressure regulator attached.

➡ **Take care not to drop the injectors when removing the delivery pipe.**

15. Remove the water outlet fitting, thermostat and gasket.

16. Remove the intake manifold.

To install:

17. Clean and inspect the intake manifold, cylinder head, surge tank and all other gasket mating surfaces. Inspect the intake manifold and surge tank for cracks. Check the coolant passages for restrictions.

18. Install the intake manifold using a new gasket. Tighten intake manifold nuts to 11–14 ft. lbs. (15–20 Nm) starting from the center and working outwards.

19. Install the thermostat, gasket and water outlet housing. Tighten bolts to 12–14 ft. lbs. (17–20 Nm).

20. Make sure the injector holes are clean. Lubricate the injector O-rings with a drop of clean engine oil.

21. Install the fuel delivery pipe onto the intake manifold. Torque the retaining bolts to 7–9 ft. lbs. (10–13 Nm).

22. Connect the fuel injector harness connectors.

23. Install the surge tank using a new gasket. Ensure the printed surface of the gasket faces upward. Tighten bolts to 11–14 ft. lbs. (15–20 Nm).

24. Connect the intake manifold, brake and PCV vacuum hoses.

25. Install the throttle body using a new gasket. Tighten bolts to 11–16 ft. lbs. (15–22 Nm).

➡ **One throttle body bolt is shorter than the rest. This bolt is installed in the upper left hole when viewed from the front of the throttle body.**

26. Connect all wiring harnesses.

27. Connect the upper radiator hose to the outlet fitting.

28. Install the accelerator cable.

29. Install the air intake hose.

30. Connect the negative battery cable.

31. Start the engine and allow it to reach operating temperature.

32. Check for fuel and coolant leaks.

33. Adjust the accelerator and cruise control cables, as necessary.

Exhaust Manifold

Exhaust system fasteners are notorious for rusting, which makes removal them without snapping or rounding them an almost impossible task. Before working on any exhaust system component, identify which flanges, brackets, U-bolts, manifold, etc. have to be removed and inspect the material condition of the fasteners. If necessary, wire brush any rusted fastener to remove loose rust particles, then spray the area with penetrating oil and allow it to soak overnight.

REMOVAL & INSTALLATION

◆ **See Figures 29, 30 and 31 (p. 35–36)**

Except 1.5L (VIN E) Turbo and 3.0L (VIN T) Engines

1. With the exhaust manifold cool, soak all nuts, studs and bolts with a liquid penetrant. Allow the penetrant to soak in overnight.

Spraying the nuts with penetrating lubricant is a must for easy removal

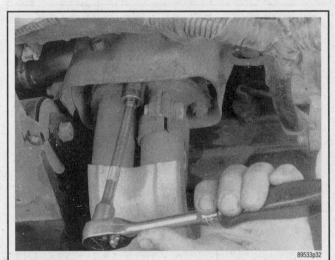

To remove the exhaust manifold, disconnect the exhaust pipe . . .

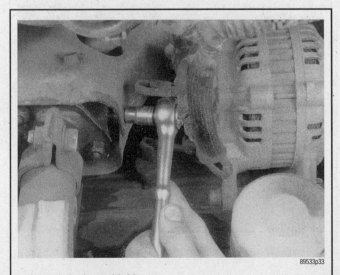

. . . and the heat shield

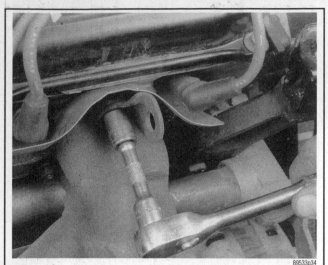

Remove the exhaust manifold attaching nut . . .

89533p34

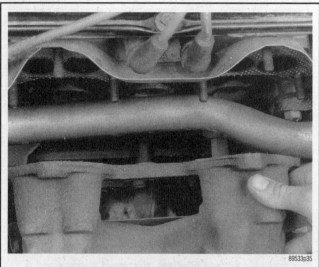

. . . and lift the manifold from the engine

89533p35

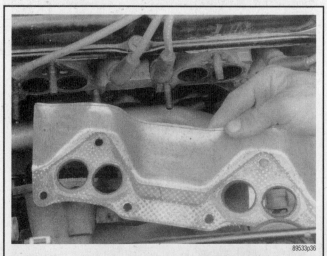

The exhaust manifold gasket is metal and incorporates a heat shield

89533p36

2. Disconnect the negative battery cable.

3. Label and disconnect the oxygen sensor electrical harness.

4. Remove the oxygen sensor.

5. Remove the heat shield on the exhaust manifold.

6. Disconnect the exhaust pipe at the exhaust manifold.

7. Support the exhaust manifold and remove all attaching nuts and washers.

8. Remove the exhaust manifold and old gasket from the cylinder head.

To install:

9. Thoroughly clean the sealing surfaces on the cylinder head and manifold.

10. Ensure all the nuts and bolts turn freely, oiling them lightly, if necessary. Also, ensure all studs are properly installed in the cylinder head. Replace any nuts, washers or studs that are excessively rusted or may have been damaged during removal.

11. Use a straightedge to check the manifold sealing surfaces for flatness. If distortion is greater than 0.006 in. (0.15mm) machine the surface or replace the exhaust manifold.

12. Install new gaskets so all bolt holes and ports are aligned.

13. Place the manifold in position and install all washers and nuts hand tight.

14. Exhaust manifold nuts should be tightened alternately and in several stages. Tighten nuts as follows:

• 1.5L (VIN E), 1.5L (VIN J) and 1.5L (VIN K): 11–15 ft. lbs. (15–20 Nm)

• 1.6L (VIN R), 1.8L (VIN M)and 2.0L (VIN P): 18–22 ft. lbs. (25–30 Nm)

• 1.6L (VIN R), 2.0L (VIN P) and 1994–95 1.8L (VIN M): 18–22 ft. lbs. (25–30 Nm)

• 2.0L (VIN F) and 1996–98 1.8L (VIN M): 32–41 ft. lbs. (43–50 Nm)

15. Connect exhaust pipe and tighten nuts to 22–29 ft. lbs. (30–40 Nm).

16. Install the heat shield and tighten bolts to 11–15 ft. lbs. (15–20 Nm).

17. Coat the oxygen sensor threads with antiseize compound and install the oxygen sensor. Tighten to 29–36 ft. lbs. (30–40 Nm).

18. Connect the oxygen sensor electrical harness.

19. Connect the negative battery cable.

20. Start the engine and allow it to reach operating temperature. Check for leaks.

1.5L (VIN E) Turbo Engine

♦ See Figure 32 (p. 36)

1. With the exhaust manifold cool, soak all nuts, studs and bolts with a liquid penetrant. Allow the penetrant to soak in overnight.

2. Disconnect the negative battery cable.

3. Label and disconnect the oxygen sensor electrical harness.

4. Remove the oxygen sensor.

5. Remove the heat shield on the exhaust manifold.

6. Remove the air intake pipe assembly.

7. Disconnect the exhaust pipe at the turbocharger discharge.

8. Support the exhaust manifold and remove all attaching nuts and washers.

9. Carefully remove the exhaust manifold (with turbocharger attached).

10. Remove the old gasket from the cylinder head.

To install:

11. Thoroughly clean the sealing surfaces on the cylinder head and manifold.

12. Ensure all the nuts and bolts turn freely, oiling them lightly, if necessary. Also, ensure all studs are properly installed in the cylinder head. Replace any nuts, washers or studs that are excessively rusted or may have been damaged during removal.

13. Use a straightedge to check the manifold sealing surfaces for flat-

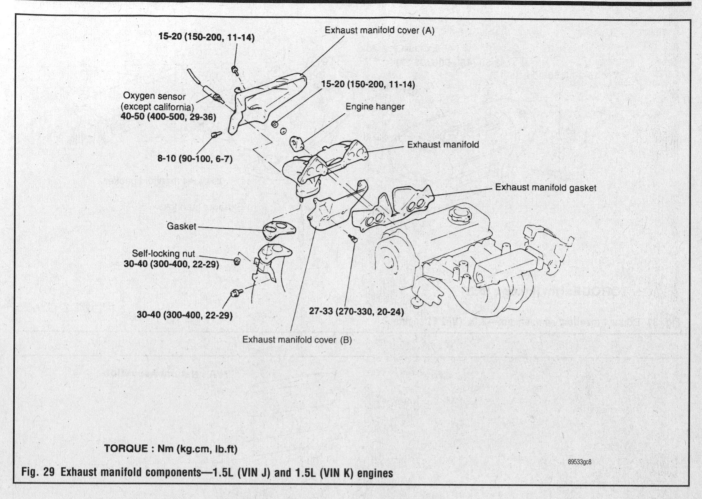

15-20 (150-200, 11-14)

Exhaust manifold cover (A)

15-20 (150-200, 11-14)

Oxygen sensor
(except california)
40-50 (400-500, 29-36)

Engine hanger

8-10 (90-100, 6-7)

Exhaust manifold

Exhaust manifold gasket

Gasket

Self-locking nut
30-40 (300-400, 22-29)

30-40 (300-400, 22-29)

27-33 (270-330, 20-24)

Exhaust manifold cover (B)

TORQUE : Nm (kg.cm, lb.ft)

89533gc8

Fig. 29 Exhaust manifold components—1.5L (VIN J) and 1.5L (VIN K) engines

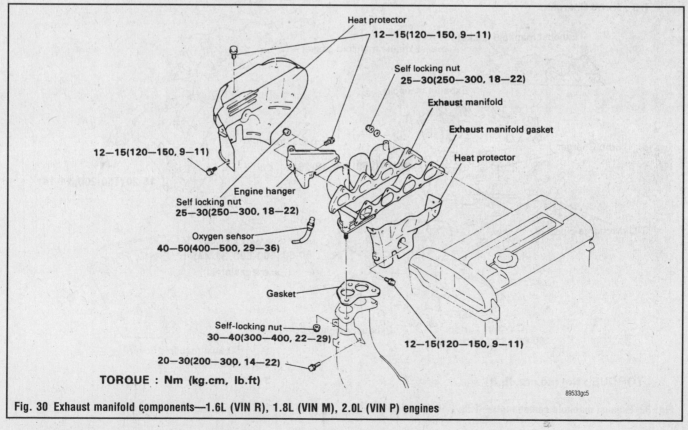

Heat protector
12—15(120—150, 9—11)

Self locking nut
25—30(250—300, 18—22)

Exhaust manifold

Exhaust manifold gasket

Heat protector

12—15(120—150, 9—11)

Engine hanger
Self locking nut
25—30(250—300, 18—22)

Oxygen sensor
40—50(400—500, 29—36)

Gasket

Self-locking nut
30—40(300—400, 22—29)

12—15(120—150, 9—11)

20—30(200—300, 14—22)

TORQUE : Nm (kg.cm, lb.ft)

89533gc5

Fig. 30 Exhaust manifold components—1.6L (VIN R), 1.8L (VIN M), 2.0L (VIN P) engines

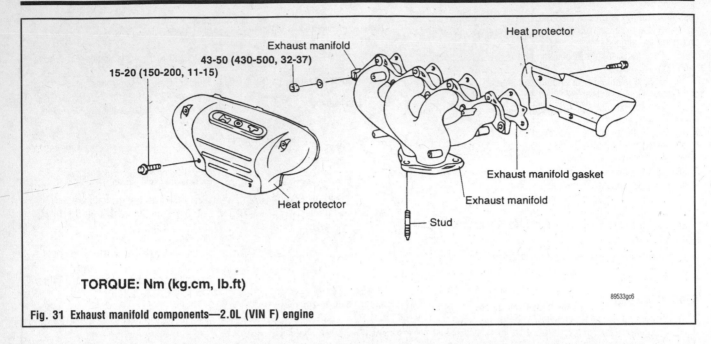

15-20 (150-200, 11-15)

43-50 (430-500, 32-37)

Exhaust manifold

Heat protector

Heat protector

Exhaust manifold gasket

Exhaust manifold

Stud

TORQUE: Nm (kg.cm, lb.ft)

89533gc6

Fig. 31 Exhaust manifold components—2.0L (VIN F) engine

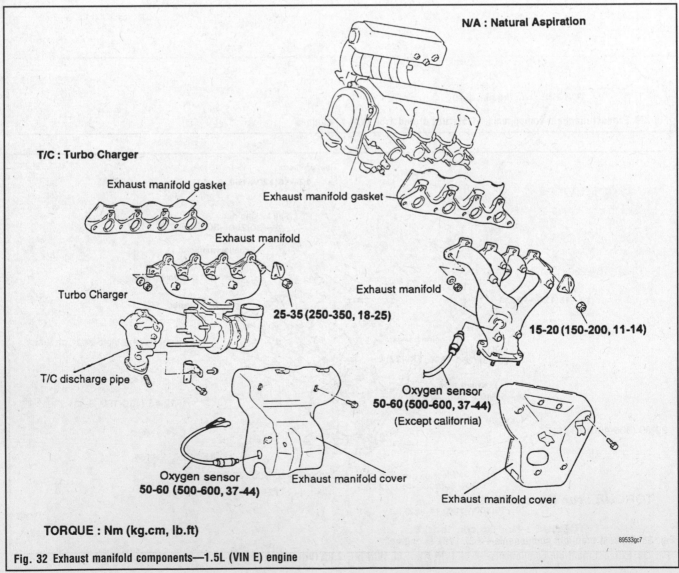

N/A : Natural Aspiration

T/C : Turbo Charger

Exhaust manifold gasket

Exhaust manifold gasket

Exhaust manifold

Turbo Charger

Exhaust manifold

25-35 (250-350, 18-25)

15-20 (150-200, 11-14)

T/C discharge pipe

Oxygen sensor
50-60 (500-600, 37-44)
(Except california)

Oxygen sensor
50-60 (500-600, 37-44)

Exhaust manifold cover

Exhaust manifold cover

TORQUE : Nm (kg.cm, lb.ft)

89533gc7

Fig. 32 Exhaust manifold components—1.5L (VIN E) engine

ness. If distortion is greater than 0.006 in. (0.15mm) machine the surface or replace the exhaust manifold. 14. Install new gaskets so all bolt holes and ports are aligned.

15. Place the manifold in position and install all washers and nuts hand tight.

16. Exhaust manifold nuts should be tightened alternately and in several stages. Tighten nuts to 18–25 ft. lbs. (25–35 Nm).

17. Connect exhaust pipe and tighten nuts to 22–29 ft. lbs. (30–40 Nm).

18. Install the air intake pipe assembly.

19. Install the heat shield and tighten bolts to 11–15 ft. lbs. (15–20 Nm).

20. Coat the oxygen sensor threads with antiseize compound and install the oxygen sensor. Tighten to 29–36 ft. lbs. (30–40 Nm).

21. Connect the oxygen sensor electrical harness.

22. Connect the negative battery cable.

23. Start the engine and allow it to reach operating temperature. Check for leaks.

3.0L (VIN T) Engine

♦ See Figure 33

REAR MANIFOLD

1. Disconnect the negative battery cable.
2. Disconnect the crossover pipe at the exhaust manifold.
3. Disconnect the EGR tube.
4. Support the exhaust manifold and remove all attaching nuts and washers.

5. Carefully remove the exhaust manifold.

6. Remove the old gasket from the cylinder head.

To install:

7. Thoroughly clean the sealing surfaces on the cylinder head and manifold.

8. Ensure all the nuts and bolts turn freely, oiling them lightly, if necessary. Also, ensure all studs are properly installed in the cylinder head. Replace any nuts, washers or studs that are excessively rusted or may have been damaged during removal.

9. Use a straightedge to check the manifold sealing surfaces for flatness. If distortion is greater than 0.006 in. (0.15mm) machine the surface or replace the exhaust manifold.

10. Install new gaskets so all bolt holes and ports are aligned.

➡ **When installing, the numbers 1–3–5 on the gaskets are used with the rear cylinders and 2–4–6 are on the gasket for the front cylinders.**

11. Place the manifold in position and install all washers and nuts hand tight.

12. Exhaust manifold nuts should be tightened alternately and in several stages. Tighten nuts to 11–16 ft. lbs. (15–22 Nm).

13. Connect the EGR tube.

14. Connect the crossover pipe and tighten nuts to 22–29 ft. lbs. (30–40 Nm).

15. Connect the negative battery cable.

16. Start the engine and allow it to reach operating temperature. Check for leaks.

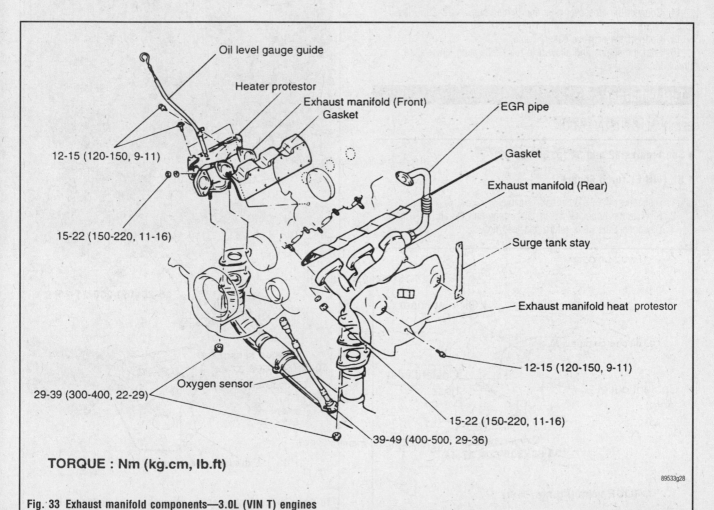

Oil level gauge guide

Heater protestor

Exhaust manifold (Front)

Gasket

EGR pipe

Gasket

Exhaust manifold (Rear)

12-15 (120-150, 9-11)

Surge tank stay

15-22 (150-220, 11-16)

Exhaust manifold heat protestor

12-15 (120-150, 9-11)

Oxygen sensor

29-39 (300-400, 22-29)

15-22 (150-220, 11-16)

39-49 (400-500, 29-36)

TORQUE : Nm (kg.cm, lb.ft)

89533g28

Fig. 33 Exhaust manifold components—3.0L (VIN T) engines

FRONT MANIFOLD

1. Disconnect the negative battery cable.
2. Disconnect the crossover pipe at the exhaust manifold.
3. Remove the oil level dipstick.
4. Support the exhaust manifold and remove all attaching nuts and washers.
5. Carefully remove the exhaust manifold.
6. Remove the old gasket from the cylinder head.

To install:

7. Thoroughly clean the sealing surfaces on the cylinder head and manifold.
8. Ensure all the nuts and bolts turn freely, oiling them lightly, if necessary. Also, ensure all studs are properly installed in the cylinder head. Replace any nuts, washers or studs that are excessively rusted or may have been damaged during removal.
9. Use a straightedge to check the manifold sealing surfaces for flatness. If distortion is greater than 0.006 in. (0.15mm) machine the surface or replace the exhaust manifold.
10. Install new gaskets so all bolt holes and ports are aligned.

➡When installing, the numbers 1–3–5 on the gaskets are used with the rear cylinders and 2–4–6 are on the gasket for the front cylinders.

11. Place the manifold in position and install all washers and nuts hand tight.
12. Exhaust manifold nuts should be tightened alternately and in several stages. Tighten nuts to 11–16 ft. lbs. (15–22 Nm).
13. Install the oil level dipstick.
14. Connect the crossover pipe and tighten nuts to 22–29 ft. lbs. (30–40 Nm).
15. Connect the negative battery cable.
16. Start the engine and allow it to reach operating temperature. Check for leaks.

Turbocharger

REMOVAL & INSTALLATION

♦ **See Figures 32 and 34 (p. 36 and 38)**

1.5L (VIN E) Turbo Engine

1. Disconnect the negative battery cable.
2. Remove the turbocharger air intake pipe and the air intake hose.
3. Disconnect the water return and feed hoses.

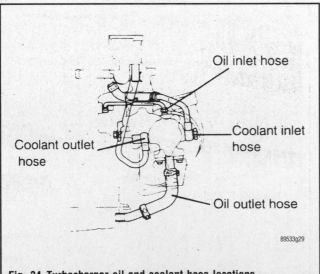

Fig. 34 Turbocharger oil and coolant hose locations

4. Disconnect the oil feed and drain pipe connectors from the turbo housing.
5. Remove the turbocharger discharge pipe and bracket from the outlet (exhaust) side of the turbo.
6. Unfasten the turbocharger mounting bolts and remove the turbocharger.

To install:

7. Install the turbocharger in position on the manifold, using a new gasket. Tighten the mounting bolts to 18–25 ft. lbs. (25–35 Nm).
8. Connect the discharge pipe and bracket to the turbocharger, and tighten the bolts to 18–25 ft. lbs. (25–35 Nm).
9. Connect the oil lines to the turbocharger housing.
10. Connect the water return and feed hoses.
11. Connect the air intake pipe and hose.
12. Connect the negative battery cable.
13. Start the engine and allow it to reach operating temperature. Check for leaks.

Radiator

REMOVAL & INSTALLATION

♦ **See Figure 35 (p. 40)**

1. Disconnect the negative battery cable.
2. Set the heater control knob to the **HOT** position.

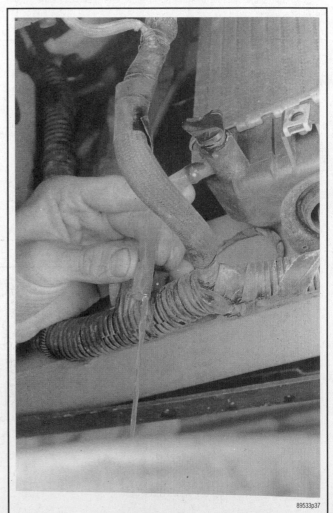

To drain the coolant, open the petcock on the bottom of the radiator

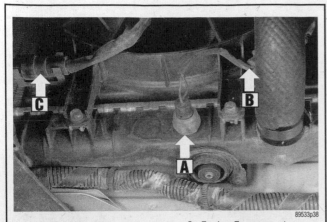

A. Thermo sensor
B. Thermo sensor connector
C. Engine Fan connector

The thermo sensor, thermo sensor connector and engine fan connector are mounted on the radiator

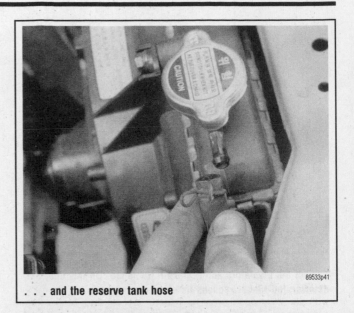

. . . and the reserve tank hose

To remove the radiator, disconnect the upper radiator hose, . . .

Next, remove the upper radiator insulator . . .

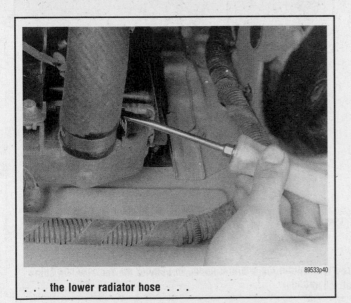

. . . the lower radiator hose . . .

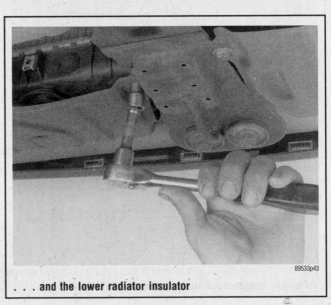

. . . and the lower radiator insulator

Inspect the insulators and replace if damaged. On this one, the deteriorated rubber reduces its effectiveness

Lift the radiator from the engine compartment, being careful not to damage the fins

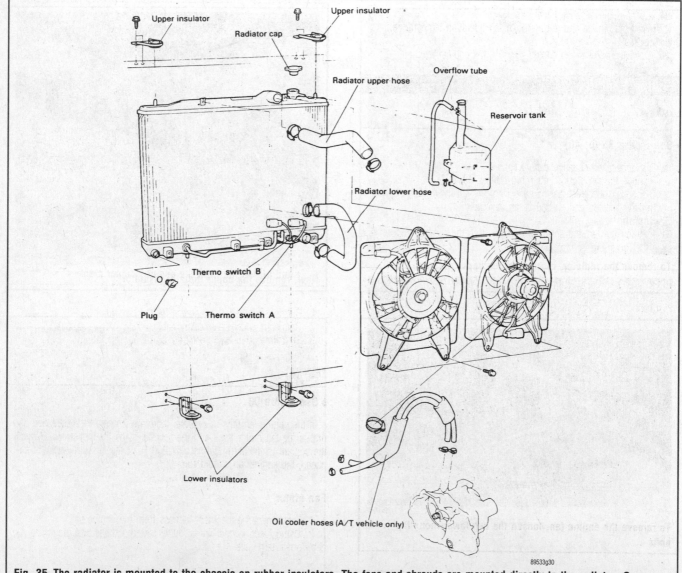

Fig. 35 The radiator is mounted to the chassis on rubber insulators. The fans and shrouds are mounted directly to the radiator. On some models, it may be possible to remove the radiator with the fans still attached

3. Drain the cooling system.

4. Raise the vehicle and support it safely.

5. Remove the splash shield from under the engine.

6. Disconenct the wiring harnesses from the fan motor and thermo sensors.

7. Remove the fan and shroud.

8. Disconnect the upper and lower radiator hoses.

9. Disconnect and plug the automatic transaxle cooler hoses, as required.

10. Disconnect the expansion tank hose.

11. Remove the radiator mounting bolts and lift out the radiator and fan assembly.

To install:

12. Install the radiator. Tighten the mounting bolts securely.

13. Connect the expansion tank hose.

14. Connect the automatic transaxle oil cooler lines.

15. Connect the upper and lower radiator hoses.

16. Install the fan and shroud.

17. Conenct the wiring harnesses for the fan motor and thermo sensors.

18. Install the splash shield under the engine.

19. Lower the vehicle.

20. Fill the engine with coolant.

21. Connect the negative battery cable.

22. Start the engine and allow it to reach operating temperature. Check for leaks.

23. Once the vehicle has cooled, recheck the coolant level.

Engine Fan

REMOVAL & INSTALLATION

▶ **See Figure 35 (p. 40)**

1. Disconnect the negative battery cable.

2. Remove the fan shroud mounting bolts.

3. Disconnect the electrical harness from the fan motor.

4. Remove the fan and shroud as an assembly.

To install:

5. Position the fan and shroud assembly onto the radiator support and tighten the mounting bolts securely.

To remove the engine fan, loosen the two lower mounting bolts . . .

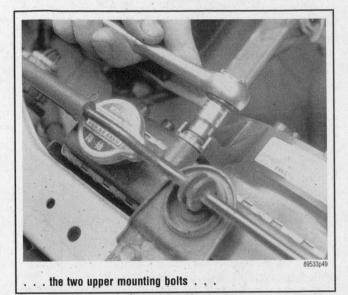

. . . the two upper mounting bolts . . .

. . . and lift the fan from the engine compartment

6. Connect the electrical harness for the fan motor.

7. Connect the negative battery cable.

8. Start the engine and check for proper fan operation.

TESTING

▶ **See Figure 36**

If the engine fan fails to operate, there are 2 items to be checked; the first is the fan motor itself and the second is the thermo switch. When the coolant temperature climbs over 200°F, or the air conditioner is engaged, the engine fan should run.

Fan Motor

1. Disconnect the electrical harness from the engine fan.

2. Using fused jumper wires, apply battery voltage and ground to the appropriate terminals.

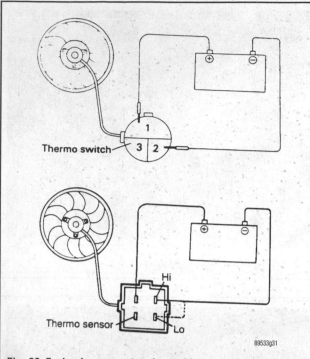

Fig. 36 Engine fan connectors have either two, three or four terminals. Apply battery voltage and ground to test the fan operation

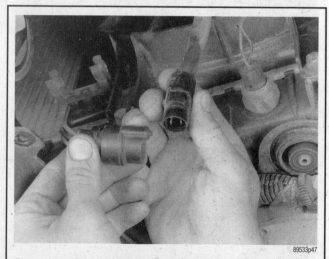

On some models, the engine fan connector is mounted to a clip at the lower left side of the radiator

3. The fan should run smoothly, without abnormal noise or vibration. Replace the fan if the fan does not run or does not function.

4. Reconnect the engine fan electrical harness.

Thermo Switch

The thermo switch, located either in the radiator or in the water pump, controls the operation of the engine fan. The switch completes an electrical circuit when the coolant temperature is above 200°F.

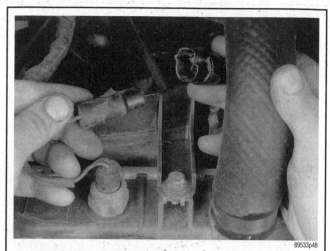

The thermo sensor electrical connector is located at the bottom of the radiator, near the sensor

1. Allow the vehicle to sit until the engine is completely cool.
2. Disconnect the switch electrical harness.
3. Using an ohmmeter, check resistance across the switch terminals.
4. Resistance should be as follows:
• Elantra, Tiburon and Accent SOHC—2.21–2.69 kilohms with a coolant temperature of 68°F (20°C).
• Excel, Scoupe, Sonata and Accent DOHC—2.27–2.73 kilohms with a coolant temperature of 68°F (20°C).
5. Start the engine and allow it to reach operating temperature.
6. Check resistance again. Resistance should be as follows:
• Elantra, Tiburon and Accent SOHC—264–328 ohms with a coolant temperature of 176°F (80°C).
• Excel, Scoupe, Sonata and Accent DOHC—290–354 ohms with a coolant temperature of 176°F (80°C).
7. If resistance is not as indicated, the switch is faulty.

Water Pump

REMOVAL & INSTALLATION

Except 3.0L (VIN T) Engine

▶ See Figures 37 thru 43 (p. 45–47)

1. Disconnect the negative battery cable.
2. Remove the water pump pulley bolts.
3. Remove the drive belt.
4. Drain the engine coolant.
5. Remove the timing belt covers.
6. Rotate the crankshaft clockwise and align the timing marks so the No. 1 piston will be at TDC of the compression stroke.
7. Remove the timing belt and tensioner.
8. Remove the water pump mounting bolts.
9. As required, remove the alternator brace.

➡Water pump bolts are three different lengths. Make a note of length and location.

10. Remove the water pump, disconnecting the water outlet pipe.
To install:
11. Clean all gasket mating surfaces thoroughly.

Loosening the water pump drive pulley bolts prior to belt removal makes breaking the bolts loose easier

Remove the upper timing belt cover . . .

Remove the drive belt . . .

. . . and lower timing belt cover

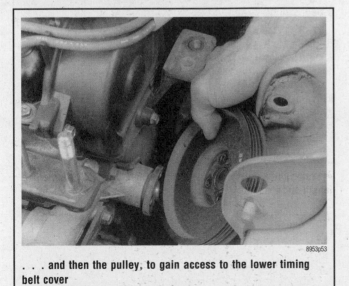

. . . and then the pulley, to gain access to the lower timing belt cover

Loosen the timing belt tensioner . . .

. . . and remove the timing belt. Note the reference marks on the cylinder head, gear and timing belt

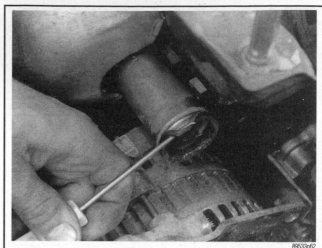

The coolant inlet O-ring should always be replaced when servicing the water pump

On some engines, the alternator bracket bolts to the water pump and must be removed

Take special care when removing old gasket material. The water pump is aluminum and is easily damaged

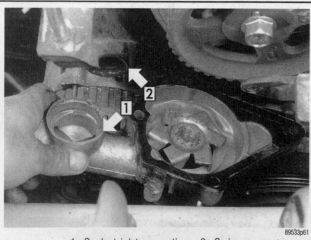

1. Coolant inlet connection   2. O-ring

When removing the water pump, pay special attention to the coolant inlet connection and O-ring

12. Install the alternator brace.
13. Install the water pump using a new O-ring and gaskets.
14. Tighten water pump bolts as follows:
• 9–11 ft. lbs. (12–15 Nm)—except 2.0L (VIN F), 3.0L (VIN T) and 1996–98 1.8L (VIN M) engines
• 14–20 ft. lbs. (20–27 Nm)—2.0L (VIN F), 3.0L (VIN T) and 1996–98 1.8L (VIN M) engines
15. Install the timing belt and tensioner. Properly tension the timing belt.
16. Install the timing belt covers.
17. Install the water pump pulley bolts and hand tighten.
18. Install and tension the drive belts.
19. Tighten the water pump pulley bolts to 6–7 ft. lbs. (8–10 Nm).
20. Fill the cooling system.
21. Start the engine and allow it to reach operating temperature. Check for leaks.
22. Once the vehicle has cooled, recheck the coolant level.

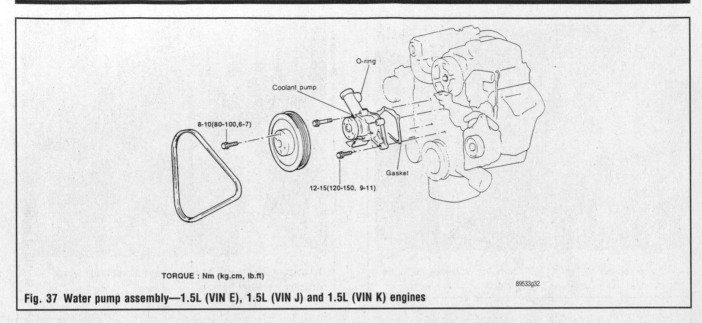

TORQUE : Nm (kg.cm, lb.ft)

Fig. 37 Water pump assembly—1.5L (VIN E), 1.5L (VIN J) and 1.5L (VIN K) engines

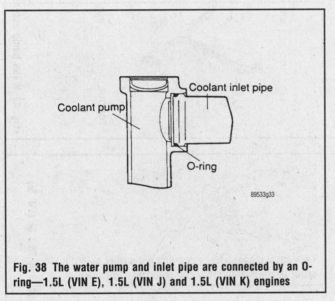

Fig. 38 The water pump and inlet pipe are connected by an O-ring—1.5L (VIN E), 1.5L (VIN J) and 1.5L (VIN K) engines

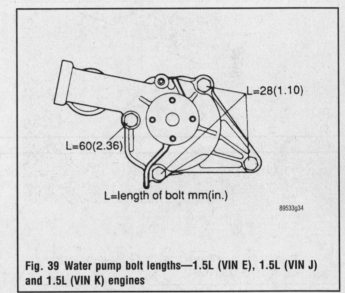

Fig. 39 Water pump bolt lengths—1.5L (VIN E), 1.5L (VIN J) and 1.5L (VIN K) engines

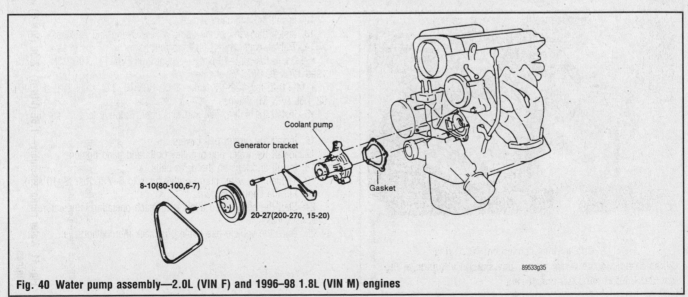

Fig. 40 Water pump assembly—2.0L (VIN F) and 1996–98 1.8L (VIN M) engines

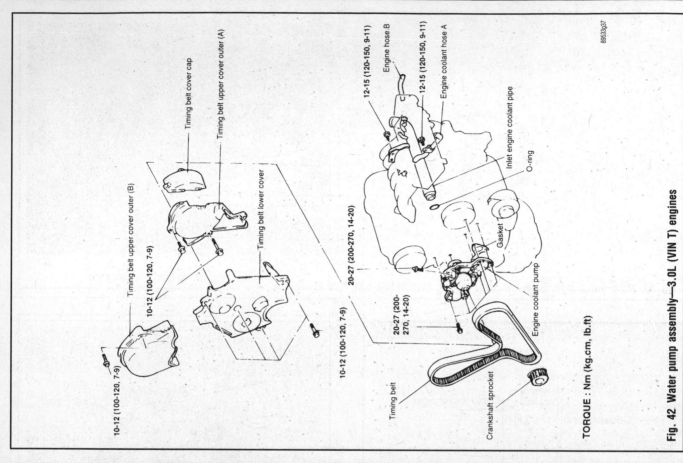

TORQUE : Nm (kg.cm, lb.ft)

Fig. 42 Water pump assembly—3.0L (VIN T) engines

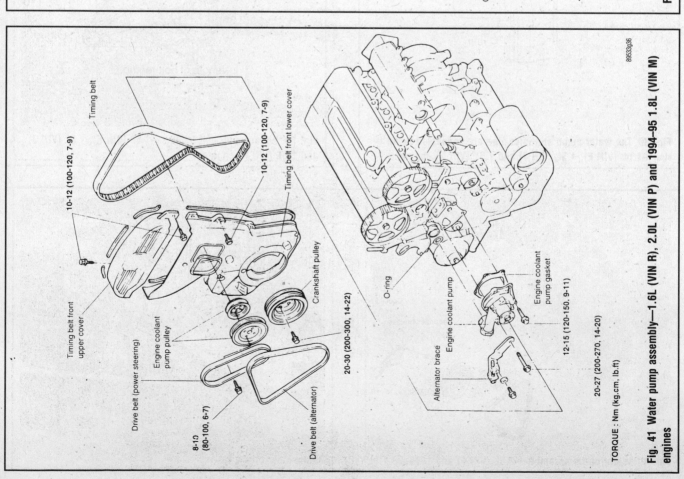

TORQUE : Nm (kg.cm, lb.ft)

Fig. 41 Water pump assembly—1.6L (VIN R), 2.0L (VIN P) and 1994–95 1.8L (VIN M) engines

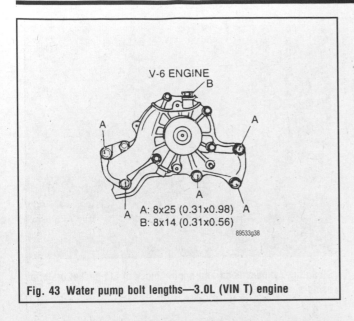

Fig. 43 Water pump bolt lengths—3.0L (VIN T) engine

. . . and ensure that the timing marks are aligned . . .

Cylinder Head

REMOVAL & INSTALLATION

➡ The cylinder heads are made of aluminum. Do not remove the cylinder head unless the engine is cold. A hot cylinder head will warp once removed from the engine.

Except 3.0L (VIN T) Engine

◆ See Figures 44, 45, 46 and 47 (p. 49)

1. Properly release fuel system pressure.
2. Disconnect the negative battery cable.
3. Drain the cooling system.
4. Disconnect the upper radiator hose and heater hoses.
5. Remove the air cleaner assembly.
6. Label and disconnect any vacuum lines running to the cylinder head.
7. Label and disconnect any electrical harnesses running to the cylinder head.

. . . then remove the timing belt

Remove the upper timing belt cover . . .

Remove the rocker cover . . .

. . . and loosen the head bolts in the proper sequence. The cylinder head must be cold prior to removal

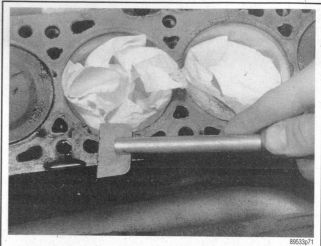

Clean the cylinder head and engine block of old gasket material using a scraper

Carefully remove the cylinder head . . .

Install the cylinder head and fasten head bolts to specification using the proper torque sequence

. . . and the head gasket

8. Label and disconnect the spark plug wires.

9. Turn the crankshaft until the No. 1 cylinder is at TDC on the compression stroke.

10. Remove the distributor or ignition coil pack.

11. Remove the power steering oil pump and bracket.

12. Remove the intake and exhaust manifolds.

13. Remove the water pump and crankshaft pulleys.

14. Remove the timing belt covers.

15. Remove the timing belt.

➡ **Do not rotate the engine with the timing belt removed.**

16. Remove the rocker cover.

17. Loosen the cylinder head bolts in proper sequence.

18. Carefully remove the cylinder head from the engine.

To install:

19. The cylinder head should be disassembled, cleaned and inspected prior to installation. Refer to Engine Reconditioning for more information. If you do not feel confident performing the inspection procedures, then take the cylinder head to a competent machinist.

20. Install the cylinder head using a new head gasket. Tighten head bolts to proper torque specification in sequence.

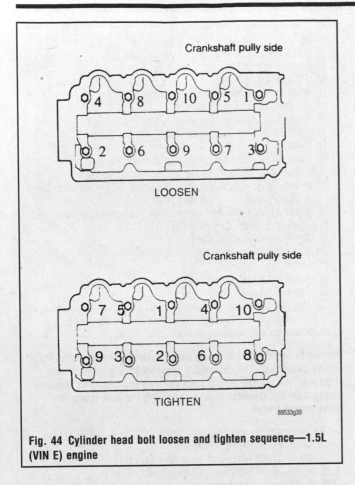

Fig. 44 Cylinder head bolt loosen and tighten sequence—1.5L (VIN E) engine

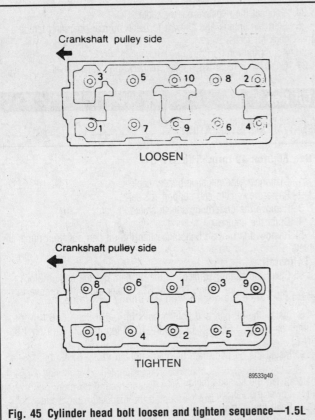

Fig. 45 Cylinder head bolt loosen and tighten sequence—1.5L (VIN J) engine

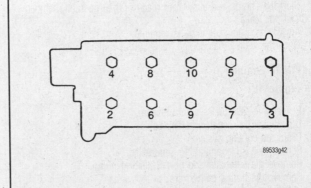

Fig. 46 Cylinder head bolt loosen AND tighten sequence—1.5L (VIN K), 1.6L (VIN R), 2.0L (VIN F) and 1996–98 1.8L (VIN M) engines

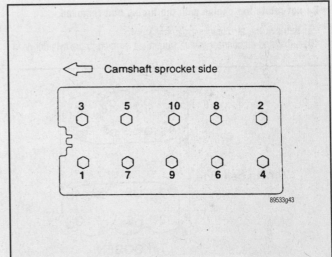

Fig. 47 Cylinder head bolt loosen AND tighten sequence—2.0L (VIN P) and 1994–95 1.6L (VIN R) and 1.8L (VIN M) engines

• 2.0L (VIN F) and 1996–98 1.8L (VIN M) engines—Tighten M10 bolts to 22 ft. lbs. (30 Nm), plus 60°–65°, plus 60°–65°. Tighten M12 bolts to 26 ft. lbs. (35 Nm), plus 60°–65°, plus 60°–65°.

• 1.5L (VIN E), 1.5L (VIN J) and 1.5L (VIN K) engines—51–54 ft. lbs. (71–75 Nm).

• 1.6L (VIN F), 2.0L (VIN P) and 1994–95 1.8L (VIN M) engines— 65–72 ft. lbs. (90–100 Nm).

21. Install the rocker cover.
22. Ensure the No. 1 cylinder is still TDC on the compression stroke.
23. Align the timing marks on the cylinder head and camshaft gear.
24. Install and properly tension the timing belt.
25. Install the timing belt covers.
26. Install the water pump and crankshaft pulleys.
27. Install the intake and exhaust manifolds.
28. Install the power steering oil pump and bracket.
29. Install the distributor or ignition coil pack.
30. Connect the spark plug wires.
31. Connect any electrical harnesses running to the cylinder head.
32. Connect any vacuum lines running to the cylinder head.
33. Install the air cleaner assembly.
34. Connect the upper radiator hose and heater hoses.

35. Refill the cooling system.
36. Connect the negative battery cable.
37. Start the engine and allow it to reach normal operating temperature. Check for leaks.
38. Adjust the ignition timing, as required.
39. Once the vehicle has cooled, recheck the coolant level.

3.0L (VIN T) Engine

♦ **See Figure 48**

1. Properly release fuel system pressure.
2. Disconnect the negative battery cable.
3. Drain the cooling system.
4. Remove the air conditioning compressor.
5. Remove the alternator and power steering pump.
6. Remove the timing belt covers.
7. Rotate the crankshaft to position the No. 1 cylinder on TDC of its compression stroke.

➡**The crankshaft sprocket timing mark should align with the oil pan timing indicator and the camshaft sprocket timing marks (triangles) should align with the rear timing belt cover timing marks.**

8. Remove the timing belts.

➡**Do not rotate the engine with the timing belt removed.**

9. Remove the air cleaner assembly.
10. Label and disconnect any vacuum lines running to the cylinder head.

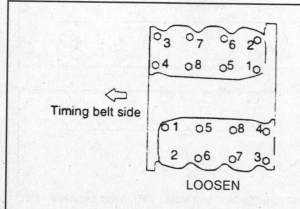

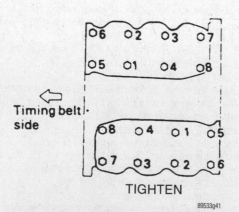

89533g41

Fig. 48 Cylinder head bolt loosen and tighten sequence—3.0L (VIN T) engine

11. Label and disconnect any electrical harnesses running to the cylinder head.
12. Label and disconnect the spark plug wires.
13. Remove the rocker covers.
14. Remove the distributor.
15. Remove the intake manifold assembly.
16. Remove the exhaust manifolds.
17. Loosen the cylinder head bolts in proper sequence.
18. Carefully remove the cylinder head from the engine.

To install:

19. The cylinder head should be disassembled, cleaned and inspected prior to installation. Refer to Engine Reconditioning for more information. If you do not feel confident performing the inspection procedures, then take the cylinder head to a competent machinist.
20. Install the cylinder head using a new head gasket. Tighten head bolts in sequence to 76–83 ft. lbs. (105–115 Nm).
21. Install the exhaust manifolds.
22. Install the intake manifold assembly.
23. Install the distributor.
24. Install the rocker covers.
25. Connect the spark plug wires.
26. Connect any electrical harnesses running to the cylinder head.
27. Connect any vacuum lines running to the cylinder head.
28. Install the air cleaner assembly.

➡**Prior to installing the timing belt, check the timing marks for proper alignment. The crankshaft sprocket timing mark should align with the oil pan timing indicator and the camshaft sprocket timing marks (triangles) should align with the rear timing belt cover timing marks.**

29. Install and tension the timing belts.
30. Install the timing belt covers.
31. Install the alternator and power steering pump.
32. Install the air conditioning compressor.
33. Refill the cooling system.
34. Connect the negative battery cable.
35. Start the engine and allow it to reach normal operating temperature. Check for leaks.
36. Adjust the ignition timing.
37. Once the vehicle has cooled, recheck the coolant level.

Oil Pan

REMOVAL & INSTALLATION

♦ **See Figures 49 thru 55 (p. 51–54)**

1. Disconnect the negative battery cable.
2. Raise the vehicle and support it safely.
3. Remove the underbody splash shield.
4. Drain the engine oil.
5. Remove the oil pan bolts and slide the oil pan out from under the vehicle.

To install:

6. Clean the mating surfaces of the oil pan and the engine block.
7. Apply a 1/8 in. (3mm) bead of RTV sealer along the groove in the oil pan.
8. Install the oil pan and tighten bolts to 4–6 ft. lbs. (6–8 Nm) on all engines except 1.5L (VIN E) and 11–16 ft. lbs. (15–22 Nm) on 1.5L (VIN E).
9. Install the oil pan drain plug and tighten to 25–33 ft. lbs. (35–45 Nm).
10. Install the splash shield
11. Lower the vehicle.
12. Refill the crankcase with oil.
13. Start the engine and allow it to reach operating temperature. Check for leaks.

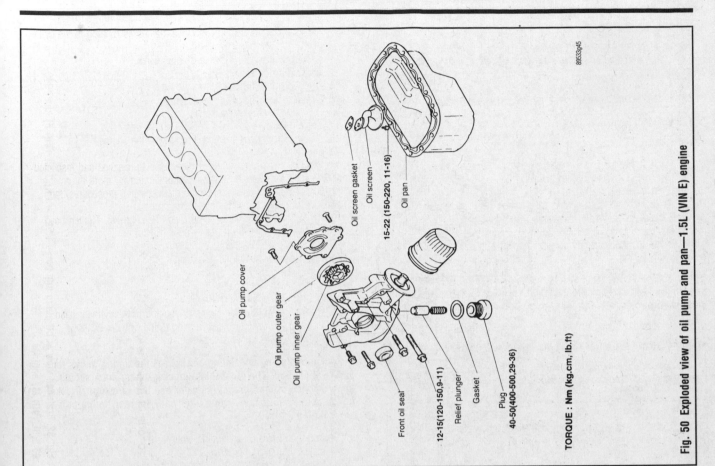

89533g45

Oil pump cover

Oil pump outer gear

Oil pump inner gear

Oil screen gasket

Oil screen

15-22 (150-220, 11-16)

Oil pan

Front oil seal

12-15(120-150,9-11)

Relief plunger

Gasket

Plug
40-50(400-500,29-36)

TORQUE : Nm (kg.cm, lb.ft)

Fig. 50 Exploded view of oil pump and pan—1.5L (VIN E) engine

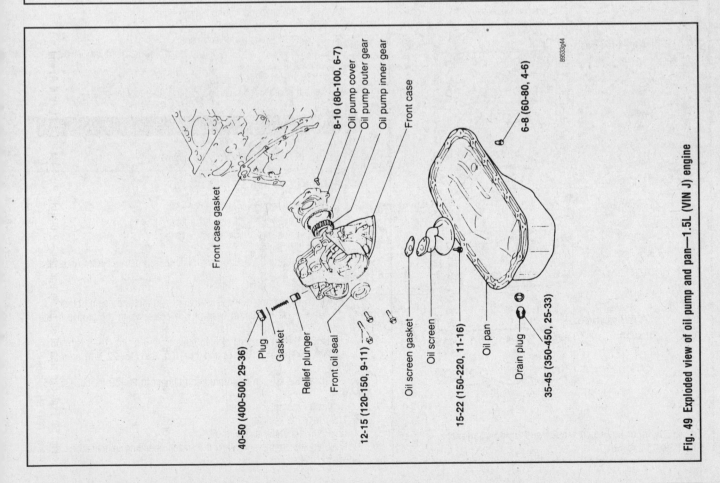

89533g44

8-10 (80-100, 6-7)

Oil pump cover

Oil pump outer gear

Oil pump inner gear

Front case

6-8 (60-80, 4-6)

Front case gasket

40-50 (400-500, 29-36)

Plug

Gasket

Relief plunger

Front oil seal

12-15 (120-150, 9-11)

Oil screen gasket

Oil screen

15-22 (150-220, 11-16)

Oil pan

Drain plug

35-45 (350-450, 25-33)

Fig. 49 Exploded view of oil pump and pan—1.5L (VIN J) engine

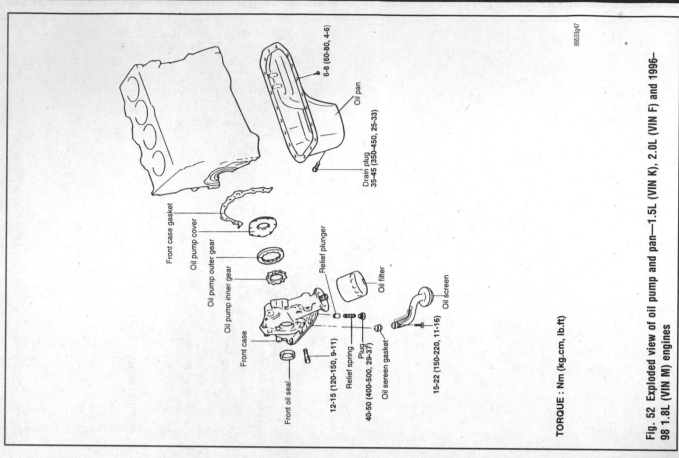

TORQUE : Nm (kg.cm, lb.ft)

Fig. 52 Exploded view of oil pump and pan—1.5L (VIN K), 2.0L (VIN F) and 1996–98 1.8L (VIN M) engines

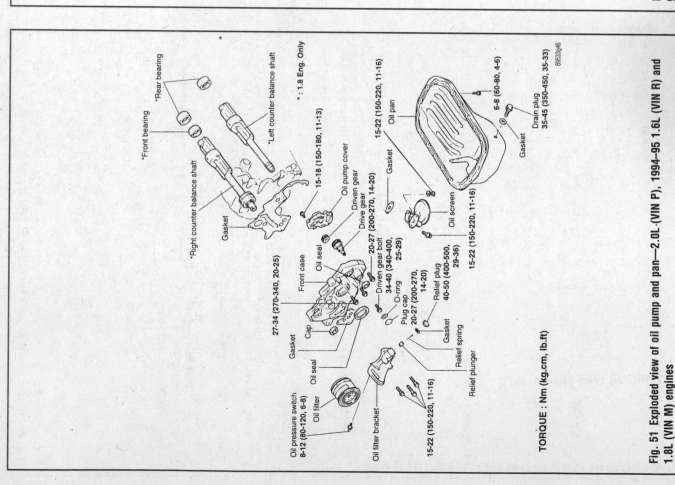

TORQUE : Nm (kg.cm, lb.ft)

Fig. 51 Exploded view of oil pump and pan—2.0L-(VIN P), 1994–95 1.6L (VIN R) and 1.8L (VIN M) engines

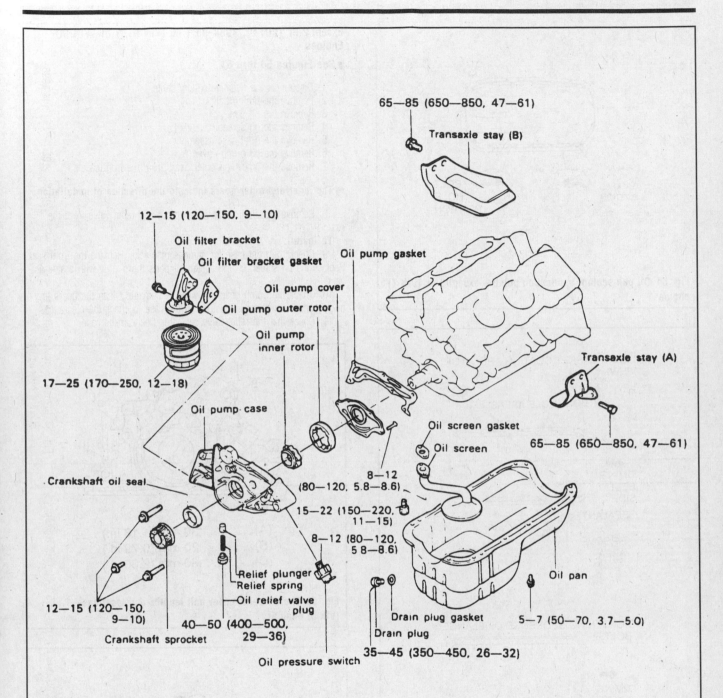

65—85 (650—850, 47—61)

Transaxle stay (B)

12—15 (120—150, 9—10)

Oil filter bracket

Oil filter bracket gasket

Oil pump gasket

Oil pump cover

Oil pump outer rotor

Oil pump inner rotor

Transaxle stay (A)

17—25 (170—250, 12—18)

Oil pump case

Oil screen gasket

Oil screen

65—85 (650—850, 47—61)

Crankshaft oil seal

8—12 (80—120, 5.8—8.6)

15—22 (150—220, 11—15)

8—12 (80—120, 5.8—8.6)

Relief plunger

Relief spring

Oil relief valve plug

Oil pan

12—15 (120—150, 9—10)

Crankshaft sprocket

40—50 (400—500, 29—36)

Drain plug gasket

Drain plug

5—7 (50—70, 3.7—5.0)

Oil pressure switch

35—45 (350—450, 26—32)

TORQUE : Nm (kg.cm, lb.ft)

89533g48

Fig. 53 Exploded view of oil pump and pan—3.0L (VIN T) engine

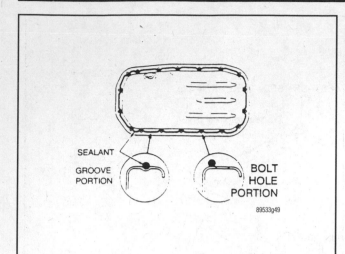

Fig. 54 Oil pan sealant application points—except 3.0L (VIN T) engine

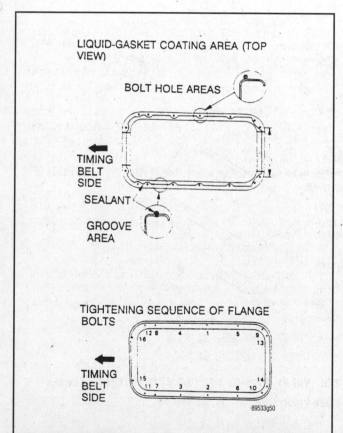

Fig. 55 Oil pan sealant application points and tightening sequence—3.0L (VIN T) engine

Oil Pump

REMOVAL & INSTALLATION

♦ See Figures 49, 50, 51, 52 and 53 (p. 51–53)

➡Whenever the oil pump is disassembled or the cover removed, the gear cavity must be filled with petroleum jelly for priming purposes. Do not use grease.

Except 2.0L (VIN P), 1994–95 1.6L (VIN R), 1.8L (VIN M) Engines

♦ See Figures 56 thru 61

1. Disconnect the negative battery cable.
2. Remove the timing belt.
3. Remove the oil pan.
4. Remove the oil screen.
5. Remove the front case assembly.
6. Remove the oil pump cover.
7. Remove the inner and outer gears from the front case.

➡The inner and outer gears indicate the direction of installation.

8. Remove the plug, relief valve spring and relief valve from the case.

To install:

9. Check the front case for damage or cracks. Replace the front seal. Replace the oil screen O-ring. Clean all parts thoroughly with a safe solvent.
10. Check the pump gears for wear or damage. Clean the gears thoroughly and place them in position in the case to check the clearances.
11. Check that the relief valve can slide freely in the case.

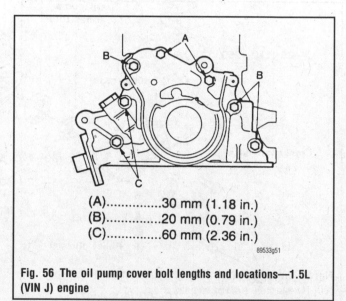

(A)..............30 mm (1.18 in.)
(B)..............20 mm (0.79 in.)
(C)..............60 mm (2.36 in.)

Fig. 56 The oil pump cover bolt lengths and locations—1.5L (VIN J) engine

Fig. 57 Align the mating marks on the oil pump gears—1.5L (VIN J) engine

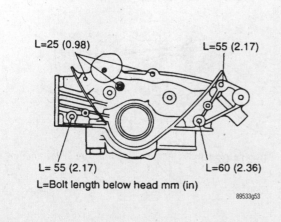

Fig. 58 Oil pump cover bolt lengths and locations—3.0L (VIN T) engine

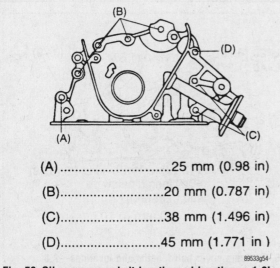

(A)	25 mm (0.98 in)
(B)	20 mm (0.787 in)
(C)	38 mm (1.496 in)
(D)	45 mm (1.771 in)

Fig. 59 Oil pump cover bolt lengths and locations—1.8L (VIN M) and 2.0L (VIN F) engines

(A)	25 mm (0.98 in.)
(B)	30 mm (1.18 in.)
(C)	45 mm (1.77 in.)
(D)	60 mm (2.36 in.)

Fig. 60 Oil pump cover bolt lengths and locations—1.5L (VIN E) and 1.5L (VIN K) engines

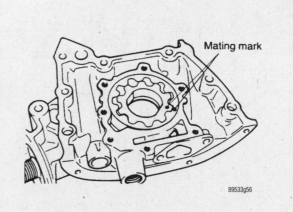

Fig. 61 Align the mating marks on the oil pump gears—1.5L (VIN E) and 1.5L (VIN K) engines

12. Check the relief valve spring for damage.

13. Thoroughly coat both oil pump gears with clean engine oil and install them in the correct direction of rotation.

14. Install the pump cover and torque the bolts as follows:
   a. 6–8 ft. lbs. (8–12 Nm)—1.5L (VIN E) and 1.5L (VIN J) engines
   b. 4–6 ft. lbs. (6–9 Nm)—except 1.5L (VIN E) and 1.5L (VIN J) engines

15. Coat the relief valve and spring with clean engine oil, install them and tighten the plug to 30–36 ft. lbs. (39–49 Nm).

16. Using a new gasket, install the front case assembly. Tighten the bolts to 8–11 ft. lbs. (12–15 Nm).

➡ **The bolts have different shank lengths. Use the illustrations to determine proper locations for each length bolt.**

17. Coat the lips of a new seal with clean engine oil and slide it along the crankshaft until it touches the front case. Drive it into place with a seal driver.

18. Install and properly tension the timing belt.

19. Install the oil screen.

20. Apply a 1/8 in. (3mm) wide bead of RTV sealer in the groove of the oil pan mating surface. Install the oil pan and tighten bolts to 60–72 inch lbs.

21. Connect the negative battery cable.

22. Start the engine and allow it to reach operating temperature. Check for leaks.

23. Check for proper oil pressure.

2.0L (VIN P), 1994–95 1.6L (VIN R), 1.8L (VIN M) Engines

♦ **See Figures 62, 63, 64, 65 and 66**

1. Disconnect the negative battery cable.

2. Remove the timing belt.

3. Remove the oil pan.

4. Remove the oil screen.

5. Remove the oil filter bracket assembly.

6. Using special tool PN 09213-33000 or equivalent, remove the plug cap from the oil pump portion of the front case.

7. Remove the left side cylinder block plug and insert a screwdriver with a 0.32 in. (8mm) diameter shaft into the plug hole. The screwdriver should be at least 2.4 in. (60mm) long.

8. Remove the oil pump drive gear and left counter balance shaft retaining bolt.

9. Remove the front case assembly.

10. Remove the oil pump cover from the front case.

11. Remove the oil pump gears.

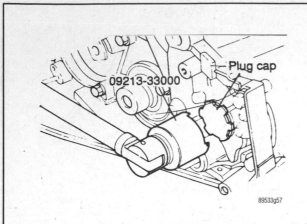

Fig. 62 A special socket is available to remove the plug cap from the oil pump portion of the case—2.0L (VIN P), 1994–95 1.6L (VIN R), 1.8L (VIN M) engines

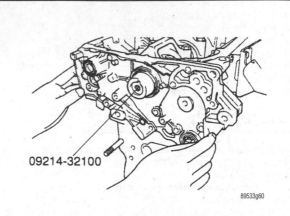

Fig. 65 A special tool is used to center the front case hole on the crankshaft—2.0L (VIN P), 1994–95 1.6L (VIN R), 1.8L (VIN M) engines

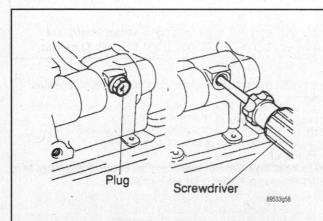

Fig. 63 Remove the left side cylinder block plug and insert a screwdriver into the hole to hold the balance shaft from turning—2.0L (VIN P), 1994–95 1.6L (VIN R), 1.8L (VIN M) engines

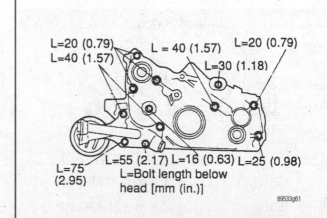

Fig. 66 Oil pump cover bolt lengths and locations—2.0L (VIN P), 1994–95 1.6L (VIN R), 1.8L (VIN M) engines

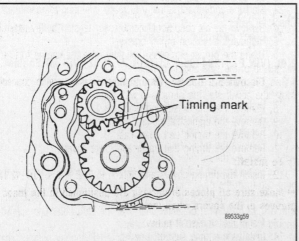

Fig. 64 Align the timing marks on the gears during assembly—2.0L (VIN P), 1994–95 1.6L (VIN R), 1.8L (VIN M) engines

To install:

12. Check the oil holes for clogging and clean as necessary.

13. Check counter balance shaft front bearing section for wear, damage or seizure. If there is any damage, replace the front case.

14. Check front case for cracks and other damage. Replace the front case as necessary.

15. Lubricate, align and install the oil pump gears.

16. Using a seal driver, install a new front case oil seal.

17. Lubricate and install special tool PN 09214-32100 or equivalent on the crankshaft.

18. Install the front case assembly using a new gasket. Install all bolts except those for the filter bracket and tighten finger tight.

19. Tighten front case bolts to specification, as per the illustration.

20. Insert a screwdriver with a 0.32 in. (8mm) diameter shaft into the left side cylinder block plug hole. The screwdriver will hold the shaft stable while tightening the oil pump drive gear retaining bolt.

21. Install the oil pump drive gear and left counter balance shaft retaining bolt. Tighten to 25–29 ft. lbs. (34–40 Nm).

22. Install a new O-ring to the groove on the front case.

23. Using special tool PN 09213-33000 or equivalent, install the plug cap on the oil pump portion of the front case. Tighten to 14–20 ft. lbs. (20–27 Nm).

24. Install the oil filter bracket assembly.
25. Install the oil screen.
26. Install the oil pan.
27. Install and properly tension the timing belt.
28. Connect the negative battery cable.
29. Start the engine and allow it to reach operating temperature. Check for leaks.
30. Check for proper oil pressure.

OIL SEAL REPLACEMENT

➡️**The front case oil seal is removed and installed from the rear of the case. The case assembly must be removed from the engine to replace the oil seal.**

1. Remove the front case assembly.
2. Using a seal remover or brass drift, drive the seal from the front case.

To install:
3. Clean the seal bore and inspect for damage. If damage is evident, replace the front case assembly.
4. Lubricate the seal bore and install the seal.
5. Using a seal driver, drive the seal into the front case.

Timing Belt Cover

REMOVAL & INSTALLATION

Except 3.0L (VIN T) Engine
◆ **See Figures 67 and 68**

1. Disconnect the negative battery cable.
2. Remove the engine undercover, as required.

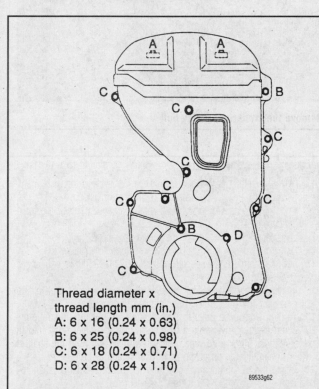

Thread diameter x
thread length mm (in.)
A: 6 x 16 (0.24 x 0.63)
B: 6 x 25 (0.24 x 0.98)
C: 6 x 18 (0.24 x 0.71)
D: 6 x 28 (0.24 x 1.10)

89533g62

Fig. 67 Timing belt cover bolts are of various lengths and sizes—except 1.5L (VIN E), 1.5L (VIN J), 1.5L (VIN K) and 3.0L (VIN T) engines

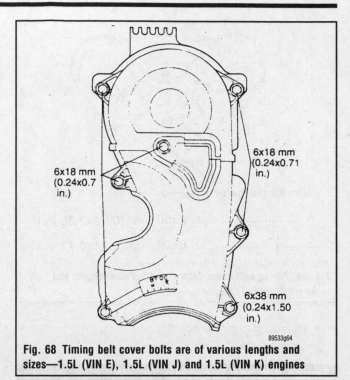

6x18 mm
(0.24x0.7
in.)

6x18 mm
(0.24x0.71
in.)

6x38 mm
(0.24x1.50
in.)

89533g64

Fig. 68 Timing belt cover bolts are of various lengths and sizes—1.5L (VIN E), 1.5L (VIN J) and 1.5L (VIN K) engines

➡️**On some engines, it is necessary to remove the side engine mount for clearance.**

3. Remove the accessory drive belts.
4. Remove the water pump pulley and crankshaft pulley.
5. Remove the upper and lower timing belt covers.

To install:
6. Install the upper and lower timing belt covers. Tighten cover bolts to 7–8 ft. lbs. (10–12 Nm).
7. Install the water pump pulley and crankshaft pulley.
8. Install and tension the accessory drive belts.
9. Install the engine undercover, as required.
10. Connect the negative battery cable.

3.0L (VIN T) Engine
◆ **See Figure 69**

1. Disconnect the negative battery cable.
2. Remove the engine undercover.
3. Remove the accessory drive belts.
4. Remove the air conditioner compressor tension pulley assembly.
5. Remove the tension pulley bracket.
6. Using the proper equipment, slightly raise the engine to take the weight off of the side engine mount.
7. Disconnect the power steering pump pressure switch connector. Move the power steering pump and wire aside.
8. Remove the engine support bracket.
9. Remove the crankshaft pulley.
10. Remove the timing belt cover cap.
11. Remove the timing belt upper and lower covers.

To install:
12. Install the timing covers and tighten to 7–8 ft. lbs. (10–12 Nm).

➡️**Make sure all pieces of packing are positioned in the inner grooves of the covers when installing.**

13. Install the crankshaft pulley.
14. Install the engine support bracket.
15. Install the power steering pump and reconnect wire harness.
16. Install the engine mounting bracket and remove the engine support fixture.
17. Install the tension pulleys and drive belts.

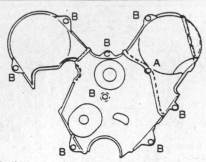

Thread diameter x height

A .... 6x60 mm (0.24x2.36 in.)

B .... 6x20 mm (0.24x0.79 in.)

89533g63

Fig. 69 Timing belt cover bolts are of various lengths and sizes—3.0L (VIN T) engines

18. Install the engine undercover.
19. Connect the negative battery cable.

Timing Belt and Sprockets

❊❊ WARNING

Timing belt maintenance is extremely important. All Hyundai models use interference-type non-freewheeling engines. Should the timing belt break in these engines, the valves in the cylinder head will likely come in contact with the pistons, causing major engine damage. The recommended replacement interval for timing belts is 60,000 miles (96,600 km).

REMOVAL & INSTALLATION

1.5L (VIN E) and 1.5L (VIN J) Engines

◗ See Figures 70, 71, 72, 73 and 74 (p. 60–61)

1. Disconnect the negative battery cable.
2. Remove the accessory drive belts.

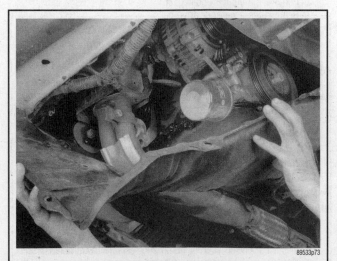

On some models, to gain access to the bottom of the engine, you must remove the engine undercover

89533p73

It is sometimes easier to loosen the crankshaft pulley bolt with the accessory belts installed

89533p74

Remove the crankshaft pulley bolt . . .

89533p75

. . . the crankshaft pulley spacer . . .

89533p76

. . . and then the crankshaft pulley

. . . the crankshaft sprocket . . .

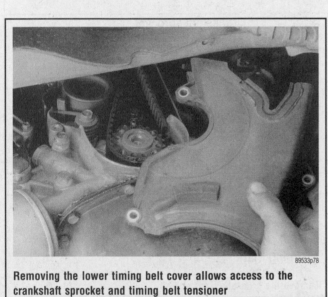

Removing the lower timing belt cover allows access to the crankshaft sprocket and timing belt tensioner

. . . and the crankshaft sprocket flange

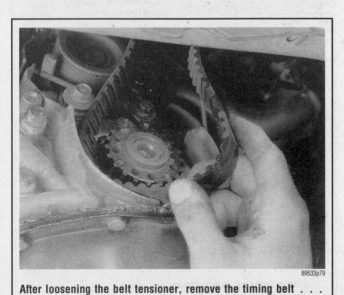

After loosening the belt tensioner, remove the timing belt . . .

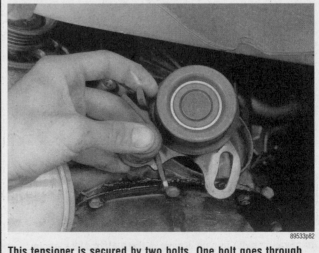

This tensioner is secured by two bolts. One bolt goes through the spring, the other in the slotted area

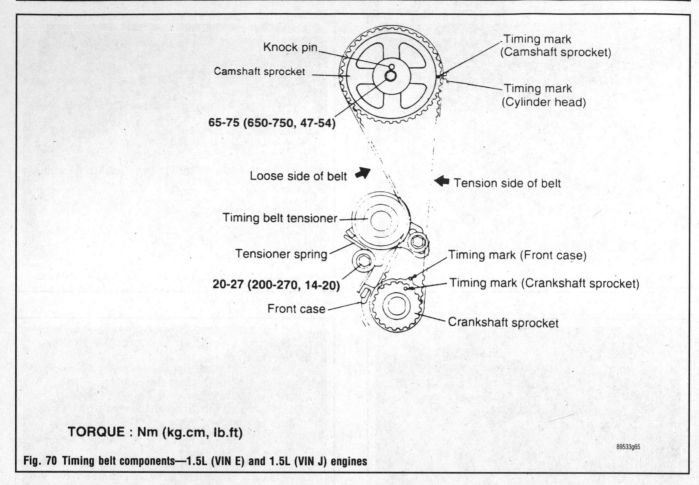

65-75 (650-750, 47-54)

20-27 (200-270, 14-20)

TORQUE : Nm (kg.cm, lb.ft)

89533g65

Fig. 70 Timing belt components—1.5L (VIN E) and 1.5L (VIN J) engines

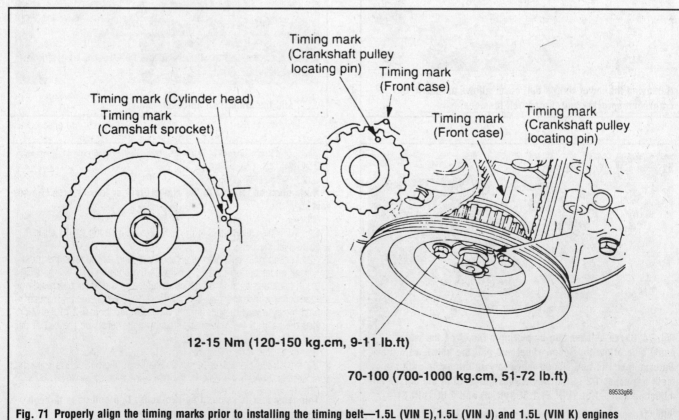

12-15 Nm (120-150 kg.cm, 9-11 lb.ft)

70-100 (700-1000 kg.cm, 51-72 lb.ft)

89533g66

Fig. 71 Properly align the timing marks prior to installing the timing belt—1.5L (VIN E),1.5L (VIN J) and 1.5L (VIN K) engines

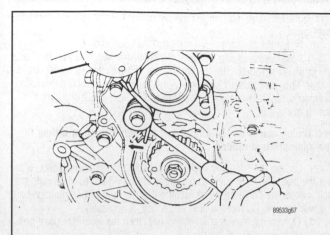

Fig. 72 Use a prybar to properly position the timing belt tensioner spring—1.5L (VIN E),1.5L (VIN J) and 1.5L (VIN K) engines

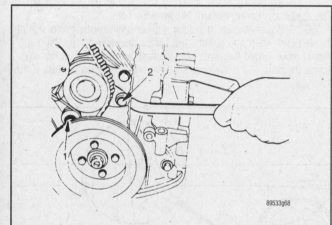

Fig. 73 When tightening the tensioner bolts, first tighten the adjuster bolt (1) and then the pivot bolt (2)—1.5L (VIN E), 1.5L (VIN J) and 1.5L (VIN K) engines

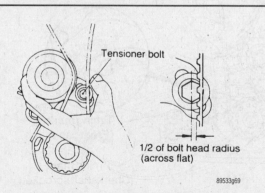

Fig. 74 Check belt tension by putting a finger on the water pump side of the tensioner wheel and pull the belt toward the water pump. The belt should move toward the pump until the teeth are about 1/2 of the way across the head of the tensioner adjusting bolt—1.5L (VIN E),1.5L (VIN J) and 1.5L (VIN K) engines

3. Remove the crankshaft and water pump pulleys.
4. Remove the timing belt cover.
5. Rotate the crankshaft clockwise and align the timing marks so No. 1 piston will be at TDC of the compression stroke.
6. Loosen the tensioning bolt and the pivot bolt on the timing belt tensioner. Move the tensioner as far as it will go toward the water pump. Tighten the adjusting bolt.
7. Mark the timing belt with an arrow showing direction of rotation.
8. Remove the timing belt.
9. Remove the camshaft sprocket as required.
10. Remove the crankshaft sprocket and flange.

➡Note the direction of installation for the crankshaft sprocket and flange.

11. Remove the timing belt tensioner.
To install:
12. Install the flange and crankshaft sprocket. Tighten bolts to 51–72 ft. lbs. (69–98 Nm).

➡The flange must go on first with the chamfered area outward. The sprocket is installed with the boss forward and the studs for the fan belt pulley outward.

13. Install the camshaft sprocket. Tighten bolt to 47–54 ft. lbs. (64–74 Nm) on 1.5L (VIN J) engines and 58–72 ft. lbs. (80–100 Nm) on 1.5L (VIN E) engines.
14. Align the timing marks of the camshaft sprocket and check that the crankshaft timing marks are still in alignment.
15. Install the timing belt tensioner, spring and spacer with the bottom end of the spring free. Tighten the adjusting bolt slightly with the tensioner moved as far as possible away from the water pump.
16. Install the free end of the spring into the locating tang on the front case.
17. Position the timing belt over the crankshaft sprocket and then over the camshaft sprocket. Slip the back of the belt over the tensioner wheel.
18. Turn the camshaft sprocket in the opposite of its normal direction of rotation until the straight side of the belt is tight and make sure the timing marks align.

➡If timing marks do not align, shift the belt 1 tooth at a time in the appropriate direction..

19. Loosen the tensioner mounting bolts so the tensioner works, without the interference of any friction, under spring pressure. Make sure the belt follows the curve of the camshaft pulley so the teeth are engaged all the way around. Correct the path of the belt, if necessary.
20. Tighten the tensioner adjusting bolt, then the tensioner pivot bolt to 15–18 ft. lbs. (20–26 Nm).

➡Bolts must be torqued in the stated order or tension won't be correct.

21. Turn the crankshaft 1 turn clockwise until timing marks again align to seat the belt.
22. Loosen both tensioner attaching bolts and let the tensioner position itself under spring tension. Retighten the bolts.
23. Check belt tension by putting a finger on the water pump side of the tensioner wheel and pull the belt toward the water pump. The belt should move toward the pump until the teeth are about 1/2 of the way across the head of the tensioner adjusting bolt. Retension the belt, if necessary.
24. Install the timing belt covers.
25. Install the crankshaft pulley, making sure the pin on the crankshaft sprocket fits through the hole in the rear surface of the pulley.
26. Install the water pump pulley.
27. Install and tension the accessory drive belts.
28. Connect the negative battery cable.

1.5L (VIN K) Engine

◆ **See Figures 71, 72, 73, 74 and 75 (p. 60–62)**

1. Disconnect the negative battery cable.
2. Remove the accessory drive belts.
3. Remove the coolant pump and crankshaft pulleys.
4. Remove the timing belt cover.
5. Rotate the crankshaft clockwise and align the timing marks so No. 1 piston will be at TDC of the compression stroke.
6. Move the timing belt tensioner toward the water pump and temporarily secure it.
7. Remove the camshaft sprocket.
8. Mark the timing belt with an arrow showing direction of rotation.
9. Remove the timing belt.
10. Remove the crankshaft sprocket and flange.

➡**Note the direction of installation for the crankshaft sprocket and flange.**

11. Remove the timing belt tensioner.
   To install:
12. Install the flange and crankshaft sprocket. Tighten crankshaft sprocket bolt to 110–118 ft. lbs. (150–160 Nm).

➡**Pay special attention to the mounting direction of the crankshaft sprocket. The flange should face the engine.**

13. Install camshaft sprocket. Tighten bolts to 59–73 ft. lbs. (80–100 Nm).
14. Align the timing marks of the camshaft sprocket and check that the crankshaft timing marks are still in alignment.
15. Install the timing belt tensioner spring and spacer. Temporarily

tighten the tensioner bolt. Install the bottom end of the spring against the front case.
16. Install the timing belt on the crankshaft sprocket.
17. Position the timing belt over the crankshaft sprocket and then over the camshaft sprocket. Slip the back of the belt over the tensioner wheel.
18. Turn the camshaft sprocket in the opposite of its normal direction of rotation until the straight side of the belt is tight and make sure the timing marks align.

➡**If timing marks do not align, shift the belt 1 tooth at a time in the appropriate direction..**

19. Loosen the tensioner mounting bolts so the tensioner works, without the interference of any friction, under spring pressure. Make sure the belt follows the curve of the camshaft pulley so the teeth are engaged all the way around. Correct the path of the belt, if necessary.
20. Tighten the tensioner adjusting bolt, then the tensioner pivot bolt to 15–18 ft. lbs. (20–26 Nm).

➡**Bolts must be tightened in the stated order or their tension won't be correct.**

21. Turn the crankshaft 1 turn clockwise until timing marks again align to seat the belt.
22. Loosen both tensioner attaching bolts and let the tensioner position itself under spring tension. Retighten the bolts
23. Check belt tension by putting a finger on the water pump side of the tensioner wheel and pull the belt toward the water pump. The belt should move toward the pump until the teeth are about 1/2 of the way across the head of the tensioner adjusting bolt. Retension the belt, if necessary.

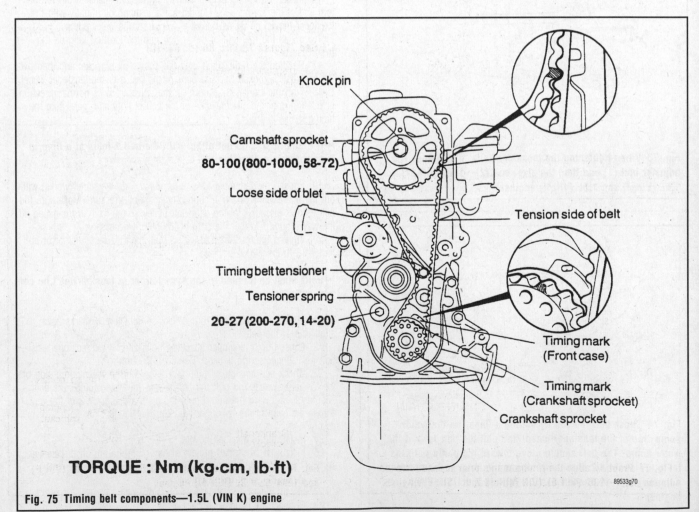

TORQUE : Nm (kg·cm, lb·ft)

Fig. 75 Timing belt components—1.5L (VIN K) engine

24. Install the timing belt covers.
25. Install the crankshaft pulley, making sure the pin on the crankshaft sprocket fits through the hole in the rear surface of the pulley.
26. Install the water pump pulley.
27. Install and tension the accessory drive belts.
28. Connect the negative battery cable.

1996–98 1.8L (VIN M) and 2.0L (VIN F) Engines

◆ **See Figures 76 and 77**

1. Disconnect the negative battery cable.
2. Remove the accessory drive belts.
3. Remove the crankshaft and water pump pulleys.
4. Remove the timing belt cover.
5. Rotate the crankshaft clockwise and align the timing marks so No. 1 piston will be at TDC of the compression stroke.
6. Remove the timing belt tensioner and idler pulley.
7. Mark the timing belt with an arrow showing direction of rotation.
8. Remove the timing belt.
9. Remove the camshaft sprocket.
10. Remove the crankshaft sprocket and flange.

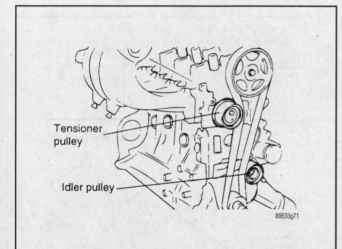

Fig. 76 The timing belt is held in place by a tensioner and an idler pulley—1996–98 1.8L (VIN M) and 2.0L (VIN F) engines

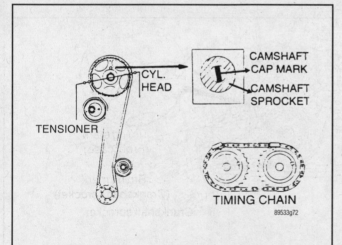

Fig. 77 Properly align the timing marks prior to installing the timing belt—1996–98 1.8L (VIN M) and 2.0L (VIN F) engines

➡**Note the direction of installation for the crankshaft sprocket and flange.**

To install:
11. Install the flange and crankshaft sprocket.

➡**Pay special attention to the mounting direction of the crankshaft sprocket. The flange should face the engine.**

12. Install camshaft sprocket. Tighten bolts to 74–89 ft. lbs. (100–120 Nm).
13. Align the timing marks of the camshaft sprocket and check that the crankshaft timing marks are still in alignment.
14. Install the timing belt tensioner.
15. Install the idler pulley, if equipped. Tighten bolt to 32–41 ft. lbs. (43–55 Nm).
16. Position the timing belt over the camshaft sprocket and then over the crankshaft sprocket.
17. Tension the timing belt and tighten the tensioner pulley bolt to 32–41 ft. lbs. (43–55 Nm). When properly tensioned, the timing belt should deflect 0.16–0.24 in. (4–6mm) when a force of 5 lbs is placed on the longest span of the belt.
18. Turn the crankshaft sprocket one turn clockwise and realign the crankshaft sprocket timing mark.
19. Recheck the belt tension and adjust as necessary.
20. Install the timing belt covers.
21. Install the crankshaft pulley, making sure the pin on the crankshaft sprocket fits through the hole in the rear surface of the pulley. Tighten pulley bolt to 125–133 ft. lbs. (170–180 Nm).
22. Install the water pump pulley.
23. Install and tension the accessory drive belts.
24. Connect the negative battery cable.

1.6L (VIN R), 2.0L (VIN P) and 1994–95 1.8L (VIN M) Engines

◆ **See Figures 78 thru 86 (p. 63–65)**

1. Disconnect the negative battery cable.
2. Remove the crankshaft pulley, water pump pulley and drive belts.
3. Remove the timing belt upper and lower covers.

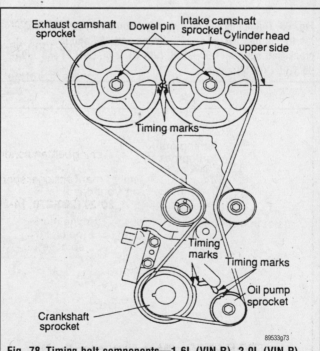

Fig. 78 Timing belt components—1.6L (VIN R), 2.0L (VIN P) and 1994–95 1.8L (VIN M) engines

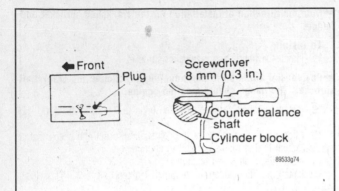

Fig. 79 Insert a screwdriver with a 0.32 in. (8mm) diameter shaft into the left side cylinder block plug hole. The screwdriver will hold the counterbalance shaft stable during timing belt service—1.6L (VIN R), 2.0L (VIN P) and 1994–95 1.8L (VIN M) engines

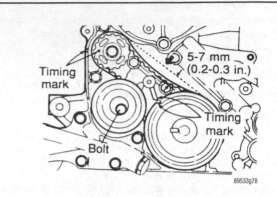

Fig. 82 Check belt for proper timing belt "B" tension by depressing the belt on its long side with your finger and noting the belt deflection. The desired reading is 0.20–0.28 in. (5–7mm) —1.6L (VIN R), 2.0L (VIN P) and 1994–95 1.8L (VIN M) engines

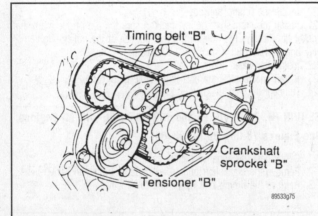

Fig. 80 Tightening the oil pump sprocket bolt after installing the timing belt tensioner "B", timing belt "B" and the crankshaft sprocket "B"—1.6L (VIN R), 2.0L (VIN P) and 1994–95 1.8L (VIN M) engines

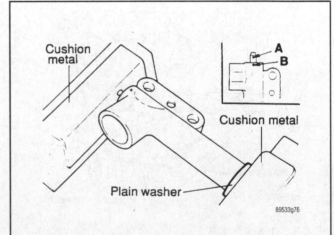

Fig. 83 Use a soft jawed vise to compress the timing belt tensioner until holes "A" and "B" align . . .

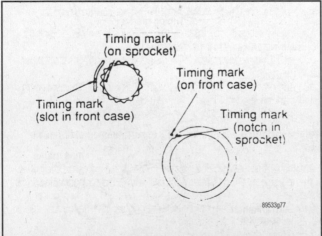

Fig. 81 Oil pump and crankshaft sprocket "B" timing mark locations—1.6L (VIN R), 2.0L (VIN P) and 1994–95 1.8L (VIN M) engines

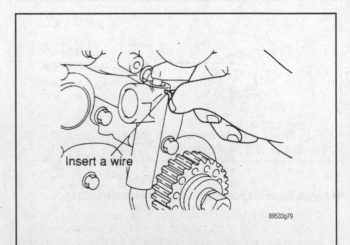

Fig. 84 . . . then insert a wire to hold the tensioner piston in place—1.6L (VIN R), 2.0L (VIN P) and 1994–95 1.8L (VIN M) engines

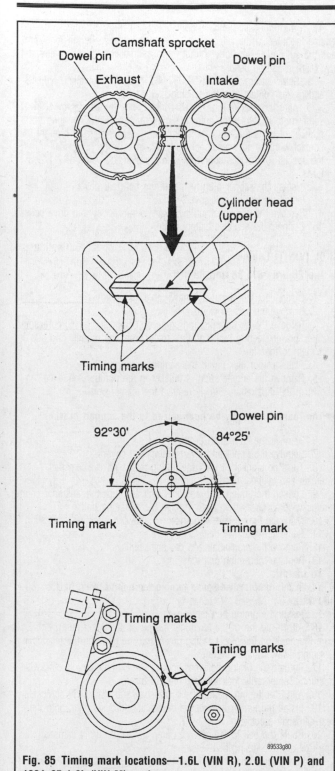

Fig. 85 Timing mark locations—1.6L (VIN R), 2.0L (VIN P) and 1994–95 1.8L (VIN M) engines

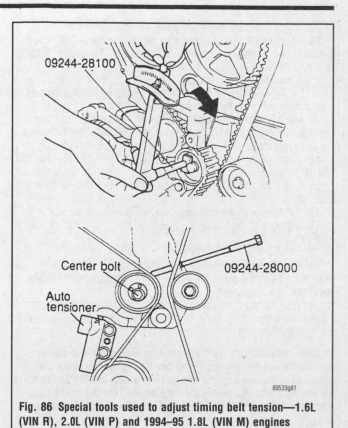

Fig. 86 Special tools used to adjust timing belt tension—1.6L (VIN R), 2.0L (VIN P) and 1994–95 1.8L (VIN M) engines

➡**Always rotate the crankshaft in a clockwise direction.**

4. Rotate the crankshaft clockwise and align the timing marks so No. 1 piston will be at TDC of the compression stroke. At this time the timing marks on the camshaft sprocket and the upper surface of the cylinder head should coincide, and the dowel pin of the camshaft sprocket should be at the upper side.

5. Remove the timing belt tensioner.

6. Mark the timing belt indicating the direction of rotation.

7. Remove the timing belt.

8. Remove the camshaft sprockets.

9. Insert a screwdriver with a 0.32 in. (8mm) diameter shaft into the left side cylinder block plug hole. The screwdriver will hold the counter balance shaft stable while removing the oil pump sprocket retaining nut.

10. Remove the oil pump sprocket.

11. Loosen the right counterbalance shaft sprocket bolt.

12. Remove the timing belt tensioner "B".

13. Remove the timing belt "B".

14. Remove the crankshaft sprocket "B".

To install:

15. Install the crankshaft sprocket "B".

➡**Pay special attention to the direction of the flange. If it is installed in the wrong direction, a broken belt could result.**

16. Lightly lubricate the outer surface of the spacer with engine oil and install with the chamfer toward the engine.

17. Install the counterbalance shaft sprocket and tighten the flange bolt finger-tight.

18. Align the timing mark on each sprocket with the corresponding timing mark on the front case.

19. Install the timing belt "B".

➡**When installing timing belt "B", ensure tension side has no slack.**

20. Install the timing belt tensioner "B" with the center of the pulley on the left side of the mounting bolt and with pulley flange facing front of engine.

21. Lift the timing belt tensioner "B" to tighten the timing belt "B" so that its tension side will be pulled tight.

22. Tighten the bolt to secure tensioner "B".

➡**When tightening the bolt of the tensioner, ensure that the tensioner pulley shaft does not rotate with the bolt. Allowing it to rotate with the bolt can cause excessive tension on the belt.**

23. Check to ensure the timing marks are in alignment.

24. Check belt for proper tension by depressing the belt on its long side with your finger and noting the belt deflection. The desired reading is 0.20–0.28 in. (5–7mm).

25. Install the flange, crankshaft sprocket and washer to the crankshaft. The flange on the crankshaft sprocket must be installed towards the inner timing belt sprocket. Tighten bolt to 80–94 ft. lbs. (110–130 Nm).

26. Insert a screwdriver with a 0.32 in. (8mm) diameter shaft into the left side cylinder block plug hole. The screwdriver will hold the counter balance shaft stable while removing the oil pump sprocket retaining nut.

27. Install the oil pump sprocket and tighten the nut to 36–43 ft. lbs. (50–60 Nm).

28. Install the camshaft sprocket and tighten the bolt to 56–72 ft. lbs. (80–100 Nm).

29. Carefully push the auto tensioner rod in until the set hole in the rod is aligned with the hole in the cylinder. Place a wire into the hole to retain the rod.

30. Install the timing belt tensioner.

31. Install the tensioner pulley onto the tensioner arm. Locate the pin-hole in the tensioner pulley shaft to the left of the center bolt. Tighten the center bolt finger-tight.

32. Turn the two camshaft sprockets so their dowel pins are located on top. Align the timing marks facing each other with the top surface of the cylinder head.

➡**Both camshaft sprockets are used for the intake and exhaust camshafts and are provided with two timing marks. When the sprocket is mounted on the exhaust camshaft, use the timing mark on the right with the dowel pin hole on top. For the intake camshaft sprocket, use the 1 on the left with the dowel pin hole on top.**

33. Align the crankshaft sprocket and oil pump sprocket timing marks.

34. Insert a screwdriver with a 0.32 in. (8mm) diameter shaft into the left side cylinder block plug hole. If the shaft can be inserted 2.4 in. deep, the silent shaft is in the correct position. If the shaft of the tool can only be inserted 0.8–1.0 in. (20–25mm) deep, turn the oil pump sprocket 1 turn and realign the marks.

➡**Keep the tool inserted in hole for the remainder of this procedure. The above step assures that the oil pump socket is in correct orientation to the silent shafts. This step must not be skipped or a vibration may develop during engine operation.**

35. Install the timing belt around the tensioner pulley and crankshaft sprocket. Hold the belt with your left hand.

36. Pulling the belt with your right hand, install it around the oil pump sprocket.

37. Install the belt around the idler pulley and intake camshaft sprocket.

38. Turn the exhaust camshaft sprocket one tooth clockwise to align it timing mark with the cylinder head top surface. Pulling the belt with both hands, install it around the exhaust camshaft sprocket.

39. Gently raise the tensioner pulley so that the belt does not sag and temporarily tighten the center bolt.

40. Turn the crankshaft 1/4 turn counterclockwise. Turn the crankshaft clockwise to move the No. 1 cylinder to TDC.

41. Loosen the center bolt and attach special tool (PN 09244-28100) or equivalent to a torque wrench. Apply a torque of 1.88–2.03 ft. lbs. (2.6–2.8 Nm). Tighten the center bolt.

42. Screw the special tool (PN 09244-28000) or equivalent into the engine left support bracket until its end makes contact with the tensioner arm. At this point, screw the special tool in some more and remove the set wire attached to the auto tensioner, if the wire was not previously removed.

43. Remove the special tool.

44. Rotate the crankshaft 2 complete turns clockwise and let it sit for approximately 15 minutes. Then, measure the auto tensioner protrusion (the distance between the tensioner arm and auto tensioner body) to ensure that it is within 0.15–0.18 in. (3.8–4.5mm).

45. If the timing belt tension adjustment is being performed with the engine mounted in the vehicle, and clearance between the tensioner arm and the auto tensioner body cannot be measured, the following alternative method can be used:

   a. Screw in special tool (PN 09244-28000) or equivalent, until its end makes contact with the tensioner arm.

   b. After the special tool makes contact with the arm, screw it in some more to retract the auto tensioner pushrod while counting the number of turns the tool makes until the tensioner arm is brought into contact with the auto tensioner body. Make sure the number of turns the special tool makes conforms with the standard value of 2 1/2–3 turns.

   c. Install the rubber plug to the timing belt rear cover.

46. Install the timing belt covers.

47. Remove the crankshaft pulley, water pump pulley and drive belts.

48. Connect the negative battery cable.

3.0L (VIN T) Engine

♦ **See Figures 87, 88 and 89**

1. Disconnect the negative battery cable.

2. Remove the accessory drive belts.

3. Remove the air conditioning compressor and the air compressor bracket, power steering pump and alternator from the mounts and support them to the side.

4. Place a floor jack under the engine to support it.

5. Remove the engine support bracket in the number sequence shown in the illustration. Slowly remove the reamer bolt.

➡**The reamer bolt may be heat seized to the support bracket.**

6. Remove the crankshaft pulley.

7. Remove the upper and lower timing belt covers.

8. Turn the crankshaft until the timing marks on the camshaft sprocket and cylinder head are aligned.

9. Loosen the timing belt tensioner bolt and turn the tensioner counterclockwise as far as it will go. Tighten the adjusting bolt.

10. Mark the timing belt with an arrow showing direction of rotation.

11. Remove the timing belt.

12. Remove the crankshaft and camshaft pulleys.

13. Remove the timing belt tensioner.

To install:

14. Install the camshaft sprockets. Tighten bolt to 58–72 ft. lbs. (80–100 Nm).

15. Install the timing belt tensioner.

16. Attach the top of the tensioner spring on the water pump pin. Ensure the hook on the pin is facing down and the hook on the tensioner is facing away from the engine.

17. Rotgate the timing belt tensioner to the extreme counterclockwise position. Temporarily lock the tensioner in place.

18. Align the timing marks of the camshaft and crankshaft sprockets.

19. Install the timing belt on the crankshaft sprocket, then onto the rear camshaft sprocket.

20. Route the belt to the coolant pump pulley, the front camshaft sprocket and the timing belt tensioner.

21. Apply force counterclockwise to the rear camshaft sprocket with tension on the tight side of the belt and check that timing marks are aligned.

22. Loosen the tensioner bolt one or two turns and tighten the timing belt to a tension of 57–84 lbs. (260–380 N).

23. Turn the crankshaft two turns clockwise.

24. Readjust the sprocket timing marks and tighten the tensioner bolts.

25. Install the timing belt covers.

26. Install the crankshaft pulley and tighten to 108–116 ft. lbs. (150–160 Nm).

27. Install the engine support bracket. The mounting bolts must be installed in the sequence shown in the illustration.

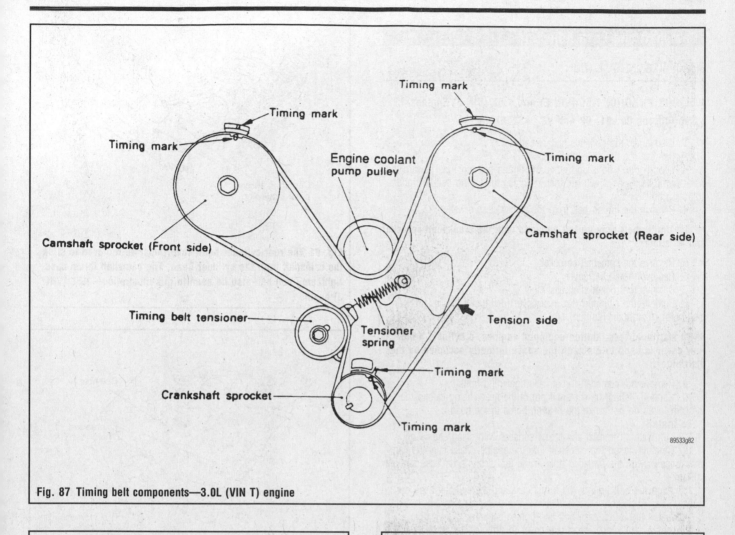

Fig. 87 Timing belt components—3.0L (VIN T) engine

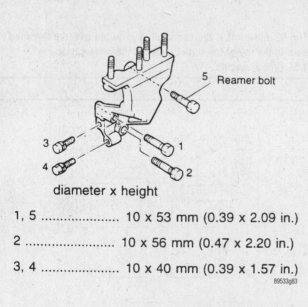

diameter x height

1, 5 .... 10 x 53 mm (0.39 x 2.09 in.)

2 .... 10 x 56 mm (0.47 x 2.20 in.)

3, 4 .... 10 x 40 mm (0.39 x 1.57 in.)

Fig. 88 Remove the engine support bracket bolts in the number sequence shown. Slowly remove the reamer bolt. The mounting bolts must also be installed in the sequence shown. When installing the reamer bolt, tighten it slowly while spraying it with penetrating lubricant—3.0L (VIN T) engine

Fig. 89 Attach the top of the tensioner spring on the water pump pin. Ensure that the hook on the pin is facing down and the hook on the tensioner is facing away from the engine— 3.0L (VIN T) engine

➡When installing the reamer bolt, tighten it slowly while spraying it with penetrating lubricant.

28. Install the air conditioning compressor bracket, compressor, power steering pump and alternator.
29. Install the accessory drive belts.
30. Connect the negative battery cable.

Camshaft and Lash Adjusters

REMOVAL & INSTALLATION

1.5L (VIN K) SOHC, 1.5L (VIN E) and 1.5L (VIN J) Engines

▶ See Figures 90, 91, 92 and 93

1. Disconnect the negative battery cable.
2. Remove the timing belt cover.
3. Loosen the 2 bolts and move the timing belt tensioner toward the water pump as far as it will go, then retighten the timing belt tensioner adjusting bolt.
4. Remove the timing belt from the camshaft sprocket

➡**The timing belt may be left engaged with the crankshaft sprocket and tensioner.**

5. Remove the camshaft sprocket.
6. Remove the rocker cover.
7. Remove the rocker shaft assembly.
8. Remove the cylinder head rear cover (distributorless ignition) or distributor (distributor ignition).

➡**On distributorless ignition equipped engines, a cylinder head rear cover is used to block off the space formerly occupied by the distributor.**

9. Remove the camshaft thrust case tightening bolt.
10. Carefully, slide the camshaft out of the head, being careful that the cam lobes do not strike the bearing bores in the head.

To install:
11. Lubricate all journal and thrust surfaces with clean engine oil.
12. Carefully insert the camshaft into the engine. Make sure the camshaft goes in with the threaded hole in the top of the thrust case straight upward.
13. Align the bolt hole in the thrust case and the cylinder head surface.
14. Install the thrust case bolt and tighten securely.
15. Install the cylinder head rear cover (distributorless ignition) with a new gasket. Tighten bolts to 6–7 ft. lbs. (8–10 Nm). Install the distributor (distributor ignition).
16. Coat the external surface of the front oil seal with engine oil.
17. Using special installer tool MD 998306-01 or equivalent, drive a new front camshaft oil seal into the clearance between the cam and head, making sure the seal seats fully.

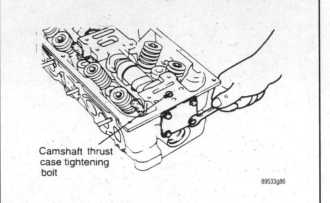

Fig. 91 The rear cylinder head cover must be removed to slide the camshaft from the cylinder head. The camshaft thrust case tightening bolt can also be seen in this illustration—1.5L (VIN J) engine

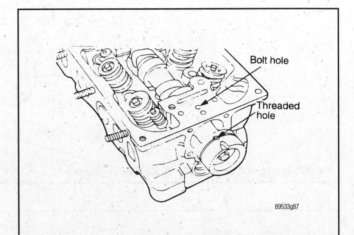

Fig. 92 Ensure that the camshaft is installed with the threaded hole in the top of the thrust case pointing straight upward—1.5L (VIN J) engine

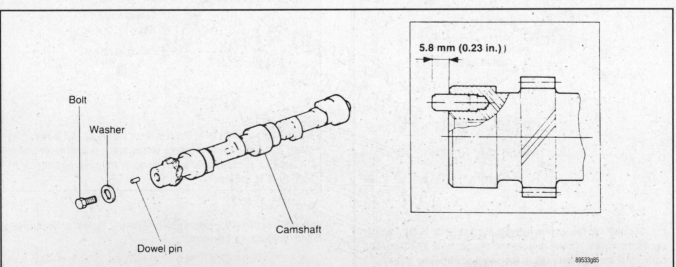

Fig. 90 The camshaft sprocket pin should protrude from the camshaft as illustrated—1.5L (VIN K) SOHC, 1.5L (VIN E) and 1.5L (VIN J) engines

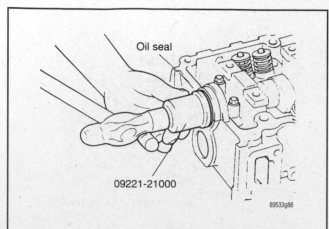

Fig. 93 Using special tool PN 09221-21000 or equivalent, drive a new front camshaft oil seal into the clearance between the camshaft and cylinder head, making sure the seal seats fully—1.5L (VIN K) SOHC, 1.5L (VIN E) and 1.5L (VIN J) engines

18. Install the rocker shaft assembly.
19. Install the camshaft sprocket and torque the bolt to 47–54 ft. lbs. (64–74 Nm).
20. Install and tension the timing belt.
21. Install the timing belt covers.
22. Temporarily adjust the valve clearance to specification with the engine cold.
23. Install the rocker cover.
24. Start the engine and allow it to reach operating temperature. Check for leaks.
25. Readjust the valve clearance with the engine warm.

1.5L (VIN K) DOHC, 2.0L (VIN F) and 1996–98 1.8L (VIN M) Engines

♦ **See Figures 94 thru 99**

1. Disconnect the negative battery cable.
2. Remove the timing belt cover.
3. Remove the timing belt tensioner and idler.
4. Remove the timing belt from the camshaft sprocket.

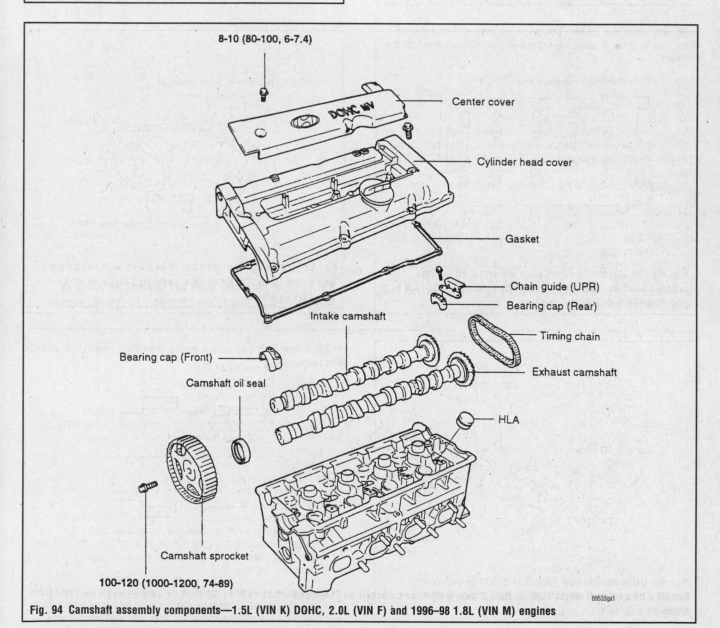

Fig. 94 Camshaft assembly components—1.5L (VIN K) DOHC, 2.0L (VIN F) and 1996–98 1.8L (VIN M) engines

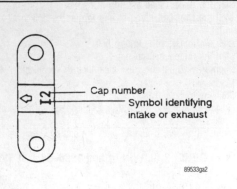

Fig. 95 The camshaft bearing caps are identified with a letter and number stamp. The letter indicates either intake or exhaust and the number is sequential from the cylinder head end opposite the timing chain—1.5L (VIN K) DOHC, 2.0L (VIN F) and 1996–98 1.8L (VIN M) engines

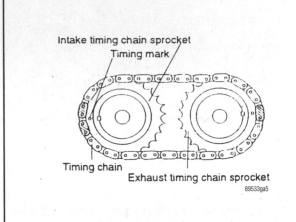

Fig. 98 Align the timing chain and camshaft sprockets as illustrated—1.5L (VIN K) DOHC engine

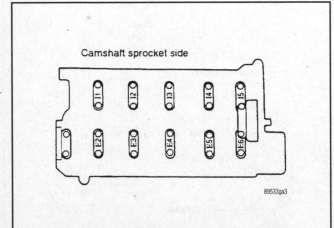

Fig. 96 The camshaft bearing caps are arranged on the cylinder head as illustrated—1.5L (VIN K) DOHC, 2.0L (VIN F) and 1996–98 1.8L (VIN M) engines

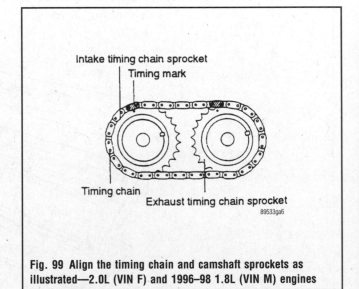

Fig. 99 Align the timing chain and camshaft sprockets as illustrated—2.0L (VIN F) and 1996–98 1.8L (VIN M) engines

➡The timing belt may be left engaged with the crankshaft sprocket and tensioner.

5. Remove the camshaft sprocket.
6. Remove the rocker cover.
7. Remove the camshaft bearing caps and timing chain.
8. Remove the camshaft from the cylinder head, being careful that the cam lobes do not strike the bearing bores in the head.
9. Remove the hydraulic lash adjusters.

To install:

10. Install the hydraulic lash adjusters.
11. Align the camshaft timing chain with the intake and exhaust camshaft sprockets as illustrated.
12. Lubricate all journal and thrust surfaces with clean engine oil.
13. Carefully insert the camshaft into the cylinder head.
14. Install the bearing caps and tighten to 9–10 ft. lbs. (12–14 Nm) in several stages. Start from the center cap and work outward to the end of the cylinder head.

➡The bearing caps are identified with a letter and number stamp. The letter indicates either intake or exhaust and the number is sequential from the cylinder head end opposite the timing chain.

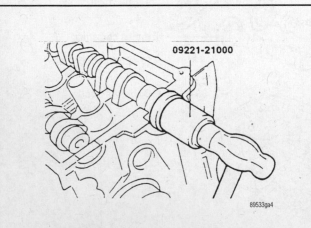

Fig. 97 Using special tool PN 09221-21000 or equivalent, install a new oil seal—1.5L (VIN K) DOHC, 2.0L (VIN F) and 1996–98 1.8L (VIN M) engines

15. Using special tool PN 09221-21000 or equivalent, install a new oil seal.

16. Install the camshaft sprocket and torque the bolt to 60–74 ft. lbs. (80–100 Nm).

17. Install and tension the timing belt.

18. Install the timing belt covers

19. Install the rocker cover.

20. Start the engine and allow it to reach operating temperature. Check for leaks.

1.6L (VIN R), 1.8L (VIN M) and 2.0L (VIN P) Engines

◆ See Figures 100 thru 106

1. Disconnect battery negative cable.
2. Remove the timing belt cover.
3. Remove the rocker cover.
4. Remove the crankshaft position sensor.
5. Loosen the bearing cap bolts in 2–3 steps.
6. Label and remove all camshaft bearing caps.

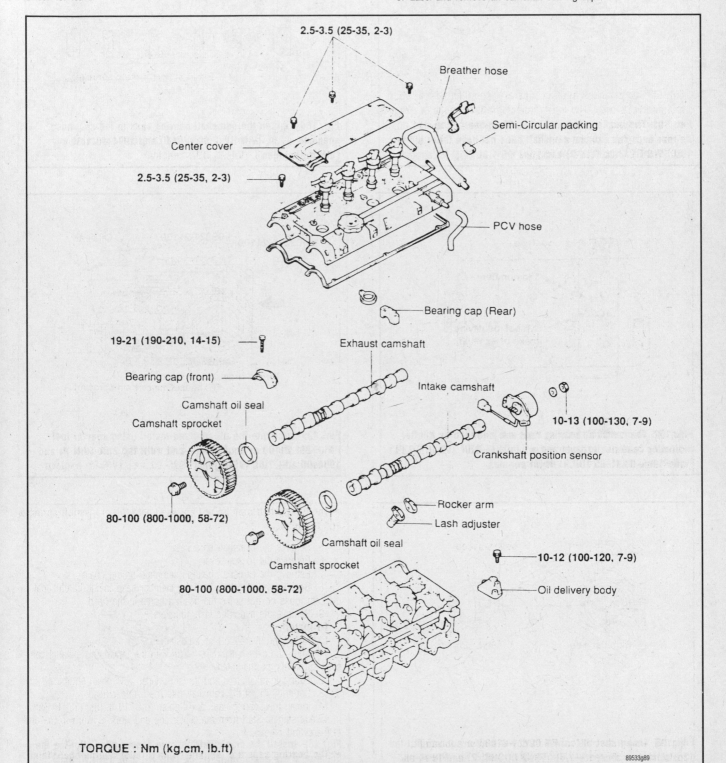

2.5-3.5 (25-35, 2-3)

Breather hose

Semi-Circular packing

Center cover

2.5-3.5 (25-35, 2-3)

PCV hose

Bearing cap (Rear)

19-21 (190-210, 14-15)

Exhaust camshaft

Bearing cap (front)

Intake camshaft

Camshaft oil seal

Camshaft sprocket

10-13 (100-130, 7-9)

Crankshaft position sensor

80-100 (800-1000, 58-72)

Rocker arm

Lash adjuster

Camshaft oil seal

10-12 (100-120, 7-9)

Camshaft sprocket

80-100 (800-1000, 58-72)

Oil delivery body

TORQUE : Nm (kg.cm, lb.ft)

89533g89

Fig. 100 Camshaft and rocker arm assembly components—1.6L (VIN R), 2.0L (VIN P) and 1994–95 1.8L (VIN M) engines

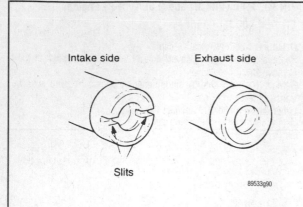

Fig. 101 The intake camshaft can be identified by the slits on its rear end. The exhaust camshaft does not have these slits—1.6L (VIN R), 2.0L (VIN P) and 1994–95 1.8L (VIN M) engines

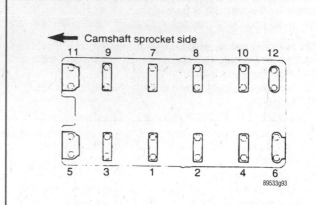

Fig. 104 Tighten the camshaft bearing caps in the sequence specified—1.6L (VIN R), 2.0L (VIN P) and 1994–95 1.8L (VIN M) engines

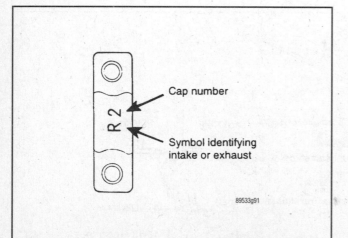

Fig. 102 The camshaft bearing caps are identified by a letter indicating intake or exhaust and a number—1.6L (VIN R), 2.0L (VIN P) and 1994–95 1.8L (VIN M) engines

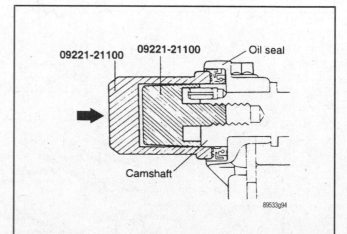

Fig. 105 Lubricate the oil seal and install using special tool PN 09221-21100 or equivalent—1.6L (VIN R), 2.0L (VIN P) and 1994–95 1.8L (VIN M) engines

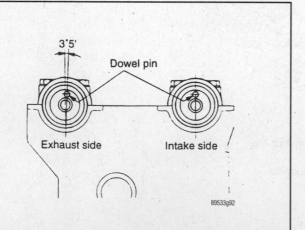

Fig. 103 Ensure that the camshaft dowel pins are located at the 12 o'clock position—1.6L (VIN R), 2.0L (VIN P) and 1994–95 1.8L (VIN M) engines

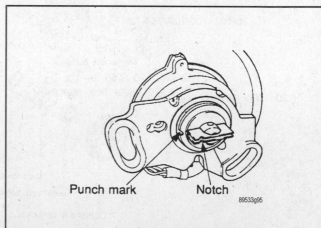

Fig. 106 Install the crankshaft position sensor after aligning the notch with the punch mark—1.6L (VIN R), 2.0L (VIN P) and 1994–95 1.8L (VIN M) engines

➡️If the bearing caps are difficult to remove, use a plastic hammer to gently tap the rear part of the camshaft.

7. Remove the intake and exhaust camshafts.

➡️The hydraulic lash adjusters can be removed without disassembling the cylinder head by using special tool PN 09246-34000 or equivalent.

8. Remove the rocker arms and lash adjusters.

To install:

9. Lubricate the components with heavy engine oil.

➡️Do not confuse the intake camshaft with the exhaust camshaft. The intake camshaft has a split on its rear end for driving the crank angle sensor.

10. Install the camshafts.

11. Install the bearing caps. Ensure the rocker arm is correctly mounted on the lash adjuster and the valve stem end. Tighten in sequence using 2 or 3 steps to 14–15 ft. lbs. (19–21 Nm).

➡️Number 2 and 5 caps are of the same shape. Check the markings on the caps to identify the cap number and intake/exhaust symbol. Only L (intake) or R (exhaust) is stamped on No. 1 bearing cap.

12. Lubricate the oil seal and install using special tool PN 09221-21100 or equivalent.

Install the camshaft sprockets and tighten to 58–72 ft. lbs. (80–100 Nm).

13. Install the rocker covers.

14. Locate the pin on the sprocket side of the intake camshaft at the 12 o'clock position.

15. Align the punch mark on the crank angle sensor housing with the notch in the plate.

16. Install the crankshaft position sensor.

17. Install and tension the timing belt.

18. Install the timing belt covers.

19. Connect the negative battery cable.

20. Start the engine and allow it to reach normal operating temperature. Check for leaks.

3.0L (VIN T) Engine

◆ See Figures 107, 108, 109 and 110

1. Disconnect the negative battery cable.
2. Remove the timing belt covers.
3. Rotate the engine until the No. 1 cylinder is at TDC on the compression stroke and the timing marks on the camshaft sprockets align.

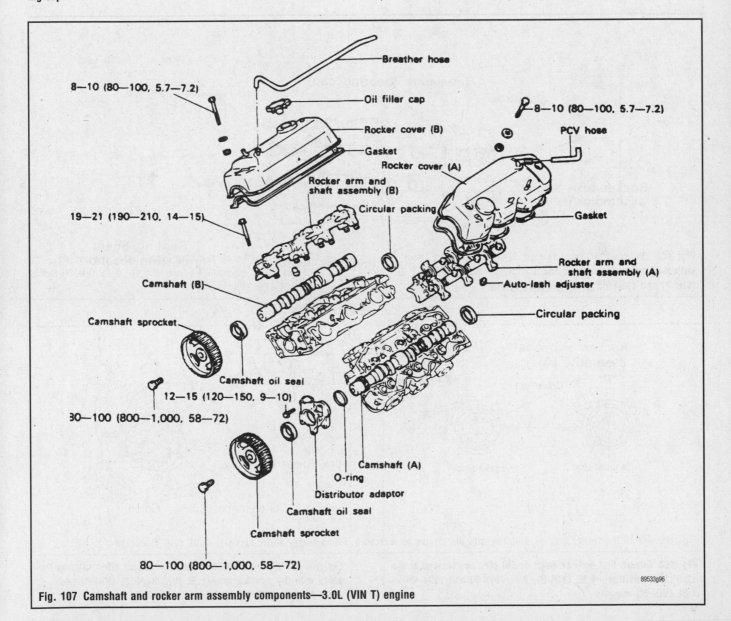

Fig. 107 Camshaft and rocker arm assembly components—3.0L (VIN T) engine

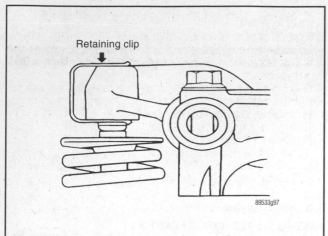

Fig. 108 Before removing the rocker arm assemblies, use the lash adjuster retaining clips (PN 09246-32000 or equivalent) to hold the lash adjusters—3.0L (VIN T) engine

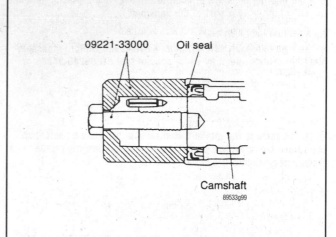

Fig. 110 Lubricate the oil seal and install using special tool PN 09221-33000 or equivalent—3.0L (VIN T) engine

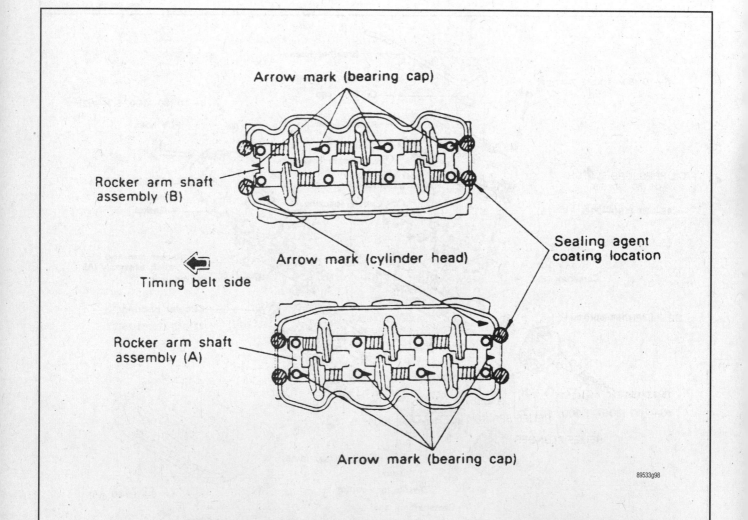

Fig. 109 Install the rocker arm assemblies with the arrows as indicated. Place sealer at the corners—3.0L (VIN T) engine

4. Remove the timing belts.

5. Remove the rocker covers.

6. Install auto lash adjuster retainer tools (PN 09246-32000) or equivalent on the rocker arms.

7. If removing the right side (front) camshaft, remove the distributor extension.

8. Remove the rocker arm and shaft assembly.

9. Remove the camshaft from the cylinder head.

To install:

10. Lubricate the camshaft journals and camshaft with clean engine oil and install the camshaft in the cylinder head.

11. Align the rocker arm and shaft assemblies. Apply sealer (Threebond No. 1324 or equivalent) at the ends of the bearing caps and install the assembly. Tighten bolts to 14–15 ft. lbs. (19–21 Nm).

12. Lubricate the oil seal and install using special tool PN 09221-33000 or equivalent.

13. Install the distributor extension, if removed.

14. Remove auto lash adjuster retainer tools.

15. Install the rocker covers.

16. Install and tension the timing belts.

17. Install the timing belt covers.

18. Connect the negative battery cable.

19. Start the engine and allow it to reach operating temperature. Check for leaks.

Balance Shafts and Bearings

REMOVAL & INSTALLATION

◆ **See Figures 111 thru 123 (p. 75–77)**

2.0L (VIN P) and 1994–95 1.8L (VIN M) Engines

You'll need a number of special tools to perform this operation. They include the following:

• Bearing puller 09212-32000—to remove the right balance shaft front bearing.

• Bearing puller 09212-32100 and holding fixture 09212-32300—to remove the left balance shaft rear bearing.

• Bearing installer 09212-32200—to install the left and right balance shaft rear bearings.

• Seal installer 90214-32100—to install the crankshaft front seal.

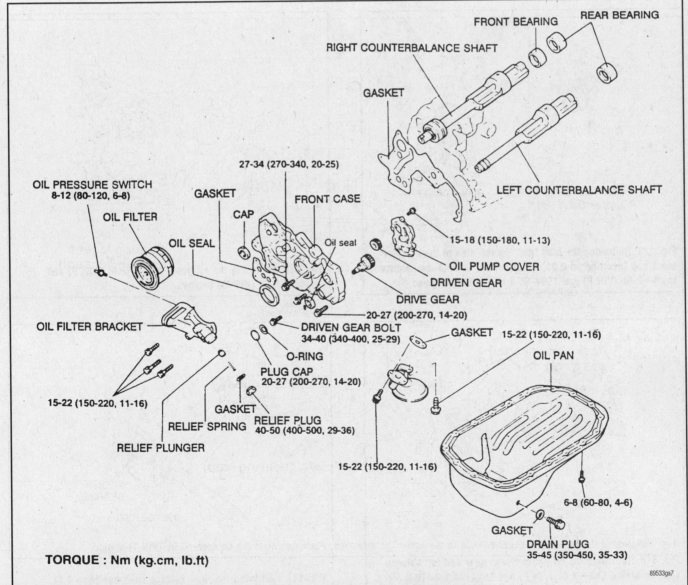

TORQUE : Nm (kg.cm, lb.ft)

89533ga7

Fig. 111 Balance shafts and related components—2.0L (VIN P) and 1994–95 1.8L (VIN M) engines

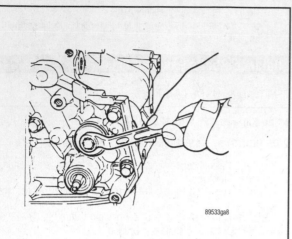

Fig. 112 Removing the plug cap from the oil pump portion of the front case—2.0L (VIN P) and 1994–95 1.8L (VIN M) engines

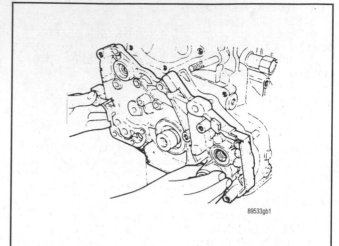

Fig. 115 Removing the front case—2.0L (VIN P) and 1994–95 1.8L (VIN M) engines

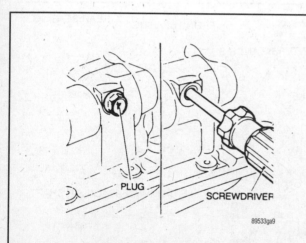

Fig. 113 Removing the plug from the left side of the cylinder block and inserting an 0.31 in. (8mm) bar to hold the balance shaft—2.0L (VIN P) and 1994–95 1.8L (VIN M) engines

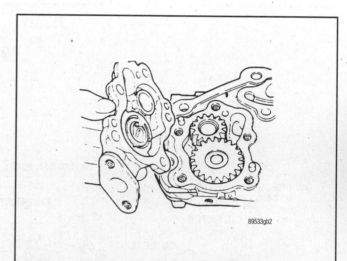

Fig. 116 Removing the oil pump cover—2.0L (VIN P) and 1994–95 1.8L (VIN M) engines

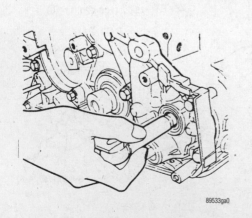

Fig. 114 Removing the oil pump driven gear and left balance shaft retaining bolt—2.0L (VIN P) and 1994–95 1.8L (VIN M) engines

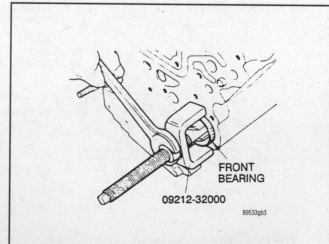

Fig. 117 Removing the right balance shaft bearing—2.0L (VIN P) and 1994–95 1.8L (VIN M) engines

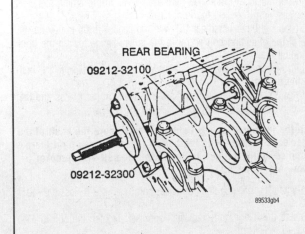

Fig. 118 Removing the left balance shaft bearing—2.0L (VIN P) and 1994–95 1.8L (VIN M) engines

Fig. 121 Balance shaft bearing oil hole alignment—2.0L (VIN P) and 1994–95 1.8L (VIN M) engines

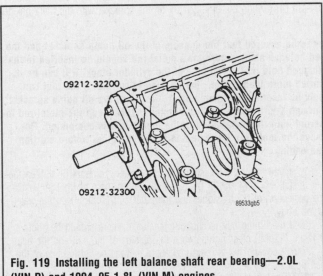

Fig. 119 Installing the left balance shaft rear bearing—2.0L (VIN P) and 1994–95 1.8L (VIN M) engines

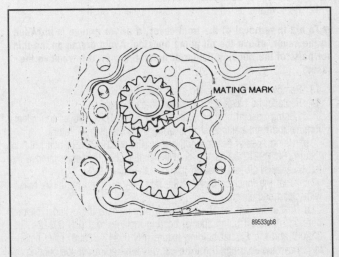

Fig. 122 Oil pump gear alignment marks—2.0L (VIN P) and 1994–95 1.8L (VIN M) engines

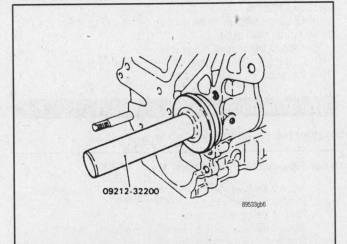

Fig. 120 Installing the right balance shaft front bearing—2.0L (VIN P) and 1994–95 1.8L (VIN M) engines

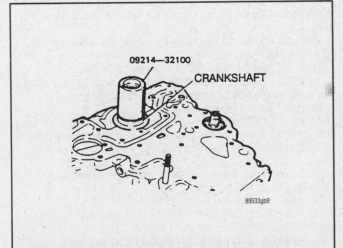

Fig. 123 Installing the oil seal guide tool—2.0L (VIN P) and 1994–95 1.8L (VIN M) engines

1. Disconnect the negative battery cable.
2. Remove the oil filter, oil pressure switch, oil gauge sending unit, oil filter mounting bracket and gasket.
3. Raise and safely support the vehicle.
4. Drain engine oil.
5. Remove engine oil pan and screen.
6. Remove the timing belts.
7. Remove the crankshaft sprocket "B" and balance shaft sprocket.
8. Remove the front engine cover which is also the oil pump cover. Different length bolts are used. Take note of their locations. Discard the shaft seal and gasket.
9. Remove the oil pump driven gear flange bolt. When loosening this bolt, first remove the plug at the bottom of the left side of the cylinder block and insert a tool approximately 3/8 in. diameter into the hole. The tool will hold the balance shaft in position. The tool must be inserted at least 2.4 in. into the hole. If depth of insertion is not correct, rotate the oil pump sprocket 1 revolution, and align the timing marks. Insert the tool again, and watch the amount of insertion, which should be at least 2.4 in.
10. Remove the oil pump gears and remove the front case assembly. Remove the threaded plug, the oil pressure relief spring and plunger.
11. Remove the shaft alignment tool, front cover and oil pump as a unit, with the left balance shaft attached.
12. Remove the oil pump gear and left balance shaft.

➡To aid in removal of the front cover, a driver groove is provided on the cover, above the oil pump housing. Avoid prying on the thinner parts of the housing flange or hammering on it to remove the case.

13. Remove the right balance shaft from the engine block.
14. Replace the balance shaft bearings as follows:
   a. Using special bearing puller tool PN 09212-32000 or equivalent, remove the right balance shaft bearing from the cylinder block.
   b. Using special bearing puller tool (PN 09212-32100) and holding fixture (PN 09212-32300) to hold the puller or equivalents, remove the left balance shaft rear bearing from the cylinder block.
   c. Coat the inner surfaces of the new bearings and the block bores with clean engine oil.
   d. Install the left rear balance shaft bearing into the cylinder block bore and install it using special bearing installer tool (PN 09212-32200) and the special holding fixture (PN 09212-32300) used before to remove the bearing. The fixture serves as a guide for the bearing installer tool.
   e. Using special bearing installer tool (PN 09212-32200) or equivalent, install the right balance shaft front bearing into the block.

To install:
15. Install a new front seal in the cover. Install the oil pump drive and driven gears in the front case, aligning the timing marks on the pump gears.
16. Install the left balance shaft in the driven gear and temporarily tighten the bolt.
17. Install the right balance shaft into the cylinder block.
18. Install an oil seal guide on the end of the crankshaft and install a new gasket on the front of the engine block for the front cover.
19. Install a new front case packing.
20. Insert the left balance shaft into the engine block and at the same time, guide the front cover into place on the front of the engine block.
21. Install an O-ring on the oil pump cover and install it on the front cover.
22. Tighten the oil pump cover bolts and the front cover bolts to 11–13 ft. lbs. (15–18 Nm).
23. Install the upper and lower under covers.
24. Install the spacer on the end of the right balance shaft, with the chamfered edge toward the rear of the engine.
25. Install the balance shaft sprocket and temporarily tighten the bolt.

26. Install the inner crankshaft sprocket and align the timing marks on the sprockets with those on the front case.
27. Install the inner tensioner "B" with the center of the pulley on the left side of the mounting bolt and with the pulley flange toward the front of the engine.
28. Lift the tensioner by hand, clockwise, to apply tension to the belt. Tighten the bolt to secure the tensioner.
29. Check that all alignment marks are in their proper places and the belt deflection is approximately 1/4–1/2 in. on the tension side.

➡When the tensioner bolt is tightened, make sure the shaft of the tensioner does not turn with the bolt. If the belt is too tight there will be noise and if the belt is too loose, the belt and sprocket may come out of mesh.

30. Tighten the balance shaft sprocket bolt to 22–29 ft. lbs. (29–40 Nm).
31. Install the flange and crankshaft sprocket. Tighten the bolt to 43–50 ft. lbs. (58–67 Nm).
32. Install the camshaft spacer and sprocket. Tighten the bolt to 44–57 ft. lbs. (61–75 Nm).
33. Align the camshaft sprocket timing mark with the timing mark on the upper inner cover.
34. Install the oil pump sprocket, tightening the nut to 25–28 ft. lbs. (34–39 Nm). Align the timing mark on the sprocket with the mark on the case.

➡To be assured that the phasing of the oil pump sprocket and the left balance shaft is correct, a metal rod should be inserted in the plugged hole on the left side of the cylinder block. If it can be inserted more than 2.4 in., the phasing is correct. If the tool can only be inserted approximately 1.0 in., turn the oil pump sprocket through 1 turn and realign the timing marks. Keep the metal rod inserted until the installation of the timing belt is completed. Remove the tool from the hole and install the plug, before starting the engine.

35. Install the tensioner spring and tensioner. Temporarily tighten the nut. Install the front end of the tensioner spring (bent at right angles) on the projection of the tensioner and the other end (straight) on the water pump body.
36. If the timing belt is correctly tensioned, there should be about 0.47 in. (12mm) clearance between the outside of the belt and the edge of the belt cover. This is measured about halfway down the side of the belt opposite the tensioner.
37. Complete the assembly by installing the oil screen, gasket and oil pan.
38. Install the crankshaft pulley, alternator and accessory belts and adjust to specifications.
39. Install the radiator, fill the cooling system with antifreeze and the crankcase with clean engine oil.
40. Connect the negative battery cable.
41. Start the engine and allow it to reach operating temperature. Check for leaks.

Rear Main Oil Seal

REMOVAL & INSTALLATION

◆ **See Figures 124, 125, 126 and 127**

1. Remove the transaxle, as described in Section 7 of this manual.
2. Remove the flywheel.
3. Remove the oil seal case.
4. Remove the separator from the case, as required.
5. Remove the seal from the case.

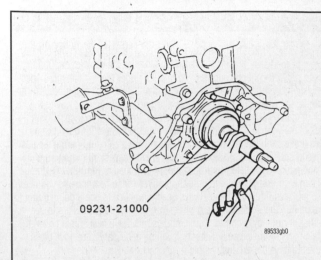

Fig. 124 Using a large diameter seal driver such as PN 09231-21000, install the seal into the case

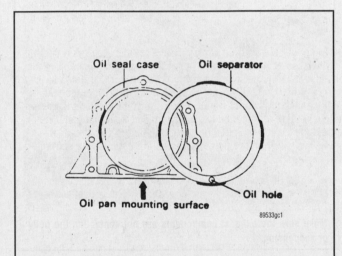

Fig. 125 Install the oil separator with the oil hole at the 6 o'clock position

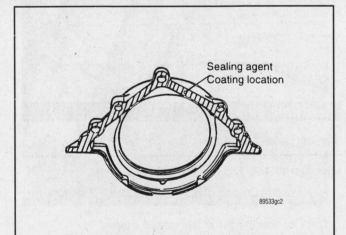

Fig. 126 If the oil seal case does not use a gasket, apply sealant to the area shown

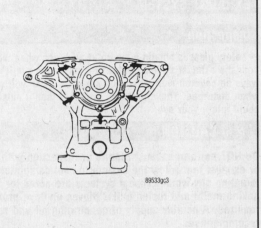

Fig. 127 The oil seal case is attached to the cylinder block by five bolts

To install:
  6. Clean the seal case and separator.
  7. Lubricate and install the new seal using a seal driver.
  8. Install the separator into the housing so that the oil hole faces down.
  9. Lubricate the lips of the seal.
  10. Apply sealer or install a new gasket on the seal case and install. Tighten case bolts to 7–9 ft. lbs. (8–10 Nm).
  11. Install the flywheel.
  12. Install the transaxle. For additional information, refer to Section 7.

Flywheel/Flexplate

REMOVAL & INSTALLATION

  1. Remove the transaxle.
  2. If equipped with a manual transaxle, remove the clutch, pressure plate and throwout bearing.
  3. Loosen the flywheel bolts a little at a time in a cross pattern to avoid warping the flywheel.
  4. On vehicles with manual transaxle, replace the pilot bearing in the end of the crankshaft.

➡ **On 1.5L (VIN E) engines with a manual transaxle, there is a crank angle sensor ring bolted to the flywheel. This ring must be removed before any repairs are done on the flywheel or ring gear.**

To install:
  5. Install the flywheel and tighten bolts a little at a time, in a cross pattern to specification.

➡ **On 1.5L (VIN E) engines with a manual transaxle, install the crank angle sensor ring and tighten the mounting bolts to 8.6–10.8 ft. lbs. (12–15 Nm).**

  6. On manual transaxle equipped vehicles, install the clutch, pressure plate and throwout bearing.
  7. Install the transaxle.

EXHAUST SYSTEM

Inspection

➡Safety glasses should be worn at all times when working on or near the exhaust system. Older exhaust systems will almost always be covered with loose rust particles which will shower you when disturbed. These particles are more than a nuisance and could injure your eye.

✳✳ CAUTION

Do NOT perform exhaust repairs or inspection with the engine or exhaust hot. Allow the system to cool completely before attempting any work. Exhaust systems are noted for sharp edges, flaking metal and rusted bolts. Gloves and eye protection are required. A healthy supply of penetrating oil and rags is highly recommended.

Your vehicle must be raised and supported safely to inspect the exhaust system properly. By placing 4 safety stands under the vehicle for support should provide enough room for you to slide under the vehicle and inspect the system completely. Start the inspection at the exhaust manifold or turbocharger pipe where the header pipe is attached and work your way to the back of the vehicle. On dual exhaust systems, remember to inspect both sides of the vehicle. Check the complete exhaust system for open seams, holes loose connections, or other deterioration which could permit exhaust fumes to seep into the passenger compartment. Inspect all mounting brackets and hangers for deterioration, some models may have rubber O-rings that can be overstretched and non-supportive. These components will need to be replaced if found. It has always been a practice to use a pointed tool to poke up into the exhaust system where the deterioration spots are to see whether or not they crumble. Some models may have heat shield covering certain parts of the exhaust system , it will be necessary to remove these shields to have the exhaust visible for inspection also.

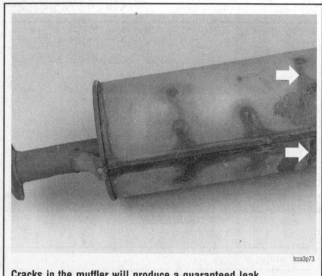

tcca3p73

Cracks in the muffler will produce a guaranteed leak

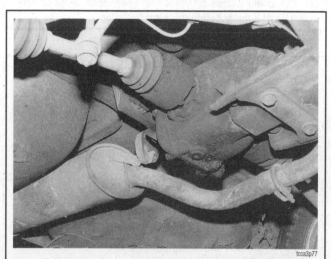

tcca3p77

Make sure the exhaust components are not contacting the body or suspension

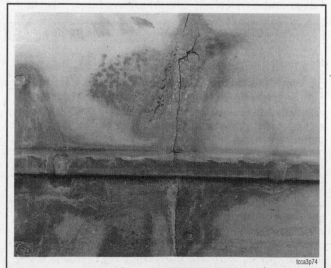

tcca3p74

Check the muffler for rotted spot welds and seams

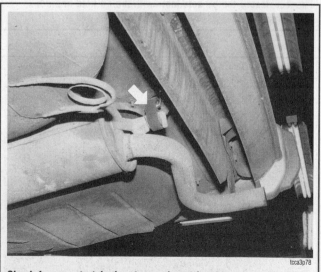

tcca3p78

Check for overstretched or torn exhaust hangers

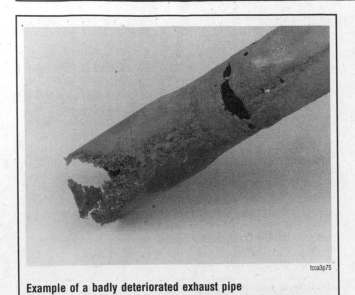

Example of a badly deteriorated exhaust pipe

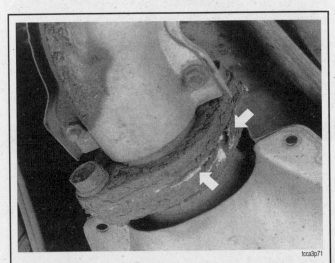

Inspect flanges for gaskets that have deteriorated and need replacement

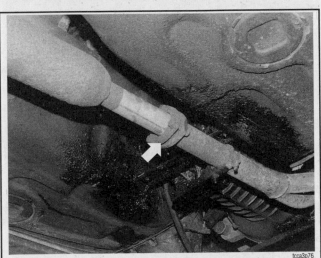

Some systems, like this one, use large O-rings (donuts) between the flanges

REPLACEMENT

There are basically two types of exhaust systems. One is the flange type where the component ends are attached with bolts and a gasket in-between. The other exhaust system is the slip joint type. These components slip into one another using clamps to retain them together.

> ☀ **CAUTION**
>
> **Allow the exhaust system to cool sufficiently before spraying a solvent exhaust fasteners. Some solvents are highly flammable and could ignite when sprayed on hot exhaust components.**

Before removing any component of the exhaust system, ALWAYS squirt a liquid rust dissolving agent onto the fasteners for ease of removal. A lot of knuckle skin will be saved by following this rule. It may even be wise to spray the fasteners and allow them to sit overnight.

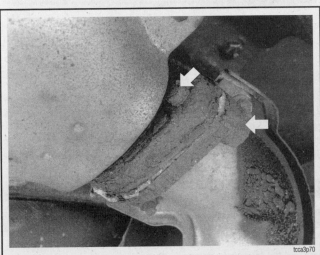

Nuts and bolts will be extremely difficult to remove when deteriorated with rust

Flange Type

> ☀ **CAUTION**
>
> **Do NOT perform exhaust repairs or inspection with the engine or exhaust hot. Allow the system to cool completely before attempting any work. Exhaust systems are noted for sharp edges, flaking metal and rusted bolts. Gloves and eye protection are required. A healthy supply of penetrating oil and rags is highly recommended. Never spray liquid rust dissolving agent onto a hot exhaust component.**

Before removing any component on a flange type system, ALWAYS squirt a liquid rust dissolving agent onto the fasteners for ease of removal. Start by unbolting the exhaust piece at both ends (if required). When unbolting the headpipe from the manifold, make sure that the bolts are free before trying to remove them. if you snap a stud in the exhaust manifold, the stud will have to be removed with a bolt extractor, which often means removal of the manifold itself. Next, disconnect the component from the mounting; slight twisting and turning may be required to remove the component completely from the vehicle. You may need to tap on the component with a rubber mallet to loosen the component. If all else fails, use a hacksaw to separate the parts. An oxy-acetylene cutting torch may be faster but the sparks are DANGEROUS near the fuel tank, and at the very least, accidents could happen, resulting in damage to the undercar parts, not to mention yourself.

Example of a flange type exhaust system joint

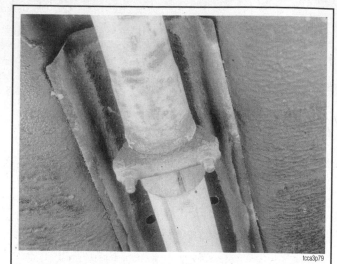

Example of a common slip joint type system

Slip Joint Type

Before removing any component on the slip joint type exhaust system, ALWAYS squirt a liquid rust dissolving agent onto the fasteners for ease of removal. Start by unbolting the exhaust piece at both ends (if required). When unbolting the headpipe from the manifold, make sure that the bolts are free before trying to remove them. If you snap a stud in the

exhaust manifold, the stud will have to be removed with a bolt extractor, which often means removal of the manifold itself. Next, remove the mounting U-bolts from around the exhaust pipe you are extracting from the vehicle. Don't be surprised if the U-bolts break while removing the nuts. Loosen the exhaust pipe from any mounting brackets retaining it to the floor pan and separate the components.

ENGINE RECONDITIONING

Determining Engine Condition

Anything that generates heat and/or friction will eventually burn or wear out (for example, a light bulb generates heat, therefore its life span is limited). With this in mind, a running engine generates tremendous amounts of both; friction is encountered by the moving and rotating parts inside the engine and heat is created by friction and combustion of the fuel. However, the engine has systems designed to help reduce the effects of heat and friction and provide added longevity. The oiling system reduces the amount of friction encountered by the moving parts inside the engine, while the cooling system reduces heat created by friction and combustion. If either system is not maintained, a break-down will be inevitable. Therefore, you can see how regular maintenance can affect the service life of your vehicle. If you do not drain, flush and refill your cooling system at the proper intervals, deposits will begin to accumulate in the radiator, thereby reducing the amount of heat it can extract from the coolant. The same applies to your oil and filter; if it is not changed often enough it becomes laden with contaminates and is unable to properly lubricate the engine. This increases friction and wear.

There are a number of methods for evaluating the condition of your engine. A compression test can reveal the condition of your pistons, piston rings, cylinder bores, head gasket(s), valves and valve seats. An oil pressure test can warn you of possible engine bearing, or oil pump failures. Excessive oil consumption, evidence of oil in the engine air intake area and/or bluish smoke from the tail pipe may indicate worn piston rings, worn valve guides and/or valve seals. As a general rule, an engine that uses no more than one quart of oil every 1,000 miles is in good condition. Engines that use one quart of oil or more in less than 1,000 miles should first be checked for oil leaks. If any oil leaks are present, have them fixed before determining how much oil is consumed by the engine, especially if blue smoke is not visible at the tail pipe.

COMPRESSION TEST

A noticeable lack of engine power, excessive oil consumption and/or poor fuel mileage measured over an extended period are all indicators of internal engine wear. Worn piston rings, scored or worn cylinder bores, blown head gaskets, sticking or burnt valves, and worn valve seats are all possible culprits. A check of each cylinder's compression will help locate the problem.

➡**A screw-in type compression gauge is more accurate than the type you simply hold against the spark plug hole. Although it takes slightly longer to use, it's worth the effort to obtain a more accurate reading.**

1. Make sure that the proper amount and viscosity of engine oil is in the crankcase, then ensure the battery is fully charged.
2. Warm-up the engine to normal operating temperature, then shut the engine **OFF.**
3. Disable the ignition system.
4. Label and disconnect all of the spark plug wires from the plugs.
5. Thoroughly clean the cylinder head area around the spark plug ports, then remove the spark plugs.
6. Set the throttle plate to the fully open (wide-open throttle) position. You can block the accelerator linkage open for this, or you can have an assistant fully depress the accelerator pedal.
7. Install a screw-in type compression gauge into the No. 1 spark plug hole until the fitting is snug.

❊❊ WARNING

Be careful not to crossthread the spark plug hole.

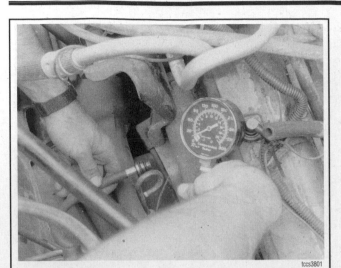

tccs3801

A screw-in type compression gauge is more accurate and easier to use without an assistant

8. According to the tool manufacturer's instructions, connect a remote starting switch to the starting circuit.

9. With the ignition switch in the **OFF** position, use the remote starting switch to crank the engine through at least five compression strokes (approximately 5 seconds of cranking) and record the highest reading on the gauge.

10. Repeat the test on each cylinder, cranking the engine approximately the same number of compression strokes and/or time as the first.

11. Compare the highest readings from each cylinder to that of the others. The indicated compression pressures are considered within specifications if the lowest reading cylinder is within 75 percent of the pressure recorded for the highest reading cylinder. For example, if your highest reading cylinder pressure was 150 psi (1,034 kPa), then 75 percent of that would be 113 psi (779 kPa). So the lowest reading cylinder should be no less than 113 psi (779 kPa).

12. If a cylinder exhibits an unusually low compression reading, pour a tablespoon of clean engine oil into the cylinder through the spark plug hole and repeat the compression test. If the compression rises after adding oil, it means that the cylinder's piston rings and/or cylinder bore are damaged or worn. If the pressure remains low, the valves may not be seating properly (a valve job is needed), or the head gasket may be blown near that cylinder. If compression in any two adjacent cylinders is low, and if the addition of oil doesn't help raise compression, there is leakage past the head gasket. Oil and coolant in the combustion chamber, combined with blue or constant white smoke from the tail pipe, are symptoms of this problem. However, don't be alarmed by the normal white smoke emitted from the tail pipe during engine warm-up or from cold weather driving. There may be evidence of water droplets on the engine dipstick and/or oil droplets in the cooling system if a head gasket is blown.

OIL PRESSURE TEST

Check for proper oil pressure at the sending unit passage with an externally mounted mechanical oil pressure gauge (as opposed to relying on a factory installed dash-mounted gauge). A tachometer may also be needed, as some specifications may require running the engine at a specific rpm.

1. With the engine cold, locate and remove the oil pressure sending unit.

2. Following the manufacturer's instructions, connect a mechanical oil pressure gauge and, if necessary, a tachometer to the engine.

3. Start the engine and allow it to idle.

4. Check the oil pressure reading when cold and record the number. You may need to run the engine at a specified rpm, so check the specifications chart located earlier in this section.

5. Run the engine until normal operating temperature is reached (upper radiator hose will feel warm).

6. Check the oil pressure reading again with the engine hot and record the number. Turn the engine **OFF**.

7. Compare your hot oil pressure reading to that given in the chart. If the reading is low, check the cold pressure reading against the chart. If the cold pressure is well above the specification, and the hot reading was lower than the specification, you may have the wrong viscosity oil in the engine. Change the oil, making sure to use the proper grade and quantity, then repeat the test.

Low oil pressure readings could be attributed to internal component wear, pump related problems, a low oil level, or oil viscosity that is too low. High oil pressure readings could be caused by an overfilled crankcase, too high of an oil viscosity or a faulty pressure relief valve.

Buy or Rebuild?

Now that you have determined that your engine is worn out, you must make some decisions. The question of whether or not an engine is worth rebuilding is largely a subjective matter and one of personal worth. Is the engine a popular one, or is it an obsolete model? Are parts available? Will it get acceptable gas mileage once it is rebuilt? Is the car it's being put into worth keeping? Would it be less expensive to buy a new engine, have your engine rebuilt by a pro, rebuild it yourself or buy a used engine from a salvage yard? Or would it be simpler and less expensive to buy another car? If you have considered all these matters and more, and have still decided to rebuild the engine, then it is time to decide how you will rebuild it.

➡**The editors at Chilton feel that most engine machining should be performed by a professional machine shop. Don't think of it as wasting money, rather, as an assurance that the job has been done right the first time. There are many expensive and specialized tools required to perform such tasks as boring and honing an engine block or having a valve job done on a cylinder head. Even inspecting the parts requires expensive micrometers and gauges to properly measure wear and clearances. Also, a machine shop can deliver to you clean, and ready to assemble parts, saving you time and aggravation. Your maximum savings will come from performing the removal, disassembly, assembly and installation of the engine and purchasing or renting only the tools required to perform the above tasks. Depending on the particular circumstances, you may save 40 to 60 percent of the cost doing these yourself.**

A complete rebuild or overhaul of an engine involves replacing all of the moving parts (pistons, rods, crankshaft, camshaft, etc.) with new ones and machining the non-moving wearing surfaces of the block and heads. Unfortunately, this may not be cost effective. For instance, your crankshaft may have been damaged or worn, but it can be machined undersize for a minimal fee.

So, as you can see, you can replace everything inside the engine, but it is wiser to replace only those parts which are really needed, and, if possible, repair the more expensive ones. Later in this section, we will break the engine down into its two main components: the cylinder head and the engine block. We will discuss each component, and the recommended parts to replace during a rebuild on each.

Engine Overhaul Tips

Most engine overhaul procedures are fairly standard. In addition to specific parts replacement procedures and specifications for your individual engine, this section is also a guide to acceptable rebuilding procedures. Examples of standard rebuilding practice are given and should be used along with specific details concerning your particular engine.

Competent and accurate machine shop services will ensure maximum performance, reliability and engine life. In most instances it is more profitable for the do-it-yourself mechanic to remove, clean and inspect the component, buy the necessary parts and deliver these to a shop for actual machine work.

Much of the assembly work (crankshaft, bearings, piston rods, and other components) is well within the scope of the do-it-yourself mechanic's tools and abilities. You will have to decide for yourself the depth of involvement you desire in an engine repair or rebuild.

TOOLS

The tools required for an engine overhaul or parts replacement will depend on the depth of your involvement. With a few exceptions, they will be the tools found in a mechanic's tool kit (see Section 1 of this manual). More in-depth work will require some or all of the following:
• A dial indicator (reading in thousandths) mounted on a universal base
• Micrometers and telescope gauges
• Jaw and screw-type pullers
• Scraper
• Valve spring compressor
• Ring groove cleaner
• Piston ring expander and compressor
• Ridge reamer
• Cylinder hone or glaze breaker
• Plastigage®
• Engine stand

The use of most of these tools is illustrated in this section. Many can be rented for a one-time use from a local parts jobber or tool supply house specializing in automotive work.

Occasionally, the use of special tools is called for. See the information on Special Tools and the Safety Notice in the front of this book before substituting another tool.

OVERHAUL TIPS

Aluminum has become extremely popular for use in engines, due to its low weight. Observe the following precautions when handling aluminum parts:
• Never hot tank aluminum parts (the caustic hot tank solution will eat the aluminum.
• Remove all aluminum parts (identification tag, etc.) from engine parts prior to the tanking.
• Always coat threads lightly with engine oil or anti-seize compounds before installation, to prevent seizure.
• Never overtighten bolts or spark plugs especially in aluminum threads.

When assembling the engine, any parts that will be exposed to frictional contact must be prelubed to provide lubrication at initial start-up. Any product specifically formulated for this purpose can be used, but engine oil is not recommended as a prelube in most cases.

When semi-permanent (locked, but removable) installation of bolts or nuts is desired, threads should be cleaned and coated with Loctite® or another similar, commercial non-hardening sealant.

CLEANING

Before the engine and its components are inspected, they must be thoroughly cleaned. You will need to remove any engine varnish, oil sludge and/or carbon deposits from all of the components to insure an accurate inspection. A crack in the engine block or cylinder head can easily become overlooked if hidden by a layer of sludge or carbon.

Most of the cleaning process can be carried out with common hand tools and readily available solvents or solutions. Carbon deposits can be chipped away using a hammer and a hard wooden chisel. Old gasket material and varnish or sludge can usually be removed using a scraper and/or cleaning solvent. Extremely stubborn deposits may require the use of a power drill with a wire brush. If using a wire brush, use extreme care

Use a gasket scraper to remove the old gasket material from the mating surfaces

around any critical machined surfaces (such as the gasket surfaces, bearing saddles, cylinder bores, etc.). USE OF A WIRE BRUSH IS NOT RECOMMENDED ON ANY ALUMINUM COMPONENTS. Always follow any safety recommendations given by the manufacturer of the tool and/or solvent. You should always wear eye protection during any cleaning process involving scraping, chipping or spraying of solvents.

An alternative to the mess and hassle of cleaning the parts yourself is to drop them off at a local garage or machine shop. They will, more than likely, have the necessary equipment to properly clean all of the parts for a nominal fee.

✳✳ CAUTION

Always wear eye protection during any cleaning process involving scraping, chipping or spraying of solvents.

Remove any oil galley plugs, freeze plugs and/or pressed-in bearings and carefully wash and degrease all of the engine components including the fasteners and bolts. Small parts such as the valves, springs, etc., should be placed in a metal basket and allowed to soak. Use pipe cleaner type brushes, and clean all passageways in the components. Use a ring expander and remove the rings from the pistons. Clean the piston

Use a ring expander tool to remove the piston rings

Clean the piston ring grooves using a ring groove cleaner tool, or . . .

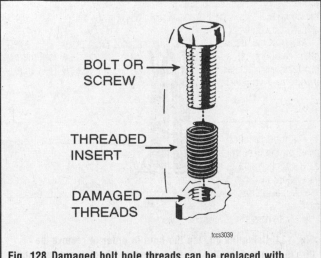

Fig. 128 Damaged bolt hole threads can be replaced with thread repair inserts

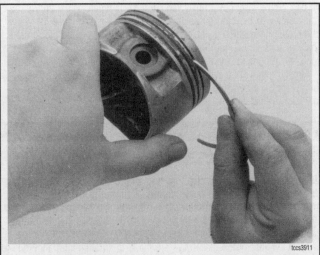

. . . use a piece of an old ring to clean the grooves. Be careful, the ring can be quite sharp

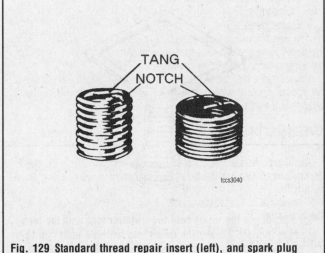

Fig. 129 Standard thread repair insert (left), and spark plug thread insert

ring grooves with a special tool or a piece of broken ring. Scrape the carbon off of the top of the piston. You should never use a wire brush on the pistons. After preparing all of the piston assemblies in this manner, wash and degrease them again.

✳✳ WARNING

Use extreme care when cleaning around the cylinder head valve seats. A mistake or slip may cost you a new seat.

When cleaning the cylinder head, remove carbon from the combustion chamber with the valves installed. This will avoid damaging the valve seats.

REPAIRING DAMAGED THREADS

◆ See Figures 128, 129, 130, 131 and 132

Several methods of repairing damaged threads are available. Heli-Coil® (shown here), Keenserts® and Microdot® are among the most widely used. All involve basically the same principle—drilling out stripped threads, tapping the hole and installing a prewound insert—making welding, plugging and oversize fasteners unnecessary.

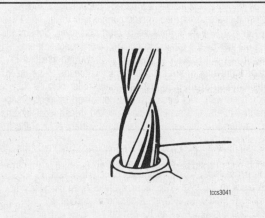

Fig. 130 Drill out the damaged threads with the specified size bit. Be sure to drill completely through the hole or to the bottom of a blind hole

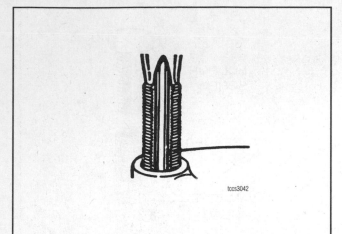

Fig. 131 Using the kit, tap the hole in order to receive the thread insert. Keep the tap well oiled and back it out frequently to avoid clogging the threads

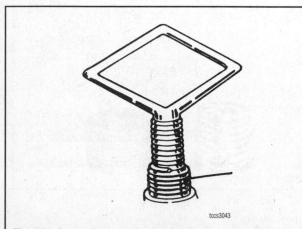

Fig. 132 Screw the insert onto the installer tool until the tang engages the slot. Thread the insert into the hole until it is 1/4– 1/2 turn below the top surface, then remove the tool and break off the tang using a punch

Two types of thread repair inserts are usually supplied: a standard type for most inch coarse, inch fine, metric course and metric fine thread sizes and a spark lug type to fit most spark plug port sizes. Consult the individual tool manufacturer's catalog to determine exact applications. Typical thread repair kits will contain a selection of prewound threaded inserts, a tap (corresponding to the outside diameter threads of the insert) and an installation tool. Spark plug inserts usually differ because they require a tap equipped with pilot threads and a combined reamer/tap section. Most manufacturers also supply blister-packed thread repair inserts separately in addition to a master kit containing a variety of taps and inserts plus installation tools.

Before attempting to repair a threaded hole, remove any snapped, broken or damaged bolts or studs. Penetrating oil can be used to free frozen threads. The offending item can usually be removed with locking pliers or using a screw/stud extractor. After the hole is clear, the thread can be repaired, as shown in the series of accompanying illustrations and in the kit manufacturer's instructions.

Engine Preparation

To properly rebuild an engine, you must first remove it from the vehicle, then disassemble and diagnose it. Ideally you should place your en-gine on an engine stand. This affords you the best access to the engine components. Follow the manufacturer's directions for using the stand with your particular engine. Remove the flywheel or flexplate before installing the engine to the stand.

Now that you have the engine on a stand, and assuming that you have drained the oil and coolant from the engine, it's time to strip it of all but the necessary components. Before you start disassembling the engine, you may want to take a moment to draw some pictures, or fabricate some labels or containers to mark the locations of various components and the bolts and/or studs which fasten them. Modern day engines use a lot of little brackets and clips which hold wiring harnesses and such, and these holders are often mounted on studs and/or bolts that can be easily mixed up. The manufacturer spent a lot of time and money designing your vehicle, and they wouldn't have wasted any of it by haphazardly placing brackets, clips or fasteners on the vehicle. If it's present when you disassemble it, put it back when you assemble, you will regret not remembering that little bracket which holds a wire harness out of the path of a rotating part.

You should begin by unbolting any accessories still attached to the engine, such as the water pump, power steering pump, alternator, etc. Then, unfasten any manifolds (intake or exhaust) which were not removed during the engine removal procedure. Finally, remove any covers remaining on the engine such as the rocker arm, front or timing cover and oil pan. Some front covers may require the vibration damper and/or crank pulley to be removed beforehand. The idea is to reduce the engine to the bare necessities (cylinder head(s), valve train, engine block, crankshaft, pistons and connecting rods), plus any other 'in block' components such as oil pumps, balance shafts and auxiliary shafts.

Finally, remove the cylinder head(s) from the engine block and carefully place on a bench. Disassembly instructions for each component follow later in this section.

Cylinder Head

There are two basic types of cylinder heads used on today's automobiles: the Overhead Valve (OHV) and the Overhead Camshaft (OHC). The latter can also be broken down into two subgroups: the Single Overhead Camshaft (SOHC) and the Dual Overhead Camshaft (DOHC). Generally, if there is only a single camshaft on a head, it is just referred to as an OHC head. Also, an engine with a OHV cylinder head is also known as a pushrod engine.

Most cylinder heads these days are made of an aluminum alloy due to its light weight, durability and heat transfer qualities. However, cast iron was the material of choice in the past, and is still used on many vehicles today. Whether made from aluminum or iron, all cylinder heads have valves and seats. Some use two valves per cylinder, while the more hi-tech engines will utilize a multi-valve configuration using 3, 4 and even 5 valves per cylinder. When the valve contacts the seat, it does so on precision machined surfaces, which seals the combustion chamber. All cylinder heads have a valve guide for each valve. The guide centers the valve to the seat and allows it to move up and down within it. The clearance between the valve and guide can be critical. Too much clearance and the engine may consume oil, lose vacuum and/or damage the seat. Too little, and the valve can stick in the guide causing the engine to run poorly if at all, and possibly causing severe damage. The last component all cylinder heads have are valve springs. The spring holds the valve against its seat. It also returns the valve to this position when the valve has been opened by the valve train or camshaft. The spring is fastened to the valve by a retainer and valve locks (sometimes called keepers). Aluminum heads will also have a valve spring shim to keep the spring from wearing away the aluminum.

An ideal method of rebuilding the cylinder head would involve replacing all of the valves, guides, seats, springs, etc. with new ones. However, depending on how the engine was maintained, often this is not necessary. A major cause of valve, guide and seat wear is an improperly tuned engine. An engine that is running too rich, will often wash the lubricating oil out of the guide with gasoline, causing it to wear rapidly. Conversely, an engine which is running too lean will place higher combustion temperatures on the valves and seats allowing them to wear or even burn. Springs fall victim to the driving habits of the individual. A driver who often runs the engine rpm to the redline will wear out or break the springs faster then one that stays well below it. Unfortunately, mileage takes it toll on all of the parts. Generally, the valves, guides, springs and seats in a cylinder head can be machined and re-used, saving you money. However, if a valve is burnt, it may be wise to replace all of the valves, since they were all operating in the same environment. The same goes for any other component on the cylinder head. Think of it as an insurance policy against future problems related to that component.

Unfortunately, the only way to find out which components need replacing, is to disassemble and carefully check each piece. After the cylinder head(s) are disassembled, thoroughly clean all of the components.

DISASSEMBLY

Whether it is a single or dual overhead camshaft cylinder head, the disassembly procedure is relatively unchanged. One aspect to pay attention to is careful labeling of the parts on the dual camshaft cylinder head. There will be an intake camshaft and followers as well as an exhaust camshaft and followers and they must be labeled as such. In some cases, the components are identical and could easily be installed incorrectly. DO NOT MIX THEM UP! Determining which is which is very simple; the intake camshaft and components are on the same side of the head as was the intake manifold. Conversely, the exhaust camshaft and components are on the same side of the head as was the exhaust manifold.

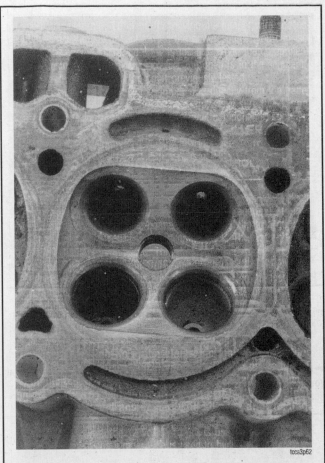

Example of a multi-valve cylinder head. Note how it has 2 intake and 2 exhaust valve ports

Cup Type Camshaft Followers

Most cylinder heads with cup type camshaft followers will have the valve spring, retainer and locks recessed within the follower's bore. You will need a C-clamp style valve spring compressor tool, an OHC spring removal tool (or equivalent) and a small magnet to disassemble the head.

Exploded view of a valve, seal, spring, retainer and locks from an OHC cylinder head

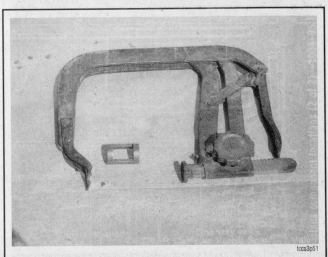

C-clamp type spring compressor and an OHC spring removal tool (center) for cup type followers

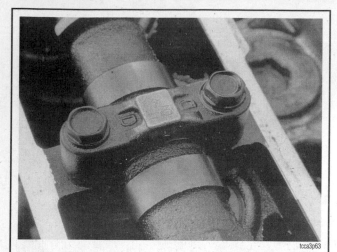

Most cup type follower cylinder heads retain the camshaft using bolt-on bearing caps

1. If not already removed, remove the camshaft(s) and/or followers. Mark their positions for assembly.

2. Position the cylinder head to allow use of a C-clamp style valve spring compressor tool.

➡️It is preferred to position the cylinder head gasket surface facing you with the valve springs facing the opposite direction and the head laying horizontal.

Position the OHC spring tool in the follower bore, then compress the spring with a C-clamp type tool

3. With the OHC spring removal adapter tool positioned inside of the follower bore, compress the valve spring using the C-clamp style valve spring compressor.

4. Remove the valve locks. A small magnetic tool or screwdriver will aid in removal.

5. Release the compressor tool and remove the spring assembly.

6. Withdraw the valve from the cylinder head.

7. If equipped, remove the valve seal.

➡️Special valve seal removal tools are available. Regular or needlenose type pliers, if used with care, will work just as well. If using ordinary pliers, be sure not to damage the follower bore. The follower and its bore are machined to close tolerances and any damage to the bore will affect this relationship.

8. If equipped, remove the valve spring shim. A small magnetic tool or screwdriver will aid in removal.

9. Repeat Steps 3 through 8 until all of the valves have been removed.

Rocker Arm Type Camshaft Followers

Most cylinder heads with rocker arm-type camshaft followers are easily disassembled using a standard valve spring compressor. However, certain

Example of the shaft mounted rocker arms on some OHC heads

Another example of the rocker arm type OHC head. This model uses a follower under the camshaft

models may not have enough open space around the spring for the standard tool and may require you to use a C-clamp style compressor tool instead.

1. If not already removed, remove the rocker arms and/or shafts and the camshaft. If applicable, also remove the hydraulic lash adjusters. Mark their positions for assembly.

2. Position the cylinder head to allow access to the valve spring.

3. Use a valve spring compressor tool to relieve the spring tension from the retainer.

➡**Due to engine varnish, the retainer may stick to the valve locks. A gentle tap with a hammer may help to break it loose.**

4. Remove the valve locks from the valve tip and/or retainer. A small magnet may help in removing the small locks.

5. Lift the valve spring, tool and all, off of the valve stem.

6. If equipped, remove the valve seal. If the seal is difficult to remove with the valve in place, try removing the valve first, then the seal. Follow the steps below for valve removal.

7. Position the head to allow access for withdrawing the valve.

Compress the valve spring . . .

Before the camshaft can be removed, all of the followers must first be removed . . .

. . . then remove the valve locks from the valve stem and spring retainer

. . . then the camshaft can be removed by sliding it out (shown), or unbolting a bearing cap (not shown)

Remove the valve spring and retainer from the cylinder head

Remove the valve seal from the guide. Some gentle prying or pliers may help to remove stubborn ones

All aluminum and some cast iron heads will have these valve spring shims. Remove all of them as well

➡Cylinder heads that have seen a lot of miles and/or abuse may have mushroomed the valve lock groove and/or tip, causing difficulty in removal of the valve. If this has happened, use a metal file to carefully remove the high spots around the lock grooves and/or tip. Only file it enough to allow removal.

8. Remove the valve from the cylinder head.

9. If equipped, remove the valve spring shim. A small magnetic tool or screwdriver will aid in removal.

10. Repeat Steps 3 though 9 until all of the valves have been removed.

INSPECTION

Now that all of the cylinder head components are clean, it's time to inspect them for wear and/or damage. To accurately inspect them, you will need some specialized tools:

• A 0–1 inch micrometer for the valves
• A dial indicator or inside diameter gauge for the valve guides
• A spring pressure test gauge

If you do not have access to the proper tools, you may want to bring the components to a shop that does.

Valves

The first thing to inspect are the valve heads. Look closely at the head, margin and face for any cracks, excessive wear or burning. The margin is the best place to look for burning. It should have a squared edge with an even width all around the diameter. When a valve burns, the margin will look melted and the edges rounded. Also inspect the valve head for any signs of tulipping. This will show as a lifting of the edges or dishing in the center of the head and will usually not occur to all of the valves. All of the heads should look the same, any that seem dished more than others are probably bad. Next, inspect the valve lock grooves and valve tips. Check for any burrs around the lock grooves, especially if you had to file them to remove the valve. Valve tips should appear flat, although slight rounding with high mileage engines is normal. Slightly worn valve tips will need to be machined flat. Last, measure the valve stem diameter with the micrometer. Measure the area that rides within the guide, especially towards the tip where most of the wear oc-

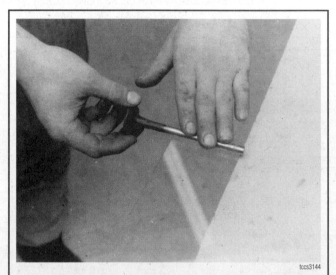
Valve stems may be rolled on a flat surface to check for bends

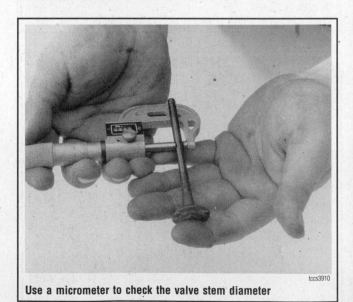
Use a micrometer to check the valve stem diameter

curs. Take several measurements along its length and compare them to each other. Wear should be even along the length with little to no taper. If no minimum diameter is given in the specifications, then the stem should not read more than 0.001 in. (0.025mm) below the specification. Any valves that fail these inspections should be replaced.

Springs, Retainers and Valve Locks

The first thing to check is the most obvious, broken springs. Next check the free length and squareness of each spring. If applicable, insure to distinguish between intake and exhaust springs. Use a ruler and/or carpenters square to measure the length. A carpenters square should be used to check the springs for squareness. If a spring pressure test gauge is available, check each springs rating and compare to the specifications chart. Check the readings against the specifications given. Any springs that fail these inspections should be replaced.

The spring retainers rarely need replacing, however they should still be checked as a precaution. Inspect the spring mating surface and the valve lock retention area for any signs of excessive wear. Also check for any signs of cracking. Replace any retainers that are questionable.

Valve locks should be inspected for excessive wear on the outside contact area as well as on the inner notched surface. Any locks which appear worn or broken and its respective valve should be replaced.

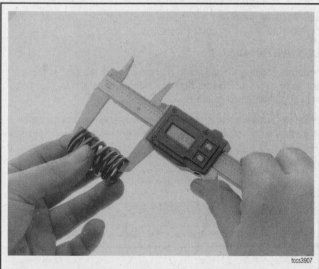

Use a caliper to check the valve spring free-length

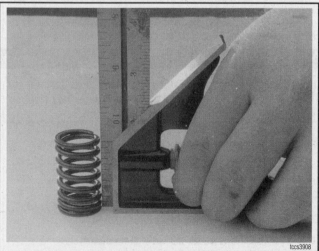

Check the valve spring for squareness on a flat surface; a carpenter's square can be used

Cylinder Head

There are several things to check on the cylinder head: valve guides, seats, cylinder head surface flatness, cracks and physical damage.

VALVE GUIDES

Now that you know the valves are good, you can use them to check the guides, although a new valve, if available, is preferred. Before you measure anything, look at the guides carefully and inspect them for any cracks, chips or breakage. Also if the guide is a removable style (as in most aluminum heads), check them for any looseness or evidence of movement. All of the guides should appear to be at the same height from the spring seat. If any seem lower (or higher) from another, the guide has moved. Mount a dial indicator onto the spring side of the cylinder head. Lightly oil the valve stem and insert it into the cylinder head. Position the dial indicator against the valve stem near the tip and zero the gauge. Grasp the valve stem and wiggle towards and away from the dial indicator and observe the readings. Mount the dial indicator 90 degrees from the initial point and zero the gauge and again take a reading. Compare the two readings for a out of round condition. Check the readings against the specifications given. An Inside Diameter (I.D.) gauge designed for valve guides will give you an accurate valve guide bore measurement. If the I.D. gauge is used, compare the readings with the specifications given. Any guides that fail these inspections should be replaced or machined.

A dial gauge may be used to check valve stem-to-guide clearance; read the gauge while moving the valve stem

VALVE SEATS

A visual inspection of the valve seats should show a slightly worn and pitted surface where the valve face contacts the seat. Inspect the seat carefully for severe pitting or cracks. Also, a seat that is badly worn will be recessed into the cylinder head. A severely worn or recessed seat may need to be replaced. All cracked seats must be replaced. A seat concentricity gauge, if available, should be used to check the seat run-out. If run-out exceeds specifications the seat must be machined (if no specification is given use 0.002 in. or 0.051mm).

CYLINDER HEAD SURFACE FLATNESS

After you have cleaned the gasket surface of the cylinder head of any old gasket material, check the head for flatness.

Place a straightedge across the gasket surface. Using feeler gauges, determine the clearance at the center of the straightedge and across the cylinder head at several points. Check along the centerline and diagonally on the head surface. If the warpage exceeds 0.003 in. (0.076mm) within a 6.0 in. (15.2cm) span, or 0.006 in. (0.152mm) over the total length of

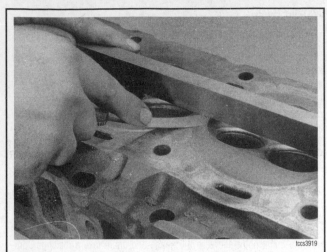

Check the head for flatness across the center of the head surface using a straightedge and feeler gauge

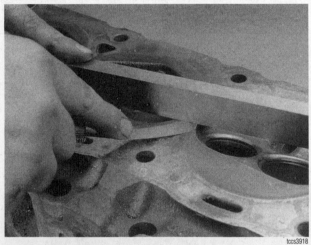

Checks should also be made along both diagonals of the head surface

the head, the cylinder head must be resurfaced. After resurfacing the heads of a V-type engine, the intake manifold flange surface should be checked, and if necessary, milled proportionally to allow for the change in its mounting position.

CRACKS AND PHYSICAL DAMAGE

Generally, cracks are limited to the combustion chamber, however, it is not uncommon for the head to crack in a spark plug hole, port, outside of the head or in the valve spring/rocker arm area. The first area to inspect is always the hottest: the exhaust seat/port area.

A visual inspection should be performed, but just because you don't see a crack does not mean it is not there. Some more reliable methods for inspecting for cracks include Magnaflux®, a magnetic process or Zyglo®, a dye penetrant. Magnaflux® is used only on ferrous metal (cast iron) heads. Zyglo® uses a spray on fluorescent mixture along with a black light to reveal the cracks. It is strongly recommended to have your cylinder head checked professionally for cracks, especially if the engine was known to have overheated and/or leaked or consumed coolant. Contact a local shop for availability and pricing of these services.

Physical damage is usually very evident. For example, a broken mount-

ing ear from dropping the head or a bent or broken stud and/or bolt. All of these defects should be fixed or, if unrepairable, the head should be replaced.

Camshaft and Followers

Inspect the camshaft(s) and followers as described earlier in this section.

REFINISHING & REPAIRING

Many of the procedures given for refinishing and repairing the cylinder head components must be performed by a machine shop. Certain steps, if the inspected part is not worn, can be performed yourself inexpensively. However, you spent a lot of time and effort so far, why risk trying to save a couple bucks if you might have to do it all over again?

Valves

Any valves that were not replaced should be refaced and the tips ground flat. Unless you have access to a valve grinding machine, this should be done by a machine shop. If the valves are in extremely good condition, as well as the valve seats and guides, they may be lapped in without performing machine work.

It is a recommended practice to lap the valves even after machine work has been performed and/or new valves have been purchased. This insures a positive seal between the valve and seat.

LAPPING THE VALVES

➡ **Before lapping the valves to the seats, read the rest of the cylinder head section to insure that any related parts are in acceptable enough condition to continue.**

➡ **Before any valve seat machining and/or lapping can be performed, the guides must be within factory recommended specifications.**

1. Invert the cylinder head.
2. Lightly lubricate the valve stems and insert them into the cylinder head in their numbered order.
3. Raise the valve from the seat and apply a small amount of fine lapping compound to the seat.
4. Moisten the suction head of a hand-lapping tool and attach it to the head of the valve.
5. Rotate the tool between the palms of both hands, changing the position of the valve on the valve seat and lifting the tool often to prevent grooving.
6. Lap the valve until a smooth, polished circle is evident on the valve and seat.
7. Remove the tool and the valve. Wipe away all traces of the grinding compound and store the valve to maintain its lapped location.

✳✳ WARNING

Do not get the valves out of order after they have been lapped. They must be put back with the same valve seat they were lapped with.

Springs, Retainers and Valve Locks

There is no repair or refinishing possible with the springs, retainers and valve locks. If they are found to be worn or defective, they must be replaced with new (or known good) parts.

Cylinder Head

Most refinishing procedures dealing with the cylinder head must be performed by a machine shop. Read the sections below and review your inspection data to determine whether or not machining is necessary.

VALVE GUIDE

➡If any machining or replacements are made to the valve guides, the seats must be machined.

Unless the valve guides need machining or replacing, the only service to perform is to thoroughly clean them of any dirt or oil residue.

There are only two types of valve guides used on automobile engines: the replaceable-type (all aluminum heads) and the cast-in integral-type (most cast iron heads). There are four recommended methods for repairing worn guides.

• Knurling
• Inserts
• Reaming oversize
• Replacing

Knurling is a process in which metal is displaced and raised, thereby reducing clearance, giving a true center, and providing oil control. It is the least expensive way of repairing the valve guides. However, it is not necessarily the best, and in some cases, a knurled valve guide will not stand up for more than a short time. It requires a special knurlizer and precision reaming tools to obtain proper clearances. It would not be cost effective to purchase these tools, unless you plan on rebuilding several of the same cylinder head.

Installing a guide insert involves machining the guide to accept a bronze insert. One style is the coil-type which is installed into a threaded guide. Another is the thin-walled insert where the guide is reamed oversize to accept a split-sleeve insert. After the insert is installed, a special tool is then run through the guide to expand the insert, locking it to the guide. The insert is then reamed to the standard size for proper valve clearance.

Reaming for oversize valves restores normal clearances and provides a true valve seat. Most cast-in type guides can be reamed to accept an valve with an oversize stem. The cost factor for this can become quite high as you will need to purchase the reamer and new, oversize stem valves for all guides which were reamed. Oversizes are generally 0.003 to 0.030 in. (0.076 to 0.762mm), with 0.015 in. (0.381mm) being the most common.

To replace cast-in type valve guides, they must be drilled out, then reamed to accept replacement guides. This must be done on a fixture which will allow centering and leveling off of the original valve seat or guide, otherwise a serious guide-to-seat misalignment may occur making it impossible to properly machine the seat.

Replaceable-type guides are pressed into the cylinder head. A hammer and a stepped drift or punch may be used to install and remove the guides. Before removing the guides, measure the protrusion on the spring side of the head and record it for installation. Use the stepped drift to hammer out the old guide from the combustion chamber side of the head. When installing, determine whether or not the guide also seals a water jacket in the head, and if it does, use the recommended sealing agent. If there is no water jacket, grease the valve guide and its bore. Use the stepped drift, and hammer the new guide into the cylinder head from the spring side of the cylinder head. A stack of washers the same thickness as the measured protrusion may help the installation process.

VALVE SEATS

➡Before any valve seat machining can be performed, the guides must be within factory recommended specifications.

➡If any machining or replacements were made to the valve guides, the seats must be machined.

If the seats are in good condition, the valves can be lapped to the seats, and the cylinder head assembled. See the valves section for instructions on lapping.

If the valve seats are worn, cracked or damaged, they must be serviced by a machine shop. The valve seat must be perfectly centered to the valve guide, which requires very accurate machining.

CYLINDER HEAD SURFACE

If the cylinder head is warped, it must be machined flat. If the warpage is extremely severe, the head may need to be replaced. In some instances, it may be possible to straighten a warped head enough to allow machining. In either case, contact a professional machine shop for service.

➡Any OHC cylinder head that shows excessive warpage should have the camshaft bearing journals align bored after the cylinder head has been resurfaced.

✲✲ WARNING

Failure to align bore the camshaft bearing journals could result in severe engine damage including, but not limited to valve and piston damage, connecting rod damage, camshaft and/or crankshaft breakage.

CRACKS AND PHYSICAL DAMAGE

Certain cracks can be repaired in both cast iron and aluminum heads. For cast iron, a tapered threaded insert is installed along the length of the crack. Aluminum can also use the tapered inserts, however welding is the preferred method. Some physical damage can be repaired through brazing or welding. Contact a machine shop to get expert advice for your particular dilemma.

ASSEMBLY

The first step for any assembly job is to have a clean area in which to work. Next, thoroughly clean all of the parts and components that are to be assembled. Finally, place all of the components onto a suitable work space and, if necessary, arrange the parts to their respective positions.

OHC Engines

CUP TYPE CAMSHAFT FOLLOWERS

To install the springs, retainers and valve locks on heads which have these components recessed into the camshaft follower's bore, you will need a small screwdriver-type tool, some clean white grease and a lot of patience. You will also need the C-clamp style spring compressor and the OHC tool used to disassemble the head.

1. Lightly lubricate the valve stems and insert all of the valves into the cylinder head. If possible, maintain their original locations.

2. If equipped, install any valve spring shims which were removed.

3. If equipped, install the new valve seals, keeping the following in mind:

• If the valve seal presses over the guide, lightly lubricate the outer guide surfaces.

• If the seal is an O-ring type, it is installed just after compressing the spring but before the valve locks.

4. Place the valve spring and retainer over the stem.

5. Position the spring compressor and the OHC tool, then compress the spring.

6. Using a small screwdriver as a spatula, fill the valve stem side of the lock with white grease. Use the excess grease on the screwdriver to fasten the lock to the driver.

7. Carefully install the valve lock, which is stuck to the end of the screwdriver, to the valve stem then press on it with the screwdriver until the grease squeezes out. The valve lock should now be stuck to the stem.

8. Repeat Steps 6 and 7 for the remaining valve lock.

9. Relieve the spring pressure slowly and insure that neither valve lock becomes dislodged by the retainer.

10. Remove the spring compressor tool.

11. Repeat Steps 2 through 10 until all of the springs have been installed.

12. Install the followers, camshaft(s) and any other components that were removed for disassembly.

ROCKER ARM TYPE CAMSHAFT FOLLOWERS

1. Lightly lubricate the valve stems and insert all of the valves into the cylinder head. If possible, maintain their original locations.

2. If equipped, install any valve spring shims which were removed.

3. If equipped, install the new valve seals, keeping the following in mind:
  • If the valve seal presses over the guide, lightly lubricate the outer guide surfaces.
  • If the seal is an O-ring type, it is installed just after compressing the spring but before the valve locks.

4. Place the valve spring and retainer over the stem.

5. Position the spring compressor tool and compress the spring.

6. Assemble the valve locks to the stem.

7. Relieve the spring pressure slowly and insure that neither valve lock becomes dislodged by the retainer.

8. Remove the spring compressor tool.

9. Repeat Steps 2 through 8 until all of the springs have been installed.

10. Install the camshaft(s), rockers, shafts and any other components that were removed for disassembly.

Once assembled, check the valve clearance and correct as needed

Engine Block

GENERAL INFORMATION

A thorough overhaul or rebuild of an engine block would include replacing the pistons, rings, bearings, timing belt/chain assembly and oil pump. For OHV engines also include a new camshaft and lifters. The block would then have the cylinders bored and honed oversize (or if using removable cylinder sleeves, new sleeves installed) and the crankshaft would be cut undersize to provide new wearing surfaces and perfect clearances. However, your particular engine may not have everything worn out. What if only the piston rings have worn out and the clearances on everything else are still within factory specifications? Well, you could just replace the rings and put it back together, but this would be a very rare example. Chances are, if one component in your engine is worn, other components are sure to follow, and soon. At the very least, you should always replace the rings, bearings and oil pump. This is what is commonly called a "freshen up".

Cylinder Ridge Removal

Because the top piston ring does not travel to the very top of the cylinder, a ridge is built up between the end of the travel and the top of the cylinder bore.

Pushing the piston and connecting rod assembly past the ridge can be difficult, and damage to the piston ring lands could occur. If the ridge is not removed before installing a new piston or not removed at all, piston ring breakage and piston damage may occur.

➡ It is always recommended that you remove any cylinder ridges before removing the piston and connecting rod assemblies. If you know that new pistons are going to be installed and the engine block will be bored oversize, you may be able to forego this step. However, some ridges may actually prevent the assemblies from being removed, necessitating its removal.

There are several different types of ridge reamers on the market, none of which are inexpensive. Unless a great deal of engine rebuilding is anticipated, borrow or rent a reamer.

1. Turn the crankshaft until the piston is at the bottom of its travel.

2. Cover the head of the piston with a rag.

3. Follow the tool manufacturers instructions and cut away the ridge, exercising extreme care to avoid cutting too deeply.

4. Remove the ridge reamer, the rag and as many of the cuttings as possible. Continue until all of the cylinder ridges have been removed.

DISASSEMBLY

The engine disassembly instructions following assume that you have the engine mounted on an engine stand. If not, it is easiest to disassemble the engine on a bench or the floor with it resting on the bellhousing or transmission mounting surface. You must be able to access the connecting rod fasteners and turn the crankshaft during disassembly. Also, all engine covers (timing, front, side, oil pan, whatever) should have already been removed. Engines which are seized or locked up may not be able to be completely disassembled, and a core (salvage yard) engine should be purchased.

If not done during the cylinder head removal, remove the timing chain/belt and/or gear/sprocket assembly. Remove the oil pick-up and pump assembly and, if necessary, the pump drive. If equipped, remove any balance or auxiliary shafts. If necessary, remove the cylinder ridge from the top of the bore. See the cylinder ridge removal procedure earlier in this section.

Place rubber hose over the connecting rod studs to protect the crankshaft and cylinder bores from damage

Rotate the engine so that the crankshaft is exposed. Use a number punch or scribe and mark each connecting rod with its respective cylinder number. The cylinder closest to the front of the engine is always number 1. However, depending on the engine placement, the front of the engine could either be the flywheel or damper/pulley end. Generally the front of the engine faces the front of the vehicle. Use a number punch or scribe and also mark the main bearing caps from front to rear with the front most cap being number 1 (if there are five caps, mark them 1 through 5, front to rear).

✳✳ WARNING

Take special care when pushing the connecting rod up from the crankshaft because the sharp threads of the rod bolts/studs will score the crankshaft journal. Insure that special plastic caps are installed over them, or cut two pieces of rubber hose to do the same.

Again, rotate the engine, this time to position the number one cylinder bore (head surface) up. Turn the crankshaft until the number one piston is at the bottom of its travel, this should allow the maximum access to its connecting rod. Remove the number one connecting rods fasteners and cap and place two lengths of rubber hose over the rod bolts/studs to protect the crankshaft from damage. Using a sturdy wooden dowel and a hammer, push the connecting rod up about 1 in. (25mm) from the crankshaft and remove the upper bearing insert. Continue pushing or tapping the connecting rod up until the piston rings are out of the cylinder bore. Remove the piston and rod by hand, put the upper half of the bearing insert back into the rod, install the cap with its bearing insert installed, and hand-tighten the cap fasteners. If the parts are kept in order in this man-

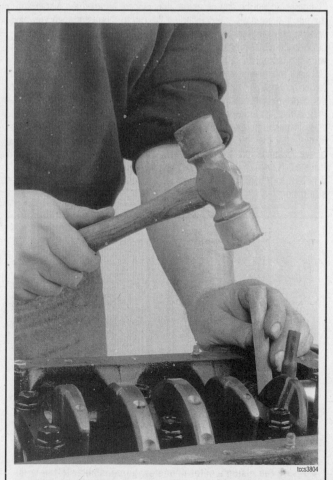

tccs3804

Carefully tap the piston out of the bore using a wooden dowel

ner, they will not get lost and you will be able to tell which bearings came form what cylinder if any problems are discovered and diagnosis is necessary. Remove all the other piston assemblies in the same manner. On V-style engines, remove all of the pistons from one bank, then reposition the engine with the other cylinder bank head surface up, and remove that banks piston assemblies.

The only remaining component in the engine block should now be the crankshaft. Loosen the main bearing caps evenly until the fasteners can be turned by hand, then remove them and the caps. Remove the crankshaft from the engine block. Thoroughly clean all of the components.

INSPECTION

Now that the engine block and all of its components are clean, it's time to inspect them for wear and/or damage. To accurately inspect them, you will need some specialized tools:

• Two or three separate micrometers to measure the pistons and crankshaft journals
• A dial indicator
• Telescoping gauges for the cylinder bores
• A rod alignment fixture to check for bent connecting rods

If you do not have access to the proper tools, you may want to bring the components to a shop that does.

Generally, you shouldn't expect cracks in the engine block or its components unless it was known to leak, consume or mix engine fluids, it was severely overheated, or there was evidence of bad bearings and/or crankshaft damage. A visual inspection should be performed on all of the components, but just because you don't see a crack does not mean it is not there. Some more reliable methods for inspecting for cracks include Magnaflux®, a magnetic process or Zyglo®, a dye penetrant. Magnaflux® is used only on ferrous metal (cast iron). Zyglo® uses a spray on fluorescent mixture along with a black light to reveal the cracks. It is strongly recommended to have your engine block checked professionally for cracks, especially if the engine was known to have overheated and/or leaked or consumed coolant. Contact a local shop for availability and pricing of these services.

Engine Block

ENGINE BLOCK BEARING ALIGNMENT

Remove the main bearing caps and, if still installed, the main bearing inserts. Inspect all of the main bearing saddles and caps for damage, burrs or high spots. If damage is found, and it is caused from a spun main bearing, the block will need to be align-bored or, if severe enough, replacement. Any burrs or high spots should be carefully removed with a metal file.

Place a straightedge on the bearing saddles, in the engine block, along the centerline of the crankshaft. If any clearance exists between the straightedge and the saddles, the block must be align-bored.

Align-boring consists of machining the main bearing saddles and caps by means of a flycutter that runs through the bearing saddles.

DECK FLATNESS

The top of the engine block where the cylinder head mounts is called the deck. Insure that the deck surface is clean of dirt, carbon deposits and old gasket material. Place a straightedge across the surface of the deck along its centerline and, using feeler gauges, check the clearance along several points. Repeat the checking procedure with the straightedge placed along both diagonals of the deck surface. If the reading exceeds 0.003 in. (0.076mm) within a 6.0 in. (15.2cm) span, or 0.006 in. (0.152mm) over the total length of the deck, it must be machined.

CYLINDER BORES

The cylinder bores house the pistons and are slightly larger than the pistons themselves. A common piston-to-bore clearance is 0.0015–0.0025 in. (0.0381mm–0.0635mm). Inspect and measure the cylinder bores. The bore should be checked for out-of-roundness, taper and size.

tccs3209

Use a telescoping gauge to measure the cylinder bore diameter—take several readings within the same bore

The results of this inspection will determine whether the cylinder can be used in its existing size and condition, or a rebore to the next oversize is required (or in the case of removable sleeves, have replacements installed).

The amount of cylinder wall wear is always greater at the top of the cylinder than at the bottom. This wear is known as taper. Any cylinder that has a taper of 0.0012 in. (0.305mm) or more, must be rebored. Measurements are taken at a number of positions in each cylinder: at the top, middle and bottom and at two points at each position; that is, at a point 90 degrees from the crankshaft centerline, as well as a point parallel to the crankshaft centerline. The measurements are made with either a special dial indicator or a telescopic gauge and micrometer. If the necessary precision tools to check the bore are not available, take the block to a machine shop and have them mike it. Also if you don't have the tools to check the cylinder bores, chances are you will not have the necessary devices to check the pistons, connecting rods and crankshaft. Take these components with you and save yourself an extra trip.

For our procedures, we will use a telescopic gauge and a micrometer. You will need one of each, with a measuring range which covers your cylinder bore size.

1. Position the telescopic gauge in the cylinder bore, loosen the gauges lock and allow it to expand.

➡**Your first two readings will be at the top of the cylinder bore, then proceed to the middle and finally the bottom, making a total of six measurements.**

2. Hold the gauge square in the bore, 90 degrees from the crankshaft centerline, and gently tighten the lock. Tilt the gauge back to remove it from the bore.

3. Measure the gauge with the micrometer and record the reading.

4. Again, hold the gauge square in the bore, this time parallel to the crankshaft centerline, and gently tighten the lock. Again, you will tilt the gauge back to remove it from the bore.

5. Measure the gauge with the micrometer and record this reading. The difference between these two readings is the out-of-round measurement of the cylinder.

6. Repeat steps 1 through 5, each time going to the next lower position, until you reach the bottom of the cylinder. Then go to the next cylinder, and continue until all of the cylinders have been measured.

The difference between these measurements will tell you all about the wear in your cylinders. The measurements which were taken 90 degrees from the crankshaft centerline will always reflect the most wear. That is because at this position is where the engine power presses the piston against the cylinder bore the hardest. This is known as thrust wear. Take your top, 90 degree measurement and compare it to your bottom, 90 de-

gree measurement. The difference between them is the taper. When you measure your pistons, you will compare these readings to your piston sizes and determine piston-to-wall clearance.

Crankshaft

Inspect the crankshaft for visible signs of wear or damage. All of the journals should be perfectly round and smooth. Slight scores are normal for a used crankshaft, but you should hardly feel them with your fingernail. When measuring the crankshaft with a micrometer, you will take readings at the front and rear of each journal, then turn the micrometer 90 degrees and take two more readings, front and rear. The difference between the front-to-rear readings is the journal taper and the first-to-90 degree reading is the out-of-round measurement. Generally, there should be no taper or out-of-roundness found, however, up to 0.0005 in. (0.0127mm) for either can be overlooked. Also, the readings should fall within the factory specifications for journal diameters.

If the crankshaft journals fall within specifications, it is recommended that it be polished before being returned to service. Polishing the crankshaft insures that any minor burrs or high spots are smoothed, thereby reducing the chance of scoring the new bearings.

Pistons and Connecting Rods

PISTONS

The piston should be visually inspected for any signs of cracking or burning (caused by hot spots or detonation), and scuffing or excessive wear on the skirts. The wristpin attaches the piston to the connecting rod. The piston should move freely on the wrist pin, both sliding and pivoting. Grasp the connecting rod securely, or mount it in a vise, and try to rock the piston back and forth along the centerline of the wristpin. There should not be any excessive play evident between the piston and the pin. If there are C-clips retaining the pin in the piston then you have wrist pin bushings in the rods. There should not be any excessive play between the wrist pin and the rod bushing. Normal clearance for the wrist pin is approx. 0.001–0.002 in. (0.025mm–0.051mm).

Use a micrometer and measure the diameter of the piston, perpendicular to the wrist pin, on the skirt. Compare the reading to its original cylinder measurement obtained earlier. The difference between the two readings is the piston-to-wall clearance. If the clearance is within specifications, the piston may be used as is. If the piston is out of specification, but the bore is not, you will need a new piston. If both are out of specification, you will need the cylinder rebored and oversize pistons installed. Generally if two or more pistons/bores are out of specification, it is best to rebore the entire block and purchase a complete set of oversize pistons.

tccs3210

Measure the piston's outer diameter, perpendicular to the wrist pin, with a micrometer

CONNECTING ROD

You should have the connecting rod checked for straightness at a machine shop. If the connecting rod is bent, it will unevenly wear the bearing and piston, as well as place greater stress on these components. Any bent or twisted connecting rods must be replaced. If the rods are straight and the wrist pin clearance is within specifications, then only the bearing end of the rod need be checked. Place the connecting rod into a vise, with the bearing inserts in place, install the cap to the rod and torque the fasteners to specifications. Use a telescoping gauge and carefully measure the inside diameter of the bearings. Compare this reading to the rods original crankshaft journal diameter measurement. The difference is the oil clearance. If the oil clearance is not within specifications, install new bearings in the rod and take another measurement. If the clearance is still out of specifications, and the crankshaft is not, the rod will need to be reconditioned by a machine shop.

➡You can also use Plastigage® to check the bearing clearances. The assembling section has complete instructions on its use.

Camshaft

Inspect the camshaft and lifters/followers as described earlier in this section.

Bearings

All of the engine bearings should be visually inspected for wear and/or damage. The bearing should look evenly worn all around with no deep scores or pits. If the bearing is severely worn, scored, pitted or heat blued, then the bearing, and the components that use it, should be brought to a machine shop for inspection. Full-circle bearings (used on most camshafts, auxiliary shafts, balance shafts, etc.) require specialized tools for removal and installation, and should be brought to a machine shop for service.

Oil Pump

➡The oil pump is responsible for providing constant lubrication to the whole engine and so it is recommended that a new oil pump be installed when rebuilding the engine.

Completely disassemble the oil pump and thoroughly clean all of the components. Inspect the oil pump gears and housing for wear and/or damage. Insure that the pressure relief valve operates properly and there is no binding or sticking due to varnish or debris. If all of the parts are in proper working condition, lubricate the gears and relief valve, and assemble the pump.

REFINISHING

Almost all engine block refinishing must be performed by a machine shop. If the cylinders are not to be rebored, then the cylinder glaze can be removed with a ball hone. When removing cylinder glaze with a ball hone, use a light or penetrating type oil to lubricate the hone. Do not allow the hone to run dry as this may cause excessive scoring of the cylinder bores and wear on the hone. If new pistons are required, they will need to be installed to the connecting rods. This should be performed by a machine shop as the pistons must be installed in the correct relationship to the rod or engine damage can occur.

Pistons and Connecting Rods

Only pistons with the wrist pin retained by C-clips are serviceable by the home-mechanic. Press fit pistons require special presses and/or heaters to remove/install the connecting rod and should only be performed by a machine shop.

All pistons will have a mark indicating the direction to the front of the engine and the must be installed into the engine in that manner. Usually it is a notch or arrow on the top of the piston, or it may be the letter F cast or stamped into the piston.

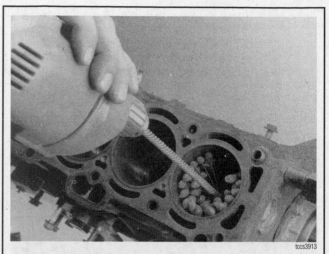
Use a ball type cylinder hone to remove any glaze and provide a new surface for seating the piston rings

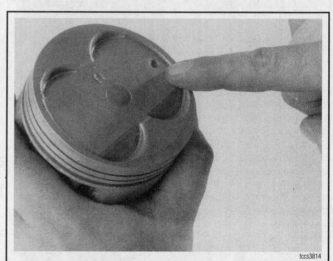
Most pistons are marked to indicate positioning in the engine (usually a mark means the side facing the front)

ASSEMBLY

Before you begin assembling the engine, first give yourself a clean, dirt free work area. Next, clean every engine component again. The key to a good assembly is cleanliness.

Mount the engine block into the engine stand and wash it one last time using water and detergent (dishwashing detergent works well). While washing it, scrub the cylinder bores with a soft bristle brush and thoroughly clean all of the oil passages. Completely dry the engine and spray the entire assembly down with an anti-rust solution such as WD-40® or similar product. Take a clean lint-free rag and wipe up any excess anti-rust solution from the bores, bearing saddles, etc. Repeat the final cleaning process on the crankshaft. Replace any freeze or oil galley plugs which were removed during disassembly.

Crankshaft

1. Remove the main bearing inserts from the block and bearing caps.
2. If the crankshaft main bearing journals have been refinished to a definite undersize, install the correct undersize bearing. Be sure that the bearing inserts and bearing bores are clean. Foreign material under inserts will distort bearing and cause failure.
3. Place the upper main bearing inserts in bores with tang in slot.

➡The oil holes in the bearing inserts must be aligned with the oil holes in the cylinder block.

    4. Install the lower main bearing inserts in bearing caps.

    5. Clean the mating surfaces of block and rear main bearing cap.

    6. Carefully lower the crankshaft into place. Be careful not to damage bearing surfaces.

    7. Check the clearance of each main bearing by using the following procedure:

      a. Place a piece of Plastigage® or its equivalent, on bearing surface across full width of bearing cap and about ¼ in. off center.

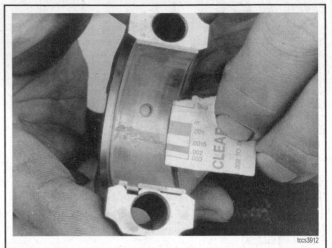

After the cap is removed again, use the scale supplied with the gauging material to check the clearance

Apply a strip of gauging material to the bearing journal, then install and torque the cap

      b. Install cap and tighten bolts to specifications. Do not turn crankshaft while Plastigage® is in place.

      c. Remove the cap. Using the supplied Plastigage® scale, check width of Plastigage® at widest point to get maximum clearance. Difference between readings is taper of journal.

      d. If clearance exceeds specified limits, try a 0.001 in. or 0.002 in.

undersize bearing in combination with the standard bearing. Bearing clearance must be within specified limits. If standard and 0.002 in. undersize bearing does not bring clearance within desired limits, refinish crankshaft journal, then install undersize bearings.

    8. After the bearings have been fitted, apply a light coat of engine oil to the journals and bearings. Install the rear main bearing cap. Install all bearing caps except the thrust bearing cap. Be sure that main bearing caps are installed in original locations. Tighten the bearing cap bolts to specifications.

    9. Install the thrust bearing cap with bolts finger-tight.

    10. Pry the crankshaft forward against the thrust surface of upper half of bearing.

    11. Hold the crankshaft forward and pry the thrust bearing cap to the rear. This aligns the thrust surfaces of both halves of the bearing.

    12. Retain the forward pressure on the crankshaft. Tighten the cap bolts to specifications.

    13. Measure the crankshaft end-play as follows:

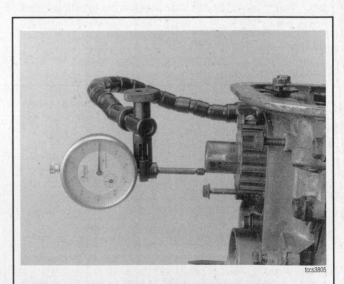

A dial gauge may be used to check crankshaft end-play

a. Mount a dial gauge to the engine block and position the tip of the gauge to read from the crankshaft end.

b. Carefully pry the crankshaft toward the rear of the engine and hold it there while you zero the gauge.

c. Carefully pry the crankshaft toward the front of the engine and read the gauge.

Carefully pry the crankshaft back and forth while reading the dial gauge for end-play

d. Confirm that the reading is within specifications. If not, install a new thrust bearing and repeat the procedure. If the reading is still out of specifications with a new bearing, have a machine shop inspect the thrust surfaces of the crankshaft, and if possible, repair it.

14. Rotate the crankshaft so as to position the first rod journal to the bottom of its stroke.

15. Install the rear main seal.

Pistons and Connecting Rods

1. Before installing the piston/connecting rod assembly, oil the pistons, piston rings and the cylinder walls with light engine oil. Install connecting rod bolt protectors or rubber hose onto the connecting rod bolts/studs. Also perform the following:

a. Select the proper ring set for the size cylinder bore.

b. Position the ring in the bore in which it is going to be used.

c. Push the ring down into the bore area where normal ring wear is not encountered.

d. Use the head of the piston to position the ring in the bore so that the ring is square with the cylinder wall. Use caution to avoid damage to the ring or cylinder bore.

e. Measure the gap between the ends of the ring with a feeler gauge. Ring gap in a worn cylinder is normally greater than specification. If the ring gap is greater than the specified limits, try an oversize ring set.

f. Check the ring side clearance of the compression rings with a feeler gauge inserted between the ring and its lower land according to specification. The gauge should slide freely around the entire ring circumference without binding. Any wear that occurs will form a step at the inner portion of the lower land. If the lower lands have high steps, the piston should be replaced.

2. Unless new pistons are installed, be sure to install the pistons in the cylinders from which they were removed. The numbers on the connecting rod and bearing cap must be on the same side when installed in the cylinder bore. If a connecting rod is ever transposed from one en-

Checking the piston ring-to-ring groove side clearance using the ring and a feeler gauge

The notch on the side of the bearing cap matches the tang on the bearing insert

gine or cylinder to another, new bearings should be fitted and the connecting rod should be numbered to correspond with the new cylinder number. The notch on the piston head goes toward the front of the engine.

3. Install all of the rod bearing inserts into the rods and caps.

4. Install the rings to the pistons. Install the oil control ring first, then the second compression ring and finally the top compression ring.

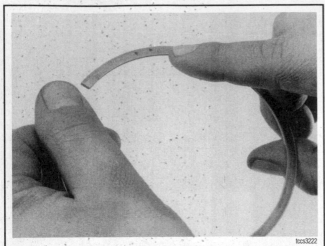

Most rings are marked to show which side of the ring should face up when installed to the piston

Install the piston and rod assembly into the block using a ring compressor and the handle of a hammer

Use a piston ring expander tool to aid in installation and to help reduce the chance of breakage.

5. Make sure the ring gaps are properly spaced around the circumference of the piston. Fit a piston ring compressor around the piston and slide the piston and connecting rod assembly down into the cylinder bore, pushing it in with the wooden hammer handle. Push the piston down until it is only slightly below the top of the cylinder bore. Guide the connecting rod onto the crankshaft bearing journal carefully, to avoid damaging the crankshaft.

6. Check the bearing clearance of all the rod bearings, fitting them to the crankshaft bearing journals. Follow the procedure in the crankshaft installation above.

7. After the bearings have been fitted, apply a light coating of assembly oil to the journals and bearings.

8. Turn the crankshaft until the appropriate bearing journal is at the bottom of its stroke, then push the piston assembly all the way down until the connecting rod bearing seats on the crankshaft journal. Be careful not to allow the bearing cap screws to strike the crankshaft bearing journals and damage them.

9. After the piston and connecting rod assemblies have been installed, check the connecting rod side clearance on each crankshaft journal.

10. Prime and install the oil pump and the oil pump intake tube.

11. If equipped, install the balance shaft(s).

12. Install the cylinder head(s) using new gaskets.

13. Install the timing sprockets/gears and the belt/chain assemblies.

Install the timing cover(s) and oil pan. Refer to your notes and drawings made prior to disassembly and install all of the components that were removed. Install the engine into the vehicle.

Engine Start-up and Break-in

STARTING THE ENGINE

Now that the engine is installed and every wire and hose is properly connected, go back and double check that all coolant and vacuum hoses are connected. Check that you oil drain plug is installed and properly tightened. If not already done, install a new oil filter onto the engine. Fill the crankcase with the proper amount and grade of engine oil. Fill the cooling system with a 50/50 mixture of coolant/water.

1. Connect the vehicle battery.

2. Start the engine. Keep your eye on your oil pressure indicator; if it does not indicate oil pressure within 10 seconds of starting, turn the vehicle off.

✴✴ WARNING

Damage to the engine can result if it is allowed to run with no oil pressure. Check the engine oil level to make sure that it is full. Check for any leaks and if found, repair the leaks before continuing. If there is still no indication of oil pressure, you may need to prime the system.

3. Confirm that there are no fluid leaks (oil or other).

4. Allow the engine to reach normal operating temperature (the upper radiator hose will be hot to the touch).

5. If necessary, set the ignition timing.

6. Install any remaining components such as the air cleaner (if removed for ignition timing) or body panels which were removed.

BREAKING IT IN

Make the first miles on the new engine, easy ones. Vary the speed but do not accelerate hard. Most importantly, do not lug the engine, and avoid sustained high speeds until at least 100 miles. Check the engine oil and coolant levels frequently. Expect the engine to use a little oil until the rings seat. Change the oil and filter at 500 miles, 1500 miles, then every 3000 miles past that.

KEEP IT MAINTAINED

Now that you have just gone through all of that hard work, keep yourself from doing it all over again by thoroughly maintaining it. Not that you may not have maintained it before, heck you could have had one to two hundred thousand miles on it before doing this. However, you may have bought the vehicle used, and the previous owner did not keep up on maintenance. Which is why you just went through all of that hard work. See?

TORQUE SPECIFICATIONS

Components	Ft. Lbs.	Nm
Balance shaft sprocket	22–29	29–40
Camshaft bearing caps		
1.5L (VIN K) DOHC, 2.0L (VIN F) and 1996-98 1.8L (VIN M)	9–10	12–14
1.6L (VIN R), 1.8L (VIN M) and 2.0L (VIN P)	14–15	19–21
3.0L (VIN T)	14–15	19–21
Camshaft sprocket		
1.5L (VIN J)	47–54	64–74
1.5L (VIN E)	58–72	80–100
1.5L (VIN K)	59–73	80–100
1.5L (VIN K) DOHC, 2.0L (VIN F) and 1996-98 1.8L (VIN M)	60–74	80–100
1.6L (VIN R), 2.0L (VIN P) and 1994-95 1.8L (VIN M)	56–72	80–100
1996-98 1.8L (VIN M) and 2.0L (VIN F)	74–89	100–120
2.0L (VIN P) and 1994-95 1.8L (VIN M)	44–57	61–75
3.0L (VIN T)	58–72	80–100
Crankshaft sprocket		
1.5L (VIN E) and 1.5L (VIN J)	51–72	69–98
1.5L (VIN K)	110–118	150–160
1996-98 1.8L (VIN M) and 2.0L (VIN F)	125–133	170–180
1.6L (VIN R), 2.0L (VIN P) and 1994-95 1.8L (VIN M)	80–94	110–130
2.0L (VIN P) and 1994-95 1.8L (VIN M)	43–50	58–67
3.0L (VIN T)	108–116	150–160
Cylinder head		
1.5L (VIN E), 1.5L (VIN J) and 1.5L (VIN K)	51–54	71–75
1.6L (VIN F), 2.0L (VIN P) and 1994-95 1.8L (VIN M)	65–72	90–100
2.0L (VIN F) and 1996-98 1.8L (VIN M)	65–74	
3.0L (VIN T)	76–83	105–115
Exhaust crossover pipe	22–29	30–40
Exhaust heat shield	11–15	15–20
Exhaust manifold		
1.5L (VIN E), 1.5L (VIN J) and 1.5L (VIN K)	11–15	15–20
1.5L (VIN E) Turbo	18–25	25–35
1.6L (VIN R), 1.8L (VIN M) and 2.0L (VIN P)	18–22	25–30
1.6L (VIN R), 2.0L (VIN P) and 1994-95 1.8L (VIN M)	18–22	25–30
2.0L (VIN F) and 1996-98 1.8L (VIN M)	32–41	43–50
3.0L (VIN T)	11–16	15–22
Exhaust pipe	22–29	30–40
Front case	8–11	12–15
Idler pulley	32–41	43–55
Intake manifold	11–14	15–20
Intake manifold stay	13–18	18–25
Oil pan		
Except 1.5L (VIN E)	4–6	6–8
1.5L (VIN E)	11–16	15–22
Oil pan drain plug	25–33	35–45
Oil pump		
1.5L (VIN E) and 1.5L (VIN J)	6–8	8–12
Except 1.5L (VIN E) and 1.5L (VIN J)	4–6	6–9
Oil pump cover	11–13	15–18

89533C11

TORQUE SPECIFICATIONS

Components	Ft. Lbs.	Nm
Oil pump drive gear		
1.6L (VIN R), 2.0L (VIN P) and 1994-95 1.8L (VIN M)	36–43	50–60
2.0L (VIN P), 1994-95 1.6L (VIN R) and 1.8L (VIN M)	25–29	34–40
Oil pump sprocket	25–28	34–39
Oxygen sensor	29–36	30–40
Rear main oil seal case	7–9	8–10
Relief valve spring plug	30–36	39–49
Rocker cover		
1.5L (VIN E), 1.5L (VIN J) and 1.5L (VIN K)	1.0–1.5	1.5–2.0
1.6L (VIN R), 1.8L (VIN M), 2.0L (VIN F) and 2.0L(VIN P)	6–7	8–10
2.0L (VIN P)	2–3	3–4
3.0L (VIN T)	6–7	8–10
Rocker center cover	6–7	8–10
Rocker shaft	14–20	20–26
Surge tank	11–14	15–20
Tensioner bolts		
Except 1996-98 1.8L (VIN M) and 2.0L (VIN F)	15–18	20–26
1996-98 1.8L (VIN M) and 2.0L (VIN F)	32–41	43–55
Thermostat housing	12–14	17–20
Throttle body	11–16	15–22
Timing belt cover	7–8	10–12
Turbocharger	18–25	25–35
Turbocharger discharge pipe	18–25	25–35
Water pump		
Except 2.0L (VIN F), 3.0L (VIN T) and 1996-98 1.8L (VIN M)	9–11	12–15
2.0L (VIN F), 3.0L (VIN T) and 1996-98 1.8L (VIN M)	14–20	20–27
Water pump pulley	6–7	8–10

Tighten M10 bolts to 22 ft. lbs. (30 Nm), plus 60°-65°, plus 60°-65°

Tighten M12 bolts to 26 ft. lbs.(35 Nm), plus 60°-65°, plus 60°-65°

89533c12

USING A VACUUM GAUGE

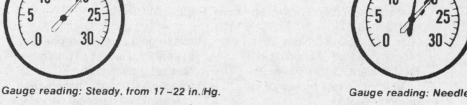

White needle = steady needle   *Dark needle = drifting needle*

The vacuum gauge is one of the most useful and easy-to-use diagnostic tools. It is inexpensive, easy to hook up, and provides valuable information about the condition of your engine.

Indication: Normal engine in good condition

Gauge reading: Steady, from 17–22 in./Hg.

Indication: Sticking valve or ignition miss

Gauge reading: Needle fluctuates from 15–20 in./Hg. at idle

Indication: Late ignition or valve timing, low compression, stuck throttle valve, leaking carburetor or manifold gasket.

Gauge reading: Low (15–20 in./Hg.) but steady

Indication: Improper carburetor adjustment, or minor intake leak at carburetor or manifold

NOTE: Bad fuel injector O-rings may also cause this reading.

Gauge reading: Drifting needle

Indication: Weak valve springs, worn valve stem guides, or leaky cylinder head gasket (vibrating excessively at all speeds).

NOTE: A plugged catalytic converter may also cause this reading.

Gauge reading: Needle fluctuates as engine speed increases

Indication: Burnt valve or improper valve clearance. The needle will drop when the defective valve operates.

Gauge reading: Steady needle, but drops regularly

Indication: Choked muffler or obstruction in system. Speed up the engine. Choked muffler will exhibit a slow drop of vacuum to zero.

Gauge reading: Gradual drop in reading at idle

Indication: Worn valve guides

Gauge reading: Needle vibrates excessively at idle, but steadies as engine speed increases

tccs3c01

Troubleshooting Engine Mechanical Problems

Problem	Cause	Solution
External oil leaks	• Cylinder head cover RTV sealant broken or improperly seated	• Replace sealant; inspect cylinder head cover sealant flange and cylinder head sealant surface for distortion and cracks
	• Oil filler cap leaking or missing	• Replace cap
	• Oil filter gasket broken or improperly seated	• Replace oil filter
	• Oil pan side gasket broken, improperly seated or opening in RTV sealant	• Replace gasket or repair opening in sealant; inspect oil pan gasket flange for distortion
	• Oil pan front oil seal broken or improperly seated	• Replace seal; inspect timing case cover and oil pan seal flange for distortion
	• Oil pan rear oil seal broken or improperly seated	• Replace seal; inspect oil pan rear oil seal flange; inspect rear main bearing cap for cracks, plugged oil return channels, or distortion in seal groove
	• Timing case cover oil seal broken or improperly seated	• Replace seal
	• Excess oil pressure because of restricted PCV valve	• Replace PCV valve
	• Oil pan drain plug loose or has stripped threads	• Repair as necessary and tighten
	• Rear oil gallery plug loose	• Use appropriate sealant on gallery plug and tighten
	• Rear camshaft plug loose or improperly seated	• Seat camshaft plug or replace and seal, as necessary
Excessive oil consumption	• Oil level too high	• Drain oil to specified level
	• Oil with wrong viscosity being used	• Replace with specified oil
	• PCV valve stuck closed	• Replace PCV valve
	• Valve stem oil deflectors (or seals) are damaged, missing, or incorrect type	• Replace valve stem oil deflectors
	• Valve stems or valve guides worn	• Measure stem-to-guide clearance and repair as necessary
	• Poorly fitted or missing valve cover baffles	• Replace valve cover
	• Piston rings broken or missing	• Replace broken or missing rings
	• Scuffed piston	• Replace piston
	• Incorrect piston ring gap	• Measure ring gap, repair as necessary
	• Piston rings sticking or excessively loose in grooves	• Measure ring side clearance, repair as necessary
	• Compression rings installed upside down	• Repair as necessary
	• Cylinder walls worn, scored, or glazed	• Repair as necessary

tccs3c02

Troubleshooting Engine Mechanical Problems

Problem	Cause	Solution
Excessive oil consumption (cont.)	• Piston ring gaps not properly staggered	• Repair as necessary
	• Excessive main or connecting rod bearing clearance	• Measure bearing clearance, repair as necessary
No oil pressure	• Low oil level	• Add oil to correct level
	• Oil pressure gauge, warning lamp or sending unit inaccurate	• Replace oil pressure gauge or warning lamp
	• Oil pump malfunction	• Replace oil pump
	• Oil pressure relief valve sticking	• Remove and inspect oil pressure relief valve assembly
	• Oil passages on pressure side of pump obstructed	• Inspect oil passages for obstruction
	• Oil pickup screen or tube obstructed	• Inspect oil pickup for obstruction
	• Loose oil inlet tube	• Tighten or seal inlet tube
Low oil pressure	• Low oil level	• Add oil to correct level
	• Inaccurate gauge, warning lamp or sending unit	• Replace oil pressure gauge or warning lamp
	• Oil excessively thin because of dilution, poor quality, or improper grade	• Drain and refill crankcase with recommended oil
	• Excessive oil temperature	• Correct cause of overheating engine
	• Oil pressure relief spring weak or sticking	• Remove and inspect oil pressure relief valve assembly
	• Oil inlet tube and screen assembly has restriction or air leak	• Remove and inspect oil inlet tube and screen assembly. (Fill inlet tube with lacquer thinner to locate leaks.)
	• Excessive oil pump clearance	• Measure clearances
	• Excessive main, rod, or camshaft bearing clearance	• Measure bearing clearances, repair as necessary
High oil pressure	• Improper oil viscosity	• Drain and refill crankcase with correct viscosity oil
	• Oil pressure gauge or sending unit inaccurate	• Replace oil pressure gauge
	• Oil pressure relief valve sticking closed	• Remove and inspect oil pressure relief valve assembly
Main bearing noise	• Insufficient oil supply	• Inspect for low oil level and low oil pressure
	• Main bearing clearance excessive	• Measure main bearing clearance, repair as necessary
	• Bearing insert missing	• Replace missing insert
	• Crankshaft end-play excessive	• Measure end-play, repair as necessary
	• Improperly tightened main bearing cap bolts	• Tighten bolts with specified torque
	• Loose flywheel or drive plate	• Tighten flywheel or drive plate attaching bolts
	• Loose or damaged vibration damper	• Repair as necessary

Troubleshooting Engine Mechanical Problems

Problem	Cause	Solution
Connecting rod bearing noise	• Insufficient oil supply	• Inspect for low oil level and low oil pressure
	• Carbon build-up on piston	• Remove carbon from piston crown
	• Bearing clearance excessive or bearing missing	• Measure clearance, repair as necessary
	• Crankshaft connecting rod journal out-of-round	• Measure journal dimensions, repair or replace as necessary
	• Misaligned connecting rod or cap	• Repair as necessary
	• Connecting rod bolts tightened improperly	• Tighten bolts with specified torque
Piston noise	• Piston-to-cylinder wall clearance excessive (scuffed piston)	• Measure clearance and examine piston
	• Cylinder walls excessively tapered or out-of-round	• Measure cylinder wall dimensions, rebore cylinder
	• Piston ring broken	• Replace all rings on piston
	• Loose or seized piston pin	• Measure piston-to-pin clearance, repair as necessary
	• Connecting rods misaligned	• Measure rod alignment, straighten or replace
	• Piston ring side clearance excessively loose or tight	• Measure ring side clearance, repair as necessary
	• Carbon build-up on piston is excessive	• Remove carbon from piston
Valve actuating component noise	• Insufficient oil supply	• Check for: (a) Low oil level (b) Low oil pressure (c) Wrong hydraulic tappets (d) Restricted oil gallery (e) Excessive tappet to bore clearance
	• Rocker arms or pivots worn	• Replace worn rocker arms or pivots
	• Foreign objects or chips in hydraulic tappets	• Clean tappets
	• Excessive tappet leak-down	• Replace valve tappet
	• Tappet face worn	• Replace tappet; inspect corresponding cam lobe for wear
	• Broken or cocked valve springs	• Properly seat cocked springs; replace broken springs
	• Stem-to-guide clearance excessive	• Measure stem-to-guide clearance, repair as required
	• Valve bent	• Replace valve
	• Loose rocker arms	• Check and repair as necessary
	• Valve seat runout excessive	• Regrind valve seat/valves
	• Missing valve lock	• Install valve lock
	• Excessive engine oil	• Correct oil level

tccs3c04

Troubleshooting Engine Performance

Problem	Cause	Solution
Hard starting (engine cranks normally)	• Faulty engine control system component	• Repair or replace as necessary
	• Faulty fuel pump	• Replace fuel pump
	• Faulty fuel system component	• Repair or replace as necessary
	• Faulty ignition coil	• Test and replace as necessary
	• Improper spark plug gap	• Adjust gap
	• Incorrect ignition timing	• Adjust timing
	• Incorrect valve timing	• Check valve timing; repair as necessary
Rough idle or stalling	• Incorrect curb or fast idle speed	• Adjust curb or fast idle speed (If possible)
	• Incorrect ignition timing	• Adjust timing to specification
	• Improper feedback system operation	• Refer to Chapter 4
	• Faulty EGR valve operation	• Test EGR system and replace as necessary
	• Faulty PCV valve air flow	• Test PCV valve and replace as necessary
	• Faulty TAC vacuum motor or valve	• Repair as necessary
	• Air leak into manifold vacuum	• Inspect manifold vacuum connections and repair as necessary
	• Faulty distributor rotor or cap	• Replace rotor or cap (Distributor systems only)
	• Improperly seated valves	• Test cylinder compression, repair as necessary
	• Incorrect ignition wiring	• Inspect wiring and correct as necessary
	• Faulty ignition coil	• Test coil and replace as necessary
	• Restricted air vent or idle passages	• Clean passages
	• Restricted air cleaner	• Clean or replace air cleaner filter element
Faulty low-speed operation	• Restricted idle air vents and passages	• Clean air vents and passages
	• Restricted air cleaner	• Clean or replace air cleaner filter element
	• Faulty spark plugs	• Clean or replace spark plugs
	• Dirty, corroded, or loose ignition secondary circuit wire connections	• Clean or tighten secondary circuit wire connections
	• Improper feedback system operation	• Refer to Chapter 4
	• Faulty ignition coil high voltage wire	• Replace ignition coil high voltage wire (Distributor systems only)
	• Faulty distributor cap	• Replace cap (Distributor systems only)
Faulty acceleration	• Incorrect ignition timing	• Adjust timing
	• Faulty fuel system component	• Repair or replace as necessary
	• Faulty spark plug(s)	• Clean or replace spark plug(s)
	• Improperly seated valves	• Test cylinder compression, repair as necessary
	• Faulty ignition coil	• Test coil and replace as necessary

Troubleshooting Engine Performance

Problem	Cause	Solution
Faulty acceleration (cont.)	• Improper feedback system operation	• Refer to Chapter 4
Faulty high speed operation	• Incorrect ignition timing • Faulty advance mechanism	• Adjust timing (if possible) • Check advance mechanism and repair as necessary (Distributor systems only)
	• Low fuel pump volume • Wrong spark plug air gap or wrong plug • Partially restricted exhaust manifold, exhaust pipe, catalytic converter, muffler, or tailpipe • Restricted vacuum passages • Restricted air cleaner	• Replace fuel pump • Adjust air gap or install correct plug • Eliminate restriction • Clean passages • Cleaner or replace filter element as necessary
	• Faulty distributor rotor or cap • Faulty ignition coil • Improperly seated valve(s) • Faulty valve spring(s) • Incorrect valve timing • Intake manifold restricted • Worn distributor shaft • Improper feedback system operation	• Replace rotor or cap (Distributor systems only) • Test coil and replace as necessary • Test cylinder compression, repair as necessary • Inspect and test valve spring tension, replace as necessary • Check valve timing and repair as necessary • Remove restriction or replace manifold • Replace shaft (Distributor systems only) • Refer to Chapter 4
Misfire at all speeds	• Faulty spark plug(s) • Faulty spark plug wire(s) • Faulty distributor cap or rotor • Faulty ignition coil • Primary ignition circuit shorted or open intermittently • Improperly seated valve(s) • Faulty hydraulic tappet(s) • Improper feedback system operation • Faulty valve spring(s) • Worn camshaft lobes • Air leak into manifold • Fuel pump volume or pressure low • Blown cylinder head gasket • Intake or exhaust manifold passage(s) restricted	• Clean or relace spark plug(s) • Replace as necessary • Replace cap or rotor (Distributor systems only) • Test coil and replace as necessary • Troubleshoot primary circuit and repair as necessary • Test cylinder compression, repair as necessary • Clean or replace tappet(s) • Refer to Chapter 4 • Inspect and test valve spring tension, repair as necessary • Replace camshaft • Check manifold vacuum and repair as necessary • Replace fuel pump • Replace gasket • Pass chain through passage(s) and repair as necessary
Power not up to normal	• Incorrect ignition timing • Faulty distributor rotor	• Adjust timing • Replace rotor (Distributor systems only)

Troubleshooting Engine Performance

Problem	Cause	Solution
Power not up to normal (cont.)	• Incorrect spark plug gap	• Adjust gap
	• Faulty fuel pump	• Replace fuel pump
	• Faulty fuel pump	• Replace fuel pump
	• Incorrect valve timing	• Check valve timing and repair as necessary
	• Faulty ignition coil	• Test coil and replace as necessary
	• Faulty ignition wires	• Test wires and replace as necessary
	• Improperly seated valves	• Test cylinder compression and repair as necessary
	• Blown cylinder head gasket	• Replace gasket
	• Leaking piston rings	• Test compression and repair as necessary
	• Improper feedback system operation	• Refer to Chapter 4
Intake backfire	• Improper ignition timing	• Adjust timing
	• Defective EGR component	• Repair as necessary
	• Defective TAC vacuum motor or valve	• Repair as necessary
Exhaust backfire	• Air leak into manifold vacuum	• Check manifold vacuum and repair as necessary
	• Faulty air injection diverter valve	• Test diverter valve and replace as necessary
	• Exhaust leak	• Locate and eliminate leak
Ping or spark knock	• Incorrect ignition timing	• Adjust timing
	• Distributor advance malfunction	• Inspect advance mechanism and repair as necessary (Distributor systems only)
	• Excessive combustion chamber deposits	• Remove with combustion chamber cleaner
	• Air leak into manifold vacuum	• Check manifold vacuum and repair as necessary
	• Excessively high compression	• Test compression and repair as necessary
	• Fuel octane rating excessively low	• Try alternate fuel source
	• Sharp edges in combustion chamber	• Grind smooth
	• EGR valve not functioning properly	• Test EGR system and replace as necessary
Surging (at cruising to top speeds)	• Low fuel pump pressure or volume	• Replace fuel pump
	• Improper PCV valve air flow	• Test PCV valve and replace as necessary
	• Air leak into manifold vacuum	• Check manifold vacuum and repair as necessary
	• Incorrect spark advance	• Test and replace as necessary
	• Restricted fuel filter	• Replace fuel filter
	• Restricted air cleaner	• Clean or replace air cleaner filter element
	• EGR valve not functioning properly	• Test EGR system and replace as necessary
	• Improper feedback system operation	• Refer to Chapter 4

tccs3c07

Troubleshooting the Serpentine Drive Belt

Problem	Cause	Solution
Tension sheeting fabric failure (woven fabric on outside circumference of belt has cracked or separated from body of belt)	• Grooved or backside idler pulley diameters are less than minimum recommended • Tension sheeting contacting (rubbing) stationary object • Excessive heat causing woven fabric to age • Tension sheeting splice has fractured	• Replace pulley(s) not conforming to specification • Correct rubbing condition • Replace belt • Replace belt
Noise (objectional squeal, squeak, or rumble is heard or felt while drive belt is in operation)	• Belt slippage • Bearing noise • Belt misalignment • Belt-to-pulley mismatch • Driven component inducing vibration • System resonant frequency inducing vibration	• Adjust belt • Locate and repair • Align belt/pulley(s) • Install correct belt • Locate defective driven component and repair • Vary belt tension within specifications. Replace belt.
Rib chunking (one or more ribs has separated from belt body)	• Foreign objects imbedded in pulley grooves • Installation damage • Drive loads in excess of design specifications • Insufficient internal belt adhesion	• Remove foreign objects from pulley grooves • Replace belt • Adjust belt tension • Replace belt
Rib or belt wear (belt ribs contact bottom of pulley grooves)	• Pulley(s) misaligned • Mismatch of belt and pulley groove widths • Abrasive environment • Rusted pulley(s) • Sharp or jagged pulley groove tips • Rubber deteriorated	• Align pulley(s) • Replace belt • Replace belt • Clean rust from pulley(s) • Replace pulley • Replace belt
Longitudinal belt cracking (cracks between two ribs)	• Belt has mistracked from pulley groove • Pulley groove tip has worn away rubber-to-tensile member	• Replace belt • Replace belt
Belt slips	• Belt slipping because of insufficient tension • Belt or pulley subjected to substance (belt dressing, oil, ethylene glycol) that has reduced friction • Driven component bearing failure • Belt glazed and hardened from heat and excessive slippage	• Adjust tension • Replace belt and clean pulleys • Replace faulty component bearing • Replace belt
"Groove jumping" (belt does not maintain correct position on pulley, or turns over and/or runs off pulleys)	• Insufficient belt tension • Pulley(s) not within design tolerance • Foreign object(s) in grooves	• Adjust belt tension • Replace pulley(s) • Remove foreign objects from grooves

Troubleshooting the Serpentine Drive Belt

Problem	Cause	Solution
"Groove jumping" (belt does not maintain correct position on pulley, or turns over and/or runs off pulleys)	• Excessive belt speed • Pulley misalignment • Belt-to-pulley profile mismatched • Belt cordline is distorted	• Avoid excessive engine acceleration • Align pulley(s) • Install correct belt • Replace belt
Belt broken (Note: identify and correct problem before replacement belt is installed)	• Excessive tension • Tensile members damaged during belt installation • Belt turnover • Severe pulley misalignment • Bracket, pulley, or bearing failure	• Replace belt and adjust tension to specification • Replace belt • Replace belt • Align pulley(s) • Replace defective component and belt
Cord edge failure (tensile member exposed at edges of belt or separated from belt body)	• Excessive tension • Drive pulley misalignment • Belt contacting stationary object • Pulley irregularities • Improper pulley construction • Insufficient adhesion between tensile member and rubber matrix	• Adjust belt tension • Align pulley • Correct as necessary • Replace pulley • Replace pulley • Replace belt and adjust tension to specifications
Sporadic rib cracking (multiple cracks in belt ribs at random intervals)	• Ribbed pulley(s) diameter less than minimum specification • Backside bend flat pulley(s) diameter less than minimum • Excessive heat condition causing rubber to harden • Excessive belt thickness • Belt overcured • Excessive tension	• Replace pulley(s) • Replace pulley(s) • Correct heat condition as necessary • Replace belt • Replace belt • Adjust belt tension

tccs3c10

Troubleshooting the Cooling System

Problem	Cause	Solution
High temperature gauge indication—overheating	• Coolant level low • Improper fan operation • Radiator hose(s) collapsed • Radiator airflow blocked	• Replenish coolant • Repair or replace as necessary • Replace hose(s) • Remove restriction (bug screen, fog lamps, etc.)
	• Faulty pressure cap • Ignition timing incorrect • Air trapped in cooling system • Heavy traffic driving	• Replace pressure cap • Adjust ignition timing • Purge air • Operate at fast idle in neutral intermittently to cool engine • Install proper component(s)
	• Incorrect cooling system component(s) installed • Faulty thermostat • Water pump shaft broken or impeller loose • Radiator tubes clogged • Cooling system clogged • Casting flash in cooling passages	• Replace thermostat • Replace water pump • Flush radiator • Flush system • Repair or replace as necessary. Flash may be visible by removing cooling system components or removing core plugs.
	• Brakes dragging • Excessive engine friction • Antifreeze concentration over 68% • Missing air seals • Faulty gauge or sending unit	• Repair brakes • Repair engine • Lower antifreeze concentration percentage • Replace air seals • Repair or replace faulty component
	• Loss of coolant flow caused by leakage or foaming • Viscous fan drive failed	• Repair or replace leaking component, replace coolant • Replace unit
Low temperature indication—undercooling	• Thermostat stuck open • Faulty gauge or sending unit	• Replace thermostat • Repair or replace faulty component
Coolant loss—boilover	• Overfilled cooling system • Quick shutdown after hard (hot) run • Air in system resulting in occasional ''burping'' of coolant • Insufficient antifreeze allowing coolant boiling point to be too low • Antifreeze deteriorated because of age or contamination • Leaks due to loose hose clamps, loose nuts, bolts, drain plugs, faulty hoses, or defective radiator	• Reduce coolant level to proper specification • Allow engine to run at fast idle prior to shutdown • Purge system • Add antifreeze to raise boiling point • Replace coolant • Pressure test system to locate source of leak(s) then repair as necessary

tccs3c11

4

DRIVEABILITY AND EMISSIONS CONTROLS

AIR POLLUTION

The earth's atmosphere, at or near sea level, consists approximately of 78 percent nitrogen, 21 percent oxygen and 1 percent other gases. If it were possible to remain in this state, 100 percent clean air would result. However, many varied sources allow other gases and particulates to mix with the clean air, causing our atmosphere to become unclean or polluted.

Some of these pollutants are visible while others are invisible, with each having the capability of causing distress to the eyes, ears, throat, skin and respiratory system. Should these pollutants become concentrated in a specific area and under certain conditions, death could result due to the displacement or chemical change of the oxygen content in the air. These pollutants can also cause great damage to the environment and to the many man made objects that are exposed to the elements.

To better understand the causes of air pollution, the pollutants can be categorized into 3 separate types: natural, industrial and automotive.

Natural Pollutants

Natural pollution has been present on earth since before man appeared and continues to be a factor when discussing air pollution, although it causes only a small percentage of the overall pollution problem. It is the direct result of decaying organic matter, wind born smoke and particulates from such natural events as plain and forest fires (ignited by heat or lightning), volcanic ash, sand and dust which can spread over a large area of the countryside.

Such a phenomenon of natural pollution has been seen in the form of volcanic eruptions, with the resulting plume of smoke, steam and volcanic ash blotting out the sun's rays as it spreads and rises higher into the atmosphere. As it travels into the atmosphere the upper air currents catch and carry the smoke and ash, while condensing the steam back into water vapor. As the water vapor, smoke and ash travel on their journey, the smoke dissipates into the atmosphere while the ash and moisture settle back to earth in a trail hundreds of miles long. In some cases, lives are lost and millions of dollars of property damage result.

Industrial Pollutants

Industrial pollution is caused primarily by industrial processes, the burning of coal, oil and natural gas, which in turn produce smoke and fumes. Because the burning fuels contain large amounts of sulfur, the principal ingredients of smoke and fumes are sulfur dioxide and particulate matter. This type of pollutant occurs most severely during still, damp and cool weather, such as at night. Even in its less severe form, this pollutant is not confined to just cities. Because of air movements, the pollutants move for miles over the surrounding countryside, leaving in its path a barren and unhealthy environment for all living things.

Working with Federal, State and Local mandated regulations and by carefully monitoring emissions, big business has greatly reduced the amount of pollutant introduced from its industrial sources, striving to obtain an acceptable level. Because of the mandated industrial emission clean up, many land areas and streams in and around the cities that were formerly barren of vegetation and life, have now begun to move back in the direction of nature's intended balance.

Automotive Pollutants

The third major source of air pollution is automotive emissions. The emissions from the internal combustion engines were not an appreciable problem years ago because of the small number of registered vehicles and the nation's small highway system. However, during the early 1950's, the trend of the American people was to move from the cities to the surrounding suburbs. This caused an immediate problem in transportation because the majority of suburbs were not afforded mass transit conveniences. This lack of transportation created an attractive market for the automobile manufacturers, which resulted in a dramatic increase in the number of vehicles produced and sold, along with a marked increase in

highway construction between cities and the suburbs. Multi-vehicle families emerged with a growing emphasis placed on an individual vehicle per family member. As the increase in vehicle ownership and usage occurred, so did pollutant levels in and around the cities, as suburbanites drove daily to their businesses and employment, returning at the end of the day to their homes in the suburbs.

It was noted that a smoke and fog type haze was being formed and at times, remained in suspension over the cities, taking time to dissipate. At first this "smog," derived from the words "smoke" and "fog," was thought to result from industrial pollution but it was determined that automobile emissions shared the blame. It was discovered that when normal automobile emissions were exposed to sunlight for a period of time, complex chemical reactions would take place.

It is now known that smog is a photo chemical layer which develops when certain oxides of nitrogen (NOx) and unburned hydrocarbons (HC) from automobile emissions are exposed to sunlight. Pollution was more severe when smog would become stagnant over an area in which a warm layer of air settled over the top of the cooler air mass, trapping and holding the cooler mass at ground level. The trapped cooler air would keep the emissions from being dispersed and diluted through normal air flows. This type of air stagnation was given the name "Temperature Inversion."

TEMPERATURE INVERSION

In normal weather situations, surface air is warmed by heat radiating from the earth's surface and the sun's rays. This causes it to rise upward, into the atmosphere. Upon rising it will cool through a convection type heat exchange with the cooler upper air. As warm air rises, the surface pollutants are carried upward and dissipated into the atmosphere.

When a temperature inversion occurs, we find the higher air is no longer cooler, but is warmer than the surface air, causing the cooler surface air to become trapped. This warm air blanket can extend from above ground level to a few hundred or even a few thousand feet into the air. As the surface air is trapped, so are the pollutants, causing a severe smog condition. Should this stagnant air mass extend to a few thousand feet high, enough air movement with the inversion takes place to allow the smog layer to rise above ground level but the pollutants still cannot dissipate. This inversion can remain for days over an area, with the smog level only rising or lowering from ground level to a few hundred feet high. Meanwhile, the pollutant levels increase, causing eye irritation, respiratory problems, reduced visibility, plant damage and in some cases, even disease.

This inversion phenomenon was first noted in the Los Angeles, California area. The city lies in terrain resembling a basin and with certain weather conditions, a cold air mass is held in the basin while a warmer air mass covers it like a lid.

Because this type of condition was first documented as prevalent in the Los Angeles area, this type of trapped pollution was named Los Angeles Smog, although it occurs in other areas where a large concentration of automobiles are used and the air remains stagnant for any length of time.

HEAT TRANSFER

Consider the internal combustion engine as a machine in which raw materials must be placed so a finished product comes out. As in any machine operation, a certain amount of wasted material is formed. When we relate this to the internal combustion engine, we find that through the input of air and fuel, we obtain power during the combustion process to drive the vehicle. The by-product or waste of this power is, in part, heat and exhaust gases with which we must dispose.

The heat from the combustion process can rise to over 4000°F (2204°C). The dissipation of this heat is controlled by a ram air effect, the use of cooling fans to cause air flow and a liquid coolant solution surrounding the combustion area to transfer the heat of combustion through the cylinder walls and into the coolant. The coolant is then directed to a thin-finned, multi-tubed radiator, from which the excess heat is transferred to the atmosphere by 1 of the 3 heat transfer methods, conduction, convection or radiation.

The cooling of the combustion area is an important part in the control of exhaust emissions. To understand the behavior of the combustion and transfer of its heat, consider the air/fuel charge. It is ignited and the flame front burns progressively across the combustion chamber until the burning charge reaches the cylinder walls. Some of the fuel in contact with the walls is not hot enough to burn, thereby snuffing out or quench-

ing the combustion process. This leaves unburned fuel in the combustion chamber. This unburned fuel is then forced out of the cylinder and into the exhaust system, along with the exhaust gases.

Many attempts have been made to minimize the amount of unburned fuel in the combustion chambers due to quenching, by increasing the coolant temperature and lessening the contact area of the coolant around the combustion area. However, design limitations within the combustion chambers prevent the complete burning of the air/fuel charge, so a certain amount of the unburned fuel is still expelled into the exhaust system, regardless of modifications to the engine.

AUTOMOTIVE EMISSIONS

Before emission controls were mandated on internal combustion engines, other sources of engine pollutants were discovered along with the exhaust emissions. It was determined that engine combustion exhaust produced approximately 60 percent of the total emission pollutants, fuel evaporation from the fuel tank and carburetor vents produced 20 percent, with the final 20 percent being produced through the crankcase as a by-product of the combustion process.

Exhaust Gases

The exhaust gases emitted into the atmosphere are a combination of burned and unburned fuel. To understand the exhaust emission and its composition, we must review some basic chemistry.

When the air/fuel mixture is introduced into the engine, we are mixing air, composed of nitrogen (78 percent), oxygen (21 percent) and other gases (1 percent) with the fuel, which is 100 percent hydrocarbons (HC), in a semi-controlled ratio. As the combustion process is accomplished, power is produced to move the vehicle while the heat of combustion is transferred to the cooling system. The exhaust gases are then composed of nitrogen, a diatomic gas (N_2), the same as was introduced in the engine, carbon dioxide (CO_2), the same gas that is used in beverage carbonation, and water vapor (H_2O). The nitrogen (N_2), for the most part, passes through the engine unchanged, while the oxygen (O_2) reacts (burns) with the hydrocarbons (HC) and produces the carbon dioxide (CO_2) and the water vapors (H_2O). If this chemical process would be the only process to take place, the exhaust emissions would be harmless. However, during the combustion process, other compounds are formed which are considered dangerous. These pollutants are hydrocarbons (HC), carbon monoxide (CO), oxides of nitrogen (NOx) oxides of sulfur (SOx) and engine particulates.

HYDROCARBONS

Hydrocarbons (HC) are essentially fuel which was not burned during the combustion process or which has escaped into the atmosphere through fuel evaporation. The main sources of incomplete combustion are rich air/fuel mixtures, low engine temperatures and improper spark timing. The main sources of hydrocarbon emission through fuel evaporation on most vehicles used to be the vehicle's fuel tank and carburetor float bowl.

To reduce combustion hydrocarbon emission, engine modifications were made to minimize dead space and surface area in the combustion chamber. In addition, the air/fuel mixture was made more lean through the improved control which feedback carburetion and fuel injection offers and by the addition of external controls to aid in further combustion of the hydrocarbons outside the engine. Two such methods were the addition of air injection systems, to inject fresh air into the exhaust manifolds and the installation of catalytic converters, units that are able to burn traces of hydrocarbons without affecting the internal combustion process or fuel economy.

To control hydrocarbon emissions through fuel evaporation, modifications were made to the fuel tank to allow storage of the fuel vapors during periods of engine shut-down. Modifications were also made to the air intake system so that at specific times during engine operation, these va-

pors may be purged and burned by blending them with the air/fuel mixture.

CARBON MONOXIDE

Carbon monoxide is formed when not enough oxygen is present during the combustion process to convert carbon (C) to carbon dioxide (CO_2). An increase in the carbon monoxide (CO) emission is normally accompanied by an increase in the hydrocarbon (HC) emission because of the lack of oxygen to completely burn all of the fuel mixture.

Carbon monoxide (CO) also increases the rate at which the photo chemical smog is formed by speeding up the conversion of nitric oxide (NO) to nitrogen dioxide (NO_2). To accomplish this, carbon monoxide (CO) combines with oxygen (O_2) and nitric oxide (NO) to produce carbon dioxide (CO_2) and nitrogen dioxide (NO_2). ($CO + O_2 + NO = CO_2 + NO_2$).

The dangers of carbon monoxide, which is an odorless and colorless toxic gas are many. When carbon monoxide is inhaled into the lungs and passed into the blood stream, oxygen is replaced by the carbon monoxide in the red blood cells, causing a reduction in the amount of oxygen supplied to the many parts of the body. This lack of oxygen causes headaches, lack of coordination, reduced mental alertness and, should the carbon monoxide concentration be high enough, death could result.

NITROGEN

Normally, nitrogen is an inert gas. When heated to approximately 2500°F (1371°C) through the combustion process, this gas becomes active and causes an increase in the nitric oxide (NO) emission.

Oxides of nitrogen (NOx) are composed of approximately 97–98 percent nitric oxide (NO). Nitric oxide is a colorless gas but when it is passed into the atmosphere, it combines with oxygen and forms nitrogen dioxide (NO_2). The nitrogen dioxide then combines with chemically active hydrocarbons (HC) and when in the presence of sunlight, causes the formation of photo-chemical smog.

Ozone

To further complicate matters, some of the nitrogen dioxide (NO_2) is broken apart by the sunlight to form nitric oxide and oxygen. (NO_2 + sunlight = NO + O). This single atom of oxygen then combines with diatomic (meaning 2 atoms) oxygen (O_2) to form ozone (O_3). Ozone is one of the smells associated with smog. It has a pungent and offensive odor, irritates the eyes and lung tissues, affects the growth of plant life and causes rapid deterioration of rubber products. Ozone can be formed by sunlight as well as electrical discharge into the air.

The most common discharge area on the automobile engine is the secondary ignition electrical system, especially when inferior quality spark plug cables are used. As the surge of high voltage is routed through the secondary cable, the circuit builds up an electrical field around the wire, which acts upon the oxygen in the surrounding air to form the ozone. The faint glow along the cable with the engine running that may be visible on a dark night, is called the "corona discharge." It is the result of the electrical field passing from a high along the cable, to a low in the surrounding air, which forms the ozone gas. The combination of corona and ozone has been a major cause of cable deterioration. Recently, different and better quality insulating materials have lengthened the life of the electrical cables.

Although ozone at ground level can be harmful, ozone is beneficial to the earth's inhabitants. By having a concentrated ozone layer called the "ozonosphere," between 10 and 20 miles (16–32 km) up in the atmosphere, much of the ultra violet radiation from the sun's rays are absorbed and screened. If this ozone layer were not present, much of the earth's surface would be burned, dried and unfit for human life.

OXIDES OF SULFUR

Oxides of sulfur (SOx) were initially ignored in the exhaust system emissions, since the sulfur content of gasoline as a fuel is less than $\frac{1}{10}$ of 1 percent. Because of this small amount, it was felt that it contributed very little to the overall pollution problem. However, because of the difficulty in solving the sulfur emissions in industrial pollutions and the introduction of catalytic converter to the automobile exhaust systems, a change was mandated. The automobile exhaust system, when equipped with a catalytic converter, changes the sulfur dioxide (SO_2) into sulfur trioxide (SO_3).

When this combines with water vapors (H_2O), a sulfuric acid mist (H_2SO_4) is formed and is a very difficult pollutant to handle since it is extremely corrosive. This sulfuric acid mist that is formed, is the same mist that rises from the vents of an automobile battery when an active chemical reaction takes place within the battery cells.

When a large concentration of vehicles equipped with catalytic converters are operating in an area, this acid mist may rise and be distributed over a large ground area causing land, plant, crop, paint and building damage.

PARTICULATE MATTER

A certain amount of particulate matter is present in the burning of any fuel, with carbon constituting the largest percentage of the particulates. In gasoline, the remaining particulates are the burned remains of the various other compounds used in its manufacture. When a gasoline engine is in good internal condition, the particulate emissions are low but as the engine wears internally, the particulate emissions increase. By visually inspecting the tail pipe emissions, a determination can be made as to where an engine defect may exist. An engine with light gray or blue smoke emitting from the tail pipe normally indicates an increase in the oil consumption through burning due to internal engine wear. Black smoke would indicate a defective fuel delivery system, causing the engine to operate in a rich mode. Regardless of the color of the smoke, the internal part of the engine or the fuel delivery system should be repaired to prevent excess particulate emissions.

Diesel and turbine engines emit a darkened plume of smoke from the exhaust system because of the type of fuel used. Emission control regulations are mandated for this type of emission and more stringent measures are being used to prevent excess emission of the particulate matter. Electronic components are being introduced to control the injection of the fuel at precisely the proper time of piston travel, to achieve the optimum in fuel ignition and fuel usage. Other particulate after-burning components are being tested to achieve a cleaner emission.

Good grades of engine lubricating oils should be used, which meet the manufacturers specification. Cut-rate oils can contribute to the particulate emission problem because of their low flash or ignition temperature point. Such oils burn prematurely during the combustion process causing emission of particulate matter.

The cooling system is an important factor in the reduction of particulate matter. The optimum combustion will occur, with the cooling system operating at a temperature specified by the manufacturer. The cooling system must be maintained in the same manner as the engine oiling system, as each system is required to perform properly in order for the engine to operate efficiently for a long time.

Crankcase Emissions

Crankcase emissions are made up of water, acids, unburned fuel, oil fumes and particulates. These emissions are classified as hydrocarbons (HC) and are formed by the small amount of unburned, compressed air/fuel mixture entering the crankcase from the combustion area (between the cylinder walls and piston rings) during the compression and power strokes. The head of the compression and combustion help to form the remaining crankcase emissions.

Since the first engines, crankcase emissions were allowed into the atmosphere through a road draft tube, mounted on the lower side of the engine block. Fresh air came in through an open oil filler cap or breather. The air passed through the crankcase mixing with blow-by gases. The motion of the vehicle and the air blowing past the open end of the road draft tube caused a low pressure area (vacuum) at the end of the tube. Crankcase emissions were simply drawn out of the road draft tube into the air.

To control the crankcase emission, the road draft tube was deleted. A hose and/or tubing was routed from the crankcase to the intake manifold so the blow-by emission could be burned with the air/fuel mixture. However, it was found that intake manifold vacuum, used to draw the crankcase emissions into the manifold, would vary in strength at the wrong time and not allow the proper emission flow. A regulating valve was needed to control the flow of air through the crankcase.

Testing, showed the removal of the blow-by gases from the crankcase as quickly as possible, was most important to the longevity of the engine. Should large accumulations of blow-by gases remain and condense, dilution of the engine oil would occur to form water, soots, resins, acids and lead salts, resulting in the formation of sludge and varnishes. This condensation of the blow-by gases occurs more frequently on vehicles used in numerous starting and stopping conditions, excessive idling and when the engine is not allowed to attain normal operating temperature through short runs.

Evaporative Emissions

Gasoline fuel is a major source of pollution, before and after it is burned in the automobile engine. From the time the fuel is refined, stored, pumped and transported, again stored until it is pumped into the fuel tank of the vehicle, the gasoline gives off unburned hydrocarbons (HC) into the atmosphere. Through the redesign of storage areas and venting systems, the pollution factor was diminished, but not eliminated, from the refinery standpoint. However, the automobile still remained the primary source of vaporized, unburned hydrocarbon (HC) emissions.

Fuel pumped from an underground storage tank is cool but when exposed to a warmer ambient temperature, will expand. Before controls were mandated, an owner might fill the fuel tank with fuel from an underground storage tank and park the vehicle for some time in warm area, such as a parking lot. As the fuel would warm, it would expand and should no provisions or area be provided for the expansion, the fuel would spill out of the filler neck and onto the ground, causing hydrocarbon (HC) pollution and creating a severe fire hazard. To correct this condition, the vehicle manufacturers added overflow plumbing and/or gasoline tanks with built in expansion areas or domes.

However, this did not control the fuel vapor emission from the fuel tank. It was determined that most of the fuel evaporation occurred when the vehicle was stationary and the engine not operating. Most vehicles carry 5–25 gallons (19–95 liters) of gasoline. Should a large concentration of vehicles be parked in one area, such as a large parking lot, excessive fuel vapor emissions would take place, increasing as the temperature increases.

To prevent the vapor emission from escaping into the atmosphere, the fuel systems were designed to trap the vapors while the vehicle is stationary, by sealing the system from the atmosphere. A storage system is used to collect and hold the fuel vapors from the carburetor (if equipped) and the fuel tank when the engine is not operating. When the engine is started, the storage system is then purged of the fuel vapors, which are drawn into the engine and burned with the air/fuel mixture.

EMISSION CONTROLS

Crankcase Ventilation System

▶ See Figure 1

OPERATION

A Positive Crankcase Ventilation (PCV) system is used to prevent pollutants (blow-by gasses) from being released into the atmosphere. The PCV system supplies fresh air to the crankcase through the air cleaner. The fresh air mixes with the gases and is passed through the PCV valve to the intake manifold. the gasses are then reburned in the combustion process. The PCV system should be inspected every 52,000 miles (84,000 km).

TESTING

1. Remove the PCV valve.
2. Shake the valve. If a rattle is heard, the valve is operational.
3. If a rattle is not heard, insert a thin stick into the PCV valve from the threaded end and push to check if the plunger moves.
4. If the plunger does not move, the valve is clogged and should be cleaned or replaced.
5. Install the hose on the valve and start the engine.
6. Place a finger over the threaded end of the valve and check for vacuum. If vacuum is not present, check the hose for obstructions and replace as necessary.
7. Install the PCV valve.

REMOVAL & INSTALLATION

1. Disconnect the ventilation ho
2. Remove the valve from the ro
3. Thread the new valve into the
lbs. (8–12 Nm).
4. Connect the ventilation hose

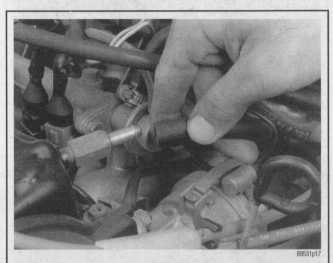

When removing the PCV hose, check it for obstructions by blowing through the hose

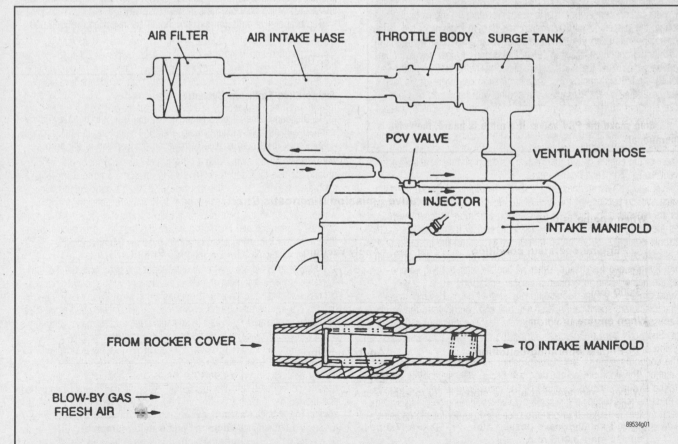

Fig. 1 Diagram of the Positive Crankcase Ventilation (PCV) system

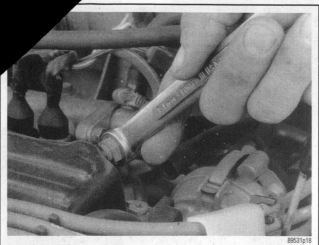

Carefully loosen the PCV valve with a wrench and remove from the rocker cover . . .

. . . then shake the PCV valve. If a rattle is heard, the valve is operational

Evaporative Emission Controls

OPERATION

◆ See Figures 2 and 3

The evaporative emission control system prevents the uncontrolled release of gasoline vapors (hydrocarbons) into the atmosphere. These vapors are produced when fuel evaporates in the sealed fuel tank. The system includes a charcoal canister, canister purge solenoid valve, fuel check valve, overfill limiter, fuel cap and on some late model vehicles, a Fuel Tank Pressure (FTP) sensor and a Canister Close Valve (CCV).

The main component of the system is the charcoal canister. The activated charcoal in the canister absorbs and stores fuel vapors generated inside the fuel tank while the engine is inoperative. When the engine is running, the vapors are drawn through the electronically controlled purge control valve and into the intake manifold. The vapors enter the air/fuel mixture and are burned in the combustion process.

The overfill limiter (two-way valve) consists of a pressure valve and a vacuum valve. The pressure valve is designed to open when the fuel tank's internal pressure has increased over the preset pressure limit. The vacuum valve opens when a vacuum is produced in the tank.

The fuel check valve is used to prevent fuel leakage should the vehicle roll over. The valve is connected in the fuel vapor line between canister and overfill limiter. The fuel check valve contains 2 balls and under normal conditions the gasoline vapor passage in the valve is open; if a vehicle rollover occurs, one of the balls closes the fuel passage thus preventing fuel leaks.

A special fuel cap is installed on these vehicles which prevents vapors from escaping through the filler neck.

An FTP sensor and a CCV are used on 2.0L (VIN F) and 1996–98 1.8L (VIN M) engines. The sensor monitors differential pressure between the inside and outside of fuel tank. It signals the Electronic Control Module (ECM) which controls the canister close valve.

The evaporative emission system should be inspected every 52,000 miles (84,000 km).

TESTING

Evaporative Emission System

1. Disconnect the vacuum hose (red stripe) from the throttle body and connect a hand-held vacuum pump. Plug the nipple on the throttle body.
2. Check if vacuum is held or released as specified in the accompanying chart.

Evaporative Emission Diagnostic Chart

When engine is cold

Engine operating condition	Apply vacuum	Result
Idling	50 kPa (7.3 psi)	Vacuum is held
3,000 rpm		

When engine is warm

Engine operating condition	Apply vacuum	Result
Idling	50 kPa (7.3 psi)	Vacuum is held
Within 3 minutes after engine start 3,000 rpm	Try to apply vacuum	Vacuum is released
After 3 minutes have passed after engine start 3,000 rpm	50 kPa (7.3 psi)	Vacuum will be held momentarily, after which, it will be released.

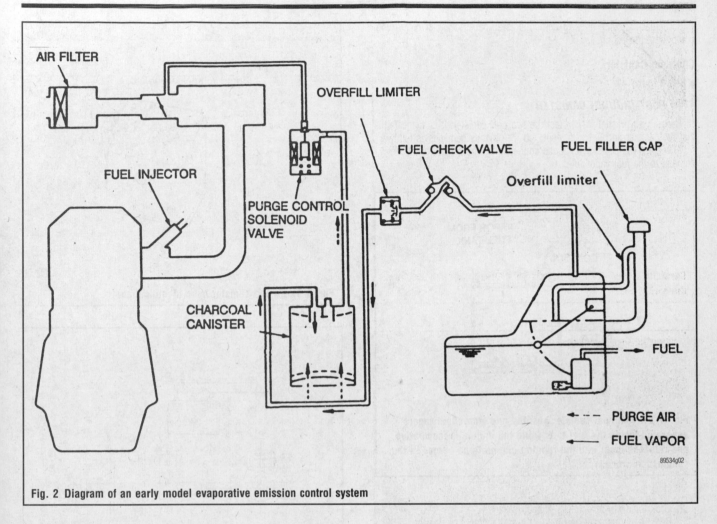

Fig. 2 Diagram of an early model evaporative emission control system

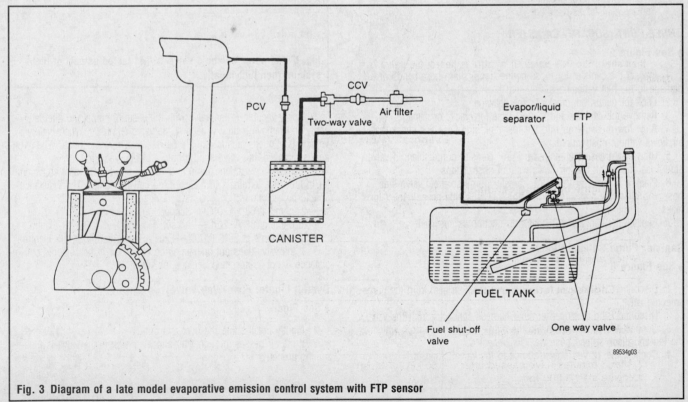

Fig. 3 Diagram of a late model evaporative emission control system with FTP sensor

3. Replace vacuum lines or components as necessary after performing component inspection.

Charcoal Canister

◆ See Figure 4

TWO PORT (ROUND) CANISTER

There is no practial way to test the two port canister. It is suggested that the canister and lines be inspected for obvious damages as follows:

1. Inspect the canister for loose connections, sharp hose bends or damage to the fuel vapor lines.

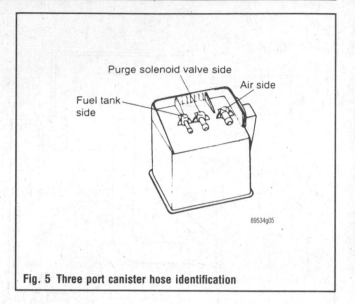

Fig. 5 Three port canister hose identification

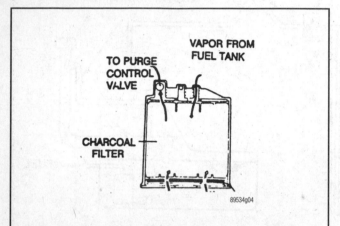

Fig. 4 The charcoal canister absorbs and stores fuel vapors generated inside the fuel tank while the engine is inoperative, and releases them into the running engine to be burned in the combustion process

2. Look for distortion, cracks or fuel leakage.
3. Remove the canister and inspect case for cracks or damage.
4. Replace canister as required.

THREE PORT (SQUARE) CANISTER

◆ See Figure 5

1. Inspect the canister for loose connections, sharp hose bends or damage to the fuel vapor lines.
2. Look for distortion, cracks or fuel leakage.
3. Remove the canister and inspect case for cracks or damage.
4. Blow low pressure air into the fuel tank side hose and check that air flows without obstructions.
5. Blow low pressure air into the EVAP canister purge solenoid valve side hose and check that air flows without obstructions.
6. Place a finger over the EVAP canister purge solenoid valve side hose and blow low pressure air into the fuel tank side hose. Inspect for leaks.
7. Replace the canister if it does not function as specified.

Canister Purge Solenoid Valve

◆ See Figure 6

1. Disconnect the vacuum hose (red and black striped) from the purge solenoid valve.
2. Disconnect the electrical terminal harness connector from the valve.
3. Connect the vacuum pump to the nipple on the valve from which the red and black striped hose was disconnected.
4. Connect the 12 volt power source to the valve terminals.

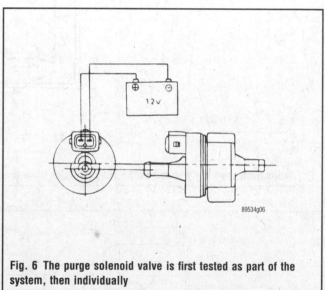

Fig. 6 The purge solenoid valve is first tested as part of the system, then individually

5. Apply vacuum to the valve with the vacuum pump and alternately apply and remove battery voltage at the valve terminals. When battery voltage is applied, vacuum should be released from the valve. When voltage is removed, the valve should hold a steady vacuum.
6. Remove the vacuum pump and voltage source. Connect an ohmmeter to the valve terminals to measure the coil resistance. The resistance should be as follows:
   • 45 ohms at 68°F (20°C)—Scoupe
   • 26 ohms at 68°F (20°C)—Accent, Tiburon and 1996–98 Elantra
   • 36–44 ohms at 68°F (20°C)—Excel, Sonata and 1994–95 Elantra
7. If the valve does not operate as described, or if the solenoid coil resistance is not as specified, replace the valve.

Overfill Limiter (Two-Way Valve)

◆ See Figure 7

1. Lightly breathe into the inlet and outlet.
2. If the air passes through after slight resistance, the valve is functioning properly.

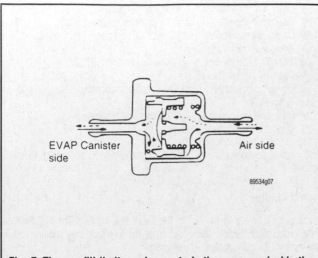

Fig. 7 The overfill limiter valve controls the pressure inside the fuel tank. It contains both a pressure valve and a vacuum valve

Fuel Filler Cap

♦ See Figure 8

1. Check the cap gasket and the cap for damage or deformation.
2. Replace the fuel cap as necessary.

Fuel Tank Pressure (FTP) Sensor

♦ See Figure 9

1. Disconnect the FTP electrical harness.
2. Connect a voltmeter to FTP terminals 2 and 3.
3. Start the engine and allow it to idle for 20 minutes.
4. Voltmeter should read 5 volts at idle and drop to 0.5–4.5 volts when the engine is accelerated.
5. If voltage is not as specified, there is a leak in the system.

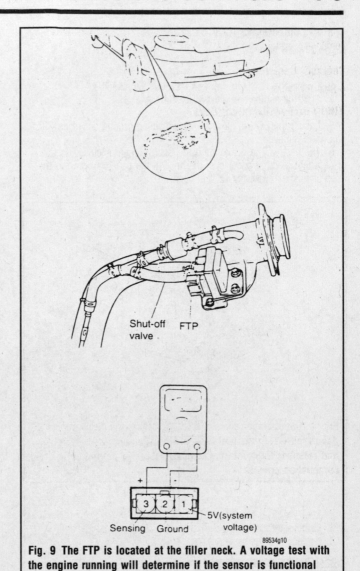

Fig. 9 The FTP is located at the filler neck. A voltage test with the engine running will determine if the sensor is functional

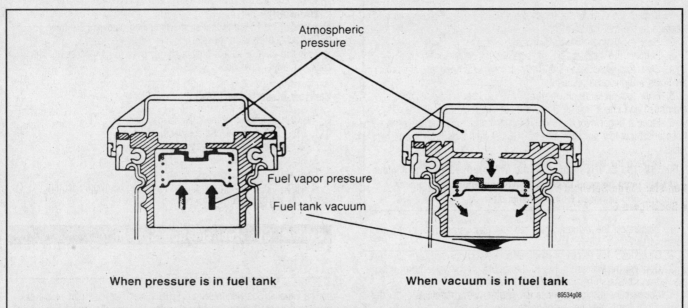

Fig. 8 The fuel cap is an important part of the evaporative emission system. It works in conjunction with the overfill limiter valve to control pressure inside the fuel tank

Canister Close Valve (CCV)

▶ **See Figure 10**

1. Disconnect the CCV electrical harness.
2. Connect the CCV to a power source as illustrated.
3. Start the engine and allow it to idle.
4. Disconnect the CCV connector.
5. Ensure the CCV is closed when providing ground and open when ground is removed.
6. The best way to determine if the CCV is open or closed, is to place a thin piece of paper over the hose. If the paper is drawn to the hose or pushed away, the CCV is open.

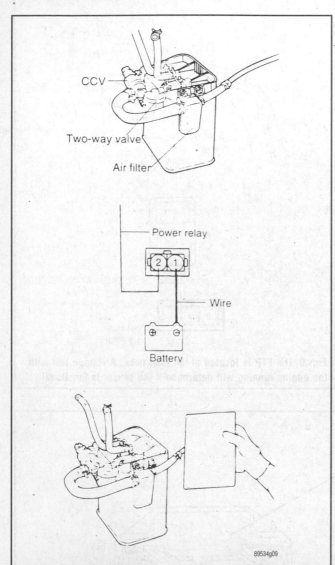

Fig. 10 The CCV is located on the evaporative canister. A piece of paper can be used to check valve operation when power is applied and removed from the connector

REMOVAL & INSTALLATION

Charcoal Canister

The canister is located either in the engine compartment at either the left or right front, near the headlights.
1. Remove any components necessary to gain access to the canister.
2. Label and disconnect the vacuum lines.
3. Label and disconnect the electrical harness.
4. On round canisters, loosen the canister retaining strap.
5. On square canisters, remove the canister mounting hardware.
6. Remove the canister.
To install:
7. Position the canister.
8. On square canisters, install the canister mounting hardware and tighten securely.
9. On round canisters, tighten the canister retaining strap.
10. Connect the electrical harness.
11. Connect the vacuum lines.
12. Install any components previously removed to gain access to the canister.

Overfill Limiter

The overfill limiter is located in the vapor line either at the fuel tank or at the charcoal canister. Valves located at the fuel tank may require fuel tank removal to gain access to the valve.
1. Remove the fuel tank, as required.
2. Loosen the hose clamps.
3. Disconnect the valve from the vapor line.
To install:
4. Connect the valve to the vapor line.
5. Tighten the hose clamps.
6. Install the fuel tank, as required.

Fuel Cap

The fuel cap screws on to the end of the fuel filler pipe. It has a special ratcheting action when tightening to prevent the cap from being over-tightented. When removing the fuel cap, caution should be taken to loosen it slowly. This will allow any pressure build-up in the fuel tank to be released.

Fuel Tank Pressure (FTP) Sensor

The FTP is located at the filler neck.
1. Remove interior panels necessary to gain access to the back of the fuel filler neck.
2. Label and disconnect the vapor hose.
3. Remove the FTP mounting hardware.
4. Remove the FTP.
To install:
5. Install the FTP and tighten the mounting hardware securely.
6. Connect the vapor hose.
7. Install interior panels previously removed to gain access to the back of the fuel filler neck.

Canister Close Valve (CCV)

The CCV is located at the charcoal canister.
1. Label and disconnect the vapor hose.
2. Remove the CCV mounting hardware.
3. Remove the CCV.
To install:
4. Install the CCV and tighten the mounting hardware securely.
5. Connect the vapor hose.

Exhaust Gas Recirculation System

OPERATION

The Exhaust Gas Recirculation (EGR) system recycles part of the exhaust gases into the combustion chamber to lower the peak combustion temperatures. By lowering peak temperatures, a reduction in Oxides of Nitrogen (NOx) is obtained.

The system consists of an EGR valve, thermo valve, and a catalytic converter. California models use an EGR Control Solenoid Valve and an EGR Temperature Sensor.

The EGR valve is operated by engine vacuum. It receives exhaust gasses through one port and as indicated by the ECM, allows exhaust gasses to flow into the combustion chambers through a second port.

The Thermo Vacuum Valve (TVV) is connected inline between the EGR valve and the vacuum supply. The valve is threaded into the intake manifold coolant passage. The valve functions as a temperature switch to stop the vacuum signal to the EGR valve.

The control solenoid valve functions much like the thermo valve but is controlled by the ECM instead of coolant temperature. The valve functions to stop the vacuum signal to the EGR valve.

TESTING

EGR Valve

◢ See Figure 11

1. Inspect the EGR valve for sticking or carbon deposits.
2. Clean the valve with solvent and ensure that the valve is fully seated on the contact surface.
3. Connect a hand vacuum pump to the valve and apply 19.4 in. Hg of vacuum. Check that vacuum is held.
4. Release the vacuum and apply 1.7 in. Hg of vacuum. Blow air into one passage of the valve. Air should not blow through.
5. Increase the vacuum to 7.5 in. Hg and blow air into the passage again. Air should blow through.
6. Replace the EGR valve if it fails to function properly.

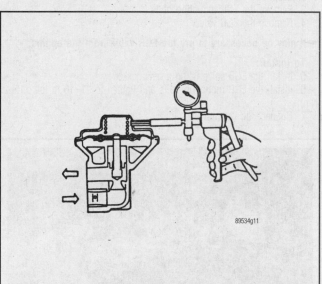

Fig. 11 Testing the EGR valve test using a hand-held vacuum pump

Thermo Valve

◢ See Figure 12

1. Connect a hand vacuum pump to the thermo valve nipple.
2. Apply vacuum with a hand-held vacuum pump.
3. At coolant temperatures below 122°F (50°C), the vacuum should not hold.

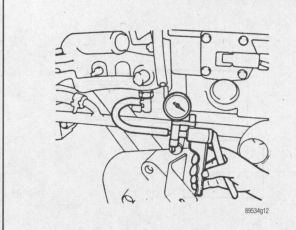

Fig. 12 The thermo valve is tested with the use of a hand-held vacuum pump. The valve can be tested on the engine or by removing it and placing it in a pot of hot water

4. At coolant temperatures above 176°F (80°C), the vacuum should hold.
5. Replace the thermo valve if not functioning properly.

EGR Control Solenoid Valve (California)

◢ See Figures 13, 14 and 15

1. Tag and disconnect the vacuum lines and harness connector from the valve.
2. Connect a hand-held vacuum pump to the nipple where the green striped hose was connected and draw vacuum.
3. Connect a 12 volt source to the solenoid and check as follows:
    a. With voltage applied, the vacuum should hold.
    b. With voltage disconnected, the vacuum should bleed off.
    c. Measure the resistance between the terminals of the solenoid valve.
    d. Resistance should be 33–44 ohms at 68°F (20°C).

Fig. 13 A functional test of the EGR control solenoid valve can be made by connecting a hand-held vacuum pump . . .

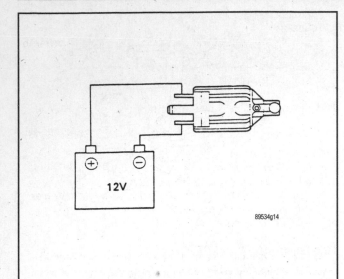

Fig. 14 . . . and applying battery voltage to the solenoid. The valve should hold vacuum when battery voltage is applied

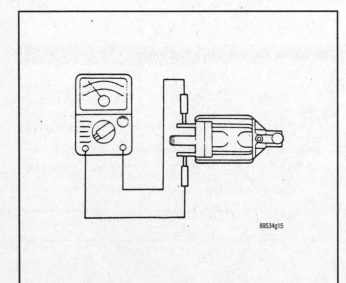

Fig. 15 EGR solenoid control valve coil resistance may also be checked with an ohmmeter

EGR Temperature Sensor (California)

♦ See Figure 16

1. Remove the EGR temperature sensor from the EGR valve and place in a bucket of water with a thermometer.
2. Heat the water to 122°F (50°C) and measure the resistance across the sensor terminals. Resistance should be 60–83 ohms.
3. Raise the temperature of the water to 212°F (100°C) and measure the resistance again. Resistance should drop to 11–14 ohms.
4. Replace the EGR temperature sensor if defective.

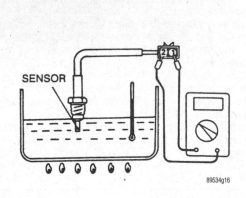

Fig. 16 The EGR temperature sensor can be tested by inserting the sensor in hot water and checking resistance across the terminals

REMOVAL & INSTALLATION

EGR Valve

1. Locate the EGR valve on the engine.
2. Label and disconnect the vacuum line.
3. Remove the EGR mounting bolts
4. Remove the EGR valve.

➡It may be necessary to pry the EGR valve from the engine.

To install:
5. Install the EGR valve using a new gasket.
6. Install the EGR mounting bolts and tighten to 11–16 ft. lbs. (15–22 Nm).
7. Connect the vacuum line.

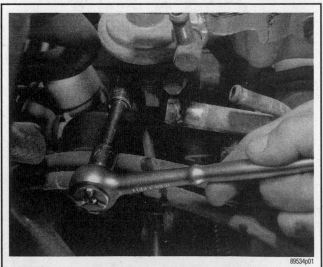

The EGR valve is mounted to the engine using two bolts

When inspecting the EGR valve, ensure the exhaust ports are free of carbon build-up

Thermo Valve

1. Drain the coolant.
2. Disconnect the thermo valve vacuum lines.
3. Remove the valve from the engine.
To install:
4. Coat the valve with sealant and install. Tighten the valve to 14–16 ft. lbs. (20–40 Nm).
5. Connect the thermo valve vacuum lines.
6. Refill the engine with coolant.

EGR Control Solenoid Valve (California)

The EGR control solenoid valve is located on the firewall, next to the purge control solenoid valve.
1. Disconnect the solenoid valve vacuum lines.
2. Remove the solenoid valve attaching screws.
3. Remove the solenoid valve from the firewall.
4. Inspect the vacuum lines for cracking or damage, and replace as necessary.
5. Installation is the reverse of removal.

EGR Temperature Sensor (California)

1. Disconnect the temperature sensor electrical harness.
2. Remove the sensor from the engine.
To install:
3. Coat the sensor with anti-seize compound and install. Tighten the sensor to 7–9 ft. lbs. (10–12 Nm).
4. Connect the temperature sensor electrical harness.

ELECTRONIC ENGINE CONTROLS

General Information

▶ **See Figures 17, 18 and 19 (p. 13–14)**

The fuel injection system used on Hyundai vehicles is classified as a Multi-port Fuel Injection (MFI) system. The basic function of the system is to control the air/fuel ratio, based on input signals from various engine sensors. The air/fuel ratio is controlled by varying the injector drive time (pulse width). The system is controlled by an Electronic Control Module (ECM), which monitors the engine conditions, then calculates the injection timing and air/fuel ratio according to the signals from the sensors. The ECM consists of a microprocessor, Random Access Memory (RAM), Read Only Memory (ROM) and input and output signal interface systems.

The MFI system consists of 2 operating modes:
• Open Loop—air/fuel ratio is controlled by information programmed into the ECM by the manufacturer.

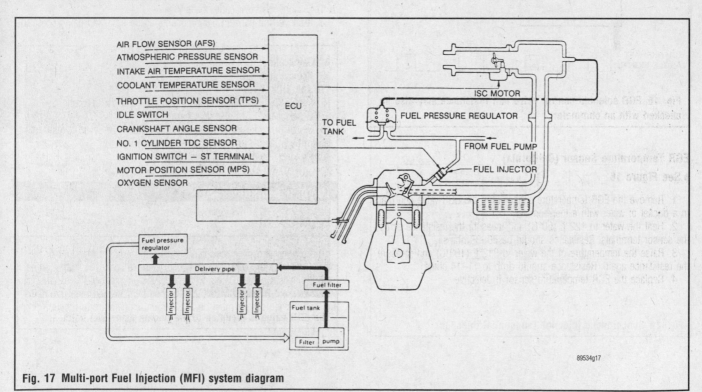

Fig. 17 Multi-port Fuel Injection (MFI) system diagram

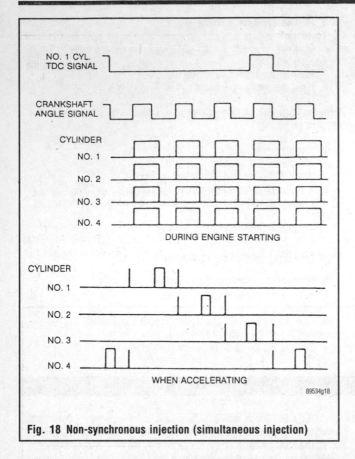

Fig. 18 Non-synchronous injection (simultaneous injection)

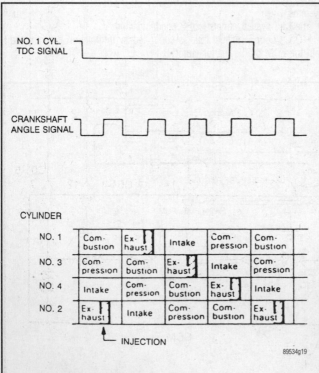

Fig. 19 Synchronous injection (sequential injection)

• Closed Loop—air/fuel ratio is varied by the ECM based on information supplied by the oxygen sensor.

An electric fuel pump supplies sufficient fuel to the injection system and the pressure regulator maintains a constant pressure to the injectors. These injectors inject a metered quantity of fuel into the intake manifold in accordance with signals from the Electronic Control Module (ECM) or engine computer. After pressure regulation, excess fuel is returned to the fuel tank.

The injectors have 2 modes (Injector Drive Timing) of operation:
• Non-synchronous Injection (Simultaneous Injection)
• Synchronous Injection (Sequential Injection)

Non-synchronous injection is activated during engine starting (cranking). There are 2 fuel injections, for each engine rpm, to all 4 cylinders. Also, during acceleration, fuel proportionate to the magnitude of acceleration, is injected to 2 selected cylinders during the intake and exhaust strokes.

Synchronous Injection is activated after the engine has started. The injectors are activated at the exhaust stroke of each cylinder in a sequential manner, according to crankshaft angle sensor signal. There is 1 injection per cylinder for every 2 crankshaft revolution, according to firing order.

Electronic Control Module (ECM)

OPERATION

The ECM is required to maintain exhaust emissions at acceptable levels. The module is a small, solid state computer which receives signals from various drivetrain and body sensors. It uses this data to calculate vehicle and engine operating conditions and then sends output signals to the fuel and emission control systems. The ECM is pre-programmed to recognize acceptable ranges or combinations while providing good driveability and economy.

The ECM is located under the left side of the dash on all vehicles except Sonata. On Sonata, the ECM is located in the right side kick panel.

REMOVAL & INSTALLATION

1. Disconnect the negative battery cable.
2. Remove trim panels or components as necessary to gain access to the ECM.
3. Label and disconnect the ECM electrical harnesses.
4. Remove the ECM mounting hardware.
5. Remove the ECM.
To install:
6. Install the ECM. Tighten the mounting hardware securely.
7. Connect the ECM electrical harnesses.
8. Install trim panels or components previously removed to gain access to the ECM.
9. Connect the negative battery cable.

Oxygen Sensor (O₂S)

OPERATION

The oxygen sensor is mounted either in the exhaust manifold or the exhaust pipe. Some vehicles use two oxygen sensors. The output signal from the sensor, which varies with the oxygen content of the exhaust gas stream, is sent to the ECM for use in controlling closed loop fuel delivery. The oxygen sensor must be at a certain temperature to function properly. Some sensors contain an internal heater to boost sensor temperature during cold starts.

TESTING

▶ **See Figures 20, 21 and 22**

1. Start the engine and allow it to reach operating temperature.
2. Unfasten the oxygen sensor electrical connector.
3. Measure resistance between the sensor signal and ground terminals.

    a. With the engine idling, voltage should be 400 millivolts or less.

    b. When the engine is suddenly accelerated, voltage should be 600–1000 millivolts.

    c. When the engine is suddenly decelerated from 4000 rpm, voltage should be 200 millivolts or less.

4. If the sensor is equipped with a heater (3 or 4 terminal connector), measure resistance between the heater positive and negative terminals.

    a. With the heater at 750°F (400°C), resistance should be 30 ohms or more.

5. If voltage or resistance is not within specifications, the sensor is faulty.

6. If voltage and resistance are within specifications, check power and ground circuits.

REMOVAL & INSTALLATION

1. Disconnect the negative battery cable.
2. Remove the exhaust heat shield as necessary to gain access to the sensor.
3. Label and disconnect the sensor electrical harness.

➡ **Special oxygen sensor wrenches are available from local tool suppliers.**

4. Carefully remove the sensor using an appropriate wrench.
To install:
5. Lubricate the sensor threads with anti-seize compound.

➡ **Take care to allow the anti-seize compound to only contact the sensor threads.**

6. Carefully install the sensor and tighten to 29–36 ft. lbs. (40–50 Nm) on all engines except the 1.5L (VIN K), 1.8L (VIN M) and 2.0L (VIN F). Tighten the 1.5L (VIN K), 1.8L (VIN M) and 2.0L (VIN F) engines' sensors to 37–44 ft. lbs. (50–60 Nm).
7. Connect the sensor electrical harness.

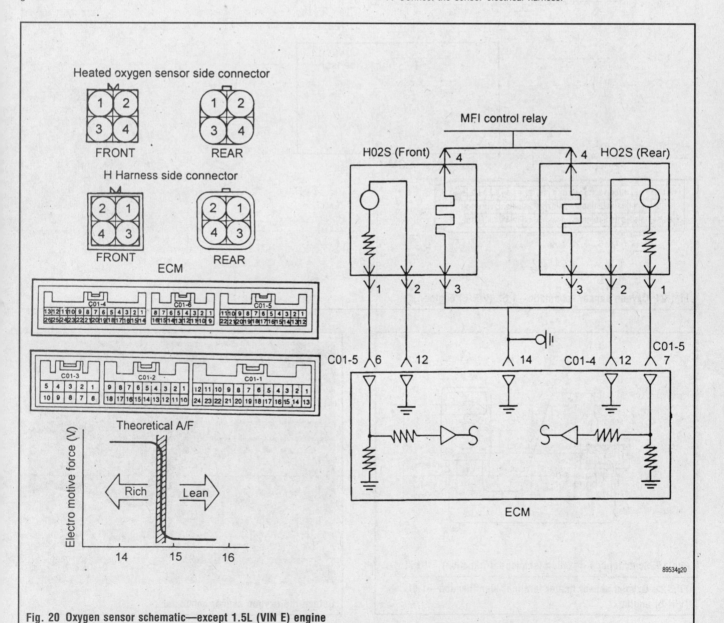

Fig. 20 Oxygen sensor schematic—except 1.5L (VIN E) engine

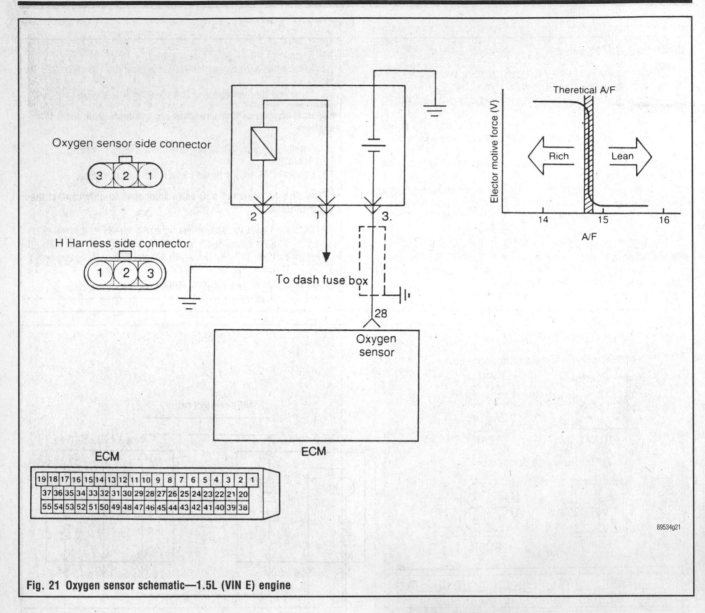

Fig. 21 Oxygen sensor schematic—1.5L (VIN E) engine

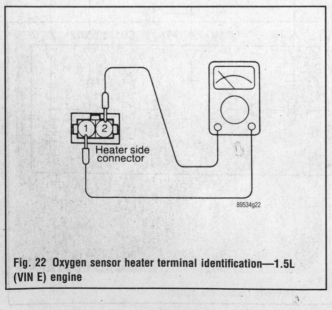

Fig. 22 Oxygen sensor heater terminal identification—1.5L (VIN E) engine

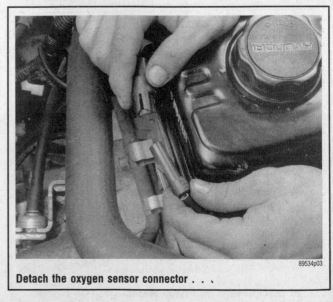

Detach the oxygen sensor connector . . .

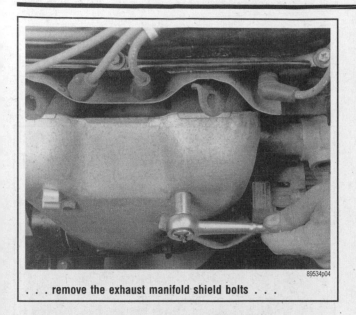

. . . remove the exhaust manifold shield bolts . . .

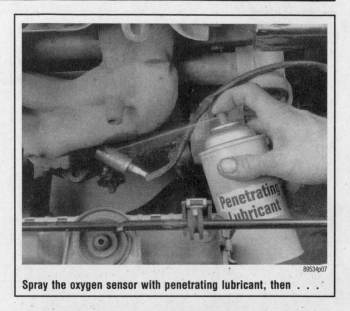

Spray the oxygen sensor with penetrating lubricant, then . . .

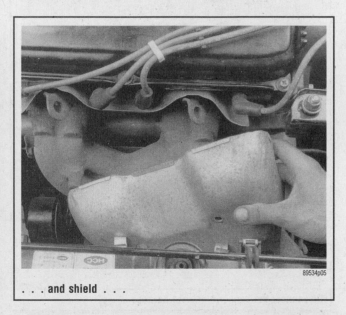

. . . and shield . . .

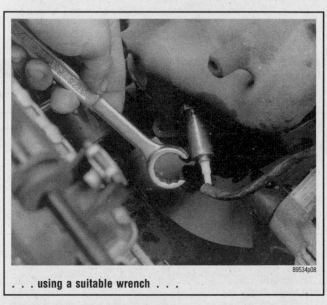

. . . using a suitable wrench . . .

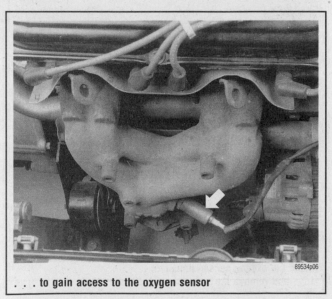

. . . to gain access to the oxygen sensor

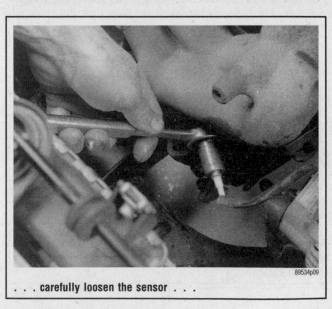

. . . carefully loosen the sensor . . .

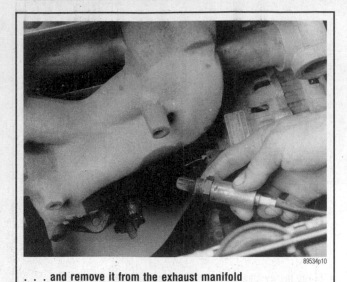

. . . and remove it from the exhaust manifold

8. Install trim panels or components previously removed to gain access to the ECM.
9. Connect the negative battery cable.

Engine Coolant Temperature (ECT) Sensor

OPERATION

The ECT is a thermistor (a resistor which changes value based on the temperature it encounters) that is mounted near the thermostat housing on the engine. Low temperatures create high resistance in the sensor, while high temperatures produce low resistance. Coolant temperature is an important parameter and will affect most calculations made by the ECM.

TESTING

1. Disconnect the sensor electrical harness.
2. Measure resistance between the sensor terminals.
3. Resistance should be high when the engine is cold and steadily drop as the engine warms.
4. If resistance does not drop steadily or resistance values do not match those in the coolant temperature resistance chart, the sensor is faulty.

Coolant Temperature Resistance Chart

Temperature °C(°F)	Resistance (kΩ)
-30 (-22)	22.22-31.78
-10 (14)	8.16-10.74
0 (32)	5.18-6.60
20 (68)	2.27-2.73
40 (104)	1.059-1.281
60 (140)	0.538-0.650
80 (176)	0.298-0.322
90 (194)	0.219-0.243

89534c02

5. If resistance is within specification, check power and ground circuits.

REMOVAL & INSTALLATION

1. Disconnect the negative battery cable.
2. Drain the engine coolant.

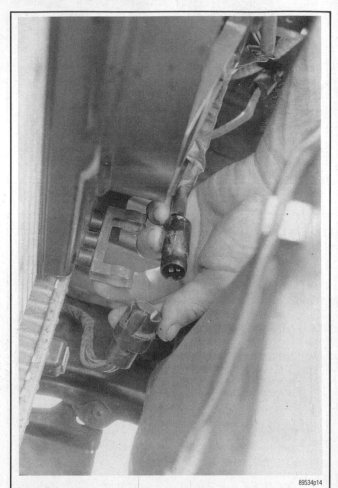

Disconnect the sensor electrical harness . . .

. . . and remove the sensor from the radiator

3. Label and disconnect the sensor electrical harness.
4. Carefully remove the sensor.

To install:

5. Coat the sensor threads with Teflon® sealant.
6. Carefully install the sensor and tighten to 14–29 ft. lbs. (20–40 Nm) on all engines except the 1.5L (VIN K), 1.8L (VIN M) and 2.0L (VIN F). Tighten 1.5L (VIN K), 1.8L (VIN M) and 2.0L (VIN F) engines' sensors to 11–15 ft. lbs. (15–20 Nm).
7. Connect the sensor electrical harness.
8. Fill the engine with coolant.
9. Connect the negative battery cable.

Intake Air Temperature (IAT) Sensor

OPERATION

The IAT is a thermistor (resistor) which changes valve based on the temperature it encounters. The IAT is mounted on the MAF sensor or air cleaner. Intake air temperature is an important parameter in fuel delivery calculations made by the ECM.

TESTING

Early Model With Six-Terminal Connector

▶ See Figure 23

The early model IAT sensor is an integral part of the VAF sensor.
1. Disconnect the sensor electrical harness.
2. Measure resistance between sensor terminals 4 and 6.

Intake Air Temperature Resistance Chart

Temperature [C° (°F)]	Resistance (kΩ)
0 (32)	6.0
20 (68)	2.7
80 (176)	0.4

89534c03

3. Resistance should be high when the ambient air is cold and steadily drop as the air warms.

➡**A hair dryer may be used to gently warm the sensor for testing purposes.**

4. If resistance does not drop steadily or resistance values do not match those in the intake air temperature resistance chart, the sensor is faulty.
5. If resistance is within specification, check power and ground circuits.

Late Model With Two-Terminal Connector

▶ See Figure 24

1. Disconnect the sensor electrical harness.
2. Measure voltage between the sensor terminals.
3. Voltage should be high when the engine is cold and steadily drop as the engine warms.

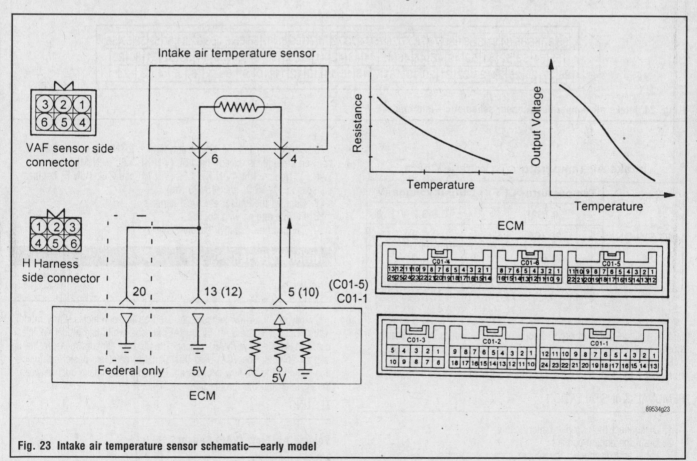

Fig. 23 Intake air temperature sensor schematic—early model

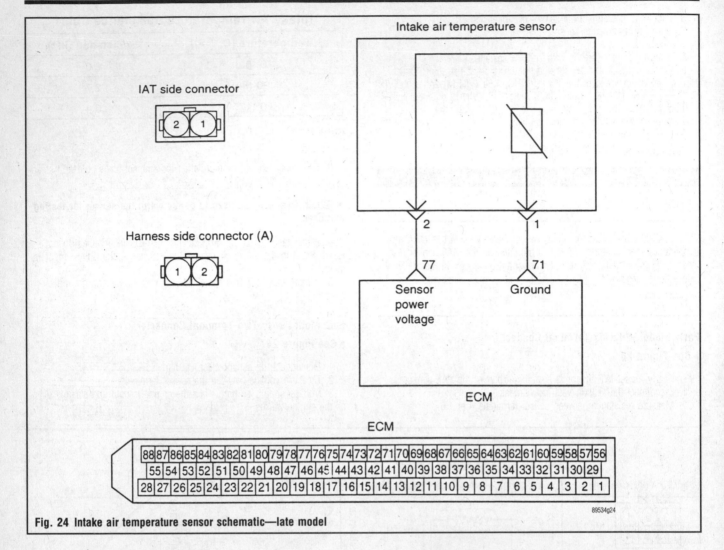

Fig. 24 Intake air temperature sensor schematic—late model

Intake Air Temperature To Voltage Chart

	Temperature °C(°F)	Output voltage (V)
IG.SW.ON	0 (32)	3.3-3.7 V
	20 (68)	2.4-2.8 V
	40 (104)	1.6-2.0 V
	80 (176)	0.5-0.9 V

89534c04

4. If voltage does not drop steadily or voltage values do not match those in the intake air temperature voltage chart, the sensor is faulty.

5. If voltage is within specification, check power and ground circuits.

REMOVAL & INSTALLATION

1. Disconnect the negative battery cable.
2. Drain the engine coolant.
3. Label and disconnect the sensor electrical harness
4. Carefully remove the sensor.

To install:

5. Coat the sensor threads with Teflon® sealant.

6. Carefully install the sensor and tighten to 14–29 ft. lbs. (20–40 Nm) on all engines except the 1.5L (VIN K), 1.8L (VIN M) and 2.0L (VIN F). Tighten 1.5L (VIN K), 1.8L (VIN M) and 2.0L (VIN F) engines' sensors to 11–15 ft. lbs. (15–20 Nm).

7. Connect the sensor electrical harness.
8. Fill the engine with coolant.
9. Connect the negative battery cable.

Airflow Sensor

OPERATION

Two types of airflow sensors are used on these vehicles. Early model vehicles use a Volume Air Flow (VAF) sensor, while late model vehicles use a Mass Air Flow (MAF) sensor. The air flow sensors measure the intake air volume. The ECM uses this signal to calculate basic fuel injection timing. The air flow sensors are located in the intake tract between the air filter and the throttle body.

TESTING

Volume Air Flow (VAF) Sensor

♦ See Figure 25

VAF sensors can be identified by the presence of a six terminal square connector.

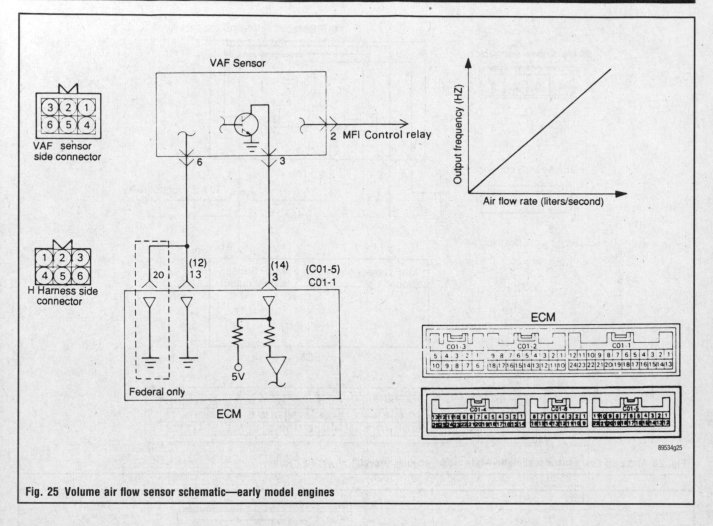

Fig. 25 Volume air flow sensor schematic—early model engines

➡️**This test requires the use of a multimeter capable of measuring frequency.**

1. Start the engine and allow it to reach operating temperature.
2. Backprobe the sensor electrical harness between terminals 3 and 6.
3. Frequency should be 27–33 Hz at idle and rise steadily to 60–80 Hz as engine speed is increased to 2000 rpm.
4. If frequency is not within specification, check the sensor power and ground circuit.
5. If power and ground circuits are functional, the sensor is faulty.

Mass Air Flow (MAF) Sensor

▶ **See Figures 26 and 27**

MAF sensors can be identified by the presence of either a four terminal or six terminal flat connector.

1. Start the engine and allow it to reach operating temperature.
2. On all engines except the 1.5L (VIN E), backprobe the sensor electrical harness between terminal 1 and ground.
   a. Voltage should be 0.7–1.1 volts at idle and rise steadily to 1.3–2.0 as engine speed is increased to 3000 rpm.
3. On 1.5L (VIN E) normally aspirated engines, backprobe the sensor electrical harness between terminal 4 and ground.
   a. Voltage should be 0.94–0.98 volts at idle and rise steadily to 1.76–1.79 as engine speed is increased to 3000 rpm.
4. On 1.5L (VIN E) turbocharged engines, backprobe the sensor electrical harness between terminal 3 and ground.

   a. Voltage should be 2.0–2.6 volts at idle and rise steadily to 2.6–3.3 as engine speed is increased to 3000 rpm.
5. If voltage is not within specification, check the sensor power and ground circuit.
6. If power and ground circuits are functional, the sensor is faulty.

REMOVAL & INSTALLATION

1. Disconnect the negative battery cable.
2. Label and disconnect the sensor electrical harness.
3. Loosen the hose clamps attaching the sensor to the intake duct.
4. Carefully remove the sensor.
To install:
5. Carefully install the sensor and tighten the hose clamps securely.
6. Connect the sensor electrical harness.
7. Connect the negative battery cable.

Barometric Pressure (BARO) Sensor

OPERATION

The BARO sensor is an integral part of the VAF. The sensor signal is used by the ECM to compute the altitude at which the vehicle is running and corrects the ignition timing and air/fuel ratio for best driveability and performance.

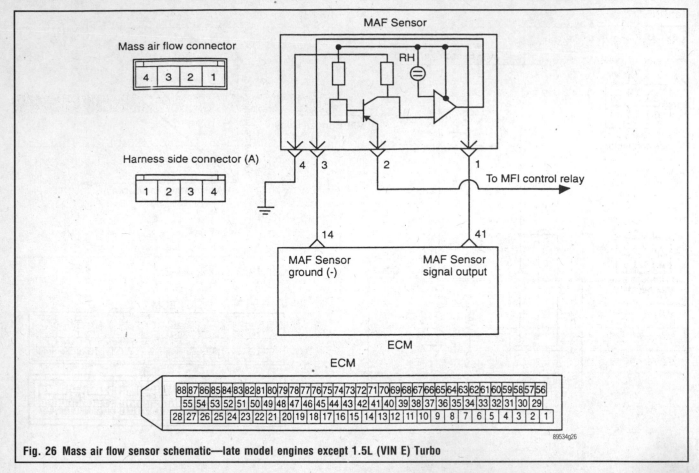

Fig. 26 Mass air flow sensor schematic—late model engines except 1.5L (VIN E) Turbo

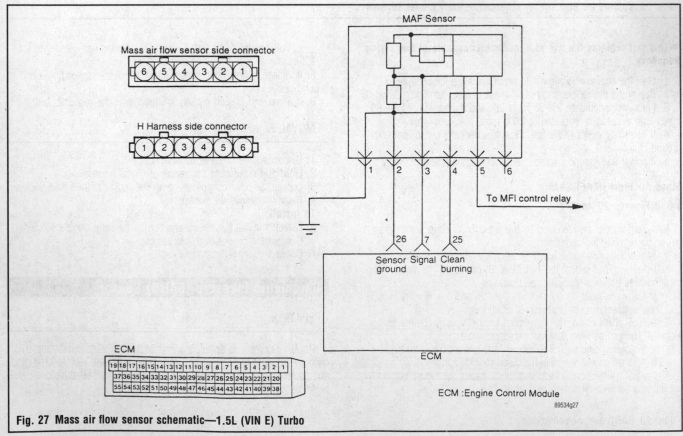

Fig. 27 Mass air flow sensor schematic—1.5L (VIN E) Turbo

TESTING

◆ **See Figure 28**

➡ **Testing of the BARO sensor requires the use of a scan tool.**

1. Connect the scan tool as per the manufacturer's instructions.
2. Note the elevation in feet of the site where the test is being performed.
3. The signal from the barometric pressure sensor should correspond with the actual altitude, as per the barometric pressure sensor specification chart.
4. If the sensor is not within specification, check the power and ground circuits.
5. If the power and ground circuits are functional, the sensor is faulty.

Barometric Pressure Sensor Specification Chart

Altitude	Test specification
When 0 m (0 ft.)	760 mmHg (29.92 in. Hg)
When 600 m (1,969 ft.)	710 mmHg (27.95 in. Hg)
When 1,200 m (3,937 ft.)	660 mmHg (25.98 in. Hg)
When 1,800 m (5,906 ft.)	610 mmHg (24.02 in. Hg)

89534c05

REMOVAL & INSTALLATION

The BARO sensor is an integral part of the VAF sensor and cannot be serviced separately. If the sensor is found to be defective, the VAF sensor must be replaced.

Throttle Position Sensor (TPS)

OPERATION

The TPS is a variable resistor that rotates with the throttle body shaft to sense the throttle valve opening. Based on TPS voltage signals, the ECM computes the throttle valve opening and accordingly corrects fuel for engine acceleration. The TPS is located on the throttle body, attached to the throttle shaft.

TESTING

◆ **See Figures 29 and 30 (p. 24–25)**

Early Model Engines

1. Backprobe the sensor electrical harness with the ignition **ON**.
2. Measure voltage between sensor terminals 1 and 3.
3. Voltage should be 0.45–0.55 volts with the throttle at idle position and increase steadily and smoothly to 4.5–5.5 volts with the throttle in the wide open throttle position.

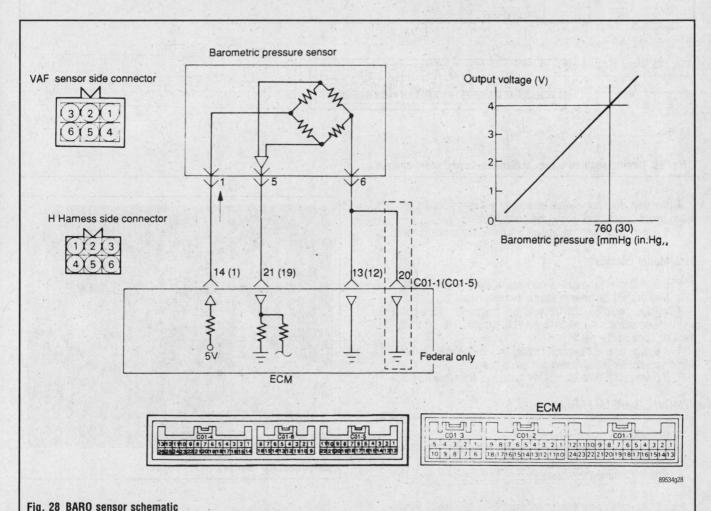

Fig. 28 BARO sensor schematic

89534g28

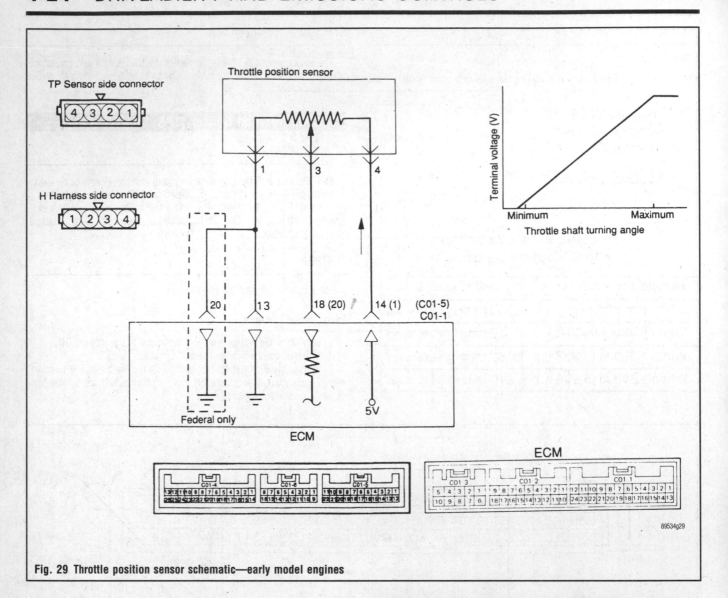

Fig. 29 Throttle position sensor schematic—early model engines

4. If voltage does not increase steadily or voltage values are not within specification, check power and ground circuits.

5. If power and ground circuits are functional, the sensor is faulty.

Late Model Engines

1. Backprobe the sensor electrical harness with the ignition **ON.**
2. Measure voltage between sensor terminals 1 and 2.
3. Voltage should be 0.25–0.8 volts with the throttle at idle position and increase steadily and smoothly to 4.25–4.8 volts with the throttle in the wide open throttle position.
4. If voltage does not increase steadily or voltage values are not within specification, check power and ground circuits.
5. If power and ground circuits are functional, the sensor is faulty.

REMOVAL & INSTALLATION

1. Disconnect the negative battery cable.
2. Label and disconnect the sensor electrical harness.
3. Loosen the sensor mounting bolts.
4. Carefully remove the sensor.

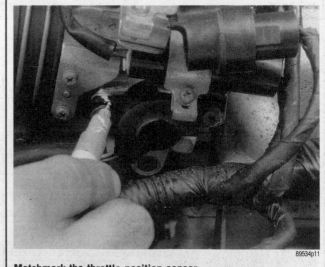

Matchmark the throttle position sensor . . .

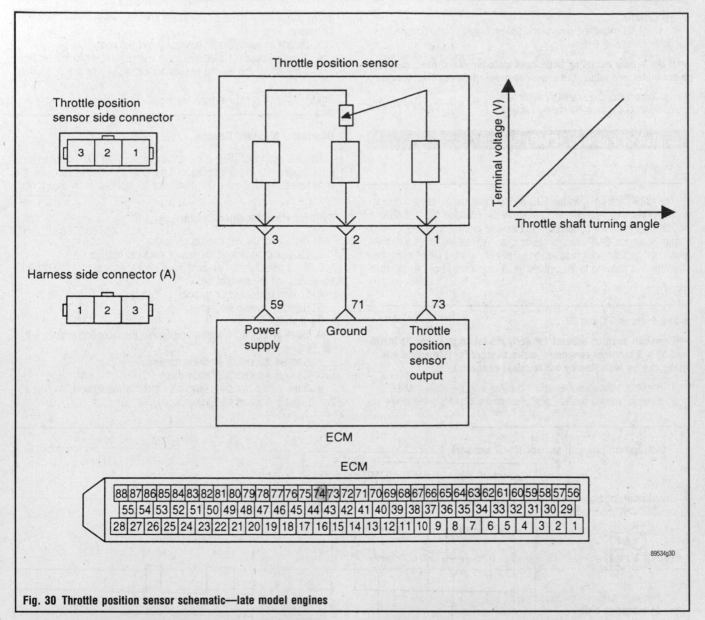

Fig. 30 Throttle position sensor schematic—late model engines

. . . loosen the mounting bolts . . .

. . . and remove the sensor from the throttle body

To install:

5. Carefully install the sensor and tighten the mounting bolts to 12–24 inch lbs. (1.5–2.5 Nm).

➡**If the sensor mounting bolts have slots for adjustment, connect a voltmeter and adjust the sensor to proper idle position voltage.**

6. Connect the sensor electrical harness.
7. Connect the negative battery cable.

Camshaft Position (CMP) Sensor

OPERATION

The CMP (also know as the TDC or Top Dead Center sensor) detects top dead center on the compression stroke for cylinders No. 1 and No. 4. The signal is used by the ECM to calculate fuel injection and ignition timing sequence. CMP sensors are used on vehicles equipped with both distributor and distributorless ignition. They are located either inside the distributor or attached to the cylinder head near the end of the camshaft.

TESTING

◆ **See Figures 31 and 32**

➡**Camshaft position sensors for early model engines can be identified by a 4 terminal connector, while sensors for late model engines can be identified by a 3 terminal connector.**

1. Backprobe the sensor electrical harness with the ignition **ON**.
2. Measure voltage between sensor terminals 1 and 3 (early model engines) or terminals 1 and 2 (late model engines) while slowly cranking the engine.
3. Voltage should alternate between 0 and 5.0 volts.
4. If voltage does not alternate, check the power and ground circuits.
5. If the power and ground circuits are functional, the sensor is faulty.

REMOVAL & INSTALLATION

Distributor Mounted Sensor

Removal and installation of the distributor mounted CMP requires complete disassembly of the distributor. If the CMP is found to be faulty, it is recommended that the entire distributor be replaced as an assembly.

Cylinder Head Mounted Sensor

1. Disconnect the negative battery cable.
2. Label and disconnect the sensor electrical harness.
3. If the sensor mounting bolts have slots for adjustment, matchmark the sensor and the cylinder head.
4. Loosen sensor mounting bolts.
5. Carefully remove the sensor.
To install:
6. Carefully install the sensor and tighten the mounting bolts to 6 ft. lbs. (8 Nm).
7. Connect the sensor electrical harness.
8. Connect the negative battery cable.
9. If the sensor mounting bolts have slots for adjustment, connect a timing light and adjust the ignition timing.

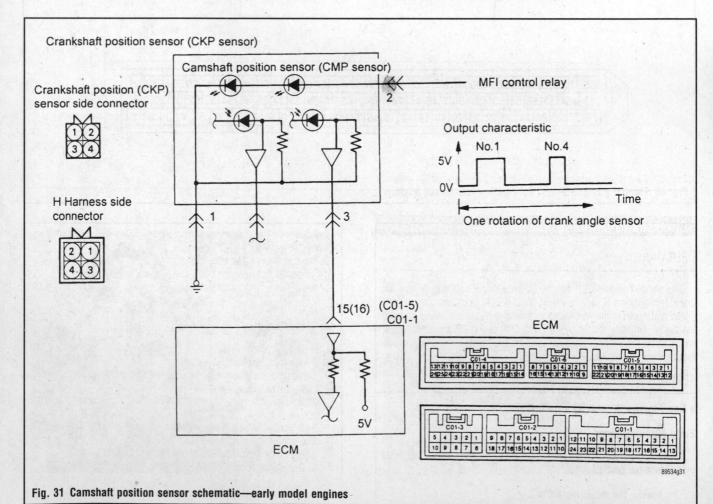

Fig. 31 Camshaft position sensor schematic—early model engines

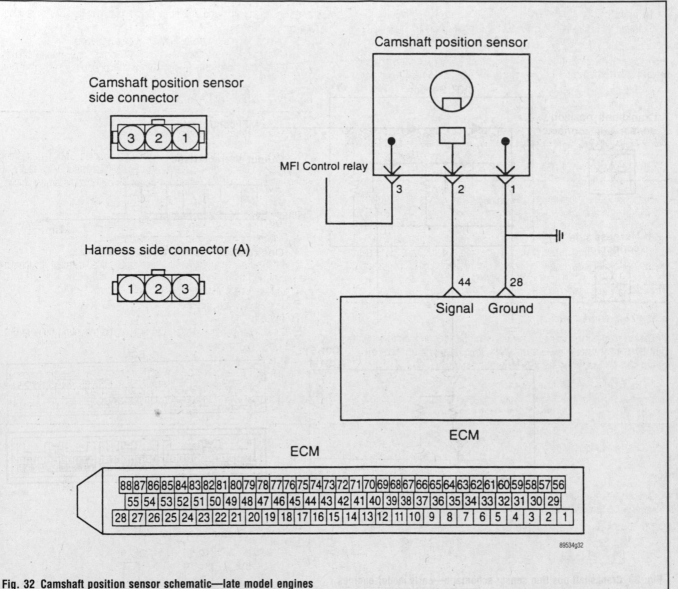

Camshaft position sensor

Camshaft position sensor side connector

MFI Control relay

Harness side connector (A)

Signal Ground

ECM

ECM

89534g32

Fig. 32 Camshaft position sensor schematic—late model engines

Crankshaft Position (CKP) Sensor

OPERATION

The signal from the CKP sensor which provides both engine rpm and crankshaft position is sent to the ECM. The ECM computes the engine speed and controls the fuel injection timing and ignition timing based on the signal. On early model engines, the CKP and CMP are combined and mounted on the cylinder head. On late model engines, the CKP is mounted on the engine near the flywheel.

TESTING

▶ **See Figures 33 and 34 (p. 28–29)**

Early Model Engines

Crankshaft position sensors for early model engines can be identified by a 4 terminal connector.

1. Backprobe the sensor electrical harness with the ignition **ON.**
2. Measure voltage between sensor terminals 1 and 4 while slowly cranking the engine.
3. Voltage should alternate between 0–5.0 volts.
4. If voltage does not alternate, check power and ground circuits.
5. If the power and ground circuits are functional, the sensor is faulty.

Late Model Engines

Crankshaft position sensors for early model engines can be identified by a 3 terminal connector.

1. Backprobe the sensor electrical harness between sensor terminals 2 and 3 with the engine running.
   a. Voltage should be greater than 0.1 volts and increase with engine rpm.
   b. If voltage is not within specification, check sensor resistance.
2. Disconnect the sensor electrical harness.
3. Measure the resistance between sensor terminals 2 and 3.
   a. Resistance should be 4.8–5.6 ohms @ 68°F (20°C).

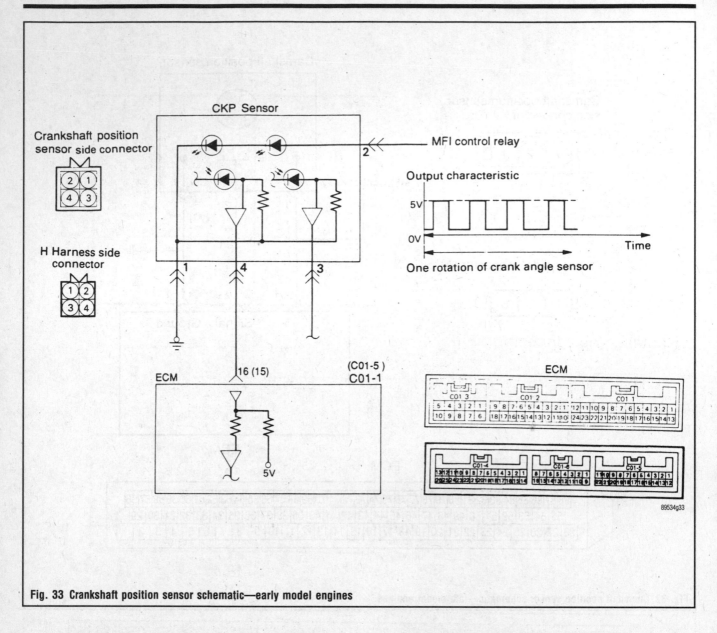

Fig. 33 Crankshaft position sensor schematic—early model engines

b. If resistance is not within specification, ensure that clearance between the CKP sensor and flywheel is 0.020–0.059 in . (0.5–1.5mm). Adjust sensor clearance as necessary.

c. If sensor resistance or voltage is still not within specification, sensor is faulty.

REMOVAL & INSTALLATION

Flywheel Mounted Sensor

1. Disconnect the negative battery cable.
2. Label and disconnect the sensor electrical harness.
3. Loosen sensor mounting bolts.
4. Carefully remove the sensor.
To install:
5. Carefully install the sensor.
6. Check sensor to flywheel clearance. Clearance should be 0.020–0.059 in. (0.5–1.5mm). Adjust as necessary.

7. Tighten mounting bolts to 6–8 ft. lbs. (9–11 Nm).
8. Connect the sensor electrical harness.
9. Connect the negative battery cable.

Cylinder Head Mounted Sensor

1. Disconnect the negative battery cable.
2. Label and disconnect the sensor electrical harness.
3. If the sensor mounting bolts have slots for adjustment, matchmark the sensor and the cylinder head.
4. Loosen the sensor mounting bolts.
5. Carefully remove the sensor.
To install:
6. Carefully install the sensor and tighten the mounting bolts to 6 ft. lbs. (8 Nm).
7. Connect the sensor electrical harness.
8. Connect the negative battery cable.
9. If the sensor mounting bolts have slots for adjustment, connect a timing light and adjust the ignition timing.

Crankshaft position sensor side connector

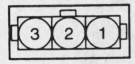

Harness side connector (A)

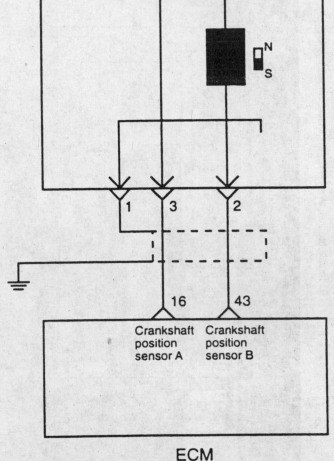

Fig. 34 Crankshaft position sensor schematic—late model engines

89534g34

COMPONENT LOCATIONS

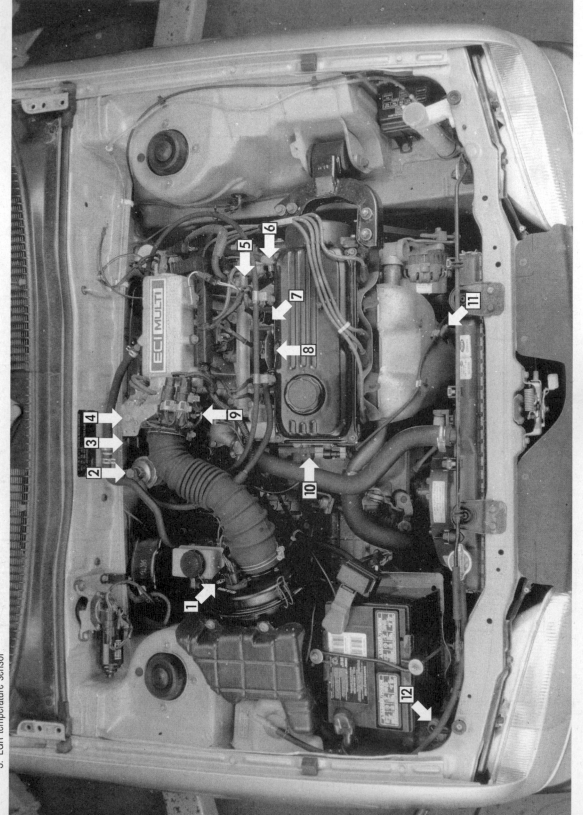

FUEL AND EMISSION SYSTEM COMPONENT LOCATIONS—SOHC ENGINE

1. Air flow sensor (includes intake air temperature and barometric pressure sensors)
2. Fuel filter
3. EGR temperature sensor
4. Purge control solenoid valve
5. Fuel pressure regulator and fuel rail
6. PCV valve
7. Fuel injector
8. Power transistor
9. Throttle position sensor
10. Engine coolant temperature sensor
11. Oxygen sensor
12. Evaporative emission canister

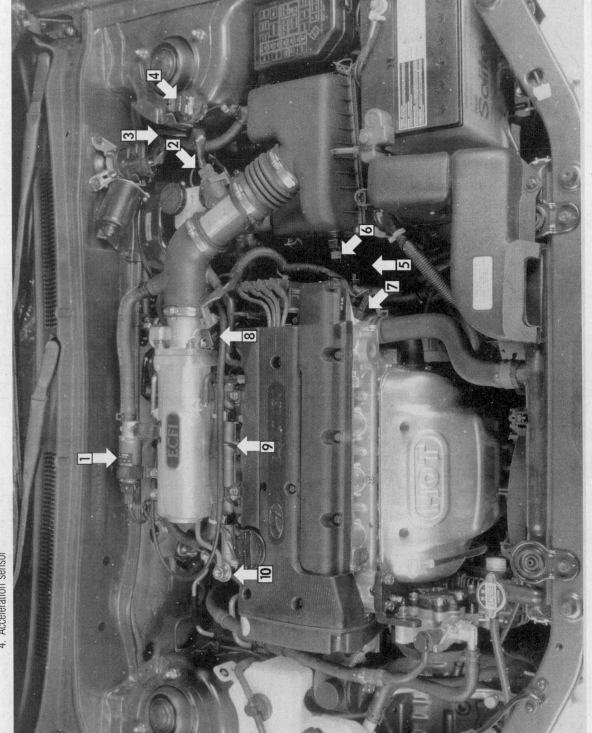

FUEL AND EMISSION SYSTEM COMPONENT LOCATIONS—DOHC ENGINE

1. Idle speed control actuator
2. Mass Air Flow (MAF) sensor
3. Canister purge solenoid valve
4. Acceleration sensor
5. Transaxle range switch
6. Intake air temperature sensor
7. Engine coolant temperature sensor
8. Throttle position sensor
9. Fuel injector
10. Fuel pressure regulator and fuel rail

89534p17

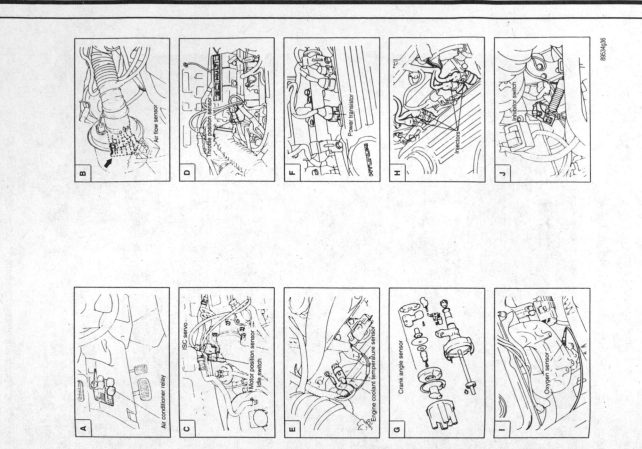

Fig. 36 Electronic engine control component locations (2 of 3)—Excel

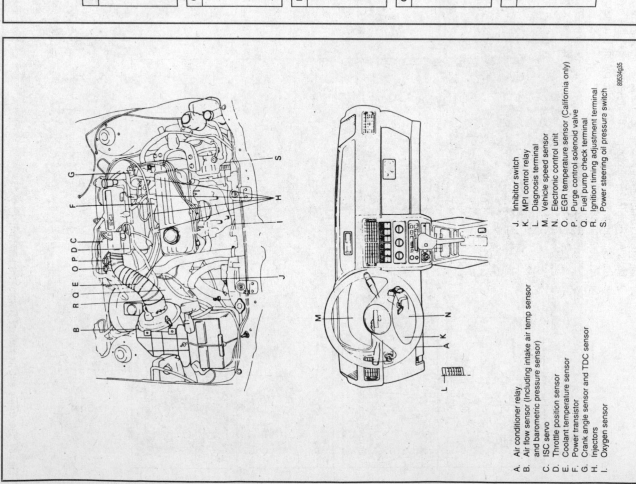

A. Air conditioner relay
B. Air flow sensor (Including intake air temp sensor and barometric pressure sensor)
C. ISC servo
D. Throttle position sensor
E. Coolant temperature sensor
F. Power transistor
G. Crank angle sensor and TDC sensor
H. Injectors
I. Oxygen sensor
J. Inhibitor switch
K. MPI control relay
L. Diagnosis terminal
M. Vehicle speed sensor
N. Electronic control unit
O. EGR temperature sensor (California only)
P. Purge control solenoid valve
Q. Fuel pump check terminal
R. Ignition timing adjustment terminal
S. Power steering oil pressure switch

Fig. 35 Electronic engine control component locations (1 of 3)—Excel

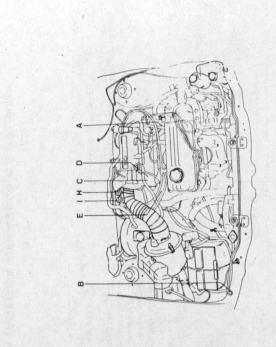
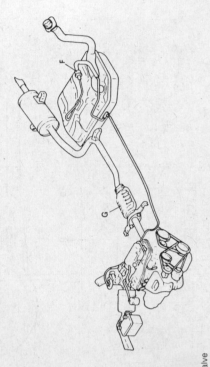

A. PCV valve
B. Canister
C. EGR valve
D. EGR temperature sensor (California only)
E. Thermo valve
F. 2-way valve
G. Catalytic converter
H. Purge control solenoid valve
I. EGR control solenoid valve (California only)

Fig. 38 Emissions component locations (1 of 2)—Excel

Self-diagnostic connector

ECU

Fuel pump check terminal

Power steering oil pressure switch

Fig. 37 Electronic engine control component locations (3 of 3)—Excel

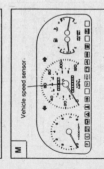
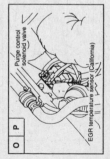

MPI control relay

Vehicle speed sensor

Purge control solenoid valve (California)

EGR temperature sensor (California)

Ignition timing adjustment terminal

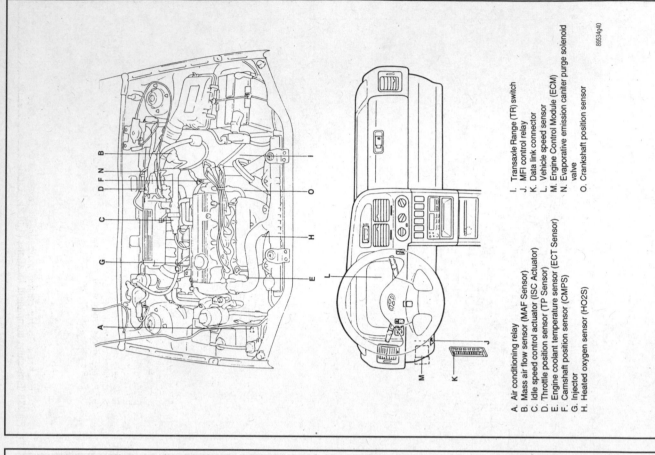

A. Air conditioning relay
B. Mass air flow sensor (MAF Sensor)
C. Idle speed control actuator (ISC Actuator)
D. Throttle position sensor (TP Sensor)
E. Engine coolant temperature sensor (ECT Sensor)
F. Camshaft position sensor (CMPS)
G. Injector
H. Heated oxygen sensor (HO2S)

I. Transaxle Range (TR) switch
J. MFI control relay
K. Data link connector
L. Vehicle speed sensor
M. Engine Control Module (ECM)
N. Evaporative emission caniter purge solenoid valve
O. Crankshaft position sensor

Fig. 40 Electronic engine control component locations (1 of 3)—Scoupe

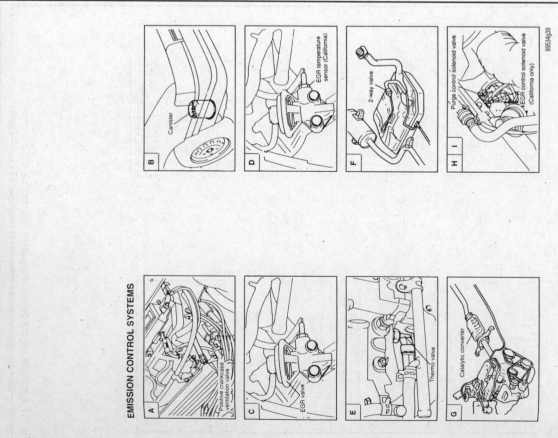

Fig. 39 Emissions component locations (2 of 2)—Excel

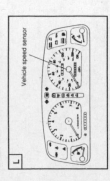

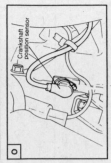

Fig. 42 Electronic engine control component locations (3 of 3)—Scoupe

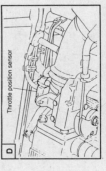

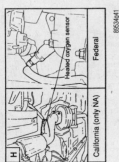
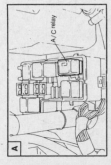
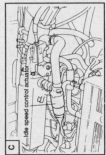

Fig. 41 Electronic engine control component locations (2 of 3)—Scoupe

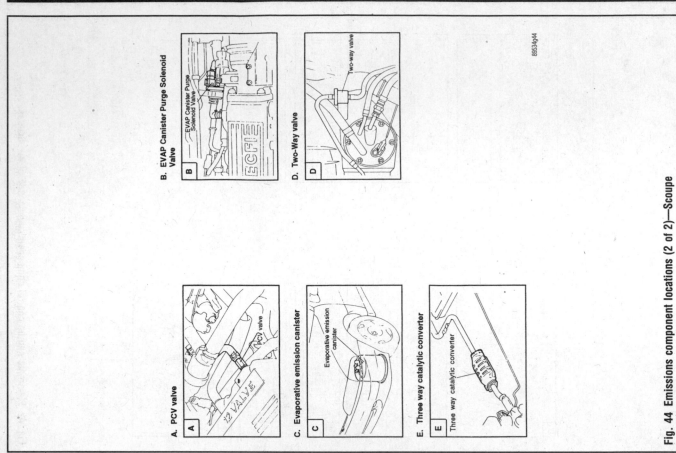

B. EVAP Canister Purge Solenoid Valve

D. Two-Way valve

A. PCV valve

C. Evaporative emission canister

E. Three way catalytic converter

Fig. 44 Emissions component locations (2 of 2)—Scoupe

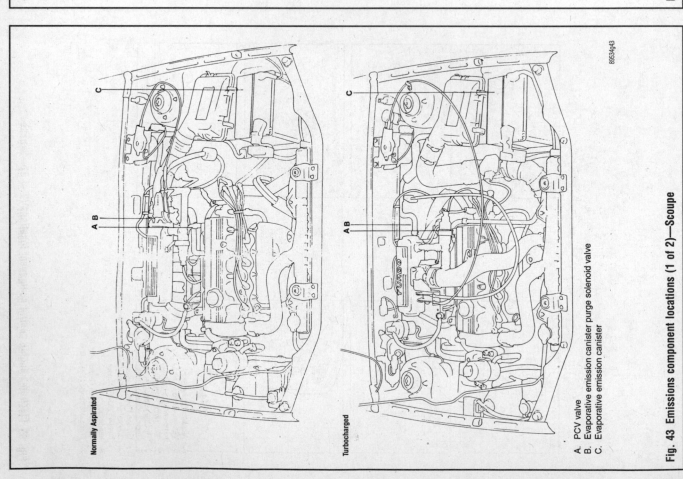

Normally Aspirated

Turbocharged

A. PCV valve
B. Evaporative emission canister purge solenoid valve
C. Evaporative emission canister

Fig. 43 Emissions component locations (1 of 2)—Scoupe

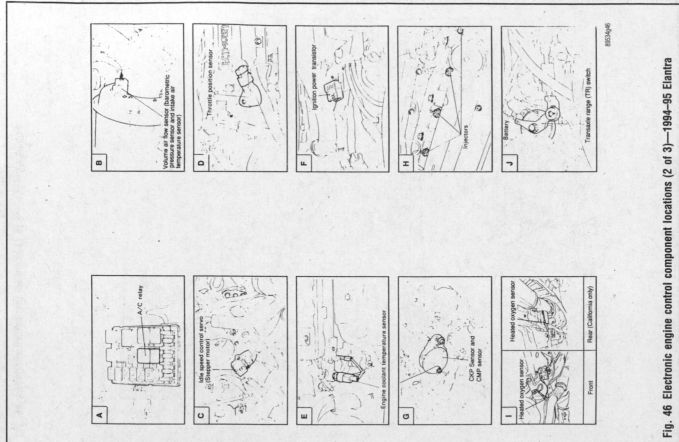

Fig. 46 Electronic engine control component locations (2 of 3)—1994–95 Elantra

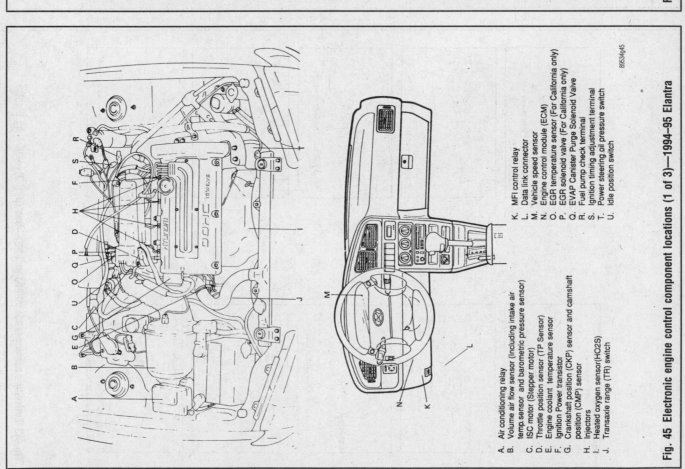

A. Air conditioning relay
B. Volume air flow sensor (including intake air temp.sensor and barometric pressure sensor)
C. ISC motor (Stepper motor)
D. Throttle position sensor (TP Sensor)
E. Engine coolant temperature sensor
F. Ignition Power transistor
G. Crankshaft position (CKP) sensor and camshaft position (CMP) sensor
H. Injectors
I. Heated oxygen sensor(HO2S)
J. Transaxle range (TR) switch
K. MFI control relay
L. Data link connector
M. Vehicle speed sensor
N. Engine control module (ECM)
O. EGR temperature sensor (For California only)
P. EGR solenoid valve (For California only)
Q. EVAP Canister Purge Solenoid Valve
R. Fuel pump check terminal
S. Ignition timing adjustment terminal
T. Power steering oil pressure switch
U. Idle position switch

Fig. 45 Electronic engine control component locations (1 of 3)—1994–95 Elantra

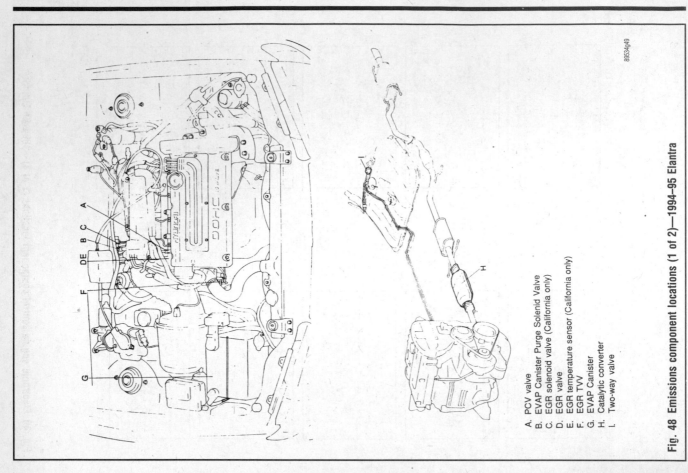

A. PCV valve
B. EVAP Canister Purge Solenid Valve
C. EGR solenoid valve (California only)
D. EGR valve
E. EGR temperature sensor (California only)
F. EGR TVV
G. EVAP Canister
H. Catalytic converter
I. Two-way valve

Fig. 48 Emissions component locations (1 of 2)—1994-95 Elantra

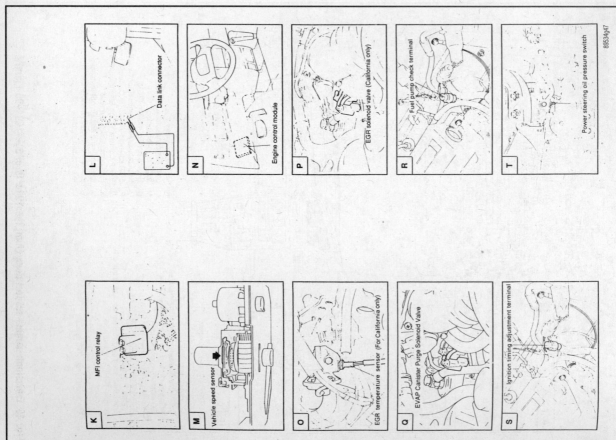

Fig. 47 Electronic engine control component locations (3 of 3)—1994-95 Elantra

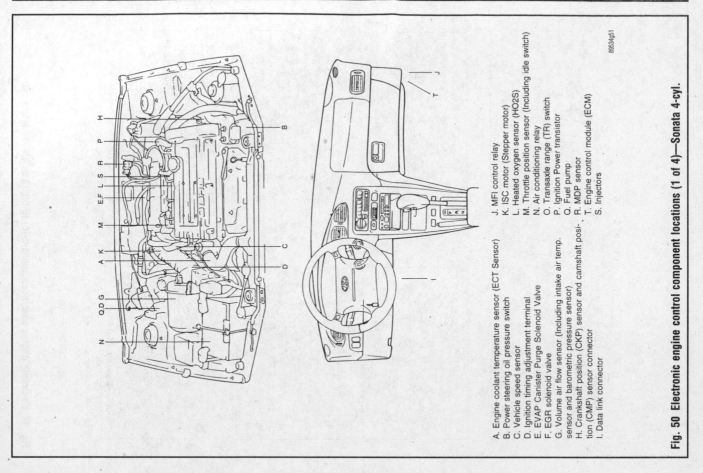

A. Engine coolant temperature sensor (ECT Sensor)
B. Power steering oil pressure switch
C. Vehicle speed sensor
D. Ignition timing adjustment terminal
E. EVAP Canister Purge Solenoid Valve
F. EGR solenoid valve
G. Volume air flow sensor (Including intake air temp. sensor and barometric pressure sensor)
H. Crankshaft position (CKP) sensor and camshaft position (CMP) sensor connector
I. Data link connector
J. MFI control relay
K. ISC motor (Stepper motor)
L. Heated oxygen sensor (HO2S)
M. Throttle position sensor (Including idle switch)
N. Air conditioning relay
O. Transaxle range (TR) switch
P. Ignition Power transistor
Q. Fuel pump
R. MDP sensor
S. Injectors
T. Engine control module (ECM)

Fig. 50 Electronic engine control component locations (1 of 4)—Sonata 4-cyl.

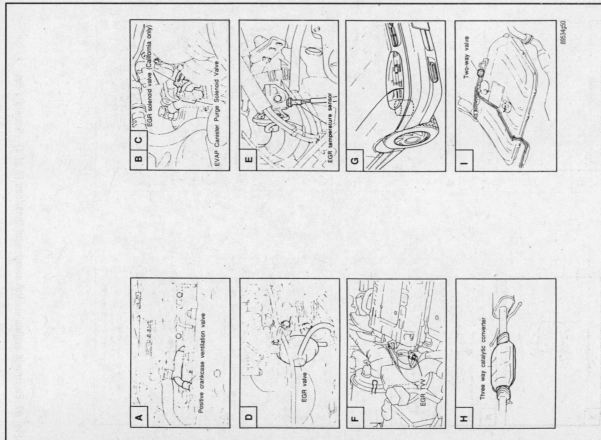

Fig. 49 Emissions component locations (2 of 2)—1994–95 Elantra

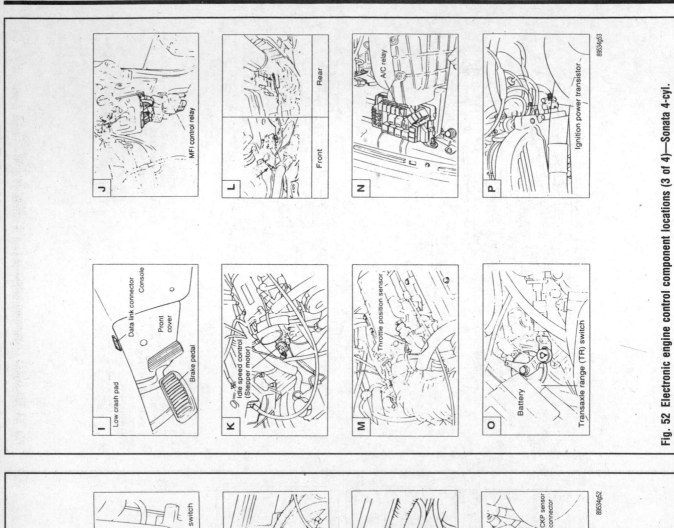

Fig. 52 Electronic engine control component locations (3 of 4)—Sonata 4-cyl.

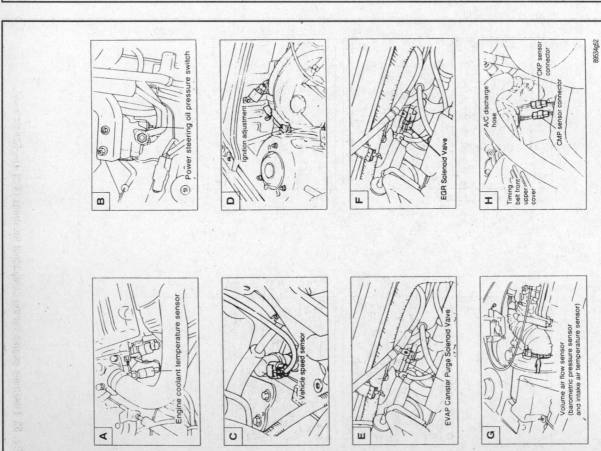

Fig. 51 Electronic engine control component locations (2 of 4)—Sonata 4-cyl.

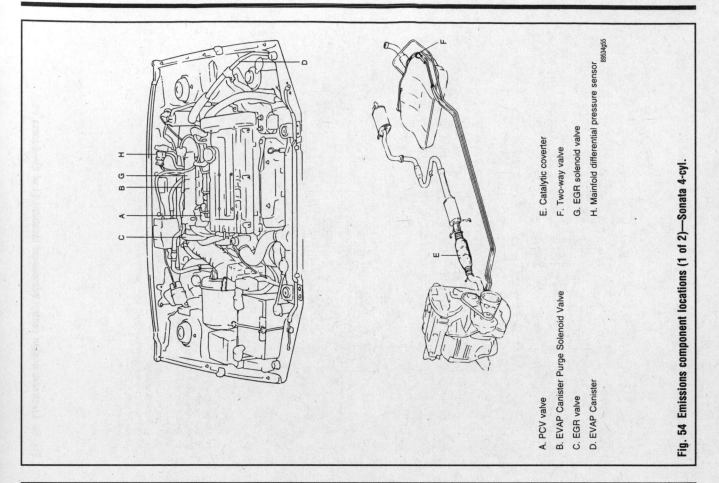

A. PCV valve
B. EVAP Canister Purge Solenoid Valve
C. EGR valve
D. EVAP Canister

E. Catalytic coverter
F. Two-way valve
G. EGR solenoid valve
H. Mainfold differential pressure sensor

Fig. 54 Emissions component locations (1 of 2)—Sonata 4-cyl.

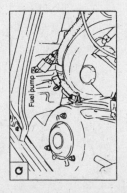

Fig. 53 Electronic engine control component locations (4 of 4)—Sonata 4-cyl.

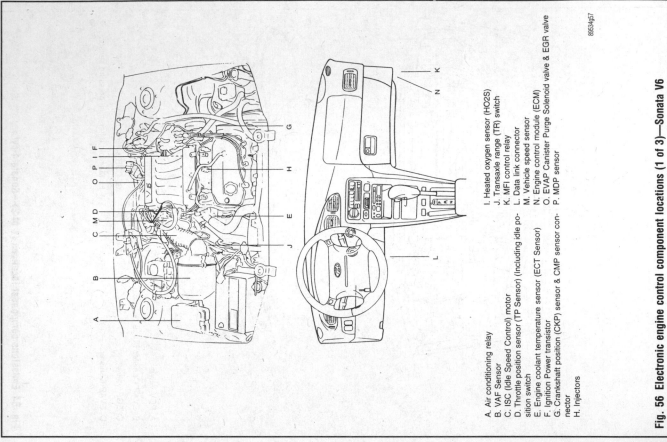

A. Air conditioning relay
B. VAF Sensor
C. ISC (Idle Speed Control) motor
D. Throttle position sensor (TP Sensor) (including position switch
E. Engine coolant temperature sensor (ECT Sensor)
F. Ignition Power transistor
G. Crankshaft position (CKP) sensor & CMP sensor connector
H. Injectors
I. Heated oxygen sensor (HO2S)
J. Transaxle range (TR) switch
K. MFI control relay
L. Data link connector
M. Vehicle speed sensor
N. Engine control module (ECM)
O. EVAP Canister Purge Solenoid valve & EGR valve
P. MDP sensor

Fig. 56 Electronic engine control component locations (1 of 3)—Sonata V6

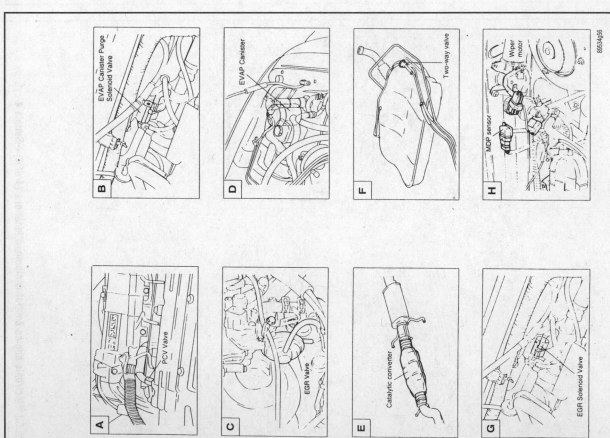

Fig. 55 Emissions component locations (2 of 2)—Sonata 4-cyl.

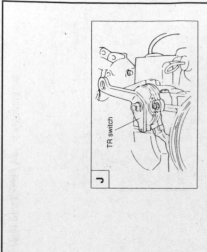

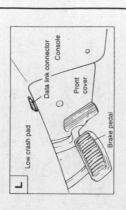

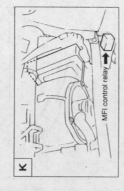

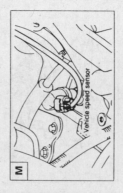

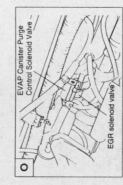

Fig. 58 Electronic engine control component locations (3 of 3)—Sonata V6

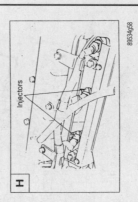

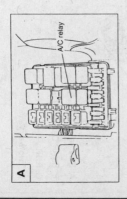

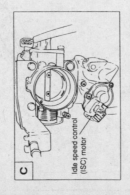

Fig. 57 Electronic engine control component locations (2 of 3)—Sonata V6

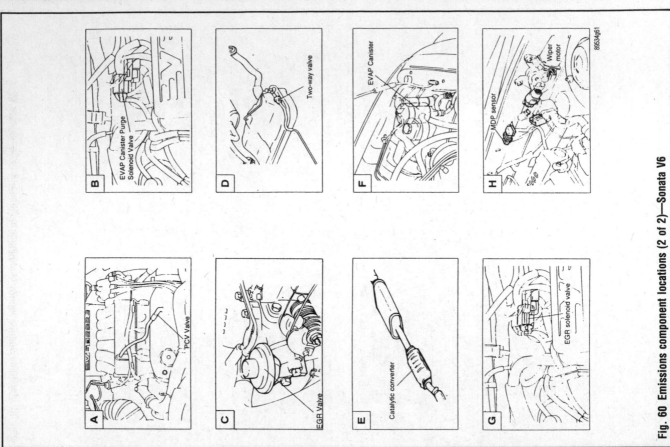

Fig. 60 Emissions component locations (2 of 2)—Sonata V6

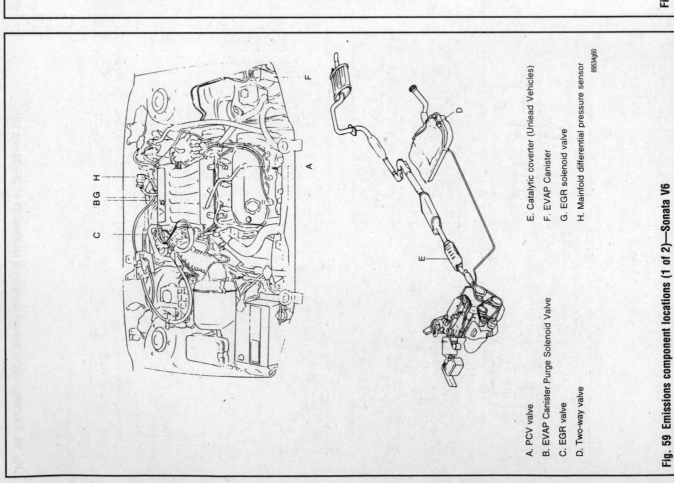

A. PCV valve
B. EVAP Canister Purge Solenoid Valve
C. EGR valve
D. Two-way valve
E. Catalytic coverter (Unlead Vehicles)
F. EVAP Canister
G. EGR solenoid valve
H. Mainfold differential pressure sensor

Fig. 59 Emissions component locations (1 of 2)—Sonata V6

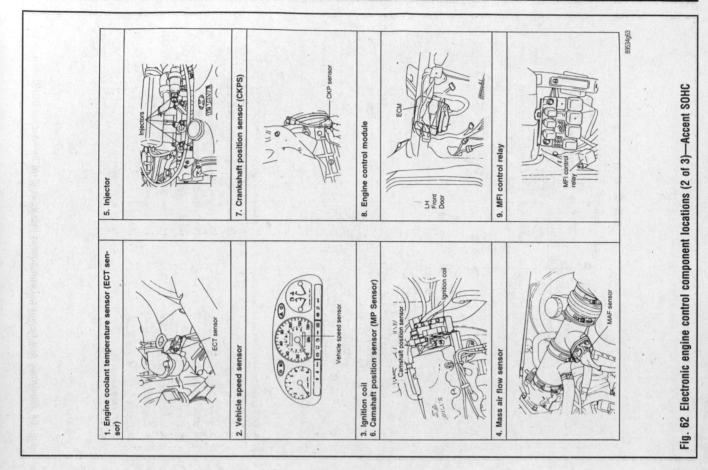

89534g63

5. Injector

7. Crankshaft position sensor (CKPS)

CKP sensor

8. Engine control module

ECM

LH
Front
Door

9. MFI control relay

MFI control
relay

1. Engine coolant temperature sensor (ECT sensor)

ECT sensor

2. Vehicle speed sensor

Vehicle speed sensor

3. Ignition coil
6. Camshaft position sensor (MP Sensor)

Ignition coil

Camshaft position sensor

4. Mass air flow sensor

MAF sensor

Fig. 62 Electronic engine control component locations (2 of 3)—Accent SOHC

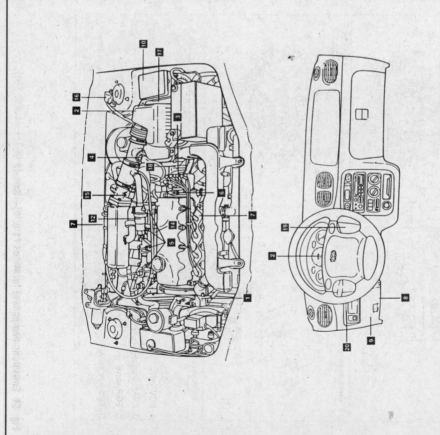

89534g62

1. Engine coolant temperature sensor (ECT sensor)
2. Vehicle speed sensor
3. Ignition coil
4. Mass air flow sensor
5. Injector
6. Camshaft position sensor (CMP)
7. Crankshaft position sensor (CKP)
8. Engine Control Module (ECM)
9. MFI control relay
10. Air conditioning relay

11. Headed oxygen sensor (H2OS)
12. Idle speed control actuator (ISC Actuator)
13. Intake air temp. sensor
14. Knock sensor
15. Throttle position sensor (TPS)
16. Acceleration sensor
17. Evaporative emission canister purge solenoid valve
18. Transaxle Range (TR) switch
19. Ignition switch
20. Data link connector

Fig. 61 Electronic engine control component locations (1 of 3)—Accent SOHC

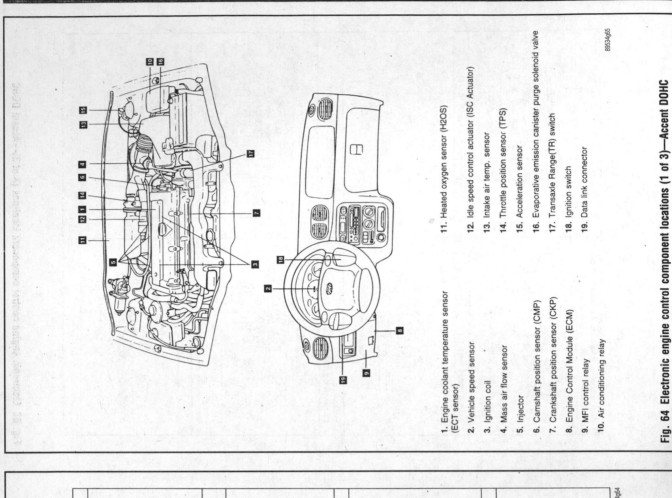

1. Engine coolant temperature sensor (ECT sensor)
2. Vehicle speed sensor
3. Ignition coil
4. Mass air flow sensor
5. Injector
6. Camshaft position sensor (CMP)
7. Crankshaft position sensor (CKP)
8. Engine Control Module (ECM)
9. MFI control relay
10. Air conditioning relay
11. Heated oxygen sensor (H2OS)
12. Idle speed control actuator (ISC Actuator)
13. Intake air temp. sensor
14. Throttle position sensor (TPS)
15. Acceleration sensor
16. Evaporative emission canister purge solenoid valve
17. Transaxle Range(TR) switch
18. Ignition switch
19. Data link connector

Fig. 64 Electronic engine control component locations (1 of 3)—Accent DOHC

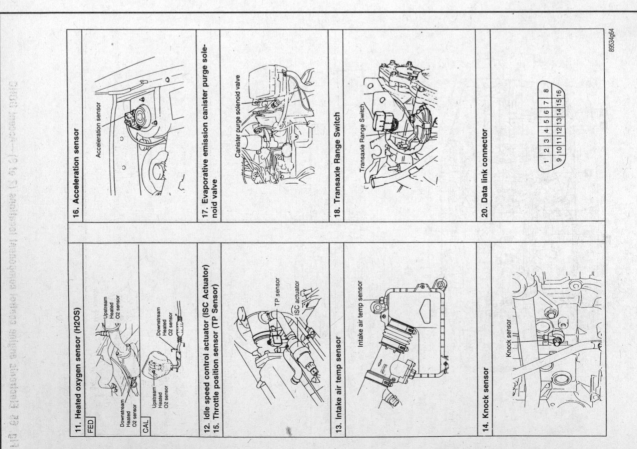

11. Heated oxygen sensor (H2OS)
12. Idle speed control actuator (ISC Actuator)
15. Throttle position sensor (TP Sensor)
13. Intake air temp sensor
14. Knock sensor
16. Acceleration sensor
17. Evaporative emission canister purge solenoid valve
18. Transaxle Range Switch
20. Data link connector

Fig. 63 Electronic engine control component locations (3 of 3)—Accent SOHC

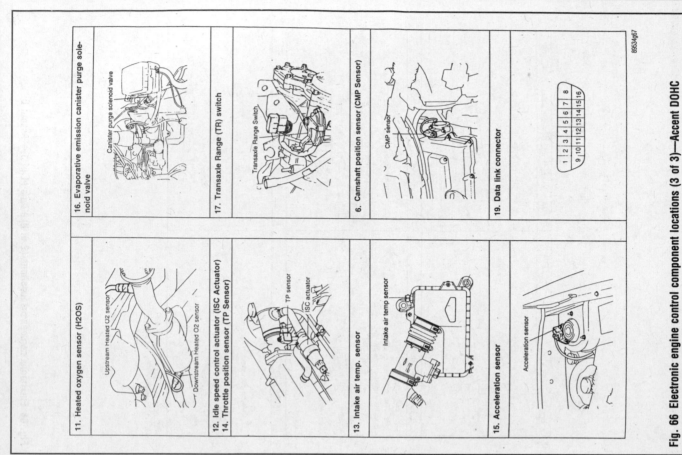

Fig. 66 Electronic engine control component locations (3 of 3)—Accent DOHC

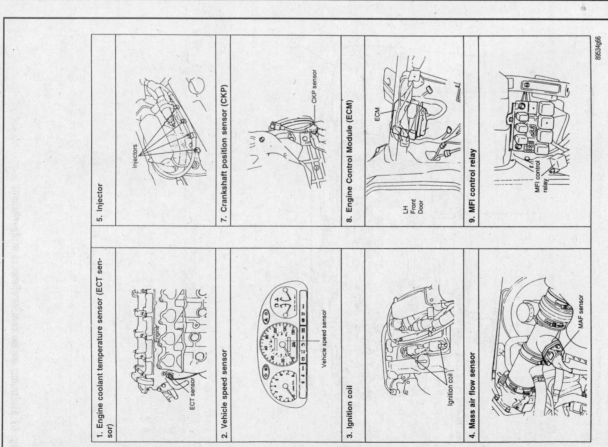

Fig. 65 Electronic engine control component locations (2 of 3)—Accent DOHC

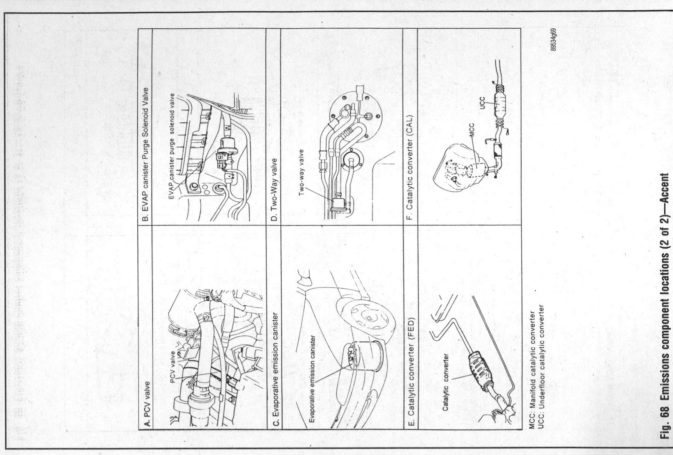

Fig. 68 Emissions component locations (2 of 2)—Accent

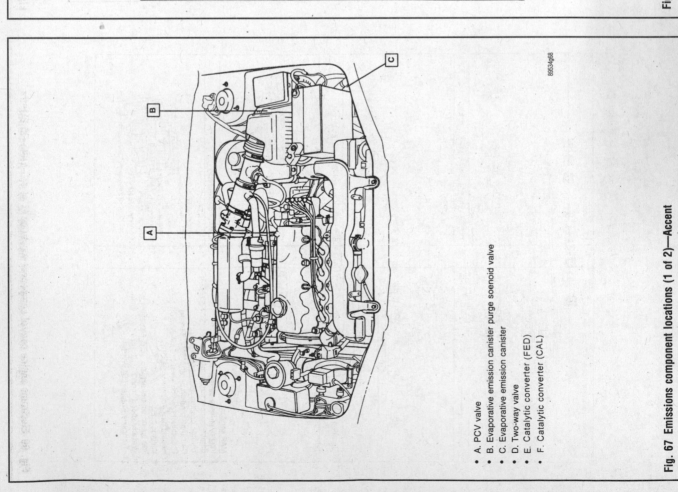

- A. PCV valve
- B. Evaporative emission canister purge soenoid valve
- C. Evaporative emission canister
- D. Two-way valve
- E. Catalytic converter (FED)
- F. Catalytic converter (CAL)

Fig. 67 Emissions component locations (1 of 2)—Accent

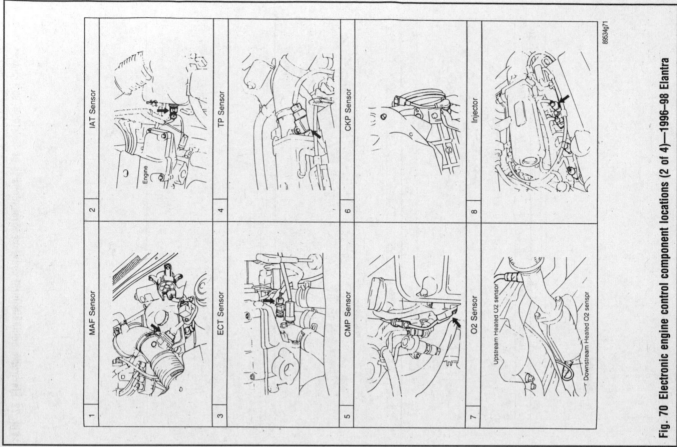

89534g71

Fig. 70 Electronic engine control component locations (2 of 4)—1996–98 Elantra

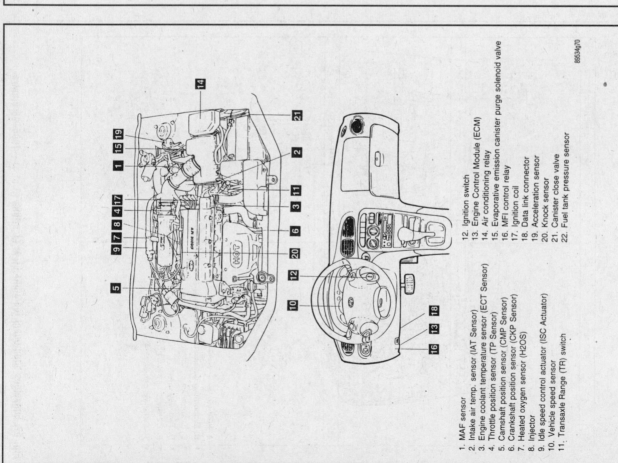

89534g70

Fig. 69 Electronic engine control component locations (1 of 4)—1996–98 Elantra

1. MAF sensor
2. Intake air temp. sensor (IAT Sensor)
3. Engine coolant temperature sensor (ECT Sensor)
4. Throttle position sensor (TP Sensor)
5. Camshaft position sensor (CMP Sensor)
6. Crankshaft position sensor (CKP Sensor)
7. Heated oxygen sensor (H2OS)
8. Injector
9. Idle speed control actuator (ISC Actuator)
10. Vehicle speed sensor
11. Transaxle Range (TR) switch

12. Ignition switch
13. Engine Control Module (ECM)
14. Air conditioning relay
15. Evaporative emission canister purge solenoid valve
16. MFI control relay
17. Ignition coil
18. Data link connector
19. Acceleration sensor
20. Knock sensor
21. Canister close valve
22. Fuel tank pressure sensor

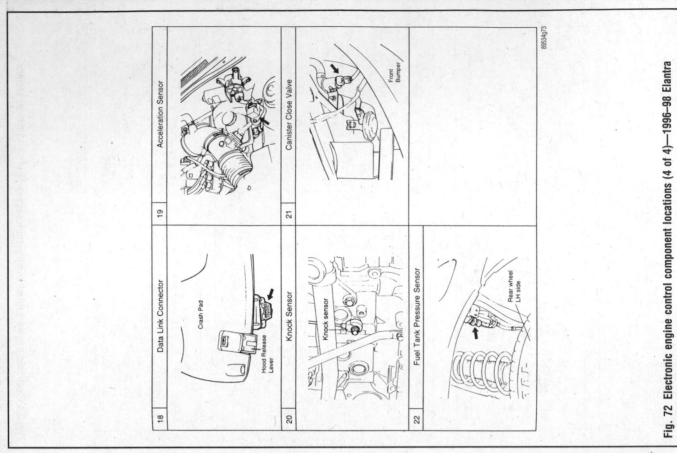

Fig. 72 Electronic engine control component locations (4 of 4)—1996–98 Elantra

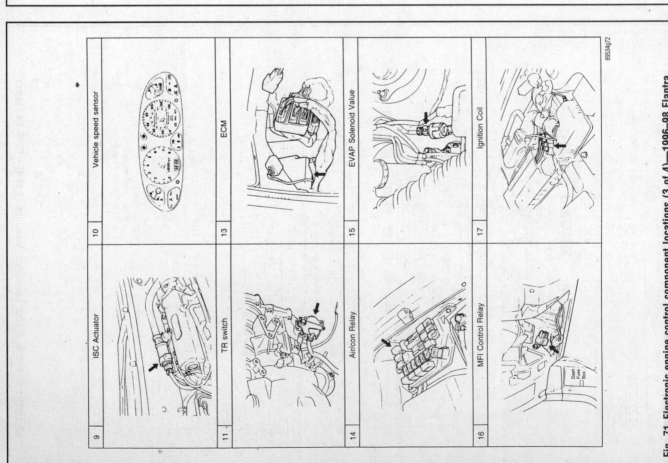

Fig. 71 Electronic engine control component locations (3 of 4)—1996–98 Elantra

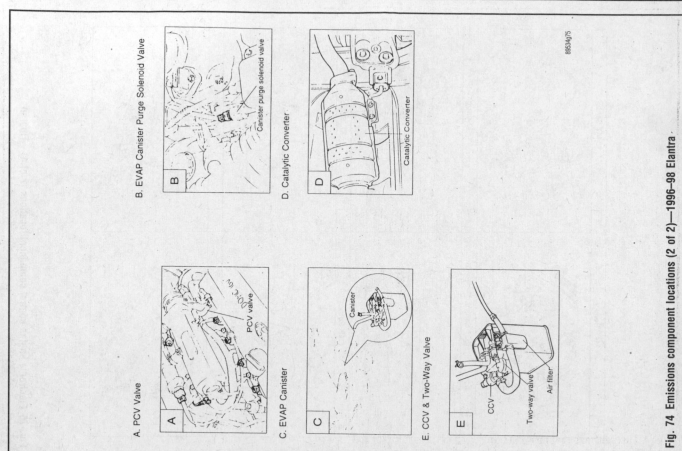

A. PCV Valve

B. EVAP Canister Purge Solenoid Valve

C. EVAP Canister

D. Catalytic Converter

E. CCV & Two-Way Valve

Fig. 74 Emissions component locations (2 of 2)—1996–98 Elantra

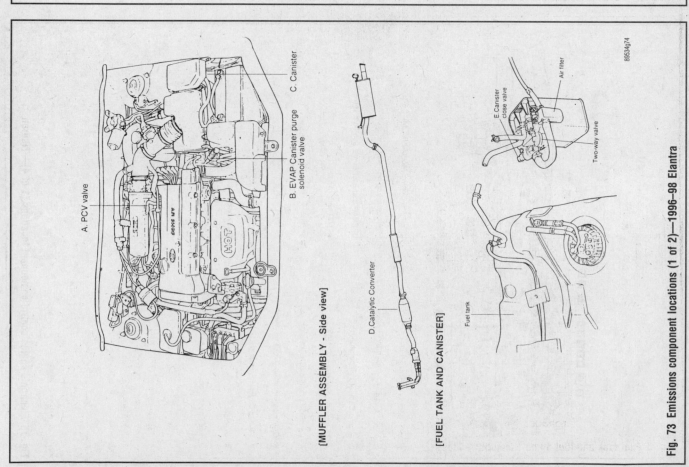

[MUFFLER ASSEMBLY - Side view]

[FUEL TANK AND CANISTER]

A. PCV valve

B. EVAP Canister purge solenoid valve

C. Canister

D. Catalytic Converter

E. Canister close valve

Fig. 73 Emissions component locations (1 of 2)—1996–98 Elantra

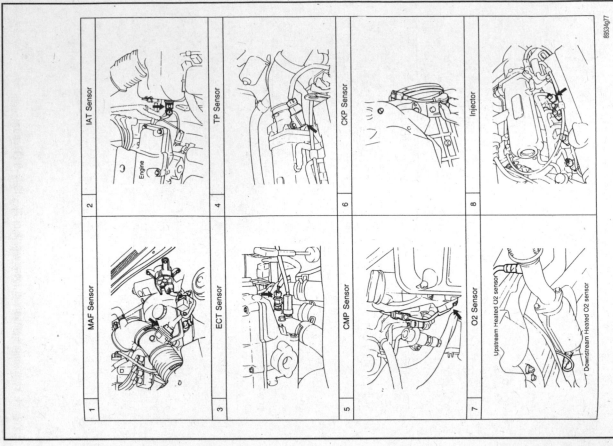

Fig. 76 Electronic engine control component locations (2 of 4)—Tiburon

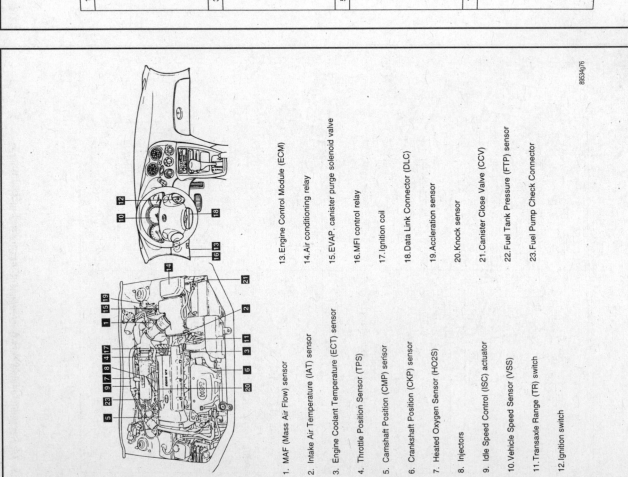

1. MAF (Mass Air Flow) sensor
2. Intake Air Temperature (IAT) sensor
3. Engine Coolant Temperature (ECT) sensor
4. Throttle Position Sensor (TPS)
5. Camshaft Position (CMP) sensor
6. Crankshaft Position (CKP) sensor
7. Heated Oxygen Sensor (HO2S)
8. Injectors
9. Idle Speed Control (ISC) actuator
10. Vehicle Speed Sensor (VSS)
11. Transaxle Range (TR) switch
12. Ignition switch
13. Engine Control Module (ECM)
14. Air conditioning relay
15. EVAP. canister purge solenoid valve
16. MFI control relay
17. Ignition coil
18. Data Link Connector (DLC)
19. Acceleration sensor
20. Knock sensor
21. Canister Close Valve (CCV)
22. Fuel Tank Pressure (FTP) sensor
23. Fuel Pump Check Connector

Fig. 75 Electronic engine control component locations (1 of 4)—Tiburon

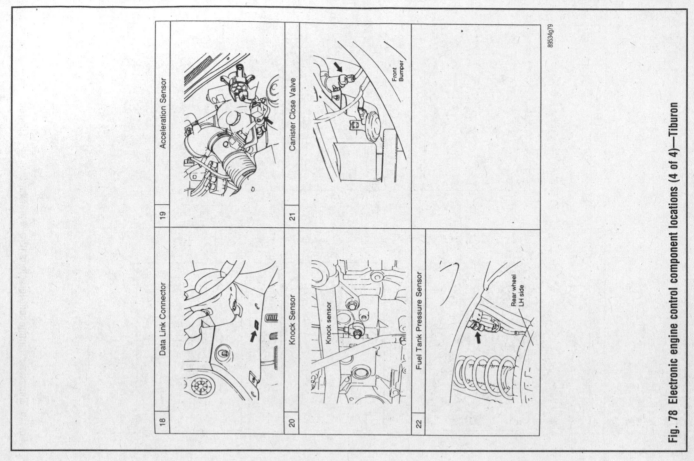

Fig. 78 Electronic engine control component locations (4 of 4)—Tiburon

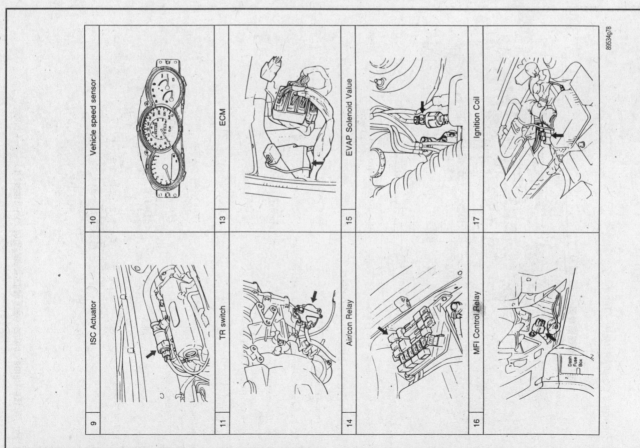

Fig. 77 Electronic engine control component locations (3 of 4)—Tiburon

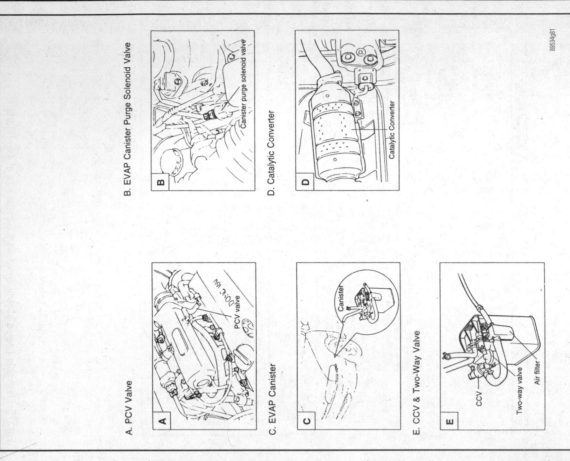

A. PCV Valve

B. EVAP Canister Purge Solenoid Valve

C. EVAP Canister

D. Catalytic Converter

E. CCV & Two-Way Valve

Fig. 80 Emissions component locations (2 of 2)—Tiburon

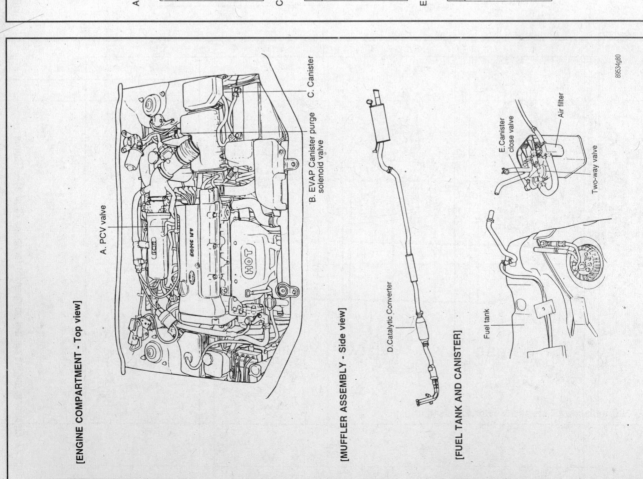

[ENGINE COMPARTMENT - Top view]

[MUFFLER ASSEMBLY - Side view]

[FUEL TANK AND CANISTER]

Fig. 79 Emissions component locations (1 of 2)—Tiburon

TROUBLE CODES

General Information

OBD I

Except Scoupe

The Engine Control Module (ECM) is capable of monitoring both input and output signals. When the ECM detects an irregularity, it sets a Diagnostic Trouble Code (DTC) and outputs the signal to the self-diagnosis output terminal. There are 14 two-digit diagnosis codes, including the normal state. DTC's can be read out by using an analog voltmeter or a generic scan tool. DTC's stay in the ECM as long as battery power is maintained.

Scoupe

The Engine Control Module (ECM) is capable of monitoring both input and output signals. When the ECM detects an irregularity, it sets a Diagnostic Trouble Code (DTC) and outputs the signal to the self-diagnosis output terminal. There are 29, two-digit codes, including the normal state. DTC's can be read out by using the Maintenance Indicator Lamp (MIL) or a generic scan tool. DTC's stay in the ECM as long as battery power is maintained.

General Information

OBD II

The Engine Control Module (ECM) monitors both input and output signals (some signals all the time and others under specified conditions). When the ECM detects an irregularity, it sets a Diagnostic Trouble Code (DTC) and outputs the signal to the self-diagnosis output terminal.. DTC's are 5-digit alpha numeric codes consisting of a "P" and a 4-digit identifier. The trouble codes can only be read out by using a generic scan tool. DTC's stay in the ECM as long as battery power is maintained.

Diagnostic Connector

▶ See Figures 81 and 82

The diagnostic connector for all vehicles is located under the left side of the dash. OBD I connectors use 12 pins, while OBD II connectors use 16 pins.

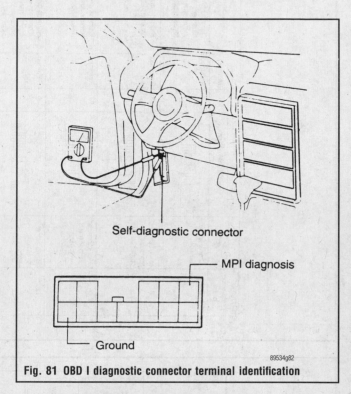

Fig. 81 OBD I diagnostic connector terminal identification

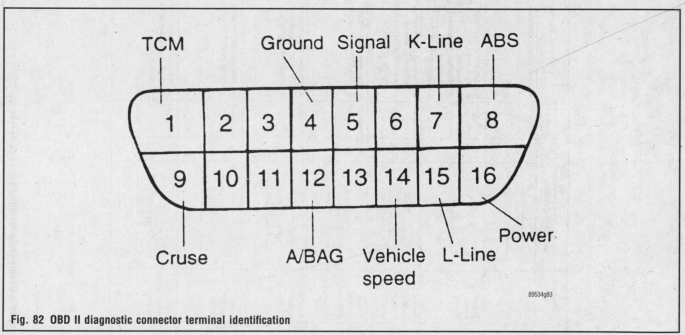

Fig. 82 OBD II diagnostic connector terminal identification

Reading Codes

Output preference order	Diagnosis item	Trouble code: Output signal pattern	Trouble code: No.	Trouble code: Memory	Check item (Remedy)
1	Engine control unit		-	-	(Replace engine control unit)
2	Oxygen sensor (Front)		11	Retained	o Harness and connector o Fuel pressure o Injectors (Replace if defective.) o Intake air leaks o Oxygen sensor (Front)
3	Air flow sensor		12	Retained	o Harness and connector (If harness and connector are normal, replace air flow sensor assembly.)
4	Air temperature sensor		13	Retained	o Harness and connector o Air temperature sensor
5	Throttle position sensor		14	Retained	o Harness and connector o Throttle position sensor o Idle position switch
6	Motor position sensor		15	Retained	o Harness and connector o Motor position sensor
7	Coolant temperature sensor		21	Retained	o Harness and connector o Coolant temperature sensor

89534g84

Fig. 83 Diagnostic trouble code identification (1 of 3)—Excel

Output preference order	Diagnosis item	Trouble code: Output signal pattern	Trouble code: No.	Trouble code: Memory	Check item (Remedy)
8	Crank angle sensor		22	Retained	o Harness and connector If harness and connector are normal, replace distributor assembly.)
9	No.1 cylinder top dead center sensor		23	Retained	o Harness and connector If harness and connector are normal, replace distributor assembly.)
10	Vehiclespeed sensor (reed switch)		24	Retained	o Harness and connector o Vehicle-speed sensor (reed switch)
11	Barometric pressure sensor		25	Retained	o Harness and connector If harness and connector are normal, replace barometric pressure sensor assembly.)
12	Injector		41	Retained	o Harness and connector o Injector coil resistance
13	Fuel pump		42	Retained	o Harness and connector o Control relay
14	EGR*		43	Retained	o Harness and connector o EGR temperature sensor o EGR valve o EGR control solenoid valve o EGR valve control vacuum
15	Oxygen sensor		59	Retained	o Harness and connector o Fuel pressure o Injectors o Intake air leaks o Oxygen sensor (Rear)

89534g85

Fig. 84 Diagnostic trouble code identification (2 of 3)—Excel

Output preference order	Diagnosis item	Trouble code			Check item (Remedy)
		Output signal pattern	No.	Memory	
16	Normal state	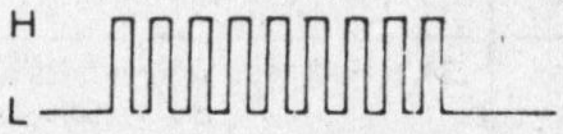 H ⊓⊓⊓⊓⊓⊓⊓⊓ L	-	-	-

NOTE

1. **Replace the engine control unit if a trouble code is read although the inspection reveals that there are no problems with the diagnosis item.**
2. **The diagnostic item marked* is applicable to the California vehicles only.**

89534g86

Fig. 85 Diagnostic trouble code identification (3 of 3)—Excel

Output preference order	Diagnosis item	Diagnostic trouble code			Check item (Remedy)
		Output signal pattern	No.	Memory	
1	Engine control module	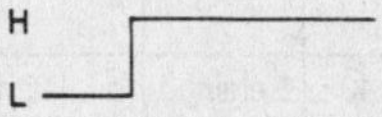 H ⌐‾‾‾‾ L	-	-	(Replace engine control module)
2	Heated oxygen sensor (Front)	 H ⊓⊓ ⊓ L	11	Retained	o Harness and connector o Fuel pressure o Injectors (Replace if defective.) o Intake air leaks o Oxygen sensor (Front)
3	Volume air flow sensor	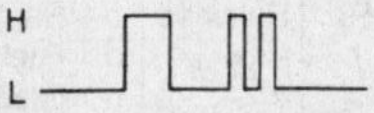 H ⊓ ⊓⊓ L	12	Retained	o Harness and connector (If harness and connector are normal, replace volume air flow sensor assembly.)
4	Intake air temperature sensor	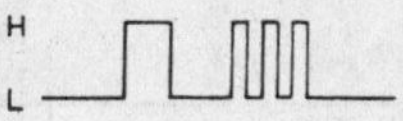 H ⊓ ⊓⊓⊓ L	13	Retained	o Harness and connector o Intake air temperature sensor
5	Throttle position sensor	 H ⊓ ⊓⊓⊓⊓ L	14	Retained	o Harness and connector o Throttle position sensor o Idle position switch
6	Engine coolant temperature sensor	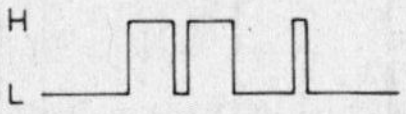 H ⊓⊓⊓ ⊓ L	21	Retained	o Harness and connector o Engine coolant temperature sensor
7	Crankshaft position sensor	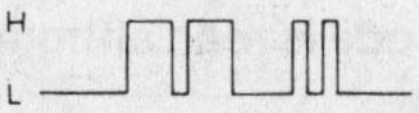 H ⊓⊓ ⊓⊓ L	22	Retained	o Harness and connector If harness and connector are normal, replace crankshaft position sensor assembly.)

89534g87

Fig. 86 Diagnostic trouble code identification (1 of 3)—1994–95 Elantra

Output preference order	Diagnosis item	Diagnostic trouble code			Check item (Remedy)
		Output signal pattern	No.	Memory	
8	Camshaft position sensor	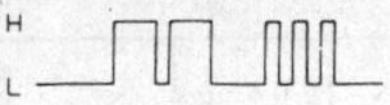	23	Retained	o Harness and connector If harness and connector are normal, replace crankshaft position sensor.)
9	Vehiclespeed sensor (reed switch)	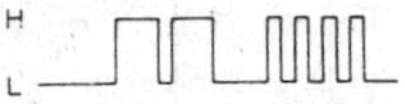	24	Retained	o Harness and connector o Vehicle-speed sensor (reed switch)
10	Barometric pressure sensor	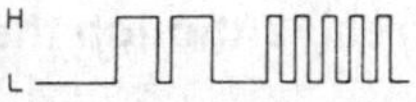	25	Retained	o Harness and connector If harness and connector are normal, replace barometric pressure sensor assembly.)
11	Injector	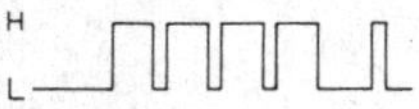	41	Retained	o Harness and connector o Injector coil resistance
12	Fuel pump	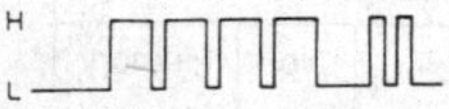	42	Retained	o Harness and connector o Control relay
13	EGR*	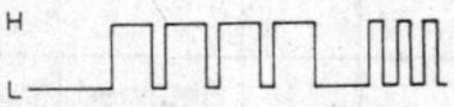	43	Retained	o Harness and connector o EGR temperature sensor o EGR valve o EGR solenoid valve o EGR valve control vacuum
14	Ignition coil	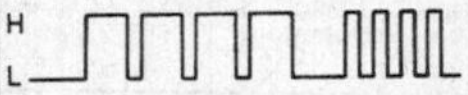	44	Retained	o Harness and connector o Ignition coil o Ignition power transistor
15	Heated * oxygen sensor (Rear)	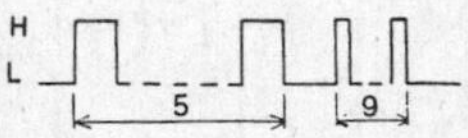	59	Retained	o Harness and connector o Fuel pressure o Injectors o Intake air leaks o Heated oxygen sensor (Rear)

89534g88

Fig. 87 Diagnostic trouble code identification (2 of 3)—1994–95 Elantra

Output preference order	Diagnosis item	Trouble code			Check item (Remedy)
		Output signal pattern	No.	Memory	
16	Normal state	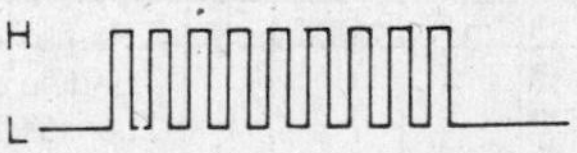	-	-	-

NOTE
1. **Replace the engine control unit if a diagnostic trouble code is read although the inspection reveals that there are no problems with the diagnosis item.**
2. **The diagnostic item marked* is applicable to the California vehicles only.**

89534g89

Fig. 88 Diagnostic trouble code identification (3 of 3)—1994–95 Elantra

Diagnosis item	Scan tool display	NA UL	NA L	TC	Description
Engine Control Module (ECM)	13.ECU-ROM	O	O	-	ECM Failure-ROM
	14. ECU-RAM	O	O	-	ECM Failure-RAM
	16.ECU-ROM/RAM	-	-	O	ECM Failure-ROM/RAM
	17. ECU-KNOCK EVA	-	-	O	ECM Failure-Knock control
	19.ECU-KNOCK	O	O	O	ECM Failure-Knock evaluation circuit
	61.INJ./PURGE VALVE	O	O	-	ECM Failure-injector or Purge control sol. valve
	62.ISA/AC RLY	O	O	-	ECM Failure idle speed actuator or air con. relay
	63.ECU-DRIVE (A)	O	O	-	ECM Failure-Driving circuit (A)
	65.ACTUATORS	-	-	O	ECM-Failure inj. or PCV or ISA or AC/relay
	69.ECU-DRIVE (B)	O	O	O	ECM Failure-Driving circuit (B)
Oxygen sensor	21.O2 SENSOR	O	-	O	Oxygen sensor failure
Mass air flow sensor	22. AFS	O	O	O	Mass air flow sensor failure
Engine coolant temperature sensor	23. WTS	O	O	O	Engine coolant temperature sensor failure
Camshaft position sensor	24.PHASE SENSOR	O	O	O	Camshaft position sensor failure
Crankshaft position sensor	25. CRANK P.SNSR	O	O	O	Crankshaft position sensor failure
Throttle position sensor	26.TPS	O	O	O	Throttle position sensor failure
Knock sensor	27.KNOCK.SNSR	O	O	O	Knock sensor failure
Vehicle speed sensor	29. VEH. SPD. SNSR	O	O	O	Vehicle speed sensor failure
Battery	31.BATTERY	O	O	O	Battery voltage & generator failure
Air conditioning compressor	33. A/C COMPRESR.	O	O	O	Air conditioning compressor failure

Fig. 89 Diagnostic trouble code identification (1 of 2)—Scoupe

Diagnosis item	Scan tool display	NA UL	NA L	TC	Description
ECM-Map sensor	36. BOOST-HIGH	-	-	O	ECM Map sensor-too high failure
	37. BOOST-CNTL.	-	-	O	ECM Map sensor-control deviation failure
	38. BOOST-C. VLV.	-	-	O	ECM Map sensor-control valve failure
	39. BOOST-P. SNSR	-	-	O	ECM Map sensor-Pressure sensor failure
Injector	41. NO.1 INJECTOR	O	O	O	No.1 Injector failure
	42. NO.2 INJECTOR	O	O	O	No.2 Injector failure
	43. NO.3 INJECTOR	O	O	O	No.3 Injector failure
	44. NO.4 INJECTOR	O	O	O	No.4 Injector failure
EVAP Canister Purge Solenoid Valve	45. PURGE VALVE	O	O	O	EVAP Canister Purge Solenoid Valve
Idle speed control actuator	47. ISA-OPEN'G	O	O	O	Idle speed control actuator-opening failure
	48. ISA-CLOS'G	O	O	O	Idle speed control actuator-closing failure
Fuel pump relay	53.FUEL PUMP RLY	O	O	-	Fuel pump relay failure
Air/Fuel ratio	81. A/F CTRL-INTG.	O	-	O	Air/Fuel control failure
	82.A/F ADAP.-MUL*	O	-	O	Air/Fuel adaptive failure-multiplicative
	83.A/F ADAP.-A/N*	O	-	O	Air/Fuel adaptive failure-A/N
	84.A/F ADAP.-ADD*	O	-	O	Air/Fuel adaptive failure-additive

Fig. 90 Diagnostic trouble code identification (2 of 2)—Scoupe

Fault Code No.	Comment	Component	MIL on
P0300	Random misfire detected	Non catalyst damage	Yes
P0301	Misfire at cylinder 1 detected		
P0302	Misfire at cylinder 2 detected	Catalyst damage (you should repair immediately)	Yes and Blinking
P0303	Misfire at cylinder 3 detected		
P0304	Misfire at cylinder 4 detected		
P0326	Knock sensor circuit range	Knock Sensor	No
P0335	Crankshaft position sensor circuit malfunction	Crankshaft Position Sensor	Yes
P0336	Crankshaft position sensor circuit range		
P0342	Camshaft position sensor circuit low input	Camshaft Position Sensor	Yes
P0343	Camshaft position sensor circuit high input		
P0421(CAL SOHC)	Manfiold catalyst efficiency, below threshold	Catalyst	Yes
P0422 (Except CAL SOHC)	Main catalyst efficiency, below threshold		
P0441	Evaporative emission control system, incorrect purge flow	Evaporative Emission Control System	Yes
P0444	Purge control valve circuit open	Evaporative Emission Control System	Yes
P0445	Purge control valve circuit shorted		
P0501	Vehicle speed sensor range	Vehicle Speed Sensor	Yes
P0506	Idle rpm lower than expected	Idle Control Valve	Yes
P0507	Idle rpm higher than expected		
P0562	System voltage low	Power Supply	Yes
P0563	System voltage highter		
P0605	Internal control module ROM error	ECM	Yes
P1123	Long term fuel trim additive air, system too rich	Fuel System	Yes
P1124	Long term fuel trim additive, air system too lean		
P1127	Long term fuel trim multiplicative, system too rich		
P1128	Long term fuel trim multiplicative, system too lean		

Fig. 92 Diagnostic trouble code identification (2 of 3)—Accent

Fault Code No.	Comment	Component	MIL on
P0102	Mass air flow circuit low input	Mass Air Flow Sensor	Yes
P0103	Mass air flow circuit high input		
P0112	Intake air temp. circuit low input	Intake Air Temperature Sensor	Yes
P0113	Intake air temp. circuit high input		
P0116	Eng.coolant temp.circuit range	Engine Coolant Temperature Sensor	Yes
P0117	Eng.coolant temp.circuit low input		
P0118	Eng.coolant temp.circuit high input		
P0121	TPS circuit range (TPS voltage does not agree with MAFS)	Throttle Position Sensor	Yes
P0122	TPS circuit low input		
P0123	TPS circuit high input		
P0130	O2 sensor circuit malfunction	Upstream Oxygen Sensor	Yes
P0131	O2 sensor circuit low voltage		
P0132	O2 sensor circuit high voltage		
P0133	O2 sensor circuit slow response		
P0134	O2 sensor circuit no activity detected		
P0135	O2 sensor heater circuit malfunction	Upstream Oxygen Sensor Heater	Yes
P0136	O2 sensor circuit malfunction	Downstream Oxygen Sensor	Yes
P0137	O2 sensor circuit low voltage		
P0138	O2 sensor circuit high voltage		
P0141	O2 sensor heater circuit malfunction	Downstream oxygen Sensor Heater	Yes
P0201	Injector cyl. 1, circuit malfunction	Injector	Yes
P0202	Injector cyl. 2, circuit malfunction		
P0203	Injector cyl. 3, circuit malfunction		
P0204	Injector cyl. 4, circuit malfunction		

Fig. 91 Diagnostic trouble code identification (1 of 3)—Accent

Fault Code No.	Comment	Component	MIL on
P1510	Idle control valve opening coil circuit shorted	Idle Control Valve	Yes
P1513	Idle control valve opening coil circuit open		
P1552	Idle control valve closing coil circuit shorted		
P1553	Idle control valve closing coil circuit open		
P1586	Encording signal circuit not rationale	MT/AT Encording	Yes
P1605	Rough road sensor circuit malfunction	Acceleration Sensor	Yes
P1606	Rough road sensor not rationale		
P1611	MIL request signal circuit low input	MIL-on Request Line	Yes
P1614	MIL request signal circuit high input		
P1624	Malfunction of TCM component	TCM	Yes
P1665	Power stage group A, malfunction	Wiring Harness ECM	Yes
P1670	Power stage group B, malfunction		

89534g94

Fig. 93 Diagnostic trouble code identification (3 of 3)—Accent

Fault Code No.	Comment	Component	MIL on
P0102	Mass air flow circuit low input	Mass Air Flow Sensor	Yes
P0103	Mass air flow circuit high input		
P0112	Intake air temp. circuit low input	Intake Air Temperature Sensor	Yes
P0113	Intake air temp. circuit high input		
P0116	Eng.coolant temp.circuit range	Engine Coolant Temperature Sensor	Yes
P117	Eng.coolant temp.circuit low input		
P118	Eng.coolant temp.circuit high input		
P0122	TPS circuit low input	Throttle Position Sensor	Yes
P0123	TPS circuit high input		
P0130	O2 sensor circuit malfunction	Upstream Oxygen Sensor	Yes
P0131	O2 sensor circuit low voltage		
P0132	O2 sensor circuit high voltage		
P0133	O2 sensor circuit slow response		
P0134	O2 sensor circuit no activity detected		
P0135	O2 sensor heater circuit malfunction	Upstream Oxygen Sensor Heater	Yes
P0136	O2 sensor circuit malfunction	Downstream Oxygen Sensor	Yes
P0137	O2 sensor circuit low voltage		
P0138	O2 sensor circuit high voltage		
P0141	O2 sensor heater circuit malfunction	Downstream Oxygen Sensor Heater	Yes
P0201	Injector cyl. 1, circuit malfunction	Injector	Yes
P0202	Injector cyl. 2, circuit malfunction		
P0203	Injector cyl. 3, circuit malfunction		
P0204	Injector cyl. 4, circuit malfunction		

89534g95

Fig. 94 Diagnostic trouble code identification (1 of 3)—Tiburon and 1996–98 Elantra

Fault Code No.	Comment	Component	MIL on
P0300	Random misfire detected	Non catalyst damage	Yes
P0301	Misfire at cylinder 1 detected		
P0302	Misfire at cylinder 2 detected	Catalyst damage (you should repair immediately)	Yes and Blinking
P0303	Misfire at cylinder 3 detected		
P0304	Misfire at cylinder 4 detected		
P0326	Knock sensor circuit range	Knock Sensor	No
P0335	Crankshaft position sensor circuit malfunction	Crankshaft Position Sensor	Yes
P0336	Crankshaft position sensor circuit range		
P0342	Camshaft position sensor circuit low input	Camshaft Position Sensor	Yes
P0343	Camshaft position sensor circuit high input		
P0420	Catalyst efficiency, below threshold	Catalyst	Yes
P0442	Evap. emission control system small leakage detected	Evaporative Emission Control System	Yes
P0443	Evap. emission control system purge valve permanently open		
P0444	Purge control valve circuit open	Evaporative Emission Control Valve	Yes
P0445	Purge control valve circuit shorted		
P0446	Evap. emission control system canister close valve permanently closed	Evaporative Emission Control System	Yes
P0447	Evap. emission control system, ventilation control valve, short circuit to ground		Yes
P0448	Evap. emission control system, ventilation control valve, short circuit to battery voltage		
P0452	Evap. emission control system, pressure sensor, signal low	Tank Pressure Sensor	Yes
P0453	Evap. emission control system, pressure sensor, signal high		
P0451	Evap. emission control system, pressure sensor, signal not plausible		
P0455	Evap. emission control system incorrect purge flow	Evaporative Emission Control System	Yes

89534g96

Fig. 95 Diagnostic trouble code identification (2 of 3)—Tiburon and 1996–98 Elantra

Fault Code No.	Comment	Component	MIL on
P0501	Vehicle speed sensor range	Vehicle Speed Sensor	Yes
P0506	Idle rpm lower than expected	Idle Control Valve	Yes
P0507	Idle rpm highter than expected		
P0562	System voltage low	Power Supply	Yes
P0563	System voltage high		
P0605	Internal control module ROM error	ECM	Yes
P1123	Long term fuel trim additive, air system too rich	Fuel System	Yes
P1124	Long term fuel trim additive, air system too lean		
P1127	Long term fuel trim multiplicative, system too rich		
P1128	Long term fuel trim multiplicative, system too lean		
P1140	Load montioring signal not plausible (Ratio-nale)	Load Detection Sensor (MAF Sensor & TP Sensor)	Yes
P1510	Idle control valve opening coil circuit shorted	Idle Control Valve	Yes
P1513	Idle control valve opening coil circuit open		
P1552	Idle control valve closing coil circuit shorted		
P1553	Idle control valve closing coil circuit open		
P1586	Encording signal circuit not rationale	MT/AT Encording	Yes
P1605	Rough road sensor circuit malfunction	Acceleration Sensor	Yes
P1606	Rough road sensor not rationale		
P1611	MIL request signal circuit low input	MIL-on Request Line	Yes
P1613	MIL request signal circuit high input		
P1665	Power stage group A, malfunction	Wiring Harness ECM	Yes
P1670	Power stage group B, malfunction		

89534g97

Fig. 96 Diagnostic trouble code identification (3 of 3)—Tiburon and 1996–98 Elantra

FAULT CODE NO.	COMMENT	COMPONENT	MIL ON
P0170	Fuel Trim Malfunction	Fuel System	YES
P0130	O2 Sensor Circuit Malfunction	Upstream Oxygen Sensor	YES
P0136	O2 Sensor Circuit Malfunction	Downstream Oxygen Sensor	YES
P0135	O2 Sensor Heater Curcuit Malfunction	Upstream Oxygen Sensor Heater	YES
P0141	O2 Sensor Heater Curcuit Malfunction	Downstream Oxygen Sensor Heater	YES
P0400	Exhaust Gas Recirculation Flow Malfunction	EGR system	YES
P0403	Exhaust Gas Recirculation Circuit Malfunction	EGR Solenoid Circuit	YES
P0125	Insufficient Coolant Temperature for Closed Loop Fuel Control	Air Fuel Ratio Feedback	YES
P0100	Mass or Volume Air Flow Circuit Malfunction	Volume Air Flow Sensor	YES
P0110	Intake Air Temperature Circuit Malfunction	Intake Air Temperature Sensor	YES
P0120	Throttle Position Sensor a Circuit Malfunction	Throttle Position Sensor	YES
P0115	Engine Coolant Temperature Circuit	Engine Coolant Temperature Sensor	YES
P0201	Injector Circuit Malfunction - Cylinder 1	Injector	YES
P0202	Injector Circuit Malfunction - Cylinder 2		
P0203	Injector Circuit Malfunction - Cylinder 3		
P0204	Injector Circuit Malfunction - Cylinder 4		
P0205	Injector Circuit Malfunction - Cylinder 5 (V6 only)		
P0206	Injector Circuit Malfunction - Cylinder 6 (V6 only)		
P1715	Open-Circuited Purse Generator A	Pluse Generator A	YES
	Open-Circuited Purse Generator B	Pluse Generator B	YES
P1750	Open-Circuited or Shorted Shift Control Solenoid Valve A	Shift Control Solenoid Valve A	YES
	Open-Circuited or Shorted Shift Control Solenoid Valve B	Shift Control Solenoid Valve B	YES
	Open-Circuited or Shorte Pressure Control Solenoid Valve	Pressure Control Solenoid Valve	YES
	Open-Circuited or Shorted Damper Clutch Control Solenoid Valve	Damper Clutch Control Solenoid Valve	YES
P0705	Inhibitor Switch Signals Malfunction	Inhibitor Switch	YES

89534g98

Fig. 97 Diagnostic trouble code identification (1 of 2)—Sonata

FAULT CODE NO.	COMMENT	COMPONENT	MIL ON
P0505	Idle Control System Malfunction	Idle Speed Control	YES
P0105	Barometric Pressure Circuit Malfunction	Barometric Pressure Sensor	YES
P0300	Random Misfire Detected	Misfire Detected Cylinder	YES
P0301	Cylinder 1 Misfire Detected		
P0302	Cylinder 2 Misfire Detected		
P0303	Cylinder 3 Misfire Detected		
P0304	Cylinder 4 Misfire Detected		
P0305	Cylinder 5 Misfire Detected (V6 only)		
P0306	Cylinder 5 Misfire Detected (V6 only)		
P0335	Crankshaft Position Sensor Circuit Malfunction	Crankshaft Position Sensor	YES
P0340	Camshaft Position Sensor Circuit Malfunction	Camshaft Position Sensor	YES
P0420	Catalyst System Efficiency Below Threshold	Catalyst	YES
P0440	Evaporative Emission Control System Malfunction	Evaporative Emission Control System	YES
P0443	Evaporative Emission Control System Purge Control Valve Circuit Malfunction	Evaporative Emission Control System Purge Control Valve	YES
P0500	Vehicle Speed Sensor Malfunction	Vehicle Speed Sensor	YES
P0510	Closed Throttle Position Switch Malfunction	Idle Switch	YES
P1400	EGR System Monitor Malfunction	Manifold Differential Pressure Sensor	YES

89534g99

Fig. 98 Diagnostic trouble code identification (2 of 2)—Sonata

VOLTMETER

▶ **See Figure 81 (p. 55)**

1. Connect the voltmeter between the MFI diagnosis pin and ground pin.
2. Turn the ingition switch **ON.**
3. The codes will be read out in sequence.

MAINTENANCE INTERVAL LAMP

▶ **See Figure 99**

1. Turn the ignition switch **ON.**
2. Ground the L-wire (pin 10) in the diagnostic connector for 2.5 seconds.
3. The first output is the stored code or the code "no fault detected (4444)".
4. Ground the L-wire (pin 10) in the diagnostic connector for an additional 2.5 seconds to obtain the next code.

➡ **Codes will repeat infinitely until the next step is ordered by grounding the L-wire.**

5. Continue pulling codes until the "end of output (3333)" code is reached.

GENERIC SCAN TOOL

When using a generic scan tool, always follow the manufacturer's instructions for hook-up and diagnosis.

Clearing Codes

1. Turn the ignition switch **OFF.**
2. Disconnect the negative battery cable for approximately 15 seconds.
3. Reconnect the negative battery cable.
4. Check that no further trouble codes are displayed.

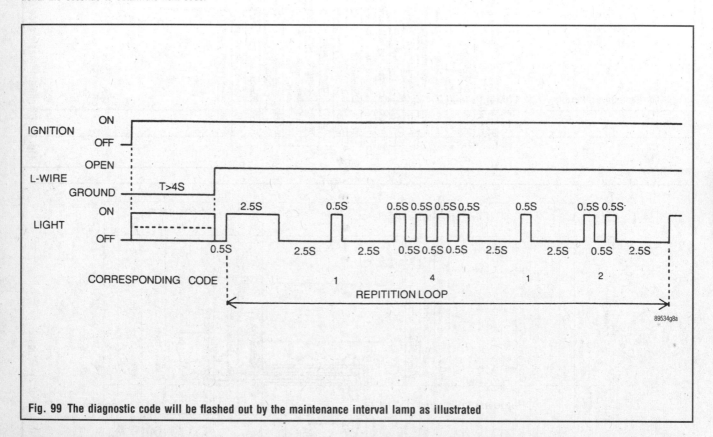

Fig. 99 The diagnostic code will be flashed out by the maintenance interval lamp as illustrated

VACUUM DIAGRAMS

Following are vacuum diagrams for most of the engine and emissions package combinations covered by this manual. Because vacuum circuits will vary based on various engine and vehicle options, always refer first to the vehicle emission control information label, if present. Should the label be missing, or should the vehicle be equipped with a different engine from the vehicle's original equipment, refer to the diagrams below for the same or similar configuration.

If you wish to obtain a replacement emissions label, most manufacturers make the labels available for purchase. The labels can usually be ordered from a local dealer.

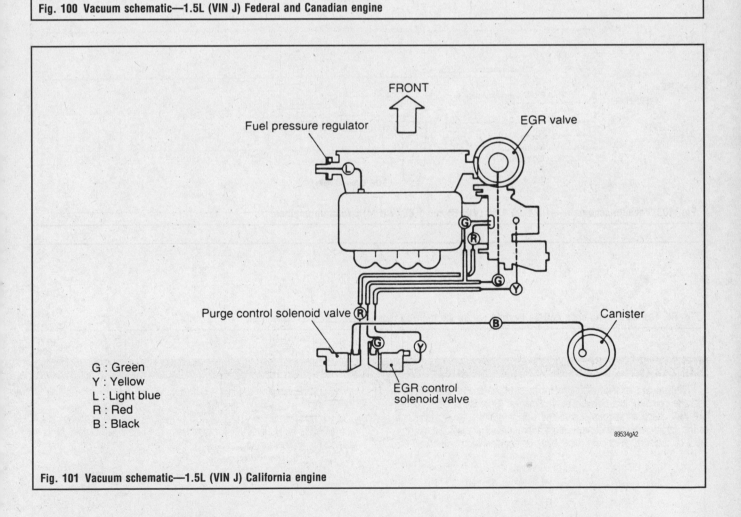

G : Green
Y : Yellow
L : Light blue
R : Red
B : Black

Fig. 100 Vacuum schematic—1.5L (VIN J) Federal and Canadian engine

G : Green
Y : Yellow
L : Light blue
R : Red
B : Black

Fig. 101 Vacuum schematic—1.5L (VIN J) California engine

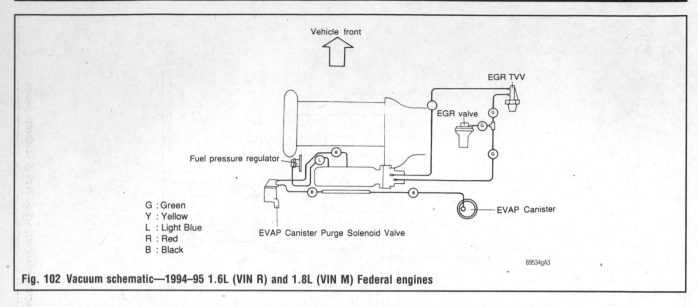

Fig. 102 Vacuum schematic—1994–95 1.6L (VIN R) and 1.8L (VIN M) Federal engines

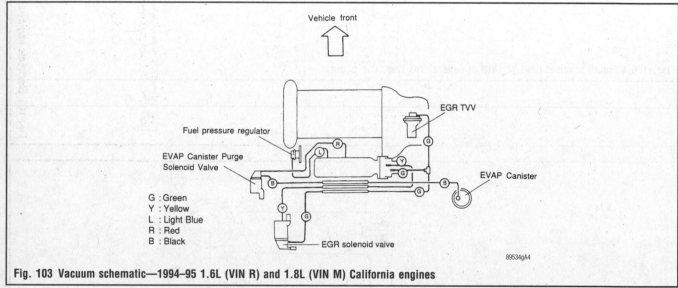

Fig. 103 Vacuum schematic—1994–95 1.6L (VIN R) and 1.8L (VIN M) California engines

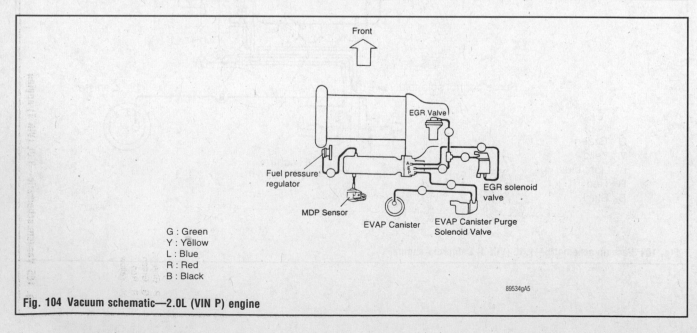

Fig. 104 Vacuum schematic—2.0L (VIN P) engine

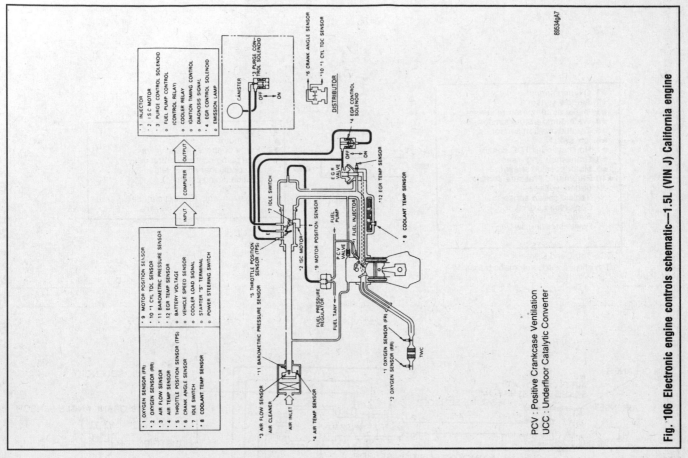

Fig. 106 Electronic engine controls schematic—1.5L (VIN J) California engine

* 1 OXYGEN SENSOR (FR)
* 2 OXYGEN SENSOR (RR)
* 3 AIR FLOW SENSOR
* 4 AIR TEMP SENSOR
* 5 THROTTLE POSITION SENSOR (TPS)
* 6 CRANK ANGLE SENSOR
* 7 IDLE SWITCH
* 8 COOLANT TEMP SENSOR
* 9 MOTOR POSITION SENSOR
* 10 *1 CYL TDC SENSOR
* 11 BAROMETRIC PRESSURE SENSOR
* 12 EGR TEMP SENSOR
* o BATTERY VOLTAGE
* o VEHICLE SPEED SENSOR
* o COOLER LOAD SIGNAL
* o STARTER "S" TERMINAL
* o POWER STEERING SWITCH

* 1 INJECTOR
* 2 ISC MOTOR
* 3 PURGE CONTROL SOLENOID
* 4 FUEL PUMP CONTROL
    (CONTROL RELAY)
* o COOLER RELAY
* o IGNITION TIMING CONTROL
* o DIAGNOSIS SIGNAL
* 4 EGR CONTROL SOLENOID
* o EMISSION LAMP

INPUT → COMPUTER → OUTPUT

PCV : Positive Crankcase Ventilation
UCC : Underfloor Catalytic Converter

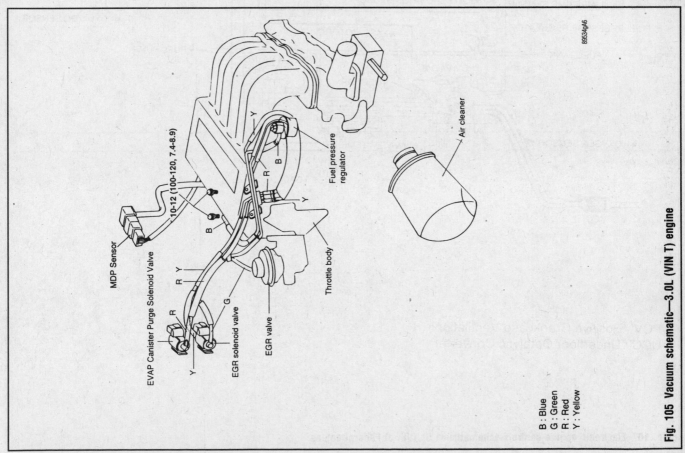

Fig. 105 Vacuum schematic—3.0L (VIN T) engine

B : Blue
G : Green
R : Red
Y : Yellow

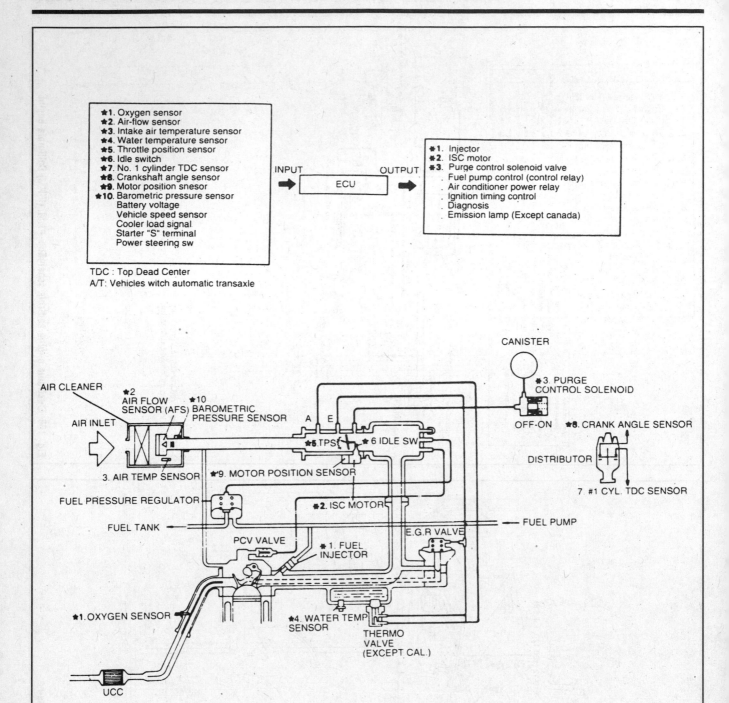

★1. Oxygen sensor
★2. Air-flow sensor
★3. Intake air temperature sensor
★4. Water temperature sensor
★5. Throttle position sensor
★6. Idle switch
★7. No. 1 cylinder TDC sensor
★8. Crankshaft angle sensor
★9. Motor position snesor
★10. Barometric pressure sensor
Battery voltage
Vehicle speed sensor
Cooler load signal
Starter "S" terminal
Power steering sw

INPUT → ECU → OUTPUT

★1. Injector
★2. ISC motor
★3. Purge control solenoid valve
. Fuel pump control (control relay)
. Air conditioner power relay
. Ignition timing control
. Diagnosis
. Emission lamp (Except canada)

TDC : Top Dead Center
A/T: Vehicles witch automatic transaxle

CANISTER

★3. PURGE CONTROL SOLENOID

OFF-ON

★8. CRANK ANGLE SENSOR

DISTRIBUTOR

7. #1 CYL. TDC SENSOR

AIR CLEANER

★2 AIR FLOW SENSOR (AFS)   ★10 BAROMETRIC PRESSURE SENSOR

AIR INLET

A   E

★5 TPS   ★6 IDLE SW

3. AIR TEMP SENSOR   ★9. MOTOR POSITION SENSOR

FUEL PRESSURE REGULATOR

★2. ISC MOTOR

FUEL TANK

FUEL PUMP

PCV VALVE

★1. FUEL INJECTOR

E.G.R VALVE

★1. OXYGEN SENSOR

4. WATER TEMP SENSOR

THERMO VALVE (EXCEPT CAL.)

UCC

PCV : Positive Crankcase Ventilation
UCC : Underfloor Catalytic Converter

89534gA8

Fig. 107 Electronic engine controls schematic—1.5L (VIN J) Federal engine

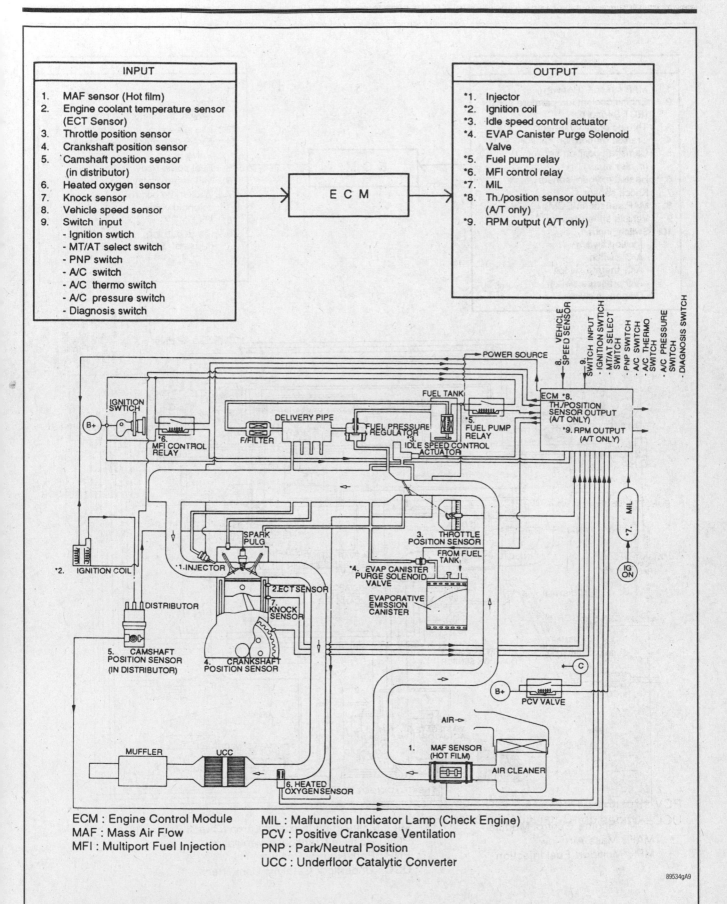

INPUT

1. MAF sensor (Hot film)
2. Engine coolant temperature sensor (ECT Sensor)
3. Throttle position sensor
4. Crankshaft position sensor
5. Camshaft position sensor (in distributor)
6. Heated oxygen sensor
7. Knock sensor
8. Vehicle speed sensor
9. Switch input
   - Ignition swtich
   - MT/AT select switch
   - PNP switch
   - A/C switch
   - A/C thermo switch
   - A/C pressure switch
   - Diagnosis switch

ECM

OUTPUT

*1. Injector
*2. Ignition coil
*3. Idle speed control actuator
*4. EVAP Canister Purge Solenoid Valve
*5. Fuel pump relay
*6. MFI control relay
*7. MIL
*8. Th./position sensor output (A/T only)
*9. RPM output (A/T only)

ECM : Engine Control Module
MAF : Mass Air Flow
MFI : Multiport Fuel Injection

MIL : Malfunction Indicator Lamp (Check Engine)
PCV : Positive Crankcase Ventilation
PNP : Park/Neutral Position
UCC : Underfloor Catalytic Converter

89534gA9

Fig. 108 Electronic engine controls schematic—1.5L (VIN E) engine

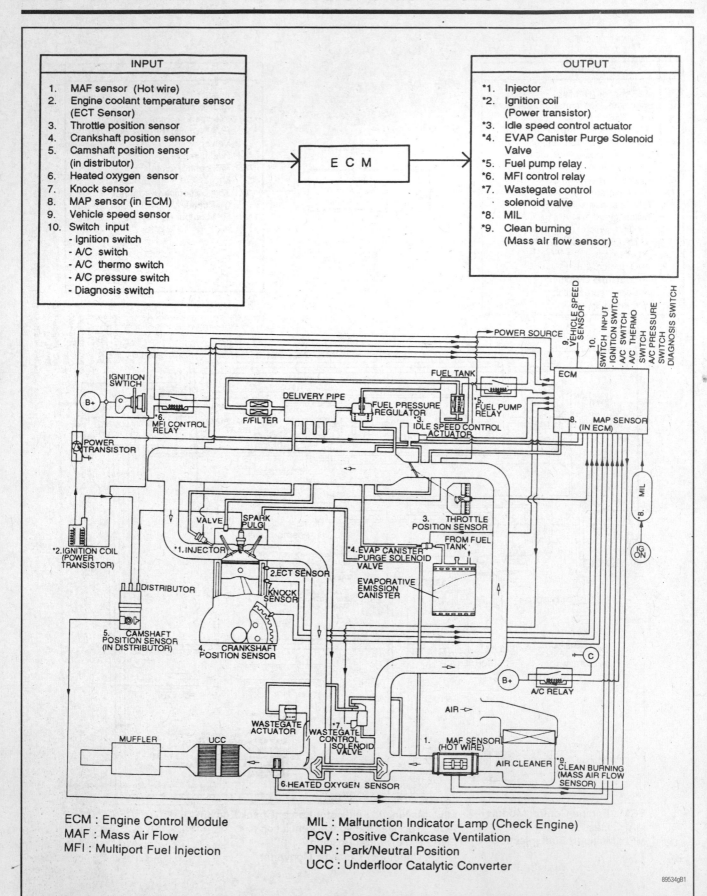

INPUT

1. MAF sensor (Hot wire)
2. Engine coolant temperature sensor (ECT Sensor)
3. Throttle position sensor
4. Crankshaft position sensor
5. Camshaft position sensor (in distributor)
6. Heated oxygen sensor
7. Knock sensor
8. MAP sensor (in ECM)
9. Vehicle speed sensor
10. Switch input
    - Ignition switch
    - A/C switch
    - A/C thermo switch
    - A/C pressure switch
    - Diagnosis switch

OUTPUT

*1. Injector
*2. Ignition coil (Power transistor)
*3. Idle speed control actuator
*4. EVAP Canister Purge Solenoid Valve
*5. Fuel pump relay
*6. MFI control relay
*7. Wastegate control solenoid valve
*8. MIL
*9. Clean burning (Mass air flow sensor)

ECM : Engine Control Module
MAF : Mass Air Flow
MFI : Multiport Fuel Injection

MIL : Malfunction Indicator Lamp (Check Engine)
PCV : Positive Crankcase Ventilation
PNP : Park/Neutral Position
UCC : Underfloor Catalytic Converter

89534gB1

Fig. 109 Electronic engine controls schematic—1.5L (VIN E) turbocharged engine

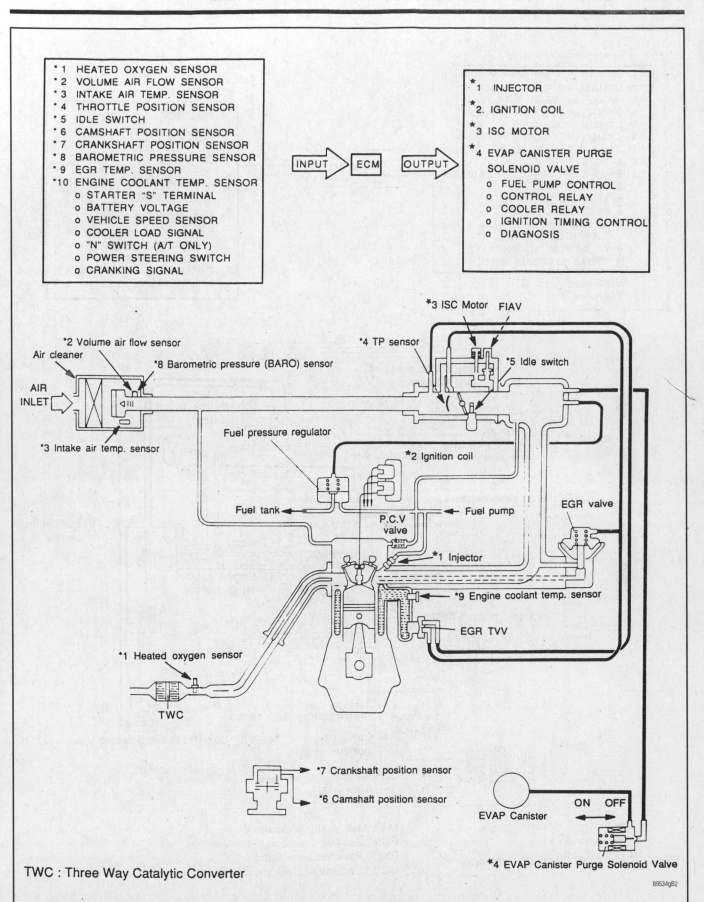

*1 HEATED OXYGEN SENSOR
*2 VOLUME AIR FLOW SENSOR
*3 INTAKE AIR TEMP. SENSOR
*4 THROTTLE POSITION SENSOR
*5 IDLE SWITCH
*6 CAMSHAFT POSITION SENSOR
*7 CRANKSHAFT POSITION SENSOR
*8 BAROMETRIC PRESSURE SENSOR
*9 EGR TEMP. SENSOR
*10 ENGINE COOLANT TEMP. SENSOR
  o STARTER "S" TERMINAL
  o BATTERY VOLTAGE
  o VEHICLE SPEED SENSOR
  o COOLER LOAD SIGNAL
  o "N" SWITCH (A/T ONLY)
  o POWER STEERING SWITCH
  o CRANKING SIGNAL

INPUT → ECM → OUTPUT

*1 INJECTOR
*2. IGNITION COIL
*3 ISC MOTOR
*4 EVAP CANISTER PURGE
   SOLENOID VALVE
  o FUEL PUMP CONTROL
  o CONTROL RELAY
  o COOLER RELAY
  o IGNITION TIMING CONTROL
  o DIAGNOSIS

*3 ISC Motor FIAV
*4 TP sensor
*5 Idle switch
*2 Volume air flow sensor
Air cleaner
*8 Barometric pressure (BARO) sensor
AIR INLET
*3 Intake air temp. sensor
Fuel pressure regulator
*2 Ignition coil
Fuel tank
Fuel pump
EGR valve
P.C.V valve
*1 Injector
*9 Engine coolant temp. sensor
EGR TVV
*1 Heated oxygen sensor
TWC
*7 Crankshaft position sensor
*6 Camshaft position sensor
EVAP Canister   ON   OFF
*4 EVAP Canister Purge Solenoid Valve

TWC : Three Way Catalytic Converter

89534g82

Fig. 110 Electronic engine controls schematic—1994-95 1.6L (VIN R) and 1.8L (VIN M) Federal engines

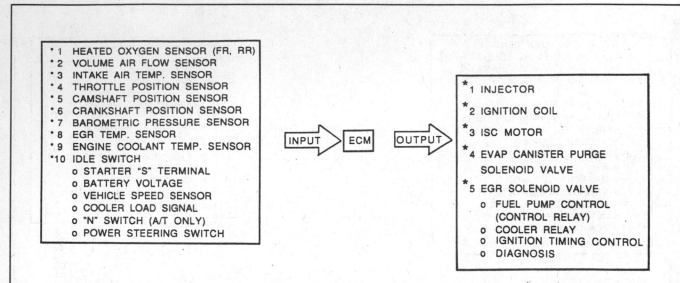

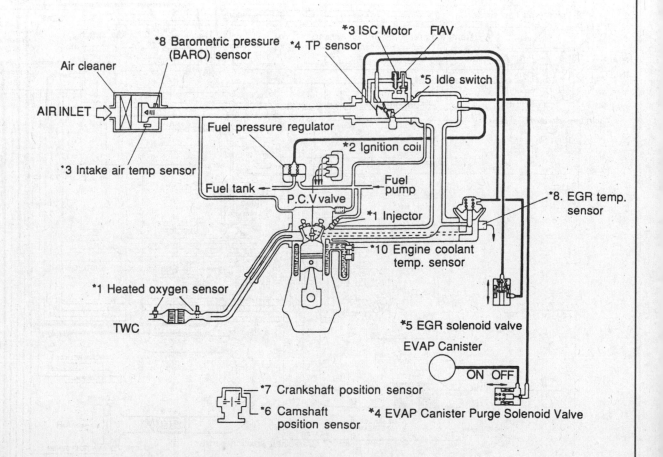

TWC : Three Way Catalytic Converter

Fig. 111 Electronic engine controls schematic—1994–95 1.6L (VIN R) and 1.8L (VIN M) California engines

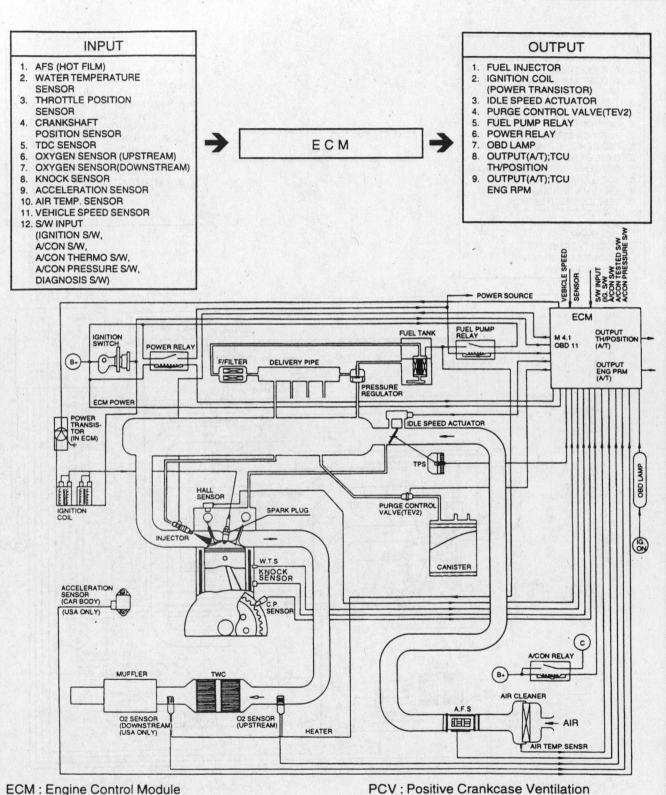

INPUT		OUTPUT
1. AFS (HOT FILM)		1. FUEL INJECTOR
2. WATER TEMPERATURE SENSOR		2. IGNITION COIL (POWER TRANSISTOR)
3. THROTTLE POSITION SENSOR		3. IDLE SPEED ACTUATOR
4. CRANKSHAFT POSITION SENSOR		4. PURGE CONTROL VALVE(TEV2)
5. TDC SENSOR		5. FUEL PUMP RELAY
6. OXYGEN SENSOR (UPSTREAM)		6. POWER RELAY
7. OXYGEN SENSOR(DOWNSTREAM)		7. OBD LAMP
8. KNOCK SENSOR		8. OUTPUT(A/T);TCU TH/POSITION
9. ACCELERATION SENSOR		9. OUTPUT(A/T);TCU ENG RPM
10. AIR TEMP. SENSOR		
11. VEHICLE SPEED SENSOR		
12. S/W INPUT (IGNITION S/W, A/CON S/W, A/CON THERMO S/W, A/CON PRESSURE S/W, DIAGNOSIS S/W)		

ECM : Engine Control Module
MAF : Mass Air Flow
MFI : Multiport Fuel Injection
MIL : Malfunction Indicator Lamp (Check Engine)

PCV : Positive Crankcase Ventilation
TR : Transaxle Range
UCC : Underfloor Catalytic Converter

89534gB4

Fig. 112 Electronic engine controls schematic—1.5L (VIN K) SOHC engine

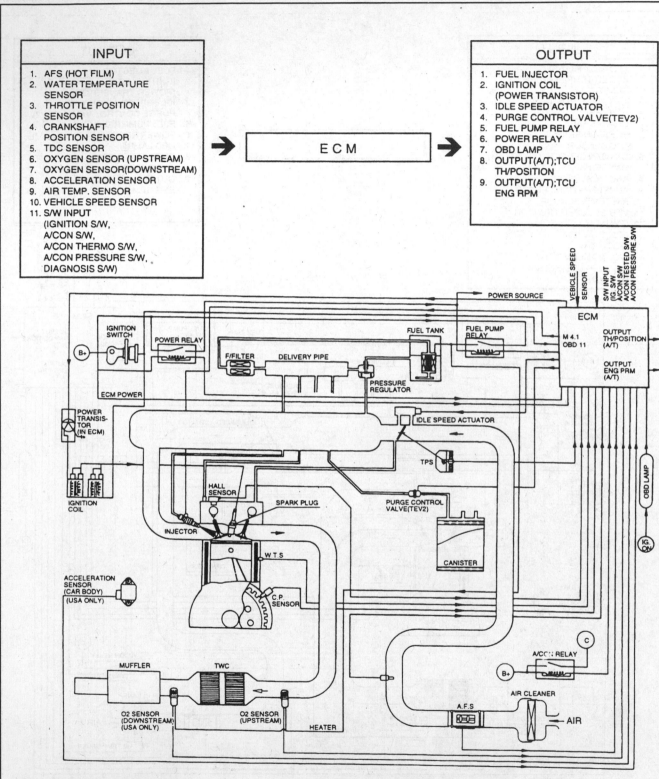

INPUT

1. AFS (HOT FILM)
2. WATER TEMPERATURE SENSOR
3. THROTTLE POSITION SENSOR
4. CRANKSHAFT POSITION SENSOR
5. TDC SENSOR
6. OXYGEN SENSOR (UPSTREAM)
7. OXYGEN SENSOR (DOWNSTREAM)
8. ACCELERATION SENSOR
9. AIR TEMP. SENSOR
10. VEHICLE SPEED SENSOR
11. S/W INPUT
    (IGNITION S/W,
    A/CON S/W,
    A/CON THERMO S/W,
    A/CON PRESSURE S/W,
    DIAGNOSIS S/W)

ECM

OUTPUT

1. FUEL INJECTOR
2. IGNITION COIL (POWER TRANSISTOR)
3. IDLE SPEED ACTUATOR
4. PURGE CONTROL VALVE(TEV2)
5. FUEL PUMP RELAY
6. POWER RELAY
7. OBD LAMP
8. OUTPUT(A/T);TCU TH/POSITION
9. OUTPUT(A/T);TCU ENG RPM

ECM : Engine Control Module
MAF : Mass Air Flow
MFI : Multiport Fuel Injection
MIL : Malfunction Indicator Lamp (Check Engine)

PCV : Positive Crankcase Ventilation
TR : Transaxle Range
UCC : Underfloor Catalytic Converter

89534gB5

Fig. 113 Electronic engine controls schematic—1.5L (VIN K) DOHC engine

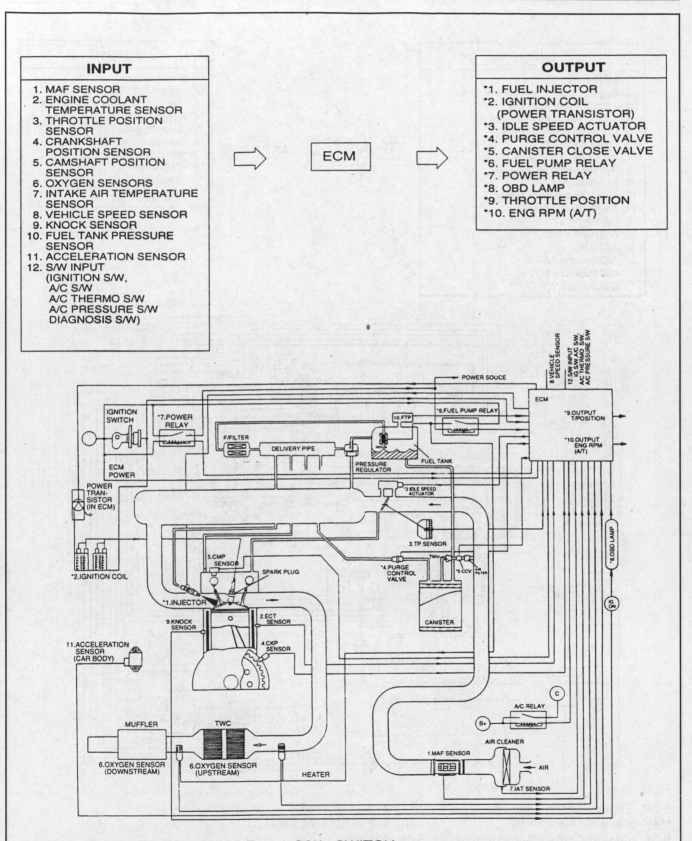

INPUT
1. MAF SENSOR
2. ENGINE COOLANT TEMPERATURE SENSOR
3. THROTTLE POSITION SENSOR
4. CRANKSHAFT POSITION SENSOR
5. CAMSHAFT POSITION SENSOR
6. OXYGEN SENSORS
7. INTAKE AIR TEMPERATURE SENSOR
8. VEHICLE SPEED SENSOR
9. KNOCK SENSOR
10. FUEL TANK PRESSURE SENSOR
11. ACCELERATION SENSOR
12. S/W INPUT
    (IGNITION S/W,
     A/C S/W
     A/C THERMO S/W
     A/C PRESSURE S/W
     DIAGNOSIS S/W)

ECM

OUTPUT
*1. FUEL INJECTOR
*2. IGNITION COIL (POWER TRANSISTOR)
*3. IDLE SPEED ACTUATOR
*4. PURGE CONTROL VALVE
*5. CANISTER CLOSE VALVE
*6. FUEL PUMP RELAY
*7. POWER RELAY
*8. OBD LAMP
*9. THROTTLE POSITION
*10. ENG RPM (A/T)

A/T : AUTOMATIC TRANSAXLE   S/W : SWITCH

Fig. 114 Electronic engine controls schematic—1996–98 1.8L (VIN M) engine

INPUT

1. MAF Sensor
2. Engine Coolant temperature sensor
3. Throttle position sensor
4. Crankshaft position sensor
5. Camshaft position sensor
6. Oxygen sensor
7. Intake Air temperature sensor
8. Vehicle speed sensor
9. Knock sensor
10. Fuel tank pressure sensor
11. Acceleration sensor
12. Switch input
   (Ingnition switch
   A/C S/W
   A/C Thermo S/W
   A/C Pressure S/W
   Diagnosis S/W)

OUTPUT

*1 Fuel injector
*2 Ignition coil (Power transistor)
*3 Idle speed control actuator
*4 Purge control valve
*5 Canister close valve
*6 Fuel pump relay
*7 MFI control relay
*8 OBD lamp
*9 Throttle position
*10 Engine RPM (A/T)

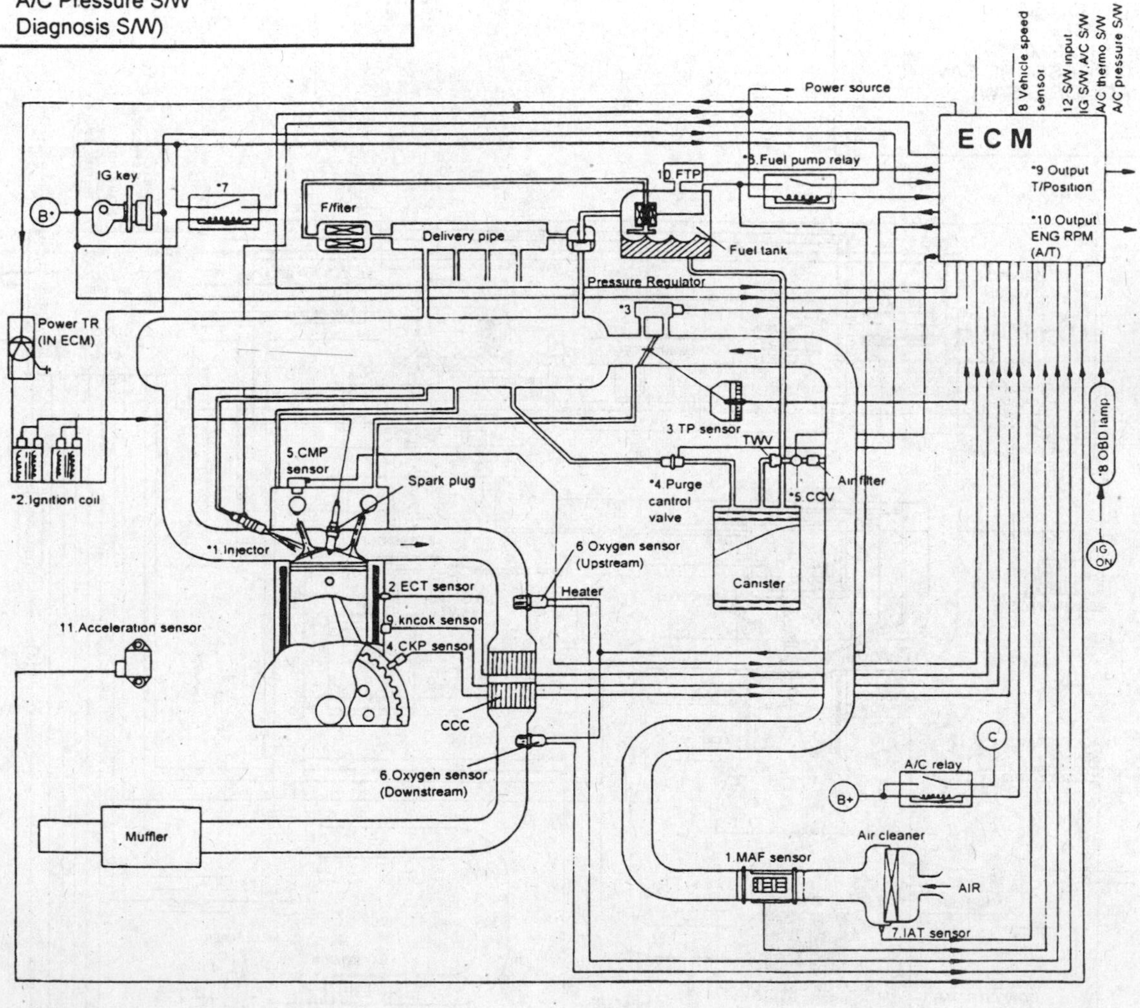

INPUT → ECM → OUTPUT

ECM: Engine Control Module
MAF: Mass Air Flow
ECT : Engine Coolant Temperature
CCC : Closed Coupled Catalyst

A/C : Air Conditioning
A/T : Automatic Transaxle
S/W : Switch

Fig. 115 Electronic engine controls schematic—2.0L (VIN F) engine

89534gB7

*1. HEATED OXYGEN SENSOR (HO2S)
*2. VOLUME AIR FLOW SENSOR
    (VAF SENSOR)
*3. INTAKE AIR TEMP.SENSOR
    (IAT SENSOR)
*4. THROTTLE POSITION SENSOR
    (TP SENSOR)
*5. CAMSHAFT POSITION SENSOR
    (CMP SENSOR)
*6. CRANKSHAFT POSITION SENSOR
    (CKP SENSOR)
*7. BAROMETRIC PRESSURE SENSOR
    (BARO SENSOR)
*8. MDP SENSOR
*9. ENGINE COOLANT TEMP. SENSOR
    (ECT Sencor)
*10.IDLE SWITCH
*11.CAM POSITION SENSOR
    (CMP) SENSOR
*12.CRANK POSITION SENSOR
    (CKP) SENSOR

o IGNITION SWITCH
o VEHICLE SPEED SENSOR
o COOLER LOAD SIGNAL
o "PNP" SWITCH (A/T ONLY)
o POWER STEERING SWITCH
o FUEL PUMP RELAY SIGNAL
o IGNITION DETECT SIGNAL

INPUT ▷ ECM OUTPUT▷

*1. FUEL INJECTOR
*2. IGNITION COIL
*3. ISC MOTOR
    (STEPPER MOTOR TYPE)
*4. EVAP Canister Purge Solenoid
    Valve
*5. EGR SOLENOID VALVE
    o FUEL PUMP CONTROL
    o MFI CONTROL RELAY
    o COOLER RELAY
    o IGNITION TIMING CONTROL
    o DIAGNOSIS

PNP : Park and Neutral Position

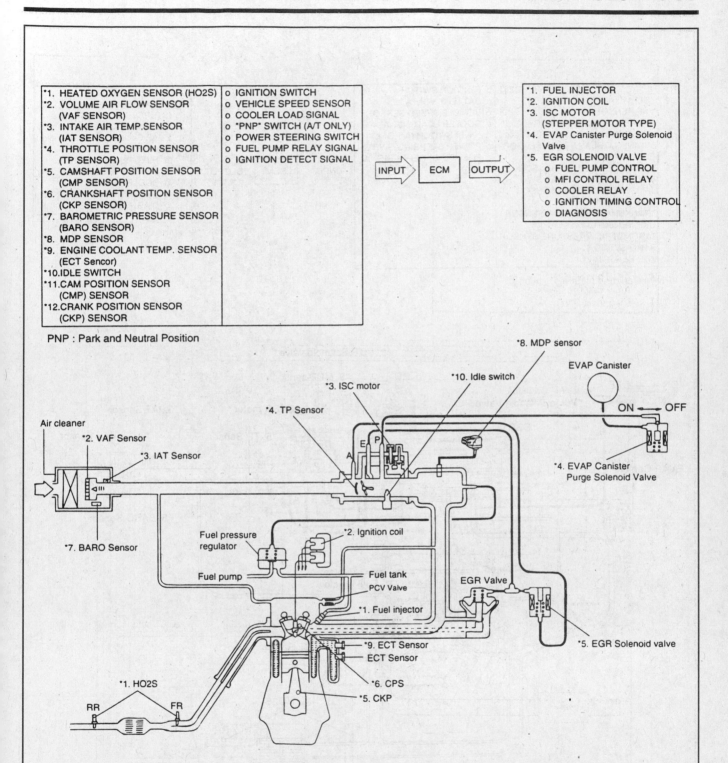

ECM : Engine Control Module
EVAP : Evaporative Emission
TWC : Three Way Catalytic Converter

89534gB8

Fig. 116 Electronic engine controls schematic—2.0L (VIN P) engine

*1. HEATED OXYGEN SENSOR (HO2S)
*2. VOLUME AIR FLOW SENSOR
(VAF SENSOR)
*3. INTAKE AIR TEMP.SENSOR
(IAT SENSOR)
*4. ENGINE COOLANT TEMP.SENSOR
(ECT SENSOR)
*5. THROTTLE POSITION SENSOR
(TP SENSOR) (WITH IDLE SWITCH)
*6. CAMSHAFT POSITION SENSOR
(CMP SENSOR)
*7. CRANKSHAFT POSITION SENSOR
(CKP SENSOR)
*8. BAROMETRIC PRESSURE SENSOR
(BARO SENSOR)
*9. MDP SENSOR

o IGNITION SWITCH
o BATTERY VOLTAGE
o VEHICLE SPEED SENSOR
o COOLER LOAD SIGNAL
o *PNP* SWITCH (A/T ONLY)
o POWER STEERING SWITCH
o FUEL PUMP RELAY SIGNAL

INPUT → ECM → OUTPUT

*1. FUEL INJECTOR
*2. ISC MOTOR
(STEPPER MOTOR TYPE)
*3. EGR SOLENOID VALVE
*4. EVAP Canister Purge Solenoid
Valve
o FUEL PUMP CONTROL
o MFI CONTROL RELAY
o COOLER RELAY
o SPARK TIMING CONTROL
o DIAGNOSIS

PNP : Park and Neutral Position

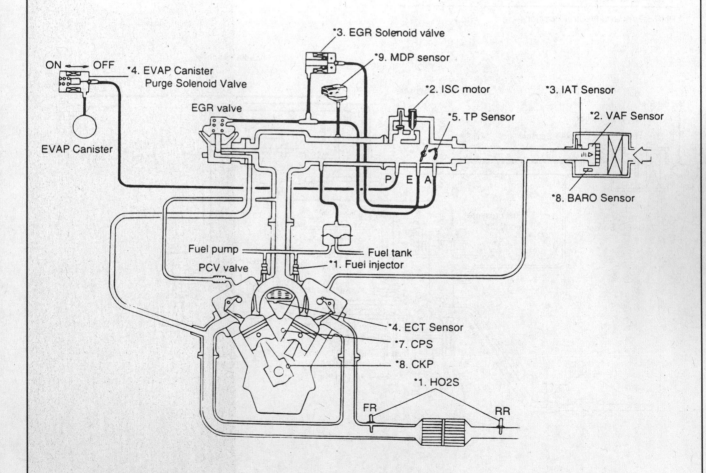

ECM : Engine Control Module
EVAP : Evaporative Emission
TWC : Three Way Catalytic Converter

89534gB9

Fig. 117 Electronic engine controls schematic—3.0L (VIN T) engine

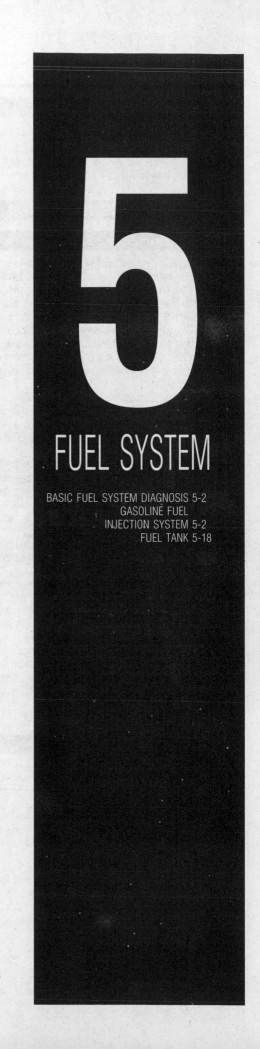

5

FUEL SYSTEM

BASIC FUEL SYSTEM DIAGNOSIS

When there is a problem starting or driving a vehicle, two of the most important checks involve the ignition and the fuel systems. The questions most mechanics attempt to answer first, "is there spark?" and "is there fuel?" will often lead to solving most basic problems. For ignition system diagnosis and testing, please refer to the information on engine electrical components and ignition systems found earlier in this manual. If the ignition system checks out (there is spark), then you must determine if the fuel system is operating properly (is there fuel?).

GASOLINE FUEL INJECTION SYSTEM

General Information

The fuel injection system used on Hyundai vehicles is classified as a Multi-port Fuel Injection (MFI) system. The basic function of the system is to control the air/fuel ratio, based on input signals from various engine sensors. The air/fuel ratio is controlled by varying the injector drive time (pulse width). The system is controlled by an Electronic Control Module (ECM), which monitors the engine conditions, then calculates the injection timing and air/fuel ratio according to the signals from the sensors. The ECM consists of a microprocessor, Random Access Memory (RAM), Read Only Memory (ROM) and input and output signal interface systems.

The MFI system consists of 2 operating modes:
• Open Loop—air/fuel ratio is controlled by information programmed into the ECM by the manufacturer.
• Closed Loop—air/fuel ratio is varied by the ECM based on information supplied by the oxygen sensor.

An electric fuel pump supplies sufficient fuel to the injection system and the pressure regulator maintains a constant pressure to the injectors. These injectors inject a metered quantity of fuel into the intake manifold in accordance with signals from the Electronic Control Module (ECM) or engine computer. After pressure regulation, excess fuel is returned to the fuel tank.

The injectors have 2 modes (Injector Drive Timing) of operation:
• Non-synchronous Injection (Simultaneous Injection)
• Synchronous Injection (Sequential Injection)

Non-synchronous injection is activated during engine starting (cranking). There are 2 fuel injections, for each engine rpm, to all 4 cylinders. Also, during acceleration, fuel proportionate to the magnitude of acceleration, is injected to 2 selected cylinders during the intake and exhaust strokes.

Synchronous Injection is activated after the engine has started. The injectors are activated at the exhaust stroke of each cylinder in a sequential manner, according to the crankshaft angle sensor signal. There is 1 injection per cylinder for every 2 crankshaft revolutions, according to firing order.

Relieving Fuel System Pressure

ACCENT, ELANTRA, SONATA AND TIBURON

▶ See Figure 1

The fuel pump connector is located at the fuel tank sending unit on top of the fuel tank. The connector is accessible through a door located under the rear seat.
1. Remove the rear seat cushion.
2. Disengage the fuel pump harness connector at the fuel tank sending unit.
3. Start the engine and allow it to run until it stalls.
4. Turn the ignition switch to the **OFF** position.
5. Disconnect the negative battery cable.
6. Reconnect the fuel pump harness connector.

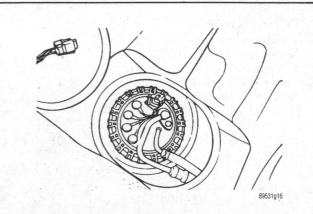

89531g16

Fig. 1 The fuel pump connector is located at the fuel tank sending unit on top of the fuel tank. The connector is accessible through a door located under the rear seat—except Excel and Scoupe

EXCEL AND SCOUPE

▶ See Figure 2

The fuel pump connector is located to the right of the fuel tank.
1. Disengage the fuel pump harness connector at the rear of the fuel tank.
2. Start the engine and allow it to run until it stalls.

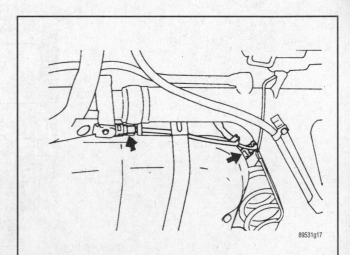

89531g17

Fig. 2 The fuel pump connector is located to the right of the fuel tank—Excel and Scoupe

3. Turn the ignition switch to the **OFF** position.
4. Disconnect the negative battery cable.
5. Reconnect the fuel pump harness connector.

Fuel Pump

♦ **See Figure 3**

REMOVAL & INSTALLATION

♦ **See Figures 4, 5, 6, 7 and 8 (p. 4–6)**

1. Relieve the fuel system pressure.
2. Raise and support the vehicle safely.
3. Remove the fuel tank drain plug and drain the fuel into an approved container.
4. Remove the fuel tank from the vehicle.
5. Label, disconnect and plug the vapor and fuel hoses at the pump.
6. Label and disconnect the electrical harness at the pump.
7. Loosen the fuel pump mounting bolts.
8. Remove the fuel pump from the tank and discard the gasket.
To install:
9. Install the fuel pump using a new gasket. Tighten the mounting bolts to 12–24 inch lbs. (3–4 Nm).

10. Connect the electrical harness at the pump.
11. Connect the vapor and fuel hoses at the pump. Tighten fuel hose connections to 22–29 ft. lbs. (29–39 Nm).
12. Install the fuel tank and fuel drain plug.
13. Lower the vehicle.
14. Fill the tank with fuel and check for proper fuel pump operation.

TESTING

Operational Check

♦ **See Figures 9, 10, 11, 12 and 13 (p. 6–7)**

1. Check the fuse.
2. Check all wiring connections.
3. Check the fuel pump relay. If the engine starts when the ignition switch is turned to **START**, but stops when it is turned to **ON**, the relay is faulty.

➡**It is sometimes hard to hear the fuel pump operate. It may be easier to hear the pump operate by removing the fuel cap and listening at the fuel filler nozzle.**

4. Jump the fuel pump test connector and the fuel pump should operate. If the pump fails to operate when the jumper is connected, the pump is faulty.

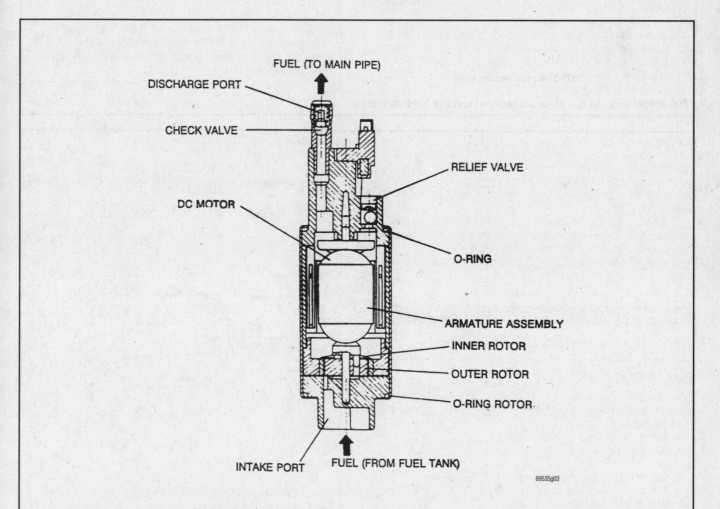

FUEL (TO MAIN PIPE)
DISCHARGE PORT
CHECK VALVE
DC MOTOR
RELIEF VALVE
O-RING
ARMATURE ASSEMBLY
INNER ROTOR
OUTER ROTOR
O-RING ROTOR
INTAKE PORT
FUEL (FROM FUEL TANK)
89535g03

Fig. 3 Cutaway view of the electric fuel pump

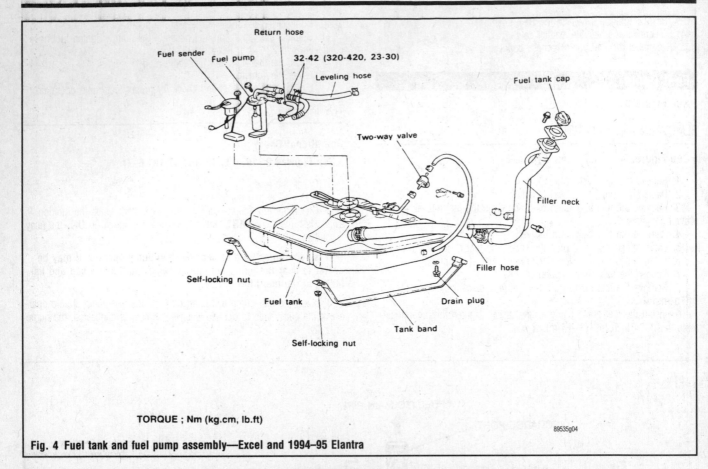

TORQUE ; Nm (kg.cm, lb.ft)

89535g04

Fig. 4 Fuel tank and fuel pump assembly—Excel and 1994–95 Elantra

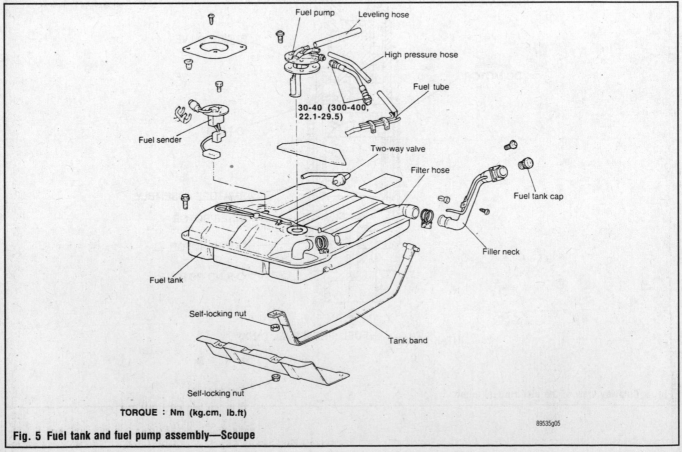

TORQUE : Nm (kg.cm, lb.ft)

89535g05

Fig. 5 Fuel tank and fuel pump assembly—Scoupe

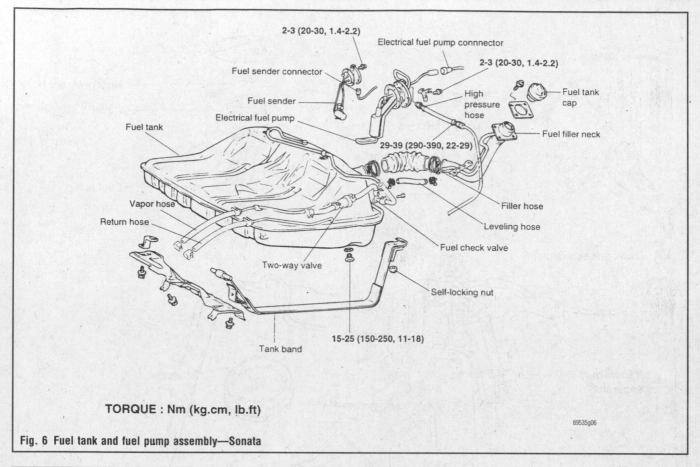

Fig. 6 Fuel tank and fuel pump assembly—Sonata

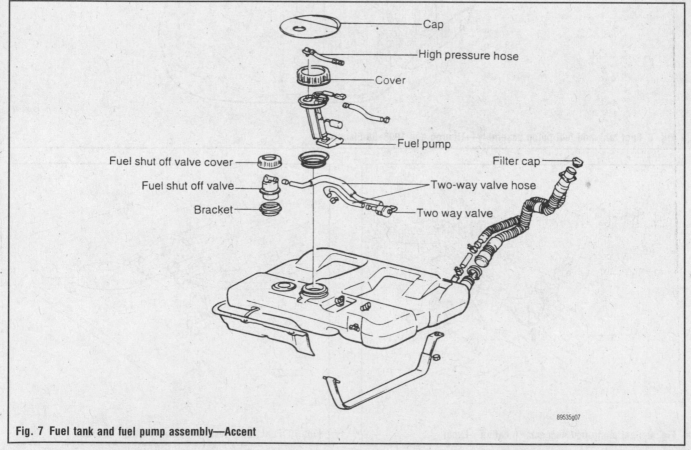

Fig. 7 Fuel tank and fuel pump assembly—Accent

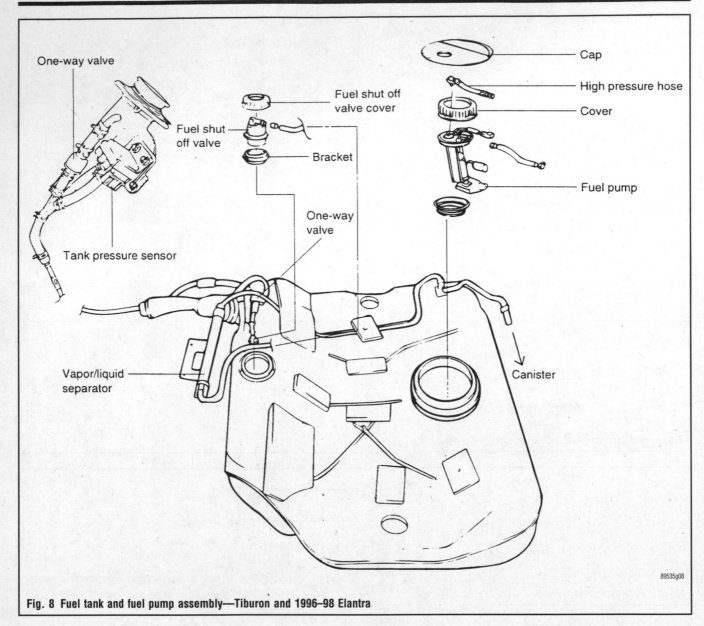

Fig. 8 Fuel tank and fuel pump assembly—Tiburon and 1996–98 Elantra

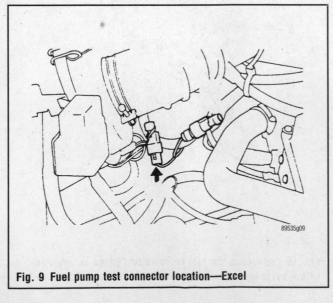

Fig. 9 Fuel pump test connector location—Excel

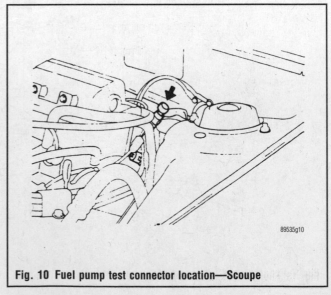

Fig. 10 Fuel pump test connector location—Scoupe

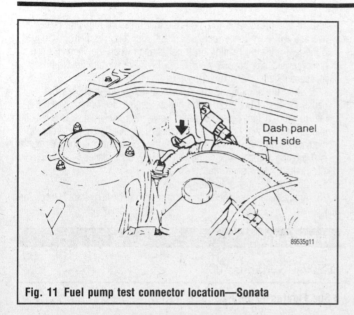

Fig. 11 Fuel pump test connector location—Sonata

Pressure Check
◢ **See Figures 14, 15 and 16**

1. Relieve fuel system pressure.
2. Disconnect the battery negative cable.
3. Disconnect the inlet fuel hose from the fuel filter.
4. Connect a fuel pressure gauge with the appropriate adapters.
5. Connect the negative battery terminal.
6. Apply battery voltage to the fuel pump test connector located in the engine compartment, which will energize the fuel pump. With pressure applied, check for fuel leakage at the gauge. If no leaks are present, continue with the test procedure.
7. Start the engine and run at curb idle speed.
8. Measure the fuel pressure and compare to specifications.
9. Locate and disconnect the vacuum hose running to the fuel pressure regulator. Plug the end of the hose and record the fuel pressure again. The fuel pressure should have increased approximately 10 psi.
10. If the pressure readings were not at the desired specifications, perform the following diagnostic procedure:
   a. If fuel pressure is too low, check for a clogged fuel filter, a defective fuel pressure regulator or a defective fuel pump, any of which will require replacement.

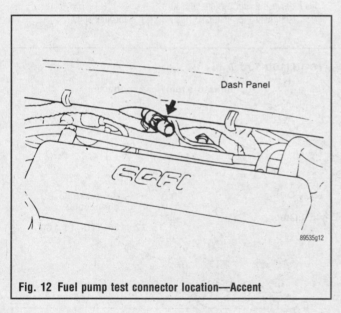

Fig. 12 Fuel pump test connector location—Accent

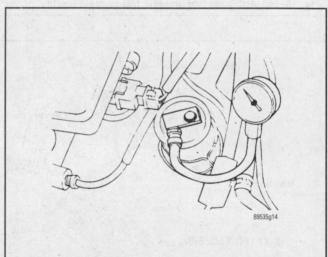

Fig. 14 Connecting the fuel pressure test gauge on vehicles with a fuel block connection on the filter—except Sonata

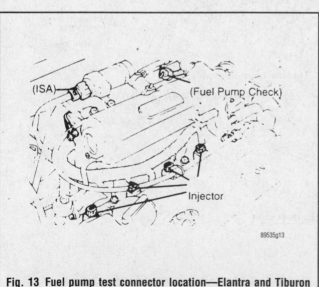

Fig. 13 Fuel pump test connector location—Elantra and Tiburon

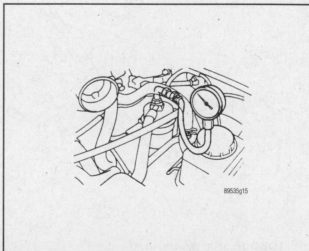

Fig. 15 Connecting the fuel pressure test gauge on vehicles with a banjo type connection on the filter—except Sonata

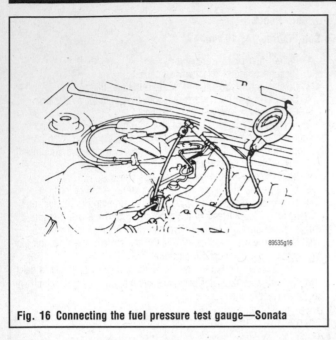

Fig. 16 Connecting the fuel pressure test gauge—Sonata

b. If fuel pressure is too high, the fuel pressure regulator is defective and will have to be replaced, or the fuel return is bent or clogged. If the fuel pressure reading does not change when the vacuum hose is disconnected, the hose is clogged or the valve is stuck in the fuel pressure regulator and it will have to be replaced.

c. Stop the engine and check for changes in the fuel pressure gauge. It should not drop. If the gauge reading does drop, watch the rate of drop. If fuel pressure drops slowly, the likely cause is a leaking injector, which will require replacement. If the fuel pressure drops immediately after the engine is stopped, the check valve in the fuel pump isn't closing and the fuel pump will have to be replaced.

11. Relieve fuel system pressure.

12. Remove the fuel pressure gauge.

13. Apply battery voltage to the fuel pump check connector. Check for leaks.

Throttle Body

REMOVAL & INSTALLATION

♦ See Figures 17 thru 22 (p. 8–11)

1. Relieve the fuel system pressure.
2. Disconnect the air intake hose from the throttle body.

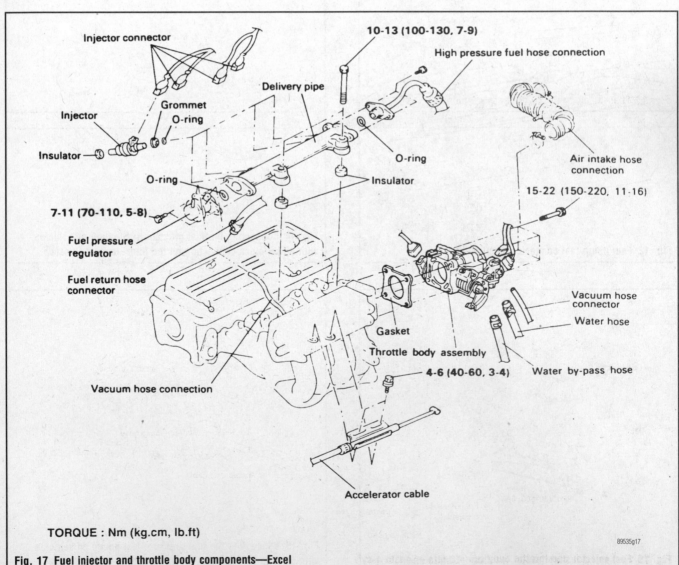

TORQUE : Nm (kg.cm, lb.ft)

Fig. 17 Fuel injector and throttle body components—Excel

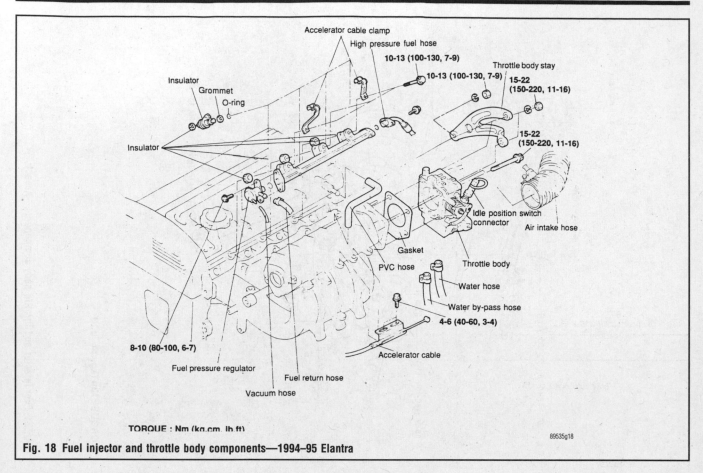

Fig. 18 Fuel injector and throttle body components—1994–95 Elantra

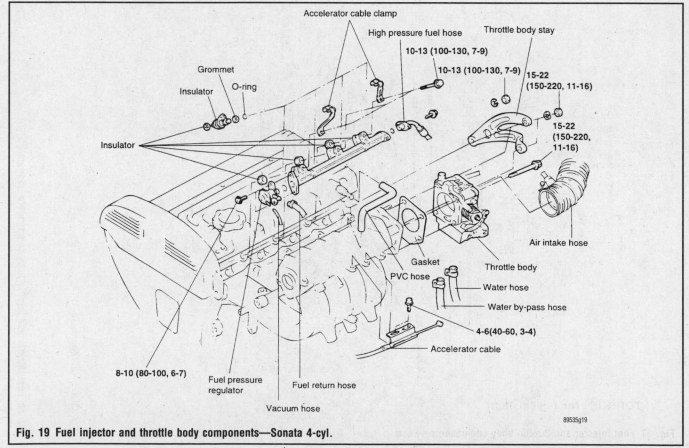

Fig. 19 Fuel injector and throttle body components—Sonata 4-cyl.

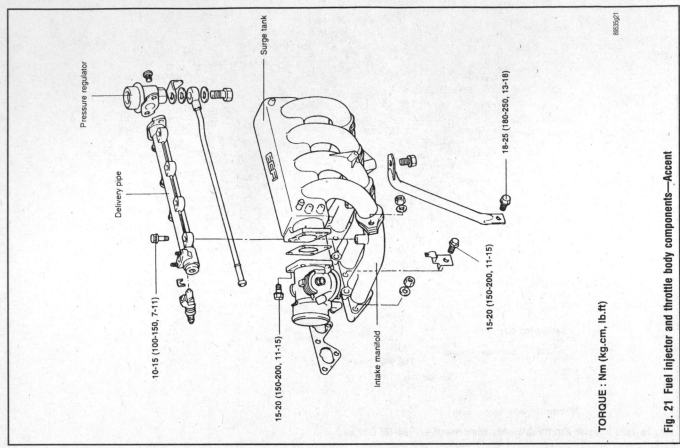

Fig. 21 Fuel injector and throttle body components—Accent

TORQUE : Nm (kg.cm, lb.ft)

Pressure regulator

Surge tank

Delivery pipe

18-25 (180-250, 13-18)

10-15 (100-150, 7-11)

15-20 (150-200, 11-15)

15-20 (150-200, 11-15)

Intake manifold

89535g21

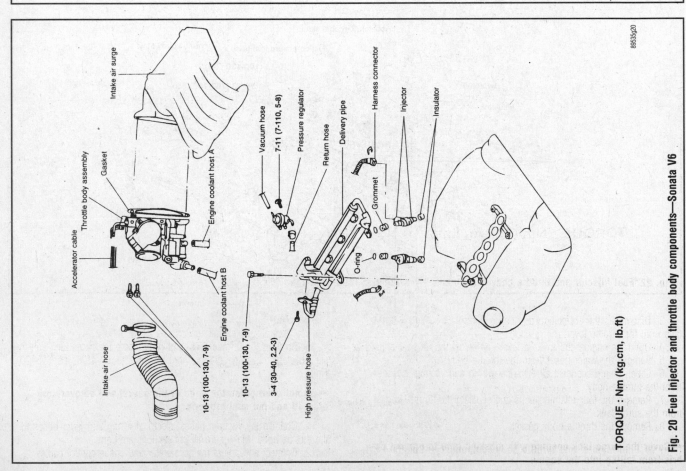

Fig. 20 Fuel injector and throttle body components—Sonata V6

TORQUE : Nm (kg.cm, lb.ft)

Intake air surge

Throttle body assembly

Gasket

Accelerator cable

Engine coolant host A

Engine coolant host B

Vacuum hose

7-11 (7-110, 5-8)

Pressure regulator

Return hose

Delivery pipe

Harness connector

Injector

Insulator

Grommet

O-ring

High pressure hose

3-4 (30-40, 2.2-3)

10-13 (100-130, 7-9)

10-13 (100-130, 7-9)

Intake air hose

89535g20

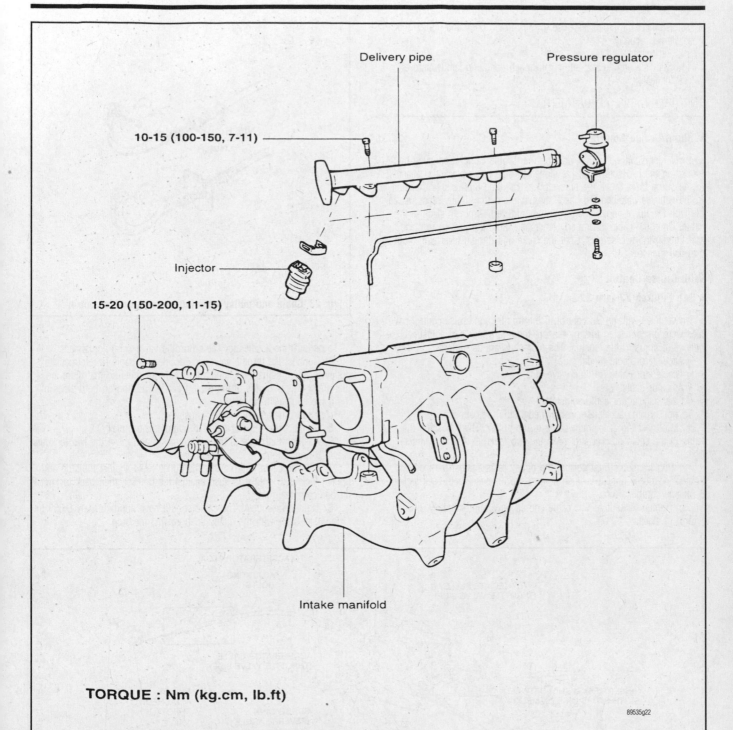

Delivery pipe

Pressure regulator

10-15 (100-150, 7-11)

Injector

15-20 (150-200, 11-15)

Intake manifold

TORQUE : Nm (kg.cm, lb.ft)

89535g22

Fig. 22 Fuel injector and throttle body components—Tiburon and 1996–98 Elantra

3. Disconnect the accelerator and cruise control (if so equipped) cables from the throttle lever.

4. Drain the engine coolant to a level just below the intake manifold.

5. Remove the water hoses from the throttle body.

6. Label, then disconnect all electrical wiring and vacuum hoses from the throttle body.

7. Remove the four retaining bolts and separate the throttle body from the surge tank.

8. Remove the throttle body gasket.

➡ **Cover the surge tank opening with masking tape to prevent debris from falling into the engine.**

To install:

9. Clean all gasket mating surfaces thoroughly.

10. Position the throttle body and gasket onto the surge tank and install the four retaining bolts. Tighten the bolts to 11–15 ft. lbs. (15–20 Nm).

➡ **Do not overtighten the bolts or the gasket will be over-compressed and not seal properly.**

11. Connect the vacuum hoses, electrical wiring and water hoses to the throttle body. Make sure all connections are tight.

12. Connect and adjust the accelerator and cruise control cables.

13. Connect the air intake hose to the throttle body and tighten the hose clamp securely.

14. Fill the cooling system.

15. Start the engine and allow it to reach operating temperature. Check for leaks.

THROTTLE CABLE ADJUSTMENT

Without Cruise Control

On vehicles without cruise control, the throttle cable is adjusted by loosening the two screws on the slotted throttle cable bracket(s) attached to the surge tank. Move the bracket(s) as required until a slight tension in the cable is obtained. To check the cable tension, lightly press the cable with the tip of your finger. There should be 0–1mm of slack in the cable. Once the cable is properly tensioned, hold the bracket in place and tighten the two screws. Coat the cable and throttle lever with multi-purpose grease.

With Cruise Control

▶ See Figures 23 thru 29

On vehicles with cruise control, if the throttle and cruise control cables were disconnected for any reason, there is a four part adjustment sequence to adjust cable tension. The four parts are as follows:

• Accelerator cable (pedal side)
• Accelerator cable (throttle valve side)
• Actuator cable
• Final accelerator cable adjustment

To perform the accelerator cable (pedal side) adjustment:

1. Connect the accelerator cable to the pulley. Then, position the cable in the cable bracket and make the two locknuts A and B finger-tight.

2. Pull the cable tight so that the pulley rests against the stop and tighten locknut B until it is flush against the bracket. Then, back locknut B off one complete turn.

3. Tighten locknut A. The cable should have approximately 0.03 in. (1mm) of slack.

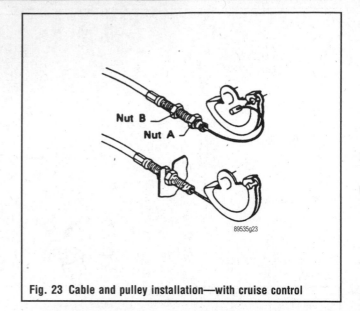

Fig. 23 Cable and pulley installation—with cruise control

To perform the accelerator cable (throttle valve side) adjustment:

4. Connect the throttle valve side accelerator cable to intermediate pulley B. Then, adjust and tighten the cable locknuts so that there are just about equal lengths of the cable threaded portion on both sides of the cable housing bracket.

To perform the actuator cable adjustment:

5. Connect the actuator cable to intermediate pulley C.

6. Position the cable in the cable bracket and make the two locknuts A and B finger-tight.

7. Pull the cable tight so that the pulley rests against the stop and tighten locknut B until it is flush against the bracket, then back locknut B off one complete turn.

8. Tighten locknut A. The cable should have approximately 0.059 in. (1.5mm) of slack with the pulley flush against the stop.

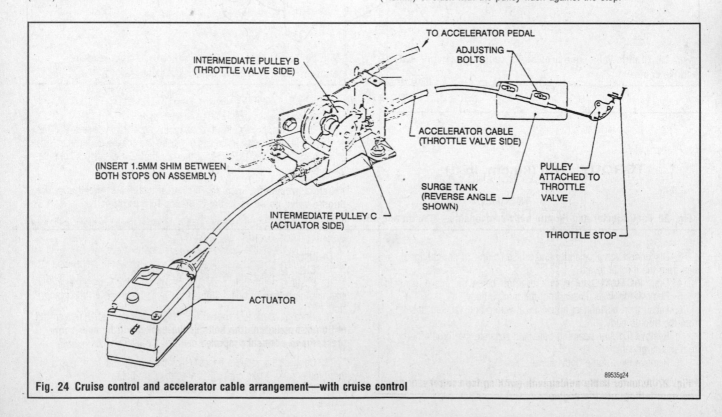

Fig. 24 Cruise control and accelerator cable arrangement—with cruise control

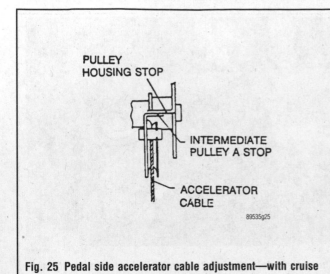

Fig. 25 Pedal side accelerator cable adjustment—with cruise control

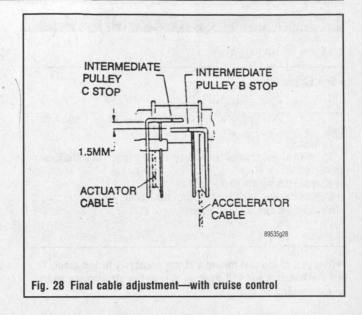

Fig. 28 Final cable adjustment—with cruise control

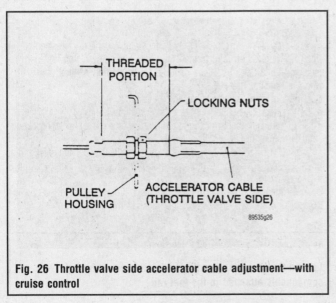

Fig. 26 Throttle valve side accelerator cable adjustment—with cruise control

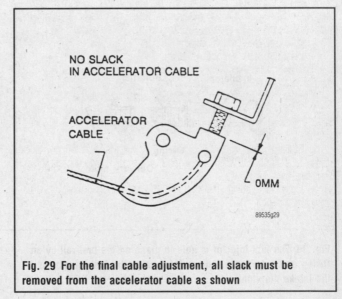

Fig. 29 For the final cable adjustment, all slack must be removed from the accelerator cable as shown

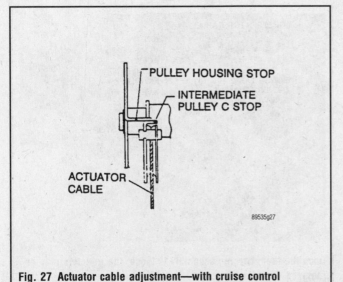

Fig. 27 Actuator cable adjustment—with cruise control

To perform the final cable adjustment:

9. If not already completed, connect the accelerator cable to the throttle valve pulley and attach the cable and slotted bracket to the rear side of the surge tank. DO NOT tighten the two bracket mounting screws at this time.

➡ Before proceeding with any further adjustments, make sure the throttle valve pulley is in the NORMAL idle position.

10. Insert a 0.059 in. (1.5mm) shim or feeler gauge between intermediate pulley stops B and C and hold it there.

11. Adjust the cable casing at the rear side of the surge tank until all slack is removed from the cable. If all slack is removed, the throttle stop bolt should be contacting the throttle valve lever. Make sure the throttle valve pulley does not deviate from the normal idle position during the adjustment.

12. Once all slack is removed from the accelerator cable, tighten the two bracket mounting screws at this time.

13. Remove the shim installed between the intermediate pulleys.

Fuel Injectors

REMOVAL & INSTALLATION

◆ **See Figure 30**

1. Remove the fuel charging assembly.
2. Remove the injectors from the rail by pulling gently. Discard the lower insulator.

To install:

3. Install a new grommet and O-ring to the injector. Coat the O-ring with light oil.
4. Install the injector to the fuel rail.
5. Install a new insulator in the intake manifold.
6. Install the fuel charging assembly.

TESTING

➡Removal of the fuel injectors is not necessary to test them. To test the injectors you will need an automotive stethoscope and/or an ohmmeter.

On some models, the injector harness is held onto the injector with a small clip (arrow)

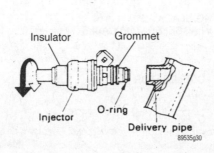
Fig. 30 The fuel injector is held in place on the fuel rail by an O-ring and a grommet. An insulator holds the fuel injector on the intake manifold

Loosen the fuel rail mounting bolts after detaching all components attached to the fuel rail

Label the injector wiring harnesses prior to removing them from the injectors

Once the fuel charging assembly is loose, the injectors may be removed one at a time . . .

. . . or the whole charging assembly may be removed as an assembly

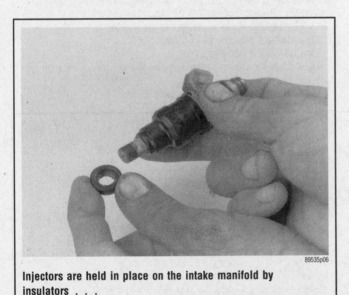

Injectors are held in place on the intake manifold by insulators . . .

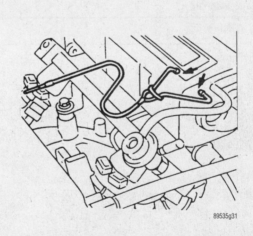

. . . and on the fuel charging assembly by O-rings

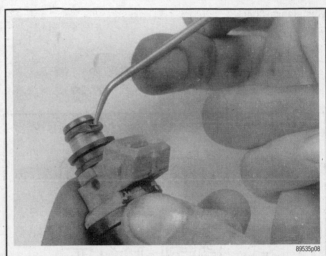

The O-rings are easily damaged and should be replaced each time the injectors are removed

Operational Check
◗ **See Figure 31**

1. Start the engine and allow it to idle.
2. Using a mechanic's stethoscope, touch the injector body and listen for the injector operating sound at idle speed. You should hear a distinct "ticking" sound at a steady interval as the solenoid valve opens and closes. Listen to all injectors.
3. Have the assistant increase the engine speed and listen again. The ticking interval should increase in proportion to the increase in engine speed. Again, perform this test on all injectors.

➡Sometimes the sound from an adjacent injector will be transmitted to another injector across the delivery pipe. In this case, a bad injector will appear to be working fine. To avoid this, make sure the tip of the stethoscope is placed directly on the injector body and does not bridge the delivery pipe. .

Fig. 31 Using a mechanic's stethoscope, touch the injector body and listen for the injector operating sound at idle speed. You should hear a distinct "ticking" sound at a steady interval as the solenoid valve opens and closes

Resistance Check

♦ **See Figure 32**

1. Disconnect the fuel injector electrical harness.
2. Measure resistance across the injector terminals.
3. Resistance should be 13–16 ohms @ 68°F (20°C).
4. If the resistance reading is not as specified, the injector may be faulty.

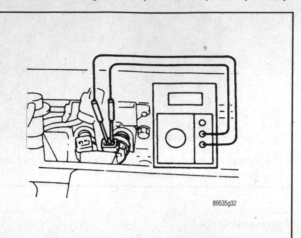

89535g32

Fig. 32 Measure resistance between injector terminals. If the resistance reading is not as specified, the injector may be faulty

Fuel Charging Assembly

REMOVAL & INSTALLATION

Except 3.0 (VIN T) Engine

♦ **See Figures 17, 18, 19 and 33 (p. 8, 9 and 16)**

1. Relieve the fuel system pressure.
2. Disconnect the negative battery cable.
3. Wrap the connection with a shop towel and disconnect the high pressure fuel line at the fuel rail.
4. Disconnect the fuel return hose.
5. Disconnect the vacuum hose from the fuel pressure regulator.
6. Disconnect and remove the PCV hose.
7. Label and disconnect the electrical harnesses from each injector.
8. Remove the injector rail retaining bolts. Make sure the rubber mounting bushings do not get lost.
9. Lift the rail assembly up and away from the engine.

To install:

10. Install the fuel rail and injectors to the manifold. Make sure the rubber bushings are in place before tightening the mounting bolts. Tighten the retaining bolts to 7–11 ft. lbs. (11–13 Nm).
11. Connect the electrical harness to the injectors.
12. Install and connect the PCV hose.
13. Connect the fuel return hose.
14. Replace the O-ring, lightly lubricate it and connect the high pressure fuel line.
15. Connect the negative battery cable

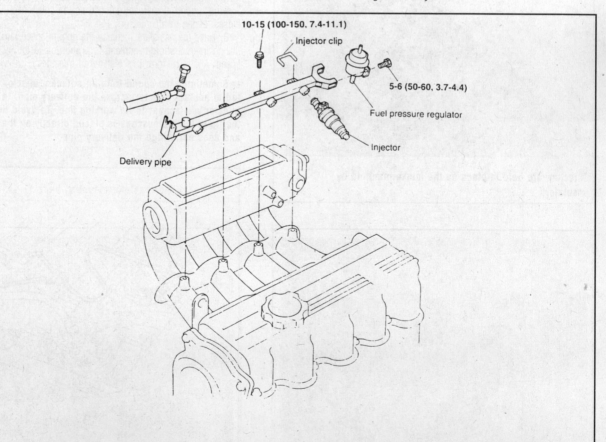

10-15 (100-150, 7.4-11.1)

Injector clip

5-6 (50-60, 3.7-4.4)

Fuel pressure regulator

Injector

Delivery pipe

TORQUE : Nm (ka.cm. lb.ft)

89535g33

Fig. 33 Fuel charging assembly and injectors—Scoupe

16. Start the engine and check the entire system for proper operation and leaks.

3.0L (VIN T) Engine

♦ See Figure 33 (p. 16)

1. Relieve the fuel system pressure.
2. Disconnect the negative battery cable.
3. Drain the cooling system.
4. Disconnect all components from the air intake plenum and remove the plenum from the intake manifold. Discard the gaskets.
5. Wrap the connection with a shop towel and disconnect the high pressure fuel line at the fuel rail.
6. Disconnect the fuel return hose and remove the O-ring.
7. Disconnect the vacuum hose from the fuel pressure regulator. Remove the fuel pressure regulator and O-ring.
8. Disconnect the electrical connectors from each injector.
9. Remove the injector rail retaining bolts. Make sure the rubber mounting bushings do not get lost.
10. Lift the rail assemblies up and away from the engine.

To install:

11. Replace the insulators in the intake manifold, if equipped.
12. Install the fuel charging assemblies on the manifold. Make sure the rubber bushings are in place before tightening the mounting bolts. Tighten the retaining bolts to 5–8 ft. lbs. (7–11 Nm).
13. Install the fuel pipe with new gasket.
14. Connect the electrical harness to the injectors.
15. Connect the fuel return hose.
16. Replace the O-ring, lightly lubricate it and connect the high pressure fuel line.
17. Using new gaskets, install the intake plenum and all related items. Tighten the plenum mounting bolts to 13 ft. lbs. (18 Nm).
18. Fill the cooling system.
19. Connect the negative battery cable
20. Start the engine and check the entire system for proper operation and leaks.

Fuel Pressure Regulator

REMOVAL & INSTALLATION

♦ See Figures 17 thru 22 and 33 (p. 8–11 and 16)

1. Relieve the fuel system pressure.
2. Disconnect the negative battery cable.

. . . remove the fuel return hose . . .

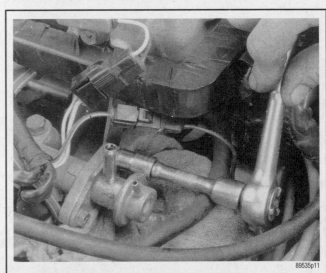

. . . loosen the regulator mounting bolts . . .

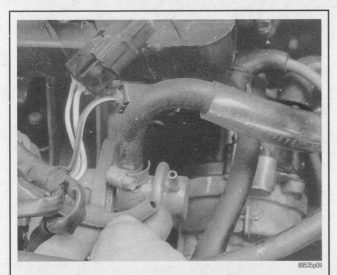

Disconnect the vacuum line from the regulator . . .

. . . and remove the regulator from the fuel rail assembly

3. Disconnect the vacuum line at the regulator.

4. Wrap the fuel return line connection with a shop towel and disconnect from the regulator.

5. Remove the regulator from the fuel rail. Discard the O-ring.

To install:

6. Install and lubricate a new O-ring.

7. Install the regulator and tighten bolts to 6–7 ft. lbs. (8–10 Nm).

8. Connect the fuel return line.

9. Connect the vacuum line.

10. Start the engine and allow it to idle. Check for leaks.

FUEL TANK

Tank Assembly

REMOVAL & INSTALLATION

◆ See Figures 34, 35, 36, 37 and 38 (p. 18–22)

✳✳ CAUTION

Take all applicable cautions when working around the fuel tank. Always disconnect the negative battery cable after relieving fuel system pressure.

1. Release the fuel system pressure. Leave the fuel pump connector disconnected.

2. Disconnect the negative battery cable.

3. Remove the fuel tank cap.

4. Raise and support the vehicle safely.

5. Position a suitable drain pan under the fuel tank.

6. Remove the fuel tank drain plug and drain all the fuel from the tank.

7. Label and disconnect the fuel return and vapor hoses from the fuel tank.

8. Label and disconnect the electrical harness from the sending unit.

9. Loosen the flare nut fitting and disconnect the high pressure hose from the fuel tank.

10. Disconnect the fuel filler and leveling hoses from the fuel tank.

11. Loosen the two self-locking nuts that hold the tank bands to the tank.

12. Support the fuel tank from underneath and swing the tank bands down away from the tank.

13. Disconnect the fuel vapor hose.

14. Lower and remove the tank.

To install:

15. Raise the fuel tank into position and connect the vapor hose.

16. Make sure the band is bonded fully to the tank and tighten the band until the end of the band contacts the body.

17. Connect the leveling hose to the tank and the filler neck. Make sure the hose is pushed at least 1.6 in. (40mm) onto the filler neck.

18. Connect the filler hose so that the end of the hose with the shorter straight pipe is connected to the tank side.

19. Connect the fuel vapor and return hoses. Make sure the hoses are pushed at least 1.0–1.2 in. (25–30mm) onto their connections.

20. Connect the high pressure hose to the tank by making the flare nut hand tight. Hold the stationary nut with a wrench and torque the flare nut to 23–30 ft. lbs. (34–40 Nm).

➡**Make sure that the fuel hose does not twist when the flare fitting is being tightened.**

21. Connect the fuel pump and sending unit harnesses.

22. Install the drain plug and tighten to 11–18 ft. lbs. (15–24 Nm).

23. Lower the vehicle.

24. Fill the fuel tank to the proper level.

25. Connect the negative battery cable.

26. Start the engine and allow it to idle.

27. Check for proper fuel pump operation and leaks.

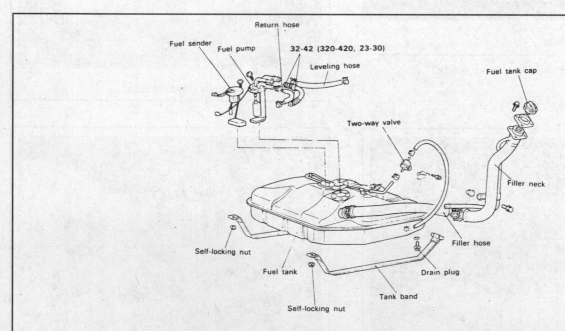

TORQUE ; Nm (kg.cm, lb.ft)

89535g04

Fig. 34 Fuel tank and fuel pump assembly—Excel and 1994–95 Elantra

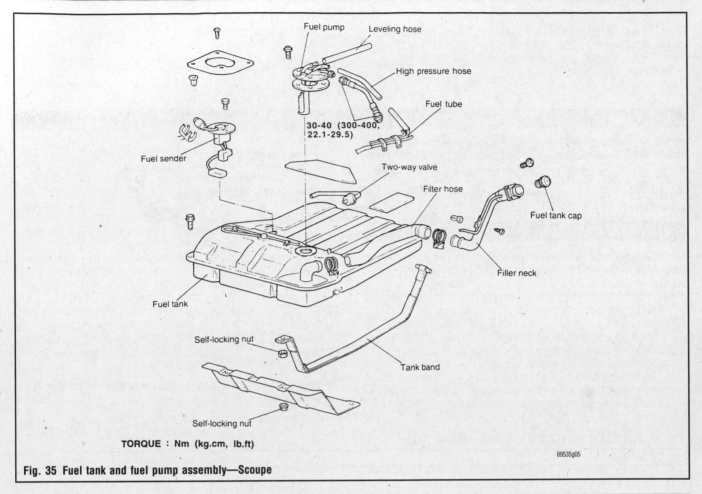

Fig. 35 Fuel tank and fuel pump assembly—Scoupe

Fuel pump
Leveling hose
High pressure hose
Fuel tube
30-40 (300-400, 22.1-29.5)
Fuel sender
Two-way valve
Filter hose
Fuel tank cap
Fuel tank
Filler neck
Self-locking nut
Tank band
Self-locking nut
TORQUE : Nm (kg.cm, lb.ft)
89535g05

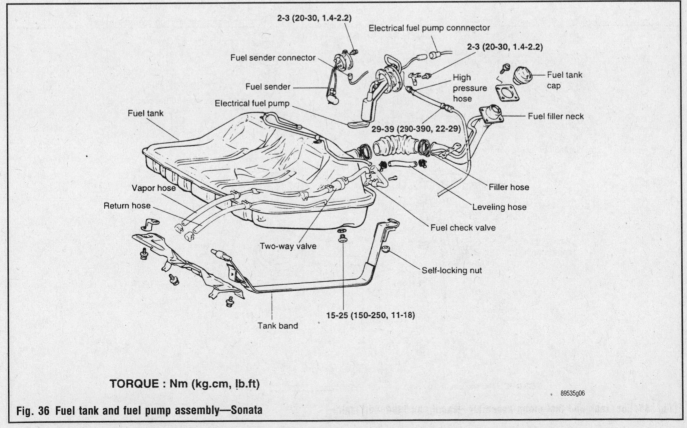

Fig. 36 Fuel tank and fuel pump assembly—Sonata

2-3 (20-30, 1.4-2.2)
Electrical fuel pump connnector
2-3 (20-30, 1.4-2.2)
Fuel sender connector
Fuel tank cap
Fuel sender
High pressure hose
Electrical fuel pump
Fuel tank
Fuel filler neck
29-39 (290-390, 22-29)
Vapor hose
Filler hose
Return hose
Leveling hose
Fuel check valve
Two-way valve
Self-locking nut
Tank band
15-25 (150-250, 11-18)
TORQUE : Nm (kg.cm, lb.ft)
89535g06

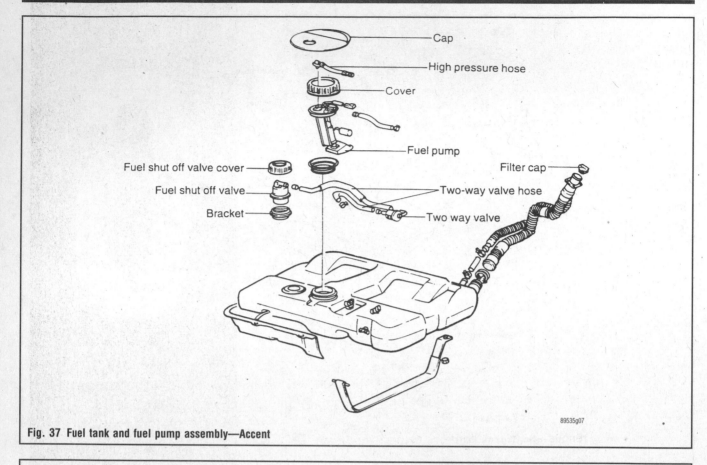

Fig. 37 Fuel tank and fuel pump assembly—Accent

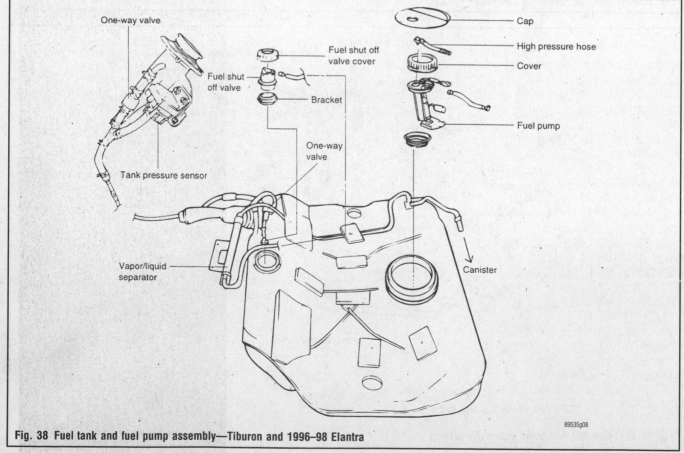

Fig. 38 Fuel tank and fuel pump assembly—Tiburon and 1996–98 Elantra

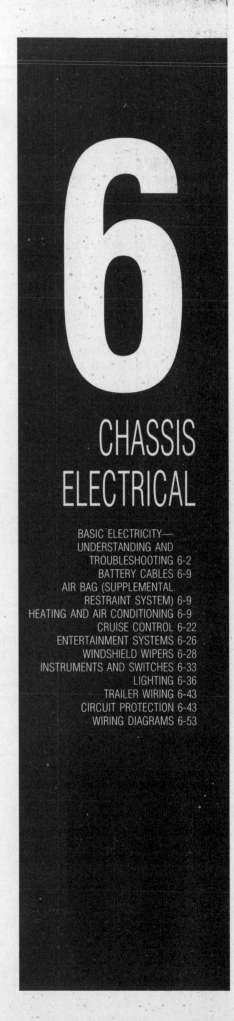

6

CHASSIS ELECTRICAL

BASIC ELECTRICITY—UNDERSTANDING AND TROUBLESHOOTING

Basic Electrical Theory

♦ See Figure 1

For any 12 volt, negative ground, electrical system to operate, the electricity must travel in a complete circuit. This simply means that current (power) from the positive terminal (+) of the battery must eventually return to the negative terminal (−) of the battery. Along the way, this current will travel through wires, fuses, switches and components. If, for any reason, the flow of current through the circuit is interrupted, the component fed by that circuit will cease to function properly.

Perhaps the easiest way to visualize a circuit is to think of connecting a light bulb (with two wires attached to it) to the battery—one wire attached to the negative (−) terminal of the battery and the other wire to the positive (+) terminal. With the two wires touching the battery terminals, the circuit would be complete and the light bulb would illuminate. Electricity would follow a path from the battery to the bulb and back to the battery. It's easy to see that with longer wires on our light bulb, it could be mounted anywhere. Further, one wire could be fitted with a switch so that the light could be turned on and off.

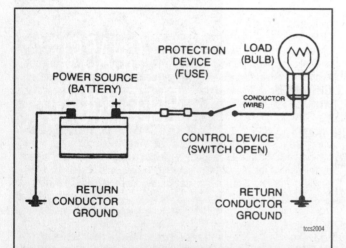

tccs2004

Fig. 1 This example illustrates a simple circuit. When the switch is closed, power from the positive (+) battery terminal flows through the fuse and the switch, and then to the light bulb. The light illuminates and the circuit is completed through the ground wire back to the negative (-) battery terminal. In reality, the two ground points shown in the illustration are attached to the metal chassis of the vehicle, which completes the circuit back to the battery.

The normal automotive circuit differs from this simple example in two ways. First, instead of having a return wire from the bulb to the battery, the current travels through the chassis of the vehicle. Since the negative (−) battery cable is attached to the chassis and the chassis is made of electrically conductive metal, the chassis of the vehicle can serve as a ground wire to complete the circuit. Secondly, most automotive circuits contain multiple components which receive power from a single circuit. This lessens the amount of wire needed to power components on the vehicle.

THE WATER ANALOGY

Electricity is the flow of electrons—hypothetical particles thought to constitute the basic "stuff" of electricity. Many people have been taught electrical theory using an analogy with water. In a comparison with water flowing through a pipe, the electrons would be the water.

The flow of electricity can be measured much like the flow of water through a pipe. The unit of measurement used is amperes, frequently abbreviated as amps (a). When connected to a circuit, an ammeter will measure the actual amount of current flowing through the circuit. When relatively few electrons flow through a circuit, the amperage is low. When many electrons flow, the amperage is high.

Just as water pressure is measured in units such as pounds per square inch (psi), electrical pressure is measured in units called volts (v). When a voltmeter is connected to a circuit, it is measuring the electrical pressure. The higher the voltage, the more current will flow through the circuit. The lower the voltage, the less current will flow.

While increasing the voltage in a circuit will increase the flow of current, the actual flow depends not only on voltage, but also on the resistance of the circuit. Resistance is the amount of force necessary to push the current through the circuit. The standard unit for measuring resistance is an ohm (W or omega). Resistance in a circuit varies depending on the amount and type of components used in the circuit. The main factors which determine resistance are:

• Material—some materials have more resistance than others. Those with high resistance are said to be insulators. Rubber is one of the best insulators available, as it allows little current to pass. Low resistance materials are said to be conductors. Copper wire is among the best conductors. Most vehicle wiring is made of copper.

• Size—the larger the wire size being used, the less resistance the wire will have. This is why components which use large amounts of electricity usually have large wires supplying current to them.

• Length—for a given thickness of wire, the longer the wire, the greater the resistance. The shorter the wire, the less the resistance. When determining the proper wire for a circuit, both size and length must be considered to design a circuit that can handle the current needs of the component.

• Temperature—with many materials, the higher the temperature, the greater the resistance. This principle is used in many of the sensors on the engine.

OHM'S LAW

The preceding definitions may lead the reader into believing that there is no relationship between current, voltage and resistance. Nothing can be further from the truth. The relationship between current, voltage and resistance can be summed up by a statement known as Ohm's law.

Voltage (E) is equal to amperage (I) times resistance (R): $E = I \times R$

Other forms of the formula are $R = E/I$ and $I = E/R$

In each of these formulas, E is the voltage in volts, I is the current in amps and R is the resistance in ohms. The basic point to remember is that as the resistance of a circuit goes up, the amount of current that flows in the circuit will go down, if voltage remains the same.

Electrical Components

POWER SOURCE

The power source for 12 volt automotive electrical systems is the battery. In most modern vehicles, the battery is a lead/acid electrochemical device consisting of six 2 volt subsections (cells) connected in series, so that the unit is capable of producing approximately 12 volts of electrical pressure. Each subsection consists of a series of positive and negative plates held a short distance apart in a solution of sulfuric acid and water.

The two types of plates are of dissimilar metals. This sets up a chemical reaction, and it is this reaction which produces current flow from the battery when its positive and negative terminals are connected to an electrical load . The power removed from the battery is replaced by the alternator, which forces electrons back through the battery, reversing the normal flow, and restoring the battery to its original chemical state.

GROUND

Two types of grounds are used in automotive electric circuits. Direct ground components are grounded through their mounting points. All other components use some sort of ground wire which is attached to the body or chassis of the vehicle. The electrical current runs through the chassis of the vehicle and returns to the battery through the ground (−) cable; if you look, you'll see that the battery ground cable connects between the battery and the body or chassis of the vehicle.

➡ **It should be noted that a good percentage of electrical problems can be traced to bad grounds.**

PROTECTIVE DEVICES

It is possible for large surges of current to pass through the electrical system of your vehicle. If this surge of current were to reach the load in the circuit, it could burn it out or severely damage it. To prevent this, fuses, circuit breakers and/or fusible links are connected into the supply wires of the electrical system. These items are nothing more than a built-in weak spot in the system. When an abnormal amount of current flows through the system, these protective devices work as follows to protect the circuit:

• Fuse—when an excessive electrical current passes through a fuse, the fuse "blows" (the conductor melts) and opens the circuit, preventing the passage of current.

• Circuit Breaker—a circuit breaker is basically a self-repairing fuse. It will open the circuit in the same fashion as a fuse, but when the surge subsides, the circuit breaker can be reset and does not need replacement.

• Fusible Link—a fusible link (fuse link or main link) is a short length of special, Hypalon high temperature insulated wire that acts as a

fuse. When an excessive electrical current passes through a fusible link, the thin gauge wire inside the link melts, creating an intentional open to protect the circuit. To repair the circuit, the link must be replaced. Some newer type fusible links are housed in plug-in modules, which are simply replaced like a fuse, while older type fusible links must be cut and spliced if they melt. Since this link is very early in the electrical path, it's the first place to look if nothing on the vehicle works, but the battery seems to be charged and is properly connected.

✳✳ CAUTION

Always replace fuses, circuit breakers and fusible links with identically rated components. Under no circumstances should a component of higher or lower amperage rating be substituted.

SWITCHES AND RELAYS

▶ **See Figure 2**

Switches are used in electrical circuits to control the passage of current. The most common use is to open and close circuits between the battery and the various electric devices in the system. Switches are rated according to the amount of amperage they can handle. If a sufficient amperage rated switch is not used in a circuit, the switch could overload and cause damage.

Some electrical components which require a large amount of current to operate use a special switch called a relay. Since these circuits carry a large amount of current, the thickness of the wire in the circuit is also greater. If this large wire were connected from the load to the control switch on the dashboard, the switch would have to carry the high amperage load and the dash would be twice as large to accommodate the increased size of the wiring harness. To prevent these problems, a relay is used.

Relays are composed of a coil and a switch. These two components are linked together so that when one operates, the other operates at the same time. The large wires in the circuit are connected from the battery to one side of the relay switch and from the opposite side of the relay switch to the load. Most relays are normally open, preventing current from passing through the circuit. Additional, smaller wires are connected from the relay coil to the control switch for the circuit and from the opposite side of the relay coil to ground. When the control switch is turned on, it grounds the smaller wire to the relay coil, causing the coil to operate. The coil pulls the relay switch closed, sending power to the component without routing it through the inside of the vehicle. Some common circuits which may use relays are the horn, headlights, starter, electric fuel pump and rear window defogger systems.

tcca6p01

Most vehicles use one or more fuse panels. This one is located in the driver's side kick panel

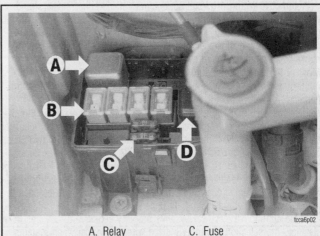

A. Relay   C. Fuse
B. Fusible Link   D. Flasher

tcca6p02

The underhood fuse and relay panel usually contains fuses, relays, flashers and fusible links

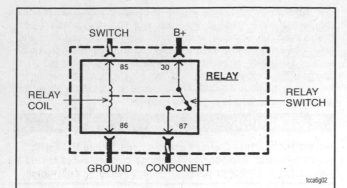

Fig. 2 Relays are composed of a coil and a switch. These two components are linked together so that when one operates, the other operates at the same time. The large wires in the circuit are connected from the battery to one side of the relay switch (B+) and from the opposite side of the relay switch to the load (component). Smaller wires are connected from the relay coil to the control switch for the circuit and from the opposite side of the relay coil to ground.

LOAD

Every complete circuit must include a "load" (something to use the electricity coming from the source). Without this load, the battery would attempt to deliver its entire power supply from one pole to another. The electricity would take a short cut to ground and cause a great amount of damage to other components in the circuit by developing a tremendous amount of heat. This condition could develop sufficient heat to melt the insulation on all the surrounding wires and reduce a multiple wire cable to a lump of plastic and copper.

WIRING AND HARNESSES

The average automobile contains about 1/2 mile of wiring, with hundreds of individual connections. To protect the many wires from damage and to keep them from becoming a confusing tangle, they are organized into bundles, enclosed in plastic or taped together and called wiring harnesses. Different harnesses serve different parts of the vehicle. Individual wires are color coded to help trace them through a harness where sections are hidden from view.

Automotive wiring or circuit conductors can be either single strand wire, multi-strand wire or printed circuitry. Single strand wire has a solid metal core and is usually used inside such components as alternators, motors, relays and other devices. Multi-strand wire has a core made of many small strands of wire twisted together into a single conductor. Most of the wiring in an automotive electrical system is made up of multi-strand wire, either as a single conductor or grouped together in a harness. All wiring is color coded on the insulator, either as a solid color or as a colored wire with an identification stripe. A printed circuit is a thin film of copper or other conductor that is printed on an insulator backing. Occasionally, a printed circuit is sandwiched between two sheets of plastic for more protection and flexibility. A complete printed circuit, consisting of conductors, insulating material and connectors for lamps or other components is called a printed circuit board. Printed circuitry is used in place of individual wires or harnesses in places where space is limited, such as behind instrument panels.

Since automotive electrical systems are very sensitive to changes in resistance, the selection of properly sized wires is critical when systems are repaired. A loose or corroded connection or a replacement wire that is too small for the circuit will add extra resistance and an additional voltage drop to the circuit.

The wire gauge number is an expression of the cross-section area of

the conductor. The most common system for expressing wire size is the American Wire Gauge (AWG) system. As gauge number increases, area decreases and the wire becomes smaller. An 18 gauge wire is smaller than a 4 gauge wire. A wire with a higher gauge number will carry less current than a wire with a lower gauge number. Gauge wire size refers to the size of the strands of the conductor, not the size of the complete wire. It is possible, therefore, to have two wires of the same gauge with different diameters because one may have thicker insulation than the other.

12 volt automotive electrical systems generally use 10, 12, 14, 16 and 18 gauge wire. Main power distribution circuits and larger accessories usually use 10 and 12 gauge wire. Battery cables are usually 4 or 6 gauge, although 1 and 2 gauge wires are occasionally used.

It is essential to understand how a circuit works before trying to figure out why it doesn't. An electrical schematic shows the electrical current paths when a circuit is operating properly. Schematics break the entire electrical system down into individual circuits. In a schematic, no attempt is made to represent wiring and components as they physically appear on the vehicle; switches and other components are shown as simply as possible. Face views of harness connectors show the cavity or terminal locations in all multi-pin connectors to help locate test points.

CONNECTORS

Three types of connectors are commonly used in automotive applications—weatherproof, molded and hard shell.

• Weatherproof—these connectors are most commonly used in the engine compartment or where the connector is exposed to the elements. Terminals are protected against moisture and dirt by sealing rings which provide a weathertight seal. All repairs require the use of a special terminal and the tool required to service it. Unlike standard blade type terminals, these weatherproof terminals cannot be straightened once they are bent. Make certain that the connectors are properly seated and all of the sealing rings are in place when connecting leads.

• Molded—these connectors require complete replacement of the connector if found to be defective. This means splicing a new connector assembly into the harness. All splices should be soldered to insure proper contact. Use care when probing the connections or replacing terminals in them, as it is possible to create a short circuit between opposite terminals. If this happens to the wrong terminal pair, it is possible to damage certain components. Always use jumper wires between connectors for circuit checking and NEVER probe through weatherproof seals.

• Hard Shell—unlike molded connectors, the terminal contacts in hard-shell connectors can be replaced. Replacement usually involves the use of a special terminal removal tool that depresses the locking tangs

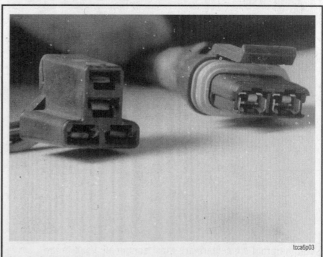

Hard shell (left) and weatherproof (right) connectors have replaceable terminals

(barbs) on the connector terminal and allows the connector to be removed from the rear of the shell. The connector shell should be replaced if it shows any evidence of burning, melting, cracks, or breaks. Replace individual terminals that are burnt, corroded, distorted or loose.

Test Equipment

Pinpointing the exact cause of trouble in an electrical circuit is most times accomplished by the use of special test equipment. The following describes different types of commonly used test equipment and briefly explains how to use them in diagnosis. In addition to the information covered below, the tool manufacturer's instructions booklet (provided with the tester) should be read and clearly understood before attempting any test procedures.

JUMPER WIRES

✳✳ CAUTION

Never use jumper wires made from a thinner gauge wire than the circuit being tested. If the jumper wire is of too small a gauge, it may overheat and possibly melt. Never use jumpers to bypass high resistance loads in a circuit. Bypassing resistances, in effect, creates a short circuit. This may, in turn, cause damage and fire. Jumper wires should only be used to bypass lengths of wire.

Jumper wires are simple, yet extremely valuable, pieces of test equipment. They are basically test wires which are used to bypass sections of a circuit. Although jumper wires can be purchased, they are usually fabricated from lengths of standard automotive wire and whatever type of connector (alligator clip, spade connector or pin connector) that is required for the particular application being tested. In cramped, hard-to-reach areas, it is advisable to have insulated boots over the jumper wire terminals in order to prevent accidental grounding. It is also advisable to include a standard automotive fuse in any jumper wire. This is commonly referred to as a "fused jumper". By inserting an in-line fuse holder between a set of test leads, a fused jumper wire can be used for bypassing open circuits. Use a 5 amp fuse to provide protection against voltage spikes.

Jumper wires are used primarily to locate open electrical circuits, on either the ground (−) side of the circuit or on the power (+) side. If an electrical component fails to operate, connect the jumper wire between the component and a good ground. If the component operates only with the jumper installed, the ground circuit is open. If the ground circuit is

good, but the component does not operate, the circuit between the power feed and component may be open. By moving the jumper wire successively back from the component toward the power source, you can isolate the area of the circuit where the open is located. When the component stops functioning, or the power is cut off, the open is in the segment of wire between the jumper and the point previously tested.

You can sometimes connect the jumper wire directly from the battery to the "hot" terminal of the component, but first make sure the component uses 12 volts in operation. Some electrical components, such as fuel injectors, are designed to operate on about 4 volts, and running 12 volts directly to these components will cause damage.

TEST LIGHTS

The test light is used to check circuits and components while electrical current is flowing through them. It is used for voltage and ground tests. To use a 12 volt test light, connect the ground clip to a good ground and probe wherever necessary with the pick. The test light will illuminate when voltage is detected. This does not necessarily mean that 12 volts (or any particular amount of voltage) is present; it only means that some voltage is present. It is advisable before using the test light to touch its ground clip and probe across the battery posts or terminals to make sure the light is operating properly.

✳✳ WARNING

Do not use a test light to probe electronic ignition spark plug or coil wires. Never use a pick-type test light to probe wiring on computer controlled systems unless specifically instructed to do so. Any wire insulation that is pierced by the test light probe should be taped and sealed with silicone after testing.

Like the jumper wire, the 12 volt test light is used to isolate opens in circuits. But, whereas the jumper wire is used to bypass the open to operate the load, the 12 volt test light is used to locate the presence of voltage in a circuit. If the test light illuminates, there is power up to that point in the circuit; if the test light does not illuminate, there is an open circuit (no power). Move the test light in successive steps back toward the power source until the light in the handle illuminates. The open is between the probe and a point which was previously probed.

The self-powered test light is similar in design to the 12 volt test light, but contains a 1.5 volt penlight battery in the handle. It is most often used in place of a multimeter to check for open or short circuits when power is isolated from the circuit (continuity test).

The battery in a self-powered test light does not provide much current.

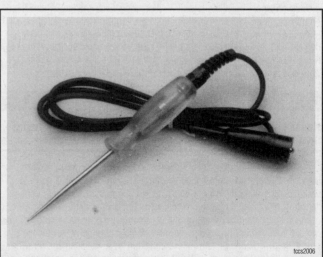

tcca6p04

Weatherproof connectors are most commonly used in the engine compartment or where the connector is exposed to the elements

tccs2006

A 12 volt test light is used to detect the presence of voltage in a circuit

A weak battery may not provide enough power to illuminate the test light even when a complete circuit is made (especially if there is high resistance in the circuit). Always make sure that the test battery is strong. To check the battery, briefly touch the ground clip to the probe; if the light glows brightly, the battery is strong enough for testing.

➡A self-powered test light should not be used on any computer controlled system or component. The small amount of electricity transmitted by the test light is enough to damage many electronic automotive components.

MULTIMETERS

Multimeters are an extremely useful tool for troubleshooting electrical problems. They can be purchased in either analog or digital form and have a price range to suit any budget. A multimeter is a voltmeter, ammeter and ohmmeter (along with other features) combined into one instrument. It is often used when testing solid state circuits because of its high input impedance (usually 10 megaohms or more). A brief description of the multimeter main test functions follows:

• Voltmeter—the voltmeter is used to measure voltage at any point in a circuit, or to measure the voltage drop across any part of a circuit. Voltmeters usually have various scales and a selector switch to allow the reading of different voltage ranges. The voltmeter has a positive and a negative lead. To avoid damage to the meter, always connect the negative lead to the negative (−) side of the circuit (to ground or nearest the ground side of the circuit) and connect the positive lead to the positive (+) side of the circuit (to the power source or the nearest power source). Note that the negative voltmeter lead will always be black and that the positive voltmeter will always be some color other than black (usually red).

• Ohmmeter—the ohmmeter is designed to read resistance (measured in ohms) in a circuit or component. All ohmmeters will have a selector switch which permits the measurement of different ranges of resistance (usually the selector switch allows the multiplication of the meter reading by 10, 100, 1,000 and 10,000). Since the meters are powered by an internal battery, the ohmmeter can be used as a self-powered test light. When the ohmmeter is connected, current from the ohmmeter flows through the circuit or component being tested. Since the ohmmeter's internal resistance and voltage are known values, the amount of current flow through the meter depends on the resistance of the circuit or component being tested.

The ohmmeter can also be used to perform a continuity test for suspected open circuits. In using the meter for making continuity checks, do not be concerned with the actual resistance readings. Zero resistance, or any ohm reading, indicates continuity in the circuit. Infinite resistance indicates an opening in the circuit. A high resistance reading where there should be none indicates a problem in the circuit. Checks for short circuits are made in the same manner as checks for open circuits, except that the circuit must be isolated from both power and normal ground. Infinite resistance indicates no continuity to ground, while zero resistance indicates a dead short to ground.

❋❋ WARNING

Never use an ohmmeter to check the resistance of a component or wire while there is voltage applied to the circuit.

• Ammeter—an ammeter measures the amount of current flowing through a circuit in units called amperes or amps. At normal operating voltage, most circuits have a characteristic amount of amperes, called "current draw" which can be measured using an ammeter. By referring to a specified current draw rating, then measuring the amperes and comparing the two values, one can determine what is happening within the circuit to aid in diagnosis. An open circuit, for example, will not allow any current to flow, so the ammeter reading will be zero. A damaged component or circuit will have an increased current draw, so the reading will be high.

The ammeter is always connected in series with the circuit being tested. All of the current that normally flows through the circuit must also flow through the ammeter; if there is any other path for the current to follow, the ammeter reading will not be accurate. The ammeter itself has very little resistance to current flow and, therefore, will not affect the circuit, but it will measure current draw only when the circuit is closed and electricity is flowing. Excessive current draw can blow fuses and drain the battery, while a reduced current draw can cause motors to run slowly, lights to dim and other components to not operate properly.

Troubleshooting

When diagnosing a specific problem, organized troubleshooting is a must. The complexity of a modern automotive vehicle demands that you approach any problem in a logical, organized manner. There are certain troubleshooting techniques which are standard:

• Establish when the problem occurs. Does the problem appear only under certain conditions? Were there any noises, odors or other unusual symptoms?

• Isolate the problem area. To do this, make some simple tests and observations, then eliminate the systems that are working properly. Check for obvious problems, such as broken wires and loose or dirty connections. Always check the obvious before assuming something complicated is the cause.

• Test for problems systematically to determine the cause once the problem area is isolated. Are all the components functioning properly? Is there power going to electrical switches and motors. Performing careful, systematic checks will often turn up most causes on the first inspection, without wasting time checking components that have little or no relationship to the problem.

• Test all repairs after the work is done to make sure that the problem is fixed. Some causes can be traced to more than one component, so a careful verification of repair work is important in order to pick up additional malfunctions that may cause a problem to reappear or a different problem to arise. A blown fuse, for example, is a simple problem that may require more than another fuse to repair. If you don't look for a problem that caused a fuse to blow, a shorted wire (for example) may go undetected.

Experience has shown that most problems tend to be the result of a fairly simple and obvious cause, such as loose or corroded connectors, bad grounds or damaged wire insulation which causes a short. This makes careful visual inspection of components during testing essential to quick and accurate troubleshooting.

Testing

OPEN CIRCUITS

1. Isolate the circuit from power and ground.
2. Connect the self-powered test light or ohmmeter ground clip to a good ground and probe sections of the circuit sequentially.
3. If the light is out or there is infinite resistance, the open is between the probe and the circuit ground.
4. If the light is on or the meter shows continuity, the open is between the probe and end of the circuit toward the power source.

SHORT CIRCUITS

➡Never use a self-powered test light to perform checks for opens or shorts when power is applied to the electrical system under test. The 12 volt vehicle power will quickly burn out the light bulb in the test light.

1. Isolate the circuit from power and ground.
2. Connect the self-powered test light or ohmmeter ground clip to a good ground and probe any easy-to-reach test point in the circuit.

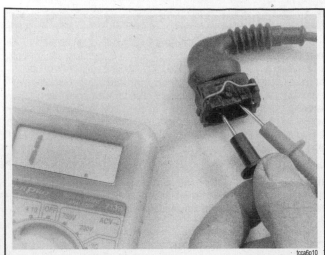

The infinite reading on this multimeter (1 .) indicates that the circuit is open

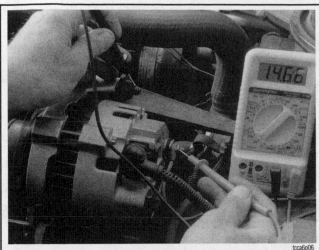

Testing voltage output between the alternator's BAT terminal and ground. This voltage reading is normal

3. If the light comes on or there is continuity, there is a short somewhere in the circuit.

4. To isolate the short, probe a test point at either end of the isolated circuit (the light should be on or the meter should indicate continuity).

5. Leave the test light probe engaged and sequentially open connectors or switches, remove parts, etc. until the light goes out or continuity is broken.

6. When the light goes out, the short is between the last two circuit components which were opened.

VOLTAGE

This test determines voltage available from the battery and should be the first step in any electrical troubleshooting procedure. Many electrical problems, especially on computer controlled systems, can be caused by a low state of charge in the battery. Excessive corrosion at the battery cable terminals can cause poor contact that will prevent proper charging and full battery current flow.

1. Set the voltmeter selector switch to the 20V position.

2. Connect the multimeter negative lead to the battery's negative (−) post or terminal and the positive lead to the battery's positive (+) post or terminal.

3. Turn the ignition switch **ON** to provide a load.

4. A well charged battery should register over 12 volts. If the meter reads below 11.5 volts, the battery power may be insufficient to operate the electrical system properly.

VOLTAGE DROP

When current flows through a load, the voltage beyond the load drops. This voltage drop is due to the resistance created by the load and also by small resistances created by corrosion at the connectors and damaged insulation on the wires. The maximum allowable voltage drop under load is critical, especially if there is more than one load in the circuit, since all voltage drops are cumulative.

1. Set the voltmeter selector switch to the 20 volt position.

2. Connect the multimeter negative lead to a good ground.

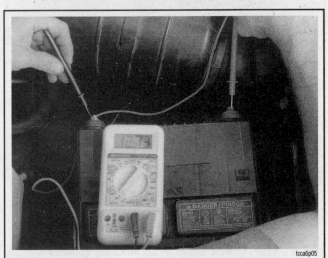

Using a multimeter to check battery voltage. This battery is fully charged

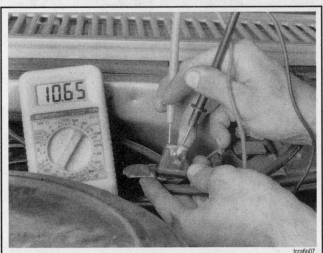

This voltage drop test revealed high resistance (low voltage) in the circuit

3. Operate the circuit and check the voltage prior to the first component (load).

4. There should be little or no voltage drop in the circuit prior to the first component. If a voltage drop exists, the wire or connectors in the circuit are suspect.

5. While operating the first component in the circuit, probe the ground side of the component with the positive meter lead and observe the voltage readings. A small voltage drop should be noticed. This voltage drop is caused by the resistance of the component.

6. Repeat the test for each component (load) down the circuit.

7. If a large voltage drop is noticed, the preceding component, wire or connector is suspect.

RESISTANCE

❋❋ WARNING

Never use an ohmmeter with power applied to the circuit. The ohmmeter is designed to operate on its own power supply. The normal 12 volt automotive electrical system current could damage the meter!

1. Isolate the circuit from the vehicle's power source.

2. Ensure that the ignition key is **OFF** when disconnecting any components or the battery.

3. Where necessary, also isolate at least one side of the circuit to be checked, in order to avoid reading parallel resistances. Parallel circuit resistances will always give a lower reading than the actual resistance of either of the branches.

4. Connect the meter leads to both sides of the circuit (wire or component) and read the actual measured ohms on the meter scale. Make sure the selector switch is set to the proper ohm scale for the circuit being tested, to avoid misreading the ohmmeter test value.

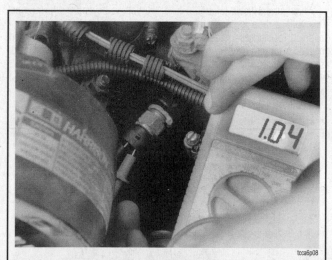

tcca6p08

Checking the resistance of a coolant temperature sensor with an ohmmeter. Reading is 1.04 kilohms

Wire and Connector Repair

Almost anyone can replace damaged wires, as long as the proper tools and parts are available. Automotive wire and terminals are available to fit almost any need. Even the specialized weatherproof, molded and hard shell connectors are now available from aftermarket suppliers.

Be sure the ends of all the wires are fitted with the proper terminal hardware and connectors. Wrapping a wire around a stud is never a permanent solution and will only cause trouble later. Replace wires one at a time to avoid confusion. Always route wires exactly the same as the factory.

➡**If connector repair is necessary, only attempt it if you have the proper tools. Weatherproof and hard shell connectors require special tools to release the pins inside the connector. Attempting to repair these connectors with conventional hand tools will damage them.**

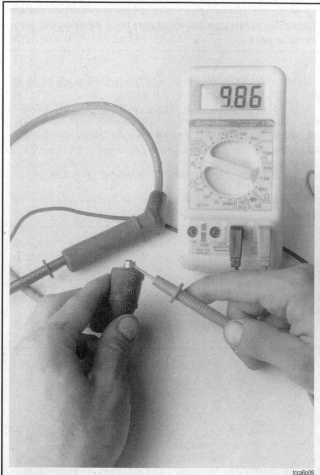

tcca6p09

Spark plug wires can be checked for excessive resistance using an ohmmeter

BATTERY CABLES

Disconnecting the Cables

When working on any electrical component on the vehicle, it is always a good idea to disconnect the negative ($-$) battery cable. This will prevent potential damage to many sensitive electrical components such as the Engine Control Module (ECM), radio, alternator, etc.

➡**Any time you disengage the battery cables, it is recommended that you disconnect the negative ($-$) battery cable first. This will prevent your accidentally grounding the positive ($+$) terminal to the body of the vehicle when disconnecting it, thereby preventing damage to the above mentioned components.**

Before you disconnect the cable(s), first turn the ignition to the **OFF** position. This will prevent a draw on the battery which could cause arcing (electricity trying to ground itself to the body of a vehicle, just like a spark plug jumping the gap) and, of course, damaging some components such as the alternator diodes.

When the battery cable(s) are reconnected (negative cable last), be sure to check that your lights, windshield wipers and other electrically operated safety components are all working correctly. If your vehicle contains an Electronically Tuned Radio (ETR), don't forget to also reset your radio stations. Ditto for the clock.

AIR BAG (SUPPLEMENTAL RESTRAINT SYSTEM)

General Information

The Supplemental Restraint System (SRS) is designed to work in conjunction with the seat belts in reducing the risk or severity of injury to the driver and passenger by activating and deploying driver and front passenger side air bags in certain frontal collisions.

The SRS (Air Bag) consists of a driver side air bag module located in the center of the steering wheel, a passenger side air bag module located in the passenger side crash pad, a control module located on the floor panel below the heater unit, an accelerometer, a service reminder lamp located on the dash, a clock spring interconnection located within the steering column, a knee bolster located under the steering column and associated wiring and connectors.

Deployment of the air bags is designed to occur in frontal or near frontal impacts of moderate or severe force. Only authorized service personnel should work on or around SRS components. Extreme care must be taken when servicing components to avoid personal injury.

SERVICE PRECAUTIONS

• Never attempt to disassemble or repair the air bag module or clock spring.
• Do not drop the air bag module or allow contact with water, grease or oil.
• Replace the module if a dent, crack, deformation or rust is evident.
• The air bag module should be stored on a flat surface and placed so that the pad surface is facing upward.
• Never place anything on top of a stored air bag.
• Do not expose the air bag module to temperatures above 200°F (93°C).
• An undeployed air bag module should only be disposed of in accordance with the proper procedures.
• Never attempt to measure the circuit resistance of the air bag module. Accidental air bag deployment could result in serious personal injury.

89536p01

Several air bag warning labels are located around the vehicle

DISARMING THE SYSTEM

The air bag system is disarmed by disconnecting the negative battery cable and waiting at least 30 seconds.

ARMING THE SYSTEM

The air bag system is armed when all appropriate system harnesses and the battery are connected.

HEATING AND AIR CONDITIONING

Blower Motor

REMOVAL & INSTALLATION

◗ **See Figures 3, 4, and 5 (p. 11–12)**

1. Disconnect the negative battery cable.
2. Remove dashboard and glove box components as necessary to gain access to the blower motor.
3. Disconnect the blower motor and blower resistor electrical harness.
4. Disconnect the blower motor cooling tube.
5. Remove the three screws that attach the blower motor to the heater unit.
6. Lower the blower motor far enough so that the FRESH/RECIRC vacuum connector can be disconnected.
7. Remove the blower motor from the car.

To install:

8. Inspect the blower wheel for damage and replace it as necessary. Replace the blower motor mounting seal.

9. Install the blower motor after attaching the FRESH/RECIRC vacuum connector.

10. Install the three screws that attach the blower motor to the heater unit and tighten securely.

11. Connect the blower motor cooling tube.

12. Connect the blower motor and blower resistor electrical harness.

13. Install dashboard and glove box components previously removed to gain access to the blower motor.

14. Connect the negative battery cable.

15. Check the blower for proper operation at all speeds.

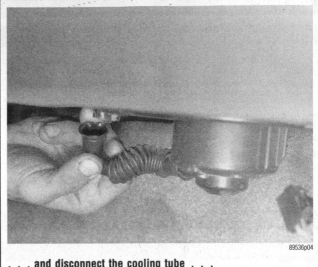

. . . and disconnect the cooling tube . . .

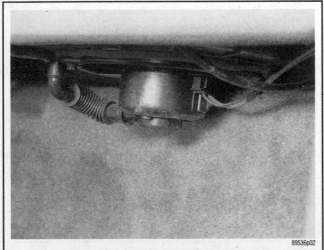

The blower motor is located under the right side of the dashboard, at the passenger's footwell

. . . then remove the three mounting screws . . .

Detach the blower motor's electrical connector . . .

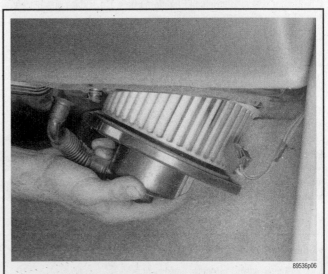

. . . and lower the blower motor assembly from the heater unit

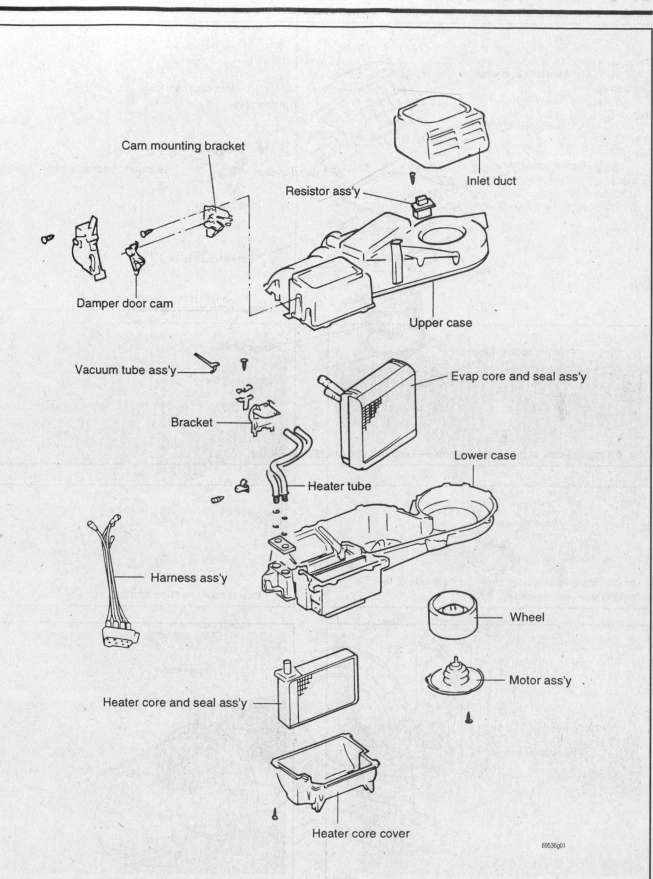

Cam mounting bracket

Resistor ass'y

Inlet duct

Damper door cam

Upper case

Vacuum tube ass'y

Evap core and seal ass'y

Bracket

Lower case

Heater tube

Harness ass'y

Wheel

Motor ass'y

Heater core and seal ass'y

Heater core cover

89536g01

Fig. 3 Exploded view of the heater unit—Sonata

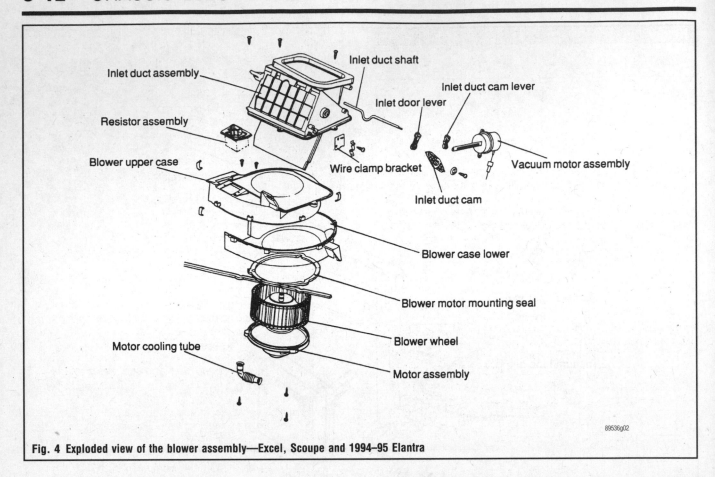

Inlet duct assembly

Inlet duct shaft

Inlet duct cam lever

Inlet door lever

Resistor assembly

Vacuum motor assembly

Blower upper case

Wire clamp bracket

Inlet duct cam

Blower case lower

Blower motor mounting seal

Blower wheel

Motor cooling tube

Motor assembly

89536g02

Fig. 4 Exploded view of the blower assembly—Excel, Scoupe and 1994–95 Elantra

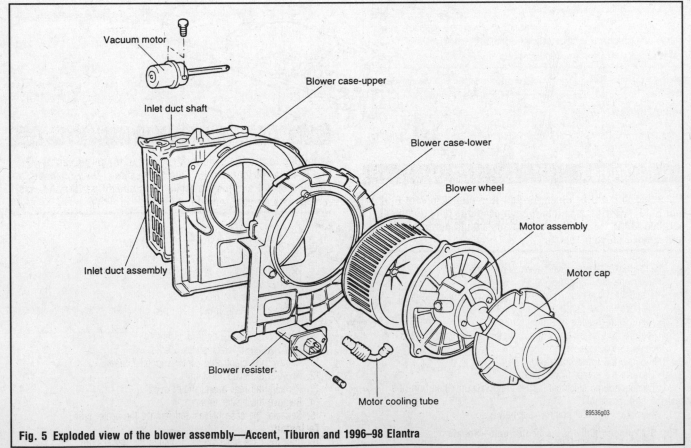

Vacuum motor

Blower case-upper

Inlet duct shaft

Blower case-lower

Blower wheel

Motor assembly

Motor cap

Inlet duct assembly

Blower resister

Motor cooling tube

89536g03

Fig. 5 Exploded view of the blower assembly—Accent, Tiburon and 1996–98 Elantra

Heater Core

REMOVAL & INSTALLATION

▶ See Figure 6

The heater core on all vehicles is contained inside the heater unit. The heater unit must be fully removed from the vehicle and then disassembled to gain access to the heater core. The following procedures outline removal, disassembly, assembly and installation of the heater unit.

➡The following procedure requires the air conditioning system, on those vehicles so equipped, to be discharged and evacuated. According to the U.S. Clean Air Act, it is illegal to vent R-12 and R-134a refrigerants into the atmosphere. Only qualified, certified MVAC automotive technicians should perform A/C system service on your vehicle.

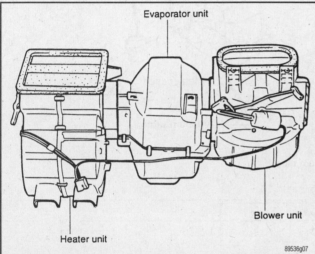

Evaporator unit

Heater unit

Blower unit

89536g07

Fig. 6 The heater unit is located under the center of the dashboard, attached to the evaporator unit and blower unit

Accent

▶ See Figure 7

1. Have the refrigerant in the air conditioning system professionally discharged and recycled.

✳✳ WARNING

According to the U.S. Clean Air Act, it is illegal to vent R-12 and R-134a refrigerants into the atmosphere. Only qualified, certified MVAC automotive technicians should perform A/C system service on your vehicle.

2. Disconnect the negative battery cable.
3. Drain the cooling system.
4. Disconnect the heater hoses and the evaporator drain hose.
5. Remove the vacuum hose from the heater unit.
6. Remove the suction and liquid tubes.
7. Remove the steering wheel and multifunction switch assembly.
8. Remove the console.
9. Remove the lower crash pad.
10. Remove the center facia panel.
11. Disconnect the electrical harness and vacuum lines from the heater control assembly.
12. Remove the heater control assembly.
13. Remove the radio.
14. Remove the glove box.

15. Remove the mounting bolts from the passenger airbag mounting bracket.
16. Remove the main crash pad assembly.
17. Disconnect the cables from the heater unit and the thermostatic switch connector from the evaporator unit.
18. Remove the main dash pad assembly.
19. Remove the evaporator unit.
20. Remove the heater unit.
21. Separate the case halves and remove the heater core.
To install:
22. Join the case halves after installing the heater core.
23. Install the heater unit.
24. Install the evaporator unit.
25. Install the main dash pad assembly.
26. Connect the cables from the heater unit and the thermostatic switch connector from the evaporator unit.
27. Install the main crash pad assembly.
28. Install the mounting bolts from the passenger airbag mounting bracket.
29. Install the glove box.
30. Install the radio.
31. Install the heater control assembly.
32. Connect the electrical harness and vacuum lines to the heater control assembly.
33. Install the center facia panel.
34. Install the lower crash pad.
35. Install the console.
36. Install the steering wheel and multi-function switch assembly.
37. Install the suction and liquid tubes.
38. Install the vacuum hose from the heater unit.
39. Connect the heater hoses and the evaporator drain hose.
40. Fill the cooling system.
41. Connect the negative battery cable.
42. Start the engine and allow it to reach operating temperature. Check for leaks.
43. Have the air conditioning system professionally evacuated, charged and leak tested.

Excel

▶ See Figure 8 (p. 15)

1. Have the refrigerant in the air conditioning system professionally discharged and recycled.

✳✳ WARNING

According to the U.S. Clean Air Act, it is illegal to vent R-12 and R-134a refrigerants into the atmosphere. Only qualified, certified MVAC automotive technicians should perform A/C system service on your vehicle.

2. Disconnect the negative battery cable.
3. Drain the cooling system.
4. Disconnect the heater hoses and the evaporator drain hose.
5. Remove the suction and liquid tubes.
6. Remove the console.
7. Remove the glove box.
8. Remove the main lower crash pad and lower crash pad center facia panel.
9. Remove the heater control assembly.
10. Remove the lower crash pad center skin.
11. Remove the crash pad center support bracket.
12. Remove the evaporator unit.
13. Remove the rear heating joint duct.
14. Remove the heater unit.
15. Separate the case halves and remove the heater core.
To install:
16. Join the case halves after installing the heater core.

* Heater Assembly

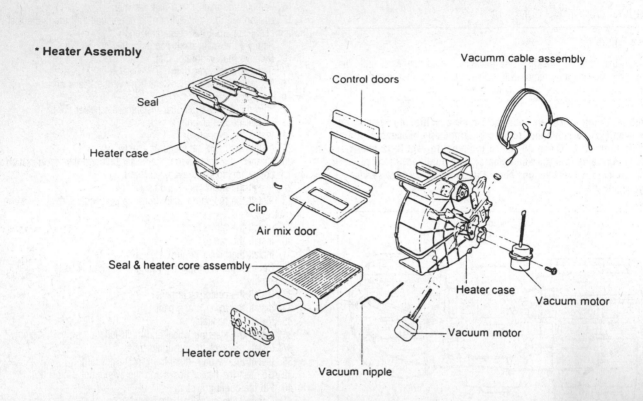

Seal

Heater case

Clip

Air mix door

Control doors

Seal & heater core assembly

Heater core cover

Vacuum nipple

Vacumm cable assembly

Heater case

Vacuum motor

Vacuum motor

* Vacuum Source Lines

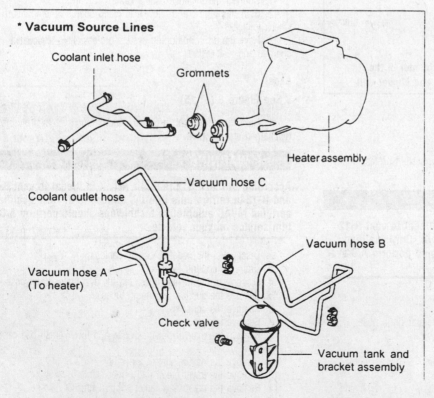

Coolant inlet hose

Grommets

Heater assembly

Coolant outlet hose

Vacuum hose C

Vacuum hose A
(To heater)

Vacuum hose B

Check valve

Vacuum tank and
bracket assembly

89536g06

Fig. 7 Exploded view of the heater unit—Accent

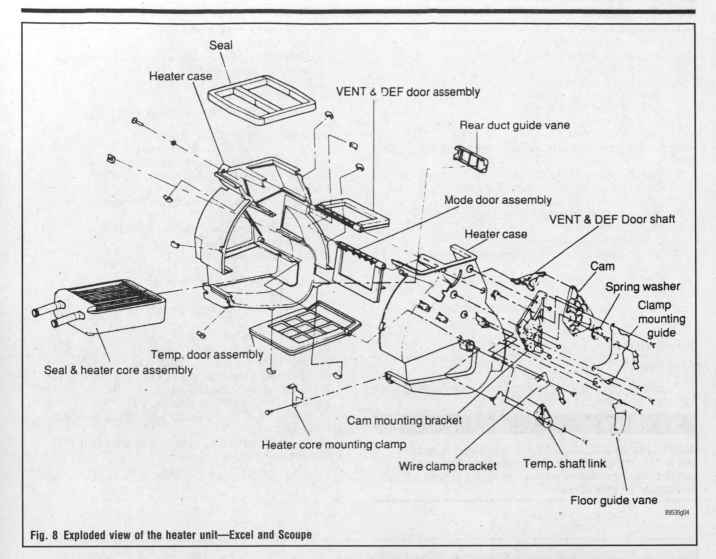

Fig. 8 Exploded view of the heater unit—Excel and Scoupe

Labels in figure:
- Seal
- Heater case
- VENT & DEF door assembly
- Rear duct guide vane
- Mode door assembly
- VENT & DEF Door shaft
- Heater case
- Cam
- Spring washer
- Clamp mounting guide
- Temp. door assembly
- Seal & heater core assembly
- Cam mounting bracket
- Heater core mounting clamp
- Wire clamp bracket
- Temp. shaft link
- Floor guide vane
- 89536g04

17. Install the heater unit.
18. Install the rear heating joint duct.
19. Install the evaporator unit.
20. Install the crash pad center support bracket.
21. Install the lower crash pad center skin.
22. Install the heater control assembly.
23. Install the main lower crash pad and lower crash pad center facia panel.
24. Install the glove box.
25. Install the console.
26. Install the suction and liquid tubes.
27. Connect the heater hoses and the evaporator drain hose.
28. Fill the cooling system.
29. Connect the negative battery cable.
30. Start the engine and allow it to reach operating temperature. Check for leaks.
31. Have the air conditioning system professionally evacuated, charged and leak tested.

Scoupe

◆ **See Figure 8**

1. Have the refrigerant in the air conditioning system professionally discharged and recycled.

2. Disconnect the negative battery cable.
3. Drain the cooling system.
4. Disconnect the heater hoses and the evaporator drain hose.
5. Remove the suction and liquid tubes.
6. Disconnect the vacuum hose for the control panel.
7. Remove the console, cluster facia and left hand lower crash pad.
8. Remove the main lower crash pad and lower crash pad center facia panel.
9. Remove the center facia panel.
10. Remove the glove box.
11. Remove the heater control assembly.
12. Remove the center skin bracket.
13. Remove the rear heating joint duct.
14. Remove the evaporator.
15. Remove the heater unit.
16. Separate the case halves and remove the heater core.

To install:

17. Join the case halves after installing the heater core.
18. Install the heater unit.
19. Install the evaporator.
20. Install the rear heating joint duct.
21. Install the center skin bracket.
22. Install the heater control assembly.
23. Install the glove box.
24. Install the center facia panel.
25. Install the main lower crash pad and lower crash pad center facia panel.
26. Install the console, cluster facia and left hand lower crash pad.
27. Connect the vacuum hose for the control panel.
28. Install the suction and liquid tubes.
29. Connect the heater hoses and the evaporator drain hose.
30. Fill the cooling system.
31. Connect the negative battery cable.
32. Start the engine and allow it to reach operating temperature. Check for leaks.
33. Check the air mix lever for ease of movement. Readjust the air mix cable as necessary.
34. Have the air conditioning system professionally evacuated, charged and leak tested.

1994–95 Elantra

♦ See Figure 9

1. Have the refrigerant in the air conditioning system professionally discharged and recycled.

❋❋ WARNING

According to the U.S. Clean Air Act, it is illegal to vent R-12 and R-134a refrigerants into the atmosphere. Only qualified, certified MVAC automotive technicians should perform A/C system service on your vehicle.

2. Disconnect the negative battery cable.
3. Drain the cooling system.
4. Disconnect the heater hoses and the evaporator drain hose.
5. Remove the suction and liquid tubes.
6. Remove the console.
7. Remove the glove box.
8. Remove the main lower crash pad and lower crash pad center facia panel.
9. Remove the heater control assembly.
10. Remove the lower crash pad center skin.
11. Remove the crash pad center support bracket.
12. Remove the rear heating joint duct.
13. Remove the heater unit.
14. Separate the case halves and remove the heater core.

To install:

15. Join the case halves after installing the heater core.
16. Install the heater unit.
17. Install the rear heating joint duct.
18. Install the crash pad center support bracket.
19. Install the lower crash pad center skin.
20. Install the heater control assembly.
21. Install the main lower crash pad and lower crash pad center facia panel.
22. Install the glove box.
23. Install the console.
24. Install the suction and liquid tubes.
25. Connect the heater hoses and the evaporator drain hose.
26. Fill the cooling system.
27. Connect the negative battery cable.
28. Start the engine and allow it to reach operating temperature. Check for leaks.
29. Have the air conditioning system professionally evacuated, charged and leak tested.

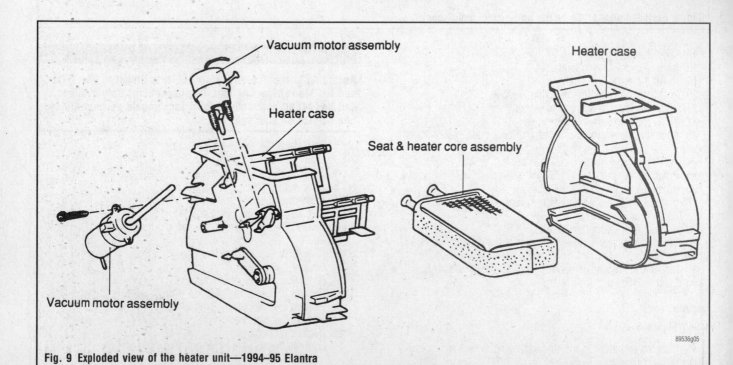

Fig. 9 Exploded view of the heater unit—1994–95 Elantra

1996–98 Elantra and Tiburon

◆ **See Figure 10**

1. Have the refrigerant in the air conditioning system professionally discharged and recycled.

> ※※ **WARNING**
>
> **According to the U.S. Clean Air Act, it is illegal to vent R-12 and R-134a refrigerants into the atmosphere. Only qualified, certified MVAC automotive technicians should perform A/C system service on your vehicle.**

2. Disconnect the negative battery cable.
3. Drain the cooling system.
4. Disconnect the heater hoses.
5. Disconnect the vacuum hose from the nipple of the heater unit.
6. Remove the main crash pad assembly.
7. Remove the right front heating side duct and turn over the carpet.
8. Remove the right console mounting bracket.
9. Remove the left front heating side duct and turn over the carpet.
10. Remove the left console mounting bracket.
11. Remove the rear heating joint duct from the heater unit.
12. Disconnect the electrical harness from the control module mounted on the center facia panel support bracket.
13. Remove the center facia panel support bracket.
14. Remove the center support bars.
15. Remove the glove box support bracket.
16. Remove the evaporator unit.
17. Remove the heater unit.
18. Separate the case halves and remove the heater core.

To install:

19. Join the case halves after installing the heater core.
20. Install the heater unit.
21. Install the evaporator unit.
22. Install the glove box support bracket.
23. Install the center support bars.
24. Install the center facia panel support bracket.
25. Connect the electrical harness to the control module mounted on the center facia panel support bracket.
26. Install the rear heating joint duct to the heater unit.

27. Install the left console mounting bracket.
28. Install the left front heating side duct and replace the carpet.
29. Install the right console mounting bracket.
30. Install the right front heating side duct and replace the carpet.
31. Install the main crash pad assembly.
32. Connect the vacuum hose from the nipple of the heater unit.
33. Connect the heater hoses.
34. Fill the cooling system.
35. Connect the negative battery cable.
36. Start the engine and allow it to reach operating temperature. Check for leaks.
37. Have the air conditioning system professionally evacuated, charged and leak tested.

Sonata

◆ **See Figure 11**

1. Have the refrigerant in the air conditioning system professionally discharged and recycled.

> ※※ **WARNING**
>
> **According to the U.S. Clean Air Act, it is illegal to vent R-12 and R-134a refrigerants into the atmosphere. Only qualified, certified MVAC automotive technicians should perform A/C system service on your vehicle.**

2. Disconnect the negative battery cable.
3. Drain the cooling system.
4. Disconnect the heater hoses and the evaporator drain hose.
5. Remove the suction and liquid tubes.
6. Remove the console and side covers.
7. Remove the glove box.
8. Remove the center crash pad cover, center crash pad and cassette assembly.
9. Remove the lower crash pad.
10. Remove the console mounting bracket and center support bracket.
11. Remove the rear heating duct assembly and rear heating joint duct.
12. Remove the heater control assembly.
13. Remove the heater assembly.
14. Separate the case halves and remove the heater core.

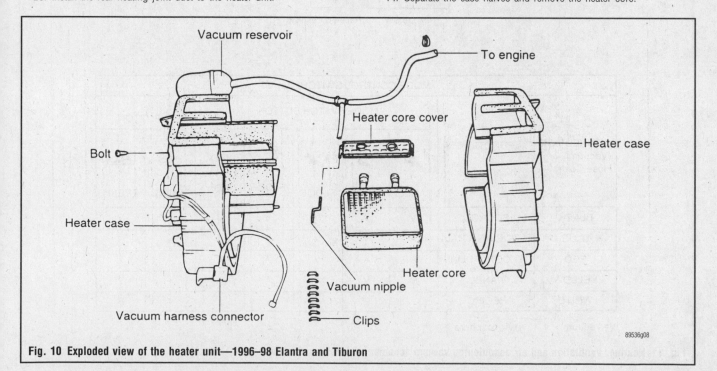

Fig. 10 Exploded view of the heater unit—1996–98 Elantra and Tiburon

89536g08

To install:

15. Join the case halves after installing the heater core.
16. Install the heater unit.
17. Install the heater control assembly.
18. Install the rear heating duct assembly and rear heating joint duct.
19. Install the console mounting bracket and center support bracket.
20. Install the lower crash pad.
21. Install the center crash pad cover, center crash pad and cassette assembly.
22. Install the glove box.
23. Install the side covers and console.
24. Install the suction and liquid tubes.
25. Connect the heater hoses and the evaporator drain hose.
26. Fill the cooling system.

27. Connect the negative battery cable.
28. Start the engine and allow it to reach operating temperature. Check for leaks.
29. Have the air conditioning system professionally evacuated, charged and leak tested.

Control Cables

♦ **See Figures 11, 12, 13 and 14 (p. 18–20)**

The heating, ventilation and air conditioning system ducts are controlled by a series of vacuum motors. A main vacuum source is drawn from the engine and distributed through the system by vacuum hose harnesses. The control panel contains vacuum switches to control where vacuum is applied.

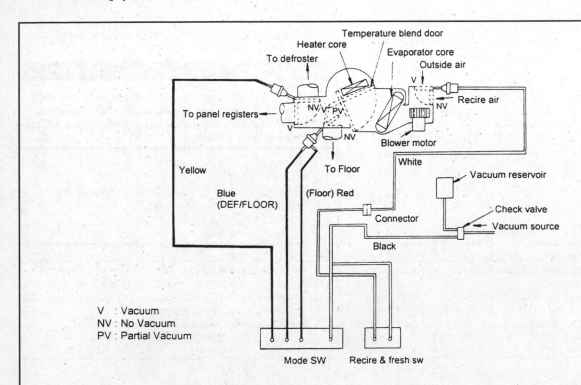

MODE CONTROL SWITCHING							
		MODE SWITCH BUTTON				FRESH/REC-BUTTON	
CONNECTION (Vacuum Hose Color)	FUNCTION	PANEL	PANEL FLOOR	FLOOR	FLOOR DEF	DEF	RECIRC	FRESH
BLACK	SOURCE	V	V	V	V	V	V	V
BLUE	FLOOR (PARTIAL)	A	V	V	V	A	-	-
RED	FLOOR (FULL)	A	A	V	A	A	-	-
YELLOW	PANEL	V	V	A	A	A	-	-
WHITE	RECIRC	-	-	-	-	-	V	A

V=Vacuum   A=Atmosphere

89536g09

Fig. 11 Heating, ventilation and air conditioning vacuum schematic—Excel and Sonata

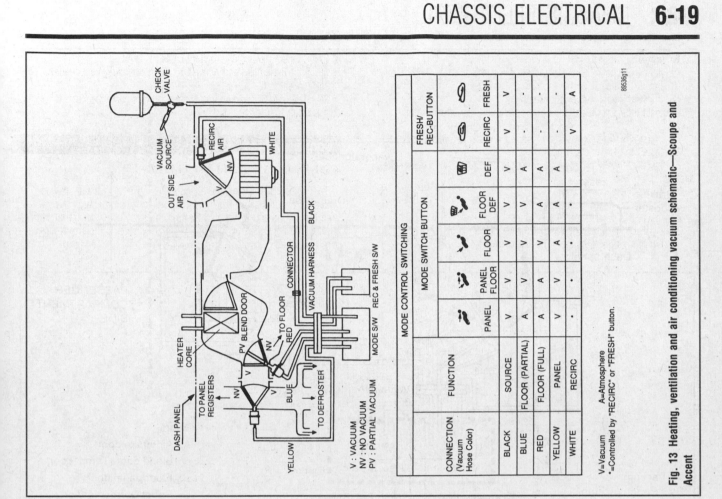

MODE CONTROL SWITCHING

CONNECTION (Vacuum Hose Color)	FUNCTION	MODE SWITCH BUTTON						FRESH/ REC-BUTTON	
		PANEL	PANEL FLOOR	FLOOR	FLOOR DEF	DEF	FRESH	RECIRC	FRESH
BLACK	SOURCE	V	V	V	V	V	V	V	V
BLUE	FLOOR (PARTIAL)	A	V	V	V	A	·	·	·
RED	FLOOR (FULL)	A	A	V	A	A	·	·	·
YELLOW	PANEL	V	V	A	A	A	·	·	·
WHITE	RECIRC	·	·	·	·	·	V	A	A

V=Vacuum   A=Atmosphere
*=Controlled by "RECIRC" or "FRESH" button.

Fig. 13 Heating, ventilation and air conditioning vacuum schematic—Scoupe and Accent

V : VACUUM
NV : NO VACUUM
PV : PARTIAL VACUUM

89536g11

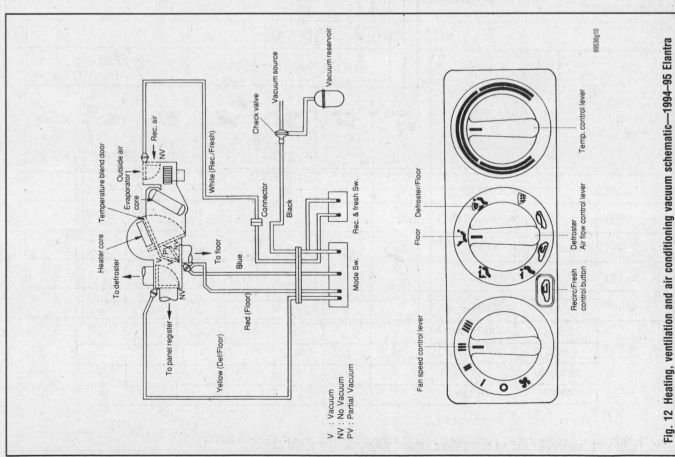

V : Vacuum
NV : No Vacuum
PV : Partial Vacuum

89536g10

Fig. 12 Heating, ventilation and air conditioning vacuum schematic—1994–95 Elantra

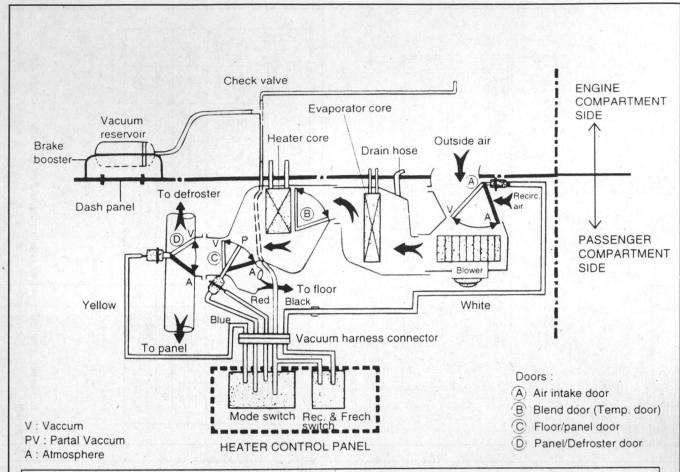

V : Vaccum
PV : Partal Vaccum
A : Atmosphere

Doors :
Ⓐ Air intake door
Ⓑ Blend door (Temp. door)
Ⓒ Floor/panel door
Ⓓ Panel/Defroster door

CONNECTION (Vacuum Hose Color)	FUNCTION	MODE SWITCH BUTTON					FRESH/ REC-BUTTON	
		PANEL	PANEL FLOOR (BI-LEVEL)	FLOOR	FLOOR DEF	DEF.	RECIRC.	FRESH
BLACK	SOURCE	V	V	V	V	V	V	V
BLUE	FLOOR (PARTIAL)	A	V	V	V	A	-	-
RED	FLOOR (FULL)	A	A	V	A	A	-	-
YELLOW	PANEL	V	V	A	A	A	-	-
WHITE	RECIRC	*	*	*	*		V	V

MODE CONTROL SWITCHING

V = Vacuum   A = Atmosphere
* = Controlled by "RECIRC" or " FRESH" button.

89536g12

Fig. 14 Heating, ventilation and air conditioning vacuum schematic—Tiburon and 1996–98 Elantra

A mechanical cable is used to control the air mix. This cable must be properly adjusted each time it is disconnected.

ADJUSTMENT

1. Slide the temperature control lever to the **HOT** position.
2. Turn the air mix door shaft arm to the left and connect the end of the cable to the arm.
3. Gently slide the cable outer housing back from the end enough to take up any slack in the cable, but not enough to make the temperature control lever move.
4. Snap the cable housing into the clamp.

Control Panel

REMOVAL & INSTALLATION

1. Disconnect the negative battery cable.
2. Remove the ashtray.
3. Remove the screws at the bottom of the facia panel behind the ashtray.

Remove the dummy switches to gain access to the upper retaining screws . . .

Remove the ashtray to gain access to the lower retaining screws . . .

. . . then unfasten the upper screws . . .

. . . then unfasten the lower screws

. . . and pull the fascia from the dashboard

4. Remove the dummy switches at the top of the panel, as illustrated.

5. Remove the screws at the bottom of the facia panel.

6. Remove the facia panel.

7. Remove the control panel screws and pull the panel out far enough to disconnect the electrical harness, vacuum line and temperature control cable.

8. Remove the control panel.

To install:

9. Connect the control panel electrical harness, vacuum line and temperature control cable.

10. Install the control panel and tighten screws securely.

11. Install the facia panel.

12. Install the screws at the bottom of the facia panel.

13. Install the dummy switches at the top of the panel, as illustrated.

14. Install the screws at the bottom of the facia panel behind the ashtray.

15. Install the ashtray.

16. Check all the heater control panel functions for proper operation.

Air Conditioning Components

REMOVAL & INSTALLATION

Repair or service of air conditioning components is not covered by this manual, because of the risk of personal injury or death, and because of the legal ramifications of servicing these components without the proper EPA certification and experience. Cost, personal injury or death, environmental damage, and legal considerations (such as the fact that it is a federal crime to vent refrigerant into the atmosphere), dictate that the A/C components on your vehicle should be serviced only by a Motor Vehicle Air Conditioning (MVAC) trained, and EPA certified automotive technician.

CRUISE CONTROL

▶ **See Figures 15 thru 20 (p. 23–25)**

The Hyundai Automatic Speed Control (ASC) system is an electronically controlled, vacuum operated system. The cruise control module receives inputs from the driver's control switches, brake switch, clutch or inhibitor switch, and vehicle speed sensor. Output signals are sent to the transaxle control module, the cruise control/release valve and the diagnostic connector.

CRUISE CONTROL TROUBLESHOOTING

Problem	Possible Cause
Will not hold proper speed	Incorrect cable adjustment
	Binding throttle linkage
	Leaking vacuum servo diaphragm
	Leaking vacuum tank
	Faulty vacuum or vent valve
	Faulty stepper motor
	Faulty transducer
	Faulty speed sensor
	Faulty cruise control module
Cruise intermittently cuts out	Clutch or brake switch adjustment too tight
	Short or open in the cruise control circuit
	Faulty transducer
	Faulty cruise control module
Vehicle surges	Kinked speedometer cable or casing
	Binding throttle linkage
	Faulty speed sensor
	Faulty cruise control module
Cruise control inoperative	Blown fuse
	Short or open in the cruise control circuit
	Faulty brake or clutch switch
	Leaking vacuum circuit
	Faulty cruise control switch
	Faulty stepper motor
	Faulty transducer
	Faulty speed sensor
	Faulty cruise control module

Note: Use this chart as a guide. Not all systems will use the components listed.

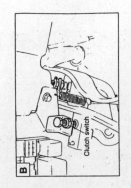
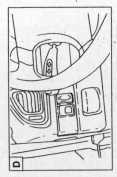
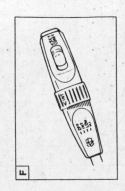

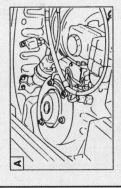
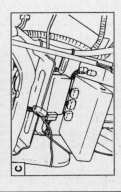
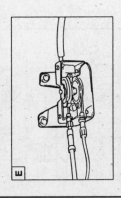
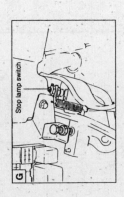
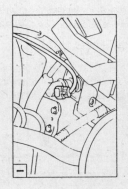

Fig. 16 Cruise control components locations (2 of 2)—Sonata

INTERIOR

ENGINE COMPARTMENT

NAME	SYMBOL	NAME	SYMBOL
Actuator	A	Speed control switch (in multi function switch)	F
Clutch switch	B	Stop lamp switch	G
Cruise control moduel	C	Vacuum motor	H
Cruise main switch	D	Vehicle speed sensor	I
Pulley-assembly	E		

Fig. 15 Cruise control components locations (1 of 2)—Sonata

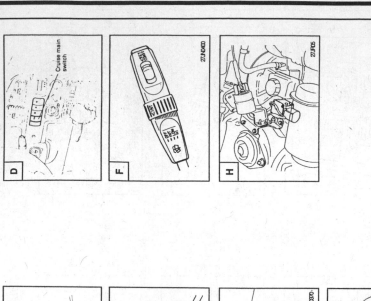

Fig. 18 Cruise control components locations (2 of 2)—1994–95 Elantra

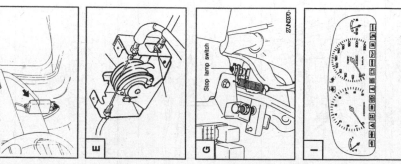

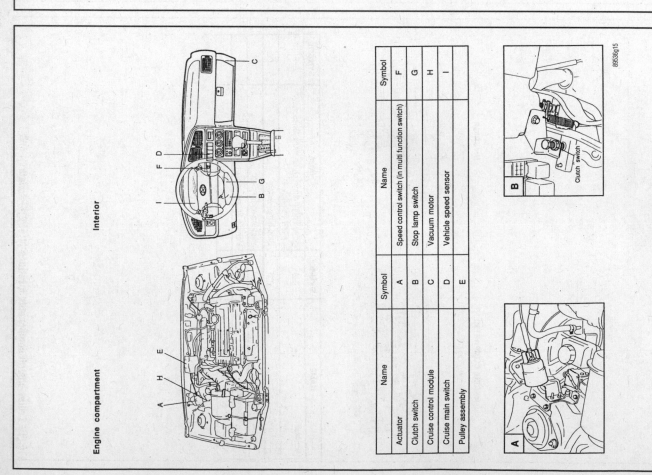

Name	Symbol	Name	Symbol
Actuator	A	Speed control switch (in multi function switch)	F
Clutch switch	B	Stop lamp switch	G
Cruise control module	C	Vacuum motor	H
Cruise main switch	D	Vehicle speed sensor	I
Pulley assembly	E		

Fig. 17 Cruise control components locations (1 of 2)—1994–95 Elantra

89536g18

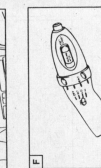

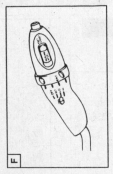

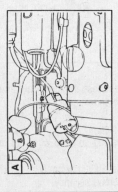

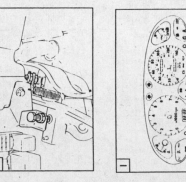

Fig. 20 Cruise control components locations (2 of 2)—Tiburon and 1996–98 Elantra

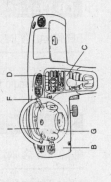

SYMBOL	NAME
F	Speed control switch (in multi function switch)
G	Stop lamp switch
H	Vacuum motor
I	Vehicle speed sensor

89536g17

INTERIOR

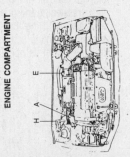

ENGINE COMPARTMENT

NAME	SYMBOL
Actuator	A
Clutch switch	B
Cruise control module	C
Cruise main switch	D
Pulley assembly	E

Fig. 19 Cruise control components locations (1 of 2)—Tiburon and 1996–98 Elantra

ENTERTAINMENT SYSTEMS

Radio Receiver

REMOVAL & INSTALLATION

1. Disconnect the negative battery cable.
2. Remove the fascia panel. This may involve removing other trim panels, the ashtray, emblems or switches to gain access to the necessary screws.
3. Remove the radio mounting screws.

➡**On some models, the radio is attached to the fascia plate.**

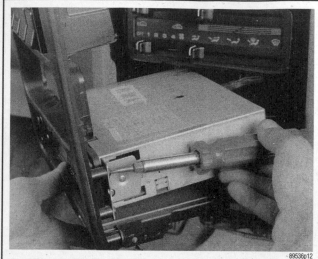

On some models, the radio is attached to the fascia plate

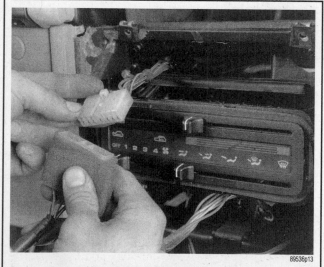

Disconnect the radio multi-pin harness . . .

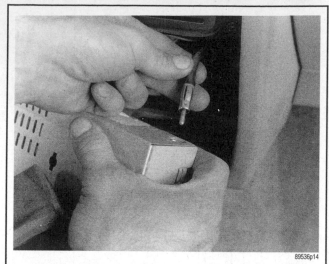

. . . and the radio antenna

4. Pull the radio from the dashboard to access the electrical harness.
5. Disconnect the electrical harness and antenna.

To install:

6. Connect the electrical harness and antenna.
7. Install the radio in the dashboard, making sure the wires are properly routed and the radio fits properly.
8. Install the radio mounting screws and tighten securely.
9. Install the fascia panel and tighten screws securely.
10. Install any components previously removed to gain access to the fascia panel screws.
11. Connect the negative battery cable.

CD Player

REMOVAL & INSTALLATION

For vehicles equipped with a compact disc player, it is removed the same as the radio head unit. The CD player is mounted below the radio.

Speakers

REMOVAL & INSTALLATION

◆ **See Figures 21 and 22**

While the location of the stereo speakers varies from vehicle to vehicle, the removal of the speakers is the same. Speakers are removed by either unfastening the grille cover (in most cases it just snaps in position) and then removing the speaker mounting screws, or by removing the speaker mounting screws from behind the speaker. The speaker can then be pulled from its opening and the wires disconnected.

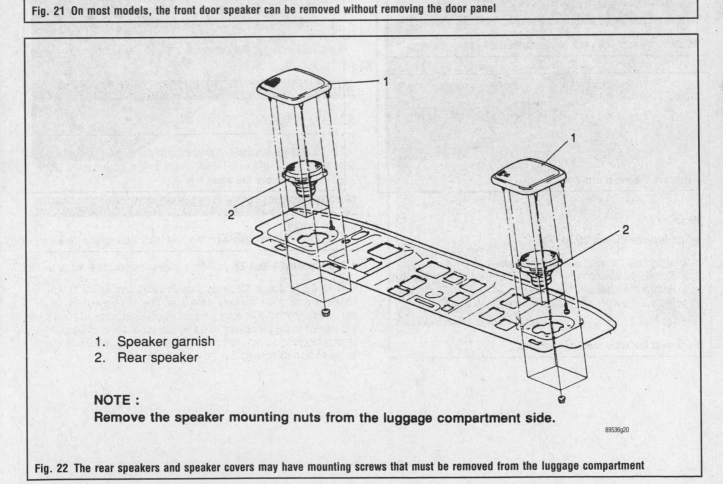

1. Door trim
2. Speaker garnish
3. Door speaker
4. Speaker cover

89536g19

Fig. 21 On most models, the front door speaker can be removed without removing the door panel

1. Speaker garnish
2. Rear speaker

NOTE :
Remove the speaker mounting nuts from the luggage compartment side.

89536g20

Fig. 22 The rear speakers and speaker covers may have mounting screws that must be removed from the luggage compartment

WINDSHIELD WIPERS

Windshield Wiper Blade and Arm

REMOVAL & INSTALLATION

Front

◆ **See Figures 23 and 24**

1. Matchmark the wiper arm and wiper arm stud.
2. Remove the wiper arm nut cap and pivot it up on the wiper shaft.
3. Remove the wiper arm nut.

➡**When removing the wiper arm nut, be careful not to scratch the hood.**

4. Remove the wiper arm and blade assembly from the pivot housing.
To install:
5. Align and install the wiper arm and blade assembly to the wiper arm stud.
6. Once the blade is in position, tighten the wiper blade nut to 7–11 ft. lbs. (10–16 Nm).
7. Operate the wipers and check for proper function.

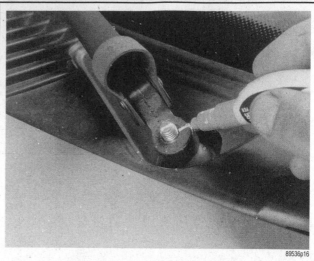

. . . then matchmark the wiper arm to the stud . . .

Remove the wiper arm nut . . .

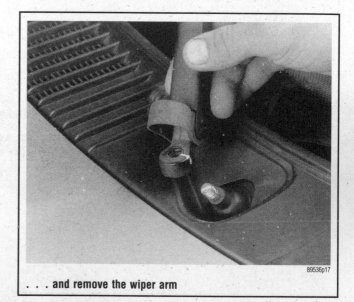

. . . and remove the wiper arm

Rear

◆ **See Figures 25 and 26 (p. 30)**

1. Matchmark the wiper arm and wiper arm stud.
2. Remove the wiper arm nut cap and pivot it up on the wiper shaft.
3. Remove the wiper arm nut.
4. Remove the wiper arm and blade assembly.

To install:
5. Align and install the wiper arm and blade assembly to the wiper arm stud.
6. Once the blade is in position, tighten the wiper blade nut to 5–9 ft. lbs. (8–12 Nm).
7. Operate the wiper and check for proper function.

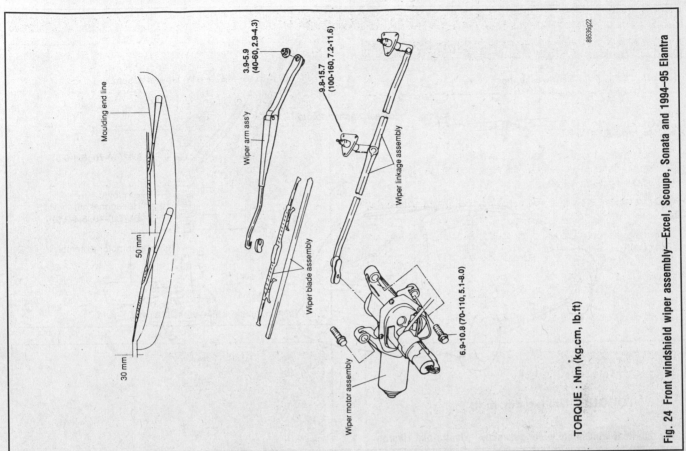

TORQUE : Nm (kg·cm, lb·ft)

Fig. 24 Front windshield wiper assembly—Excel, Scoupe, Sonata and 1994–95 Elantra

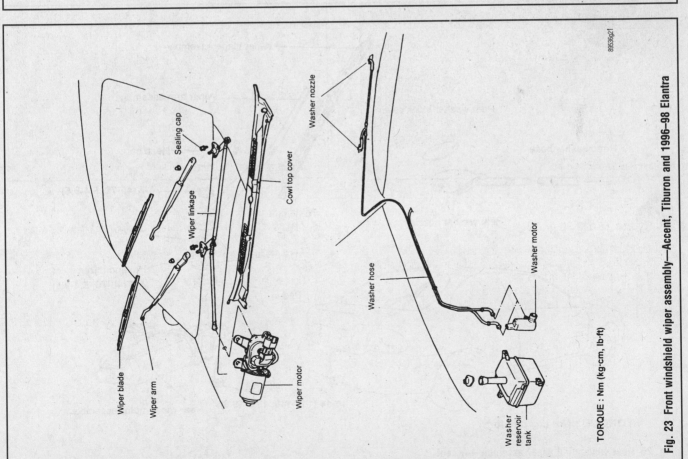

TORQUE : Nm (kg·cm, lb·ft)

Fig. 23 Front windshield wiper assembly—Accent, Tiburon and 1996–98 Elantra

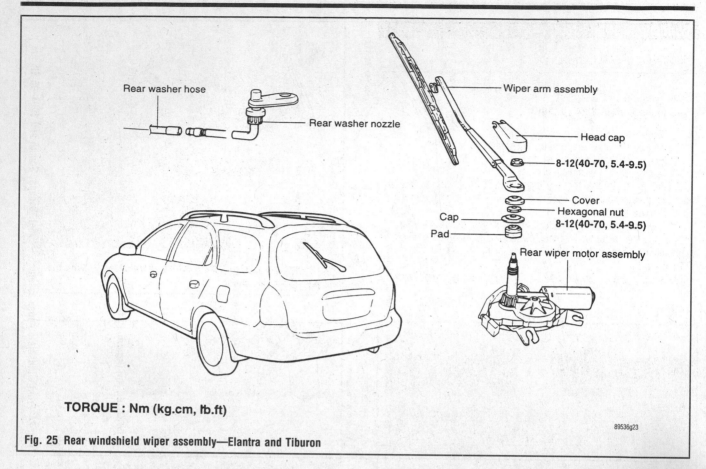

TORQUE : Nm (kg.cm, lb.ft)

Fig. 25 Rear windshield wiper assembly—Elantra and Tiburon

89536g23

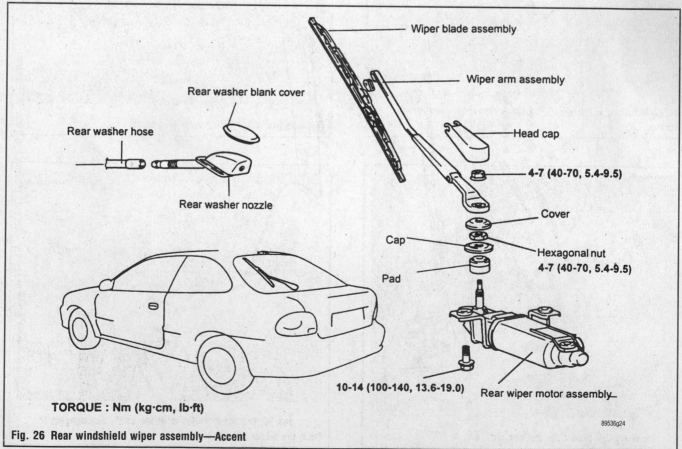

TORQUE : Nm (kg·cm, lb·ft)

Fig. 26 Rear windshield wiper assembly—Accent

89536g24

Windshield Wiper Motor

REMOVAL & INSTALLATION

Front

♦ See Figures 23 and 24 (p. 29)

1. Disconnect the negative battery cable.
2. Remove the wiper arm and blade assemblies.
3. Remove the cowl trim panel.
4. Remove the motor mounting bolts.
5. Pull the motor into the best possible position for access and remove the linkage from the motor crank arm.
6. Remove the wiper motor.
7. If the motor is being replaced, matchmark the position of the crank arm of the motor shaft of the new motor and then remove the nut and crank arm, transferring both to the new motor.

   To install:
8. Position the motor and connect the linkage to the motor crank arm.

Disconnect the wiper motor electrical harness and unclip the harness from the motor

To gain access to the wiper linkage, remove the cowl trim screws . . .

Remove the wiper motor mounting bolts . . .

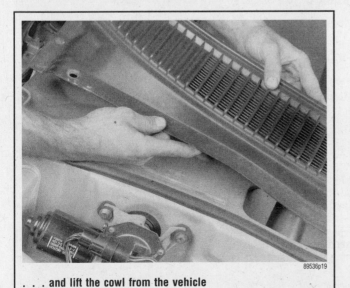

. . . and lift the cowl from the vehicle

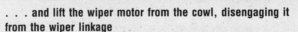

. . . and lift the wiper motor from the cowl, disengaging it from the wiper linkage

9. Install the wiper motor and tighten the bolts to 5–8 ft. lbs. (7–11 Nm).
10. Install the cowl trim panel.
11. Install the wiper arm and blade assemblies.
12. Connect the negative battery cable.
13. Check the wipers for proper operation.

Rear

♦ **See Figures 25 and 26 (p. 30)**

1. Disconnect the negative battery cable.
2. Remove the wiper arm and blade assembly.
3. Remove the lift gate trim panel.
4. Disconnect the motor electrical harness.
5. Remove the shaft nut and motor mounting bolts.
6. Remove the wiper motor.

To install:

7. Install the wiper motor.
8. Install the shaft nut and motor mounting bolts. tighten to 5–10 ft. lbs. (8–12 Nm).
9. Connect the motor electrical harness.
10. Install the lift gate trim panel.
11. Install the wiper arm and blade assembly.
12. Connect the negative battery cable.
13. Check the wiper for proper operation.

Wiper Linkage

REMOVAL & INSTALLATION

♦ **See Figures 23 and 24 (p. 29)**

1. Remove the wiper arms and blade assemblies.
2. Remove the cowl panel.
3. Remove the pivot shaft mounting nuts and push the pivot shaft toward the inside.

4. Remove the wiper motor mounting bolts.
5. Disconnect the linkage from the motor and remove.

To install:

6. Lubricate the wiper linkage.
7. Connect the wiper linkage to the motor.
8. Install the wiper motor to the firewall.
9. Pull the pivot shaft into position and install the pivot shaft mounting nuts. Tighten to 7–11 ft. lbs. (10–15 Nm).
10. Install the cowl panel.
11. Install the wiper arm and blade assemblies.
12. Check the wipers for proper operation.

Washer Fluid Reservoir and Washer Pumps

REMOVAL & INSTALLATION

♦ **See Figure 27**

1. Disconnect the negative battery cable.
2. Disconnect the electrical leads from the washer pump motor.
3. Disconnect a washer pump hose and drain the washer fluid into a suitable container.
4. Disconnect the all other hoses from the reservoir.
5. Remove the washer fluid reservoir.
6. Remove the washer pump from the reservoir.

To install:

7. Install the washer pump and tighten securely.

➡ **The washer fluid reservoir is plastic. Take care not to overtighten the washer pump.**

8. Install the reservoir and tighten mounting bolts to 7 ft. lbs. (10 Nm).
9. Connect the electrical lead and the hoses.
10. Connect the negative battery cable.
11. Refill the reservoir and test the operation of the system.

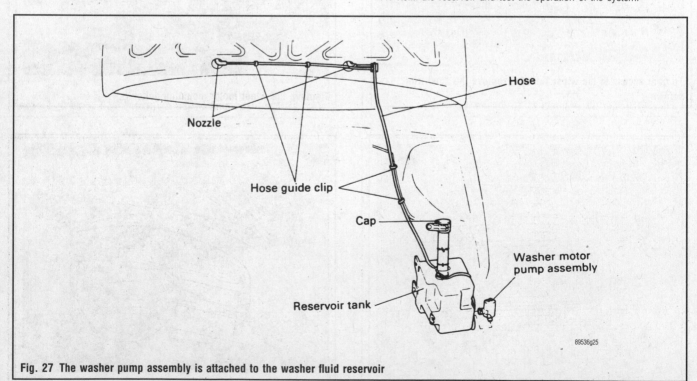

Fig. 27 The washer pump assembly is attached to the washer fluid reservoir

INSTRUMENTS AND SWITCHES

Instrument Cluster

REMOVAL & INSTALLATION

♦ See Figures 28 thru 41 (p. 33–35)

1. Disconnect the negative battery cable.
2. Remove the cluster fascia panel.
3. Remove the instrument panel mounting screws and carefully pull the panel from the dashboard.
4. Label and disconnect all electrical harnesses.
5. Disconnect the speedometer cable.
6. Remove the instrument panel.

To install:

7. Connect the speedometer cable and all electrical harnesses.
8. Install the instrument panel and tighten screws securely.
9. Install the cluster fascia panel and tighten the screws securely.
10. Connect the negative battery cable.

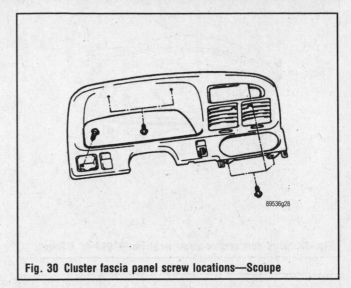

Fig. 30 Cluster fascia panel screw locations—Scoupe

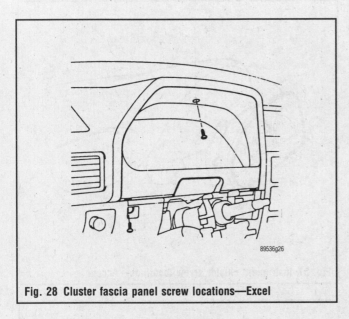

Fig. 28 Cluster fascia panel screw locations—Excel

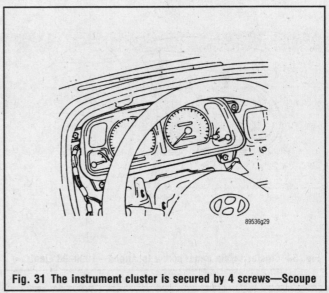

Fig. 31 The instrument cluster is secured by 4 screws—Scoupe

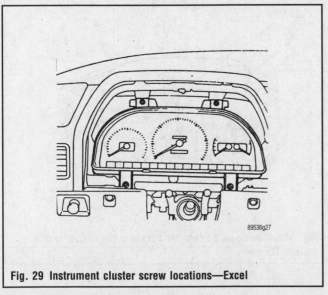

Fig. 29 Instrument cluster screw locations—Excel

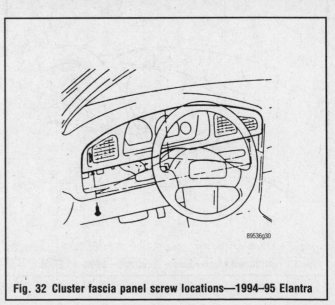

Fig. 32 Cluster fascia panel screw locations—1994–95 Elantra

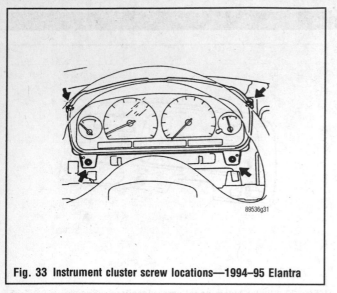

Fig. 33 Instrument cluster screw locations—1994–95 Elantra

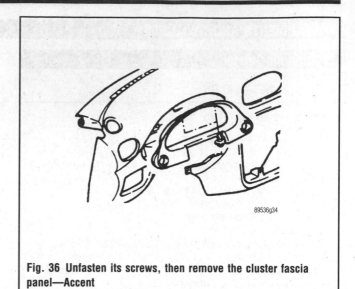

Fig. 36 Unfasten its screws, then remove the cluster fascia panel—Accent

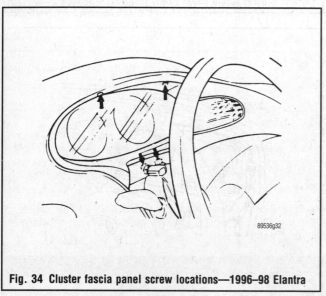

Fig. 34 Cluster fascia panel screw locations—1996–98 Elantra

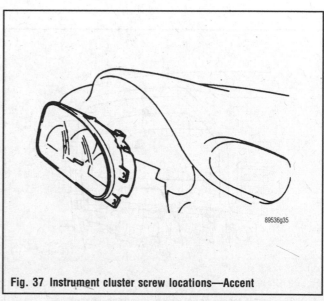

Fig. 37 Instrument cluster screw locations—Accent

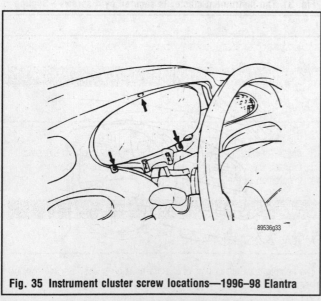

Fig. 35 Instrument cluster screw locations—1996–98 Elantra

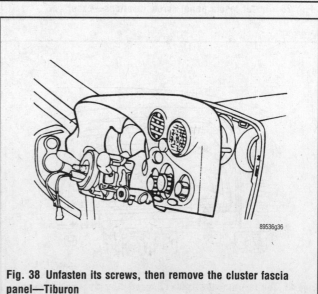

Fig. 38 Unfasten its screws, then remove the cluster fascia panel—Tiburon

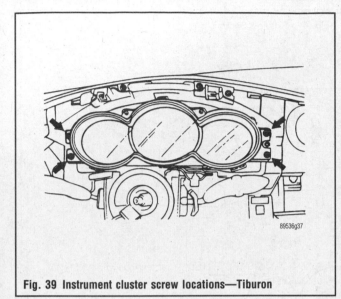

Fig. 39 Instrument cluster screw locations—Tiburon

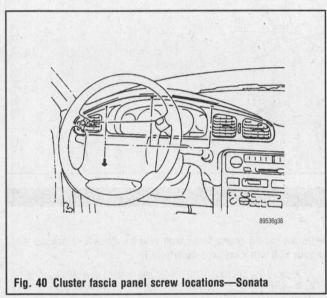

Fig. 40 Cluster fascia panel screw locations—Sonata

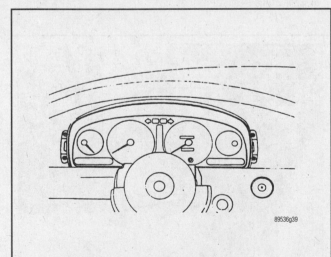

Fig. 41 The instrument cluster is secured by 4 screws—Sonata

Gauges

REMOVAL & INSTALLATION

◆ See Figure 42

1. Disconnect the negative battery cable.
2. Remove the instrument cluster from the instrument panel.
3. Place the instrument cluster on clean work area.
4. Remove the instrument cluster lens retaining screws from the side of the cluster and remove the lens.
5. Remove the gauge retaining screws and carefully remove the gauge from the cluster assembly.

To install:

6. Install the gauge into the cluster and install the retaining screws.
7. Install the instrument cluster lens and tighten retaining screws.
8. Position the cluster assembly to the dash, while inserting the speedometer cable into the speedometer, push in securely.
9. Install the instrument cluster.
10. Connect the negative battery cable.

Speedometer Cable

REMOVAL & INSTALLATION

1. Remove the instrument cluster far enough to disconnect the speedometer cable.
2. Raise and support the front end on jackstands.
3. Disconnect the speedometer cable at the transmission or transaxle.
4. Installation is the reverse of removal. Insert the cable into the speedometer until the stopper engages with the groove. Install the firewall grommet so that the attachment and projecting portions are horizontal. Route the cable in the engine compartment so that the radius of the cable bend does not exceed 6 in. (150mm). Use wire ties to control the bend of the cable as required.

➡Improper installation or bend radius of the speedometer cable will cause a fluctuation of the pointer needle, noise or a damaged wiring harness inside the instrument panel.

Windshield Wiper Switch

REMOVAL & INSTALLATION

The windshield wiper switch is part of a multi-function switch. For information on removal and installation, refer to Section 8 of this manual.

Rear Window Wiper Switch

REMOVAL & INSTALLATION

1. Pry the switch bezel from the panel.
2. Reach behind the panel and disconnect the wiring from the switch.
3. Depress the two retainers and pull the switch from the panel.
4. Installation is the reverse of removal.

Headlight Switch

REMOVAL & INSTALLATION

The headlight switch is part of a multi-function switch. For information on removal and installation, refer to Section 8 of this manual.

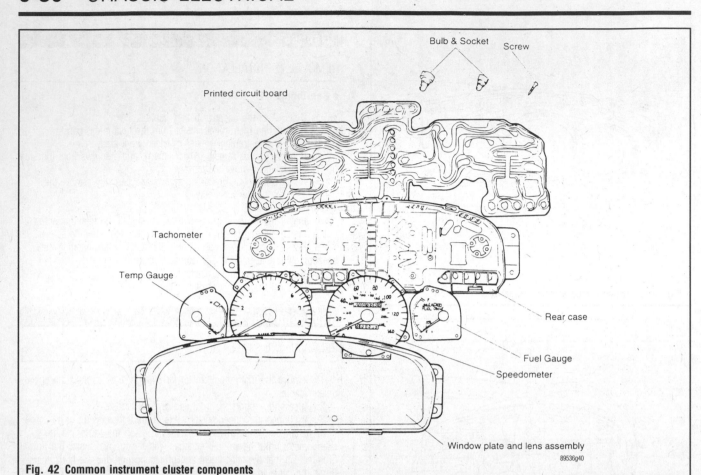

Fig. 42 Common instrument cluster components

LIGHTING

Headlight Bulbs

REMOVAL & INSTALLATION

1. Twist the lockring and slide it back on the electrical harness.
2. Disconnect the electrical harness and pull the bulb holder from the headlight housing.

➡Do not handle quartz bulbs with your bare hands, since the oils in your skin will cause the bulb to fail.

3. Remove the bulb from the holder and insert the replacement bulb.
4. Reinsert the holder into the housing and turn the lockring.
5. Connect the electrical harness.

The headlight bulb holder is secured in the headlight assembly by a lockring

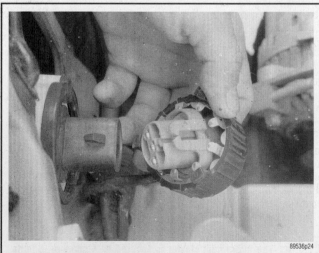

Once the lockring is loose, the electrical harness can be disconnected from the bulb holder

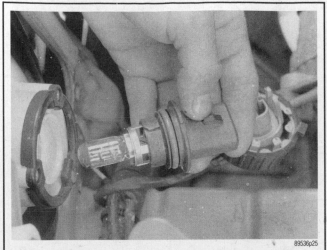

Always handle the bulb by the holder. Oil from your skin will shorten the life of the bulb

AIMING

▶ **See Figures 43, 44, 45, 46 and 47**

The headlights must be properly aimed to provide the best, safest road illumination. The lights should be checked for proper aim and adjusted as necessary. Certain state and local authorities have requirements for headlight aiming; these should be checked before adjustment is made.

✳✳ CAUTION

About once a year, when the headlights are replaced or any time front end work is performed on your vehicle, the headlight should be accurately aimed by a reputable repair shop using the proper equipment. Headlights not properly aimed can make it virtually impossible to see and may blind other drivers on the road, possibly causing an accident. Note that the following procedure is a temporary fix, until you can take your vehicle to a repair shop for a proper adjustment.

Headlight adjustment may be temporarily made using a wall, as described below, or on the rear of another vehicle. When adjusted, the lights should not glare in oncoming car or truck windshields, nor should they illuminate the passenger compartment of vehicles driving in front of you. These adjustments are rough and should always be fine-tuned by a repair shop which is equipped with headlight aiming tools. Improper adjustments may be both dangerous and illegal.

For most of the vehicles covered by this manual, horizontal and vertical aiming of each sealed beam unit is provided by two adjusting screws which move the retaining ring and adjusting plate against the tension of a coil spring. There is no adjustment for focus; this is done during headlight manufacturing.

➡**Because the composite headlight assembly is bolted into position, no adjustment should be necessary or possible. Some applications, however, may be bolted to an adjuster plate or may be retained by adjusting screws. If so, follow this procedure when adjusting the lights, BUT always have the adjustment checked by a reputable shop.**

Before removing the headlight bulb or disturbing the headlamp in any way, note the current settings in order to ease headlight adjustment upon reassembly. If the high or low beam setting of the old lamp still works, this can be done using the wall of a garage or a building:

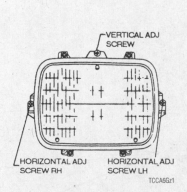

Fig. 43 Location of the aiming screws on most vehicles with sealed beam headlights

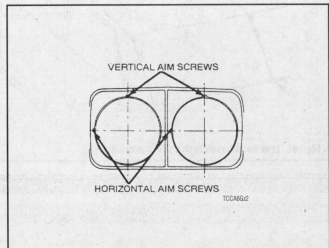

Fig. 44 Dual headlight adjustment screw locations—one side shown here (other side should be mirror image)

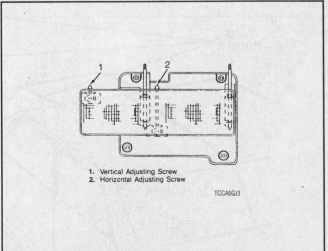

1. Vertical Adjusting Screw
2. Horizontal Adjusting Screw

Fig. 45 Example of headlight adjustment screw location for composite headlamps

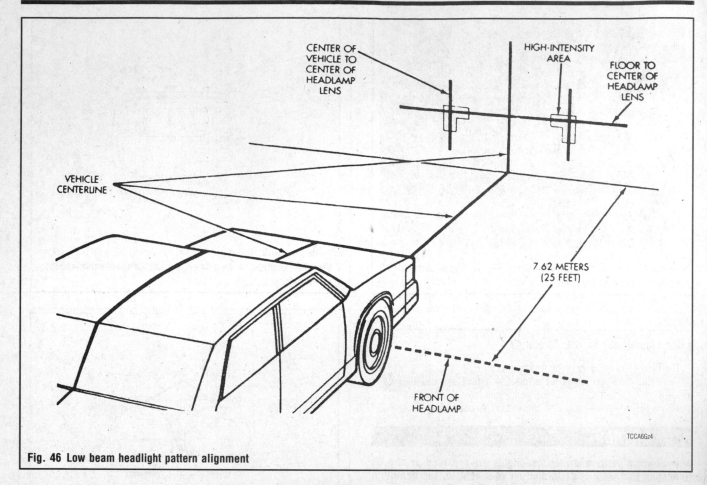

Fig. 46 Low beam headlight pattern alignment

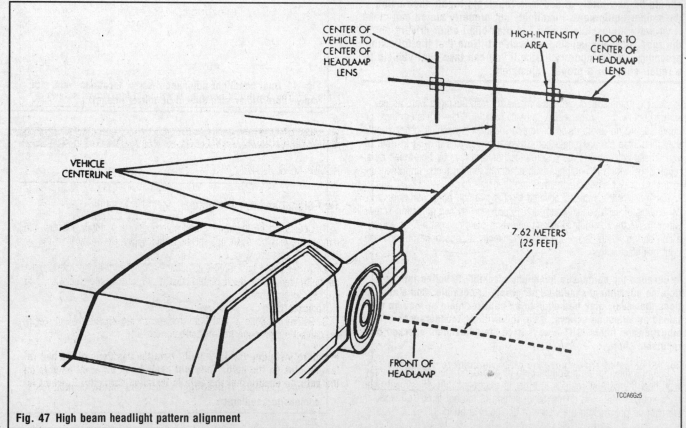

Fig. 47 High beam headlight pattern alignment

1. Park the vehicle on a level surface, with the fuel tank about ½full and with the vehicle empty of all extra cargo (unless normally carried). The vehicle should be facing a wall which is no less than 6 feet (1.8m) high and 12 feet (3.7m) wide. The front of the vehicle should be about 25 feet from the wall.

2. If aiming is to be performed outdoors, it is advisable to wait until dusk in order to properly see the headlight beams on the wall. If done in a garage, darken the area around the wall as much as possible by closing shades or hanging cloth over the windows.

3. Turn the headlights **ON** and mark the wall at the center of each light's low beam, then switch on the brights and mark the center of each light's high beam. A short length of masking tape which is visible from the front of the vehicle may be used. Although marking all four positions is advisable, marking one position from each light should be sufficient.

4. If neither beam on one side is working, and if another like-sized vehicle is available, park the second one in the exact spot where the vehicle was and mark the beams using the same-side light. Then switch the vehicles so the one to be aimed is back in the original spot. It must be parked no closer to or farther away from the wall than the second vehicle.

5. Perform any necessary repairs, but make sure the vehicle is not moved, or is returned to the exact spot from which the lights were marked. Turn the headlights **ON** and adjust the beams to match the marks on the wall.

6. Have the headlight adjustment checked as soon as possible by a reputable repair shop.

Headlight Housing

REMOVAL & INSTALLATION

▶ See Figures 48, 49 and 50

1. Remove the grille.
2. Remove the screws that retain the turn signal/marker lamp housing and remove the housing.
3. Remove the screws that retain the headlight housing and remove the housing.
4. Installation is the reverse of removal.
5. When installing the housing, be careful not to overtighten the screws.
6. Check the headlight alignment. Have it corrected if necessary.

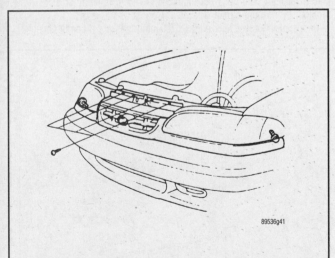

Fig. 48 Unfasten and remove the grille, in order to access the headlight housing

Fig. 49 The parking lamp is usually retained by a single screw. It must be removed to gain access to the headlight housing's outer screws

Fig. 50 The headlight housing is retained by several screws

Signal and Marker Lights

REMOVAL & INSTALLATION

Turn Signal and Brake Lights

1. Depending on the vehicle and bulb application, either unscrew and remove the lens or disengage the bulb and socket assembly from the rear of the lens housing.
2. To remove a light bulb with retaining pins from its socket, grasp the bulb, then gently depress and twist it 1/8 turn counterclockwise, and pull it from the socket.
To install:
3. Before installing a light bulb into the socket, ensure that all electrical contact surfaces are free of corrosion or dirt.

➡Before installing the light bulb, note the positions of the two retaining pins on the bulb. They will likely be at different heights on the bulb, to ensure that the bulb is installed correctly. If, when in-

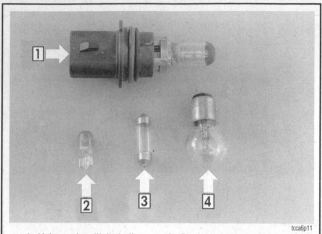

1. Halogen headlight bulb
2. Side marker light bulb
3. Dome light bulb
4. Turn signal/brake light bulb

Examples of various types of automotive light bulbs

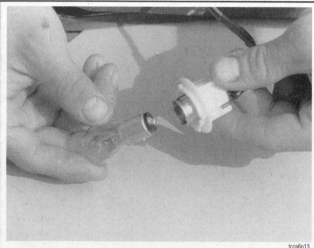

Depress and twist this type of bulb counterclockwise, then pull the bulb straight from its socket

stalling the bulb, it does not turn easily, do not force it. Remove the bulb and rotate it 180 degrees from its former position, then reinsert it into the bulb socket.

4. Insert the light bulb into the socket and, while depressing the bulb, twist it 1/8 turn clockwise until the two pins on the light bulb are properly engaged in the socket.

5. To ensure that the replacement bulb functions properly, activate the applicable switch to illuminate the bulb which was just replaced. If the replacement light bulb does not illuminate, either it too is faulty or there is a problem in the bulb circuit or switch. Correct if necessary.

6. If applicable, install the socket and bulb assembly into the rear of the lens housing; otherwise, install the lens over the bulb.

Side Marker Light

1. Disengage the bulb and socket assembly from the lens housing.
2. Gently grasp the light bulb and pull it straight out of the socket.
To install:
3. Before installing the light bulb into the socket, ensure that all electrical contact surfaces are free of corrosion or dirt.
4. Line up the base of the light bulb with the socket, then insert the light bulb into the socket until it is fully seated.
5. To ensure that the replacement bulb functions properly, activate the

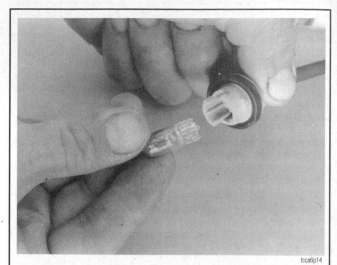

Simply pull this side marker light bulb straight from its socket

applicable switch to illuminate the bulb which was just replaced. If the replacement light bulb does not illuminate, either it too is faulty or there is a problem in the bulb circuit or switch. Correct as necessary.

6. Install the socket and bulb assembly into the lens housing.

Dome Light

1. Using a small prytool, carefully remove the cover lens from the lamp assembly.
2. Remove the bulb from its retaining clip contacts. If the bulb has tapered ends, gently depress the spring clip/metal contact and disengage the light bulb, then pull it free of the two metal contacts.
To install:
3. Before installing the light bulb into the metal contacts, ensure that all electrical conducting surfaces are free of corrosion or dirt.
4. Position the bulb between the two metal contacts. If the contacts have small holes, be sure that the tapered ends of the bulb are situated in them.
5. To ensure that the replacement bulb functions properly, activate the applicable switch to illuminate the bulb which was just replaced. If the replacement light bulb does not illuminate, either it is faulty or there is a problem in the bulb circuit or switch. Correct as necessary.
6. Install the cover lens until its retaining tabs are properly engaged.

Disengage the spring clip which retains one tapered end of this dome light bulb, then withdraw the bulb

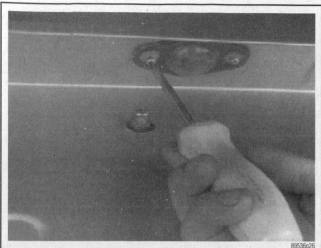

To remove the early model license plate light, first remove the light's mounting screws . . .

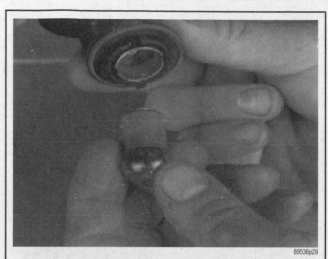

. . . then depress and twist the bulb to remove it from the socket

. . . then pull the bulb and lens assembly from the opening

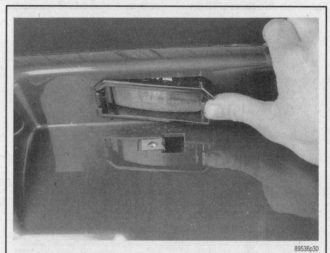

To remove the late model license plate light, squeeze the tabs to remove the lens . . .

Twist the bulb socket to remove it from the lens . . .

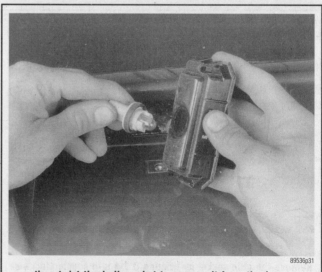

. . . then twist the bulb socket to remove it from the lens . . .

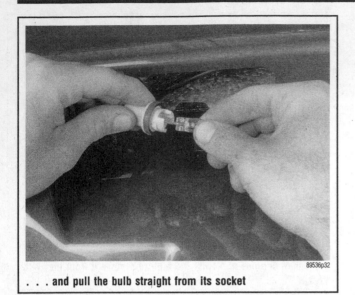

. . . and pull the bulb straight from its socket

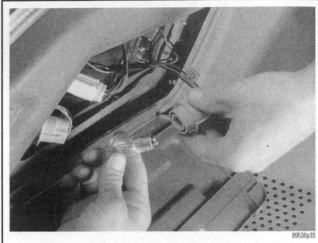

. . . then depress and twist the bulb 1/8 turn counterclockwise to remove it from the socket

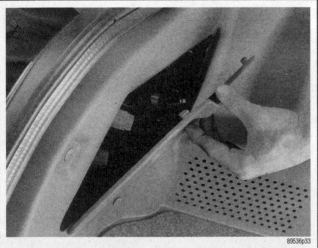

The rear turn signal, brake and parking lights are located behind an access panel in the trunk

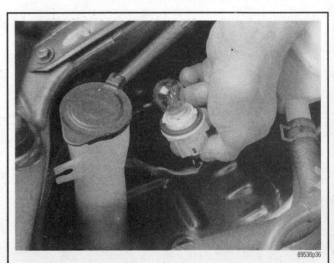

Front turn signal and parking lights are located at the front of the engine compartment

Remove the bulb socket by twisting it 1/4 turn counterclockwise and pulling . . .

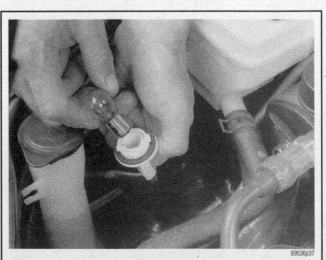

Remove the bulb socket by turning, then depress and twist the bulb to remove it from the socket

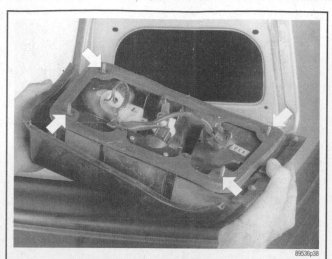

The rear turn signal, brake and parking light housing is attached to the body by four studs (arrows)

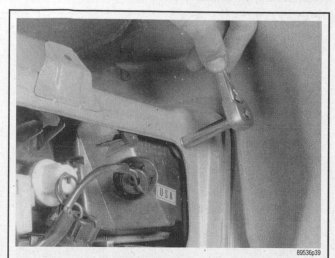

Remove the nuts and carefully push the light housing from the opening

TRAILER WIRING

Wiring the vehicle for towing is fairly easy. There are a number of good wiring kits available and these should be used, rather than trying to design your own.

All trailers will need brake lights and turn signals as well as tail lights and side marker lights. Most areas require extra marker lights for over-wide trailers. Also, most areas have recently required back-up lights for trailers, and most trailer manufacturers have been building trailers with back-up lights for several years.

Additionally, some Class I, most Class II and just about all Class III trailers will have electric brakes. Add to this number an accessories wire, to operate trailer internal equipment or to charge the trailer's battery, and you can have as many as seven wires in the harness.

Determine the equipment on your trailer and buy the wiring kit necessary. The kit will contain all the wires needed, plus a plug adapter set which includes the female plug, mounted on the bumper or hitch, and the male plug, wired into, or plugged into the trailer harness.

When installing the kit, follow the manufacturer's instructions. The color coding of the wires is usually standard throughout the industry. One point to note: some domestic vehicles, and most imported vehicles, have separate turn signals. On most domestic vehicles, however, the brake lights and rear turn signals operate with the same bulb. For those vehicles without separate turn signals, you can purchase and install an isolation unit, so that the brake lights won't blink whenever the turn signals are operated. The isolation units are simple and quick to install.

One final point—the best kits are those with a spring loaded cover on the vehicle mounted socket. This cover prevents dirt and moisture from corroding the terminals. Never let the vehicle socket hang loosely; always mount it securely to the bumper or hitch.

CIRCUIT PROTECTION

The underhood relay box contains a schematic on the cover for easy identification of relays and fuses

Remove the cover and hold it alongside the box to identify the location of the desired component

Fusible links look like giant fuses—to remove them, simply pull them straight out

To remove hard to reach fuses, a fuse tool is available at most automotive stores

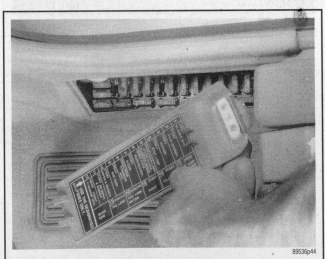

The passenger compartment fuse panel is located in the left kick panel. The lid contains a schematic

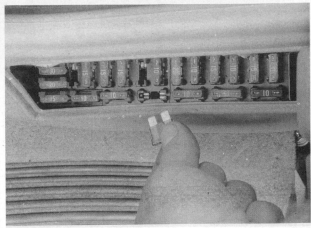

Many fuses can be removed by hand. Always inspect the fuse terminals for corrosion or damage

Fuses

REPLACEMENT

Fuses are located either in the engine compartment relay box or in the passenger compartment fuse panel. If a fuse blows, an single component or single circuit will function improperly.
  1. Remove the engine compartment relay box or fuse panel cover.
  2. Inspect the fuses to determine which is faulty. The faulty fuse will appear burned.
  3. Unplug and discard the fuse.
  4. Inspect box terminals and clean if corroded. If terminals are damaged, replace the terminals.
  5. Plug in a new fuse of the same amperage rating.
  6. Check for proper operation.

Fusible Links

The fusible links are located either in the engine compartment relay box or in a separate box located near the battery. If a fusible link blows, an entire circuit or several circuits will function improperly.

REPLACEMENT

  1. Remove the engine compartment relay box cover or fusible link box cover.
  2. Inspect the fusible links to determine which is faulty. The faulty fusible link will appear burned.
  3. Unplug and discard the fusible link.
  4. Inspect box terminals and clean if corroded. If terminals are damaged, replace the terminals.
  5. Plug in a new fusible link of the same amperage rating.
  6. Check for proper operation.

Flashers

The flashers are located passenger compartment relay box. If the turn signals operate in only one direction, a bulb is probably burned out. If they do not operate in either direction, a bulb on each side may be burned out, or the flasher may be defective.

REPLACEMENT

1. Remove the passenger compartment relay box cover, noting which position the flasher unit occupies.
2. Unplug and discard the flasher.

3. Inspect the box terminals and clean if corroded. If terminals are damaged, replace the terminals.
4. Plug in a new flasher of the same type.
5. Operate turn signals and hazard lights. Check for proper operation.

Engine Compartment Relay Box—Excel

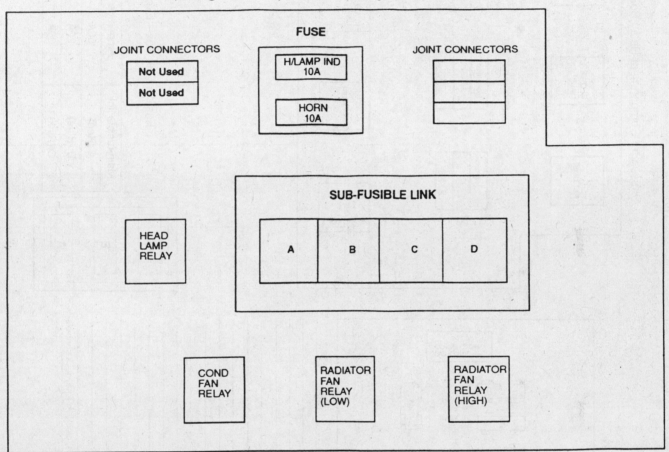

Description	Amperages	Circuit protected	Remark
Sub-fusible link			
A(Red)	50A	Fuse box	
B(Blue)	20A	MFI system controls	
C(Pink)	30A	Head lamps	
D(Pink)	30A	Ignition	
Fuse			
H/LAMP IND	10A	Headlamp indicator	
HORN	10A	Horns	

89536C02

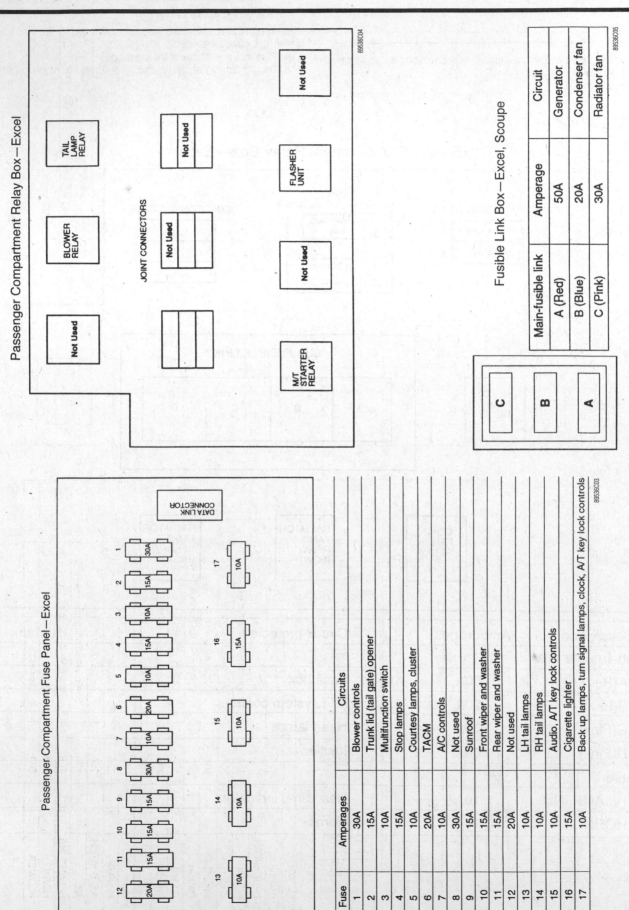

Passenger Compartment Relay Box—Excel

TAIL LAMP RELAY	BLOWER RELAY	Not Used
Not Used	Not Used	
FLASHER UNIT	Not Used	M/T STARTER RELAY

JOINT CONNECTORS

89536C04

Fusible Link Box—Excel, Scoupe

Main-fusible link	Amperage	Circuit
A (Red)	50A	Generator
B (Blue)	20A	Condenser fan
C (Pink)	30A	Radiator fan

89536C05

Passenger Compartment Fuse Panel—Excel

DATA LINK CONNECTOR

89536C03

Fuse	Amperages	Circuits
1	30A	Blower controls
2	15A	Trunk lid (tail gate) opener
3	10A	Multifunction switch
4	15A	Stop lamps
5	10A	Courtesy lamps, cluster
6	20A	TACM
7	10A	A/C controls
8	30A	Not used
9	15A	Sunroof
10	15A	Front wiper and washer
11	15A	Rear wiper and washer
12	20A	Not used
13	10A	LH tail lamps
14	10A	RH tail lamps
15	10A	Audio, A/T key lock controls
16	15A	Cigarette lighter
17	10A	Back up lamps, turn signal lamps, clock, A/T key lock controls

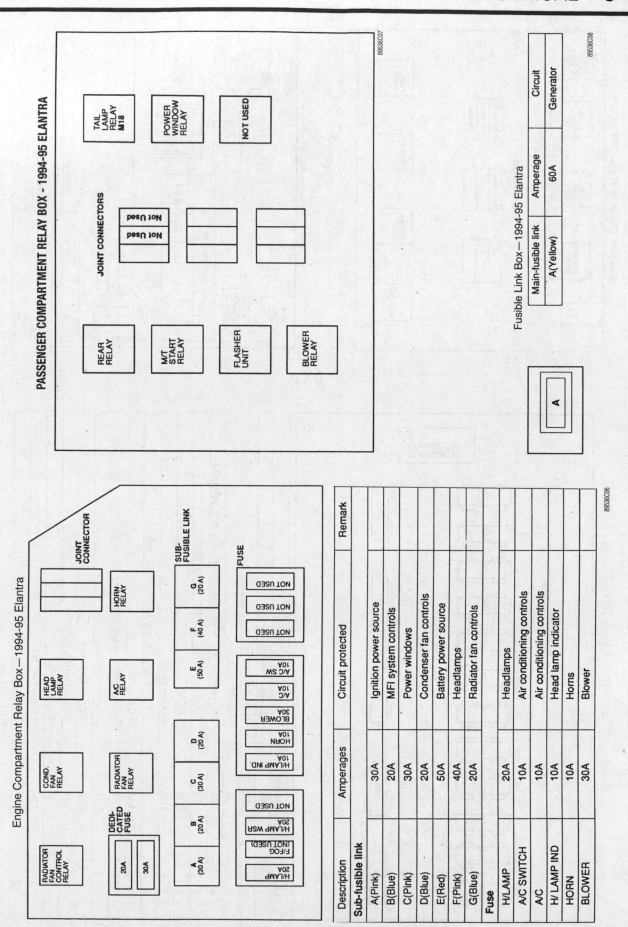

PASSENGER COMPARTMENT RELAY BOX – 1994-95 ELANTRA

| TAIL LAMP RELAY M18 | POWER WINDOW RELAY | NOT USED |

JOINT CONNECTORS

| Not Used | Not Used |

| REAR RELAY | M/T START RELAY | FLASHER UNIT | BLOWER RELAY |

Fusible Link Box—1994-95 Elantra

Main-fusible link	Amperage	Circuit
A(Yellow)	60A	Generator

A

Engine Compartment Relay Box—1994-95 Elantra

JOINT CONNECTOR

HORN RELAY

RADIATOR FAN CONTROL RELAY · COND. FAN RELAY · RADIATOR FAN RELAY · HEAD LAMP RELAY · A/C RELAY

DEDI-CATED FUSE: 20A, 30A

SUB-FUSIBLE LINK: G (20 A), F (40 A), E (50 A), D (20 A), C (30 A), B (20 A), A (30 A)

FUSE: NOT USED, NOT USED, NOT USED, A/C SW 10A, A/C 10A, BLOWER 30A, HORN 10A, H/LAMP IND. 10A, NOT USED, H/LAMP WSR 20A, F/FOG (NOT USED), H/LAMP 20A

Description	Amperages	Circuit protected	Remark
Sub-fusible link			
A(Pink)	30A	Ignition power source	
B(Blue)	20A	MFI system controls	
C(Pink)	30A	Power windows	
D(Blue)	20A	Condenser fan controls	
E(Red)	50A	Battery power source	
F(Pink)	40A	Headlamps	
G(Blue)	20A	Radiator fan controls	
Fuse			
H/LAMP	20A	Headlamps	
A/C SWITCH	10A	Air conditioning controls	
A/C	10A	Air conditioning controls	
H/ LAMP IND	10A	Head lamp indicator	
HORN	10A	Horns	
BLOWER	30A	Blower	

PASSENGER COMPARTMENT RELAY BOX - SCOUPE

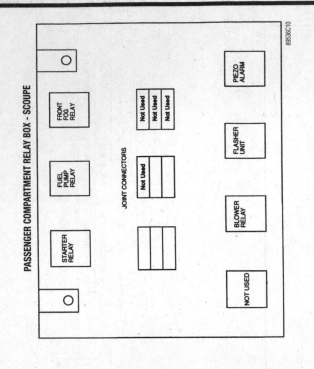

89536C10

Relays: STARTER RELAY, FUEL PUMP RELAY, FRONT FOG RELAY, PIEZO ALARM, BLOWER RELAY, FLASHER UNIT, NOT USED

JOINT CONNECTORS: Not Used

Engine Compartment Relay Box—Scoupe

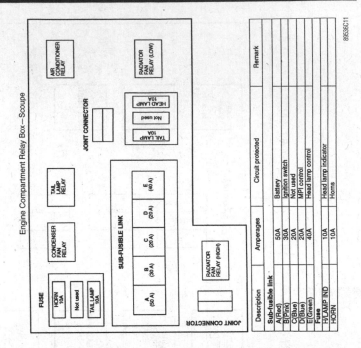

89536C11

Relays: AIR CONDITIONER RELAY, RADIATOR FAN RELAY (LOW), TAIL LAMP RELAY, CONDENSER FAN RELAY, RADIATOR FAN RELAY (HIGH)

JOINT CONNECTOR

HEAD LAMP 10A, Not used, TAIL LAMP 10A

SUB-FUSIBLE LINK: A (50 A), B (30 A), C (20 A), D (20 A), E (40 A)

FUSE: HORN 10A, Not used, TAIL LAMP 10A

Description	Amperages	Circuit protected	Remark
Sub-fusible link			
A(Red)	50A	Battery	
B(Pink)	30A	Ignition switch	
C(Blue)	20A	Not used	
D(Blue)	20A	MPI control	
E(Green)	40A	Head lamp control	
Fuse			
H/LAMP IND	10A	Head lamp indicator	
HORN	10A	Horns	

Passenger Compartment Fuse Box—Scoupe

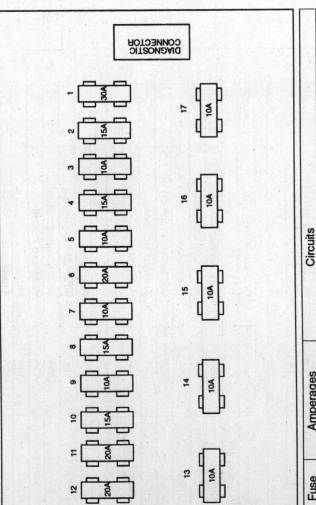

DIAGNOSTIC CONNECTOR

Fuses: 1 - 30A, 2 - 15A, 3 - 10A, 4 - 15A, 5 - 10A, 6 - 20A, 7 - 10A, 8 - 15A, 9 - 10A, 10 - 15A, 11 - 20A, 12 - 20A, 13 - 10A, 14 - 10A, 15 - 10A, 16 - 10A, 17 - 10A

89536C09

Fuse	Amperages	Circuits
1	30A	Blower controls
2	15A	Turn lid opener
3	10A	Hazard switch
4	15A	Stop lamps, A/T shift and ignition key lock solenoid
5	10A	Courtesy lamps, cluster, audio, clock
6	20A	TACM
7	10A	Audio, clock
8	15A	A/T and ignition key lock control unit
9	10A	TCM
10	15A	Wiper motor, washer motor
11	20A	Power windows
12	20A	Power windows
13	10A	Hazard/cruise controls
14	10A	A/C controls
15	10A	LH tail lamps
16	15A	Not used
17	10A	RH tail lamps

PASSENGER COMPARTMENT FUSE PANEL - SONATA

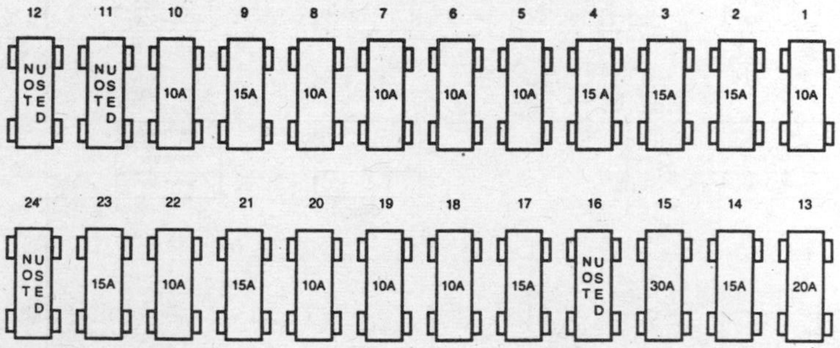

Fuse	Amperages	Circuits
1	10A	Hazard
2	15A	Stop lamp.
3	15A	Cooling control module
4	15A	Sunroof
5	10A	Audio, Power antenna, ETACS, TCM
6	10A	Courtesy lamp, A/C, Trunk room lamp
7	10A	Turn signal lamp, Back-up lamp, ETACS
8	10A	Seatbelt, A/T interlock
9	15A	Airbag
10	10A	Cluster, Clock
11	Not used	Not used
12	Not used	Not used
13	20A	Power seat
14	15A	Trunk lid opener, Power door lock
15	30A	Rear window defogger
16	Not used	Not used
17	15A	Power door mirror, Cigarette lighter
18	10A	Audio, A/T interlock
19	10A	ABS
20	10A	Cruise
21	15A	Seat warmer
22	10A	TCM, Blower, Headlamp, Power window
23	15A	Wiper and washer
24	Not used	Not used

Engine Compartment Relay and Fuse Box—Sonata

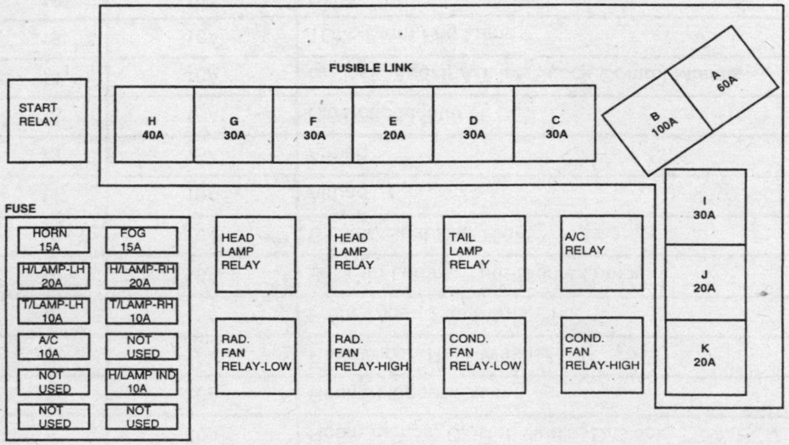

Description	Amperages	Circuit protected	Remark
Fusible link			
A (Yellow)	60A	Battery power source	
B (Dark blue)	100A	Generator	
C (Pink)	30A	Ignition power source	
D (Pink)	30A	Radiator control	
E (Blue)	20A	MFI system control	
F (Pink)	30A	Power windows	
G (Pink)	30A	Blower control	
H (Green)	40A	Lamp control	
I (Pink)	30A	ABS control	
J (Blue)	20A	ABS control	
K (Blue)	20A	A/C condenser fan control	
Fuse			
HORN	15A	Horn	
H/LAMP	20A	Head lamp	
H/LAMP	20A	Head lamp	
FOG	15A	Fog lamps	
T/LAMP-LH	10A	LH Tail lamps	
T/LAMP-RH	10A	RH Tail lamps, illuminations	
A/C	10A	A/C Compressor control	
H/LAMP IND.	10A	Head lamp indicator	

89536C13

89536C12

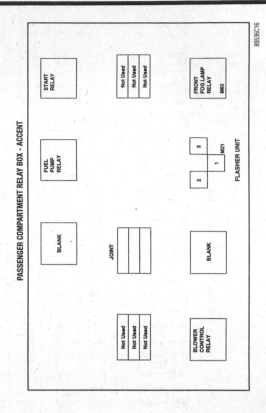

Engine Compartment Relay Box — Accent

FUSIBLE LINK

E (20 A)	D (20 A)	BLANK	B (50 A)

FUSE

- TAIL LAMP RH 10 A
- TAIL LAMP LH 10 A
- HEAD LAMP RH 10 A
- HEAD LAMP LH 10 A
- AIR CONDITIONING 10 A
- BLOWER CONTROL 30 A

FUSIBLE LINK A (60 A)

Relays: RADIATOR RELAY, HEAD LAMP RELAY, A/C RELAY, HORN RELAY, TAIL LAMP RELAY, CONDENSER RELAY

FUSIBLE LINK

I (20 A)	H (30 A)	G (30 A)	F (30 A)

FUSE: HORN 10 A, CONDENSER 20 A

Description	Amperages	Circuit protected	Remark
A (YELLOW)	60A	Generator	
B (RED)	50A	Battery	
D (BLUE)	20A	Radiator Fan Controls	
E (BLUE)	20A	ABS Controls	
F (PINK)	30A	Ignition Power Source	
G (PINK)	30A	ABS Controls	
H (PINK)	30A	Lamps	
I (BLUE)	20A	MFI System Controls	

PASSENGER COMPARTMENT RELAY BOX - ACCENT

START RELAY, Not Used, Not Used, Not Used, FRONT FOG LAMP RELAY M60

FUEL PUMP RELAY

BLANK, JOINT, BLANK

Not Used, Not Used, Not Used, BLOWER CONTROL RELAY

FLASHER UNIT: 2 1 3 M21

SPARE FUSE

30A	20A	15A	10A

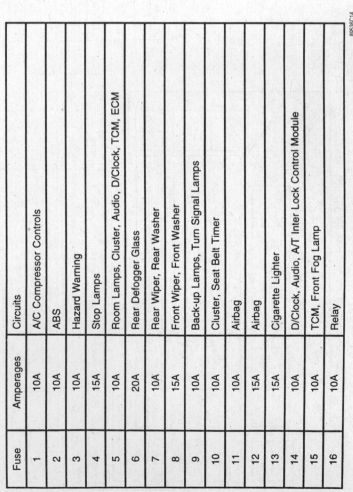

Passenger Compartment Fuse Panel — Accent

Fuses (top row): 16 (10A), 15 (10A), 14 (10A), 13 (15 A), 12 (15A), 11 (10A), 10 (10A), 9 (10A)

Fuses (bottom row): 8 (15A), 7 (10A), 6 (20A), 5 (10A), 4 (15A), 3 (10A), 2 (10A), 1 (10A)

Fuse	Amperages	Circuits
1	10A	A/C Compressor Controls
2	10A	ABS
3	10A	Hazard Warning
4	15A	Stop Lamps
5	10A	Room Lamps, Cluster, Audio, D/Clock, TCM, ECM
6	20A	Rear Defogger Glass
7	10A	Rear Wiper, Rear Washer
8	15A	Front Wiper, Front Washer
9	10A	Back-up Lamps, Turn Signal Lamps
10	10A	Cluster, Seat Belt Timer
11	10A	Airbag
12	15A	Airbag
13	15A	Cigarette Lighter
14	10A	D/Clock, Audio, A/T Inter Lock Control Module
15	10A	TCM, Front Fog Lamp
16	10A	Relay

89536C15

89536C16

89536C14

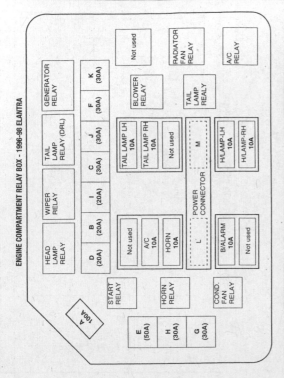

ENGINE COMPARTMENT RELAY BOX - 1996-98 ELANTRA

Description	Amperages	Circuit protected	Remark
Fusible link			
A (Dark blue)	100A	Generator	
B (Blue)	20A	MFI system control	
C (Pink)	30A	Power windows	
D (Blue)	20A	A/C condenser fan control	
E (Red)	50A	Battery power source	
F (Pink)	30A	Head lamps, Tail lamps	
G (Pink)	30A	Radiator fan control	
H (Pink)	30A	ABS control	
I (Blue)	20A	ABS control	
J (Pink)	30A	Ignition power source	
K (Pink)	30A	Blower control	
Fuse			
Not used			
A/C	10A	A/C conditioning control	
HORN	10A	Horn	
B/ALARM	10A	Audio, clock, TCM, ECM	
Not used			
TAIL LAMP (LH)	10A	Tail lamps (LH)	
TAIL LAMP (RH)	10A	Tail lamps (RH)	
Not used			
H/LAMP (LH)	10A	Head lamps (LH)	
H/LAMP (RH)	10A	Head lamps (RH)	
Power connector			
L		TCM, Audio (10A)	
M		Fuse 14 (10A)	

89536C19

FUSE BOX

Passenger Compartment Fuse Panel—1996-98 Elantra

Fuse	Amperages	Circuits
1	10A	A/C Controls
2	15A	Power door lock
3	15A	Stop lamps
4	10A	Hazard warning
5	30A	Rear defogger glass
6	15A	Sunroof
7	15A	Rear wiper
8	15A	Front wiper, ETACS
9	10A	Back-up lamps, Turn signal lamps
10	10A	Cluster
11	10A	ABS
12	15A	Airbag
13	15A	Cigarette lighter, power door mirrors
14	10A	Audio, A/T Inter lock module
15	10A	TCM
16	10A	Cruise, Sunroof, Head lamps
17		Not used

89536C17

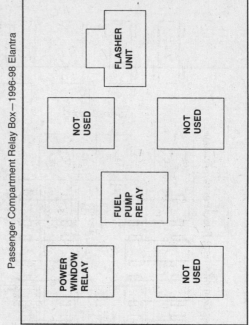

Passenger Compartment Relay Box—1996-98 Elantra

89536C18

FUSE BOX

Passenger Compartment Fuse Panel—Tiburon

1	10A
2	15A
3	15A
4	10A
5	30A
6	15A
7	15A
8	15A
9	10A
10	10A
11	10A
12	15A
13	15A
14	10A
15	10A
16	10A

17	NOT USED
SPARE	
SPARE	
SPARE	

89536C21

Fuse	Amperages	Circuits
1	10A	A/C controls
2	15A	Power door locks
3	15A	Stop lamps
4	10A	Hazard warning
5	30A	Rear defogger glass
6	15A	Room lamp
7	15A	Rear wiper
8	15A	ETACS, Front wiper & washer
9	10A	Back-up lamps, Turn signal lamps, TCM
10	10A	Instrument cluster
11	10A	ABS
12	15A	Airbag
13	15A	Cigarette lighter, Power door mirrors, clock
14	10A	Audio, Key inter lock
15	10A	EPS, Sun roof
16	10A	Cruise, Head lamps, Power window
17	Not used	

PASSENGER COMPARTMENT RELAY BOX—TIBURON

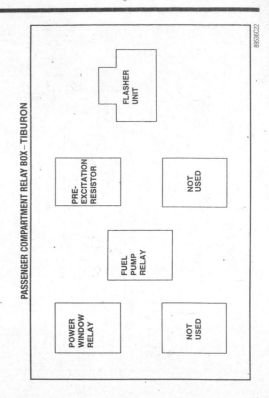

89536C22

Engine Compartment Relay and Fuse Box—Tiburon

89536C20

Description	Amperages	Circuit protected	Remark
Fusible link			
A (Dark blue)	100A	Generator	
B (Blue)	20A	MFI control relay	
C (Pink)	30A	Power windows	
D (Blue)	20A	A/C condenser fan control	
E (Red)	50A	Battery power source	
F (Green)	40A	Head lamps, Tail lamps	
G (Pink)	30A	Radiator fan control	
H (Pink)	30A	ABS control	
I (Blue)	20A	ABS control	
J (Pink)	30A	Ignition power source	
K(Pink)	30A	Blower control	
Fuse			
A/C	10A	A/C conditioning control	
HORN	10A	Horns	
AUDIO	10A	Audio, ECM, TCM	
TAIL LAMP (LH)	10A	Tail lamps (LH)	
TAIL LAMP (RH)	10A	Tail lamps (RH)	
FRONT FOG LAMP	15A	Front fog lamps	
H/LAMP (LH)	15A	Head lamps (LH)	
H/LAMP (RH)	15A	Head lamps (RH)	
Power connector			
L	-	Audio Fuse (10A) Fuse 6 (15A)	
M	-	Fuse 14 (10A)	

WIRING DIAGRAMS

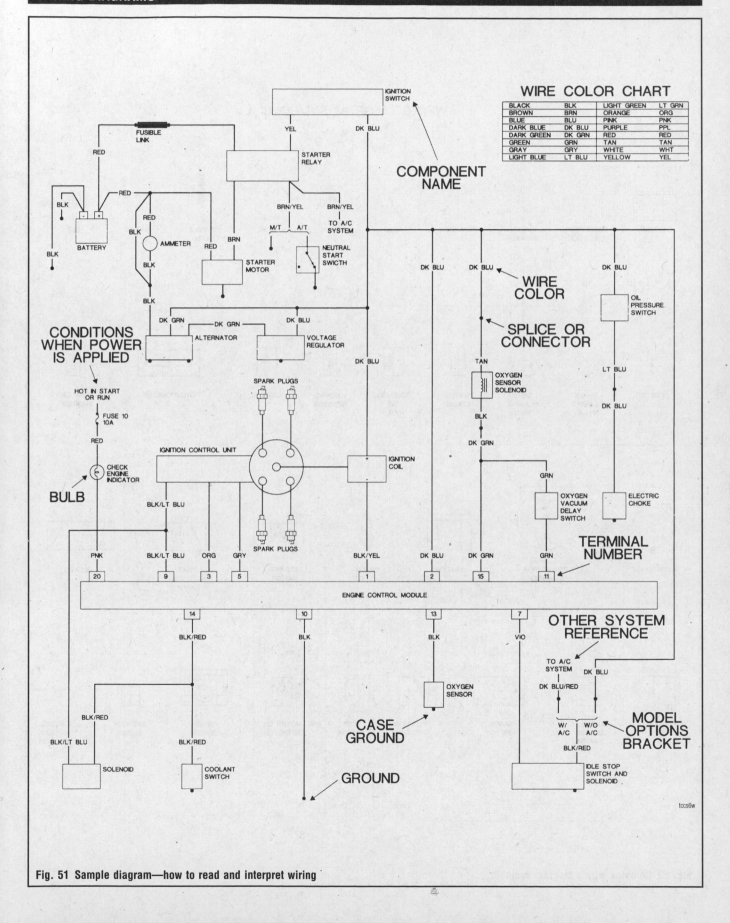

Fig. 51 Sample diagram—how to read and interpret wiring

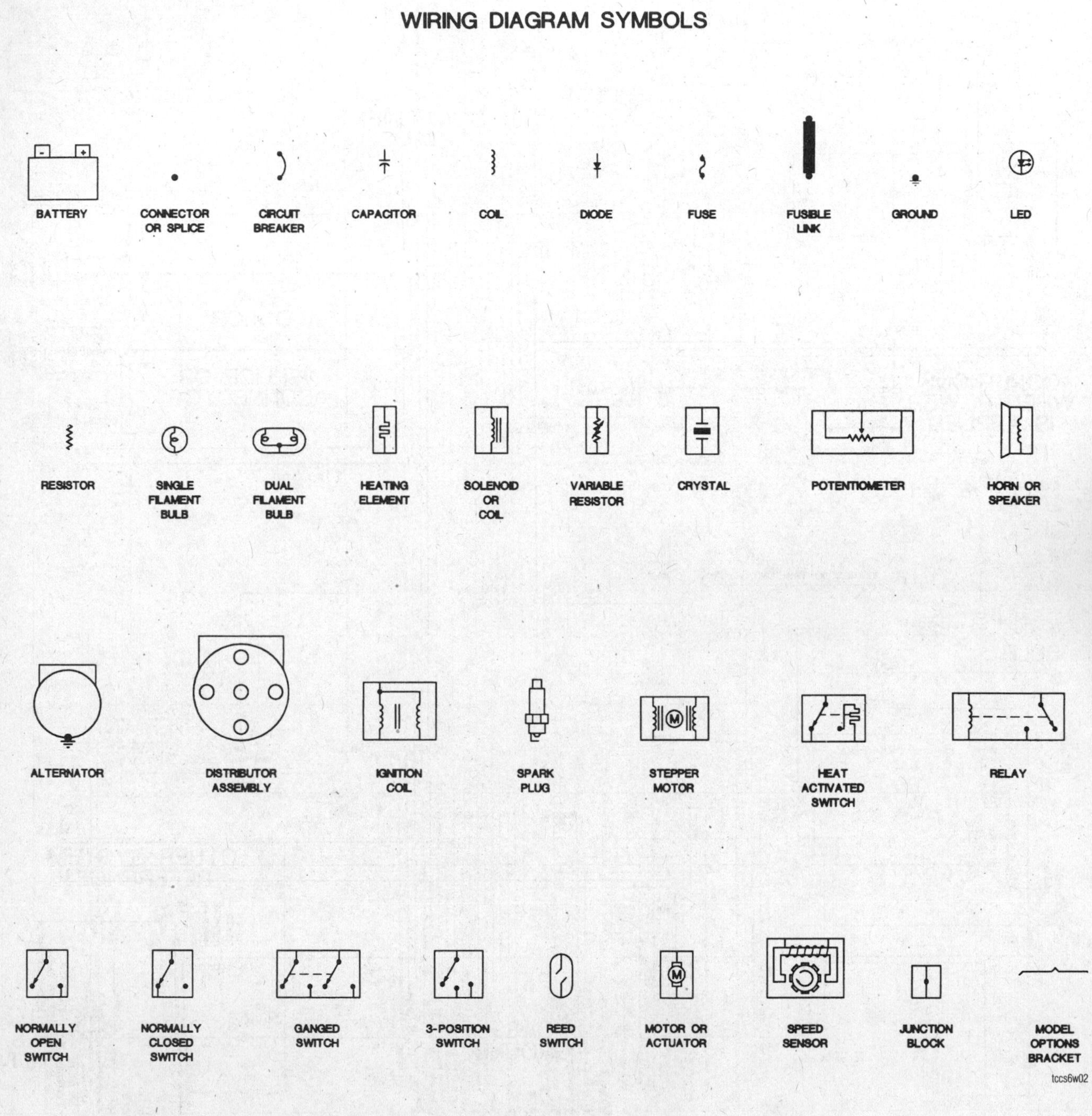

WIRING DIAGRAM SYMBOLS

BATTERY	CONNECTOR OR SPLICE	CIRCUIT BREAKER	CAPACITOR	COIL	DIODE	FUSE	FUSIBLE LINK	GROUND	LED

RESISTOR	SINGLE FILAMENT BULB	DUAL FILAMENT BULB	HEATING ELEMENT	SOLENOID OR COIL	VARIABLE RESISTOR	CRYSTAL	POTENTIOMETER	HORN OR SPEAKER

ALTERNATOR	DISTRIBUTOR ASSEMBLY	IGNITION COIL	SPARK PLUG	STEPPER MOTOR	HEAT ACTIVATED SWITCH	RELAY

NORMALLY OPEN SWITCH	NORMALLY CLOSED SWITCH	GANGED SWITCH	3-POSITION SWITCH	REED SWITCH	MOTOR OR ACTUATOR	SPEED SENSOR	JUNCTION BLOCK	MODEL OPTIONS BRACKET

tccs6w02

Fig. 52 Common wiring diagram symbols

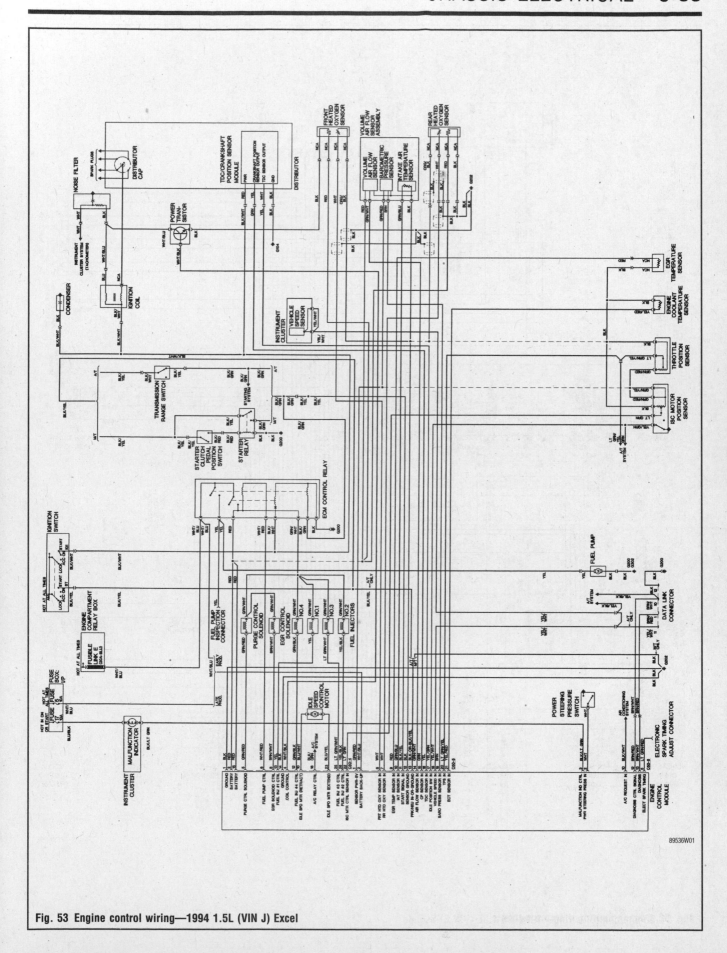

Fig. 53 Engine control wiring—1994 1.5L (VIN J) Excel

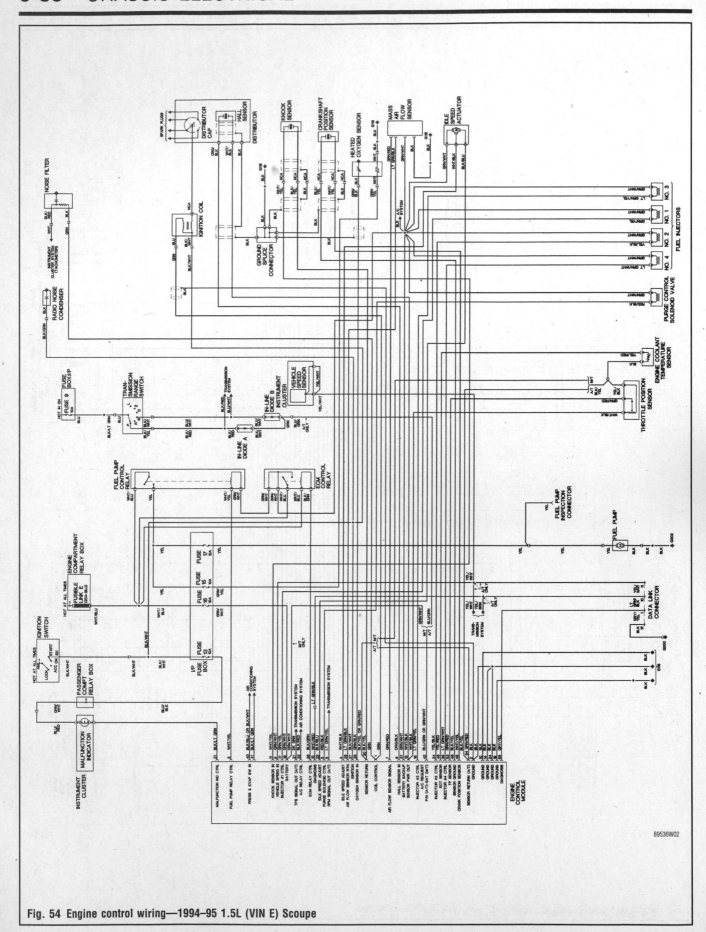

Fig. 54 Engine control wiring—1994–95 1.5L (VIN E) Scoupe

89536W02

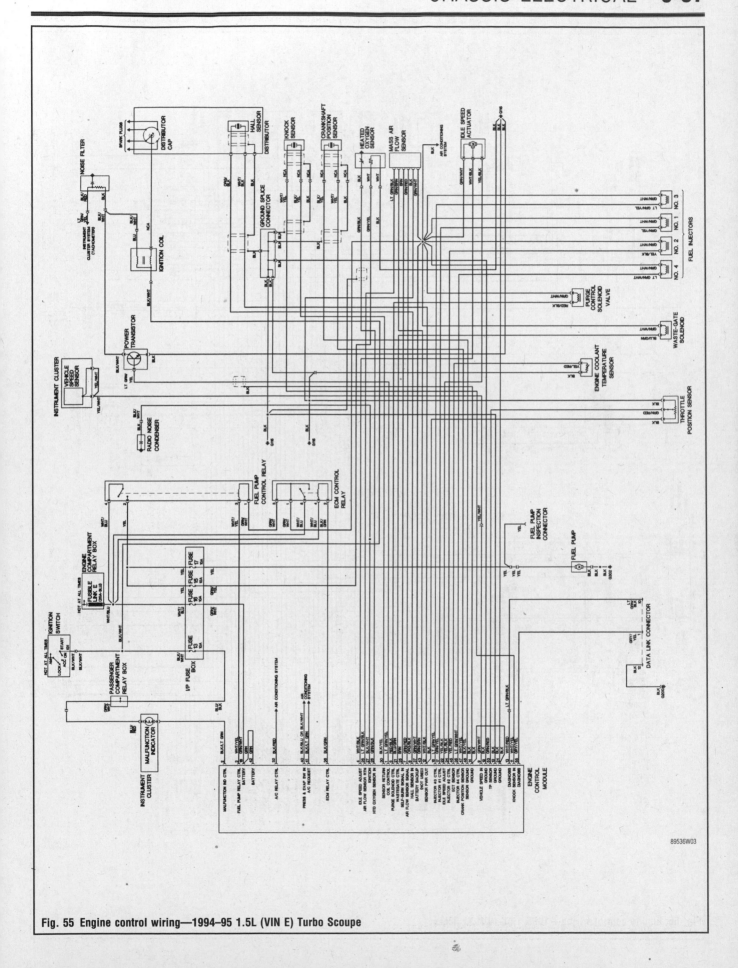

Fig. 55 Engine control wiring—1994-95 1.5L (VIN E) Turbo Scoupe

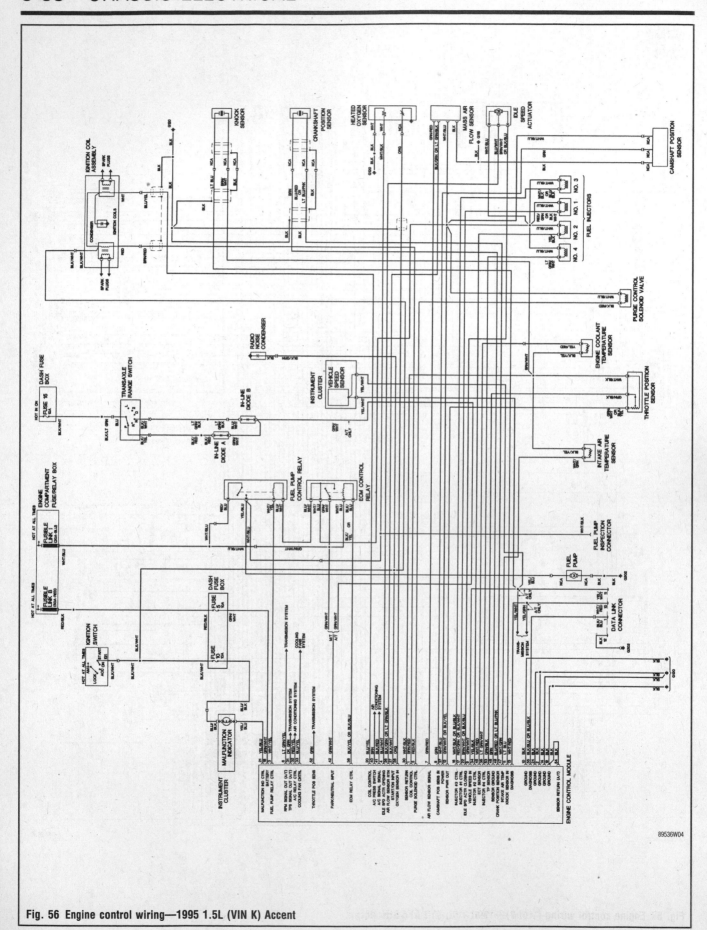

Fig. 56 Engine control wiring—1995 1.5L (VIN K) Accent

89536W04

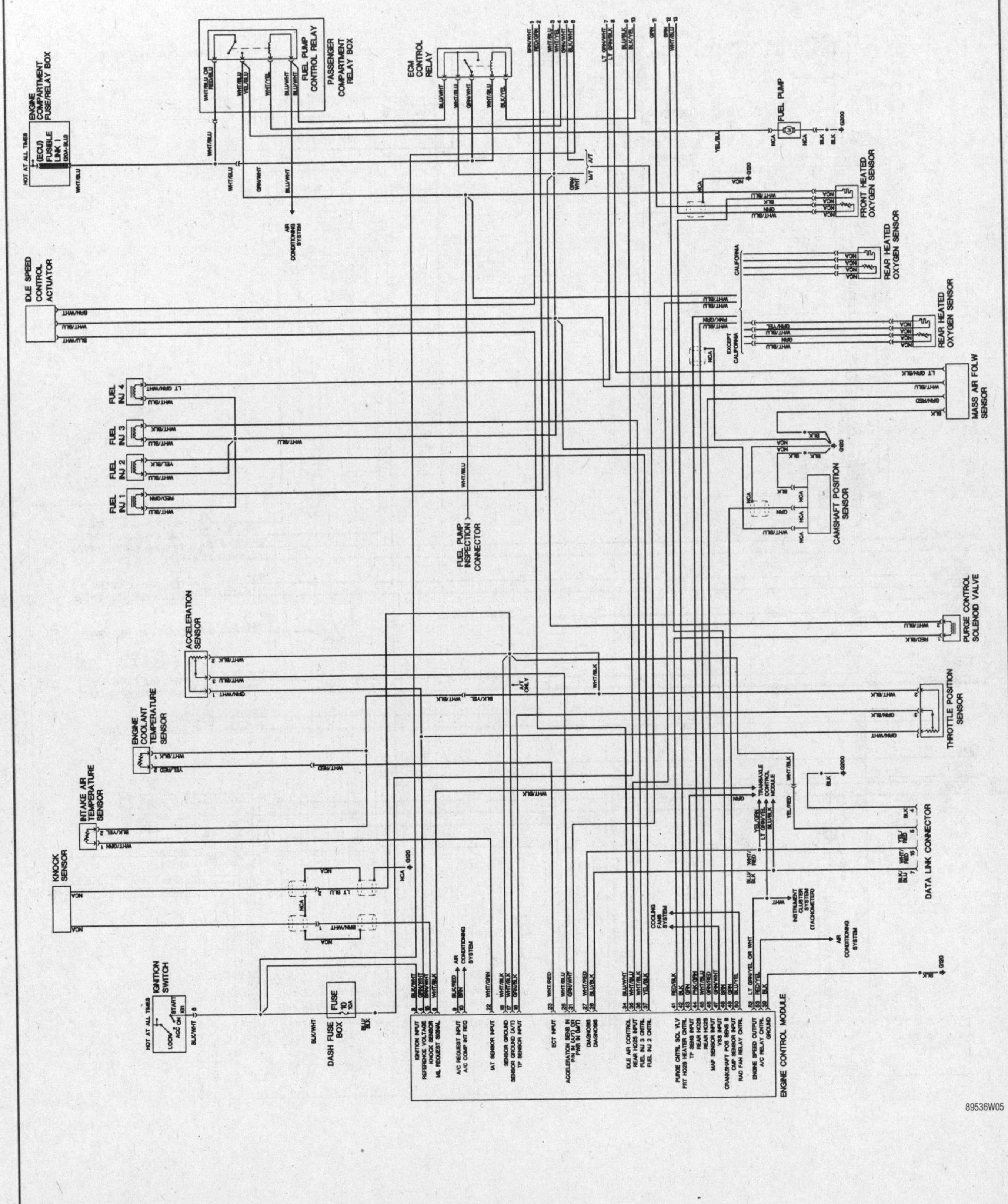

Fig. 57 Engine control wiring (1 of 2)—1996 1.5L (VIN K) SOHC Accent

89536W05

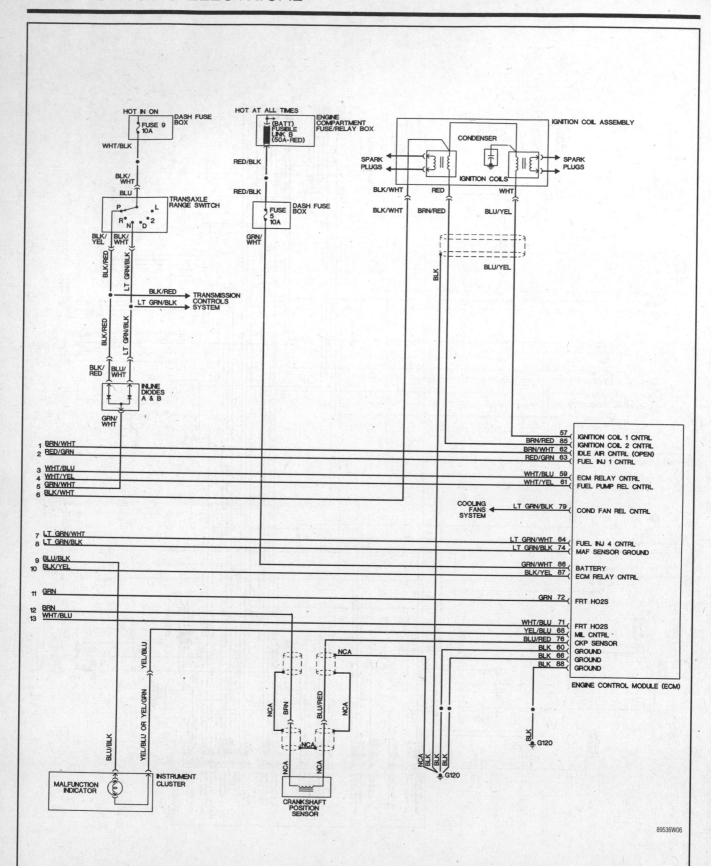

Fig. 58 Engine control wiring (2 of 2)—1996 1.5L (VIN K) SOHC Accent

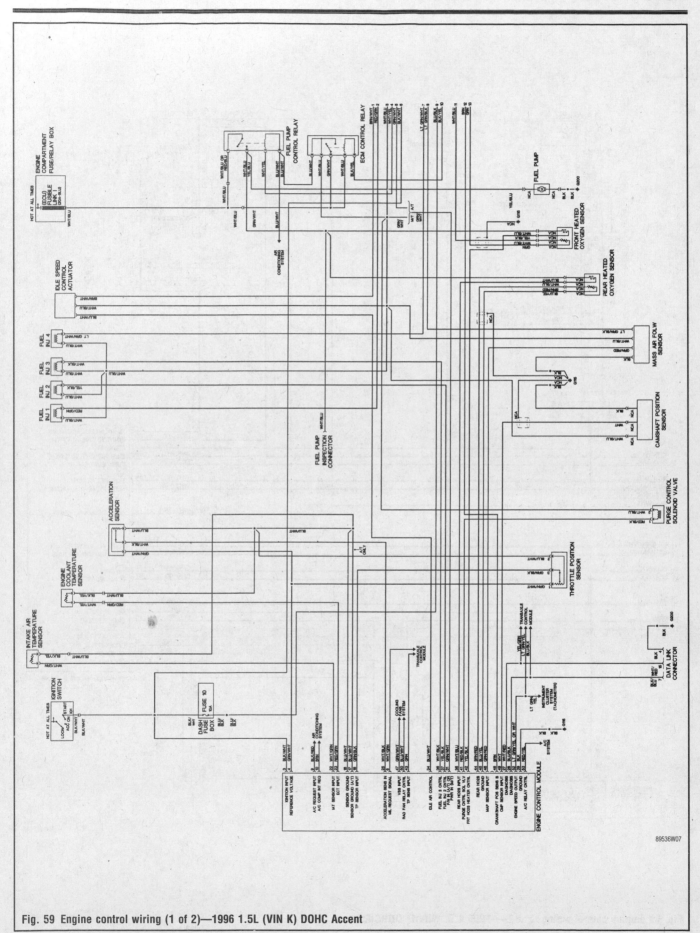

Fig. 59 Engine control wiring (1 of 2)—1996 1.5L (VIN K) DOHC Accent

89536W07

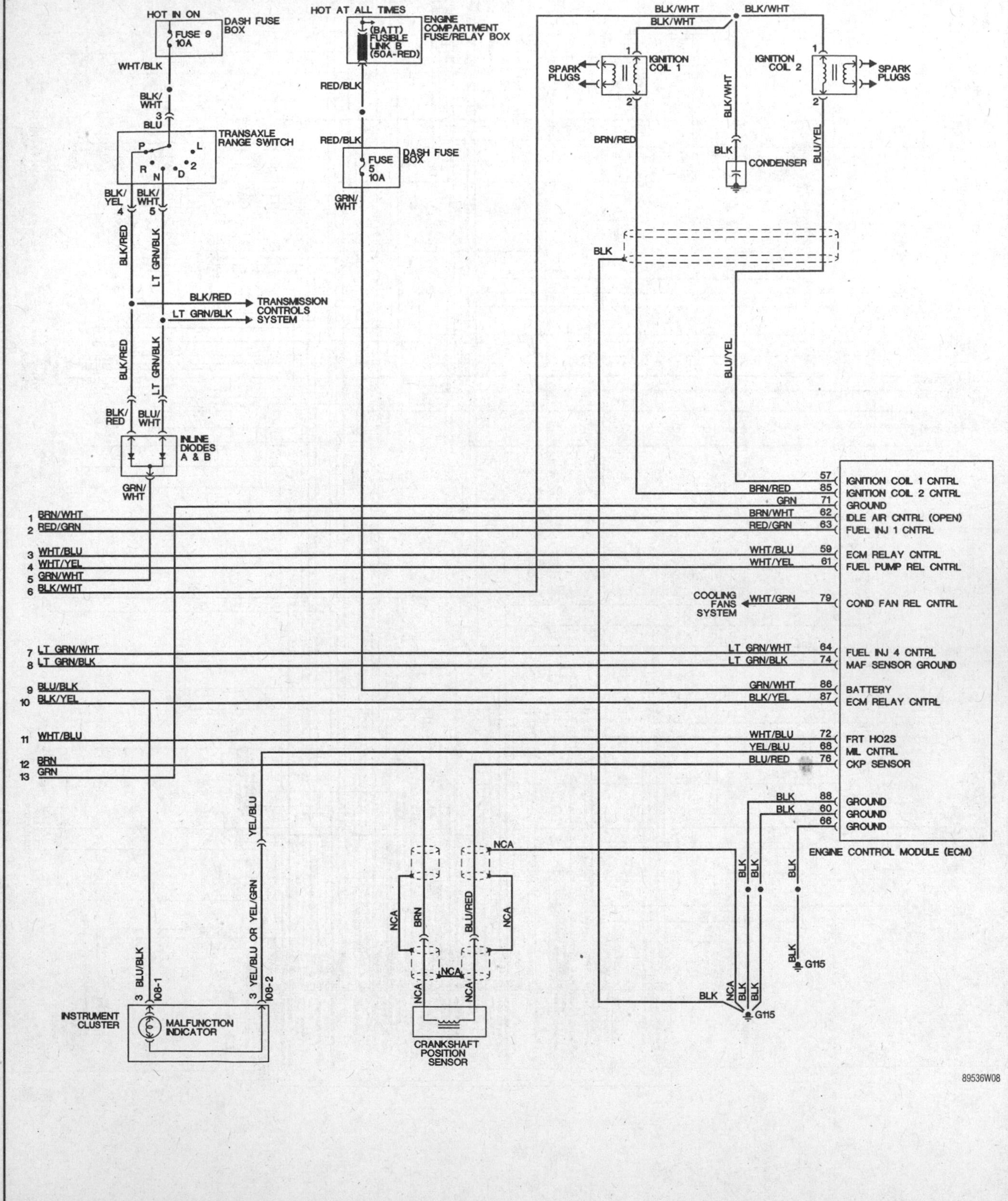

Fig. 60 Engine control wiring (2 of 2)—1996 1.5L (VIN K) DOHC Accent

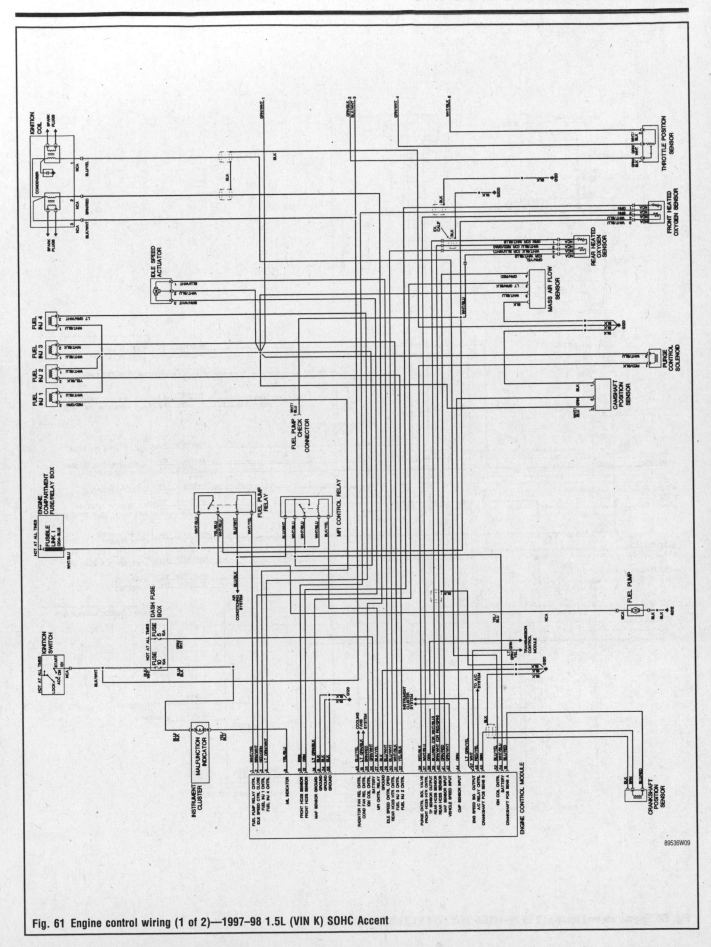

Fig. 61 Engine control wiring (1 of 2)—1997–98 1.5L (VIN K) SOHC Accent

89536W09

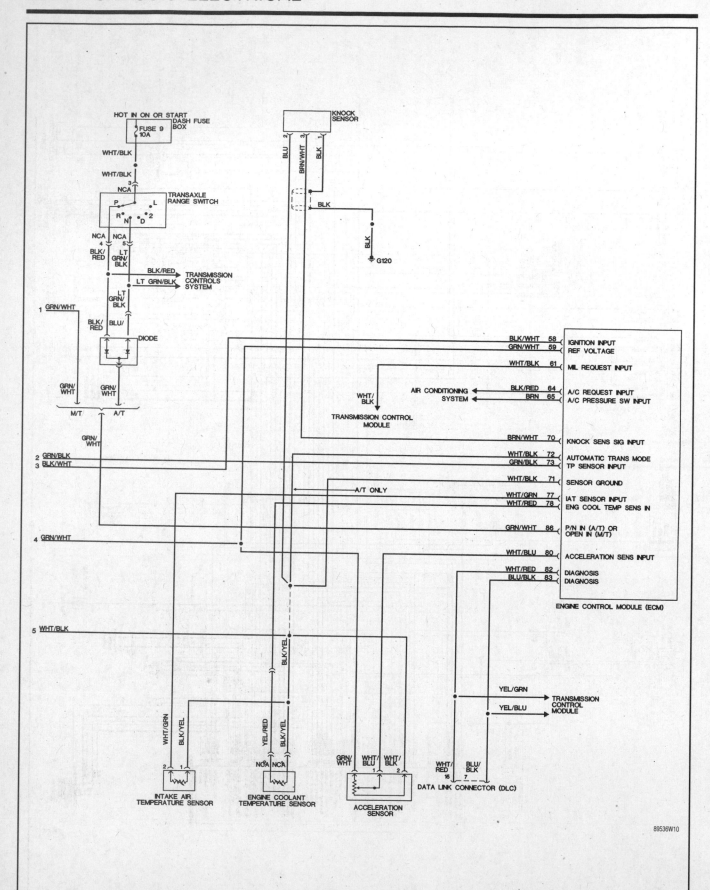

Fig. 62 Engine control wiring (2 of 2)—1997-98 1.5L (VIN K) SOHC Accent

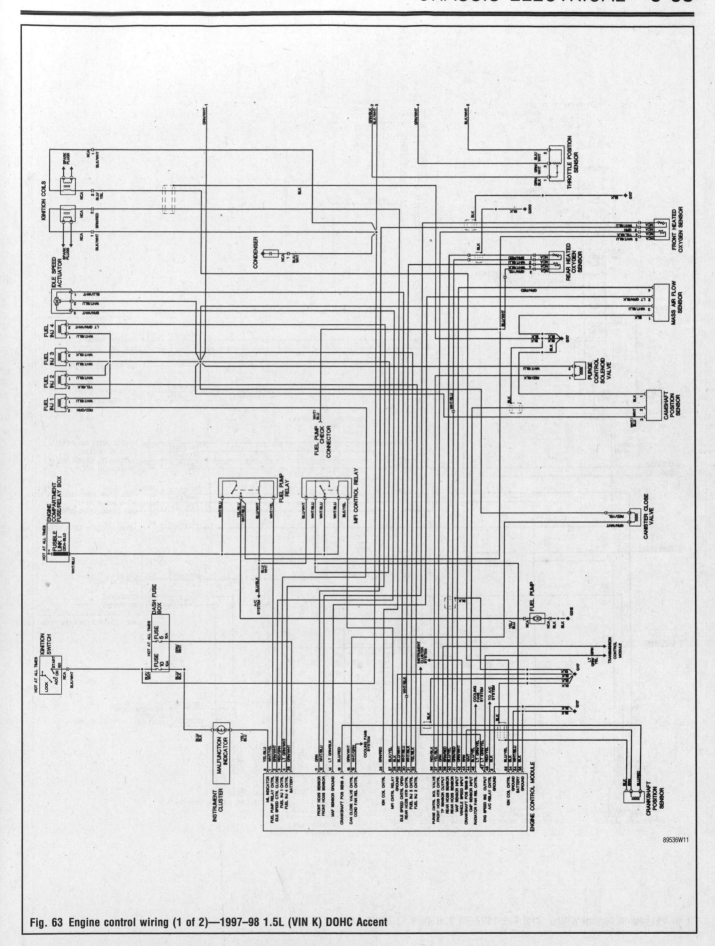

Fig. 63 Engine control wiring (1 of 2)—1997-98 1.5L (VIN K) DOHC Accent

89536W11

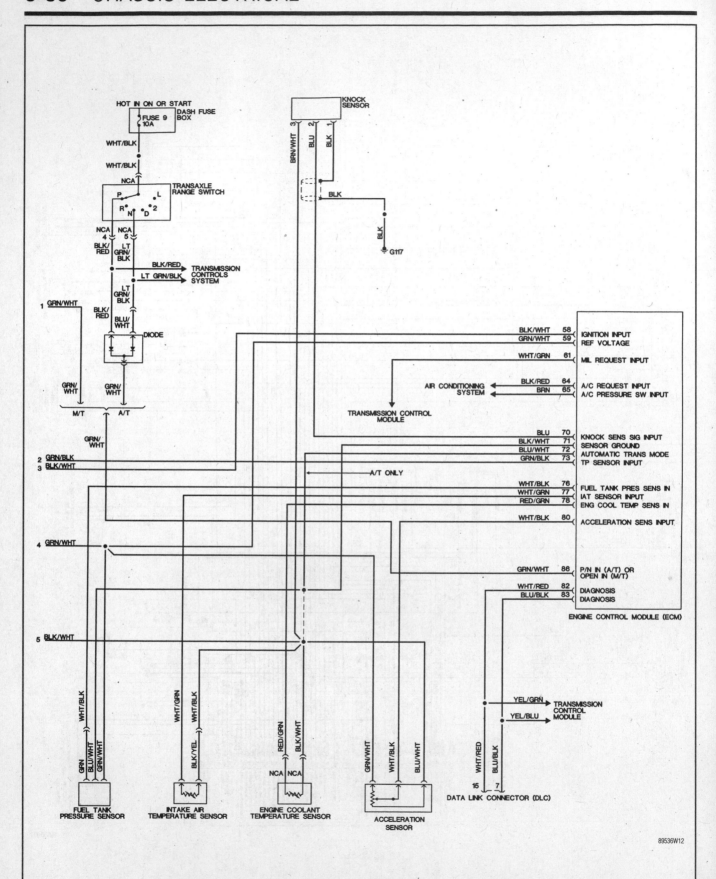

Fig. 64 Engine control wiring (2 of 2)—1997–98 1.5L (VIN K) DOHC Accent

89536W12

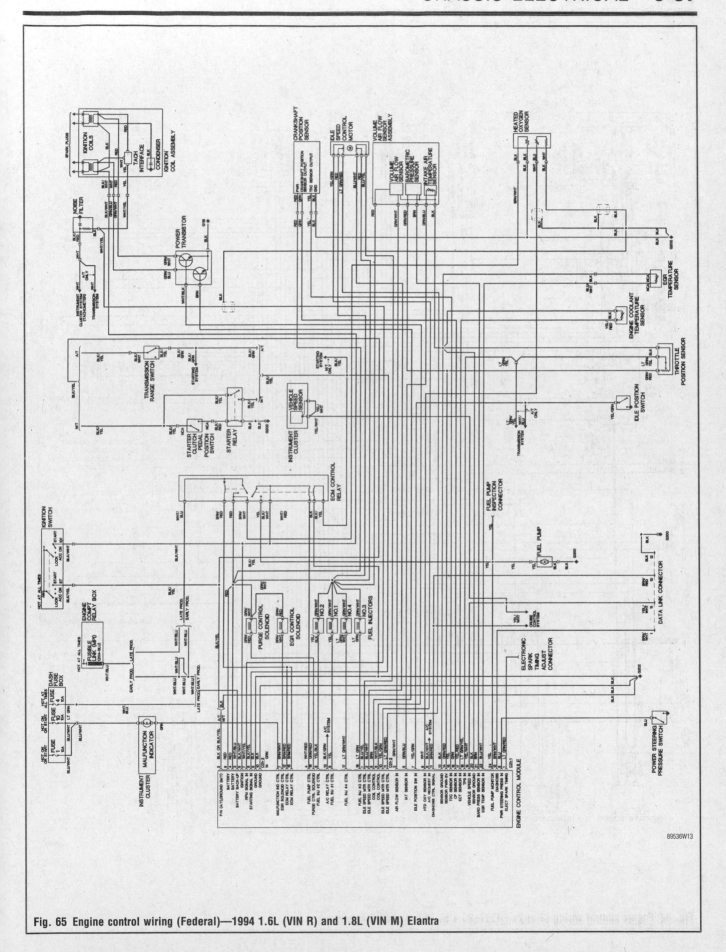

Fig. 65 Engine control wiring (Federal)—1994 1.6L (VIN R) and 1.8L (VIN M) Elantra

89536W13

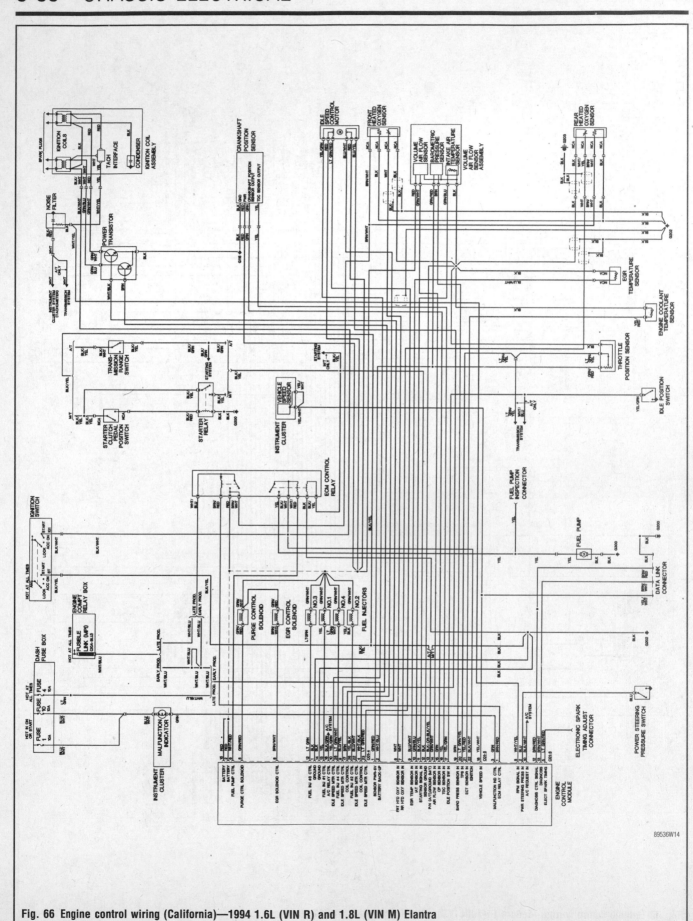

Fig. 66 Engine control wiring (California)—1994 1.6L (VIN R) and 1.8L (VIN M) Elantra

89536W14

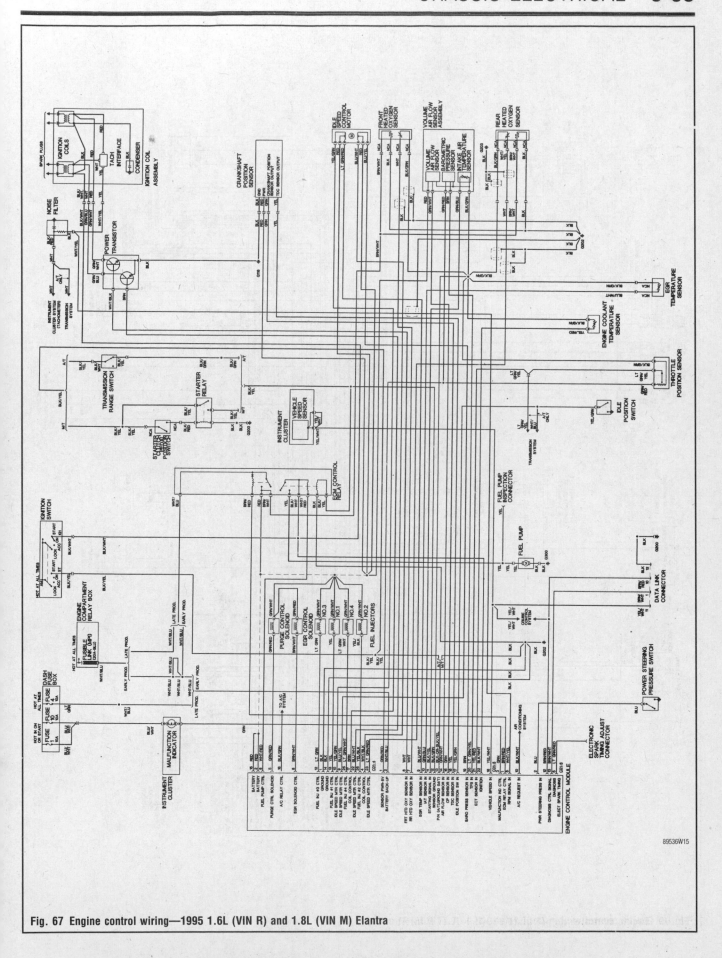

Fig. 67 Engine control wiring—1995 1.6L (VIN R) and 1.8L (VIN M) Elantra

89536W15

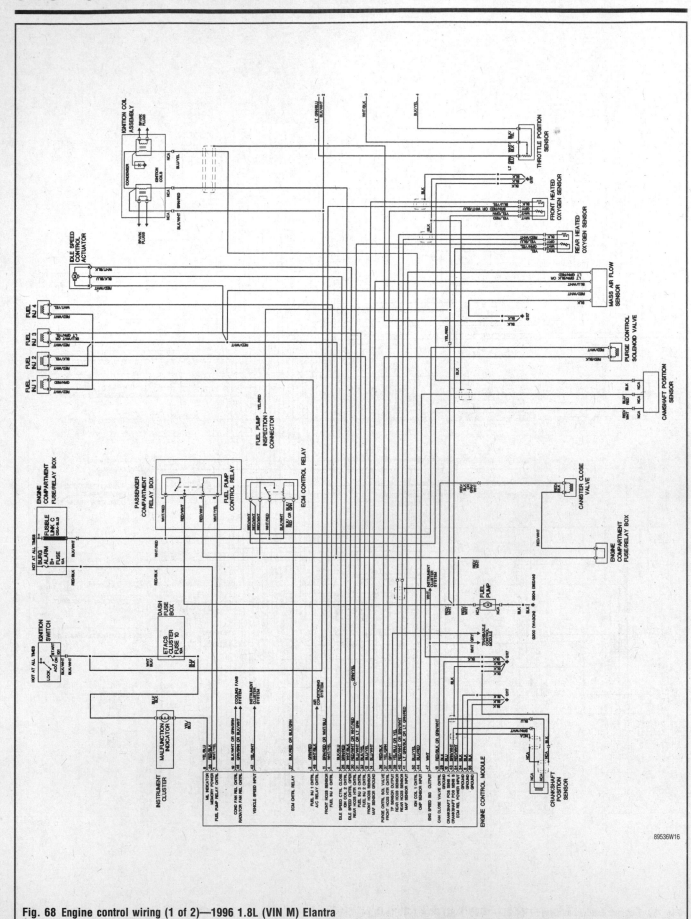

Fig. 68 Engine control wiring (1 of 2)—1996 1.8L (VIN M) Elantra

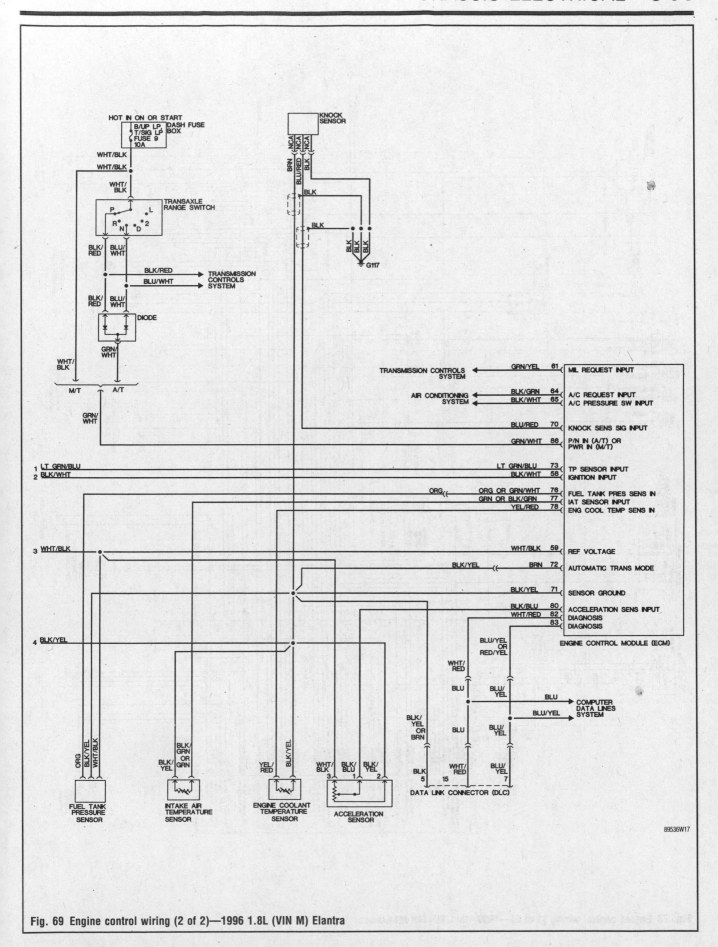

Fig. 69 Engine control wiring (2 of 2)—1996 1.8L (VIN M) Elantra

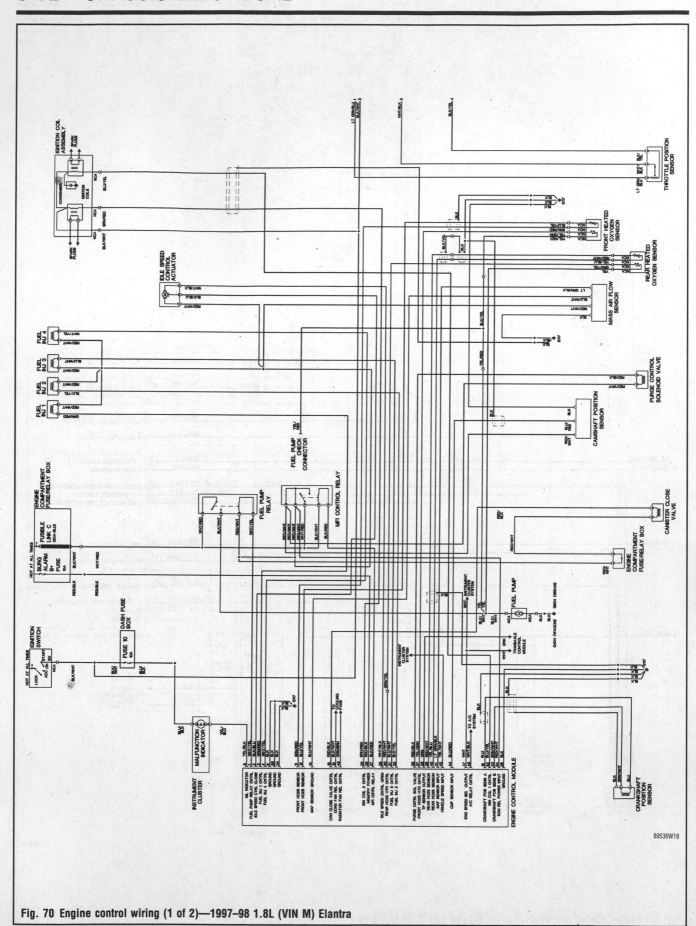

Fig. 70 Engine control wiring (1 of 2)—1997-98 1.8L (VIN M) Elantra

89536W18

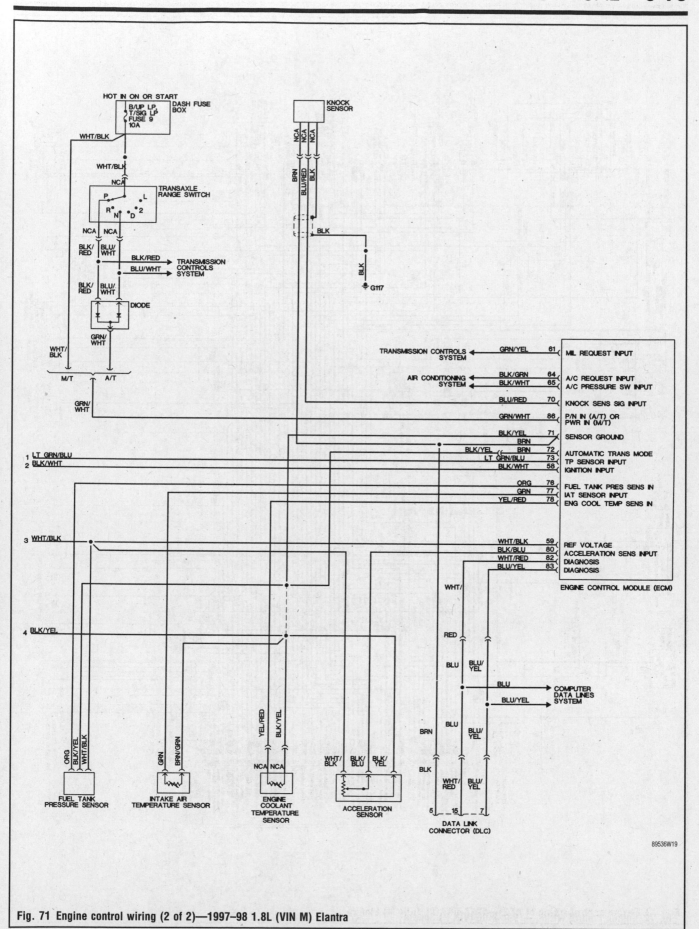

Fig. 71 Engine control wiring (2 of 2)—1997–98 1.8L (VIN M) Elantra

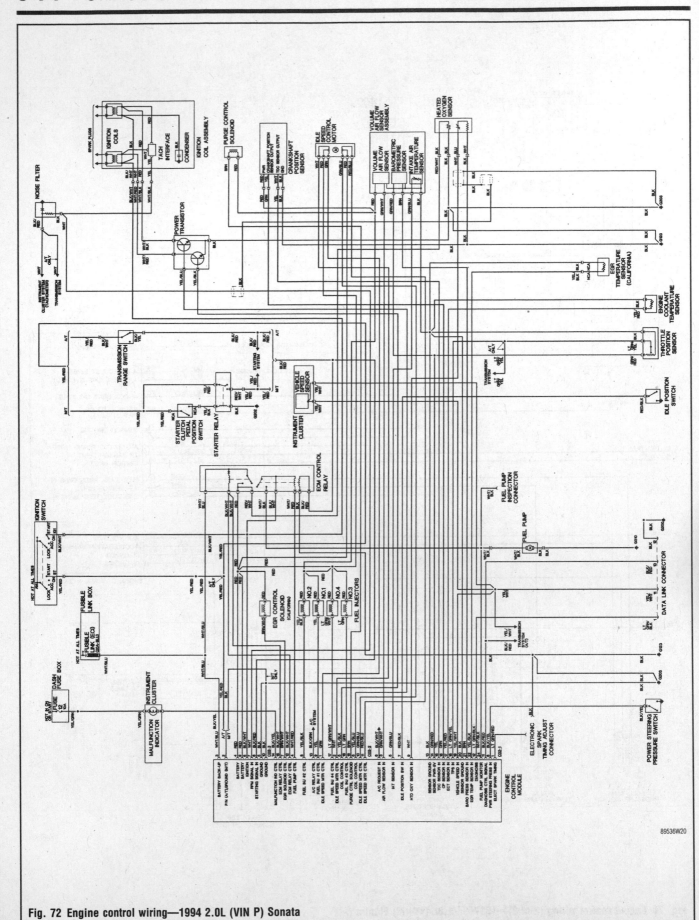

Fig. 72 Engine control wiring—1994 2.0L (VIN P) Sonata

89536W20

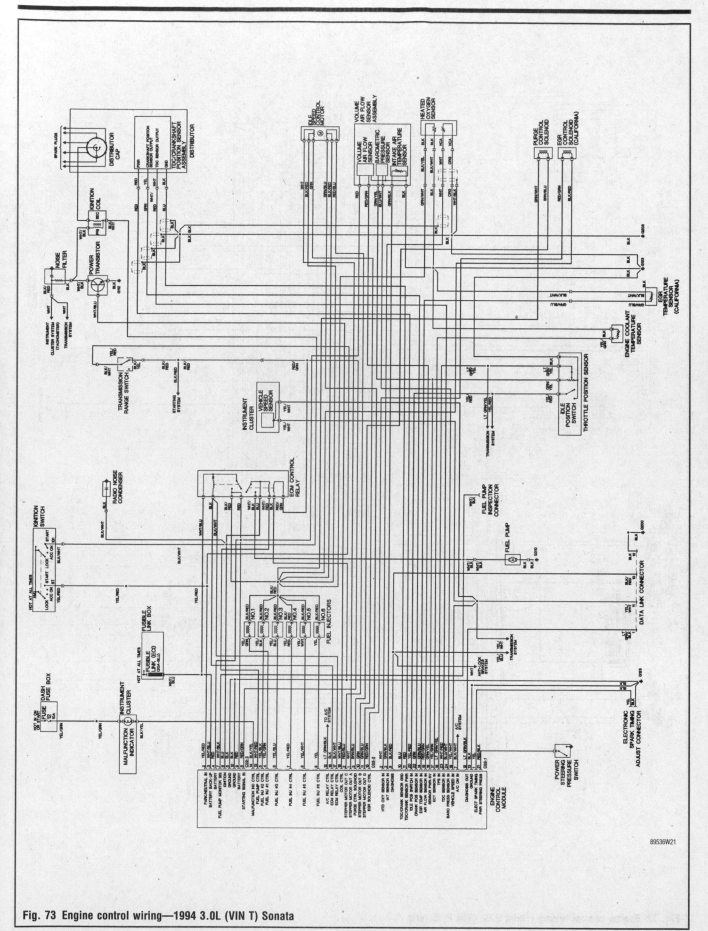

Fig. 73 Engine control wiring—1994 3.0L (VIN T) Sonata

89536W21

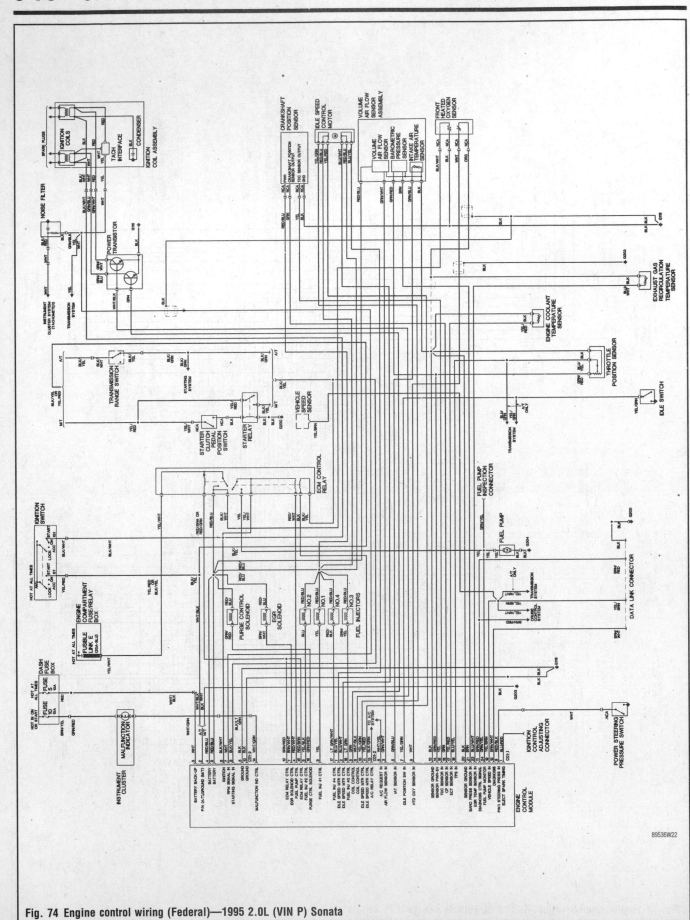

Fig. 74 Engine control wiring (Federal)—1995 2.0L (VIN P) Sonata

89536W22

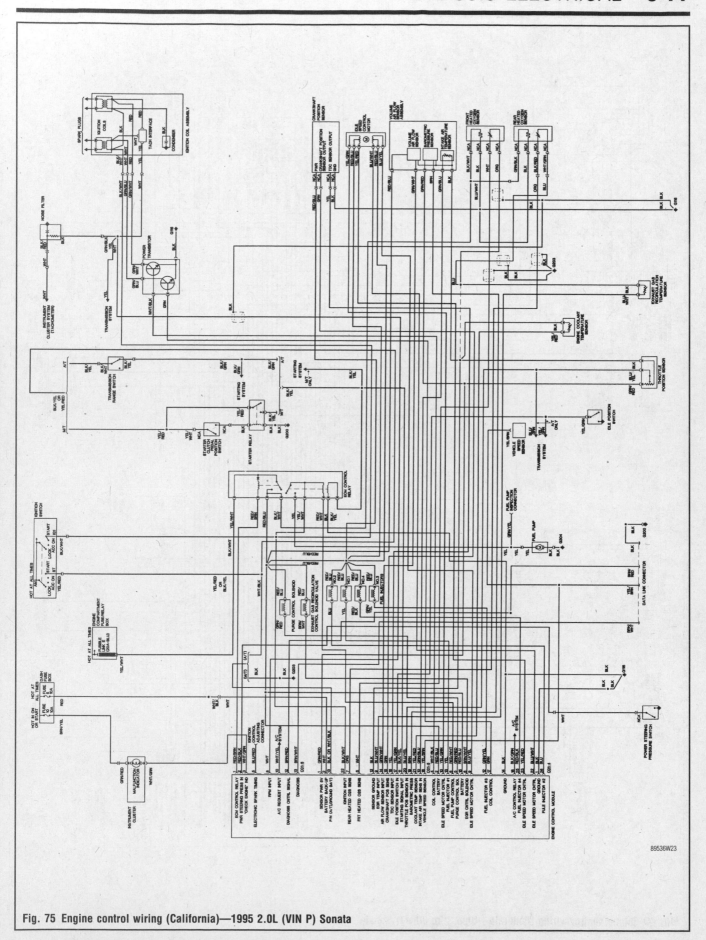

Fig. 75 Engine control wiring (California)—1995 2.0L (VIN P) Sonata

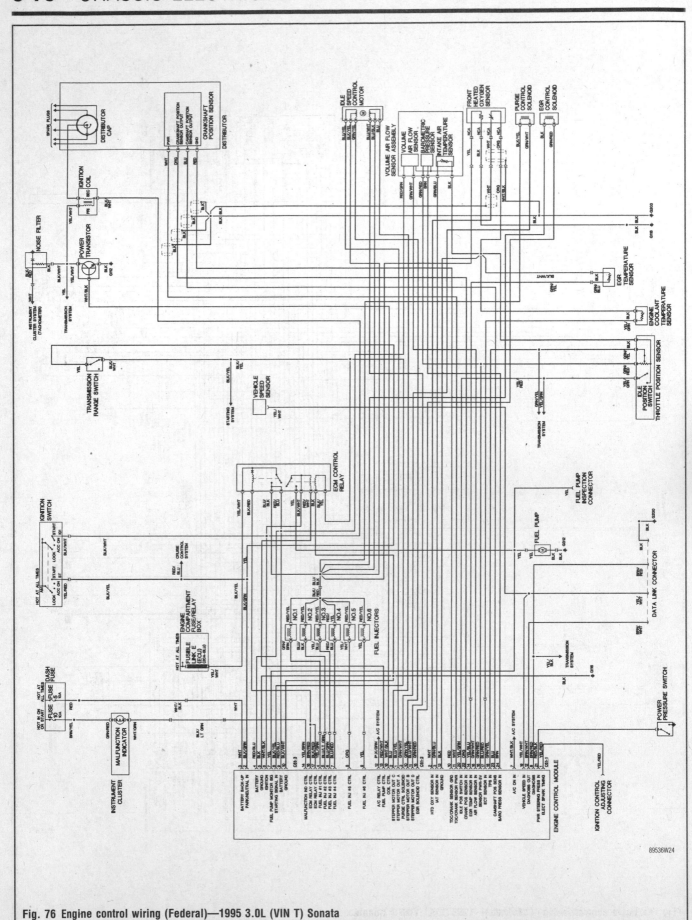

Fig. 76 Engine control wiring (Federal)—1995 3.0L (VIN T) Sonata

89536W24

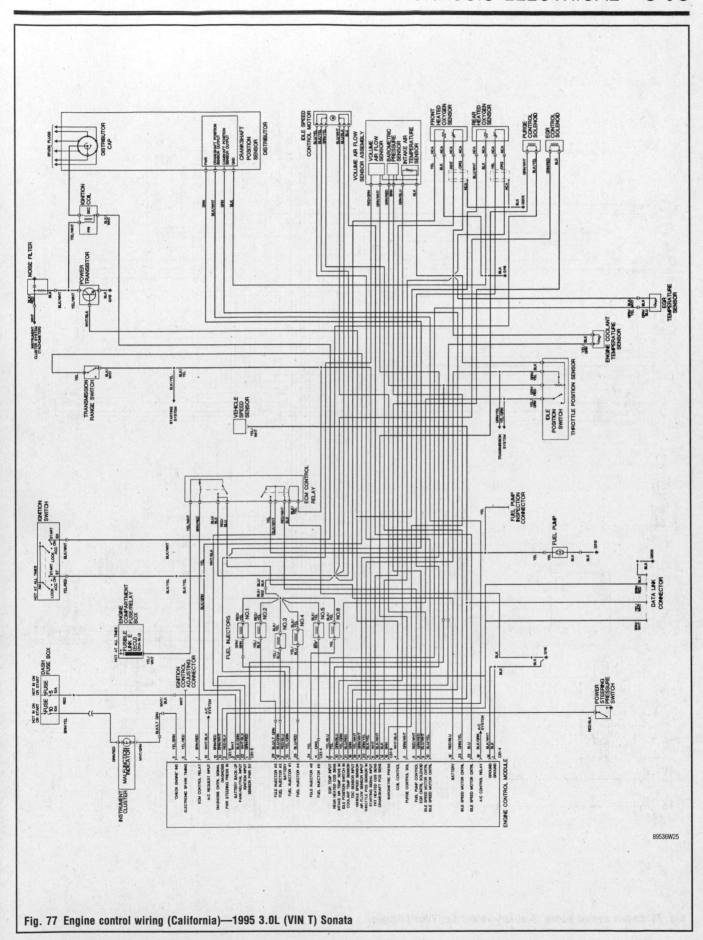

Fig. 77 Engine control wiring (California)—1995 3.0L (VIN T) Sonata

89536W25

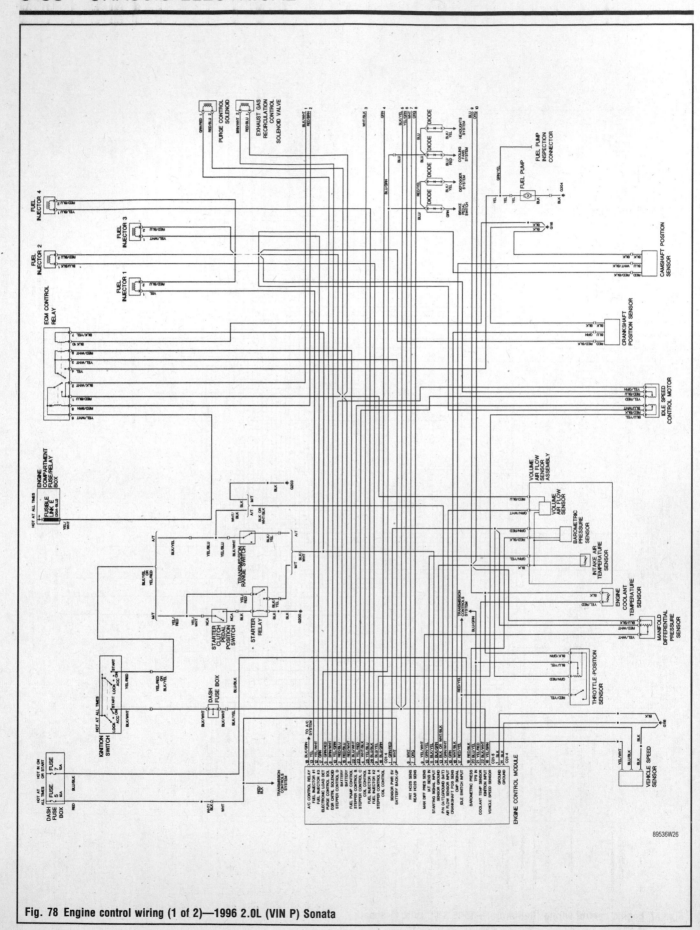

Fig. 78 Engine control wiring (1 of 2)—1996 2.0L (VIN P) Sonata

89536W26

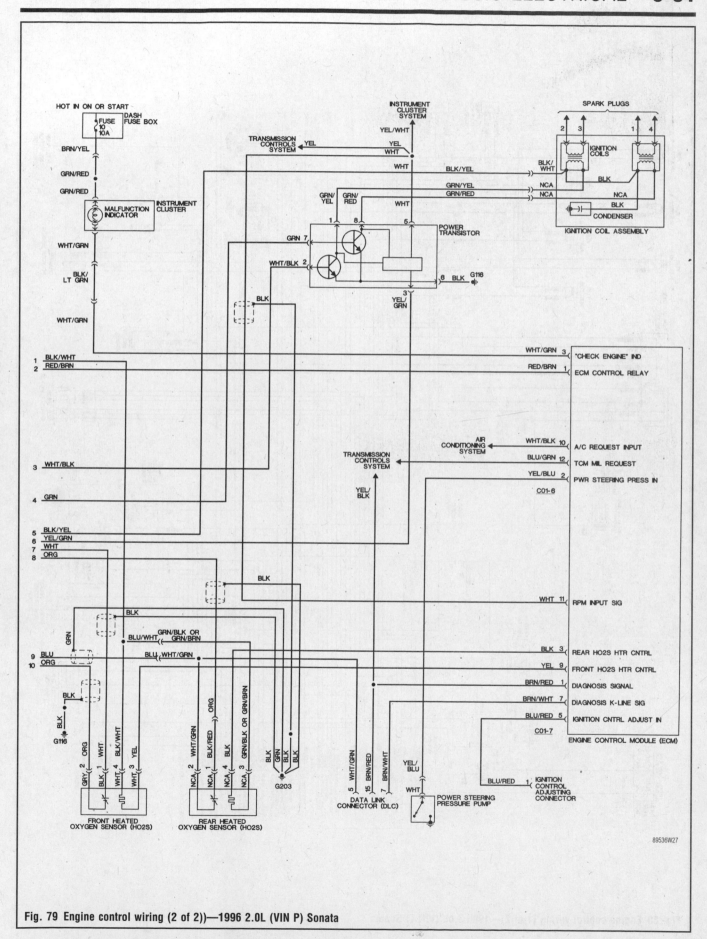

Fig. 79 Engine control wiring (2 of 2)—1996 2.0L (VIN P) Sonata

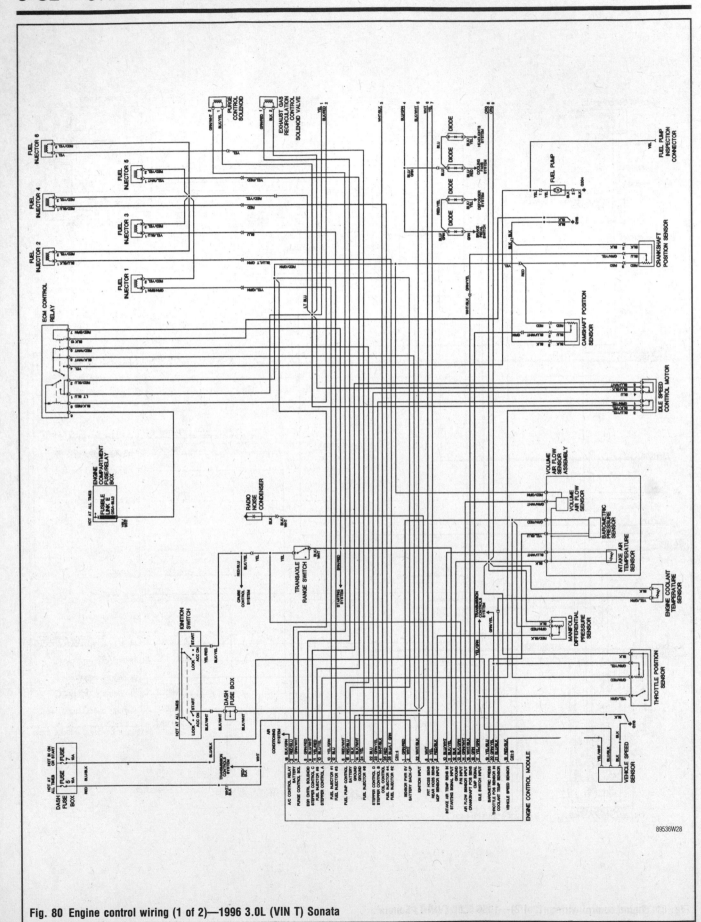

Fig. 80 Engine control wiring (1 of 2)—1996 3.0L (VIN T) Sonata

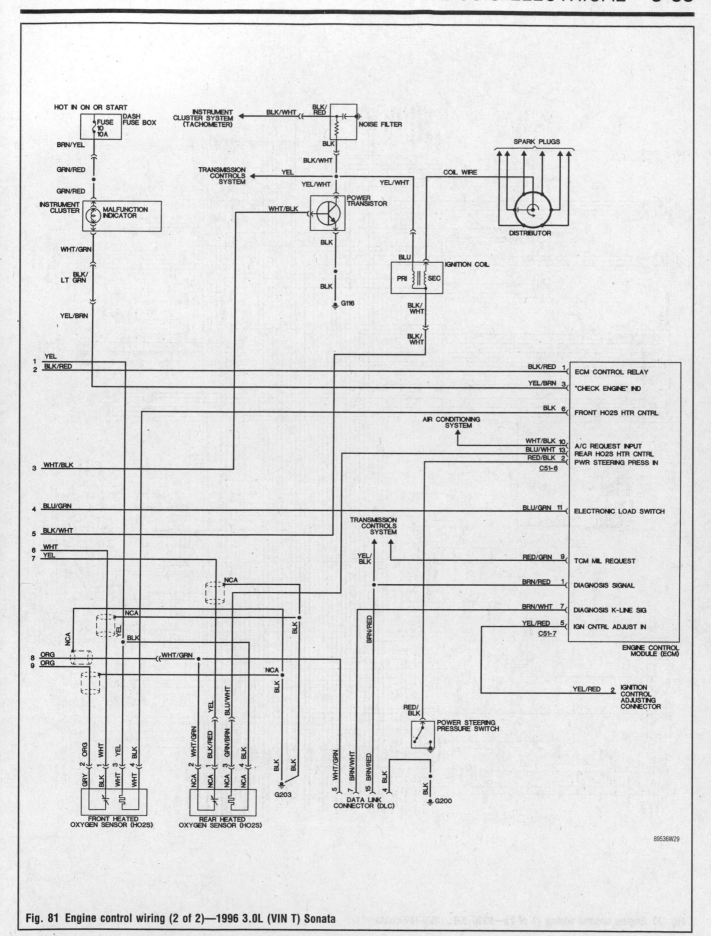

Fig. 81 Engine control wiring (2 of 2)—1996 3.0L (VIN T) Sonata

89536W29

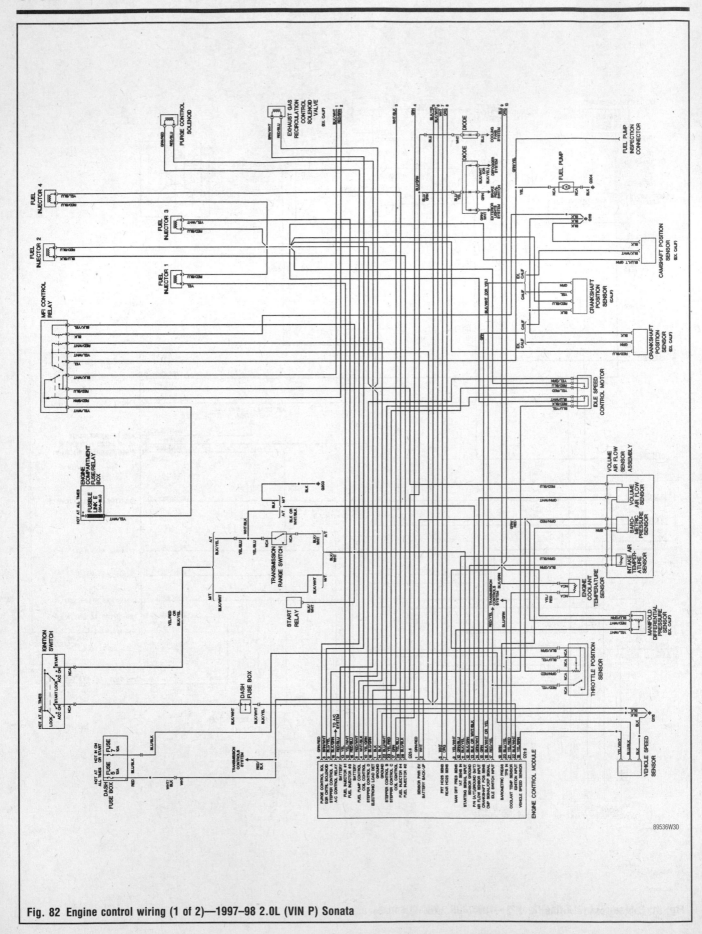

Fig. 82 Engine control wiring (1 of 2)—1997-98 2.0L (VIN P) Sonata

89536W30

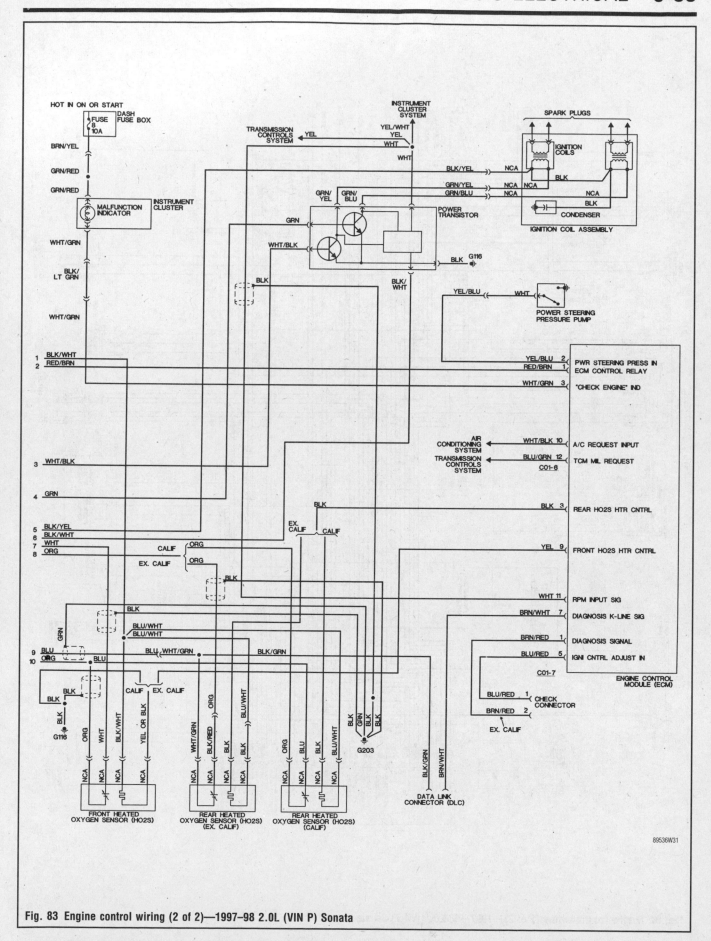

Fig. 83 Engine control wiring (2 of 2)—1997-98 2.0L (VIN P) Sonata

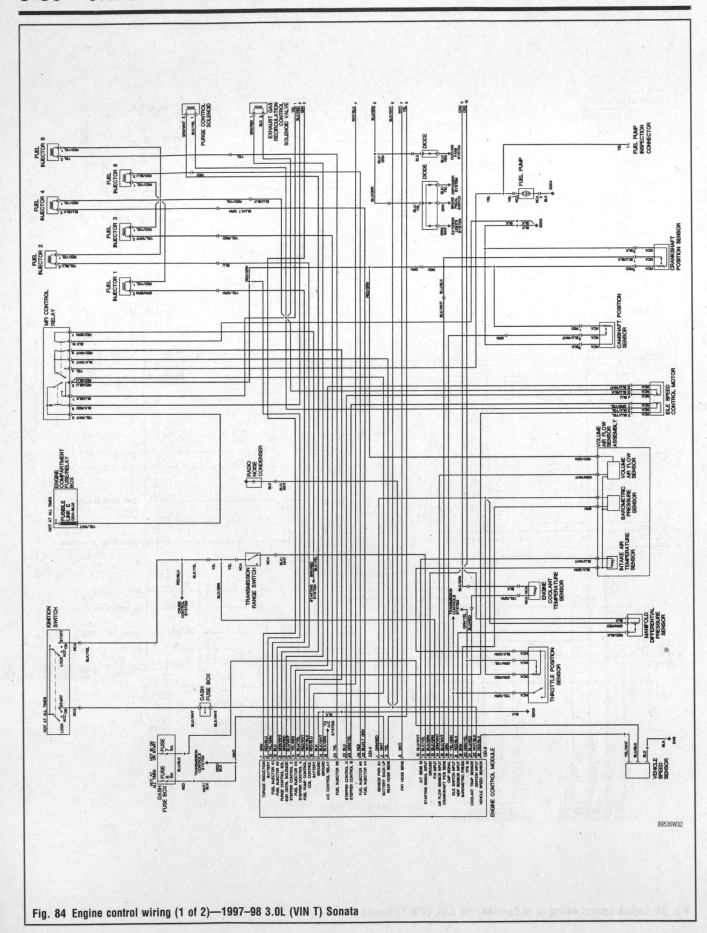

Fig. 84 Engine control wiring (1 of 2)—1997-98 3.0L (VIN T) Sonata

89536W32

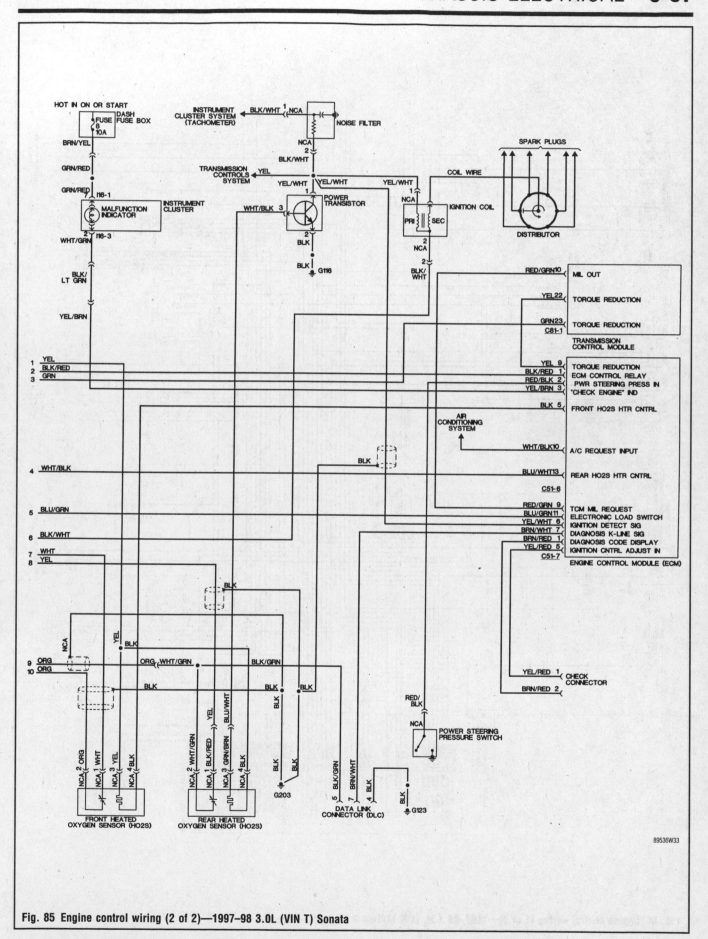

Fig. 85 Engine control wiring (2 of 2)—1997–98 3.0L (VIN T) Sonata

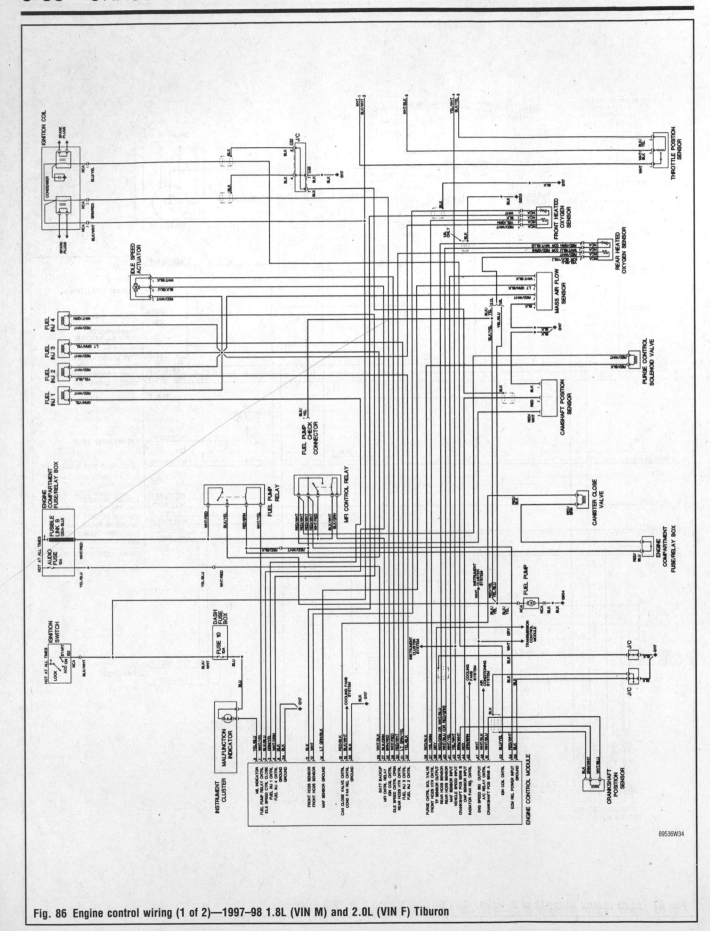

Fig. 86 Engine control wiring (1 of 2)—1997-98 1.8L (VIN M) and 2.0L (VIN F) Tiburon

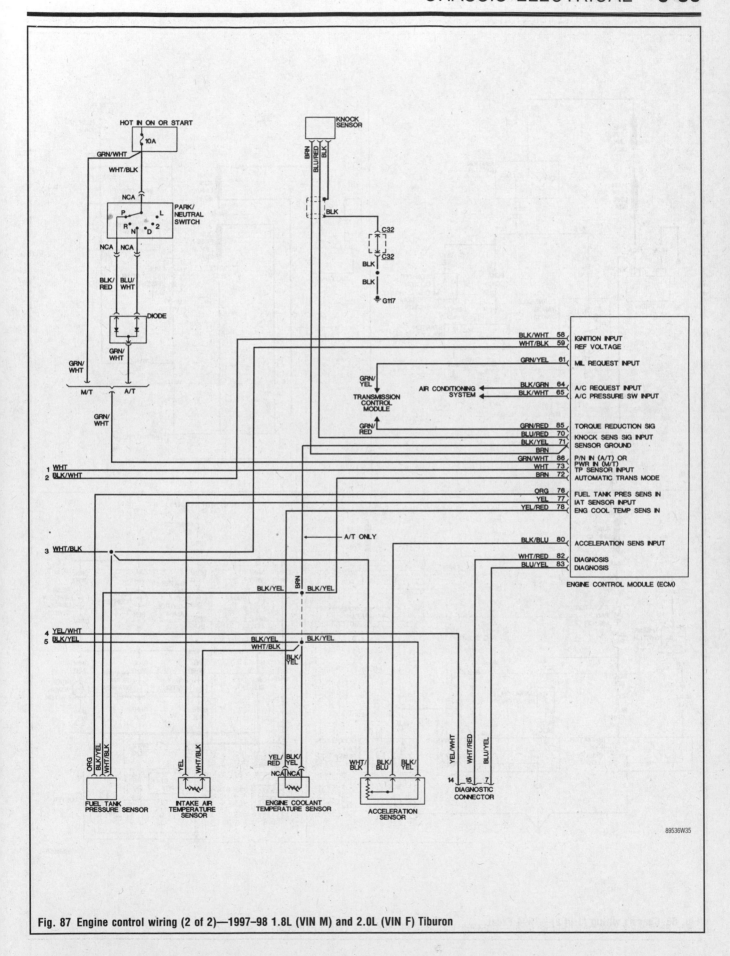

Fig. 87 Engine control wiring (2 of 2)—1997–98 1.8L (VIN M) and 2.0L (VIN F) Tiburon

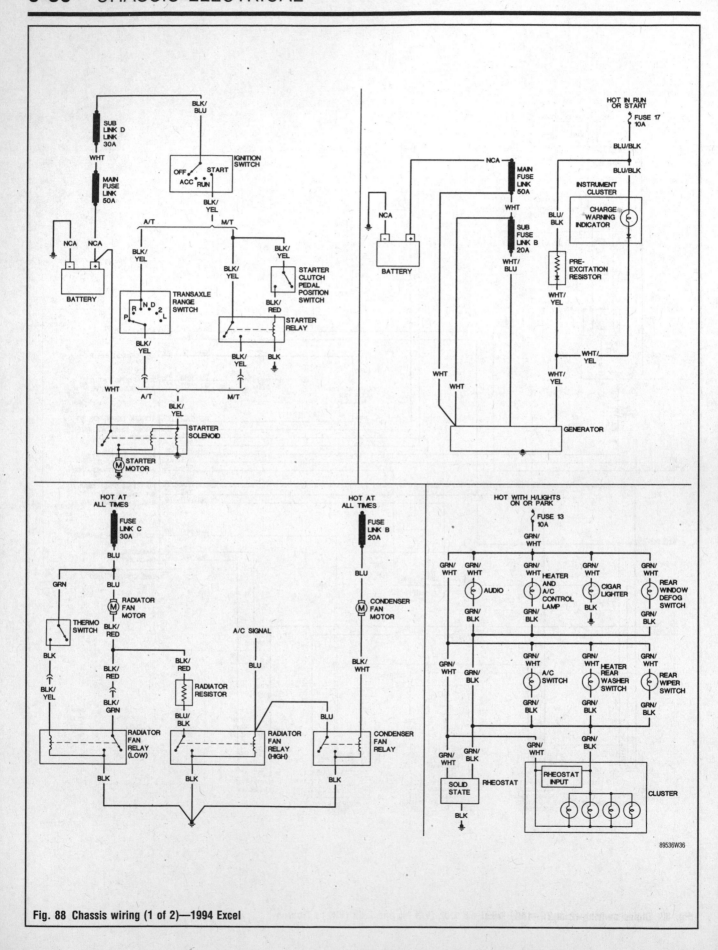

Fig. 88 Chassis wiring (1 of 2)—1994 Excel

89536W36

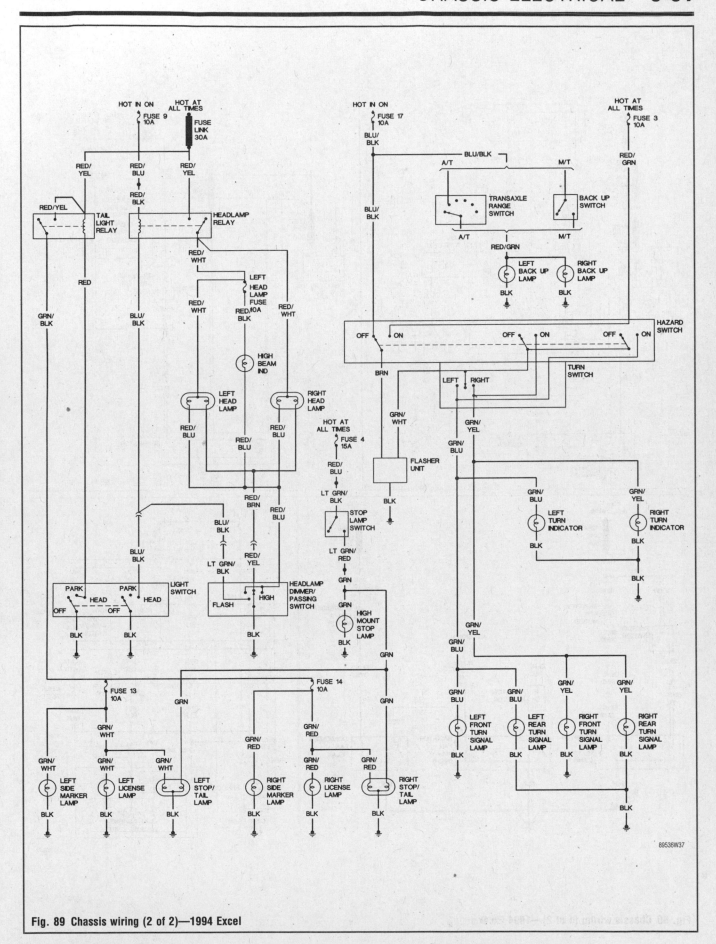

Fig. 89 Chassis wiring (2 of 2)—1994 Excel

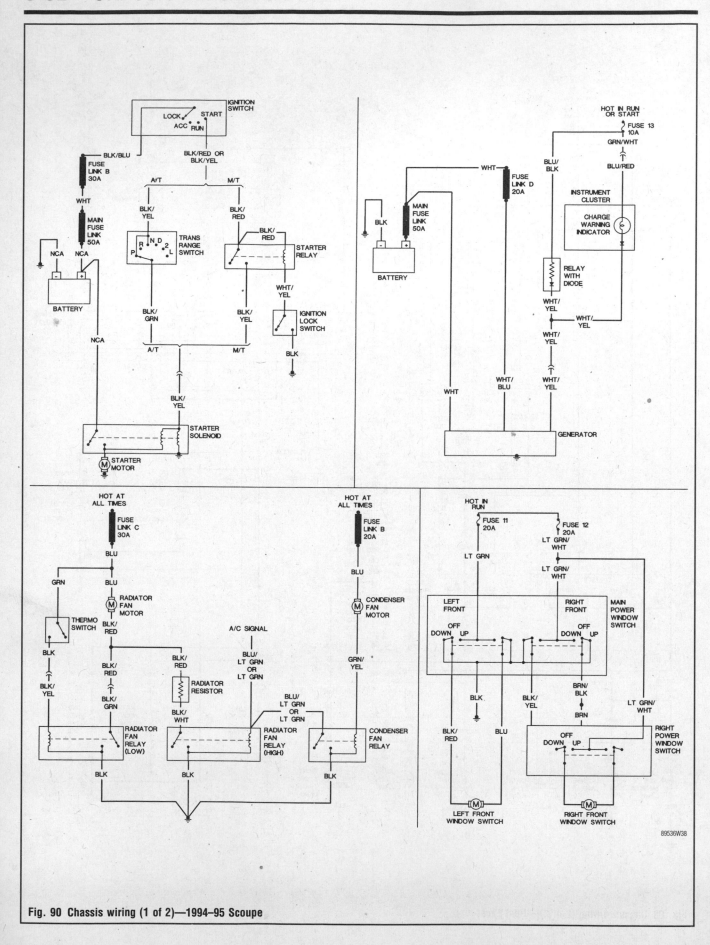

Fig. 90 Chassis wiring (1 of 2)—1994-95 Scoupe

89536W38

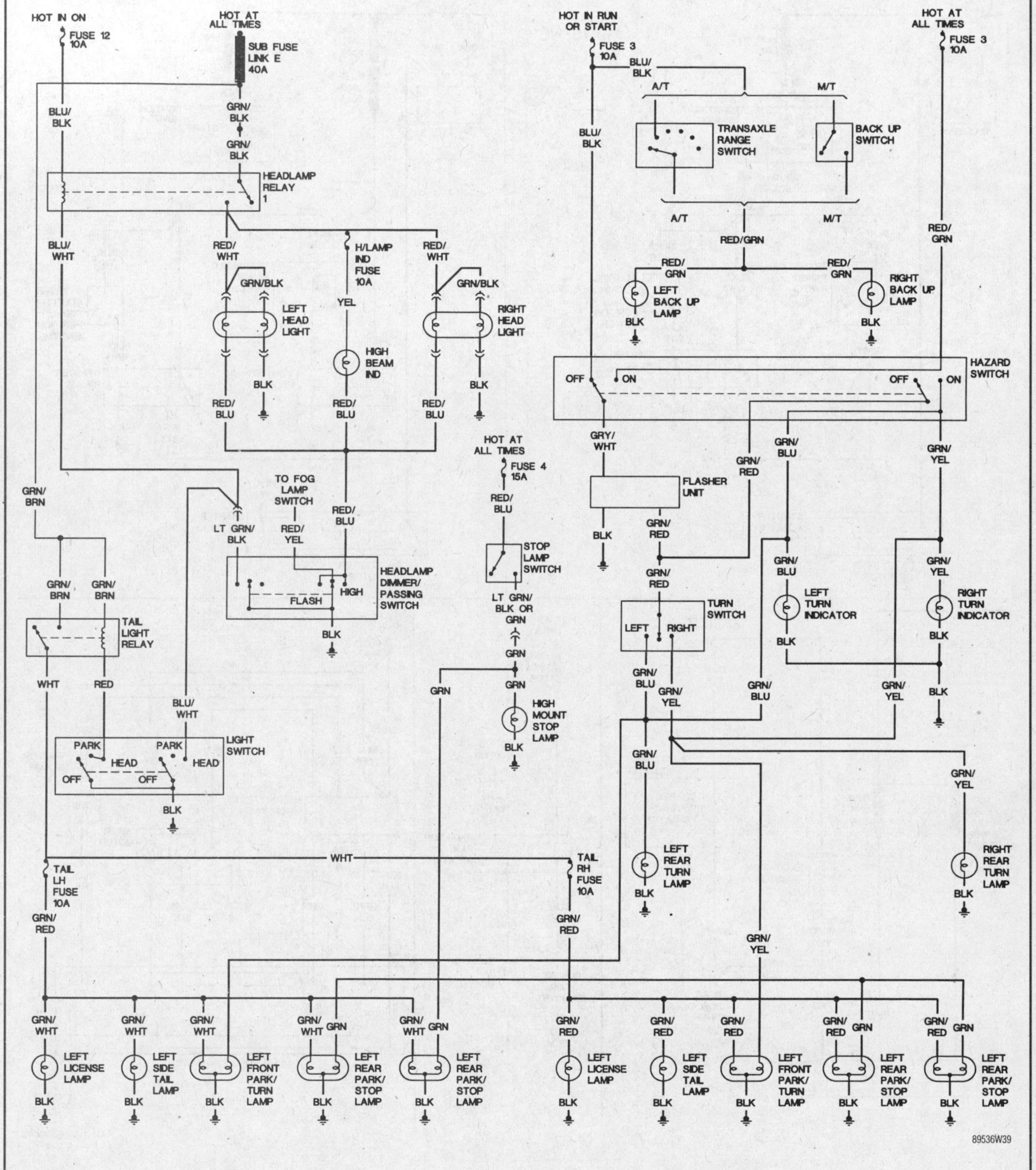

Fig. 91 Chassis wiring (2 of 2)—1994-95 Scoupe

89536W39

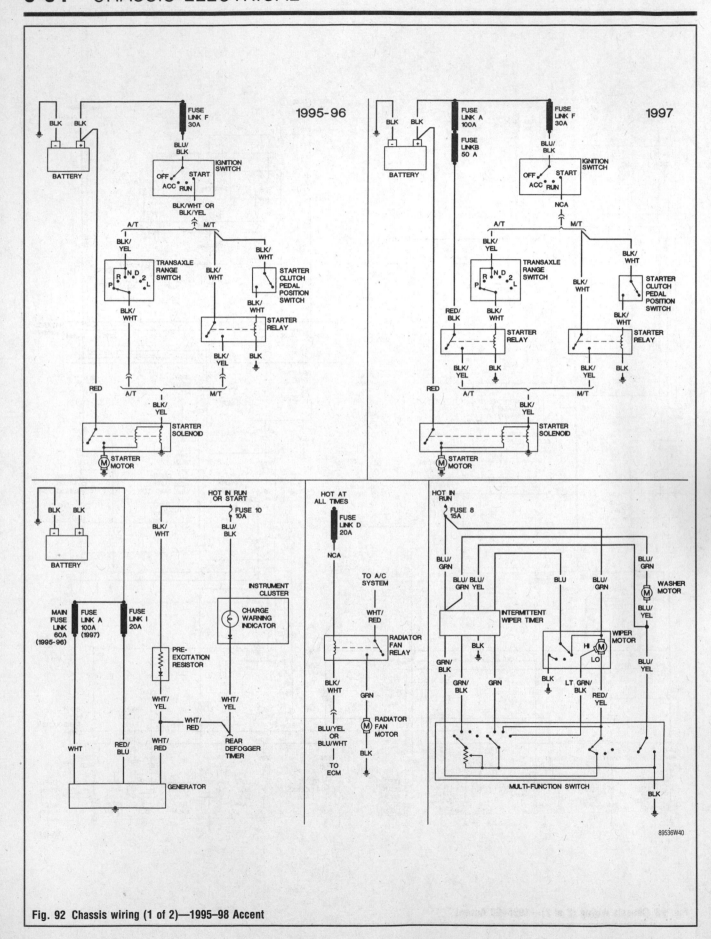

Fig. 92 Chassis wiring (1 of 2)—1995–98 Accent

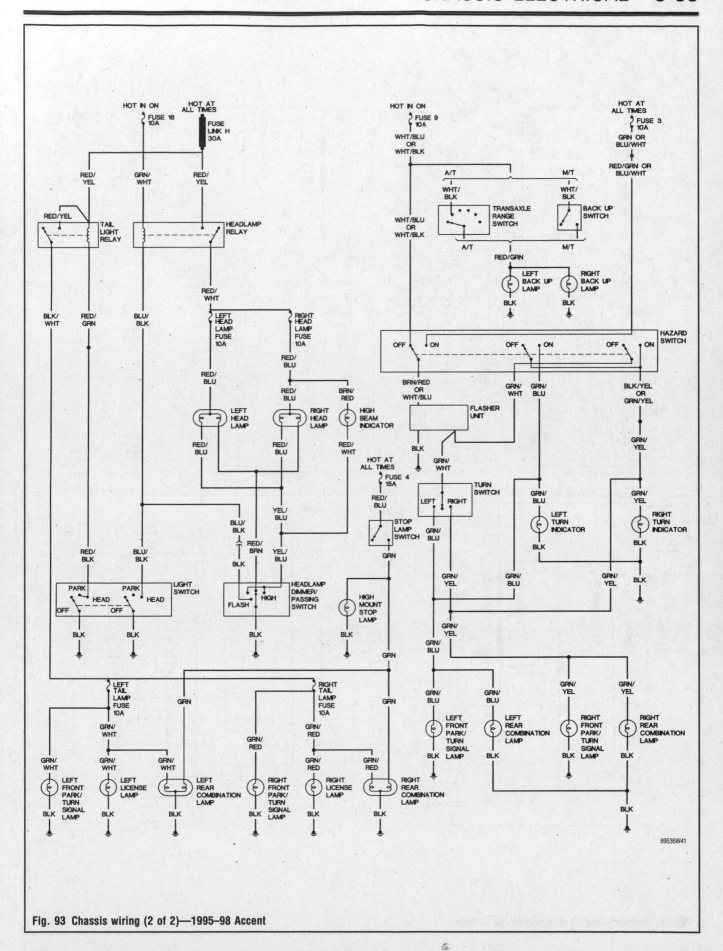

Fig. 93 Chassis wiring (2 of 2)—1995–98 Accent

89536W41

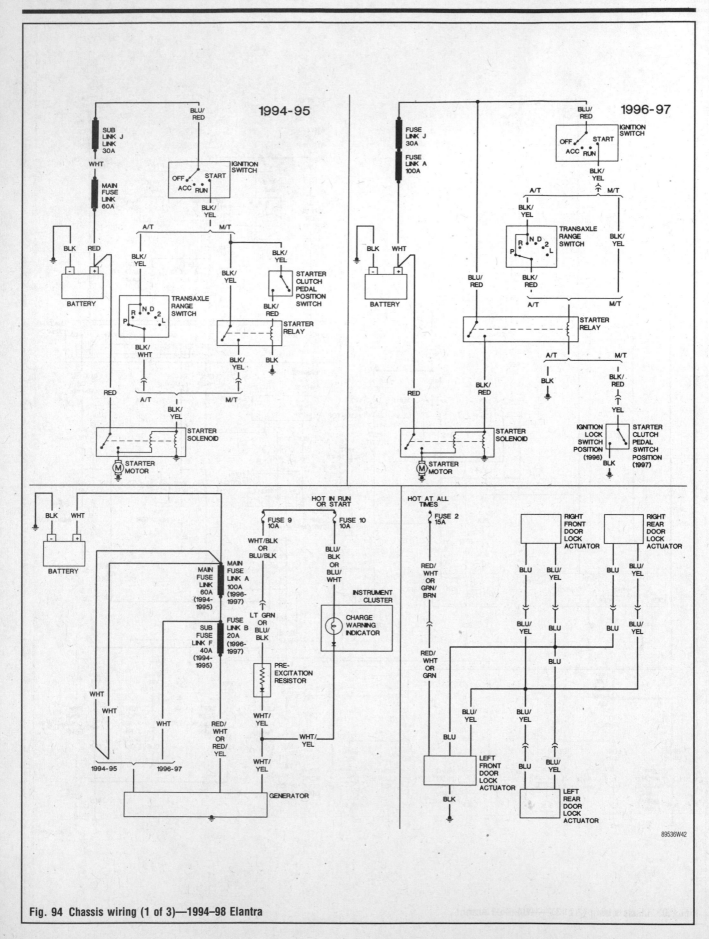

Fig. 94 Chassis wiring (1 of 3)—1994-98 Elantra

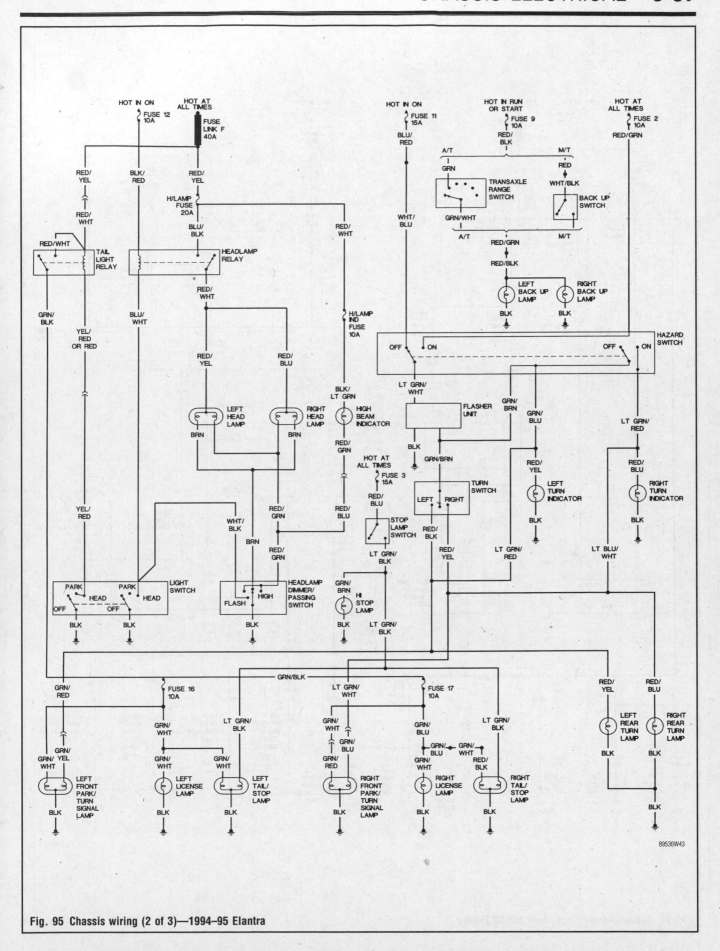

Fig. 95 Chassis wiring (2 of 3)—1994-95 Elantra

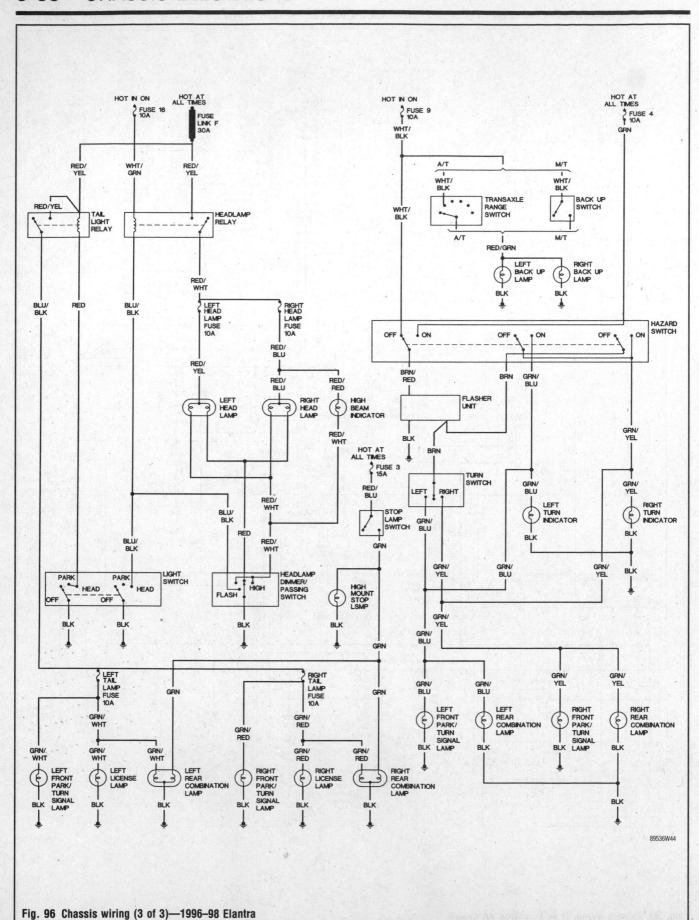

Fig. 96 Chassis wiring (3 of 3)—1996-98 Elantra

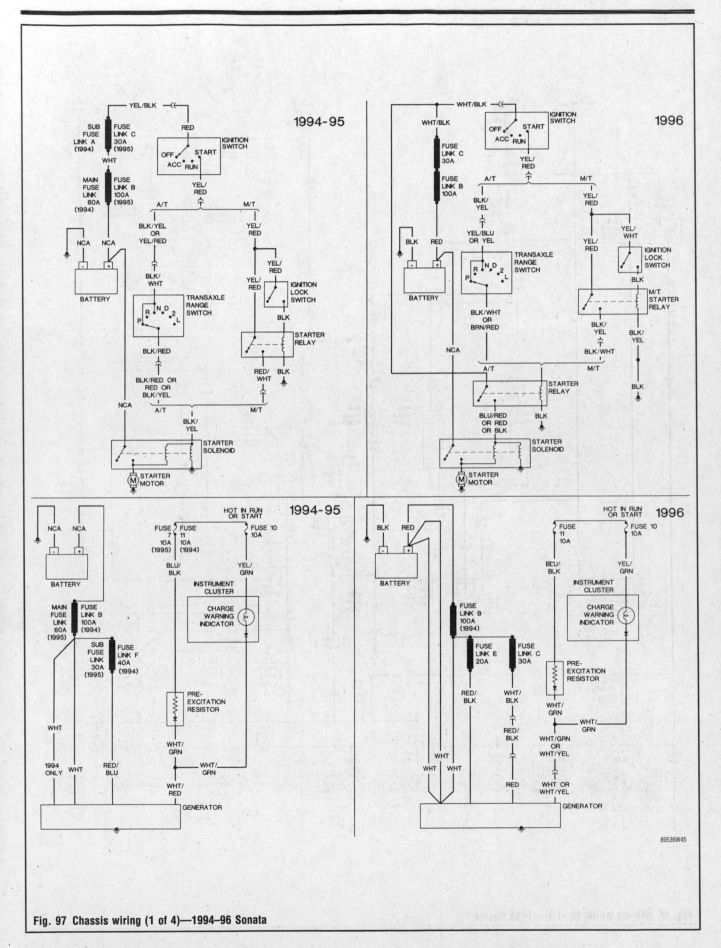

Fig. 97 Chassis wiring (1 of 4)—1994–96 Sonata

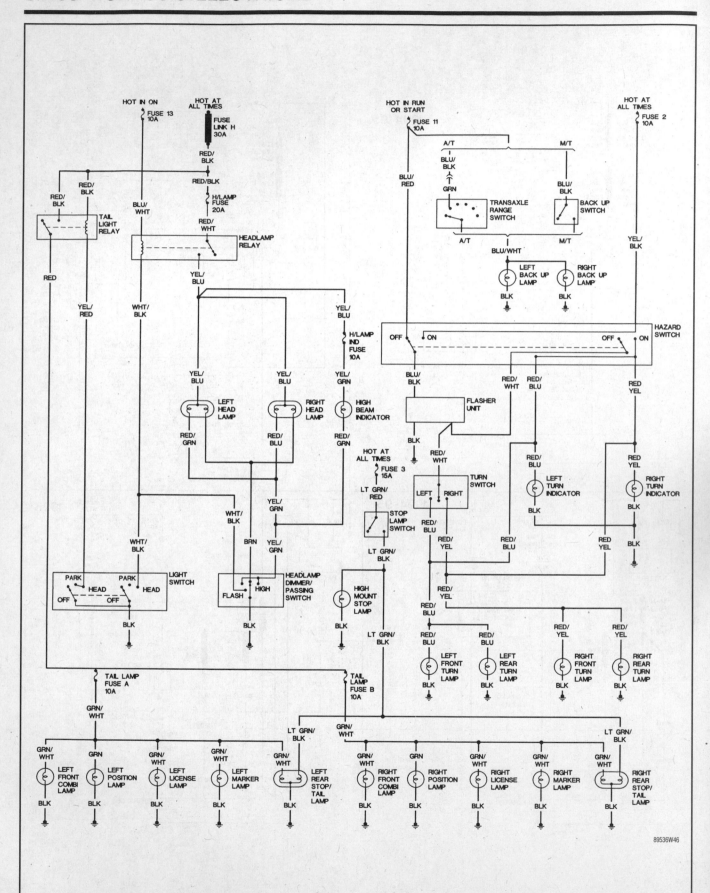

Fig. 98 Chassis wiring (2 of 4)—1994 Sonata

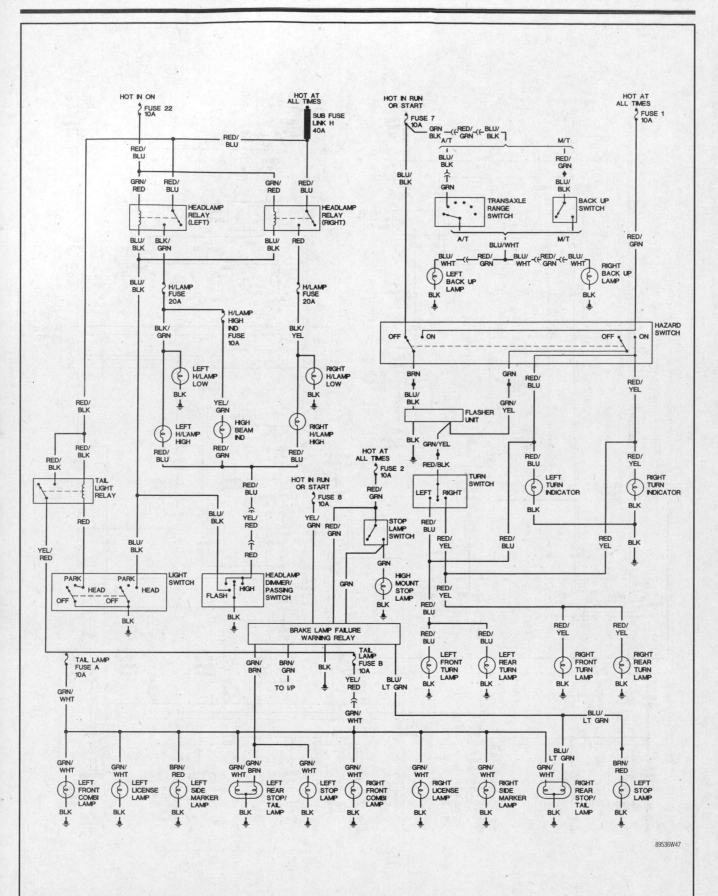

Fig. 99 Chassis wiring (3 of 4)—1995 Sonata

89536W47

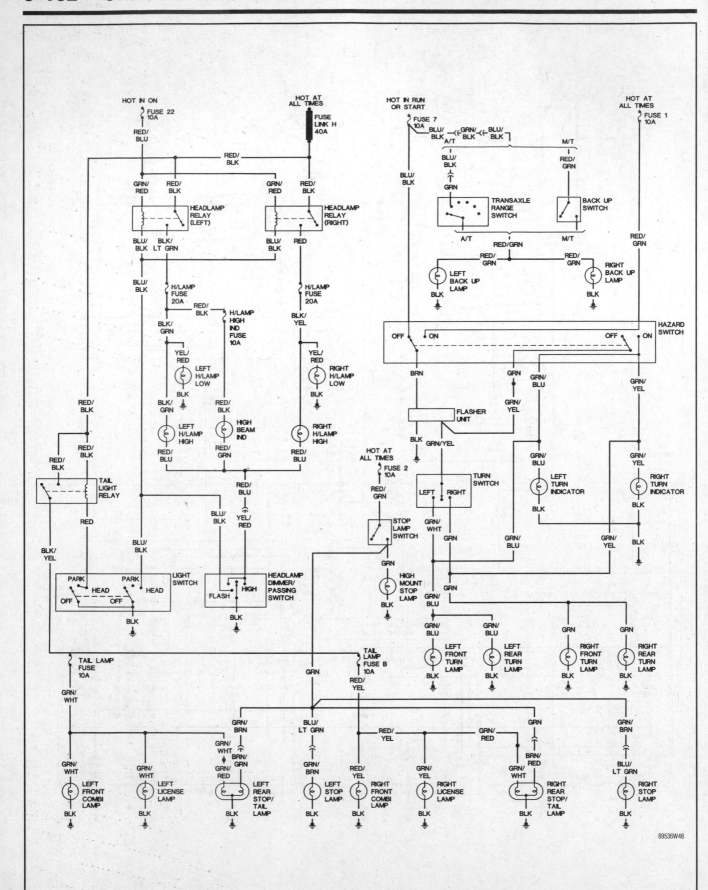

Fig. 100 Chassis wiring (4 of 4)—1996 Sonata

89536W48

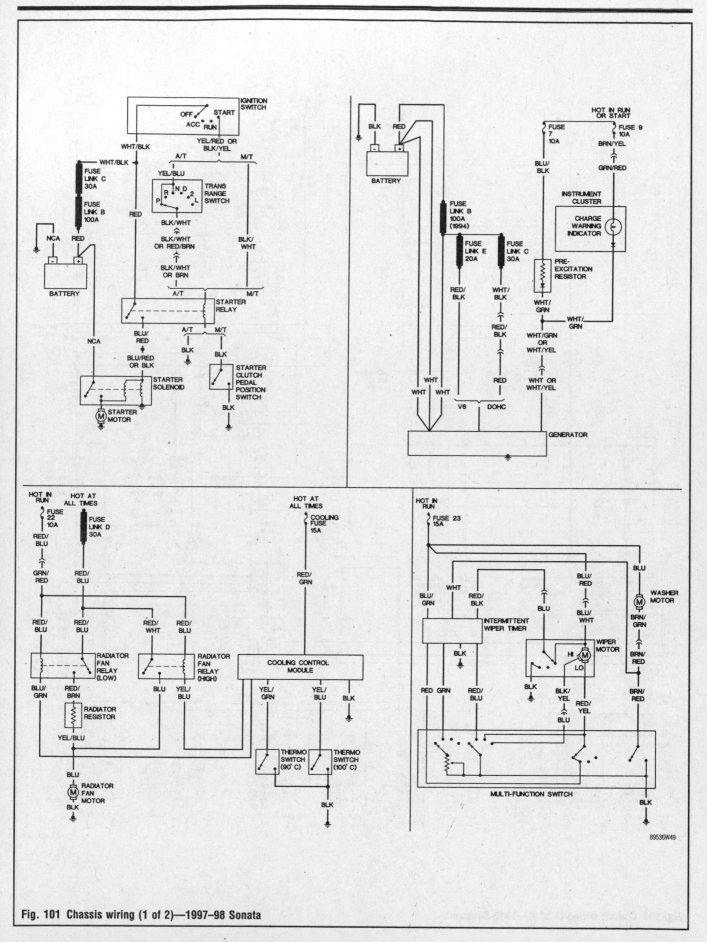

Fig. 101 Chassis wiring (1 of 2)—1997-98 Sonata

89536W49

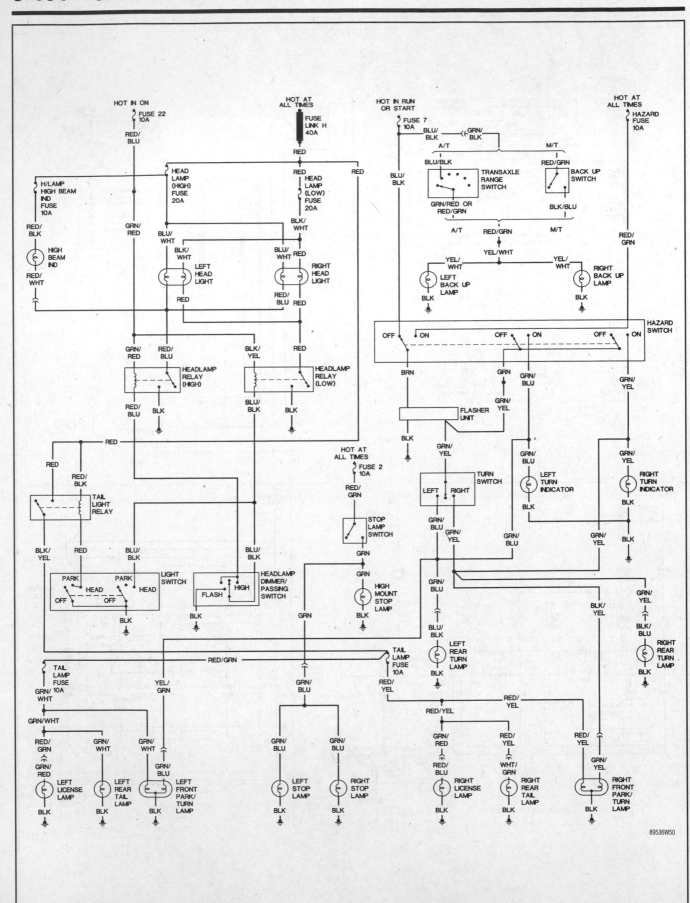

Fig. 102 Chassis wiring (2 of 2)—1997–98 Sonata

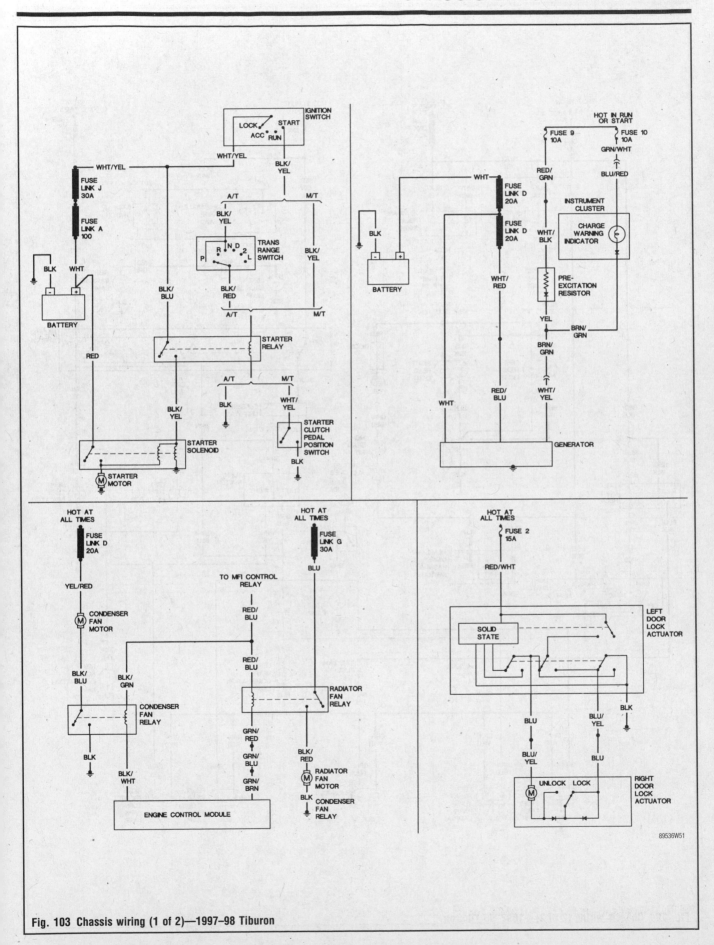

Fig. 103 Chassis wiring (1 of 2)—1997–98 Tiburon

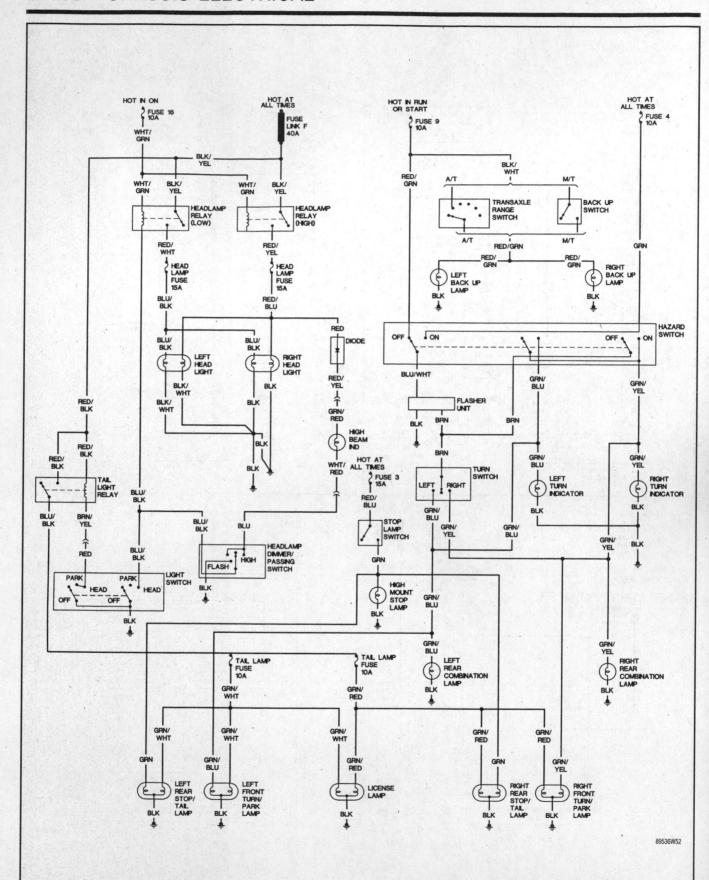

Fig. 104 Chassis wiring (2 of 2)—1997-98 Tiburon

7
DRIVE TRAIN

MANUAL TRANSAXLE

Understanding Manual Transaxles

Because of the way an internal combustion engine breathes, it can produce torque, or twisting force, only within a narrow speed range. Most modern, overhead valve pushrod engines must turn at about 2500 rpm to produce their peak torque. By 4500 rpm they are producing so little torque that continued increases in engine speed produce no power increases. The torque peak on overhead camshaft engines is generally much higher, but much narrower.

The manual transaxle and clutch are employed to vary the relationship between engine speed and the speed of the wheels so that adequate engine power can be produced under all circumstances. The clutch allows engine torque to be applied to the transaxle input shaft gradually, due to mechanical slippage. Consequently, the vehicle may be started smoothly from a full stop. The transaxle changes the ratio between the rotating speeds of the engine and the wheels by the use of gears. The gear ratios allow full engine power to be applied to the wheels during acceleration at low speeds and at highway/passing speeds.

In a front wheel drive transaxle, power is usually transmitted from the input shaft to a mainshaft or output shaft located slightly beneath and to the side of the input shaft. The gears of the mainshaft mesh with gears on the input shaft, allowing power to be carried from one to the other. All forward gears are in constant mesh and are free from rotating with the shaft unless the synchronizer and clutch is engaged. Shifting from one gear to the next causes one of the gears to be freed from rotating with the shaft and locks another to it. Gears are locked and unlocked by internal dog clutches which slide between the center of the gear and the shaft. The forward gears employ synchronizers; friction members which smoothly bring gear and shaft to the same speed before the toothed dog clutches are engaged.

Back-Up Light Switch

REMOVAL & INSTALLATION

The switch is screwed into the side of the transaxle case and is replaceable, but not adjustable.
1. Disconnect the wiring harness.
2. Unscrew the switch from the transaxle case.

➡ Do not remove the steel ball from the switch mounting bore.

3. Install the new switch and tighten to 22–25 ft. lbs. (29–33 Nm).
4. Check the new switch for proper operation.

Manual Transaxle Assembly

REMOVAL & INSTALLATION

1. Disconnect the negative battery cable.
2. Drain the transaxle oil.
3. Remove the air duct and air cleaner assembly, as required.
4. Disconnect the back-up light switch connector.
5. Disconnect the clutch release mechanism and remove the clutch release cylinder.
6. Disconnect the speedometer cable.
7. Remove the pin clips and cotter pins and disconnect the select and shift cables from the control levers.
8. Label and disconnect the starter wiring harness. Remove the starter.
9. Raise and support the vehicle safely.
10. Disconnect the halfshafts.
11. Unbolt and remove the bell housing cover.
12. Support the bottom of the transaxle with a transmission jack.
13. Support the engine by the engine lifting tabs and remove the transaxle mounting brackets and insulator.

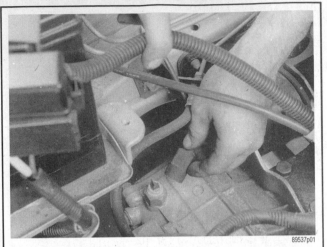

The back-up light switch connector is located at the top of the transaxle

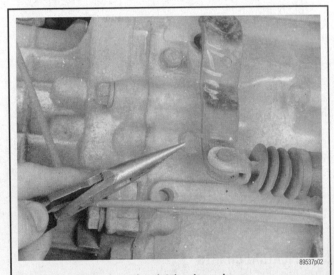

Remove the E-clip from the clutch release lever . . .

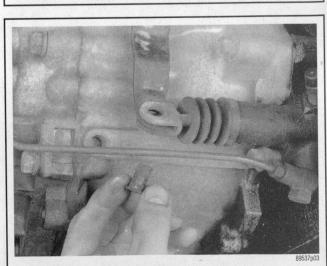

. . . then remove the pin and separate the lever from the clutch slave cylinder pushrod

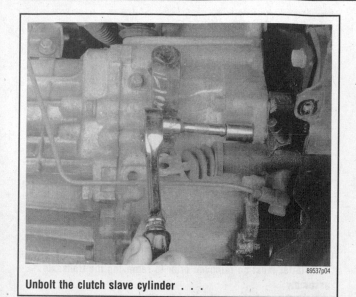

Unbolt the clutch slave cylinder . . .

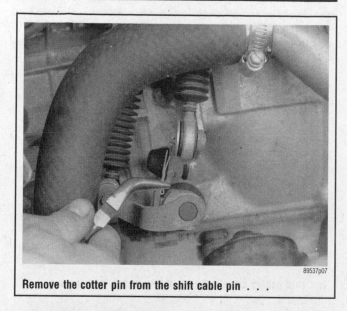

Remove the cotter pin from the shift cable pin . . .

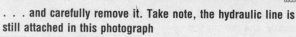

. . . and carefully remove it. Take note, the hydraulic line is still attached in this photograph

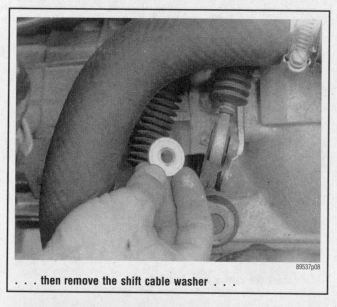

. . . then remove the shift cable washer . . .

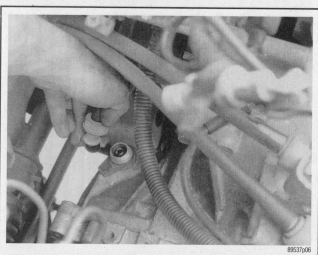

Disconnect the speedometer cable by unscrewing the attaching nut and pulling out the cable end

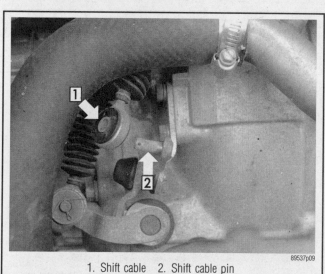

1. Shift cable   2. Shift cable pin
. . . and remove the cable from the pin

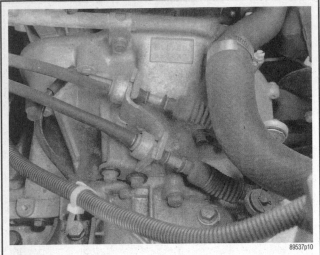

The shift cables are attached to the transaxle by a bracket

The starter must be removed prior to removing the transaxle assembly

Matchmark the cables prior to removal . . .

The transaxle mounting bracket is attached between the transaxle and the chassis

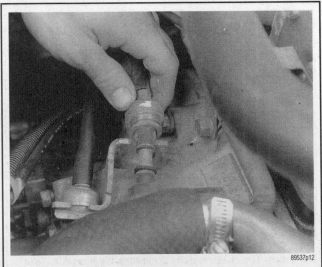

. . . then spread the bracket ends and remove the cable

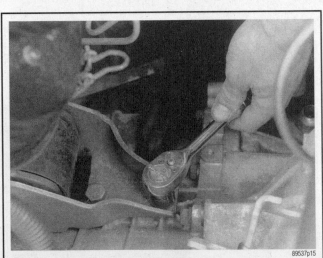

The mount-to-transaxle bolts are accessible from the top of the transaxle . . .

. . . while the mount-to-chassis bolts are hidden behind caps . . .

The transaxle also has an insulator which must be disconnected prior to removal

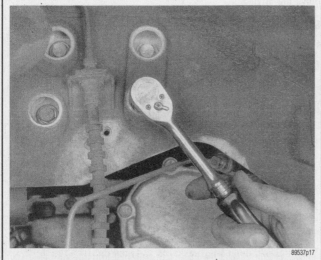

. . . and accessible from inside the fender well

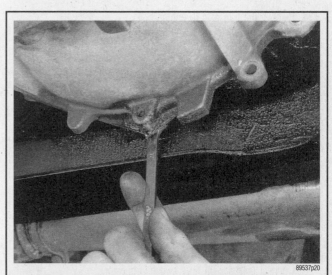

Remove the bell housing cover to gain access to the clutch

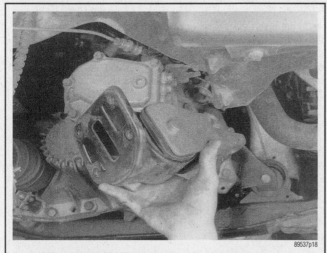

Once disconnected, the mount can be removed from the underside of the vehicle

The halfshafts can be carefully pried from the transaxle. Take care not to damage the seals

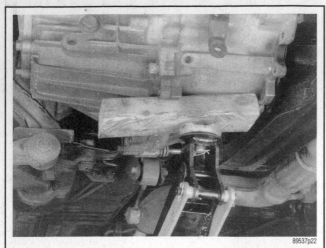

89537p22

When jacking the transaxle, insert a large block of wood under the largest part of the case for support

14. Remove the transaxle-to-engine bolts.
15. Slide the transaxle back and then lower it away from the engine.
To install:
16. Raise the transaxle into position on the engine.
17. Install the transaxle-to-engine bolts. Tighten M8 bolts to 6–7 ft. lbs. (8–10 Nm), M10 bolts to 22–25 ft. lbs. (30–35 Nm) and M12 bolts to 32–39 ft. lbs. (43–55 Nm).
18. Install the transaxle mounting brackets and tighten bolts to 65–80 ft. lbs. (90–110 Nm).
19. Install the bell housing cover and tighten bolts to 6–7 ft. lbs. (8–10 Nm).
20. Connect the halfshafts.
21. Lower the vehicle.
22. Install the starter and connect the starter wiring harness.
23. Connect the select and shift cables. Install new pin clips and cotter pins.
24. Connect the speedometer cable.
25. Install the clutch release cylinder and connect the clutch release mechanism.
26. Connect the back-up light switch connector.
27. Install the air duct and air cleaner assembly, as required.
28. Fill the transaxle with the correct grade and quantity of oil.
29. Connect the negative battery cable.

Halfshafts

REMOVAL & INSTALLATION

Except Sonata V6
♦ See Figure 1

1. Remove the hub center cap and loosen the driveshaft (axle) nut.
2. Loosen the wheel lug nuts.
3. Raise and support the front of the vehicle safely.
4. Remove the front wheels.
5. Remove the engine splash shield.
6. Remove the lower ball joint and strut bar from the lower control arm.

➡**Place the lower arm ball joint on the lower arm to prevent damage to the ball joint dust boot.**

7. Drain the transaxle fluid into a suitable waste container.
8. Insert a prybar between the transaxle case (on the raised rib) and

the driveshaft inner joint case. Move the bar to the right to withdraw the left driveshaft; to the left to remove the right driveshaft.

➡**Do not insert the prybar too deeply (beyond 7mm) or you will damage the oil seal.**

9. Plug the transaxle case with a clean rag to prevent dirt from entering the case.
10. Use a puller/driver mounted on the wheel studs to push the driveshaft from the front hub. Take care to prevent the spacer shims from falling out of place.
To install:
11. Installation is the reverse of removal. Please note the following important steps.
12. Insert the driveshaft into the hub first, then install the transaxle end.
13. Install the hub nut and washer and tighten to 144–187 ft. lbs. (195–253 Nm).
14. Tighten the lower arm-to-ball joint nuts to 43–52 ft. lbs. (58–70 Nm).
15. Tighten the lower arm-to-strut bar nuts to 54–65 ft. lbs. (73–88 Nm).
16. Tighten tie rod end-to-knuckle to 17–25 ft. lbs. (23–34 Nm).

➡**Always use a new inner joint retaining ring every time you remove the driveshaft.**

Sonata V6
♦ See Figure 2

LEFT HALFSHAFT

1. Remove the hub center cap and remove the split pin, driveshaft (axle) nut and washer. Make a mental note of how the washer is installed.
2. Loosen the wheel lug nuts.
3. Raise and support the front end on jackstands.
4. Remove the front wheels.
5. Remove the engine splash shield and drain the transaxle fluid.
6. Remove the split pin from the tie rod end and loosen the tie rod end nut but do not remove it.
7. Using special puller tool 09568-3100 or equivalent, disconnect the tie rod end from the steering knuckle. Tie the tool off to a suspension member component before using it. Remove the tie rod end nut.
8. Reposition the tool between the lower control arm and steering knuckle and disconnect the lower arm ball joint from the knuckle.
9. Using puller tool 09526-11001 or equivalent, pull the left driveshaft from the wheel hub.
10. Insert a prybar between the center bearing bracket and the driveshaft. Separate the driveshaft from the center bracket as shown.

➡**Do not insert the prybar any deeper than 7mm or you will puncture the oil seal and also damage the joint. When separating the driveshaft, do not allow the full weight of the vehicle to be placed on the wheel bearing. If the weight of the vehicle must be applied for any reason, support the wheel bearing with holding tool 09517-21500 or equivalent.**

11. Remove the oxygen sensor connector from the center bearing bracket. One screw holds the connector to the bracket.
12. Remove the two center bracket mounting bolts. Insert a prybar between the center bearing bracket, inner shaft and cylinder block. Then, pull the center bracket and inner shaft assembly from the transaxle case. Plug the transaxle case with a clean rag to prevent dirt from entering the case.
To install:

➡**Always use a new inner joint retaining ring every time you remove the driveshaft.**

13. Insert the inner shaft and bracket assembly into the transaxle case and install the center bracket mounting bolts. Tighten the bolts to 26–33 ft. lbs. (35–45 Nm).

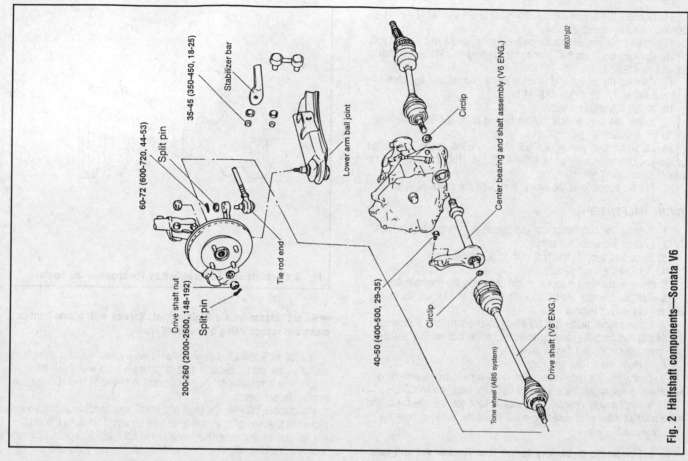

89537g02

Fig. 2 Halfshaft components—Sonata V6

Stabilizer bar

35-45 (350-450, 18-25)

Lower arm ball joint

60-72 (600-720, 44-53)

Split pin

Split pin

Tie rod end

Drive shaft nut
200-260 (2000-2600, 148-192)

Split pin

Circlip

Center bearing and shaft assembly (V6 ENG.)

Circlip

40-50 (400-500, 29-35)

Drive shaft (V6 ENG.)

Tone wheel (ABS system)

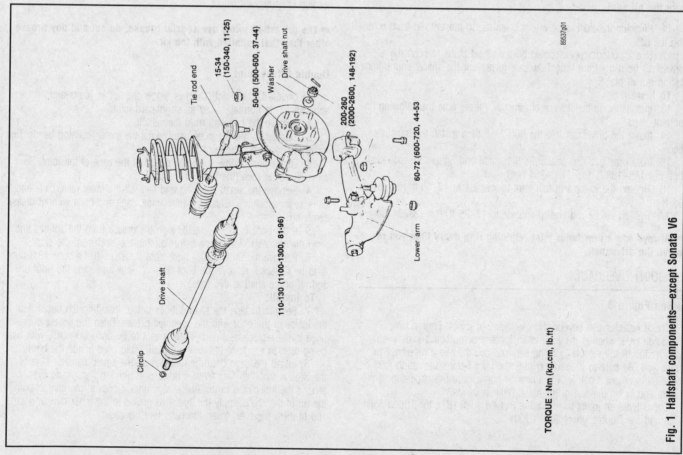

89537g01

Fig. 1 Halfshaft components—except Sonata V6

Tie rod end

15-34 (150-340, 11-25)

50-60 (500-600, 37-44)

Washer

Drive shaft nut

200-260 (2000-2600, 148-192)

60-72 (600-720, 44-53)

110-130 (1100-1300, 81-96)

Lower arm

Drive shaft

Circlip

TORQUE : Nm (kg.cm, lb.ft)

14. Connect the oxygen sensor connector to the center mounting bracket with the mounting screw.

15. Insert the driveshaft into the center bearing, then into the wheel hub.

16. Connect the lower ball joint to the steering knuckle and tighten the nut to 43–52 ft. lbs. (58–71 Nm).

17. Connect the tie rod end to the steering knuckle and tighten the tie rod end nut to 17–25 ft. lbs. (23–34 Nm).

18. Install the splash shield.

19. Mount the front wheels, tighten the lug nuts, and lower the vehicle to the ground.

20. Install the axle washer and nut. Make sure the washer is installed properly. Tighten the axle nut to 145–188 ft. lbs. (196–254 Nm) and secure the nut with a new split pin.

21. Fill the transaxle to the proper level with the specified fluid.

RIGHT HALFSHAFT

1. Remove the hub center cap and loosen the driveshaft (axle) nut.
2. Loosen the wheel lug nuts.
3. Raise and support the front end on jackstands.
4. Remove the front wheels.
5. Remove the engine splash shield and drain the transaxle fluid.
6. Remove the split pin from the tie rod end and loosen the tie rod end nut but do not remove it.
7. Using special puller tool 09568-3100 or equivalent, disconnect the tie rod end from the steering knuckle. Tie the tool off to a suspension member component before using it.
8. Remove the tie rod end nut.
9. Reposition the tool between the lower control arm and steering knuckle and disconnect the lower arm ball joint from the knuckle.
10. Insert a prybar between the transaxle case (on the raised rib) and the driveshaft inner joint case, Move the bar to the left to remove the right driveshaft.

➡Do not insert the prybar any deeper than 7mm or you will puncture the oil seal.

11. Plug the transaxle case with a clean rag to prevent dirt from entering the case.
12. Use a puller/driver mounted on the wheel studs to push the driveshaft from the front hub. Take care to prevent the spacer shims from falling out of place.

To install:

13. Installation is the reverse of removal. Please note the following important steps.
14. Insert the driveshaft into the hub, first, then install the transaxle end.
15. Install the hub nut washer as illustrated and tighten the axle shaft hub nut 145–188 ft. lbs. (196–254 Nm).
16. Tighten the lower arm ball joint-to-knuckle to 42–50 ft. lbs. (57–68 Nm)
17. Tighten the tie rod end-to-knuckle to 17–25 ft. lbs. (23–34 Nm).

➡Always use a new inner joint retaining ring every time you remove the driveshaft.

CV-JOINT OVERHAUL

◆ See Figure 3

These vehicles use several different types of joints. Engine size, transaxle type, whether the joint is an inboard or outboard joint, even which side of the vehicle is being serviced could make a difference in joint type. Be sure to properly identify the joint before attempting joint or boot replacement. Look for identification numbers at the large end of the boots and/or on the end of the metal retainer bands.

The 3 types of joints used are the Birfield Joint (BJ), the Tripod Joint (TJ) and the Double Offset Joint (DOJ).

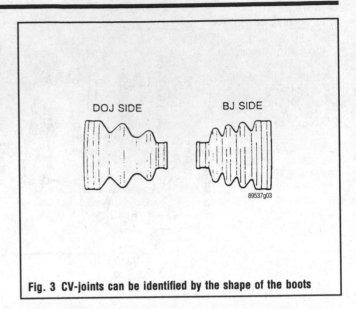

Fig. 3 CV-joints can be identified by the shape of the boots

DOJ SIDE   BJ SIDE

89537g03

➡Do not disassemble a Birfield joint. Service with a new joint or clean and repack using a new boot kit.

In addition, some left side shafts will have a round dynamic damper installed on the shaft. Special grease is generally used with these joints and is often supplied with the replacement joint and/or boot. Do not use regular chassis grease.

The distance between the large and small boot bands is important and should be checked prior to and after boot service. This is so the boot will not be installed either too loose or too tight, which could cause early wear and cracking, allowing the grease to get out and water and dirt in, leading to early joint failure.

➡The driveshaft joints use special grease, do not add any grease other than that supplied with the kit.

Double Offset Joint

The Double Offset Joint (DOJ) is bigger than other joints and, in these applications, is normally used as an inboard joint.

1. Remove the halfshaft from the vehicle.
2. Side cutter pliers can be used to cut the metal retaining bands. Remove the boot from the joint outer race.
3. Locate and remove the large circlip at the base of the joint. Remove the outer race (the body of the joint).
4. Remove the small snaping and take off the inner race, cage and balls as an assembly. Clean the inner race, cage and balls without disassembling.
5. If the boot is to be reused, wipe the grease from the splines and wrap the splines in vinyl tape before sliding the boot from the shaft.
6. Remove the inner (DOJ) boot from the shaft. If the outer (BJ) boot is to be replaced, remove the boot retainer rings and slide the boot down and off of the shaft at this time.

To install:

7. Be sure to tape the shaft splines before installing the boots. Fill the inside of the boot with the specified grease. Often the grease supplied in the replacement parts kit is meant to be divided in half, with half being used to lubricate the joint and half being used inside the boot.
8. Install the cage onto the halfshaft so the small diameter side of the cage is installed first. With a brass drift pin, tap lightly and evenly around the inner race to install the race until it comes into contact with the rib of the shaft. Apply the specified grease to the inner race and cage and fit them together. Insert the balls into the cage.

9. Install the outer race (the body of the joint) after filling with the specified grease. The outer race should be filled with this grease.

10. Tighten the boot bands securely. Make sure the distance between the boot bands is correct.

11. Install the halfshaft to the vehicle.

Except Double Offset Joint

1. Disconnect the negative battery cable. Remove the halfshaft.

2. Use side cutter pliers to remove the metal retaining bands from the boot(s) that will be removed. Slide the boot from the TJ case.

3. Remove the snapring and the tripod joint spider assembly from the halfshaft. Do not disassemble the spider and use care in handling.

4. If the boot is be reused, wrap vinyl tape around the spline part of the shaft so the boot(s) will not be damaged when removed. Remove the dynamic damper, if used, and the boots from the shaft.

To install:

5. Double check that the correct replacement parts are being installed. Wrap vinyl tape around the splines to protect the boot and install the boots and damper, if used, in the correct order.

6. Install the joint spider assembly to the shaft and install the snapring.

7. Fill the inside of the boot with the specified grease. Often the grease supplied in the replacement parts kit is meant to be divided in half, with half being used to lubricate the joint and half being used inside the boot. Keep grease off the rubber part of the dynamic damper (if used).

8. Secure the boot bands with the halfshaft in a horizontal position. Make sure distance between boot bands is correct.

9. Install the halfshaft to the vehicle and reconnect the negative battery cable.

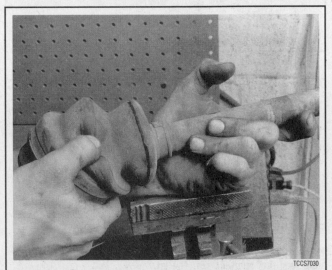

Check the CV-boot for wear

TCCS7030

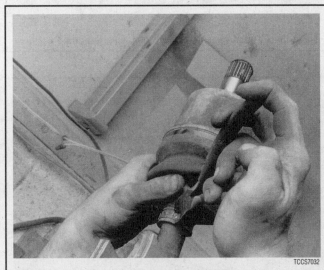

Removing the inner band from the CV-boot

TCCS7032

Removing the outer band from the CV-boot

TCCS7031

Removing the CV-boot from the joint housing

TCCS7033

Clean the CV-joint housing prior to removing the boot

Inspecting the CV-joint housing

Removing the CV-joint housing assembly

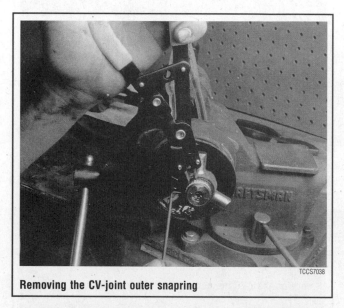

Removing the CV-joint outer snapring

Removing the CV-joint

Checking the CV-joint snapring for wear

CV-joint snapring

TCCS7040

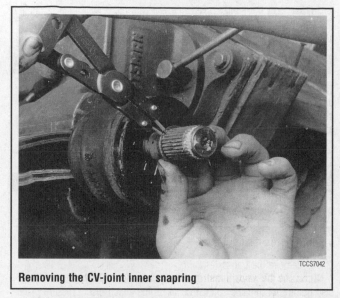

Removing the CV-joint inner snapring

TCCS7042

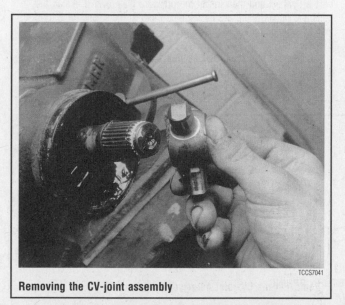

Removing the CV-joint assembly

TCCS7041

Installing the CV-joint assembly

TCCS7043

CLUTCH

Understanding the Clutch

The purpose of the clutch is to disconnect and connect engine power at the transaxle. A vehicle at rest requires a lot of engine torque to get all that weight moving. An internal combustion engine does not develop a high starting torque (unlike steam engines) so it must be allowed to operate without any load until it builds up enough torque to move the vehicle. Torque increases with engine rpm. The clutch allows the engine to build up torque by physically disconnecting the engine from the transaxle, relieving the engine of any load or resistance. The transfer of engine power to the transaxle (the load) must be smooth and gradual; if it weren't, drive line components would wear out or break quickly. This gradual power transfer is made possible by gradually releasing the clutch pedal. The clutch disc and pressure plate are the connecting link between the engine and transaxle. When the clutch pedal is released, the disc and plate contact each other (the clutch is engaged) physically joining the engine and transaxle. When the pedal is pushed inward, the disc and plate separate (the clutch is disengaged) disconnecting the engine from the transaxle.

Most clutches utilize a single plate, dry friction disc with a diaphragm-style spring pressure plate. The clutch disc has a splined hub which attaches the disc to the input shaft. The disc has friction material where it contacts the flywheel and pressure plate. Torsion springs on the disc help absorb engine torque pulses. The pressure plate applies pressure to the clutch disc, holding it tight against the surface of the flywheel. The clutch operating mechanism consists of a release bearing, fork and cylinder assembly.

The release fork and actuating linkage transfer pedal motion to the release bearing. In the engaged position (pedal released) the diaphragm spring holds the pressure plate against the clutch disc, so engine torque is transmitted to the input shaft. When the clutch pedal is depressed, the release bearing pushes the diaphragm spring center toward the flywheel. The diaphragm spring pivots the fulcrum, relieving the load on the pressure plate. Steel spring straps riveted to the clutch cover lift the pressure plate from the clutch disc, disengaging the engine drive from the transaxle and enabling the gears to be changed.

The clutch is operating properly if:

• It will stall the engine when released with the vehicle held stationary
• The shift lever can be moved freely between 1st and reverse gears when the vehicle is stationary and the clutch disengaged

✳✳ CAUTION

The clutch driven disc may contain asbestos, which has been determined to be a cancer causing agent. Never clean the clutch surfaces with compressed air! Avoid inhaling dust from any clutch surface. When cleaning clutch surfaces, use a commercially available brake cleaning fluid.

Driven Disc and Pressure Plate

REMOVAL & INSTALLATION

▶ See Figures 4 and 5

1. Remove the transaxle.
2. Insert the forward end of an old transaxle input shaft or a clutch disc guide tool into the splined center of the clutch disc, pressure plate and the pilot bearing in the crankshaft. This will keep the disc from dropping when the pressure plate is removed from the flywheel.
3. Loosen the clutch mounting bolts alternately and diagonally in very small increments, no more than 2 turns at a time, so as to avoid warping the cover flange.
4. Remove the pressure plate and disc.
5. Remove the return clip and the clutch release bearing.

6. On early model clutches, insert tool 09414-24000, or equivalent, in the spring pin and attach the round nut to the end of the tool. While holding the shaft of the special tool, rotate the sleeve with a wrench to force the spring pin out.
7. Remove the clutch release shaft, packings, return spring and the release fork.
   To install:
8. Apply a light coating of high temperature grease to the release fork shaft and the clutch release bearing contact surfaces.
9. On early model clutches, align the lock pin holes of the release fork and shaft and drive 2 new spring pins into the holes. Make sure the spring pin slot is at right angles to the centerline of the control shaft.
10. Apply grease into the groove in the release bearing and install the bearing into the front bearing retainer in the transaxle. Install the return clip to the release bearing and fork.
11. Make sure the surfaces of the pressure plate and flywheel are wiped clean of grease and lightly sand them with crocus cloth. Lightly grease the clutch disc and transaxle input shaft splines, making sure not to allow any grease to contact the clutch disc material or clutch slippage may result.
12. Locate the clutch disc on the flywheel with the stamped mark facing outward. Use a clutch disc guide or old input shaft to center the disc on the flywheel and then install the pressure plate over it. Install the bolts and tighten them evenly. Tighten them in increments of 2 turns or less to avoid warping the pressure plate. Tighten to 11–15 ft. lbs. (15–21 Nm).
13. Remove the clutch disc centering tool.
14. Install the transaxle.
15. Adjust the clutch free-play.

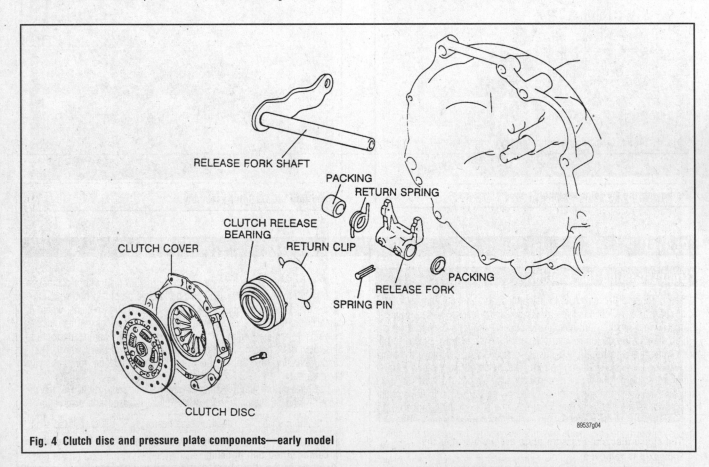

RELEASE FORK SHAFT
PACKING
RETURN SPRING
CLUTCH RELEASE BEARING
RETURN CLIP
CLUTCH COVER
SPRING PIN
RELEASE FORK
PACKING
CLUTCH DISC

89537g04

Fig. 4 Clutch disc and pressure plate components—early model

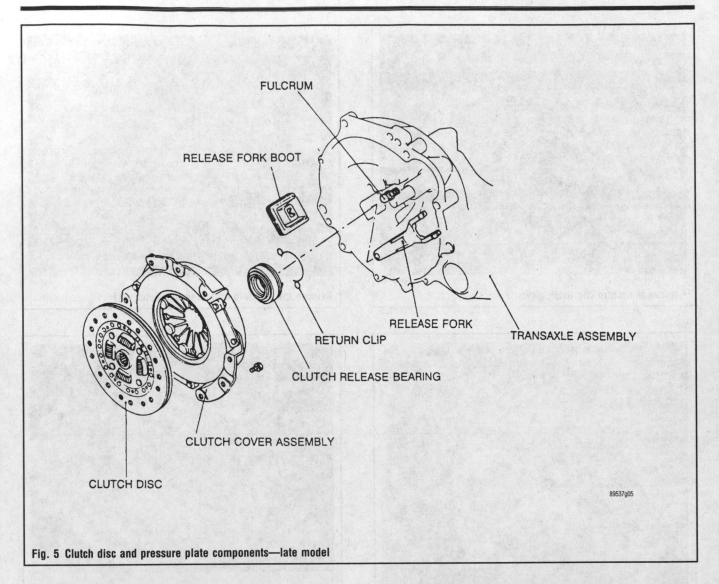

Fig. 5 Clutch disc and pressure plate components—late model

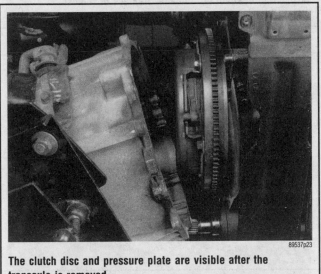

The clutch disc and pressure plate are visible after the transaxle is removed

1. Input shaft   2. Clutch release bearing   3. Clutch release shaft
The clutch release bearing and release shaft can be seen at the center of the bell housing

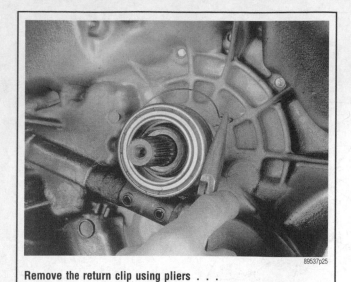

Remove the return clip using pliers . . .

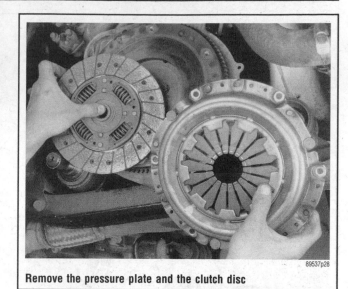

Remove the pressure plate and the clutch disc

. . . and slide the clutch release bearing off the input shaft

Inspect the flywheel for damage. Replace or refinish as necessary

Loosen the pressure plate bolts evenly. When tightening, use a flywheel tool to hold the engine

Always clean the flywheel with an evaporative brake cleaner. This prevents contamination of the clutch

The bolt pattern in the flywheel is staggered for easy alignment with the crankshaft flange

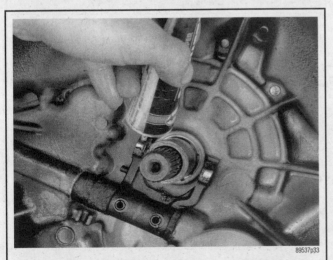

Attach a flywheel tool to lock the engine, then evenly tighten the flywheel bolts to the proper torque

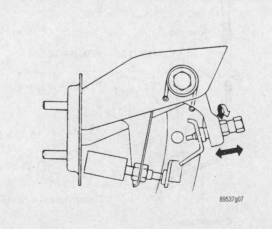

Prior to installing the clutch release bearing, lubricate the clutch release fork with hi-temp grease

ADJUSTMENTS

Pedal Height and Free-Play

◆ See Figures 6, 7 and 8

1. Measure the clutch pedal height (from the face of the pedal pad to the floorboard). The distance should be 7.0 in. (178mm).
2. Measure the clutch pedal clevis pin play (measured at the face of the pedal pad). The distance should be 0.04–0.11 in. (1–3mm).
3. If either measurement is not within specification, adjust as follows:
4. Turn and adjust the stop bolt so that the pedal height is within specification. and secure with the locknut.
5. When the pedal height is lower than specification, loosen the bolt or clutch pedal position switch and turn the pushrod to make the adjustment. Turn the bolt or clutch pedal position switch until it reaches the pedal stopper and then lock with the locknut.

➡ When adjusting clutch pedal height or pedal clevis pin play, be careful not to push the clutch master cylinder rod toward the master cylinder.

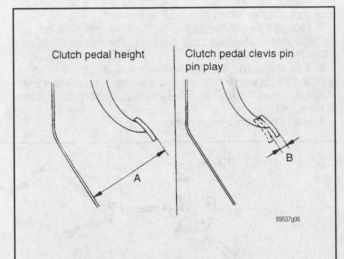

Fig. 6 Measuring clutch pedal height (A) and clutch pedal clevis pin play (B)

Fig. 7 Loosen the stop bolt or clutch pedal position switch and turn the pushrod to make the adjustment

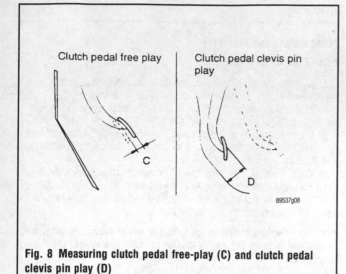

Clutch pedal free play

Clutch pedal clevis pin play

89537g08

Fig. 8 Measuring clutch pedal free-play (C) and clutch pedal clevis pin play (D)

6. Measure the clutch pedal free-play (measured at the face of the pedal pad). Distance should be 0.2–0.5 in. (6–13mm).

7. Measure the clutch pedal clevis pin play (measured at the face of the pedal pad with the clutch pedal depressed). The distance should be 2.8 in. (90mm).

8. If the clutch pedal free-play and the distance between the clutch pedal and the firewall when the clutch is disengaged are not within specification, it may be the result of air in the hydraulic line or a faulty hydraulic component.

9. Bleed the hydraulic clutch system.

Clutch Master Cylinder

REMOVAL & INSTALLATION

◆ **See Figures 9 and 10**

1. Unscrew the reservoir cap.
2. Loosen the bleeder plug and drain the clutch fluid into a suitable container.
3. Disconnect and plug the hydraulic line at the release cylinder.
4. From inside the vehicle, remove the split pin, clevis pin and washer from the clutch pedal to release the master cylinder pushrod.
5. Remove the clutch fluid reservoir tank mounting bolt.
6. Loosen the hydraulic line clamps to permit movement of the clutch tube.
7. Disconnect the hydraulic line from the master cylinder.
8. Remove the two nuts and pull the master cylinder and gasket from the firewall.
9. Inspect the gasket for damage and replace as required.

To install:

10. Position the master cylinder assembly with gasket onto the firewall and tighten mounting nuts and bolts to 7–10 ft. lbs. (9–14 Nm).
11. Connect the hydraulic line to the master cylinder and tighten to 9–12 ft. lbs. (13–17 Nm).
12. Connect the pushrod to the clutch pedal and insert the clevis pin. Secure the clevis pin with the split pin.
13. Fill and bleed the system.
14. Adjust the clutch pedal height and free-play.
15. When the pin play adjustment is complete, lubricate the clevis pin with a small amount of wheel bearing or multi-purpose grease.
16. Check the clutch for proper performance.

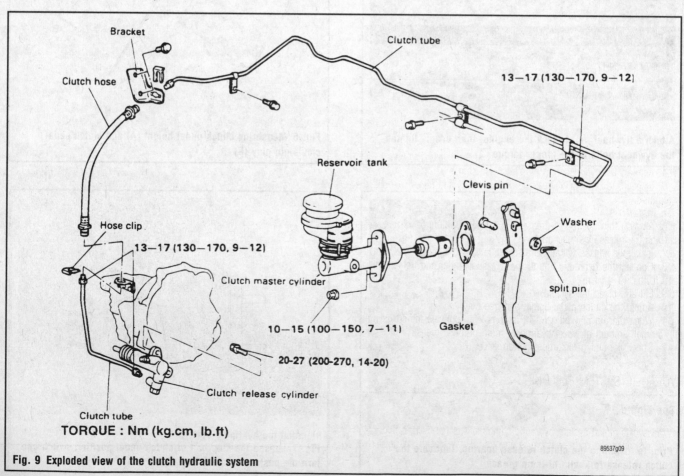

TORQUE : Nm (kg.cm, lb.ft)

89537g09

Fig. 9 Exploded view of the clutch hydraulic system

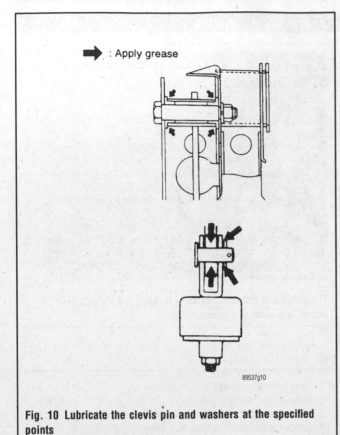

: Apply grease

Fig. 10 Lubricate the clevis pin and washers at the specified points

Clutch Release Cylinder

REMOVAL & INSTALLATION

♦ **See Figures 9 and 10**

1. Unscrew the reservoir cap.
2. Loosen the bleeder plug and drain the clutch fluid into a suitable container.
3. Disconnect and plug the hydraulic line at the release cylinder.
4. Remove the cylinder from the clutch housing.
5. Inspect the cylinder for leakage or torn boots and repair or replace as required.

To install:

6. Apply a thin coating of grease to the contact points of the release shaft and the release cylinder pushrod.
7. Install the release cylinder and tighten to 14–20 ft. lbs. (20–27 Nm).
8. Connect the hydraulic line to the release cylinder and tighten to 7–10 ft. lbs. (9–14 Nm).
9. Fill and bleed the system.
10. Adjust the clutch pedal height and free-play.
11. When the pin play adjustment is complete, lubricate the clevis pin with a small amount of wheel bearing or multi-purpose grease.
12. Check the clutch for proper performance.

HYDRAULIC SYSTEM BLEEDING

♦ **See Figure 11**

Whenever a clutch system hydraulic component is removed, a hydraulic line disconnected or the system is opened for any reason, the system

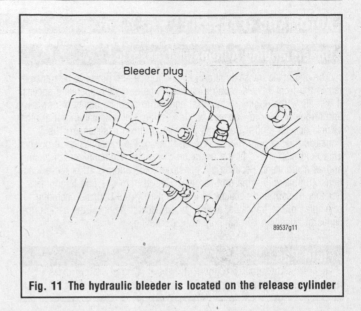

Fig. 11 The hydraulic bleeder is located on the release cylinder

must be bled to remove any air that may be trapped inside the system.

To bleed the system you will need: a good supply of brake fluid that meets or exceeds DOT 3 specifications, a small transparent plastic container, a wrench to loosen and tighten the bleeder screw, a small length of clear plastic hose to attach to the bleeder screw and an assistant to work the clutch pedal.

1. Unscrew the clutch fluid reservoir cap.
2. Loosen the bleeder screw just so fluid starts to leak out of the bleeder hole.
3. Fill the plastic container halfway with brake fluid.
4. Connect the hose to the bleeder screw and place the other end of hose into the container of brake fluid.
5. Fill the reservoir to the MAX fill line and have the assistant pump the clutch pedal slowly. You will notice air bubbles rising to the top of the fluid container. Keep the reservoir full at all times.
6. Repeat the previous step until all the air bubbles are gone.
7. Tighten the bleeder screw and check the fluid level. Add fluid as necessary until the proper level is reached.
8. Install the reservoir cap.

Bleeding the hydraulic system

AUTOMATIC TRANSAXLE

Understanding Automatic Transaxles

The automatic transaxle allows engine torque and power to be transmitted to the front wheels within a narrow range of engine operating speeds. It will allow the engine to turn fast enough to produce plenty of power and torque at very low speeds, while keeping it at a sensible rpm at high vehicle speeds (and it does this job without driver assistance). The transaxle uses a light fluid as the medium for the transmission of power. This fluid also works in the operation of various hydraulic control circuits and as a lubricant. Because the transaxle fluid performs all of these functions, trouble within the unit can easily travel from one part to another. For this reason, and because of the complexity and unusual operating principles of the transaxle, a very sound understanding of the basic principles of operation will simplify troubleshooting.

Fluid Pan

REMOVAL & INSTALLATION

1. Raise the front of the vehicle and support it safely.
2. Remove the drain plug from the bottom of the transaxle and allow the fluid to drain.
3. Position a large drain pan under the transaxle pan and have plenty of rags on hand.
4. Slightly loosen all the pan bolts. Tap one corner of the pan with a soft hammer to break the seal.
5. Once the pan is broken loose, support it, remove all the bolts, and then tilt it to one side to drain the remaining fluid.

To install:

6. Clean all the gasket surfaces and the inside of the pan thoroughly. Then, raise the pan and gasket in position with bolt holes lined up.
7. Support the pan and replace the bolts, tightening them only very gently with your fingers.
8. Tighten the pan bolts diagonally in several stages to 7.5–8.5 ft. lbs. (10–12 Nm).
9. Install the drain plug and torque to 22–25 ft. lbs. (30–35 Nm).
10. Refill the transaxle carefully through the dipstick. Check the fluid level several times until it reaches the lower mark on the dipstick.
11. Start the engine and allow to idle for about two minutes so that the fluid has a chance to warm to normal operating temperature.
12. Check the fluid level and add fluid as necessary.

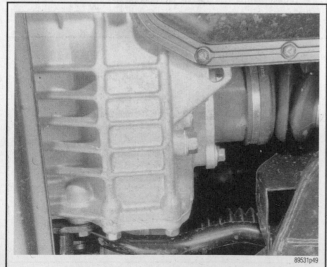

Some models have the drain plug located in the transaxle case

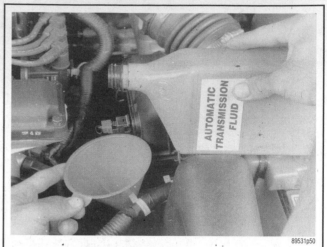

The automatic transaxle is filled through the dipstick tube. A funnel is a must to prevent spills

PAN & FILTER SERVICE

1. Drain the transaxle fluid.
2. Remove the transaxle pan.
3. Remove the filter.
4. Check the filter for clogging and damage and replace as necessary.
5. Install a new filter as necessary.
6. Install the transaxle pan.
7. Refill the transaxle with fluid.

Inhibitor Switch

REMOVAL & INSTALLATION

1. Place the selector lever in the **N** position.
2. Loosen the control cable to the manual control lever. Separate the cable and the lever.
3. Place the manual control lever in the **N** position.
4. Remove the manual control lever.
5. Loosen the switch attaching bolts.
6. Remove the switch.
7. Installation is the reverse of removal. Please note the following important steps.
8. Tighten the inhibitor switch mounting bolts to 7–9 ft. lbs. (10–12 Nm).
9. When setting up the switch body, be careful not to drop the O-ring from the switch body. Tighten the switch body carefully.
10. Tighten the manual lever nut to 13–15 ft. lbs. (17–21 Nm).

ADJUSTMENT

▶ See Figures 12 and 13

The inhibitor (transaxle range) switch is located at the top of the transaxle case. It functions as a neutral safety switch that will prevent the vehicle from starting in any gear except P or N. The inhibitor switch also completes the reverse light circuit when the selector lever is placed in reverse.

1. Place the selector lever in the **N** position.
2. Loosen the control cable to the manual control lever. Separate the cable and the lever.

3. Place the manual control lever in the **N** position.
4. Loosen the switch attaching bolts.
5. Turn the inhibitor switch body until the 0.47 in. (12mm) wide end of the manual control lever aligns with the switch body flange. Tighten the mounting bolts to 7–9 ft. lbs. (10–12 Nm).

➡**When setting up the switch body, be careful not to drop the O-ring from the switch body. Tighten the switch body carefully.**

6. Ensure the selector lever is in the **N** position.
7. Adjust the flange nut so there is no slack in the control cable.
8. Ensure the selector lever operates smoothly.
9. Operate the vehicle and confirm the transaxle is set in each range when the selector lever is shifted into each position.
10. Ensure the vehicle starts only in the **P** and **N** position.
11. Ensure the back-up lights are functional in the **R** position.

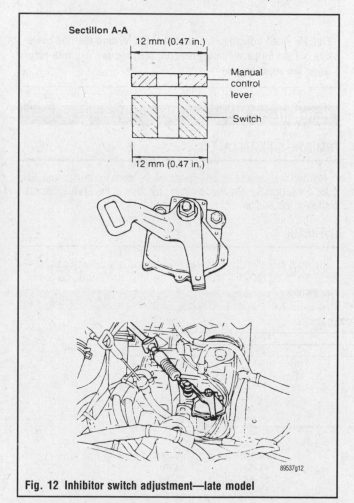

Fig. 12 Inhibitor switch adjustment—late model

Automatic Transaxle Assembly

REMOVAL & INSTALLATION

◆ **See Figure 14**

1. Disconnect the negative battery cable.
2. Drain the transmission fluid.
3. Remove the air duct and air cleaner assembly, as required.
4. Disconnect and plug the transaxle cooler lines.
5. Disconnect the control cable.
6. Disconnect the speedometer cable.
7. Label and disconnect the pulse generator, inhibitor, kickdown servo, solenoid valve and oil temperature sensor electrical harnesses.

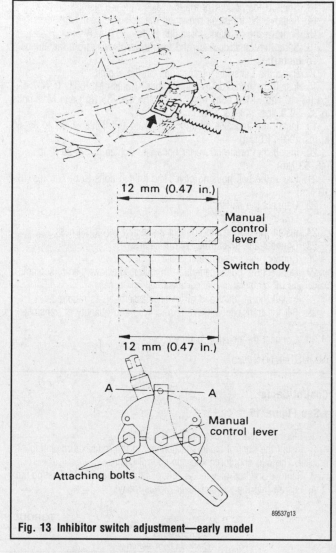

Fig. 13 Inhibitor switch adjustment—early model

8. Label and disconnect the starter wiring harness. Remove the starter.
9. Raise and support the vehicle safely.
10. Disconnect the halfshafts.
11. Unbolt and remove the bell housing cover.
12. Remove the torque converter bolts.

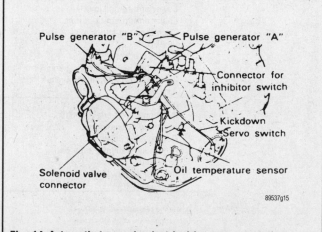

Fig. 14 Automatic transaxle electrical harness connections

13. Support the bottom of the transaxle with a transmission jack.
14. Remove the transaxle mounting brackets and center member.
15. Remove the transaxle-to-engine bolts.
16. Slide the transaxle back and then lower it away from the engine.

To install:

17. Raise the transaxle into position on the engine.
18. Install the transaxle-to-engine bolts. Tighten M8 bolts to 6–7 ft. lbs. (8–10 Nm), M10 bolts to 22–25 ft. lbs. (30–35 Nm) and M12 bolts to 32–39 ft. lbs. (43–55 Nm).
19. Install the transaxle mounting brackets and tighten bolts to 65–80 ft. lbs. (90–110 Nm).
20. Install the torque converter bolts and tighten to 34–39 ft. lbs. (46–53 Nm).
21. Install the bell housing cover and tighten bolts to 6–7 ft. lbs. (8–10 Nm).
22. Connect the halfshafts.
23. Lower the vehicle.
24. Install the starter and connect the starter wiring harness.
25. Connect and adjust the control cables.
26. Connect the speedometer cable.
27. Connect the pulse generator, inhibitor, kickdown servo, solenoid valve and oil temperature sensor electrical harnesses.
28. Install the air duct and air cleaner assembly, as required.
29. Fill the transaxle with the correct type and quantity of transmission fluid.
30. Connect the negative battery cable.

ADJUSTMENTS

Control Cable

♦ **See Figure 15**

1. Place the selector lever in the **N** position.
2. Install the control cable and connect to the transaxle mounting bracket. The clip should contact the control cable.
3. Remove any free-play in the control cable by using the adjusting nut.
4. Ensure that the selector lever moves freely.

Fig. 15 When adjusting the control cable, ensure that the cable clip is tight in the mounting bracket, then remove any free-play using the adjusting nut

Halfshafts

REMOVAL & INSTALLATION

Removal and installation procedures are the same for manual and automatic transaxles. Refer to the Halfshaft procedure in the Manual Transaxle portion of this section.

OVERHAUL

Overhaul procedures are the same for manual and automatic transaxles. Refer to the Halfshaft procedure in the Manual Transaxle portion of this section.

TORQUE SPECIFICATIONS

Components	Ft. Lbs.	Nm
Back-up light switch	22–25	29–33
Clutch		
Master cylinder	7–10	9–14
Master cylinder hydraulic line	9–12	13–17
Pressure plate bolts	11–15	15–21
Release cylinder	14–20	20–27
Release cylinder hydraulic line	7–10	9–14
Halfshafts		
Except Sonata V6		
Axle nut	144-187	195–253
Lower arm-to-ball joint	43–52	58–70
Lower arm-to-strut bar nuts	54–65	73–88
Tie rod end-to-knuckle	17–25	23–34
Sonata V6		
Center bracket	26–33	35–45
Lower ball joint-to-steering knuckle	43–52	58–71
Tie rod end-to-steering knuckle	17–25	23–34
Axle nut	145-188	196–254
Transaxle		
Bell housing-to-engine bolts	①	
Mounting brackets	65–80	90–110
Bell housing cover	6–7	8–10
Automatic transaxle fluid pan	7.5–8.5	10–12
Drain plug	22–25	30–35
Inhibitor switch	7–9	10–12
Manual lever	13–15	17–21

① Tighten M12 bolts to 32–39 (43–55 Nm).
   Tighten M10 bolts to 22–25 (30–35 Nm)
   Tighten M8 bolts to 6–7 (8–10 Nm)

89537c01

8

SUSPENSION AND STEERING

WHEELS

Wheels

REMOVAL & INSTALLATION

◆ **See Figure 1**

1. Park the vehicle on a level surface.
2. Remove the jack, tire iron and, if necessary, the spare tire from their storage compartments.
3. Check the owner's manual or refer to Section 1 of this manual for the jacking points on your vehicle. Then, place the jack in the proper position.

Place the jack at the proper lifting point on your vehicle

4. If equipped with lug nut trim caps, remove them by either unscrewing or pulling them off the lug nuts, as appropriate. Consult the owner's manual, if necessary.
5. If equipped with a wheel cover or hub cap, insert the tapered end of the tire iron in the groove and pry off the cover.

Before jacking the vehicle, block the diagonally opposite wheel with one or, preferably, two chocks

6. Apply the parking brake and block the diagonally opposite wheel with a wheel chock or two.

➡**Wheel chocks may be purchased at your local auto parts store, or a block of wood cut into wedges may be used. If possible, keep one or two of the chocks in your tire storage compartment, in case any of the tires has to be removed on the side of the road.**

7. If equipped with an automatic transmission/transaxle, place the selector lever in **P** or Park; with a manual transmission/transaxle, place the shifter in Reverse.
8. With the tires still on the ground, use the tire iron/wrench to break the lug nuts loose.

With the vehicle still on the ground, break the lug nuts loose using the wrench end of the tire iron

➡**If a nut is stuck, never use heat to loosen it or damage to the wheel and bearings may occur. If the nuts are seized, one or two heavy hammer blows directly on the end of the bolt usually loosens the rust. Be careful, as continued pounding will likely damage the brake drum or rotor.**

After the lug nuts have been loosened, raise the vehicle using the jack until the tire is clear of the ground

Remove the lug nuts from the studs

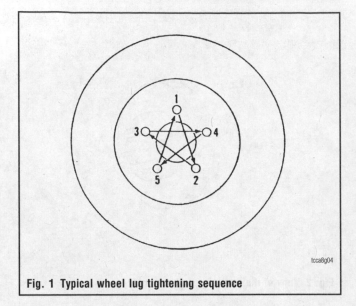

Fig. 1 Typical wheel lug tightening sequence

Remove the wheel and tire assembly from the vehicle

9. Using the jack, raise the vehicle until the tire is clear of the ground. Support the vehicle safely using jackstands.

10. Remove the lug nuts, then remove the tire and wheel assembly.

To install:

11. Make sure the wheel and hub mating surfaces, as well as the wheel lug studs, are clean and free of all foreign material. Always remove rust from the wheel mounting surface and the brake rotor or drum. Failure to do so may cause the lug nuts to loosen in service.

12. Install the tire and wheel assembly and hand-tighten the lug nuts.

13. Using the tire wrench, tighten all the lug nuts, in a crisscross pattern, until they are snug.

14. Raise the vehicle and withdraw the jackstand, then lower the vehicle.

15. Using a torque wrench, tighten the lug nuts in a crisscross pattern to 65–80 ft. lbs. (88–108 Nm). Check your owner's manual or refer to Section 1 of this manual for the proper tightening sequence.

✳✳ WARNING

Do not overtighten the lug nuts, as this may cause the wheel studs to stretch or the brake disc (rotor) to warp.

16. If so equipped, install the wheel cover or hub cap. Make sure the valve stem protrudes through the proper opening before tapping the wheel cover into position.

17. If equipped, install the lug nut trim caps by pushing them or screwing them on, as applicable.

18. Remove the jack from under the vehicle, and place the jack and tire iron/wrench in their storage compartments. Remove the wheel chock(s).

19. If you have removed a flat or damaged tire, place it in the storage compartment of the vehicle and take it to your local repair station to have it fixed or replaced as soon as possible.

INSPECTION

Inspect the tires for lacerations, puncture marks, nails and other sharp objects. Repair or replace as necessary. Also check the tires for treadwear and air pressure as outlined in Section 1 of this manual.

Check the wheel assemblies for dents, cracks, rust and metal fatigue. Repair or replace as necessary.

Wheel Lug Studs

REPLACEMENT

With Disc Brakes

◆ See Figures 2, 3 and 4

1. Raise and support the appropriate end of the vehicle safely using jackstands, then remove the wheel.

2. Remove the brake pads and caliper. Support the caliper aside using wire or a coat hanger. For details, please refer to Section 9 of this manual.

3. Remove the outer wheel bearing and lift off the rotor. For details on wheel bearing removal, installation and adjustment, please refer to Section 1 of this manual.

4. Properly support the rotor using press bars, then drive the stud out using an arbor press.

➡If a press is not available, **CAREFULLY** drive the old stud out using a blunt drift. **MAKE SURE** the rotor is properly and evenly supported or it may be damaged.

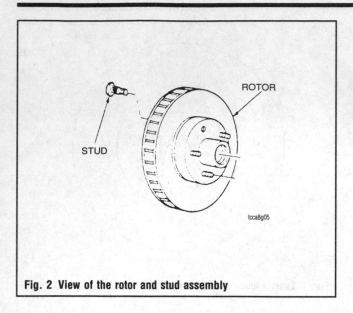

Fig. 2 View of the rotor and stud assembly

To install:

5. Clean the stud hole with a wire brush and start the new stud with a hammer and drift pin. Do not use any lubricant or thread sealer.

6. Finish installing the stud with the press.

➡️If a press is not available, start the lug stud through the bore in the hub, then position about 4 flat washers over the stud and thread the lug nut. Hold the hub/rotor while tightening the lug nut, and the stud should be drawn into position. **MAKE SURE THE STUD IS FULLY SEATED, then remove the lug nut and washers.**

7. Install the rotor and adjust the wheel bearings.

8. Install the brake caliper and pads.

9. Install the wheel, then remove the jackstands and carefully lower the vehicle.

10. Tighten the lug nuts to the proper torque.

With Drum Brakes

♦ **See Figures 5, 6 and 7**

1. Raise the vehicle and safely support it with jackstands, then remove the wheel.

2. Remove the brake drum.

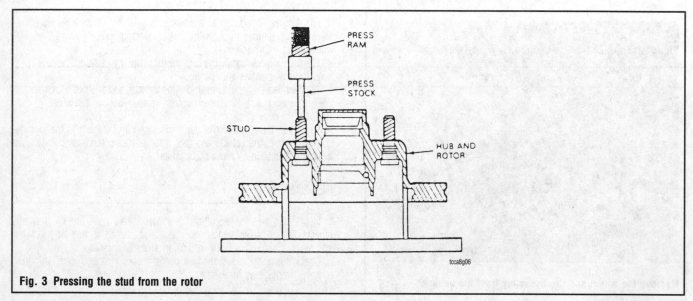

Fig. 3 Pressing the stud from the rotor

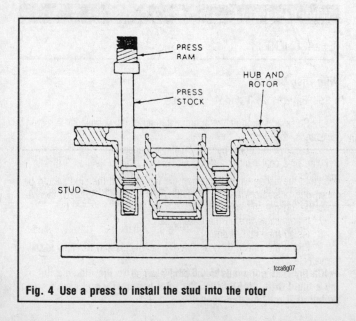

Fig. 4 Use a press to install the stud into the rotor

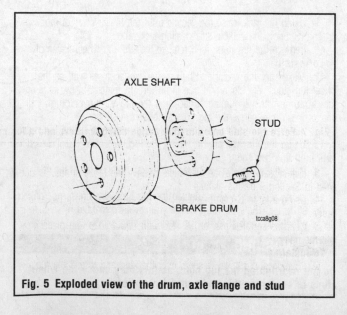

Fig. 5 Exploded view of the drum, axle flange and stud

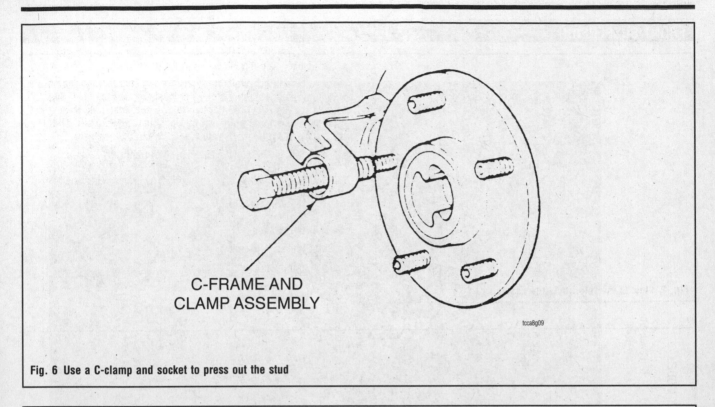

**C-FRAME AND
CLAMP ASSEMBLY**

tcca8g09

Fig. 6 Use a C-clamp and socket to press out the stud

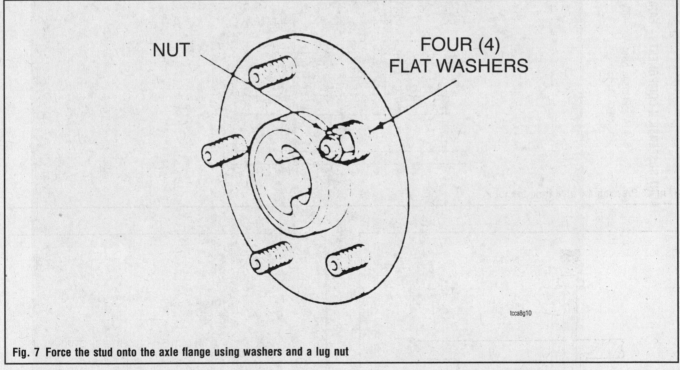

NUT

**FOUR (4)
FLAT WASHERS**

tcca8g10

Fig. 7 Force the stud onto the axle flange using washers and a lug nut

3. If necessary to provide clearance, remove the brake shoes, as outlined in Section 9 of this manual.

4. Using a large C-clamp and socket, press the stud from the axle flange.

5. Coat the serrated part of the stud with liquid soap and place it into the hole.

To install:

6. Position about 4 flat washers over the stud and thread the lug nut. Hold the flange while tightening the lug nut, and the stud should be drawn into position. MAKE SURE THE STUD IS FULLY SEATED, then remove the lug nut and washers.

7. If applicable, install the brake shoes.

8. Install the brake drum.

9. Install the wheel, then remove the jackstands and carefully lower the vehicle.

10. Tighten the lug nuts to the proper torque.

FRONT SUSPENSION

FRONT SUSPENSION COMPONENTS—EARLY MODEL

1. Jacking Point
2. Halfshaft
3. Halfshaft Damper
4. MacPherson Strut Assembly
5. Sway Bar Link
6. Lower Arm
7. Sway Bar

89538p01

FRONT SUSPENSION COMPONENTS—LATE MODEL

1. Crossmember
2. MacPherson Strut Assembly
3. Sway Bar Link
4. Sway Bar
5. Lower Arm
6. Crossmember
7. CV-Boot
8. Halfshaft
9. Halfshaft Damper

89538p02

The front suspension consists of MacPherson struts, and lower arms. The strut assembly performs several suspension functions: it provides the steering knuckle mounting, the concentric coil acts as the spring medium, the integral shock absorber provides dampening and the strut assembly locates the wheel. The stabilizer bar minimizes body roll when cornering. The lower arm acts to longitudinally locate the suspension/wheel.

MacPherson Struts

REMOVAL & INSTALLATION

▶ **See Figure 8**

1. Raise and support the vehicle safely.
2. Remove the front wheels.

3. Detach the brake hose from the clip on the strut.
4. Unbolt the strut from the knuckle.
5. Remove the four strut-to-fender nuts.
6. Pull the strut away from the steering knuckle and wheelhouse and out from the car.

➡**On some models, it is helpful to raise the lower arm with a jack and attach the brake hose, brake line, front speed sensor harness and halfshaft to the steering knuckle with a piece of rope or wire after the strut is separated from the knuckle.**

To install:

7. Before installing the strut, make sure the surface where the strut attaches to the knuckle is clean. This ensures a good connection.
8. Position the strut onto the knuckle and inside fender apron and install the upper and lower attaching hardware.
9. Observe the following torque specifications:

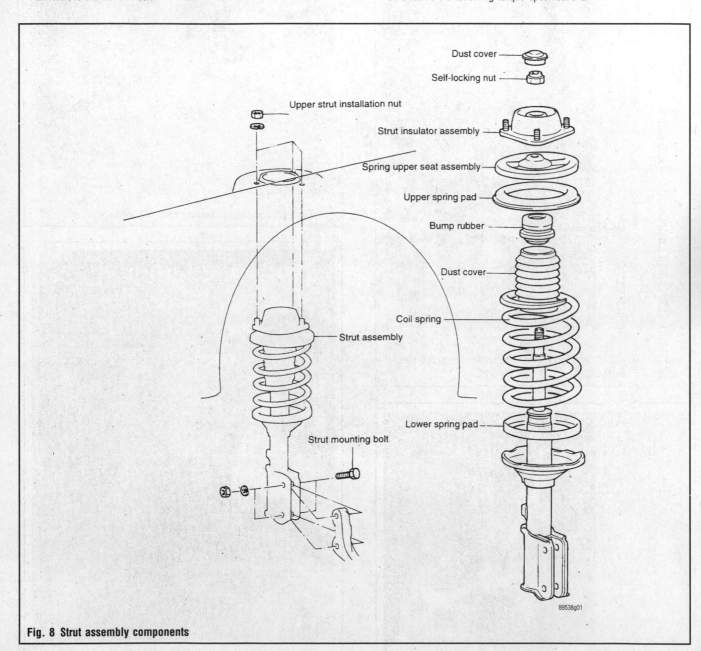

Dust cover
Self-locking nut
Upper strut installation nut
Strut insulator assembly
Spring upper seat assembly
Upper spring pad
Bump rubber
Dust cover
Coil spring
Strut assembly
Lower spring pad
Strut mounting bolt

89538g01

Fig. 8 Strut assembly components

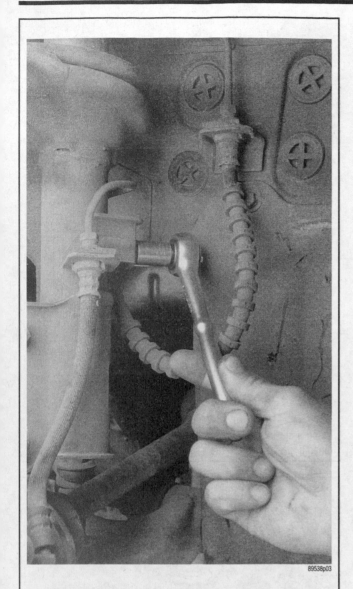

To remove the strut assembly, first disconnect the brake hose mount from the strut . . .

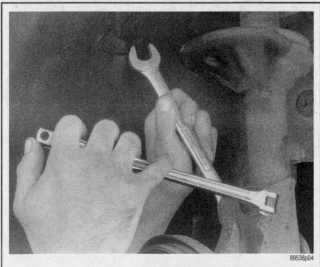

. . . then remove the strut-to-steering knuckle bolts . . .

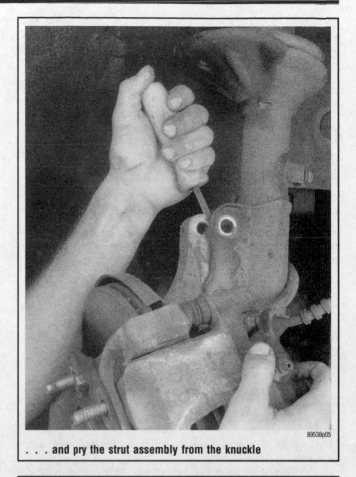

. . . and pry the strut assembly from the knuckle

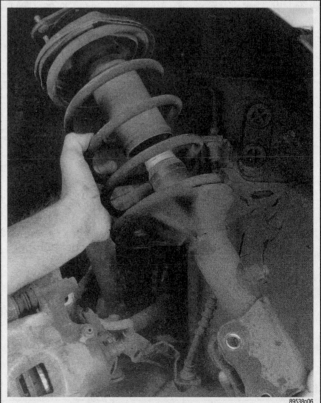

Remove the strut from the vehicle after unbolting it from the wheelhouse

- Strut-to-knuckle bolts—65–76 ft. lbs. (95–105 Nm) for Accent, Excel, Scoupe and Sonata.
- Strut-to-knuckle bolts—80–94 ft. lbs. (110–130 Nm) for Elantra and Tiburon.
- Strut-to-fender nuts—11–14 ft. lbs. (15–20 Nm) for Excel and Scoupe.
- Strut-to-fender nuts—14–22 ft. lbs. (20–30 Nm) for Accent.
- Strut-to-fender nuts—25–33 ft. lbs. (35–45 Nm) for Elantra and Tiburon.
- Strut-to-fender nuts—18–25 ft. lbs. (25–34 Nm) for Sonata.
10. Install the tire and wheel and lower the vehicle.

OVERHAUL

▶ See Figure 9

➡Hyundai does not recommend strut overhaul for late model vehicles. If determined to be faulty, the strut should be replaced as an assembly. The strut spring can be serviced as follows:

1. The strut assembly must be removed from the vehicle to remove the spring.
2. Using a spring compressor, compress the coil spring.
3. Hold the upper spring seat with spanner wrench (PN 09546-21000), or equivalent, loosen the nut at the top end of the strut and remove the insulator.
4. Remove the spring seat, spring and rubber bumper.

To install:
5. Install the coil spring with the identification mark toward the steering knuckle.
6. Install the rubber bumper, upper rubber seat, upper seat assembly, insulator and washer.
7. Align the "D" shaped hole in the spring seat upper assembly with the indentation on the piston rod.
8. After seating the upper and lower ends of the coil spring in the upper and lower spring seat grooves, tighten the locknut to 29–36 ft. lbs. (40–50 Nm).
9. Pack grease in the strut upper bearing and install the cap.

➡Ensure that grease does not contact the insulator rubber.

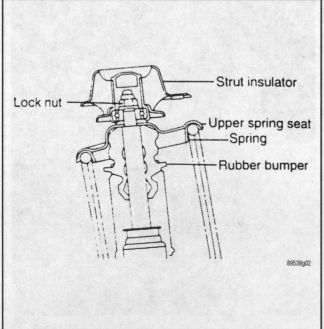

Fig. 9 The upper strut components must be assembled in a specific order for the strut to function properly

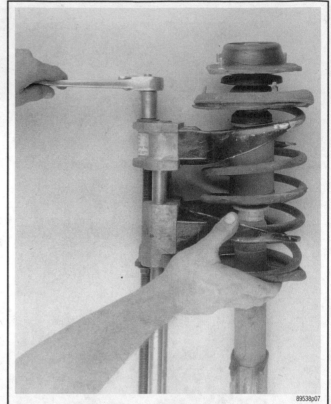

Using a spring compressor, relieve the strut spring's tension . . .

. . . then remove the strut insulator cap . . .

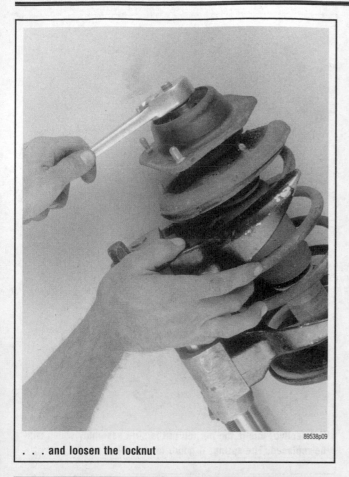

89538p09

. . . and loosen the locknut

89538p11

. . . and washer . . .

89538p10

Remove the strut's locknut . . .

89538p12

. . . then remove the insulator

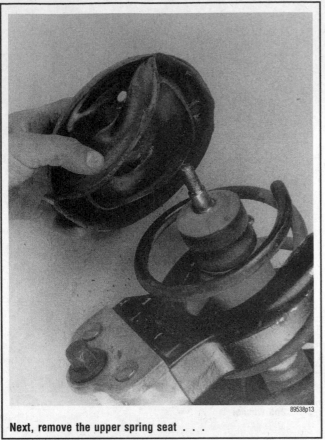

Next, remove the upper spring seat . . .

. . . and rubber bumper

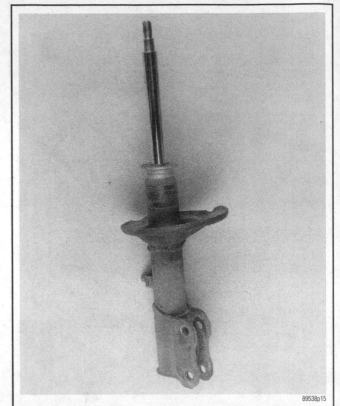

If defective, this is the portion of the strut assembly which will be replaced. The spring, if good, is reusable

Ball Joints

INSPECTION

▶ **See Figure 10**

1. Raise the vehicle and support it safely.
2. Disconnect the ball joint at the lower end of the strut.
3. Install the nut back onto the ball stud.
4. Using an inch lbs. torque wrench, measure the torque required to

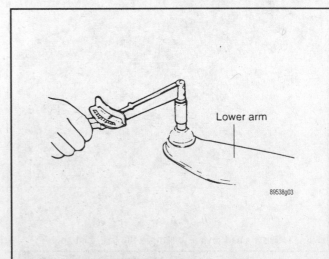

Fig. 10 Using an inch lbs. torque wrench, measure the torque required to start the ball joint rotating

start the ball joint rotating. The specification is 1.4–7.0 ft. lbs. (2.0–9.5 Nm).

5. If torque is within the specification, the ball joint is functional.

6. If torque is higher than the specification, the joint is faulty.

7. If torque is below specification, the joint may be reused provided its rotation is smooth and even.

8. If the joint exhibits any roughness or play, it is faulty and should be replaced.

9. Inspect the dust cover for cracks and check all bolts for straightness. Replace any damaged components.

REMOVAL & INSTALLATION

Bolt-On Type

1. Raise the vehicle and support it safely.
2. Remove the front wheel.
3. Disconnect the stabilizer bar from the lower arm.
4. Remove the ball joint-to-steering knuckle nut and separate the ball joint from the knuckle.
5. Remove the ball joint-to-lower arm mounting bolts and remove the joint from the arm.
6. Remove the dust cover from the ball joint.

To install:

7. Lubricate the ball joint with grease and install the dust cover.
8. Install the joint to the lower arm. Tighten the ball joint mounting bolts to 69–87 ft. lbs. (95–120 Nm).
9. Connect the ball joint to the steering knuckle and tighten the nut to 43–52 ft. lbs. (60–72 Nm).
10. Connect the stabilizer bar to the lower arm.
11. Install the front wheel.
12. Lower the vehicle

Press-In Type

▶ **See Figures 11, 12 and 13**

1. Raise the vehicle and support it safely.
2. Remove the front wheel.
3. Remove the lower arm from the vehicle.
4. Remove the ball joint dust cover.
5. Using special tools (PN 09221-21000, 09545-11000A and 09545-11000B), press the ball joint from the control arm.

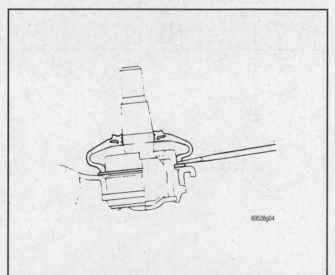

Fig. 11 Use a small prybar to remove the ball joint boot

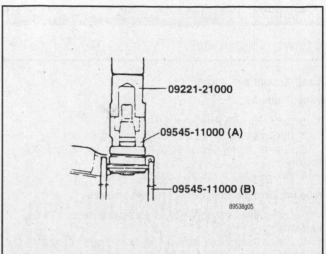

Fig. 12 The ball joint is removed from the lower arm using the special tools illustrated and a hydraulic press

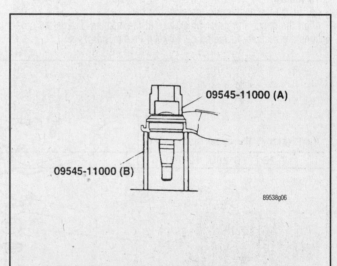

Fig. 13 The ball joint is installed in the lower arm using the special tools illustrated and a hydraulic press

To install:

6. Apply grease to the lip of the control arm and to the ball joint contact surfaces.
7. Place the ball joint in the control arm.
8. Using a special tools (PN 09545-11000A and 09545-11000B), press the ball joint into the control arm.

➡ **The ball joint must be pressed evenly into the control arm.**

9. Install a new dust cover on the ball joint.
10. Install the control arm assembly into the vehicle.
11. Tighten the ball joint-to-steering knuckle retaining nut to 43–52 ft. lbs. (60–72 Nm).
12. Install the front wheel.
13. Lower the vehicle.

Stabilizer Bar

REMOVAL & INSTALLATION

Excel, Scoupe and Accent

♦ See Figure 14

1. Raise and support the vehicle safely.
2. Disconnect the tie rod end from the steering knuckle.
3. Remove rear roll stopper bolts and rear roll bracket assembly mounting bolt.
4. Pull the rear roll bracket assembly forward.

➡**Do not disconnect the center member assembly.**

5. Loosen the stabilizer link bolt, then separate the bar from the lower arm.
6. Loosen the stabilizer bar mounting bolts through the steering gear box access opening provided on the body.
7. Remove the stabilizer bar through the access opening.
8. Remove the upper and lower brackets and remove the bushing.

To install:

9. Install the bushing to the stabilizer bar.
Align the upper and lower brackets with the bushing. Ensure the projections are securely in the space between the brackets.

➡**Distinguish the side the fixtures are to be installed by locating the identification marks stamped on each; R will denote the right side and L will denote the left side fixture. They are not the same and should be installed as labeled.**

10. Using the access opening, temporarily tighten the bushing brackets, then position the opposite side bushing.
11. Securely tighten the stabilizer bar mounts to 12–19 ft. lbs. (17–26 Nm).
12. Install the stabilizer link to the lower arm making sure that the stabilizer bar mounting spacer, bushing and cup are aligned properly. Tighten the link bolt locknut until 0.945–1.024 in. (22–26mm) of the bolt threads are showing through the lower arm.
13. Install the rear roll bracket assembly.
14. Connect the tie rod end to the steering knuckle.
15. Lower the vehicle.

Elantra and Tiburon

♦ See Figures 15 and 16

1. Raise and support the vehicle safely.
2. Disconnect the tie rod end from the steering knuckle.
3. Remove the stabilizer link self locking nut.
4. Remove the stabilizer bar through the access opening.
5. Detach the upper and the lower fixtures; then remove the bushings.

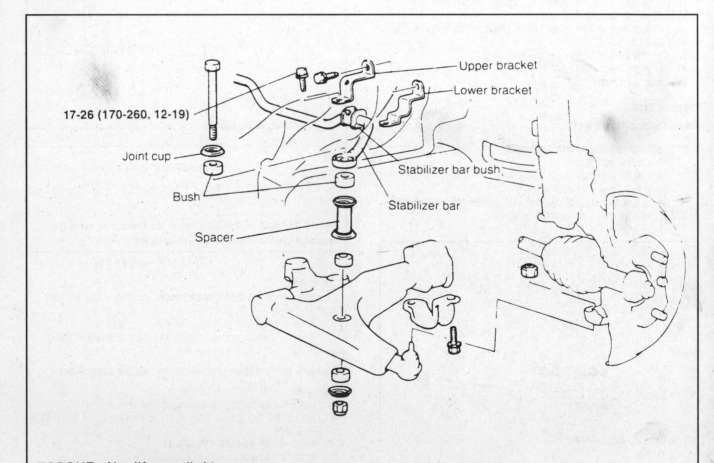

17-26 (170-260, 12-19)

Joint cup

Bush

Spacer

Upper bracket

Lower bracket

Stabilizer bar bush

Stabilizer bar

TORQUE : Nm (Kg.cm, lb.ft)

89538g12

Fig. 14 Stabilizer bar components—Excel, Scoupe and Accent

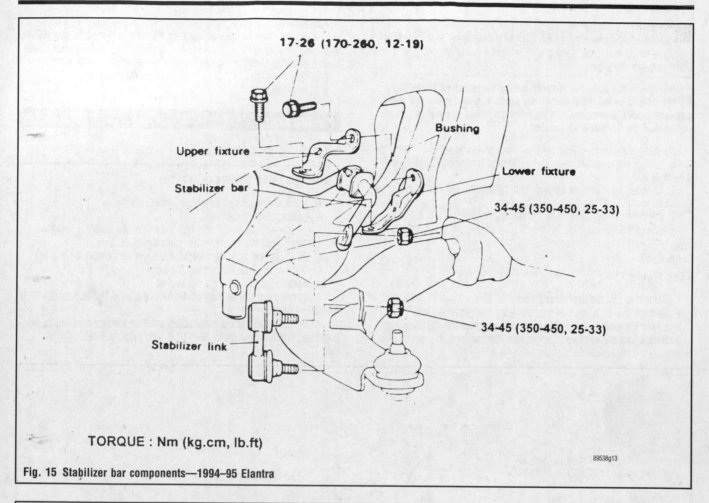

17-26 (170-260, 12-19)

Upper fixture

Bushing

Stabilizer bar

Lower fixture

34-45 (350-450, 25-33)

34-45 (350-450, 25-33)

Stabilizer link

TORQUE : Nm (kg.cm, lb.ft)

89538g13

Fig. 15 Stabilizer bar components—1994–95 Elantra

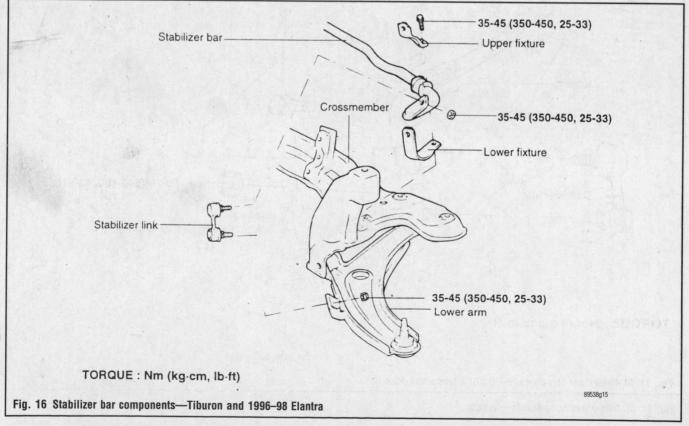

Stabilizer bar

35-45 (350-450, 25-33)

Upper fixture

Crossmember

35-45 (350-450, 25-33)

Lower fixture

Stabilizer link

35-45 (350-450, 25-33)

Lower arm

TORQUE : Nm (kg·cm, lb·ft)

89538g15

Fig. 16 Stabilizer bar components—Tiburon and 1996–98 Elantra

To install:

6. Install the bushings onto the bar. Align the upper and the lower fixtures with the bushings making sure the projections are securely in the space between the fixtures.

➡**Distinguish the side the fixtures are to be installed by locating the identification marks stamped on each; R will denote the right side and L will denote the left side fixture. They are not the same and should be installed as labeled.**

7. Using the access opening, install the rod to the vehicle. Temporarily tighten the bushing fixtures. Final tightening torque is 12–19 ft. lbs. (17–26 Nm).
8. Connect the stabilizer bar link and tighten the self-locking nuts to 25–33 ft. lbs. (34–45 Nm).
9. Connect the tie rod end to the steering knuckle.
10. Lower the vehicle.

Sonata

▶ **See Figure 17**

1. Raise and support the vehicle safely.
2. Remove the stabilizer bar brackets from the crossmember.
3. Lower the rear of the center member and lower the stabilizer bar.
4. Disconnect the end links and remove the stabilizer.

To install:

5. Connect the end links and tighten the nuts to 43–51 ft. lbs. (60–70 Nm).
6. Install the stabilizer bar and raise the rear of the center member.
7. Install the stabilizer bar brackets and tighten securely.
8. Lower the vehicle.

Lower Arm

REMOVAL & INSTALLATION

▶ **See Figures 18 thru 24 (p. 17–19)**

1. Raise and support the vehicle safely.
2. Remove the front wheels.
3. Disconnect the lower arm ball joint from the steering knuckle.
4. Disconnect the stabilizer bar from the lower arm.
5. On Excel and Scoupe, remove the lower arm mounting bracket.
6. Remove the lower arm from the frame.

To install:

7. Install the lower arm to the frame and tighten the bolt to 69–87 ft. lbs. (95–120 Nm).
8. On 1994–95 Elantra and Accent, position the rear bushing as illustrated and tighten the bolt to 90–112 ft. lbs. (125–155 Nm).

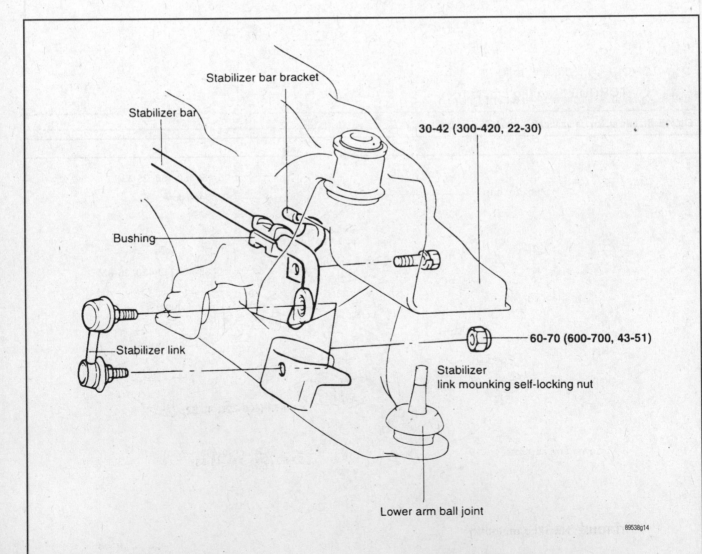

Stabilizer bar bracket

Stabilizer bar

30-42 (300-420, 22-30)

Bushing

60-70 (600-700, 43-51)

Stabilizer link

Stabilizer link mounking self-locking nut

Lower arm ball joint

89538g14

Fig. 17 Stabilizer bar components—Sonata

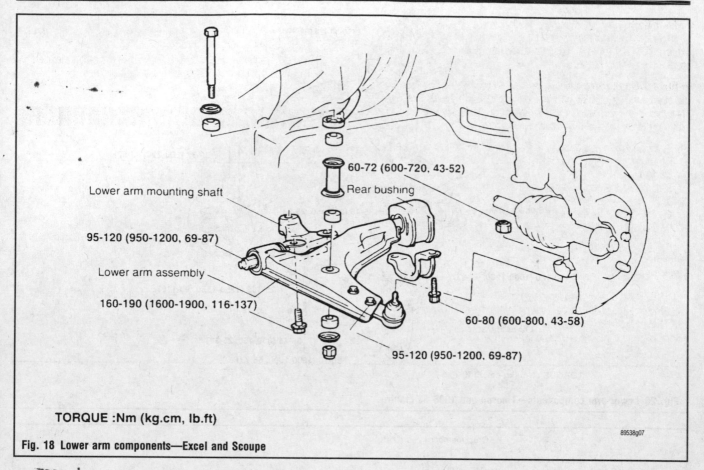

TORQUE :Nm (kg.cm, lb.ft)

Fig. 18 Lower arm components—Excel and Scoupe

89538g07

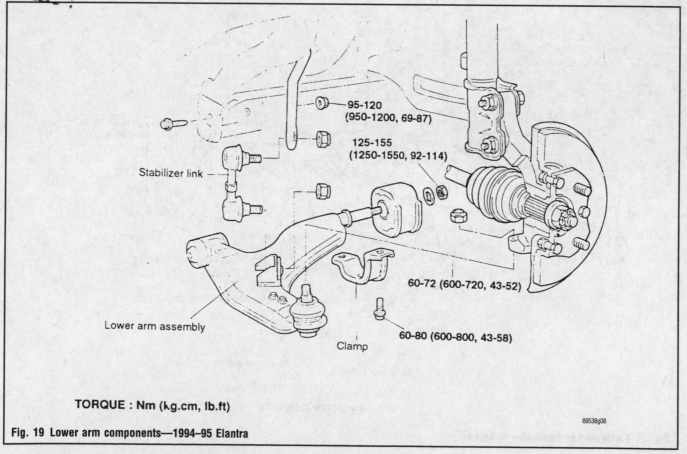

TORQUE : Nm (kg.cm, lb.ft)

Fig. 19 Lower arm components—1994–95 Elantra

89538g08

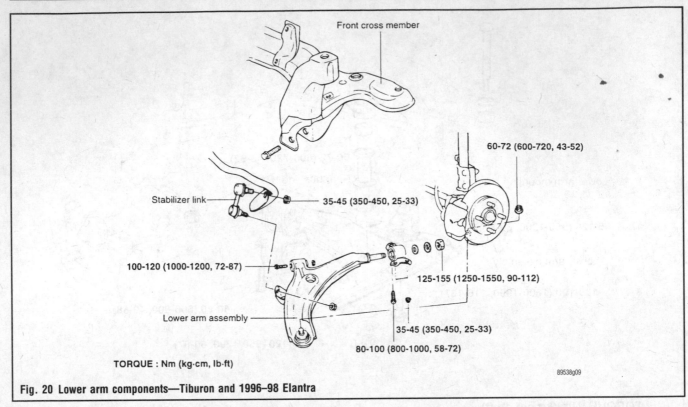

Front cross member

60-72 (600-720, 43-52)

Stabilizer link

35-45 (350-450, 25-33)

100-120 (1000-1200, 72-87)

125-155 (1250-1550, 90-112)

Lower arm assembly

35-45 (350-450, 25-33)

80-100 (800-1000, 58-72)

TORQUE : Nm (kg·cm, lb·ft)

89538g09

Fig. 20 Lower arm components—Tiburon and 1996–98 Elantra

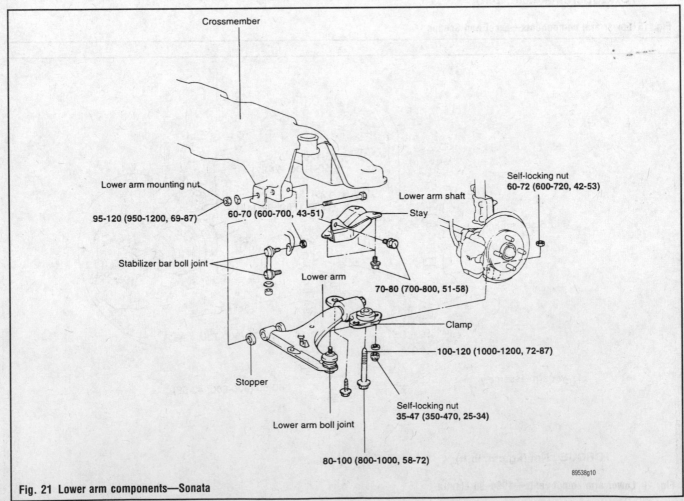

Crossmember

Lower arm mounting nut

95-120 (950-1200, 69-87)

60-70 (600-700, 43-51)

Lower arm shaft

Self-locking nut
60-72 (600-720, 42-53)

Stay

Stabilizer bar boll joint

70-80 (700-800, 51-58)

Lower arm

Clamp

100-120 (1000-1200, 72-87)

Stopper

Self-locking nut
35-47 (350-470, 25-34)

Lower arm boll joint

80-100 (800-1000, 58-72)

89538g10

Fig. 21 Lower arm components—Sonata

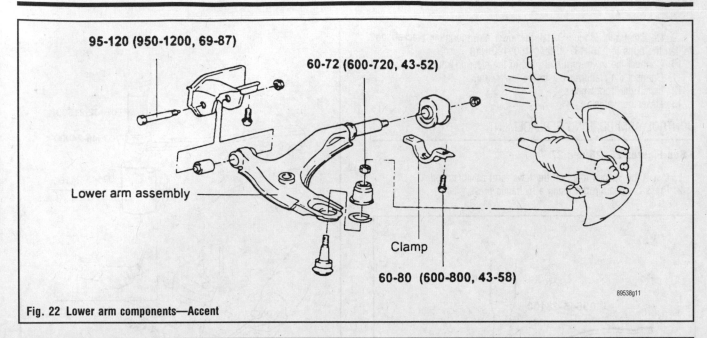

Fig. 22 Lower arm components—Accent

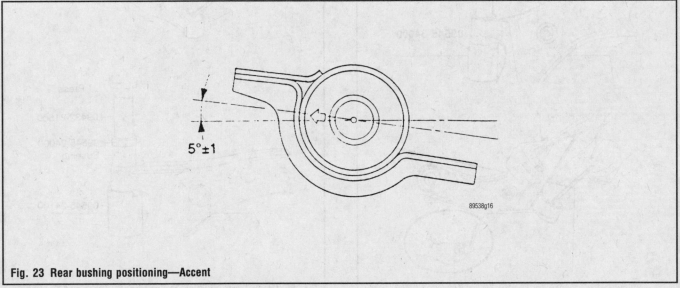

Fig. 23 Rear bushing positioning—Accent

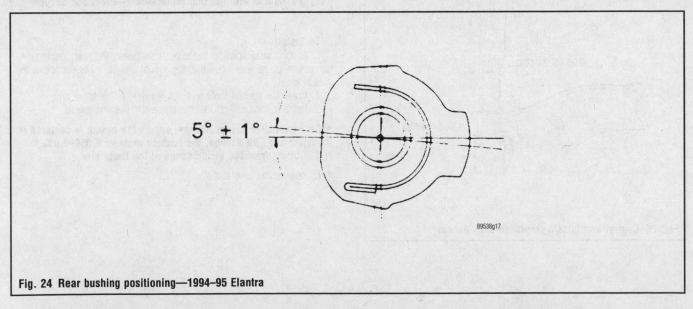

Fig. 24 Rear bushing positioning—1994-95 Elantra

9. On Excel and Scoupe, install the lower arm mounting bracket and tighten the bolts to 116–137 ft. lbs. (160–190 Nm).
10. Connect the lower arm ball joint to the steering knuckle.
11. Connect the stabilizer bar to the lower arm.
12. Install the front wheels.
13. Lower the vehicle.

CONTROL ARM BUSHING REPLACEMENT

♦ **See Figures 25, 26 and 27**

1. Install the special tools on the lower arm as illustrated.
2. Press the bearing out using a hydraulic press.

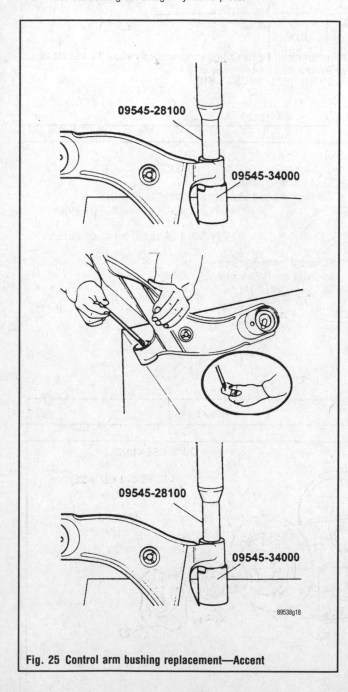

Fig. 25 Control arm bushing replacement—Accent

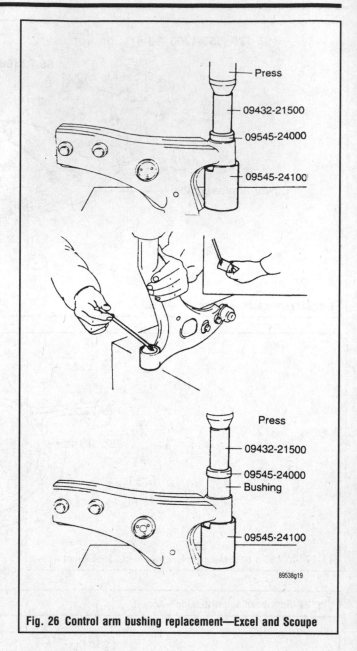

Fig. 26 Control arm bushing replacement—Excel and Scoupe

To install:

3. Apply a soap solution to the outer surface of the new bushing, inner surface of the lower arm bushing mount and the inner surface of the special tools.
4. Install the special tools and new bushing in the lower arm.
5. Press fit the bushing into the lower arm bushing mount.

➡**On all vehicles except Scoupe, ensure the busing is centered in the lower arm. On Scoupe, the bushing must be 0.059–0.098 in. (1.5–2.5mm) from the inside flange of the lower arm**

6. Remove the special tools.

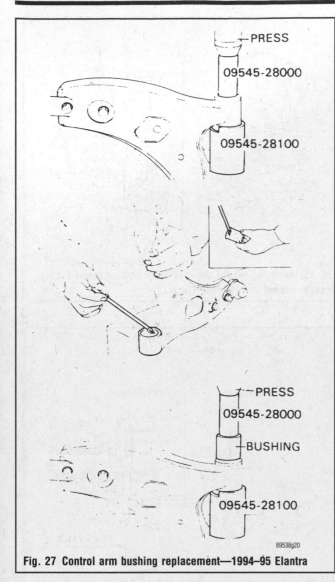

Fig. 27 Control arm bushing replacement—1994–95 Elantra

Knuckle and Spindle

REMOVAL & INSTALLATION

▶ **See Figure 28**

1. Raise and support the vehicle safely.
2. Remove the front wheels.
3. Remove the caliper and suspend it out of the way without disconnecting the brake hose.
4. Disconnect the lower ball joint from the knuckle.
5. Disconnect the tie rod end from the steering knuckle.
6. Using a two-jawed puller, press the axle shaft from the hub.
7. Unbolt the strut from the knuckle.
8. Remove the knuckle assembly.

To install:

➡**Perform final tightening of all components when the vehicle is on the ground at proper ride height.**

9. Install the knuckle assembly and tighten bolts as follows:
• Strut-to-knuckle bolts—65–76 ft. lbs. (95–105 Nm) for Accent, Excel, Scoupe and Sonata.
• Strut-to-knuckle bolts—80–94 ft. lbs. (110–130 Nm) for Elantra and Tiburon.
• Ball joint nut—43–52 ft. lbs. (60–72 Nm).
• Tie rod end—11–25 ft. lbs. (15–34 Nm).
10. Install the axle shaft into the hub.
11. Install the axle shaft nut and tighten as follows:
• 145–188 ft. lbs. (200–260 Nm) for Excel, Scoupe, Sonata and 1994–95 Elantra
• 130–159 ft. lbs. (180–220 Nm) for Accent, Tiburon and 1996–98 Elantra
12. Install the brake caliper.
13. Install the front wheels.
14. Lower the vehicle.

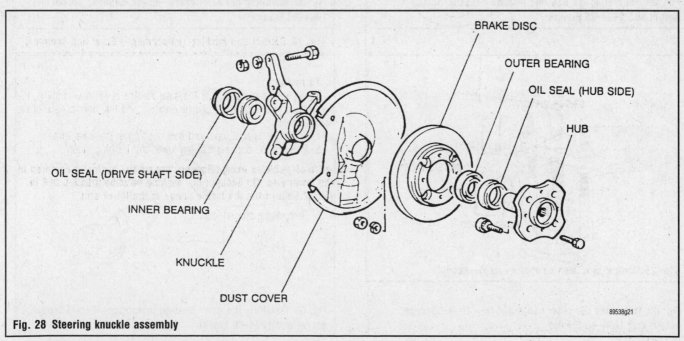

Fig. 28 Steering knuckle assembly

Front Hub and Bearing

REMOVAL & INSTALLATION

Excel, Scoupe, Accent and 1994–95 Elantra

♦ See Figures 29 thru 36

➡ The following procedure requires the use of several special tools.

1. Raise and support the vehicle safely.
2. Remove the steering knuckle assembly.
3. First install the arm, then the body of special tool (PN 09517-21600) on the knuckle and tighten the nut.
4. Using special tool (PN 09517-21500), separate the hub from the knuckle.

➡ Prying or hammering will damage the bearing. Use these special tools, or their equivalent to separate the hub and knuckle.

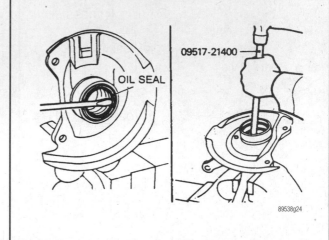

Fig. 31 Removing the oil seal and inner bearing race—Excel, Scoupe, Accent and 1994–95 Elantra

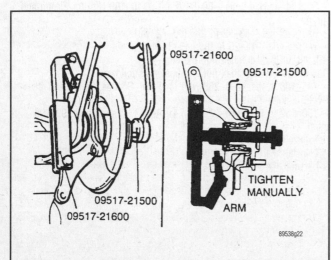

Fig. 29 Separating the hub and knuckle— Excel, Scoupe, Accent and 1994–95 Elantra

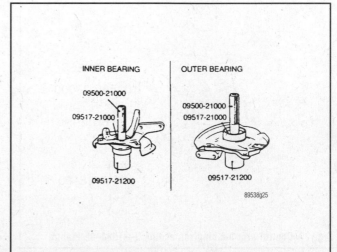

Fig. 32 Installing the outer races—Excel, Scoupe, Accent and 1994–95 Elantra

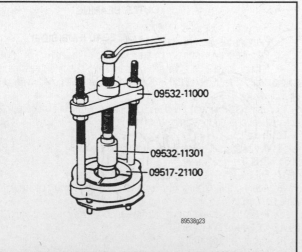

Fig. 30 Removing the outer bearing race— Excel, Scoupe, Accent and 1994–95 Elantra

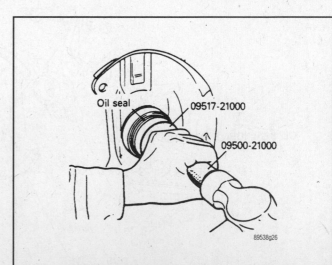

Fig. 33 Installing the outer bearing inner race—Excel, Scoupe, Accent and 1994–95 Elantra

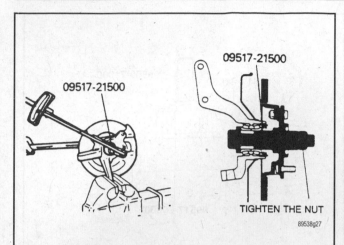

Fig. 34 Assembling the hub and knuckle—Excel, Scoupe, Accent and 1994–95 Elantra

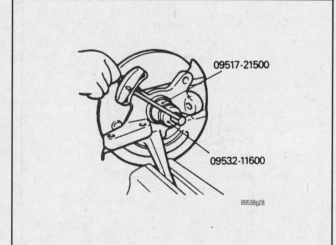

Fig. 35 Measuring bearing starting torque—Excel, Scoupe, Accent and 1994–95 Elantra

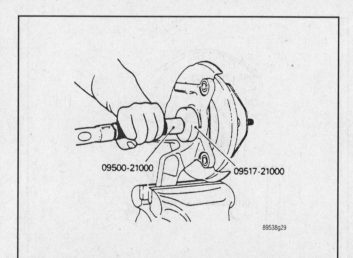

Fig. 36 Halfshaft side seal installation—Excel, Scoupe, Accent and 1994–95 Elantra

5. Place the knuckle in a protected jaw vise and separate the rotor from the hub by removing the four attaching bolts.

6. Using special tools (PN 09532-11000, 0953211301 and 09517-21100), remove the outer bearing inner race.

7. Drive the oil seal and inner bearing inner race from the knuckle with a brass drift.

8. Drive out both outer races in a similar fashion.

➡**Always replace bearings and races as a set. Never replace just an inner or outer bearing. If either is in need of replacement, both sets must be replaced.**

9. Thoroughly clean and inspect all parts. Any suspect part should be replaced.

To install:

10. Pack the wheel bearings with lithium based wheel bearing grease. Coat the inside of the knuckle with similar grease and pack the cavities in the knuckle.

➡**Apply a thin coating of grease to the outer surface of the race before installation.**

11. Using special tools (PN 09500-21000, 09517-21300, and 09517-21200), install the outer races.

12. Install the rotor on the hub and tighten the bolts to 36–43 ft. lbs. (50–60 Nm).

13. Drive the outer bearing inner race into position.

14. Coat the out ring and lip of the oil seal and drive the hub side oil seal into place, using a seal driver.

15. Place the inner bearing in the knuckle.

16. Mount the knuckle in a vise. Position the hub and knuckle together. Install tool (PN 09517-21500) and tighten the tool to 145–188 ft. lbs. (200–260 Nm). Rotate the hub to seat the bearing.

17. With the knuckle still in the vise, measure the hub starting torque with an inch lbs. torque wrench and tool (PN 09517-215000). Starting torque should be 11.5 inch lbs. If the starting torque is 0, measure the hub bearing axial play with a dial indicator. If axial play exceeds 0.11mm, while the nut is tightened to specification, the assembly has not been done correctly. Disassemble the knuckle and hub and start again.

18. Remove the special tool.

19. Place the outer bearing in the hub and drive the seal into place.

20. Install the steering knuckle assembly.

21. Lower the vehicle.

Sonata, Tiburon and 1996–98 Elantra

◆ **See Figures 37 thru 43 (p. 24–25)**

➡**The following procedure requires the use of several special tools.**

1. Raise and support the vehicle safely.

2. Remove the steering knuckle assembly.

3. Remove the snapring from the axle side of the hub.

4. Secure knuckle in a vise and separate the hub and knuckle using special tools (PN 09517-21500, 09517-29000 and 09517-33000), or equivalent.

5. Using special tool PN 09455-21000 or equivalent, remove the outer wheel bearing inner race from the hub.

To install:

6. Install the outer wheel bearing inner race using special tool PN 09517-21000 or equivalent.

7. Fill the wheel bearing with multipurpose grease.

8. Apply a thin coating of grease to the knuckle and bearing contact surfaces.

9. Press the wheel bearing into the knuckle using special tool PN 09517-215000 or equivalent.

10. Install the snapring.

11. Measure the wheel bearing starting rotation torque using a torque wrench and special tools (PN 09517-21500 and 09532-11600), or equivalent. Starting torque should be 11.5 inch lbs. (1.3 Nm).

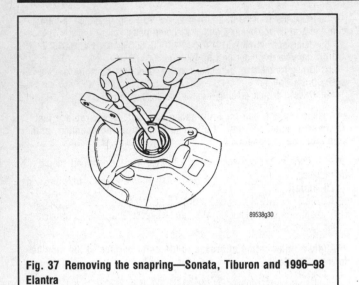

Fig. 37 Removing the snapring—Sonata, Tiburon and 1996–98 Elantra

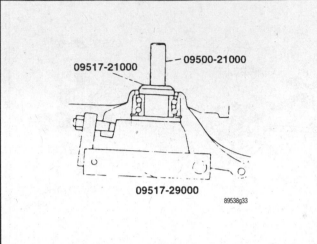

Fig. 40 Installing the outer wheel bearing inner race—Sonata, Tiburon and 1996–98 Elantra

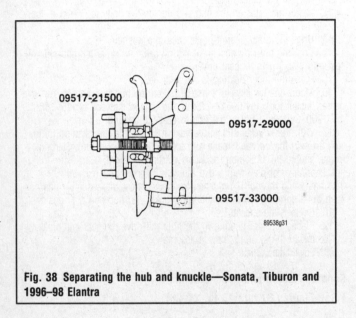

Fig. 38 Separating the hub and knuckle—Sonata, Tiburon and 1996–98 Elantra

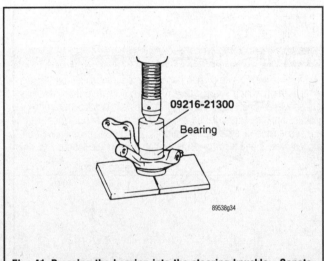

Fig. 41 Pressing the bearing into the steering knuckle—Sonata, Tiburon and 1996–98 Elantra

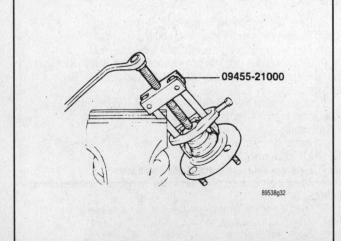

Fig. 39 Removing the outer wheel bearing inner race—Sonata, Tiburon and 1996–98 Elantra

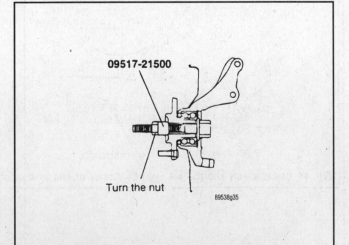

Fig. 42 Assembling the hub and steering knuckle—Sonata, Tiburon and 1996–98 Elantra

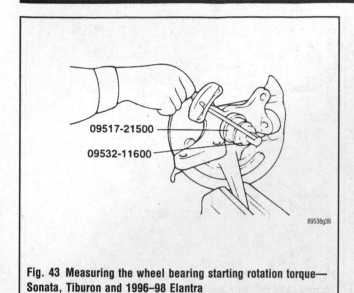

Fig. 43 Measuring the wheel bearing starting rotation torque—Sonata, Tiburon and 1996–98 Elantra

12. Install the steering knuckle.
13. Lower the vehicle.

Wheel Alignment

If the tires are worn unevenly, if the vehicle is not stable on the highway or if the handling seems uneven in spirited driving, the wheel alignment should be checked. If an alignment problem is suspected, first check for improper tire inflation and other possible causes. These can be worn suspension or steering components, accident damage or even unmatched tires. If any worn or damaged components are found, they must

be replaced before the wheels can be properly aligned. Wheel alignment requires very expensive equipment and involves minute adjustments which must be accurate; it should only be performed by a trained technician. Take your vehicle to a properly equipped shop.

Following is a description of the alignment angles which are adjustable on most vehicles and how they affect vehicle handling. Although these angles can apply to both the front and rear wheels, usually only the front suspension is adjustable.

CASTER

▶ See Figure 44

Looking at a vehicle from the side, caster angle describes the steering axis rather than a wheel angle. The steering knuckle is attached to a control arm or strut at the top and a control arm at the bottom. The wheel pivots around the line between these points to steer the vehicle. When the upper point is tilted back, this is described as positive caster. Having a positive caster tends to make the wheels self-centering, increasing directional stability. Excessive positive caster makes the wheels hard to steer, while an uneven caster will cause a pull to one side. Overloading the vehicle or sagging rear springs will affect caster, as will raising the rear of the vehicle. If the rear of the vehicle is lower than normal, the caster becomes more positive.

CAMBER

▶ See Figure 45

Looking from the front of the vehicle, camber is the inward or outward tilt of the top of wheels. When the tops of the wheels are tilted in, this is negative camber; if they are tilted out, it is positive. In a turn, a slight amount of negative camber helps maximize contact of the tire with the road. However, too much negative camber compromises straight-line stability, increases bump steer and torque steer.

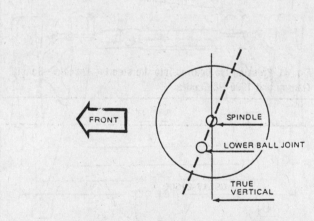

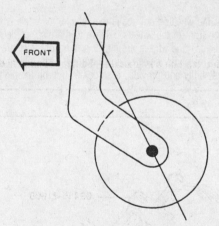

Fig. 44 Caster affects straight-line stability. Caster wheels used on shopping carts, for example, employ positive caster

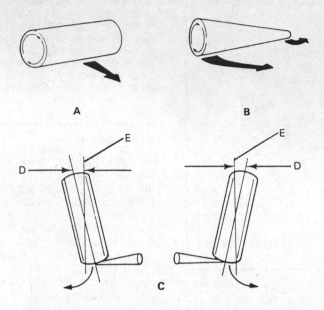

A A CYLINDER WILL ROLL STRAIGHT AHEAD
B A CONE WILL ROLL IN A CIRCLE TOWARD THE SMALL
   END
C TIRE CONTACTS THE ROAD SURFACE
D POSITIVE CAMBER ANGLE
E VERTICAL

TCCA8g02

Fig. 45 Camber influences tire contact with the road

TOE

▶ **See Figure 46**

Looking down at the wheels from above the vehicle, toe angle is the distance between the front of the wheels, relative to the distance between the back of the wheels. If the wheels are closer at the front, they are said to be toed-in or to have negative toe. A small amount of negative toe enhances directional stability and provides a smoother ride on the highway.

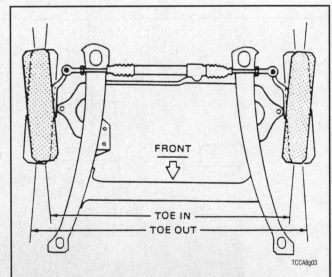

TCCA8g03

Fig. 46 With toe-in, the distance between the wheels is closer at the front than at the rear

REAR SUSPENSION

COIL SPRING INDEPENDENT REAR SUSPENSION COMPONENTS

1. Jacking Point   2. Sway Bar   3. Rear Suspension Assembly   4. Coil Spring

89538p16

MULTI-LINK INDEPENDENT REAR SUSPENSION COMPONENTS

1. Suspension Arm "A"
2. Crossmember
3. Suspension Arm "B"
4. Sway Bar
5. MacPherson Strut Assembly
6. Sway Bar Link
7. Trailing Arm

89538p17

Three types of rear suspensions are used on these vehicles. The Excel and Scoupe use an independent rear suspension with coil springs and separate shock absorbers. The Sonata and 1994–95 Elantra use a torsion rear axle with coil springs over shock absorbers. All other vehicles use a multi-link independent rear suspension with MacPherson struts.

Coil Springs

REMOVAL & INSTALLATION

♦ **See Figure 47**

1. Raise the support the vehicle safely.
2. Remove the rear wheels.
3. Support the rear suspension arm with a floor jack.

4. Remove the lower shock absorber attaching bolt, nut and lock-washer.
5. Slowly, lower the jack just to the point where the spring can be re-moved

➡**If the spring is being replaced, transfer the spring seat to the new spring.**

To install:
6. Install the spring in the reverse order of removal.

➡**Ensure that the smaller diameter of the spring is installed upward and that the spring identification and load markings match up.**

7. Tighten the lower shock mounting bolt to 47–58 ft. lbs. (64–78 Nm).

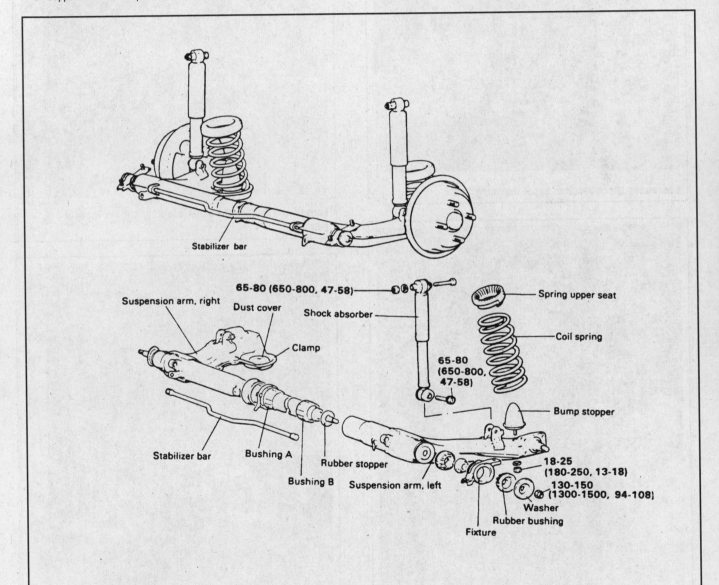

TORQUE : Nm (kg.cm, lb.ft)

89538g39

Fig. 47 Rear suspension components—Excel and Scoupe

Shock Absorbers

REMOVAL & INSTALLATION

◆ See Figures 47, 48 and 49 (p. 29–32)

1. Raise and support the vehicle safely.
2. Remove the rear wheels.

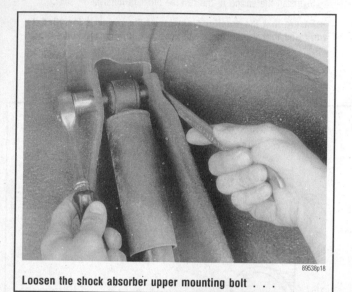

Loosen the shock absorber upper mounting bolt . . .

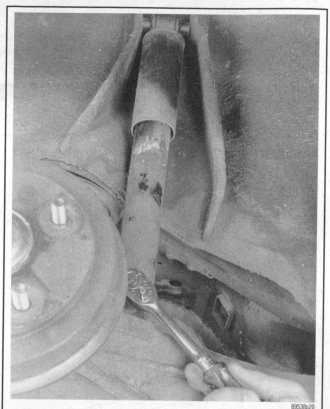

Loosen and remove the shock absorber's lower mounting bolt . . .

. . . then remove the bolt after supporting the trailing arm with a floor jack

. . . then remove the shock absorber from the vehicle

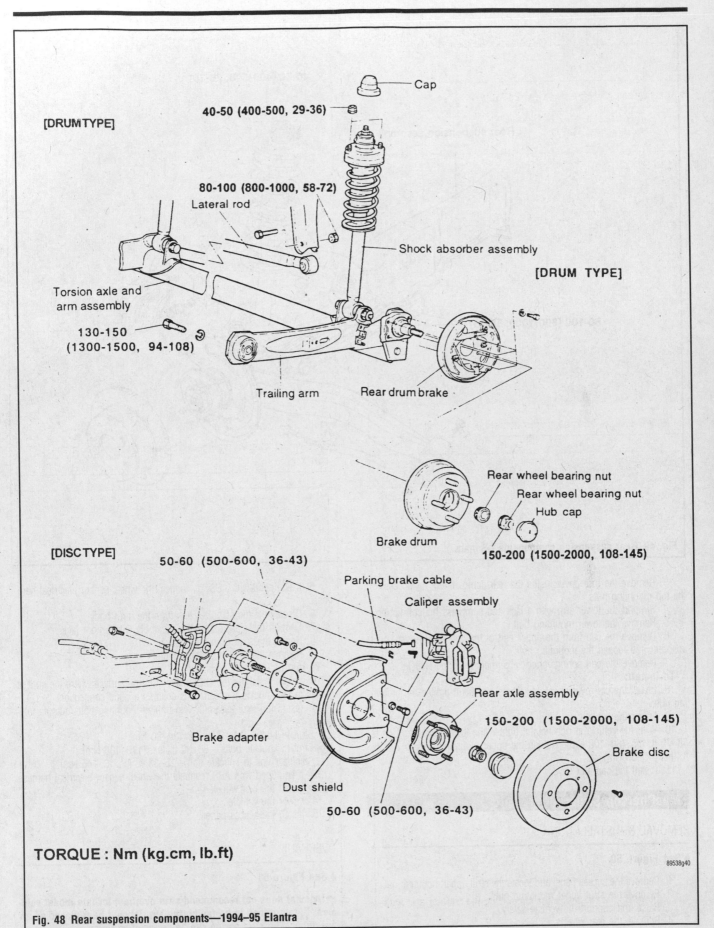

[DRUM TYPE]

Cap

40-50 (400-500, 29-36)

80-100 (800-1000, 58-72)
Lateral rod

Shock absorber assembly

[DRUM TYPE]

Torsion axle and
arm assembly

130-150
(1300-1500, 94-108)

Trailing arm

Rear drum brake

Rear wheel bearing nut

Rear wheel bearing nut

Hub cap

Brake drum

150-200 (1500-2000, 108-145)

[DISC TYPE]

50-60 (500-600, 36-43)

Parking brake cable

Caliper assembly

Rear axle assembly

150-200 (1500-2000, 108-145)

Brake adapter

Brake disc

Dust shield

50-60 (500-600, 36-43)

TORQUE : Nm (kg.cm, lb.ft)

89538g40

Fig. 48 Rear suspension components—1994–95 Elantra

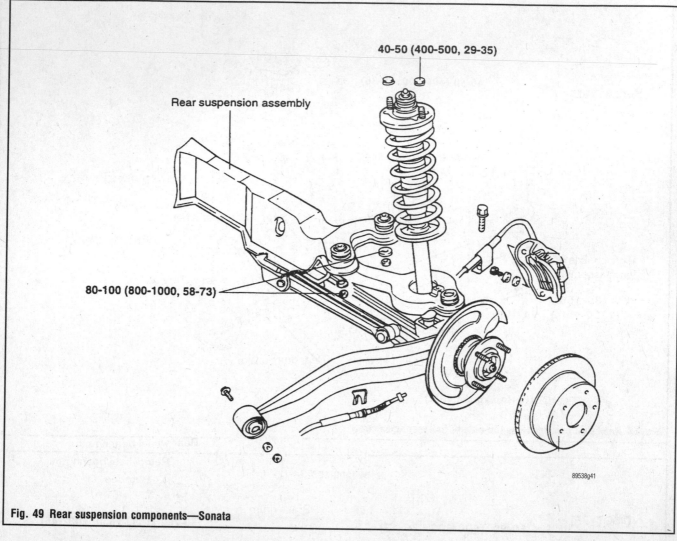

Fig. 49 Rear suspension components—Sonata

3. Remove the trim cover inside the rear compartment for access to the top mounting nuts.

4. Support the lower arm with a jack and compress the coil spring.

5. Remove the lower mounting bolt.

6. Remove the cap from the upper end of the coil spring-over-shock absorber and loosen the mounting nuts.

7. Remove the coil springs/shock absorbers from the vehicle.

To install:

8. Install the coil-over-shock absorbers and hand-tighten the mounting nuts.

9. Lower the vehicle.

10. With the vehicle at ride height, tighten the lower mounting bolt to 58–72 ft. lbs. (80–100 Nm). Tighten the upper mounting nuts to 29–36 ft. lbs. (40–50 Nm).

11. Install the cap and cover.

MacPherson Struts

REMOVAL & INSTALLATION

▶ See Figure 50

1. Remove the access panel and locate the strut upper mounting nuts.
2. Remove the strut upper mounting nuts.
3. Raise and support the vehicle safely.
4. Remove the rear wheels.

5. If equipped with ABS, disconnect the wheel sensor electrical harness.

6. Disconnect the stabilizer link from the strut body.

7. Support the rear suspension assembly with a floor jack.

8. Unbolt the strut from the knuckle.

9. Remove the strut from the vehicle.

To install:

10. Before installing the strut, make sure the surface where the strut attaches to the knuckle is clean. This ensures a good connection.

11. Install the strut assembly and tighten mounting bolts/nuts as follows:

- Strut-to-body—14–22 ft. lbs. (20–30 Nm)
- Strut-to-knuckle bolts—80–90 ft. lbs. (110–130 Nm)
- Stabilizer link-to-knuckle bolt—25–33 ft. lbs. (35–45 Nm)

12. If equipped with ABS, connect the wheel sensor electrical harness.

13. Install the rear wheels.

14. Lower the vehicle.

15. Install the access panel.

OVERHAUL

▶ See Figure 51

➡Hyundai does not recommend strut overhaul for late model vehicles. If determined to be faulty, the strut should be replaced as an assembly. The strut spring can be serviced as follows:

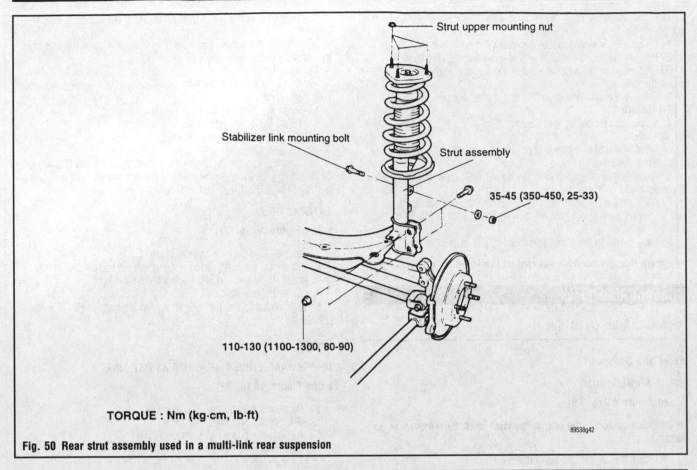

TORQUE : Nm (kg·cm, lb·ft)

89538g42

Fig. 50 Rear strut assembly used in a multi-link rear suspension

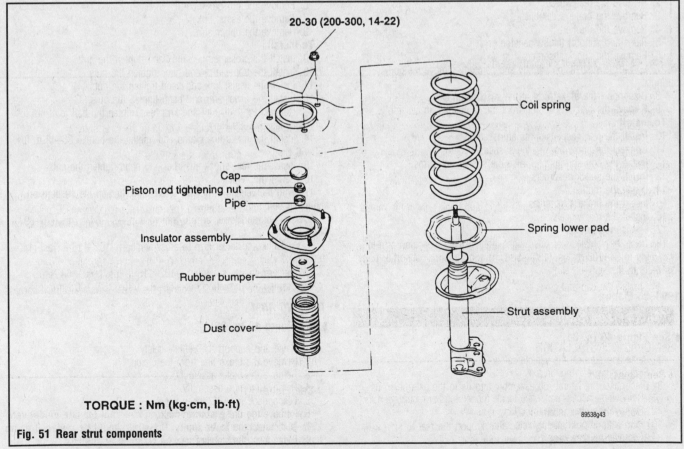

TORQUE : Nm (kg·cm, lb·ft)

89538g43

Fig. 51 Rear strut components

The strut assembly must be removed from the vehicle to remove the spring.

1. Using a spring compressor, compress the coil spring.
2. Hold the upper spring seat with spanner wrench (PN 09546-11000), or equivalent, loosen the nut at the top end of the strut and remove the insulator.
3. Remove the spring seat, spring and rubber bumper.

To install:

4. Install the coil spring with the identification mark toward the steering knuckle.
5. Install the rubber bumper, upper rubber seat, upper seat assembly, insulator and washer.
6. Align the "D" shaped hole in the spring seat upper assembly with the indentation on the piston rod.
7. After seating the upper and lower ends of the coil spring in the upper and lower spring seat grooves, tighten the locknut to 29–36 ft. lbs. (40–50 Nm).
8. Pack grease in the strut upper bearing and install the cap.

➡**Ensure that grease does not contact the insulator rubber.**

Control Arms/Links

REMOVAL & INSTALLATION

Excel and Scoupe

SPLIT SUSPENSION

♦ **See Figure 47 (p. 29)**

➡**On these vehicles, the rear suspension must be removed as an assembly.**

1. Raise the vehicle and support it safely.
2. Remove the rear wheels.
3. Remove the brake assemblies.
4. Remove the muffler.
5. Raise and support the suspension arm.
6. Remove the shock absorbers.
7. Lower the suspension slightly and carefully remove the coil springs.
8. Disconnect the brake hose at the suspension arm.
9. Remove the rear suspension from the vehicle as an assembly.

To install:

10. Install the rear suspension as an assembly.
11. Connect the brake hose at the suspension arm.
12. Install the coil springs and raise the suspension arms.
13. Install the shock absorbers.
14. Install the muffler.
15. Install the brake assemblies.
16. Install the rear wheels.
17. Lower the vehicle.
18. Once the vehicle is at ride height, tighten the suspension arm-to-body nuts to 94–108 ft. lbs. (130–150 Nm) and the shock absorber bolts to 47–58 ft. lbs. (65–80 Nm).

1994–95 Elantra

TORSION AXLE

♦ **See Figure 48 (p. 31)**

1. Raise and support the vehicle safely.
2. Support the rear torsion axle.
3. Disconnect the lateral rod assembly and tie to the axle beam using wire.
4. Remove the brake assemblies.
5. Using a floor jack, slightly raise and support the rear torsion axle.
6. Remove the shock absorber lower mounting bolt.

7. Lower the arm enough to separate the shock absorber from the axle.
8. Remove the trailing arm mounting bolts and lower the arm from the vehicle.

To install:

9. Raise the axle into position and install the trailing arm mounting bolts hand-tight.
10. Raise the axle and connect the shock absorber.
11. Install the brake assemblies.
12. Connect the lateral rod assembly.
13. Lower the vehicle.
14. With the vehicle at ride height, tighten the trailing arm bolts to 94–108 ft. lbs. (130–150 Nm), the lower shock mount bolts and lateral rod bolts to 58–72 ft. lbs. (80–100 Nm).

LATERAL ROD

♦ **See Figure 48 (p. 31)**

1. Raise and support the vehicle safely.
2. Disconnect the rod at each end and remove it from the vehicle.
3. Install the lateral rod and tighten bolts hand-tight.
4. Lower the vehicle.
5. With the vehicle at ride height, tighten the bolts to 58–72 ft. lbs. (78–97 Nm).

Sonata

UPPER ARM, LOWER ARM AND ASSIST LINK

♦ **See Figure 49 (p. 32)**

1. Raise and support the vehicle safely.
2. Remove the rear shock absorber.
3. Remove the brake line from the clamp.
4. Disconnect the ball joint and knuckle.
5. Remove the lower arm.
6. Remove the crossmember.
7. Remove the assist link.
8. Remove the upper arm.

To install:

9. Install the crossmember and hand-tighten the nuts.
10. Install the upper arm and hand-tighten the nuts.
11. Install the assist link and hand-tighten the nuts.
12. Install the lower arm and hand-tighten the nuts.
13. Connect the ball joint and knuckle. Tighten the ball joint nut to 54–64 ft. lbs. (75–89 Nm).
14. Install the brake line clamp and tighten the bolt to 36–43 ft. lbs. (50–60 Nm).
15. Install the rear shock absorber and hand-tighten the nuts.
16. Lower the vehicle.
17. With the vehicle at normal ride height, tighten the suspension mounting bolts/nuts as follows:
   • Assist link and lower arm-to-trailing arm—54–64 ft. lbs. (75–89 Nm)
   • Assist link and lower arm-to-crossmember—102–116 ft. lbs. (140–160 Nm)
   • Upper arm-to-crossmember—102–116 ft. lbs. (140–160 Nm)
   • Crossmember mounting nut—58–73 ft. lbs. (80–100 Nm)

TRAILING ARM

♦ **See Figure 49 (p. 32)**

1. Raise and support the vehicle safely.
2. Remove the brake line from the clamp.
3. Remove the brake assembly.
4. Remove the hub assembly.
5. Disconnect the ABS speed sensor.
6. Remove the brake backing plate.
7. Disconnect the lower arm.
8. Disconnect the stabilizer link.

9. Disconnect the upper arm.
10. Disconnect the assist link.
11. Remove the trailing arm.

To install:

12. Install the trailing arm and hand-tighten the bolts.
13. Connect the assist link and hand-tighten the nuts.
14. Connect the upper arm and hand-tighten the nuts.
15. Connect the stabilizer link and hand-tighten the nuts.
16. Connect the lower arm and hand-tighten the nuts.
17. Install the brake backing plate.
18. Connect the ABS speed sensor.
19. Install the hub assembly.
20. Install the brake assembly.
21. Install the brake line from the clamp.
22. Lower the vehicle.
23. With the vehicle at normal ride height, tighten the suspension mounting bolts/nuts as follows:

• Assist link and lower arm-to-trailing arm—54–64 ft. lbs. (75–89 Nm)
• Assist link and lower arm-to-crossmember—102–116 ft. lbs. (140–160 Nm)
• Upper arm-to-crossmember—102–116 ft. lbs. (140–160 Nm)
• Crossmember mounting nut—58–73 ft. lbs. (80–100 Nm)
• Trailing arm-to-chassis—102–116 ft. lbs. (140–160 Nm)

Accent, Tiburon and 1996–98 Elantra

SUSPENSION ARMS AND TRAILING ARM

♦ See Figures 52 and 53

1. Raise and support the vehicle safely.
2. Disconnect the ABS wheel sensor

3. Remove the brake assembly.
4. Remove the suspension arms and trailing arm mounting bolts from the crossmember and knuckle.
5. Remove the suspension arms and trailing arm from the vehicle.

To install:

6. Install the suspension arms and trailing arm. Hand-tighten the mounting bolts/nuts.
7. Install the brake assembly.
8. Connect the ABS wheel sensor.
9. Lower the vehicle.
10. With the vehicle at normal ride height, tighten the suspension mounting bolts/nuts as follows:

• Suspension arms (Accent)—72–87 ft. lbs. (100–120 Nm)
• Suspension arms (except Accent)—58–72 ft. lbs. (80–100 Nm)
• Trailing arm—72–87 ft. lbs. (100–120 Nm)

Sway Bar

REMOVAL & INSTALLATION

Excel and Scoupe

♦ See Figure 47 (p. 29)

1. Raise and support the vehicle safely.
2. Remove the rear suspension from the vehicle.
3. Matchmark the two halves of the rear suspension.
4. Matchmark the sway bar to the sway bar mounts.
5. Carefully separate the rear suspension halves.
6. Remove the sway bar.

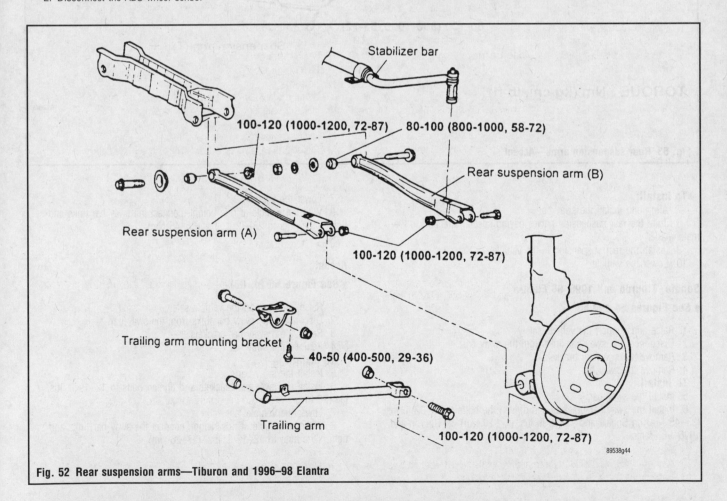

Stabilizer bar

100-120 (1000-1200, 72-87)   80-100 (800-1000, 58-72)

Rear suspension arm (B)

Rear suspension arm (A)

100-120 (1000-1200, 72-87)

Trailing arm mounting bracket

40-50 (400-500, 29-36)

Trailing arm

100-120 (1000-1200, 72-87)

89538g44

Fig. 52 Rear suspension arms—Tiburon and 1996–98 Elantra

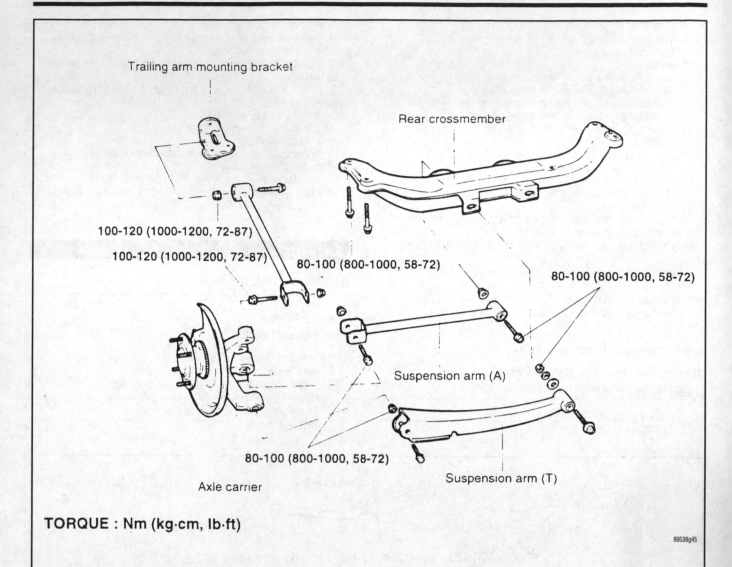

Trailing arm mounting bracket

Rear crossmember

100-120 (1000-1200, 72-87)

100-120 (1000-1200, 72-87)

80-100 (800-1000, 58-72)

80-100 (800-1000, 58-72)

Suspension arm (A)

80-100 (800-1000, 58-72)

Suspension arm (T)

Axle carrier

TORQUE : Nm (kg·cm, lb·ft)

89538g45

Fig. 53 Rear suspension arms—Accent

To install:

7. Align and install the sway bar.
8. Joint the rear suspension halves paying special attention to the matchmarks.
9. Install the rear suspension in the vehicle.
10. Lower the vehicle.

Sonata, Tiburon and 1996–98 Elantra

♦ See Figures 54 and 55

1. Raise and support the vehicle safely.
2. Disconnect the sway bar links from the sway bar.
3. Remove the sway bar brackets.
4. Remove the sway bar.
To install:
5. Install the sway bar.
6. Install the sway bar brackets and tighten the bolts to 25–32 ft. lbs. (35–45 Nm) on Sonata and 12–19 ft. lbs. (17–26 Nm) on Tiburon and 1996–98 Elantra.

7. Lower the vehicle.
8. With the vehicle at ride height, connect the sway bar links and tighten the nuts to 25–32 ft. lbs. (35–45 Nm).

Accent

♦ See Figure 56 (p. 38)

1. Raise and support the vehicle safely.
2. Disconnect the sway bar links from the sway bar.
3. Remove the sway bar brackets.
4. Remove the sway bar.
To install:
5. Install the sway bar.
6. Install the sway bar brackets and tighten bolts to 12–19 ft. lbs. (17–26 Nm).
7. Lower the vehicle.
8. With the vehicle at ride height, connect the sway bar links and tighten the nuts to 12–19 ft. lbs. (17–26 Nm).

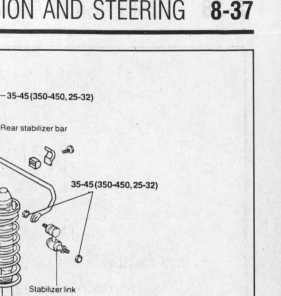

Stabilizer bar bracket

35-45 (350-450, 25-32)

Rear stabilizer bar

35-45 (350-450, 25-32)

Stabilizer link

Fig. 54 Rear sway bar components—Sonata

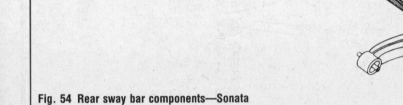

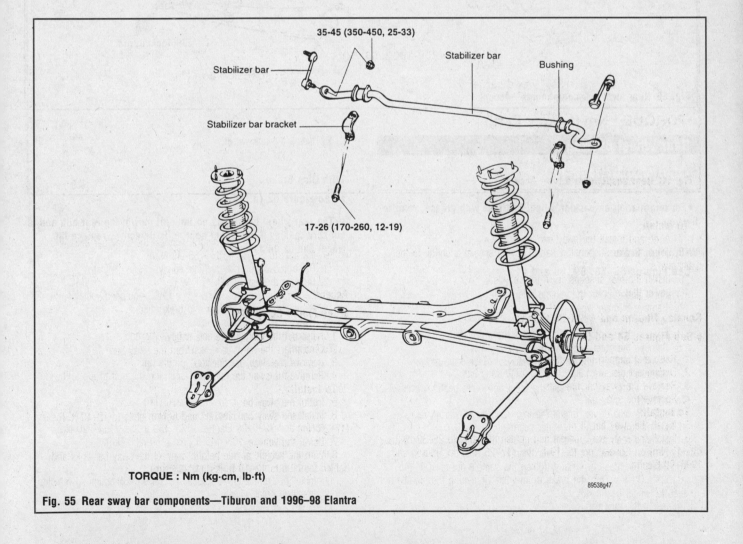

35-45 (350-450, 25-33)

Stabilizer bar

Stabilizer bar

Bushing

Stabilizer bar bracket

17-26 (170-260, 12-19)

TORQUE : Nm (kg·cm, lb·ft)

Fig. 55 Rear sway bar components—Tiburon and 1996–98 Elantra

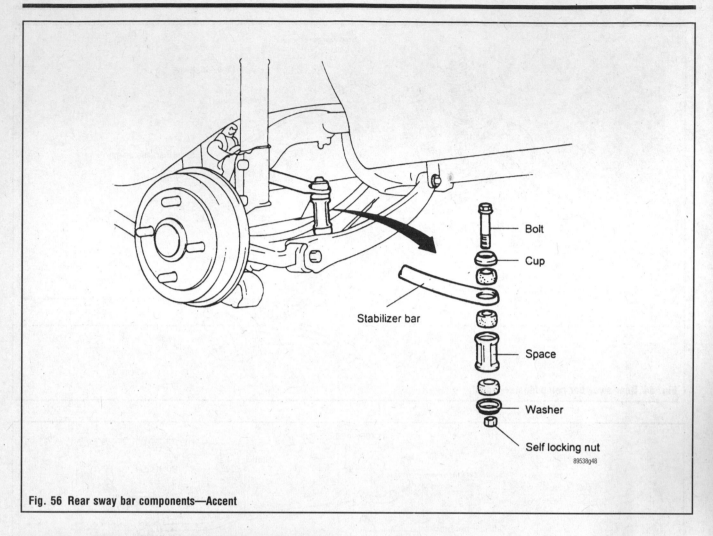

Fig. 56 Rear sway bar components—Accent

Rear Wheel Bearings

REMOVAL & INSTALLATION

➡For information on packing wheel bearings with grease, refer to Section 1.

With Drum Brakes

◆ **See Figures 57, 58, 59, 60 and 61**

1. Raise and support the vehicle safely.
2. Remove the rear wheel.
3. Remove the dust cap.
4. Loosen the spindle nut and remove the brake drum.
5. Remove the outer bearing from the drum.
6. Using a prybar, remove the oil seal from inside the drum.
7. Remove the inner bearing.
8. Using a brass drift, remove the inner and outer bearing races.

To install:

9. Using a race driver, install the inner and outer bearing races.
10. Lubricate and install the inner bearing.
11. Using a seal driver, install the oil seal on the inside of the drum.
12. Lubricate and install the outer bearing.
13. Install the brake drum and tighten the spindle nut to 108–145 ft. lbs. (150–200 Nm). Turn the brake drum while tightening the spindle nut to seat the wheel bearings.
14. Install the dust cap.

15. Install the rear wheel.
16. Lower the vehicle.

With Disc Brakes

◆ **See Figure 62 (p. 40)**

➡The rear wheel bearing is an integral part of the rear hub and is not serviceable. If the wheel bearing is defective, replace the wheel hub as an assembly.

1. Raise and support the vehicle safely.
2. Remove the rear wheel.
3. Remove the rear speed sensor on ABS equipped vehicles.
4. Remove the brake caliper and brake disc.
5. Remove the hub cap.
6. Loosen the spindle nut and remove the hub.

To install:

7. Install the hub, washer and spindle nut.
8. Tighten the spindle nut while spinning the hub to the following torque:

• Tiburon—143–164 ft. lbs. (200–230 Nm)
• Sonata—146–189 ft. lbs. (200–260 Nm)
• Accent and 1996–98 Elantra—130–159 ft. lbs. (180–220 Nm)
• 1994–95 Elantra—108–145 ft. lbs. (150–200 Nm)

9. Install the hub cap.
10. Install the brake caliper and brake disc.
11. Install and adjust the rear speed sensor on ABS equipped vehicles.
12. Install the rear wheel.
13. Lower the vehicle.

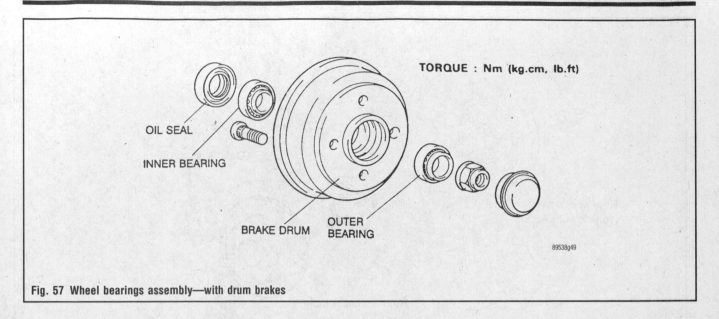

Fig. 57 Wheel bearings assembly—with drum brakes

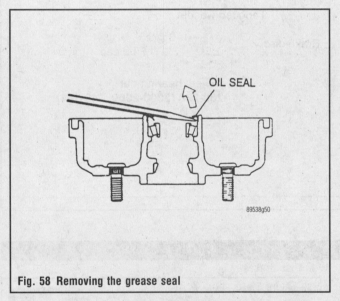

Fig. 58 Removing the grease seal

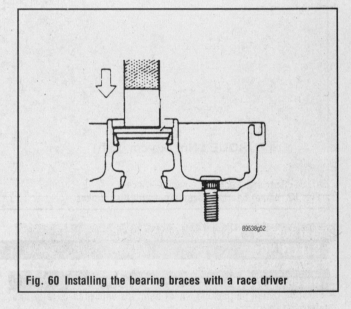

Fig. 60 Installing the bearing braces with a race driver

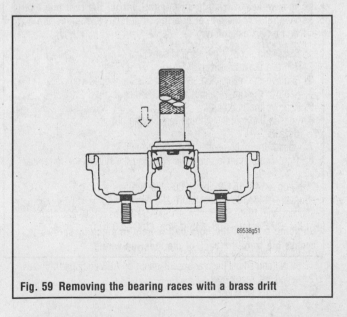

Fig. 59 Removing the bearing races with a brass drift

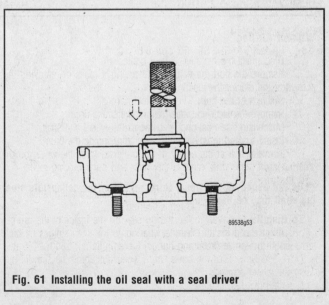

Fig. 61 Installing the oil seal with a seal driver

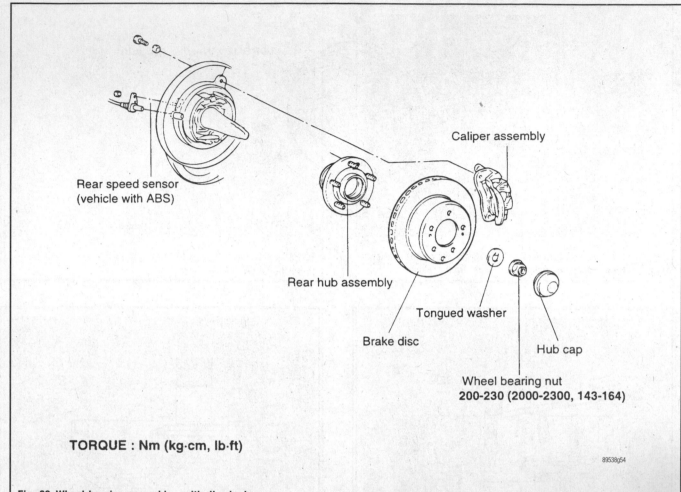

Caliper assembly

Rear speed sensor
(vehicle with ABS)

Rear hub assembly

Tongued washer

Brake disc

Hub cap

Wheel bearing nut
200-230 (2000-2300, 143-164)

TORQUE : Nm (kg·cm, lb·ft)

89538g54

Fig. 62 Wheel bearing assembly—with disc brakes

STEERING

Steering Wheel

REMOVAL & INSTALLATION

Without Air Bag

1. Disconnect the negative battery cable.
2. Remove the horn cover by either prying it loose or removing the screws at the rear of the steering wheel.
3. Disconnect the horn wire electrical harness.
4. Remove the steering wheel retaining nut.
5. Matchmark the relationship between the wheel and shaft.
6. Install a steering wheel puller on the wheel.
7. Turn the bolt at the center of the puller to force the wheel off the steering shaft.

➡**Do not pound on the wheel to remove it or the collapsible steering shaft may be damaged.**

To install:

8. Align and push the steering wheel onto the shaft splines by hand far enough to start the retaining nut.

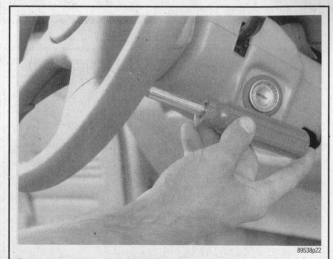

89538p22

On some models, the horn pad is held in place by screws accessible from the back of the steering wheel

On other models, the horn pad is held in place by clips and can be pried from the steering wheel

Install a steering wheel puller and tighten the center bolt to force the wheel off the shaft

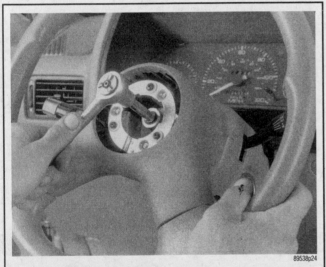

Loosen the steering shaft nut . . .

Once the steering wheel is removed, the multi-function switch assembly is easily accessed

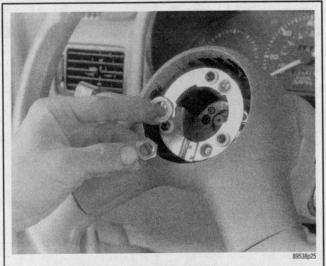

. . . then remove the shaft nut and washer

9. Install the retaining nut and tighten to 26–32 ft. lbs. (34–44 Nm).
10. Connect the horn wire electrical harness.
11. Install the horn cover.
12. Connect the negative battery cable.

With Air Bag

♦ **See Figure 63**

• Never attempt to disassemble or repair the air bag module or clock spring.
• Do not drop the air bag module or allow contact with water, grease or oil.
• Replace the module if a dent, crack, deformation or rust is evident.
• The air bag module should be stored on a flat surface and placed so that the pad surface is facing upward.
• Never place anything on top of a stored air bag.
• Do not expose the air bag module to temperature over 200°F (93°C).
• An undeployed air bag module should only be disposed of in accordance with the proper procedures.
• Never attempt to measure the circuit resistance of the air bag module. Accidental air bag deployment will result in serious personal injury.

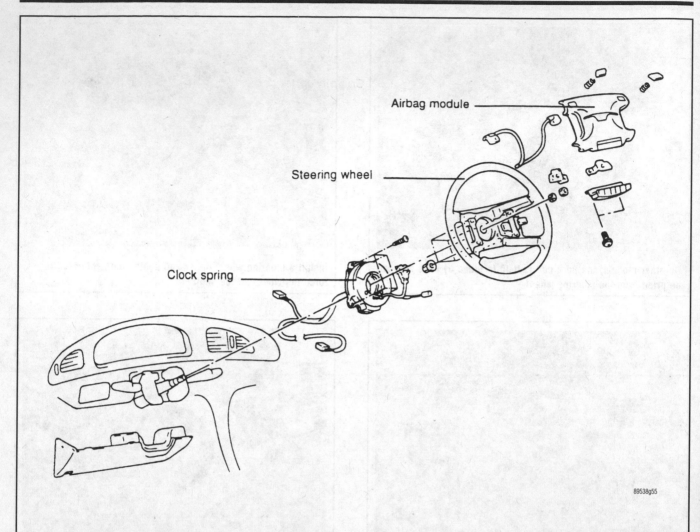

Fig. 63 Air bag system components are an integral part of the steering column assembly. Extreme caution should be taken when working around air bag components

1. Turn the steering wheel to the straight ahead position.
2. Disconnect the negative battery cable.

➡**Wait at least 30 seconds prior to the start of service. This disables the air bag system.**

3. Loosen the air bag module screws at the rear of the steering wheel.
4. Disconnect the air bag electrical harness
5. Remove the air bag and store with the cushion side upward.
6. Disconnect the horn wire electrical harness.
7. Remove the steering wheel retaining nut.
8. Matchmark the relationship between the wheel and shaft.
9. Install a steering wheel puller on the wheel.
10. Turn the bolt at the center of the puller to force the wheel off the steering shaft.

➡**Do not pound on the wheel to remove it or the collapsible steering shaft may be damaged.**

To install:
11. Align and push the steering wheel onto the shaft splines by hand far enough to start the retaining nut.
12. Install the retaining nut and torque to 29–36 ft. lbs. (40–50 Nm).
13. Connect the horn wire connector.
14. Connect the air bag electrical harness

15. Install the air bag module and tighten the screw securely.
16. Connect the negative battery cable.

Multi-Function (Combination) Switch

REMOVAL & INSTALLATION

Without Air Bag
▸ **See Figure 64**

1. Disconnect the negative battery cable.
2. Remove the steering wheel.
3. Remove the steering column covers.
4. Disconnect the horn electrical harness.
5. Remove the electrical harness retainers.
6. Remove the retaining screws and slide the switch off the steering column.

To install:
7. Install the multi-function switch and tighten the retaining screws securely.
8. Install the electrical harness retainers.
9. Connect the horn electrical harness.

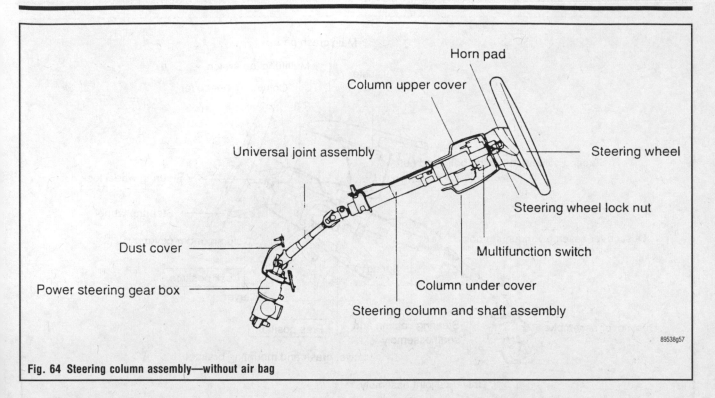

Fig. 64 Steering column assembly—without air bag

10. Install the steering column covers.
11. Install the steering wheel.
12. Connect the negative battery cable.

With Air Bag

♦ See Figure 65

1. Turn the steering wheel to the straight ahead position.
2. Disconnect the negative battery cable.

➡**Wait at least 30 seconds prior to the start of service. This disables the air bag system.**

3. Remove the air bag module.
4. Disconnect the air bag and horn electrical harnesses.
5. Remove the steering wheel.
6. Remove the steering column upper and lower shrouds.
7. Remove the clock spring.
8. Remove the multi-function switch assembly.

To install:
9. Install the multi-function switch assembly.
10. Align the mating mark and neutral position indicator of the clock spring.
11. Ensure the front wheels are in the straight ahead position.
12. Install the clock spring.
13. Install the steering column upper and lower shrouds.
14. Install the steering wheel.
15. Connect the air bag and horn electrical harnesses.
16. Install the air bag module.
17. Connect the negative battery cable.

Ignition Switch

REMOVAL & INSTALLATION

♦ See Figures 66 and 67 (p. 44–45)

1. Disconnect the negative battery cable.
2. Remove the steering wheel.
3. Remove the lower instrument panel knee protector.

4. Remove the steering column covers.
5. Disconnect the electrical harness from the mounting clip.
6. Remove the multi-function switch and harness.
7. Disconnect the electrical harness for the ignition switch.
8. Use a hacksaw to cut a slit in the top of each of the fastening bolts. An alternate method is to use a chisel to punch a groove in the top of the screw.
9. Carefully remove the screws from the ignition switch.
10. Remove the ignition switch.

To install:
11. Align the halves of the ignition switch assembly around the steering column.
12. Align the ignition switch assembly with the column boss.
13. Install the new tamper-proof screws and tighten loosely.
14. Verify proper operation of the ignition switch.
15. Tighten the tamper-proof screws until their heads break off.
16. Connect the electrical harness for the ignition switch.
17. Install the multi-function switch and harness.
18. Connect the electrical harness to the mounting clip.
19. Install the steering column covers.
20. Install the lower instrument panel knee protector.
21. Install the steering wheel.
22. Connect the negative battery cable.

Steering Linkage

REMOVAL & INSTALLATION

Tie Rod Ends

1. Raise and support the vehicle safely.
2. Remove the front wheels.
3. Loosen the tie rod end locknut.
4. Remove the castle nut cotter pin and then remove the castle nut.
5. Disconnect the tie rod ends front the steering knuckle with a separator tool (PN 09568-31000) or equivalent.
6. Count the exact number of exposed threads on the tie rod ends and unscrew the tie rod end.

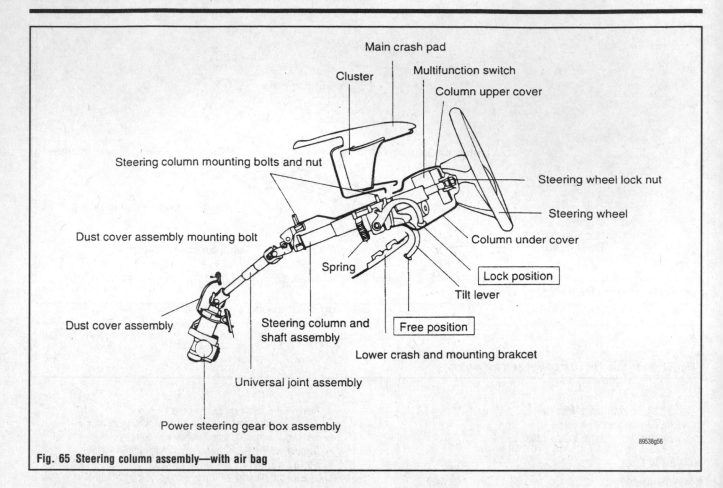

Main crash pad

Cluster

Multifunction switch

Column upper cover

Steering column mounting bolts and nut

Steering wheel lock nut

Steering wheel

Dust cover assembly mounting bolt

Column under cover

Spring

Lock position

Tilt lever

Dust cover assembly

Steering column and shaft assembly

Free position

Lower crash and mounting brakcet

Universal joint assembly

Power steering gear box assembly

89538g56

Fig. 65 Steering column assembly—with air bag

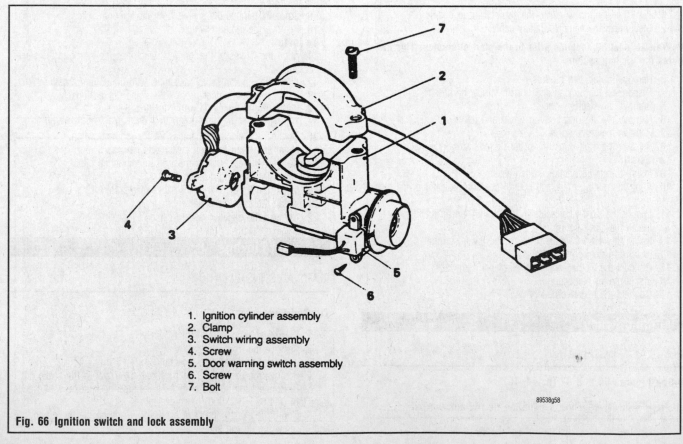

1. Ignition cylinder assembly
2. Clamp
3. Switch wiring assembly
4. Screw
5. Door warning switch assembly
6. Screw
7. Bolt

89538g58

Fig. 66 Ignition switch and lock assembly

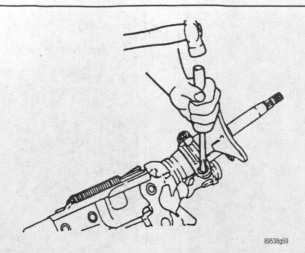

Fig. 67 Remove the ignition switch screws by either cutting a slot in the top of the screw or using a chisel to punch a groove. Then, remove the screws with a flat bladed screwdriver

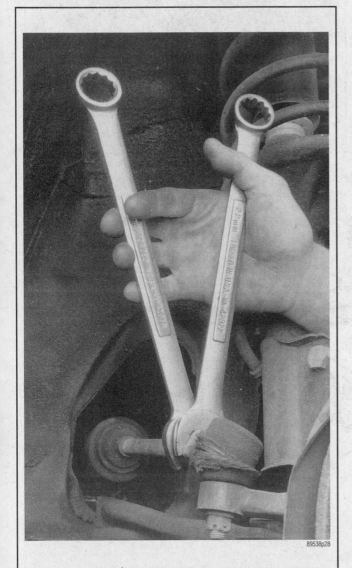

Using a pair of wrenches, loosen the tie rod end locknut . . .

. . . then remove the castle nut cotter pin . . .

. . . and remove the castle nut

Attach a ball joint separator, then tighten the center bolt to press out the ball joint from the knuckle

Remove the ball joint from the steering knuckle . . .

. . . then unthread the tie rod end from the tie rod

To install:

7. Lubricate the tie rod threads and screw the tie rod ends into place so that the previously noted number of threads are visible with the locknut tightened to 44–59 ft. lbs. (60–80 Nm).

8. Insert the tie rod ball joint stud into the steering knuckle and tighten the castle nut to 11–25 ft. lbs. (15–34 Nm).

9. Install the front wheels.

10. Lower the vehicle.

11. Check the wheel alignment.

Manual Steering Rack

REMOVAL & INSTALLATION

▶ **See Figures 68 and 69**

1. Raise and support the vehicle safely.

2. Turn the wheels to the straight ahead position.

3. Remove the wheels.

4. Remove all components necessary to gain access to the rack.

5. Matchmark the steering shaft to the pinion.

6. Remove the steering shaft-to-pinion coupling bolt.

7. Disconnect the tie rod ends from the steering knuckles.

8. Remove the clamps securing the rack to the crossmember.

9. Remove the rack from the vehicle.

To install:

10. Install the rubber mount for the rack and pinion with the slit on the downside.

11. Install the rack from the vehicle.

12. Install the clamps securing the rack to the crossmember. Tighten bolts to 44–59 ft. lbs. (60–80 Nm).

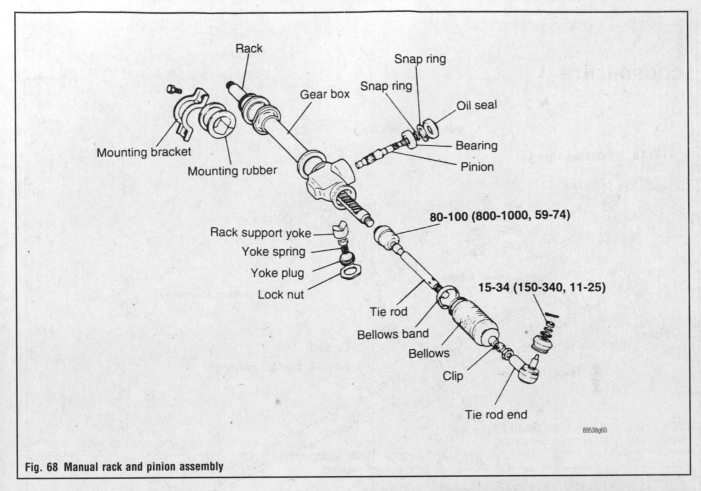

Fig. 68 Manual rack and pinion assembly

(Labels on diagram:)
- Rack
- Gear box
- Snap ring
- Snap ring
- Oil seal
- Bearing
- Pinion
- Mounting bracket
- Mounting rubber
- 80-100 (800-1000, 59-74)
- Rack support yoke
- Yoke spring
- Yoke plug
- Lock nut
- 15-34 (150-340, 11-25)
- Tie rod
- Bellows band
- Bellows
- Clip
- Tie rod end

89538g60

Fig. 69 Manual rack and pinion mounting bolt locations

89538g61

13. Install the steering shaft-to-pinion coupling bolt and tighten to 11–14 ft. lbs. (15–19 Nm).

14. Connect the tie rod ends to the steering knuckles.

15. Install all components previously removed to gain access to the rack.

16. Install the wheels.

17. Lower the vehicle.

Power Steering Rack

REMOVAL & INSTALLATION

◆ See Figures 70, 71 and 72 (p. 48–49)

1. Raise and support the vehicle safely.
2. Turn the wheels to the straight ahead position.
3. Remove the wheels.
4. Remove all components necessary to gain access to the rack.
5. Drain the fluid from the power steering system.
6. Disconnect and plug the fluid hoses.
7. Matchmark the steering shaft to the pinion.
8. Remove the steering shaft-to-pinion coupling bolt.
9. Disconnect the tie rod ends from the steering knuckles.
10. Remove the clamps securing the rack to the crossmember.
11. Remove the rack from the vehicle.

To install:

12. Install the rubber mount for the rack and pinion with the slit on the downside.

13. Install the rack from the vehicle.

14. Install the clamps securing the rack to the crossmember. Tighten bolts to 44–59 ft. lbs. (60–80 Nm).

15. Install the steering shaft-to-pinion coupling bolt and tighten to 11–14 ft. lbs. (15–19 Nm).

16. Connect the tie rod ends to the steering knuckles.

17. Connect the fluid hoses and tighten fittings to 9–13 ft. lbs. (12–18 Nm).

18. Install all components previously removed to gain access to the rack.

COMPONENTS

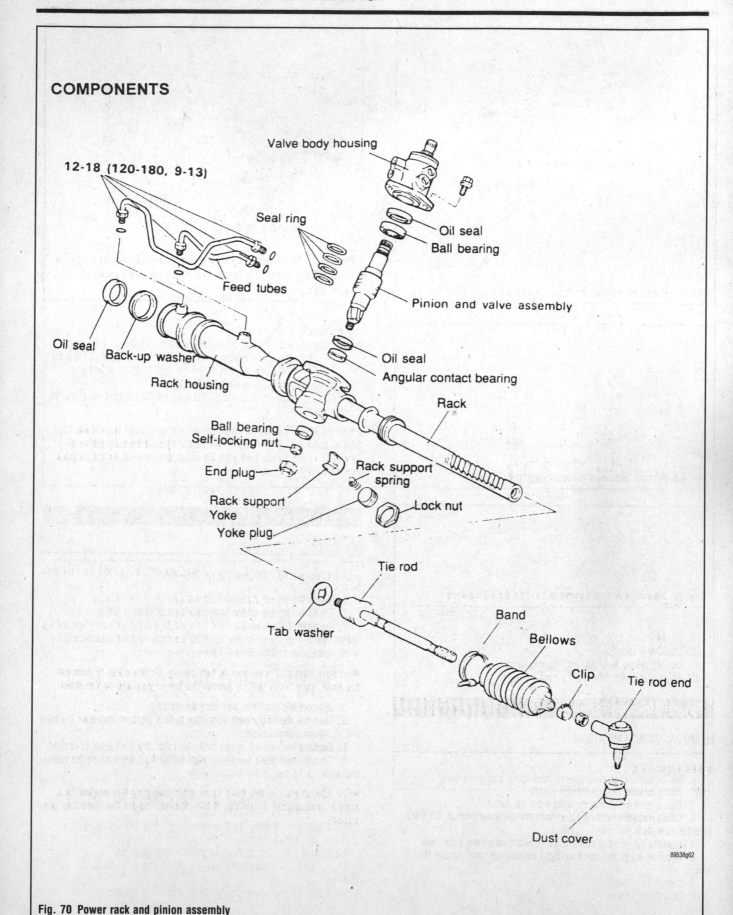

12-18 (120-180, 9-13)

Valve body housing

Seal ring

Feed tubes

Oil seal

Back-up washer

Rack housing

Oil seal

Ball bearing

Pinion and valve assembly

Oil seal

Angular contact bearing

Rack

Ball bearing
Self-locking nut

End plug

Rack support
spring

Lock nut

Rack support
Yoke

Yoke plug

Tie rod

Tab washer

Band

Bellows

Clip

Tie rod end

Dust cover

89538g62

Fig. 70 Power rack and pinion assembly

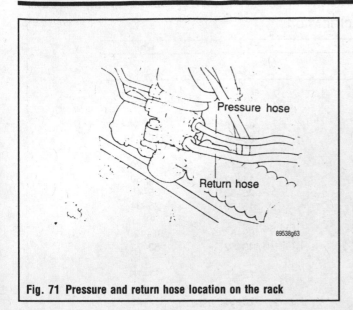

Fig. 71 Pressure and return hose location on the rack

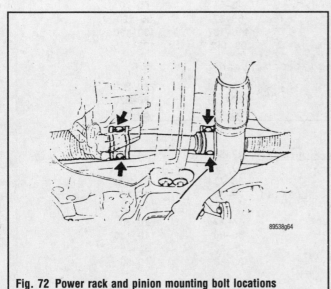

Fig. 72 Power rack and pinion mounting bolt locations

19. Install the wheels.
20. Lower the vehicle.
21. Fill the power steering system with fluid.
22. Bleed the power steering system.

Power Steering Pump

REMOVAL & INSTALLATION

♦ See Figure 73

1. Place a drain pan under the pump.
2. Disconnect the pressure hose from the pump.
3. Disconnect the suction hose from the pump and drain the fluid into the drain pan.
4. Loosen the pump mounting bolts and remove the drive belt.
5. Remove the pump-to-mounting bracket bolts and remove the pump.

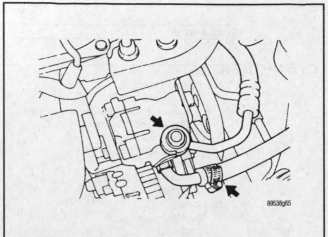

Fig. 73 On the power steering pump, the pressure hose uses a banjo fitting, while the return fitting is held in place with a hose clamp

To install:

6. Install the pump and tighten the mounting bolts as follows:
• 18–24 ft. lbs. (25–33 Nm)—except Tiburon and 1996–98 Elantra
• 26–37 ft. lbs. (35–50 Nm)—Tiburon and 1996–98 Elantra
7. Connect the suction hose to the pump.
8. Connect the pressure hose to the pump. Tighten fitting to 41–44 ft. lbs. (55–60 Nm).

➡When installing the hoses, make sure you push it at least 25–30mm onto the return tube. The hoses should be twisted or allowed to come in contact with an other component in the engine compartment.

9. Install the drive belt and adjust the tension.
10. Fill the system fluid.
11. Bleed the system.

BLEEDING

1. Ensure that the reservoir is full of Dexron®II automatic transmission fluid.
2. Raise and safely support the front wheels of the vehicle.
3. Turn the steering wheel from lock-to-lock 5 or 6 times.
4. Disconnect the coil wire and connect to a solid ground. Operate the starter motor intermittently for 15 to 20 seconds and turn the steering wheel from lock-to-lock 5 or 6 times.

➡Ensure that the reservoir is full during air bleeding to prevent the fluid level from falling below the lower position of the filter.

5. Connect the coil wire and start the engine.
6. Turn the steering wheel from lock to lock until no more air bubbles are visible in the reservoir.
7. Confirm that the oil is not milky and that the fluid level is correct.
8. Confirm that there is little change in the fluid level when the steering wheel is turned to the left and right.

➡An abrupt rise in the fluid level after stopping the engine is a sign of incomplete bleeding. If this occurs, repeat the bleeding procedure.

TORQUE SPECIFICATIONS

Components	Ft. Lbs.	Nm
Wheels		
Lug nut	65–80	88–108
Front suspension		
MacPherson struts		
Strut-to-knuckle		
Accent, Excel, Scoupe and Sonata	65–76	95–105
Elantra and Tiburon	80–94	110–130
Strut-to-fender		
Excel and Scoupe	11–14	15–20
Accent	11–22	20–30
Elantra and Tiburon	25–33	35–45
Sonata	18–25	25–34
Ball joints		
Mounting nuts	69–87	95–120
Castle nut	43–52	60–72
Stabilizer bar		
Mount bolts	12–19	17–26
Link nuts		
Elantra and Tiburon	25–33	34–45
Sonata	43–51	60–70
Lower arm-to-frame	69–87	95–120
Lower arm mounting bracket	116–137	160–190
Lower arm rear bushing	90–112	125–155
Front hub		
Axle nut		
Excel, Scoupe, Sonata and 1994–95 Elantra	145–188	200–260
Accent, Tiburon and 1996–98 Elantra	130–159	180–220
Rotor-to-hub	36–43	50–60
Rear suspension		
Shock absorber		
Except Sonata	47–58	64–78
Sonata		
Lower bolt	58–72	80–100
Upper bolt	29–36	40–50
MacPherson strut		
Strut-to-body	14–22	20–30
Strut-to-knuckle	80–90	110–130
Stabilizer link	25–33	35–45
Strut lock nut	29–36	40–50
Suspension arms		
Excel, Scoupe and 1994–95 Elantra		
Suspension-to-body	94–108	130–150
Lateral rod	58–72	80–100
Assist link and lower arm-to-trailing arm	54–64	78–89
Assist link and lower arm-to-crossmember	102–116	140–160
Crossmember mounting nuts	58–73	80–100
Upper arm-to-crossmember	102–116	140–160
Trailing arm-to-chassis	102–116	140–160
Accent	72–87	100–120
Tiburon and 1996–98 Elantra	58–72	80–100
Trailing arm	72–87	100–120
Ball joint castle nut	54–64	75–89
Steering		
Steering wheel nut	26–32	34–44
Rack and pinion mounting bolts	44–59	60–80
Steering shaft-to-pinion bolt	11–14	15–19
Tie rod end castle nut	11–25	15–34
Tie rod end locknut	44–59	60–80
Power steering pump mounting bolts		
Tiburon and 1996–98 Elantra	26–37	35–50
Except Tiburon and 1996–98 Elantra	18–24	25–33
Power steering pump fittings	9–13	12–18

89538c01

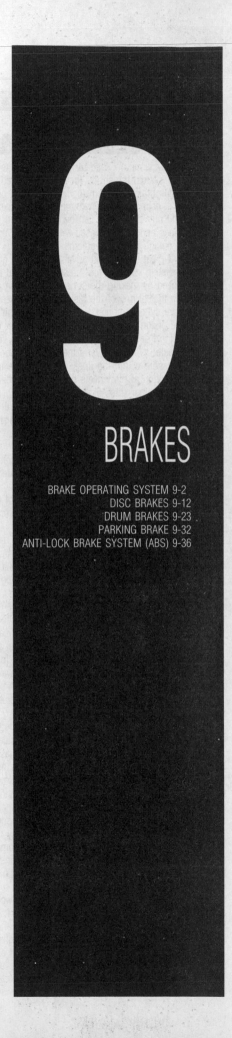

9

BRAKES

BRAKE OPERATING SYSTEM

Basic Operating Principles

Hydraulic systems are used to actuate the brakes of all modern automobiles. The system transports the power required to force the frictional surfaces of the braking system together from the pedal to the individual brake units at each wheel. A hydraulic system is used for two reasons.

First, fluid under pressure can be carried to all parts of an automobile by small pipes and flexible hoses without taking up a significant amount of room or posing routing problems.

Second, a great mechanical advantage can be given to the brake pedal end of the system, and the foot pressure required to actuate the brakes can be reduced by making the surface area of the master cylinder pistons smaller than that of any of the pistons in the wheel cylinders or calipers.

The master cylinder consists of a fluid reservoir along with a double cylinder and piston assembly. Double type master cylinders are designed to separate the front and rear braking systems hydraulically in case of a leak. The master cylinder coverts mechanical motion from the pedal into hydraulic pressure within the lines. This pressure is translated back into mechanical motion at the wheels by either the wheel cylinder (drum brakes) or the caliper (disc brakes).

Steel lines carry the brake fluid to a point on the vehicle's frame near each of the vehicle's wheels. The fluid is then carried to the calipers and wheel cylinders by flexible tubes in order to allow for suspension and steering movements.

In drum brake systems, each wheel cylinder contains two pistons, one at either end, which push outward in opposite directions and force the brake shoe into contact with the drum.

In disc brake systems, the cylinders are part of the calipers. At least one cylinder in each caliper is used to force the brake pads against the disc.

All pistons employ some type of seal, usually made of rubber, to minimize fluid leakage. A rubber dust boot seals the outer end of the cylinder against dust and dirt. The boot fits around the outer end of the piston on disc brake calipers, and around the brake actuating rod on wheel cylinders.

The hydraulic system operates as follows: When at rest, the entire system, from the piston(s) in the master cylinder to those in the wheel cylinders or calipers, is full of brake fluid. Upon application of the brake pedal, fluid trapped in front of the master cylinder piston(s) is forced through the lines to the wheel cylinders. Here, it forces the pistons outward, in the case of drum brakes, and inward toward the disc, in the case of disc brakes. The motion of the pistons is opposed by return springs mounted outside the cylinders in drum brakes, and by spring seals, in disc brakes.

Upon release of the brake pedal, a spring located inside the master cylinder immediately returns the master cylinder pistons to the normal position. The pistons contain check valves and the master cylinder has compensating ports drilled in it. These are uncovered as the pistons reach their normal position. The piston check valves allow fluid to flow toward the wheel cylinders or calipers as the pistons withdraw. Then, as the return springs force the brake pads or shoes into the released position, the excess fluid reservoir through the compensating ports. It is during the time the pedal is in the released position that any fluid that has leaked out of the system will be replaced through the compensating ports.

Dual circuit master cylinders employ two pistons, located one behind the other, in the same cylinder. The primary piston is actuated directly by mechanical linkage from the brake pedal through the power booster. The secondary piston is actuated by fluid trapped between the two pistons. If a leak develops in front of the secondary piston, it moves forward until it bottoms against the front of the master cylinder, and the fluid trapped between the pistons will operate the rear brakes. If the rear brakes develop a leak, the primary piston will move forward until direct contact with the secondary piston takes place, and it will force the secondary piston to actuate the front brakes. In either case, the brake pedal moves farther when the brakes are applied, and less braking power is available.

All dual circuit systems use a switch to warn the driver when only half of the brake system is operational. This switch is usually located in a valve body which is mounted on the firewall or the frame below the master cylinder. A hydraulic piston receives pressure from both circuits, each circuit's pressure being applied to one end of the piston. When the pressures are in balance, the piston remains stationary. When one circuit has a leak, however, the greater pressure in that circuit during application of the brakes will push the piston to one side, closing the switch and activating the brake warning light.

In disc brake systems, this valve body also contains a metering valve and, in some cases, a proportioning valve. The metering valve keeps pressure from traveling to the disc brakes on the front wheels until the brake shoes on the rear wheels have contacted the drums, ensuring that the front brakes will never be used alone. The proportioning valve controls the pressure to the rear brakes to lessen the chance of rear wheel lock-up during very hard braking.

Warning lights may be tested by depressing the brake pedal and holding it while opening one of the wheel cylinder bleeder screws. If this does not cause the light to go on, substitute a new lamp, make continuity checks, and, finally, replace the switch as necessary.

The hydraulic system may be checked for leaks by applying pressure to the pedal gradually and steadily. If the pedal sinks very slowly to the floor, the system has a leak. This is not to be confused with a springy or spongy feel due to the compression of air within the lines. If the system leaks, there will be a gradual change in the position of the pedal with a constant pressure.

Check for leaks along all lines and at wheel cylinders. If no external leaks are apparent, the problem is inside the master cylinder.

DISC BRAKES

Instead of the traditional expanding brakes that press outward against a circular drum, disc brake systems utilize a disc (rotor) with brake pads positioned on either side of it. An easily-seen analogy is the hand brake arrangement on a bicycle. The pads squeeze onto the rim of the bike wheel, slowing its motion. Automobile disc brakes use the identical principle but apply the braking effort to a separate disc instead of the wheel.

The disc (rotor) is a casting, usually equipped with cooling fins between the two braking surfaces. This enables air to circulate between the braking surfaces making them less sensitive to heat buildup and more resistant to fade. Dirt and water do not drastically affect braking action since contaminants are thrown off by the centrifugal action of the rotor or scraped off the by the pads. Also, the equal clamping action of the two brake pads tends to ensure uniform, straight line stops. Disc brakes are inherently self-adjusting. There are three general types of disc brake:

1. A fixed caliper
2. A floating caliper
3. A sliding caliper

The fixed caliper design uses two pistons mounted on either side of the rotor (in each side of the caliper). The caliper is mounted rigidly and does not move.

The sliding and floating designs are quite similar. In fact, these two types are often lumped together. In both designs, the pad on the inside of the rotor is moved into contact with the rotor by hydraulic force. The caliper, which is not held in a fixed position, moves slightly, bringing the outside pad into contact with the rotor. There are various methods of attaching floating calipers. Some pivot at the bottom or top, and some slide on mounting bolts. In any event, the end result is the same.

DRUM BRAKES

Drum brakes employ two brake shoes mounted on a stationary backing plate. These shoes are positioned inside a circular drum which rotates with the wheel assembly. The shoes are held in place by springs. This allows them to slide toward the drums (when they are applied) while keeping the linings and drums in alignment. The shoes are actuated by a wheel cylinder which is mounted at the top of the backing plate. When the brakes are applied, hydraulic pressure forces the wheel cylinder's actuating links outward. Since these links bear directly against the top of the brake shoes, the tops of the shoes are then forced against the inner side of the drum. This action forces the bottoms of the two shoes to contact the brake drum by rotating the entire assembly slightly (known as servo action). When pressure within the wheel cylinder is relaxed, return springs pull the shoes back away from the drum.

Most modern drum brakes are designed to self-adjust themselves during application when the vehicle is moving in reverse. This motion causes both shoes to rotate very slightly with the drum, rocking an adjusting lever, thereby causing rotation of the adjusting screw. Some drum brake systems are designed to self-adjust during application whenever the brakes are applied. This on-board adjustment system reduces the need for maintenance adjustments and keeps both the brake function and pedal feel satisfactory.

POWER BOOSTERS

Virtually all modern vehicles use a vacuum assisted power brake system to multiply the braking force and reduce pedal effort. Since vacuum is always available when the engine is operating, the system is simple and efficient. A vacuum diaphragm is located on the front of the master cylinder and assists the driver in applying the brakes, reducing both the effort and travel he must put into moving the brake pedal.

The vacuum diaphragm housing is normally connected to the intake manifold by a vacuum hose. A check valve is placed at the point where the hose enters the diaphragm housing, so that during periods of low manifold vacuum brakes assist will not be lost.

Depressing the brake pedal closes off the vacuum source and allows atmospheric pressure to enter on one side of the diaphragm. This causes the master cylinder pistons to move and apply the brakes. When the brake pedal is released, vacuum is applied to both sides of the diaphragm and springs return the diaphragm and master cylinder pistons to the released position.

If the vacuum supply fails, the brake pedal rod will contact the end of the master cylinder actuator rod and the system will apply the brakes without any power assistance. The driver will notice that much higher pedal effort is needed to stop the car and that the pedal feels harder than usual.

Power brake systems may be tested for hydraulic leaks just as ordinary systems are tested.

✳✳ WARNING

Clean, high quality brake fluid is essential to the safe and proper operation of the brake system. You should always buy the highest quality brake fluid that is available. If the brake fluid becomes contaminated, drain and flush the system, then refill the master cylinder with new fluid. Never reuse any brake fluid. Any brake fluid that is removed from the system should be recycled.

Brake Light Switch

REMOVAL & INSTALLATION

♦ See Figure 1

1. Disconnect the negative battery cable.
2. Locate the light switch at the brake pedal lever.
3. Disconnect the electrical harness from the switch.
4. Remove the switch.
To install:
5. Thread the brake light switch into the bracket.
6. Adjust the switch so the distance between the end of the switch plunger and the brake lever stop is 0.020–0.039 in. (0.5–1.0mm).

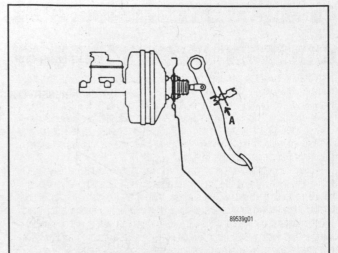

Fig. 1 The clearance between the switch plunger and the brake lever stop (A) should be 0.020–0.039 in. (0.5–1.0mm)

7. Tighten the locknut securely.
8. Connect the electrical harness to the switch.
9. Connect the negative battery cable.
10. Make sure the brake lights come on when the brake pedal is depressed and go out when the pedal is released. Also, make sure that the cruise control system operates properly.

Master Cylinder

✳✳ CAUTION

Be careful not to spill brake fluid on the painted surfaces of your car. The brake fluid will cause damage to the paint.

REMOVAL & INSTALLATION

♦ See Figures 2, 3 and 4 (p. 4–5)

1. Place a drain pan under the master cylinder to catch dripping brake fluid.
2. Disconnect the fluid level sensor.
3. Remove the cap and siphon most of the brake fluid from the reservoir.
4. Disconnect the tubes from the master cylinder.

➡**On Sonata V6 with rear disc brakes, disconnect the brake lines without removing the proportioning valves.**

5. Remove the master cylinder and gasket from the booster.
To install:
6. Inspect master cylinder gaskets and/or O-ring for damage and replace as necessary.
7. If a new or rebuilt master cylinder is being installed, the master cylinder must be bench bled prior to installation.
   a. Mount the master cylinder in a bench vice.
   b. Fill the reservoir with fluid.
   c. Install tubes on the master cylinder outlet ports and submerge the tubes in the reservoir fluid.

➡**Master cylinder bench bleeding kits are available from aftermarket suppliers. Some new and rebuilt master cylinders contain bleeding kits as part of the package.**

   a. Use a rod to slowly activate the master cylinder piston. Bubbles will appear in the reservoir fluid.

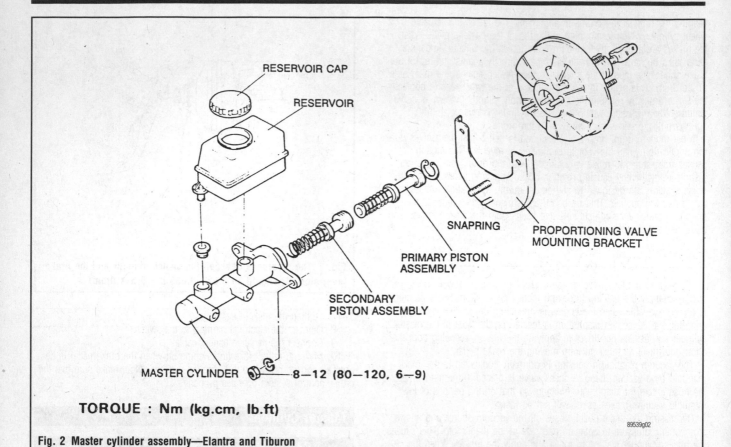

TORQUE : Nm (kg.cm, lb.ft)

Fig. 2 Master cylinder assembly—Elantra and Tiburon

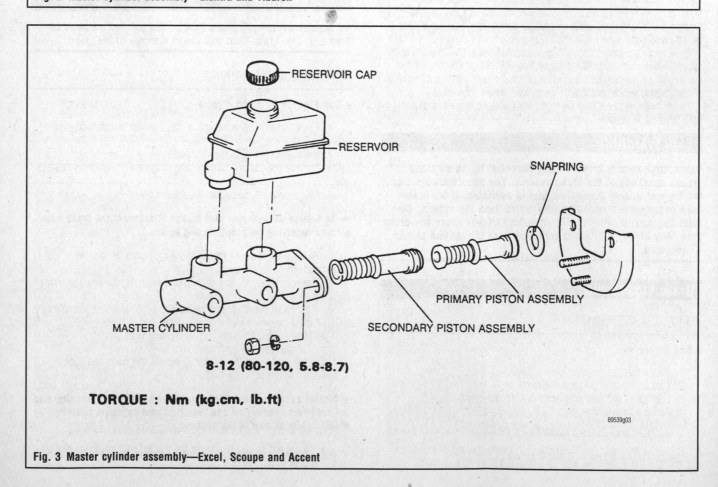

TORQUE : Nm (kg.cm, lb.ft)

Fig. 3 Master cylinder assembly—Excel, Scoupe and Accent

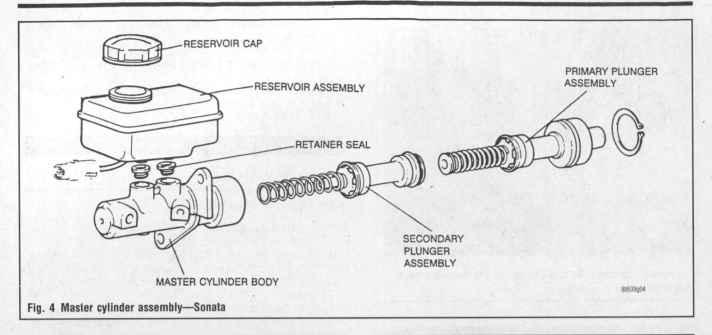

Fig. 4 Master cylinder assembly—Sonata

The master cylinder is attached to the power brake booster on the firewall

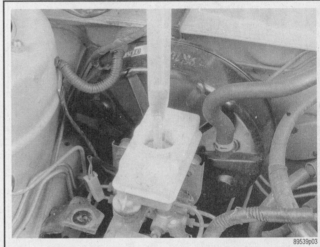

. . . then open the reservoir's cap and siphon out most of the brake fluid

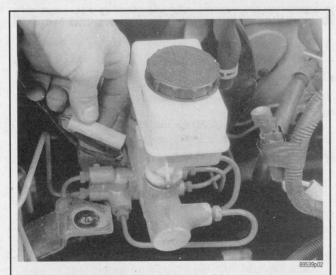

Disconnect the brake fluid level sensor . . .

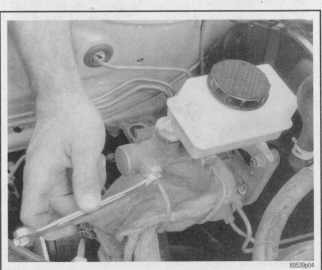

Using a flare nut wrench, loosen the brake line fittings . . .

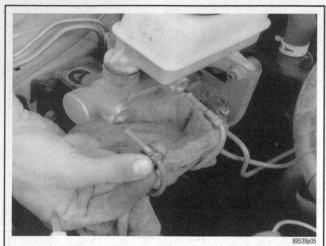

. . . then disconnect the brake lines and cap them to prevent the entry of dirt or moisture

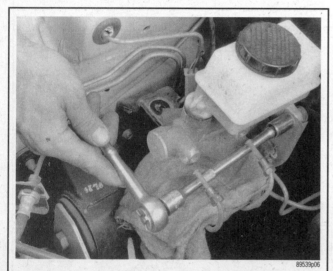

Unfasten the master cylinder mounting bolts . . .

. . . and lift the master cylinder assembly from the vehicle

b. Continue activating the master cylinder piston until no bubbles are present.

8. Position the master cylinder on the booster and tighten mounting bolts to 10–16 ft. lbs. (14–22 Nm) on Sonata or 6–9 ft. lbs. (8–12 Nm) for all others.

9. Connect the brake lines to the master cylinder. Tighten the tubes to 9–12 ft. lbs. (13–17 Nm).

10. Bleed the brake system.

Power Brake Booster

REMOVAL & INSTALLATION

♦ **See Figures 5, 6 and 7 (p. 7)**

1. Disconnect the vacuum hose from the power booster.
2. Remove the master cylinder.
3. Disconnect the pushrod at the brake pedal.
4. Remove the power booster mounting bolts
5. Carefully remove the power booster from the firewall.

To install:

6. Install the brake booster on the firewall and tighten the mounting nuts to 15–21 ft. lbs. (21–28 Nm) on Sonata and 6–9 ft. lbs. (8–12 Nm) except Sonata.

7. Connect the vacuum hose to the power booster.
8. Install the master cylinder.

TESTING

1. Operate the engine at idle with the transmission in Neutral without touching the brake pedal for at least two minutes.
2. Turn the engine off, and wait one minute.
3. Test for the presence of assist vacuum by depressing the brake pedal and releasing it several times. Light application will produce less and less pedal travel, if vacuum is present.
4. Pump the brake pedal (with engine off) until the supply vacuum is entirely gone.
5. Put a light, steady pressure on the pedal.
6. Start the engine, and allow it to idle with the transaxle in neutral (manual transaxle) or park (automatic transaxle).
7. If the brake booster is operating properly, the brake pedal should fall toward the floor when constant pressure is maintained on the pedal.
8. Power brake systems may be tested for hydraulic leaks just as ordinary systems are tested, except that the engine should be idling with the transmission in neutral (manual transaxle) or park (automatic transaxle).

Proportioning Valve

REMOVAL & INSTALLATION

♦ **See Figure 8 (p. 8)**

1. Place a drain pan under the proportioning valve to catch dripping brake fluid.
2. Label, disconnect and plug the brake lines at the proportioning valve.

➡ **Use a flare nut wrench to avoid damage to the lines and fittings.**

3. Remove the mounting bolts and remove the proportioning valve.

To install:

4. Install the proportioning valve and tighten the mounting bolts to 9–16 ft. lbs. (13–22 Nm) on Sonata or 6–9 ft. lbs. (8–12 Nm) except Sonata.

5. Connect the brake lines and tighten fittings to 9–12 ft. lbs. (13–17 Nm).

6. Refill the system with fluid and bleed the brakes.

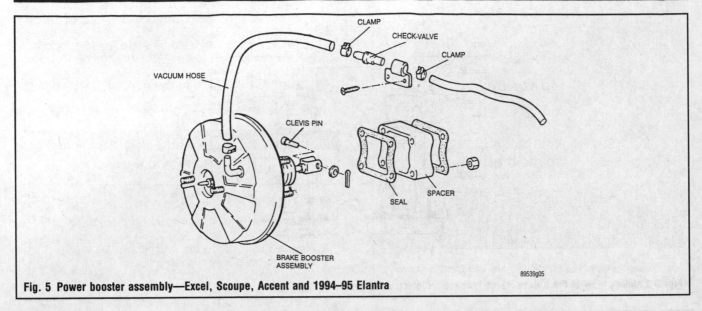

Fig. 5 Power booster assembly—Excel, Scoupe, Accent and 1994–95 Elantra

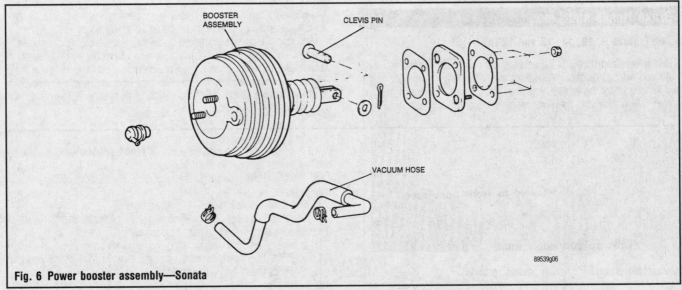

Fig. 6 Power booster assembly—Sonata

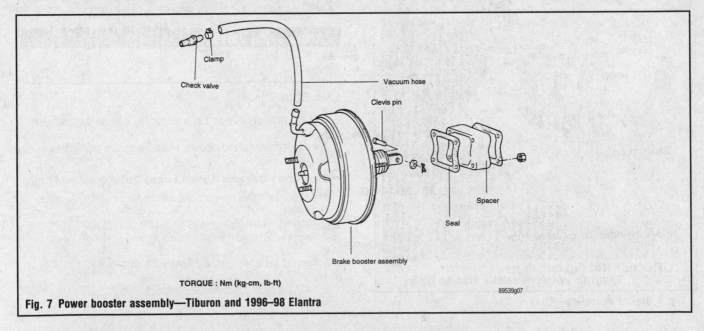

TORQUE : Nm (kg-cm, lb-ft)

Fig. 7 Power booster assembly—Tiburon and 1996–98 Elantra

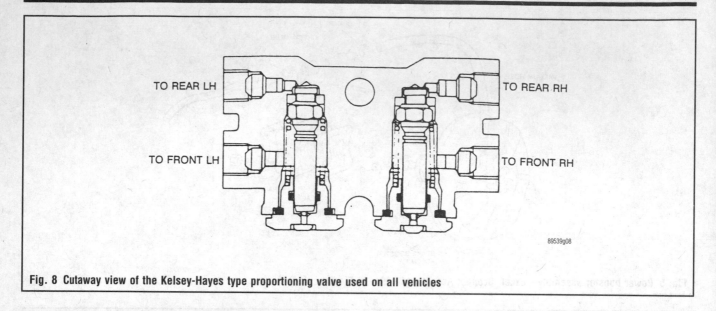

TO REAR LH

TO REAR RH

TO FRONT LH

TO FRONT RH

89539g08

Fig. 8 Cutaway view of the Kelsey-Hayes type proportioning valve used on all vehicles

Brake Hoses and Lines

▶ **See Figures 9, 10, 11, 12 and 13 (p. 8–10)**

Metal lines and rubber brake hoses should be checked frequently for leaks and external damage. Metal lines are particularly prone to crushing and kinking under the vehicle. Any such deformation can restrict the proper flow of fluid and therefore impair braking at the wheels. Rubber hoses should be checked for cracking or scraping; such damage can create a weak spot in the hose and it could fail under pressure.

Any time the lines are removed or disconnected, extreme cleanliness must be observed. Clean all joints and connections before disassembly (use a stiff bristle brush and clean brake fluid); be sure to plug the lines and ports as soon as they are opened. New lines and hoses should be flushed clean with brake fluid before installation to remove any contamination.

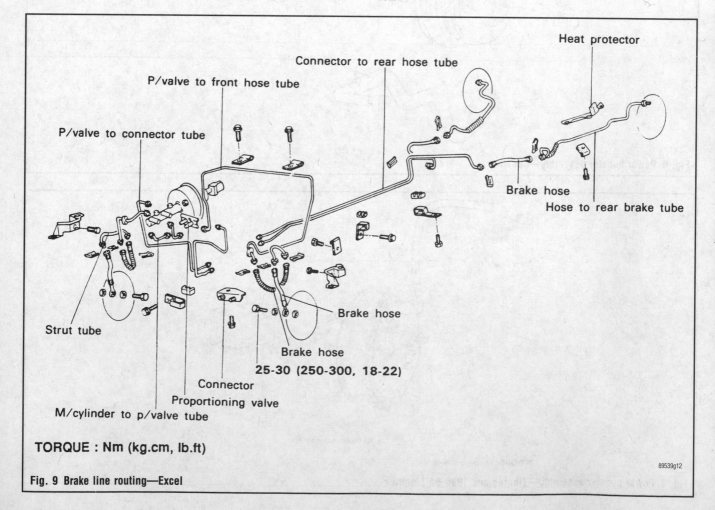

Heat protector

Connector to rear hose tube

P/valve to front hose tube

P/valve to connector tube

Brake hose

Hose to rear brake tube

Strut tube

Brake hose

Brake hose

25-30 (250-300, 18-22)

Connector

Proportioning valve

M/cylinder to p/valve tube

TORQUE : Nm (kg.cm, lb.ft)

89539g12

Fig. 9 Brake line routing—Excel

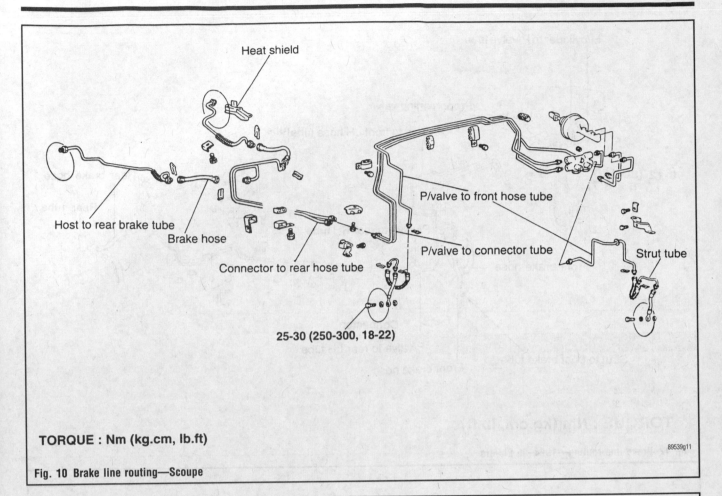

Heat shield

Host to rear brake tube

Brake hose

Connector to rear hose tube

P/valve to front hose tube

P/valve to connector tube

Strut tube

25-30 (250-300, 18-22)

TORQUE : Nm (kg.cm, lb.ft)

89539g11

Fig. 10 Brake line routing—Scoupe

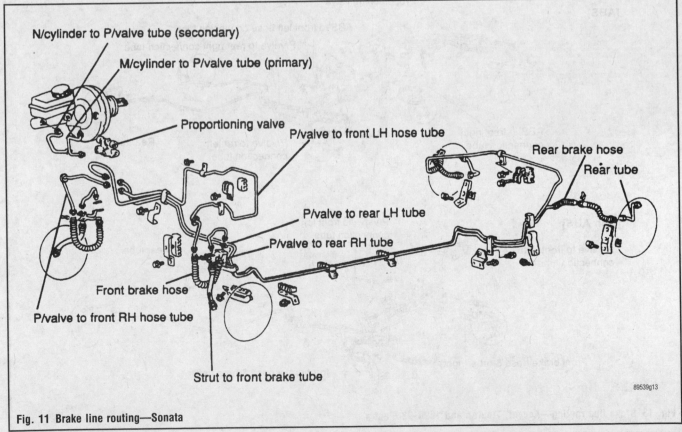

N/cylinder to P/valve tube (secondary)

M/cylinder to P/valve tube (primary)

Proportioning valve

P/valve to front LH hose tube

Rear brake hose

Rear tube

P/valve to rear LH tube

P/valve to rear RH tube

Front brake hose

P/valve to front RH hose tube

Strut to front brake tube

89539g13

Fig. 11 Brake line routing—Sonata

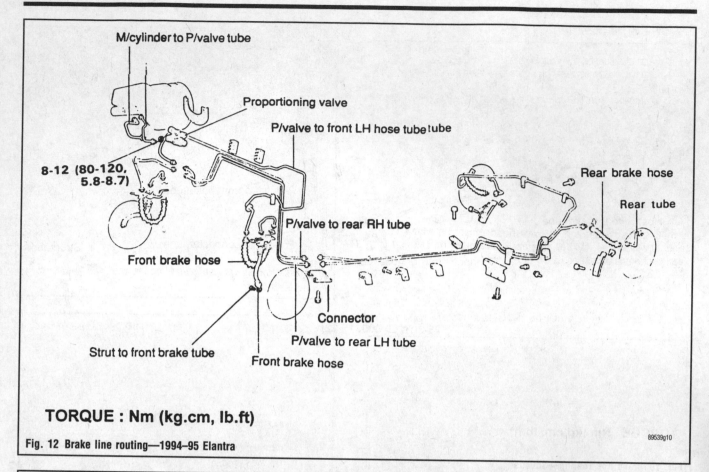

M/cylinder to P/valve tube

Proportioning valve

P/valve to front LH hose tube tube

8-12 (80-120, 5.8-8.7)

Rear brake hose

Rear tube

P/valve to rear RH tube

Front brake hose

Connector

P/valve to rear LH tube

Strut to front brake tube

Front brake hose

TORQUE : Nm (kg.cm, lb.ft)

Fig. 12 Brake line routing—1994–95 Elantra

89539g10

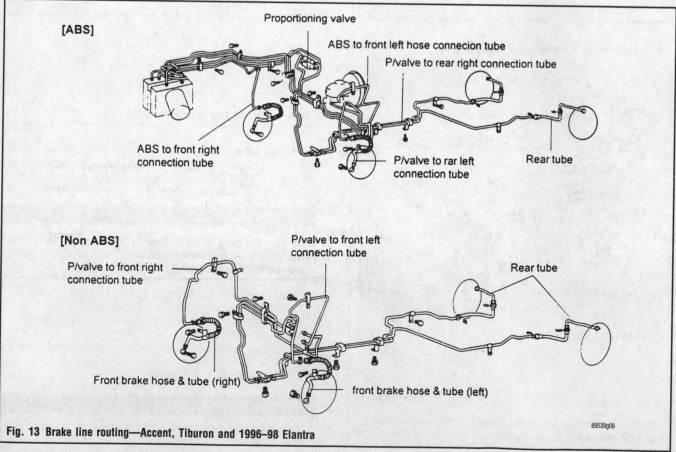

[ABS]

Proportioning valve

ABS to front left hose connecion tube

P/valve to rear right connection tube

ABS to front right connection tube

P/valve to rar left connection tube

Rear tube

[Non ABS]

P/valve to front left connection tube

P/valve to front right connection tube

Rear tube

Front brake hose & tube (right)

front brake hose & tube (left)

Fig. 13 Brake line routing—Accent, Tiburon and 1996–98 Elantra

89539g09

REMOVAL & INSTALLATION

1. Raise and support the vehicle safely.
2. Remove wheels necessary for access to the particular line you are servicing.
3. Thoroughly clean the surrounding area at the joints to be disconnected.
4. Place a suitable catch pan under the joint to be disconnected.
5. Using two wrenches (one to hold the joint and one to turn the fitting), disconnect the hose or line to be replaced.
6. Disconnect the other end of the line or hose, moving the drain pan if necessary. Always use a back-up wrench to avoid damaging the fitting.
7. Disconnect any retaining clips or brackets holding the line and remove the line from the vehicle.

➡If the brake system is to remain open for more time than it takes to swap lines, tape or plug each remaining clip and port to keep contaminants out and fluid in.

To install:

8. Install the new line or hose, starting with the end farthest from the master cylinder. Connect the other end, then confirm that both fittings are correctly threaded and turn smoothly using finger pressure. Make sure

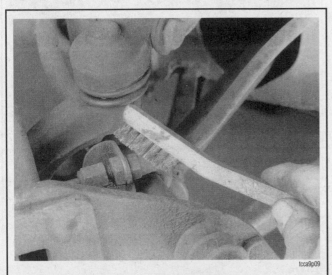

Use a brush to clean the fittings of any debris

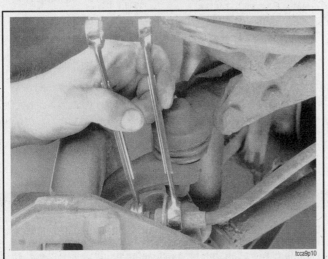

Use two wrenches to loosen the fitting. If available, use flare nut type wrenches

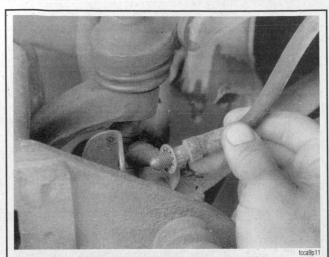

Any gaskets/crush washers should be replaced with new ones during installation

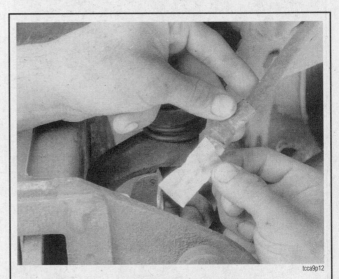

Tape or plug the line to prevent contamination

the new line will not rub against any other part. Brake lines must be at least 1/2 in. (13mm) from the steering column and other moving parts. Any protective shielding or insulators must be reinstalled in the original location.

❋❋ WARNING

Make sure the hose is NOT kinked or touching any part of the frame or suspension after installation. These conditions may cause the hose to fail prematurely.

9. Using two wrenches as before, tighten each fitting.
10. Install any retaining clips or brackets on the lines.
11. If removed, install the wheel and tire assemblies, then carefully lower the vehicle to the ground.
12. Refill the brake master cylinder reservoir with clean, fresh brake fluid, meeting DOT 3 specifications.
13. Properly bleed the brake system.

Bleeding Brake System

When any part of the hydraulic system has been disconnected for repair or replacement, air may get into the lines and cause spongy pedal action (because air can be compressed and brake fluid cannot). To correct this condition, it is necessary to bleed the hydraulic system to be sure that all air is purged.

When bleeding the brake system, bleed one brake cylinder at a time, beginning at the cylinder with the longest hydraulic line (farthest from the master cylinder) first. ALWAYS Keep the master cylinder reservoir filled with brake fluid during the bleeding operation. Never use brake fluid that has been drained from the hydraulic system, no matter how clean it is.

The primary and secondary hydraulic brake systems are separate and are bled independently. During the bleeding operation, do not allow the reservoir to run dry. Keep the master cylinder reservoir filled with brake fluid.

1. Clean all dirt from around the master cylinder fill cap, remove the cap and fill the master cylinder with brake fluid until the level is within ¼ in. (6mm) of the top edge of the reservoir.

2. Clean the bleeder screws at all 4 wheels. The bleeder screws are located on the back of the brake backing plate (drum brakes) and on the top of the brake calipers (disc brakes).

3. Attach a length of rubber hose over the bleeder screw and place the other end of the hose in a glass jar, submerged in brake fluid.

Bleeding the rear drum brakes

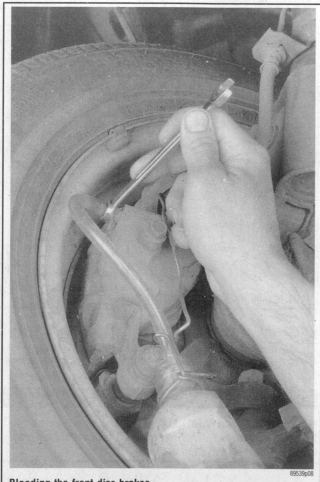

Bleeding the front disc brakes

4. Open the bleeder screw ½–¾ turn. Have an assistant slowly depress the brake pedal.

5. Close the bleeder screw and tell your assistant to allow the brake pedal to return slowly. Continue this process to purge all air from the system.

6. When bubbles cease to appear at the end of the bleeder hose, close the bleeder screw and remove the hose. Tighten the bleeder screw to the proper torque:
   - 5–7 ft. lbs. (7–9 Nm)—Tiburon and 1996–98 Elantra
   - 5–10 ft. lbs. (7–13 Nm)—Except Tiburon and 1996–98 Elantra (front)
   - 5–7 ft. lbs. (7–9 Nm)—Except Tiburon, Sonata and 1996–98 Elantra (rear)
   - 6–15 ft. lbs. (8–20 Nm)—Sonata (rear)

7. Check the master cylinder fluid level and add fluid accordingly. Do this after bleeding each wheel.

8. Repeat the bleeding operation at the remaining 3 wheels, ending with the one closet to the master cylinder.

9. Fill the master cylinder reservoir to the proper level.

DISC BRAKES

▶ See Figures 14, 15, 16 and 17 (p. 13–15)

✳✳ CAUTION

Older brake pads or shoes may contain asbestos, which has been determined to be a cancer causing agent. Never clean the brake surfaces with compressed air! Avoid inhaling any dust from any brake surface. When cleaning brake surfaces, use a commercially available brake cleaning fluid.

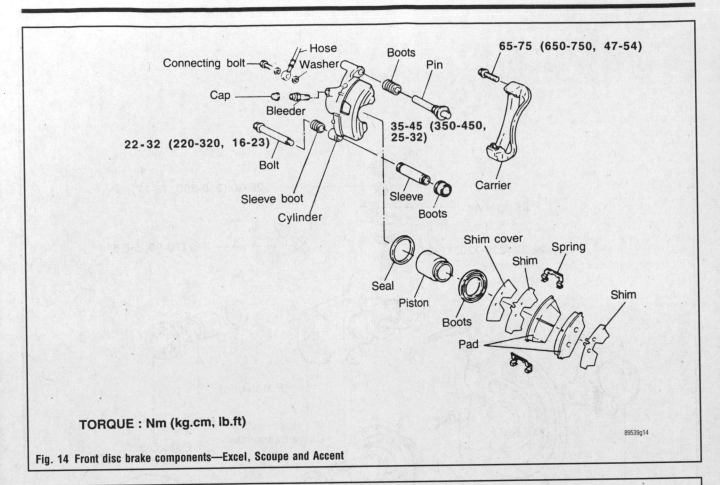

TORQUE : Nm (kg.cm, lb.ft)

89539g14

Fig. 14 Front disc brake components—Excel, Scoupe and Accent

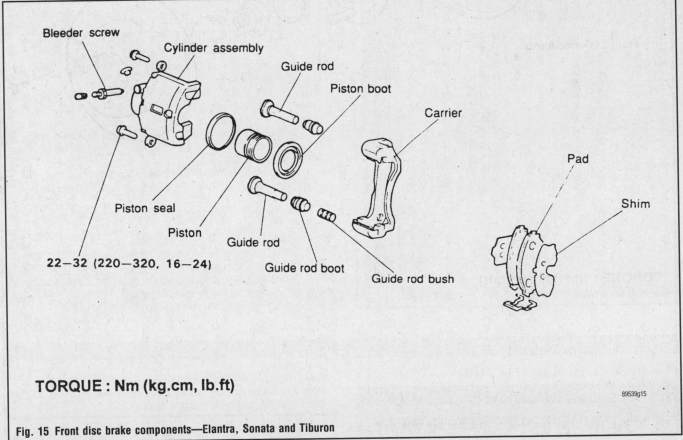

TORQUE : Nm (kg.cm, lb.ft)

89539g15

Fig. 15 Front disc brake components—Elantra, Sonata and Tiburon

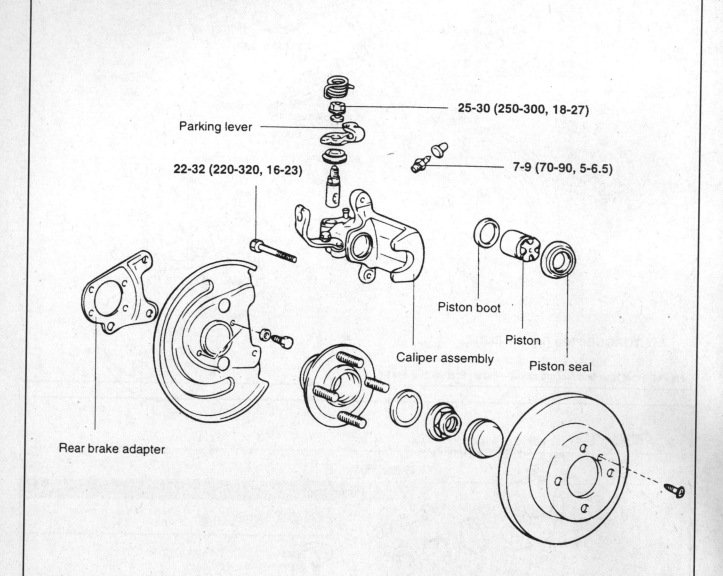

Parking lever

25-30 (250-300, 18-27)

22-32 (220-320, 16-23)

7-9 (70-90, 5-6.5)

Piston boot

Piston

Caliper assembly

Piston seal

Rear brake adapter

TORQUE : Nm (kg·cm, lb·ft)

89539g18

Fig. 16 Rear disc brake components—Tiburon and 1996–98 Elantra

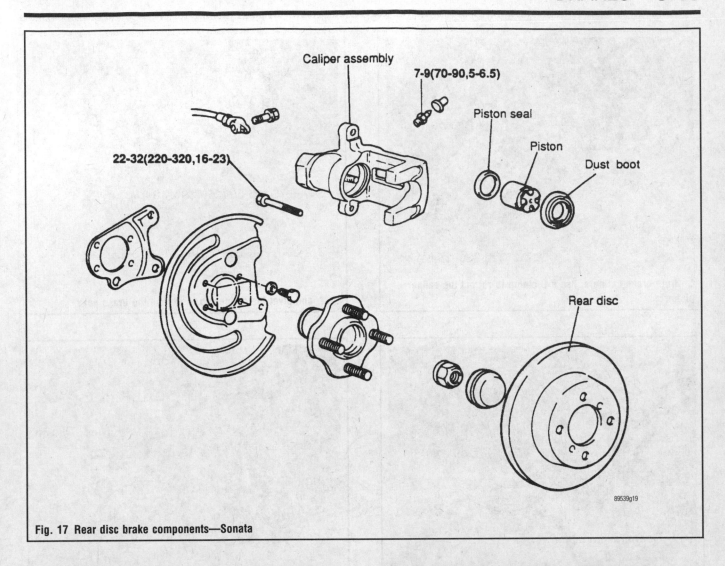

Fig. 17 Rear disc brake components—Sonata

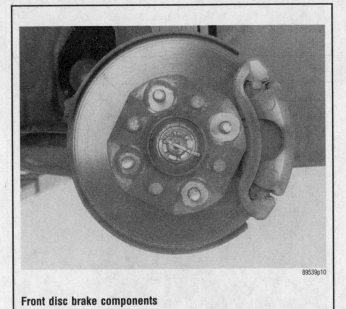

Front disc brake components

Brake Pads

REMOVAL & INSTALLATION

1. Raise and support the vehicle safely.
2. Remove the wheels.
3. Remove some of the brake fluid in the reservoir. This prevents the reservoir from overflowing when the caliper piston is retracted.
4. Using a large C-clamp, retract the piston into the caliper.
5. Loosen the caliper bolt(s) and lift the caliper out of the way. Suspend the caliper with safety wire.

➡**Don't stretch the brake hose.**

6. Remove the pads and anti-rattle clips from the carrier.
To install:
7. Install the new pads and clips on the carrier.
8. Position the caliper and tighten caliper bolts to 16–23 ft. lbs. (22–32 Nm).
9. Install the wheels.
10. Lower the vehicle.

➡**Depress the brake pedal several times prior to driving the vehicle. This will extend the caliper piston and seat the brake pads.**

On front brake calipers, use a C-clamp to retract the caliper piston

. . . and pivot the caliper up to expose the brake pads

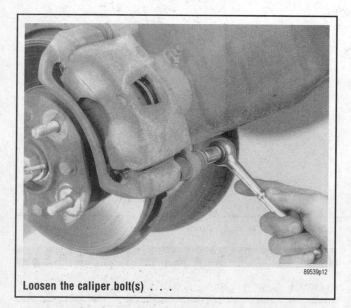

Loosen the caliper bolt(s) . . .

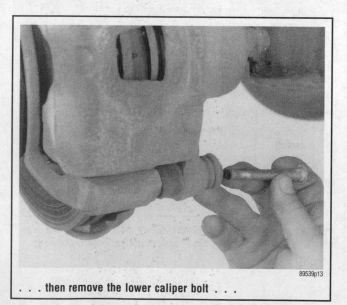

1. Wear indicator

Remove the brake pads. The inboard pad contains the wear indicator

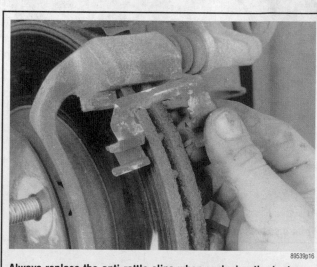

. . . then remove the lower caliper bolt . . .

Always replace the anti-rattle clips when replacing the brake pads

INSPECTION

⬧ See Figure 18

The inner brake pads are equipped with metal wear indicators which act as warning devices to alert the driver to change the brake pads. When the brake pad wears to the minimum service limit, the indicator contacts the rotor and makes a noticeable "chirping" noise while the wheels are turning. When you hear this sound, it's time to replace the front pads.

To perform a visual inspection, do the following:
1. Raise and support the vehicle safely.
2. Remove the front wheels.
3. Check the brake lining thickness through the inspection window in the caliper with a 6 in. machinist's rule. After checking the brake lining thickness, check the brake pads for oil deposits, and check the pad springs for wear and damage. Make replacements as necessary.

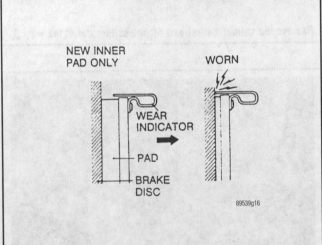

Fig. 18 Brake pad wear indicators alert the driver when the brake pad has reached its wear limit

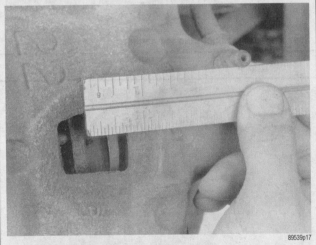

To inspect brake pad thickness, look through the end of the caliper

Brake Caliper

REMOVAL & INSTALLATION

⬧ See Figures 19 and 20

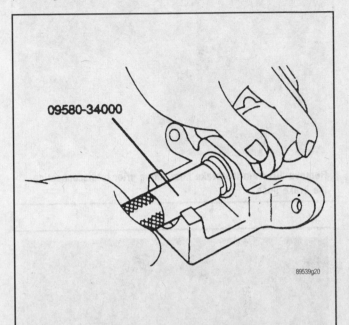

Fig. 19 On rear calipers, use special tool (PN 09580-34000) or equivalent, to screw the caliper back into the piston

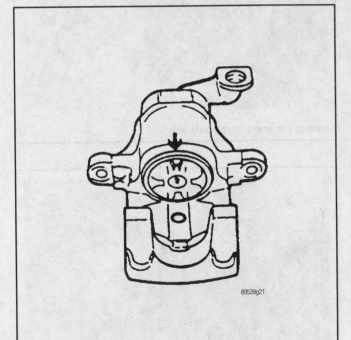

Fig. 20 Align the rear caliper piston mating mark as illustrated

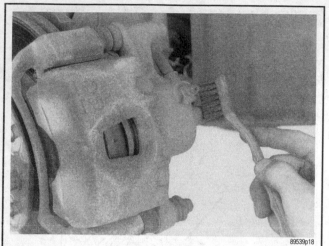

Remove dirt from the brake hose fitting prior to disconnecting the brake hose

Remove the caliper bolt(s) and lift the caliper out of the way

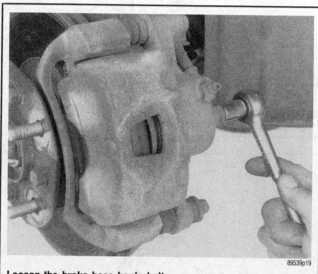

Loosen the brake hose banjo bolt . . .

Separate the dust boot from the caliper

. . . and disconnect the hose. Replace the washers during assembly

Some calipers use only one attaching bolt. The top of the caliper is positioned by a stud attached to the carrier

Front Caliper

1. Raise and support the vehicle safely.
2. Remove the wheels.
3. Remove the brake pads and clips.
4. Remove some of the brake fluid in the reservoir. This prevents the reservoir from overflowing when the caliper piston is retracted.
5. Use a large C-clamp to retract the piston into the caliper.
6. If the caliper is to be replaced, disconnect and cap the brake hose at the caliper.
7. If the caliper is not being replaced, suspend the caliper out of the way using mechanic's wire.
8. Loosen the caliper bolt(s) and lift the caliper out of the way.

To install:

9. Install the brake pads and clips on the carrier.
10. Position the caliper and tighten caliper bolts to 16–23 ft. lbs. (22–32 Nm).
11. Install the brake hose and tighten to 18–22 ft. lbs. (25–30 Nm).
12. Install the wheels.
13. Lower the vehicle.
14. Bleed the brakes.

Rear Caliper

1. Raise and support the vehicle safely.
2. Remove the wheels.
3. Remove the brake pads and clips.
4. Remove some of the brake fluid in the reservoir. This prevents the reservoir from overflowing when the caliper piston is retracted.
5. Use special tool (PN 09580-34000), or equivalent, to screw the piston back into the caliper. Align the caliper piston mating mark as illustrated.
6. If the caliper is to be replaced, disconnect and cap the brake hose at the caliper. Disconnect the parking brake cable.
7. If the caliper is not being replaced, suspend the caliper out of the way using mechanic's wire.
8. Loosen the caliper bolt(s) and lift the caliper out of the way.

To install:

9. Install the brake pads and clips on the carrier.
10. Position the caliper and tighten caliper bolts to 16–23 ft. lbs. (22–32 Nm).
11. Install the brake hose and tighten to 18–22 ft. lbs. (25–30 Nm). Connect the parking brake cable.
12. Install the wheels.
13. Lower the vehicle.
14. Bleed the brakes.

OVERHAUL

♦ See Figures 21 thru 28

➡Some vehicles may be equipped dual piston calipers. The procedure to overhaul the caliper is essentially the same, with the exception of multiple pistons, O-rings and dust boots.

1. Remove the caliper from the vehicle and place on a clean workbench.

❋❋ CAUTION

NEVER place your fingers in front of the pistons in an attempt to catch or protect the pistons when applying compressed air. This could result in personal injury!

➡Depending upon the vehicle, there are two different ways to remove the piston from the caliper. Refer to the brake pad replacement procedure to make sure you have the correct procedure for your vehicle.

2. The first method is as follows:
a. Stuff a shop towel or a block of wood into the caliper to catch the piston.

Fig. 21 Use compressed air to drive the piston out of the caliper, but make sure to keep your fingers clear

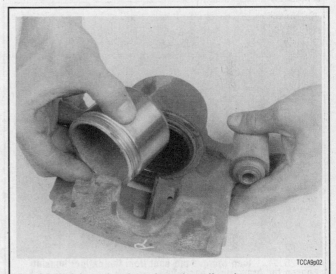

Fig. 22 Withdraw the piston from the caliper bore

Fig. 23 On some vehicles, you must remove the anti-rattle clip

Fig. 24 Use a prytool to carefully pry around the edge of the boot . . .

Fig. 27 Use the proper size driving tool and a mallet to properly seal the boots in the caliper housing

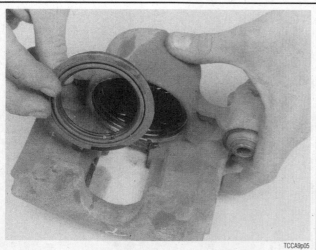

Fig. 25 . . . then remove the boot from the caliper housing, taking care not to score or damage the bore

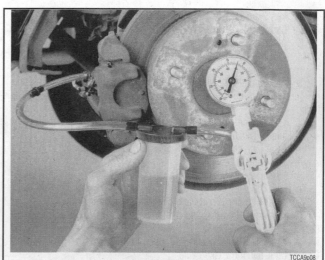

Fig. 28 There are tools, such as this Mighty-Vac, available to assist in proper brake system bleeding

Fig. 26 Use extreme caution when removing the piston seal; DO NOT scratch the caliper bore

b. Remove the caliper piston using compressed air applied into the caliper inlet hole. Inspect the piston for scoring, nicks, corrosion and/or worn or damaged chrome plating. The piston must be replaced if any of these conditions are found.

3. For the second method, you must rotate the piston to retract it from the caliper.

4. If equipped, remove the anti-rattle clip.

5. Use a prybar to remove the caliper boot, being careful not to scratch the housing bore.

6. Remove the piston seals from the groove in the caliper bore.

7. Carefully loosen the brake bleeder valve cap and valve from the caliper housing.

8. Inspect the caliper bores, pistons and mounting threads for scoring or excessive wear.

9. Use crocus cloth to polish out light corrosion from the piston and bore.

10. Clean all parts with denatured alcohol and dry with compressed air.
To assemble:

11. Lubricate and install the bleeder valve and cap.

12. Install the new seals into the caliper bore grooves, making sure they are not twisted.

13. Lubricate the piston bore.

14. Install the pistons and boots into the bores of the calipers and push to the bottom of the bores.

15. Use a suitable driving tool to seat the boots in the housing.

16. Install the caliper in the vehicle.

17. Install the wheel and tire assembly, then carefully lower the vehicle.

18. Properly bleed the brake system.

Brake Disc (Rotor)

REMOVAL & INSTALLATION

Front Rotor

1. Raise and support the vehicle safely.

2. Remove the wheels.

3. Remove the brake caliper and carrier without disconnecting the hydraulic line and suspend it out of the way with a piece of mechanic's wire.

4. Remove the axle shaft nut.

The rotor is attached to the hub and cannot be removed without first removing the hub

To remove the entire caliper assembly, loosen the carrier bolts

Attach a gear puller to the hub using the wheel studs and lug nuts

When removing the rotor, it may be easier to remove the caliper and carrier as an assembly

Place the center bolt of the puller on the axle shaft and press the hub and rotor from the axle shaft

The backing plate may now be removed for servicing or cleaning

Remove the hub-to-rotor bolts . . .

. . . then separate the hub and rotor

5. Using special tool (PN 09526-11001) or equivalent press the hub and disc from the axle shaft.

6. Matchmark the relationship between the brake disc and hub.

7. Remove the bolts attaching the rotor to the hub.

8. Remove the rotor.

To install:

9. Align and install the hub on the rotor. Tighten the attaching bolts to 36–43 ft. lbs. (50–60 Nm).

10. Install the hub on the spindle.

11. Tighten the axle shaft nut, while spinning the hub, to the following torque:

- Tiburon—143–164 ft. lbs. (200–230 Nm)
- Sonata—146–189 ft. lbs. (200–260 Nm)
- Accent and 1996–98 Elantra—130–159 ft. lbs. (180–220 Nm)
- 1994–95 Elantra—108–145 ft. lbs. (150–200 Nm)

12. Install the brake caliper.

13. Install the wheels.

14. Lower the vehicle.

Rear Rotor

1. Raise and support the vehicle safely.
2. Remove the wheels.
3. Remove the brake caliper.
4. Remove the rotor setscrew.
5. Remove the rotor.

To install:

6. Install the rotor and tighten the setscrew securely.
7. Install the brake caliper.
8. Install the front wheel.
9. Lower the vehicle.

INSPECTION

♦ See Figure 29

1. Loosen the lug nuts.
2. Raise the front end and support on jackstands.
3. Remove the front wheels.
4. Using a 0–1 inch micrometer or Vernier caliper measure the rotor thickness.
5. Mount a magnetic base dial indicator to the strut member and zero the indicator stylus on the face of the rotor. Rotate the rotor 360 degrees by hand and record the run-out.
6. Compare measurements to the brake specifications chart. If the thickness and run-out do not meet specifications, replace the rotor.

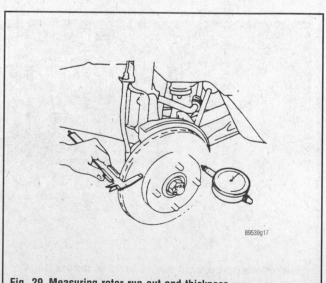

Fig. 29 Measuring rotor run-out and thickness

DRUM BRAKES

▶ See Figures 30 and 31

✳✳ CAUTION

Older brake pads or shoes may contain asbestos, which has been determined to be a cancer causing agent. Never clean the brake surfaces with compressed air! Avoid inhaling any dust from any brake surface. When cleaning brake surfaces, use a commercially available brake cleaning fluid.

COMPONENTS

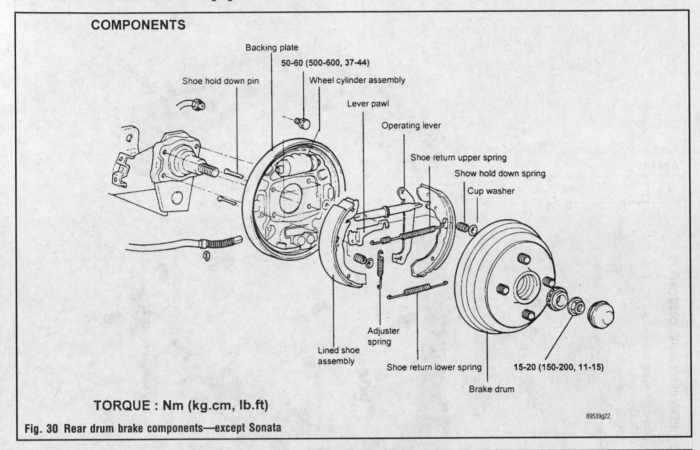

Backing plate
50-60 (500-600, 37-44)
Shoe hold down pin
Wheel cylinder assembly
Lever pawl
Operating lever
Shoe return upper spring
Show hold down spring
Cup washer
Adjuster spring
Lined shoe assembly
Shoe return lower spring
15-20 (150-200, 11-15)
Brake drum

TORQUE : Nm (kg.cm, lb.ft)

89539g22

Fig. 30 Rear drum brake components—except Sonata

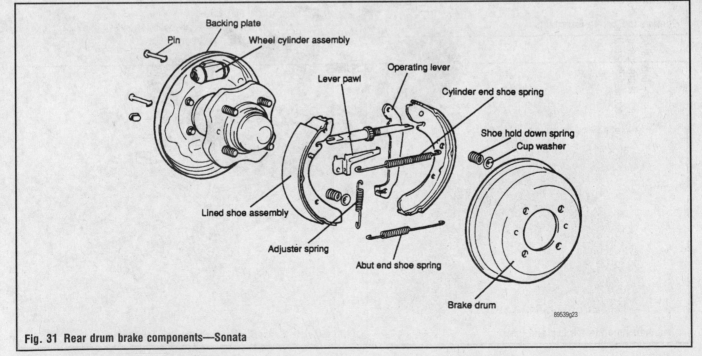

Backing plate
Pin
Wheel cylinder assembly
Operating lever
Lever pawl
Cylinder end shoe spring
Shoe hold down spring
Cup washer
Lined shoe assembly
Adjuster spring
Abut end shoe spring
Brake drum

89539g23

Fig. 31 Rear drum brake components—Sonata

REAR DRUM BRAKE COMPONENTS

1. Primary brake shoe
2. Shoe return spring
3. Secondary brake shoe
4. Hold-down spring and retainer
5. Hold-down pin
6. Adjuster level pawl
7. Clip
8. Wave washer
9. Self-adjuster
10. Shoe return spring
11. Parking brake lever

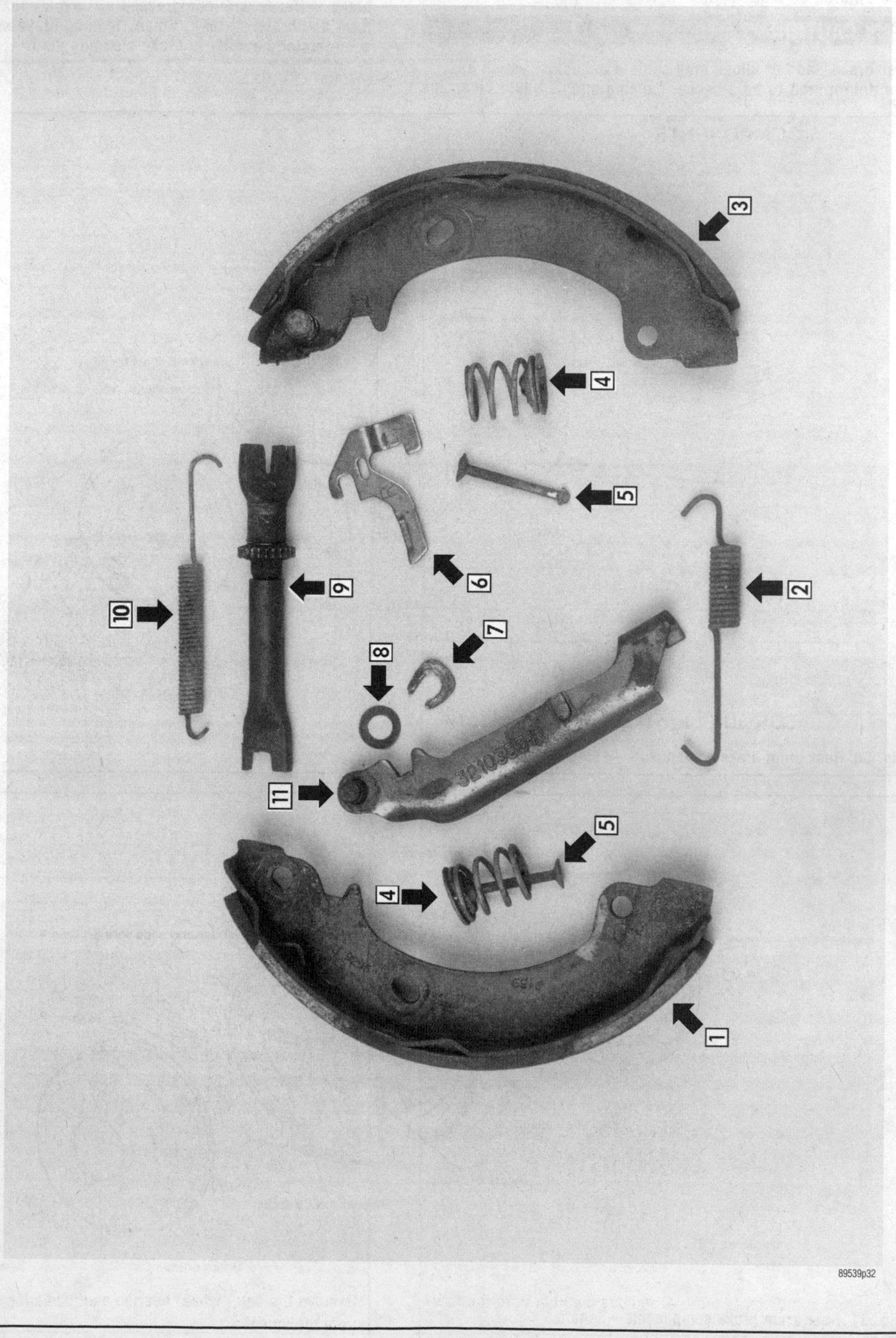

Brake Drums

REMOVAL & INSTALLATION

With Rear Hub Bearing

1. Raise the vehicle and support safely.
2. Remove the wheels.
3. Remove the dust cap and cotter pin, then loosen the locknut.
4. Remove the washer and outer wheel bearing.

Remove the dust cap from the brake drum

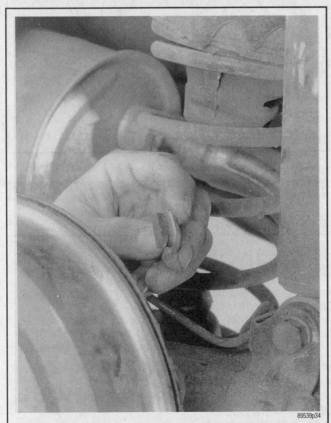

If the drum is difficult to remove, remove the plug from the rear of the backing plate . . .

. . . then push the self-adjuster lever away from the star wheel, and rotate the star wheel to retract the shoes

Remove the outer wheel bearing and then slide the brake drum from the spindle

Always use a torque wrench to tighten the spindle nut to specification

➡If the drum is difficult to remove, remove the plug from the rear of the backing plate and push the self-adjuster lever away from the star wheel. Rotate the star wheel to retract the shoes.

  5. Remove the drum with the inner wheel bearing from the spindle.
To install:
  6. Install the drum on the spindle.
  7. Install the outer wheel bearing and washer.
  8. Tighten the locknut to 108–145 ft. lbs. (150–200 Nm). Turn the brake drum while tightening the spindle nut to seat the wheel bearings.
  9. Install the cotter pin and dust cap.
  10. Install the wheels.
  11. Adjust the rear brakes.

Without Rear Hub Bearing

  1. Raise and support the vehicle safely.
  2. Remove the wheels.

➡If the drum is difficult to remove, remove the plug from the rear of the backing plate and push the self-adjuster lever away from the star wheel. Rotate the star wheel to retract the shoes.

  3. Remove the drum setscrew, as required.
  4. Remove the drum.
To install:
  5. Install the drum and tighten the setscrew securely.
  6. Install the wheels.
  7. Adjust the brake shoes.
  8. Lower the vehicle.

INSPECTION

◆ **See Figures 32 and 33**

  1. Raise the rear end and remove the brake drum as previously described.
  2. Thoroughly clean the drum with brake cleaning solvent and allow the drum to dry.
  3. Measure the brake drum inside diameter with an outside Vernier caliper. The manufacturer's minimum allowable service specifications are as follows:
   • Excel—182mm
   • Sonata—230mm.
  4. Using a dial indicator, measure the brake drum for out-of-roundness. Maximum brake drum out-of-round for all vehicles is 0.15mm.
  5. Check the brake linings for proper lining to drum contact.

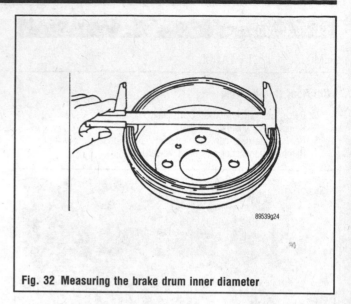

Fig. 32 Measuring the brake drum inner diameter

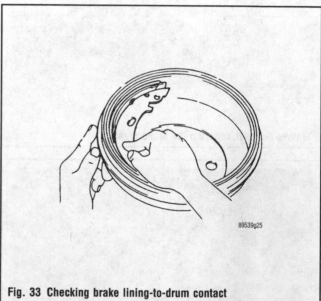

Fig. 33 Checking brake lining-to-drum contact

Brake Shoes

REMOVAL & INSTALLATION

  1. Raise and support the vehicle safely.
  2. Remove the wheels.
  3. Remove the brake drum.
  4. Thoroughly clean the brake assembly with a commercially available brake cleaner to remove all brake dust.
  5. Remove the lower brake shoe return spring.
  6. Remove the upper brake shoe return spring.
  7. Spread the brake shoes apart and remove the brake self-adjuster.
  8. Remove the self-adjuster lever pawl.
  9. Remove the brake shoe hold-down springs.
  10. Remove the brake shoes.
  11. On the primary brake shoe, remove the clip and wave washer that attach the parking brake lever.
  12. Remove the parking brake lever.
  13. Disconnect the parking brake cable from the lever.

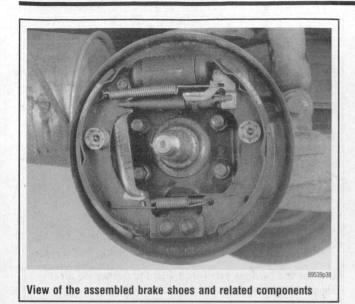

View of the assembled brake shoes and related components

This is a commercially available brake spring tool. It is used on the upper and lower shoe return springs

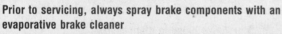

Prior to servicing, always spray brake components with an evaporative brake cleaner

Unfasten and remove the lower brake shoe return spring . . .

Make sure to remove all the old grease from the spindle

. . . as well as the upper return spring

After the return springs are removed, push apart the brake pads and remove the self-adjuster

Depress and twist the retainers 1/4 turn to release the brake shoe hold-down springs . . .

Next, remove the brake self-adjuster lever pawl

. . . then remove the hold-down pins from the rear of the backing plate

This is a commercially available brake spring tool. It is used to remove and install the hold-down springs

Perform the same procedure for the other brake shoe

Disconnect the parking brake lever by removing this clip and the wave washer beneath it

If necessary, disconnect the parking brake cable from the lever. For most brake jobs, this will not be required

After cleaning the backing plate thoroughly, lubricate the brake shoe contact points with lithium grease

To install:

14. Clean both backing plates and all brake components using a commercially available brake cleaner.

15. Lubricate all contact points on the backing plate, anchor plate, wheel cylinder-to-shoe contact and parking brake contacts with lithium based grease.

16. Connect the parking brake cable to the lever.

17. Install the parking brake lever on the primary brake shoe and retain with the wave washer and clip.

18. Install the brake shoes one at a time and fasten with the shoe hold-down springs.

19. Install the self-adjuster lever pawl.

20. Spread the brake shoes apart and install the brake self-adjuster.

21. Install the upper brake shoe return spring.

22. Install the lower brake shoe return spring.

23. Pre-adjust the brake shoes by turning the adjuster star wheel outward until the drum will just slide on over the brake shoes.

24. Before installing the drum, make sure the parking brake is not adjusted too tightly; if it is, loosen it, or the adjustment of the rear brakes will not be correct.

25. Install the brake drums.

26. Install the wheels.

27. Check and adjust the level of brake fluid in the master cylinder reservoirs.

ADJUSTMENT

1. Brakes shoes are adjusted by inserting a brake shoe adjusting tool into the slot on the backing plate and turning the star wheel until a light drag is felt when turning the wheel.

2. Adjust the parking brake stroke after the brake shoes are properly adjusted.

3. Road test the vehicle to assure proper brake operation.

4. The vehicle should always stop straight. If the vehicle pulls to one side, check the rear brake adjustment. If the brakes are properly adjusted, check the front calipers for proper operation.

Wheel Cylinders

REMOVAL & INSTALLATION

1. Remove the brake shoes.

2. Place a container or some old rags under the brake backing plate to catch the brake fluid that will run out of the wheel cylinder.

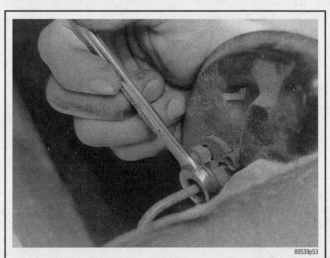

Disconnect the brake line at the wheel cylinder. Always use a flare nut wrench to prevent rounding the fitting

Unfasten the wheel cylinder attaching bolts . . .

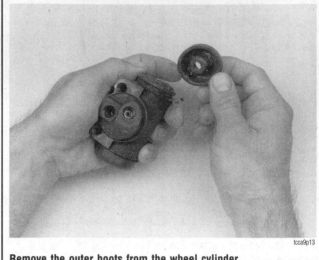

Remove the outer boots from the wheel cylinder

. . . and remove the wheel cylinder from the backing plate

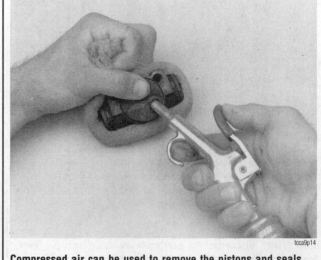

Compressed air can be used to remove the pistons and seals

3. Disconnect and plug the brake line.
4. Remove the wheel cylinder mounting bolts.
5. Remove the wheel cylinder from the backing plate.
To install:
6. Install the wheel cylinder on the backing plate and tighten the mounting bolts to 108–156 inch lbs. (7–10 Nm).
7. Connect the brake line and tighten the fitting to 9–12 ft. lbs. (13–17 Nm).
8. Install the brake shoes.
9. Refill and bleed the system.

OVERHAUL

Wheel cylinder overhaul kits may be available, but often at little or no savings over a reconditioned wheel cylinder. It often makes sense with these components to substitute a new or reconditioned part instead of attempting an overhaul.

If no replacement is available, or you would prefer to overhaul your wheel cylinders, the following procedure may be used. When rebuilding and installing wheel cylinders, avoid getting any contaminants into the system. Always use clean, new, high quality brake fluid. If dirty or im-

Remove the pistons, cup seals and spring from the cylinder

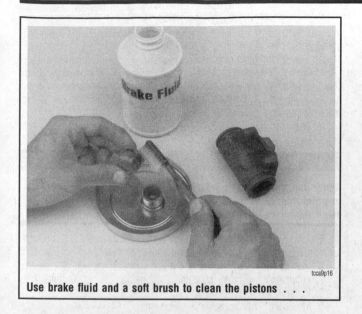

Use brake fluid and a soft brush to clean the pistons . . .

Lubricate the cup seals with brake fluid

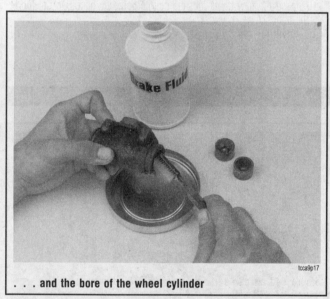

. . . and the bore of the wheel cylinder

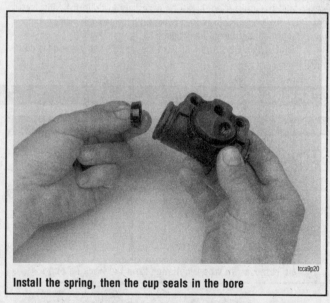

Install the spring, then the cup seals in the bore

Once cleaned and inspected, the wheel cylinder is ready for assembly

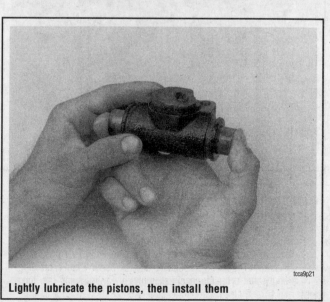

Lightly lubricate the pistons, then install them

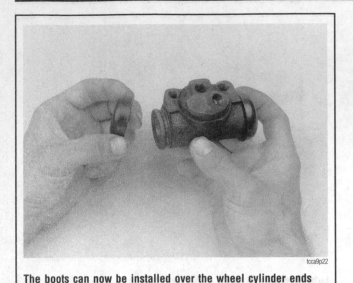

The boots can now be installed over the wheel cylinder ends

proper fluid has been used, it will be necessary to drain the entire system, flush the system with proper brake fluid, replace all rubber components, then refill and bleed the system.

1. Remove the wheel cylinder from the vehicle and place on a clean workbench.

PARKING BRAKE

Cables

REMOVAL & INSTALLATION

Remove the parking brake cable retaining clip . . .

Except Sonata

◆ **See Figures 34 and 35**

1. Raise and support the vehicle safely.
2. Remove the rear console.
3. Detach the adjusting nut and detach the parking brake cable.
4. Remove the tire and wheel assembly, brake drum and the brake shoes.

2. First remove and discard the old rubber boots, then withdraw the pistons. Piston cylinders are equipped with seals and a spring assembly, all located behind the pistons in the cylinder bore.

3. Remove the remaining inner components, seals and spring assembly. Compressed air may be useful in removing these components. If no compressed air is available, be VERY careful not to score the wheel cylinder bore when removing parts from it. Discard all components for which replacements were supplied in the rebuild kit.

4. Wash the cylinder and metal parts in denatured alcohol or clean brake fluid.

✳✳ WARNING

Never use a mineral-based solvent such as gasoline, kerosene or paint thinner for cleaning purposes. These solvents will swell rubber components and quickly deteriorate them.

5. Allow the parts to air dry or use compressed air. Do not use rags for cleaning, since lint will remain in the cylinder bore.
6. Inspect the piston and replace it if it shows scratches.
7. Lubricate the cylinder bore and seals using clean brake fluid.
8. Position the spring assembly.
9. Install the inner seals, then the pistons.
10. Insert the new boots into the counterbores by hand. Do not lubricate the boots.
11. Install the wheel cylinder.

. . . and slide the cable through the backing plate

5. Detach the parking brake cable from the parking brake lever.
6. Remove the parking brake cable retainer ring in the rear of the backing plate.
7. Remove the rear seat cushion assembly and roll up the carpet.
8. Loosen the parking brake cable clamp and remove the cable assembly.

To install:

9. Check the parking brake cables for left and right identification marks and install accordingly.
10. Install the cable to the parking brake lever. Move the adjuster lever all the way to the back when installing the shoe—to—shoe spring. Install the brake shoes and the drum.
11. Install the parking brake retainer ring to the rear of the backing

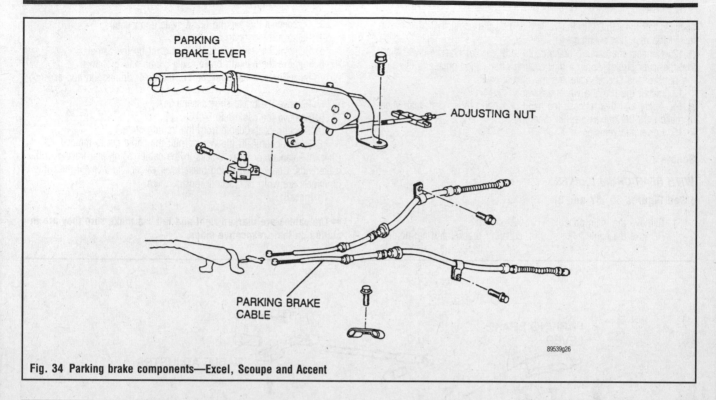

PARKING
BRAKE LEVER

ADJUSTING NUT

PARKING BRAKE
CABLE

89539g26

Fig. 34 Parking brake components—Excel, Scoupe and Accent

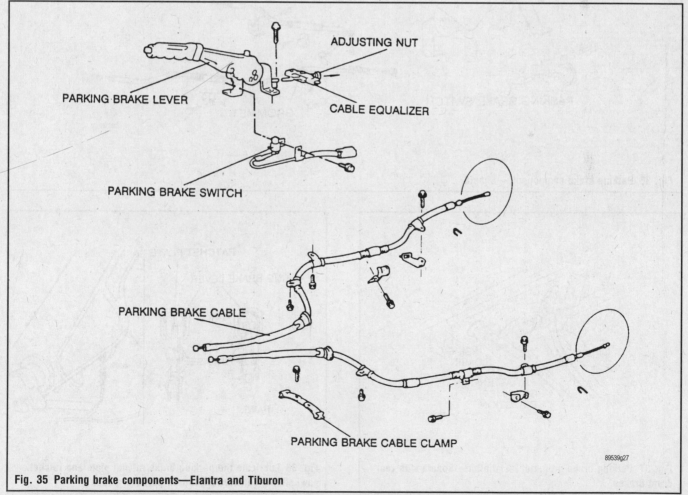

ADJUSTING NUT

PARKING BRAKE LEVER

CABLE EQUALIZER

PARKING BRAKE SWITCH

PARKING BRAKE CABLE

PARKING BRAKE CABLE CLAMP

89539g27

Fig. 35 Parking brake components—Elantra and Tiburon

plate. Install the cable into the vehicle and secure using the cable clamp. Install the rear seat cushion.

12. Connect the parking brake cable to the actuator assembly and adjust the lever stroke. Apply a thin coating of specified grease to the sliding parts of the ratchet plate and the ratchet pawl.

13. Install the tire and wheel assembly.

14. Apply and then release the hand brake and rotate each rear wheel to make sure the brakes are not dragging.

15. Lower the vehicle.

Sonata

WITH REAR DRUM BRAKES

♦ See Figures 36, 37 and 38

1. Remove the main console.
2. Remove the cable adjuster, pin, equalizer bracket and nut holder.

3. Disconnect the parking brake switch connector.
4. Remove the parking brake lever.
5. Remove the rear seat cushion and lift up the carpet.
6. Remove the parking brake cable clamp and grommet.
7. Raise the rear end and remove the tires, drums and hub assemblies.
8. Remove the brake shoe assemblies.
9. Remove the cable clip.
10. Disconnect the cable from the trailing shoe.
11. From underneath the vehicle pull the cable out to remove it.

Check the cables for wear, cracks in the cable casing and fraying in the cable ends. Check the parking brake lever ratchet for wear. If the cable grommets are worn or cracked, replace them.

To install:

➥The cables are marked right and left, so make sure they are installed on their respective sides.

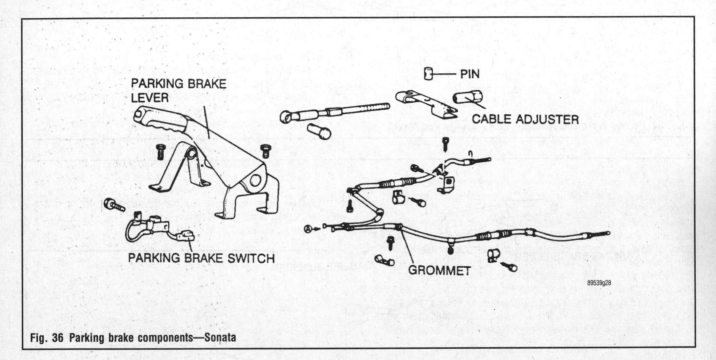

Fig. 36 Parking brake components—Sonata

Fig. 37 Parking brake grommet installation—Sonata with rear drum brakes

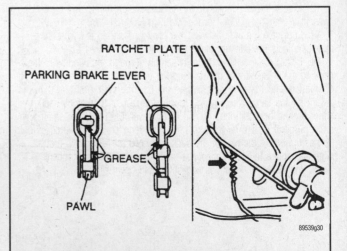

Fig. 38 Lubricate the parking brake ratchet plate and ratchet pawl sliding surfaces with multi-purpose grease

12. Route the cable up through the under body and connect the cable to the trailing shoe. Install the cable clip.

13. Install the brake shoe assemblies. Set the adjuster lever all the way back when installing the shoe-to-shoe spring.

14. Install the hub, drum and tire assemblies. Lower the rear end.

15. Install the grommets as show in the illustration. Make certain that the grommets are facing in the right direction.

16. Replace the carpet and the rear seat cushion.

17. Install the parking brake lever and connect the parking brake switch.

18. Install the nut holder, equalizer bracket, pin and cable adjuster. Lubricate the ratchet plate and ratchet pawl sliding surfaces with multi-purpose grease.

19. Adjust the parking brake lever stroke.

20. Install the main console.

21. Check the parking brake and parking brake switch for proper operation.

WITH REAR DISC BRAKES

1. Raise the rear and support safely. Remove the rear wheels.

2. Remove the rear caliper, rotor disc, hub and bearing assemblies.

3. Remove the lower shoe-to-shoe spring.

4. Remove the parking brake lever adjusters.

5. Remove the upper shoe-to-shoe return spring.

6. Disconnect the shoe hold-down pin and spring.

7. Disconnect the cable clevis from the adjusting lever. Be careful not to tear cable dust boot. Pull the lever and slider assembly out towards the outboard side of the brake and through the access window in the backing plate.

8. Remove the cable clips.

9. Unbolt the backing plate from the suspension arm.

10. Loosen the cable adjusting nut and remove the cables from the adjuster bracket.

11. Remove the cables. Check the cables for wear, cracks in the cable casing and fraying in the cable ends. Check the parking brake lever ratchet for wear. If the cable grommets are worn or cracked, replace them. Check the dust boots for rips and tears. Check the brake shoe linings for wear and oil contamination. Minimum brake lining thickness is 2mm. Check the shoe webs and adjusters for bending. Check the return springs for bent hooks, over-extension and breaks. Check the lever and slider assemblies for cracks, bending and wear. Check the drum surface for scoring, wear and oil contamination. Replace any worn or damaged component as necessary.

To install:

12. Mount the backing plate to the suspension flange and tighten the bolts in a diagonal pattern to 45–60 ft. lbs. (61–81 Nm).

13. Lubricate the area between the lever and slider and where the slider contacts the backing plate. Use multi-purpose grease.

14. Install the lever and slider assembly through the window in the backing plate. Be careful not damage the dust boot. The lever should be positioned with the long portion into the backing plate first and then the indent for the cable clevis facing toward the rear of the vehicle last. The slider should be positioned on top of the lever. Lubricate the slider with multi-purpose grease for easy rotation. The long arm of the slider should be positioned on the rear of the backing plate. The assembly should slide and rotate freely. Connect the cable clevis to the lever indent.

15. Install the brake shoes and shoe hold-down pin.

16. Shorten the adjuster assembly and install between the slots in the bottom portion of the shoes.

17. Install the upper and lower shoe-to-shoe springs. The upper portion of the shoe web should contact the anchor block. Adjust the cable as necessary to make this contact.

18. Check the lever function by pushing the end of the lever by the cable clevis and observe the movement of the brake shoes. The tab end of the lever should move against the shoe and the slider tab end should contact fully against the outer shoe.

19. Install the parking brake adjusters.

20. Install the rear hub and bearing, rotor disc and caliper assemblies.

21. Mount the rear wheels and lower the vehicle.

22. Adjust the parking brake lever stroke.

23. Check the parking brake and parking brake switch for proper operation. Lubricate the ratchet plate and ratchet pawl sliding surfaces with multi-purpose grease.

ADJUSTMENT

♦ See Figure 39

1. Fully release the brake lever.

2. Pull the parking brake upward with normal effort. Maximum travel should be 6–8 clicks.

3. Remove the console and adjust the cable length by turning the nut on the equalizer.

4. Recheck the parking brake stroke and adjust as necessary.

5. Loosen the parking brake switch mounting bolt. Adjust the switch so that when the lever is fully released, the switch lamp goes and out and when the lever is pulled one click, the switch lamp illuminates.

6. If the switch does not operate as described check the switch lamp bulb. If the bulb is good, replace the switch.

7. After the adjustment, make sure that the rear brakes do not drag when the parking brake lever is released.

8. Install the console.

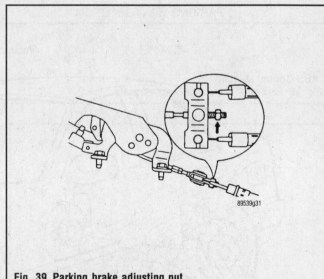

89539g31

Fig. 39 Parking brake adjusting nut

ANTI-LOCK BRAKE SYSTEM (ABS)

◆ See Figures 40 and 41

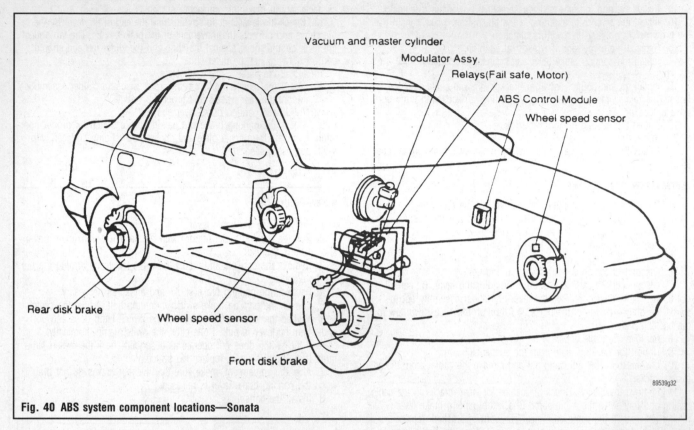

Vacuum and master cylinder
Modulator Assy.
Relays(Fail safe, Motor)
ABS Control Module
Wheel speed sensor
Rear disk brake
Wheel speed sensor
Front disk brake

89539g32

Fig. 40 ABS system component locations—Sonata

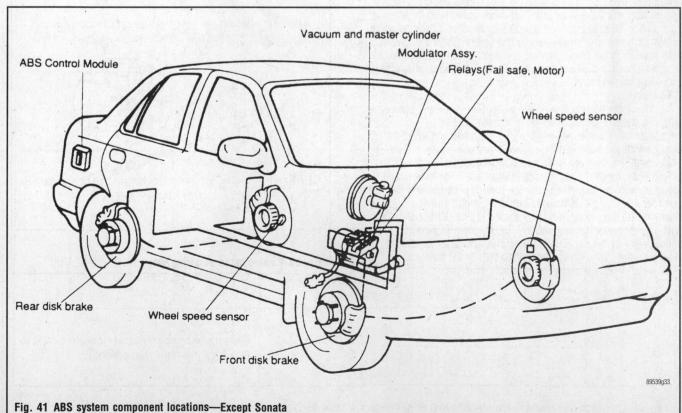

ABS Control Module
Vacuum and master cylinder
Modulator Assy.
Relays(Fail safe, Motor)
Wheel speed sensor
Rear disk brake
Wheel speed sensor
Front disk brake

89539g33

Fig. 41 ABS system component locations—Except Sonata

General Information

♦ **See Figures 42 thru 48 (p. 37–40)**

Anti-lock braking systems are designed to prevent locked-wheel skidding during hard braking or during braking on slippery surfaces. The front wheels of a vehicle cannot properly steer the vehicle if they are locked and sliding; the vehicle will continue in its previous direction of travel. The four wheel anti-lock brake system holds each wheel just below the point of locking, thereby allowing steering response and preventing the rear of the vehicle from sliding sideways.

The system monitors and compares wheel speed based on the inputs from the wheel speed sensors. The brake pressure is controlled according to the impending lock-up computations of the ABS control unit.

Diagnostic trouble code No.	SRI lamp flash pattern	Diagnosis item	Check Item
19	DEFECTIVE TONE WHEEL	CHECK THE TONE WHEELS	Check for a defective tone wheel on a wheel.
21	LF SOLENOID CIRCUIT - SHORT BATT	LEFT FRONT SOLENOID	Detection for short circuit to +12 Volt for the left front solenoid.
22	LF SOLENOID CIRCUIT - SHORT GND	LEFT FRONT SOLENOID	Detection for open circuit or short circuit to GND for the left front solenoid.
23	RF SOLENOID CIRCUIT - SHORT BATT	RIGHT FRONT SOLENOID	Detection for short circuit to +12 Volt for the right front solenoid.
24	RF SOLENOID CIRCUIT - SHORT GND	RIGHT FRONT SOLENOID	Detection for open circuit or short circuit to GND for the right front solenoid.
25	LR SOLENOID CIRCUIT - SHORT BATT	LEFT REAR SOLENOID	Detection for short circuit to +12 Volt for the left rear solenoid.
26	LR SOLENOID CIRCUIT - SHORT GND	LEFT REAR SOLENOID	Detection for open circuit or short circuit to GND for the left rear solenoid.
27	RR SOLENOID CIRCUIT - SHORT BATT	RIGHT REAR SOLENOID	Detection for short circuit to +12 Volt for the right rear solenoid.
28	RR SOLENOID CIRCUIT - SHORT GND	RIGHT REAR SOLENOID	Detection for open circuit or short circuit to GND for the right rear solenoid.

Fig. 42 ABS diagnostic trouble code identification (1 of 4)—except 1994–95 Elantra and Sonata

89539g35

Diagnostic trouble code No.	SRI lamp flash pattern	Diagnosis item	Check Item
42	FAIL SAFE RELAY CIRCUIT - OPEN	FAIL SAFE RELAY	Fail safe relay contacts are open circuit
43	FAIL SAFE RELAY COIL	FAIL SAFE RELAY COIL	The current from the fail safe relay is too high or too low
44	ABS SRI CIRCUIT - SHORT GND	SERVICE REMINDER INDICATOR	Detection of a short circuit of the Service Reminder Indicator (Permanently on)
45	ABS SRI DIODE - OPEN	SERVICE REMINDER INDICATOR DIODE	Detection for an open circuit of the diode for the Service Reminder Indicator ABS.
54	ABS SRI CIRCUIT - SHORT BATT	SERVICE REMINDER INDICATOR	Detection for a short circuit to +12V of the Service Reminder Indicator
55	ABS SRI CIRCUIT - OPEN	SERVICE REMINDER INDICATOR	Detection for an open circuit of the Service Reminder Indicator ABS.
56	BATTERY VOLTAGE - LOW	BATTERY VOLTAGE	Battery voltage out of the function range (Under voltage) for the system.
57	BATTERY VOLTAGE - HIGH	BATTERY VOLTAGE	Battery voltage out of the function range (Over voltage) for the system.
62	LF WHEEL SENSOR - CIRCUIT OPEN	LEFT FRONT SENSOR CIRCUIT	Sensor open circuit or short to 12 Volt detection for the left front wheel
63	RF WHEEL SENSOR - CIRCUIT OPEN	RIGHT FRONT SENSOR CIRCUIT	Sensor open circuit or short to 12 Volt detection for the right front wheel.

Fig. 44 ABS diagnostic trouble code identification (3 of 4)—except 1994–95 Elantra and Sonata

Diagnostic trouble code No.	SRI lamp flash pattern	Diagnosis item	Check Item
31	LF WHEEL SPEED SENSOR AIR GAP	LEFT FRONT SENSOR	Detection for the air gap of the tone wheel. This detection will be activated if all wheel speeds are zero and the ABS-function is not active.
32	RF WHEEL SPEED SENSOR AIR GAP	RIGHT FRONT SENSOR	Detection for the air gap of the tone wheel. This detection will be activated if all wheel speeds are zero and the ABS-function is not active.
33	LR WHEEL SPEED SENSOR AIR GAP	LEFT REAR SENSOR	Detection for the air gap of the tone wheel. This detection will be activated if all wheel speeds are zero and the ABS-function is not active.
34	RR WHEEL SPEED SENSOR AIR GAP	RIGHT REAR SENSOR	Detection for the air gap of the tone wheel. This detection will be activated if all wheel speeds are zero and the ABS-function is not active.
35	MOTOR PUMP	MOTOR PUMP	Check for faulty or seized up of motor pump.
36	MOTOR PUMP RELAY - SHORT GND	MOTOR RELAY CIRCUIT	Detection for a open circuit or a short circuit to GND from the motor pump relay.
37	MOTOR PUMP RELAY - SHORT BATT	MOTOR RELAY CIRCUIT	Detection for a short circuit to +12 Volt from the motor pump relay.
38	MOTOR PUMP CIRCUIT - SHORT BATT	PUMP MOTOR	Detection for a short circuit at the motor pump
39	MOTOR PUMP CIRCUIT - SHORT GND	PUMP MOTOR	Detection for a short circuit to GND at the motor pump
41	FAIL SAFE RELAY CIRCUIT - SHORT	FAIL SAFE RELAY	Fail safe relay contacts are short circuit.

Fig. 43 ABS diagnostic trouble code identification (2 of 4)—except 1994–95 Elantra and Sonata

Diagnostic trouble code No.	Scan Tool display	Diagnosis item	Description
19	TONE WHEEL	CHECK THE TONE WHEELS	Check for a defective tone wheel on a wheel.
21	SOL. LF-SHRT	LEFT FRONT SOLENOID	Detection for short circuit to +12 Volt for the left front solenoid.
22	SOL. LF-OPEN	LEFT FRONT SOLENOID	Detection for open circuit or short circuit to GND for the left front solenoid.
23	SOL. RF-SHRT	RIGHT RIGHT SOLENOID	Detection for short circuit to +12 Volt for the right front solenoid.
24	SOL. RF-OPEN	RIGHT FRONT SOLENOID	Detection for open circuit or short circuit to GND for the right front solenoid.
25	SOL. LR-SHRT	LEFT REAR SOLENOID	Detection for short circuit to +12 Volt for the left rear solenoid.
26	SOL. LR-OPEN	LEFT REAR SOLENOID	Detection for open circuit or short circuit to GND for the left rear solenoid.
27	SOL. RR-SHRT	RIGHT REAR SOLENOID	Detection for short circuit to +12 Volt for the right rear solenoid.
28	SOL. RR-OPEN	RIGHT REAR SOLENOID	Detection for open circuit or short circuit to GND for the right rear solenoid.
31	SNSR. LF-GAP	LEFT FRONT SENSOR	Detection for the air gap of the tone wheel. This detection will be activated if all wheel speeds are zero and the ABS-function is not active.
32	SNSR. RF-GAP	RIGHT FRONT SENSOR	Detection for the air gap of the tone wheel. This detection will be activated if all wheel speeds are zero and the ABS-function is not active.
33	SNSR. LR-GAP	LEFT REAR SENSOR	Detection for the air gap of the tone wheel. This detection will be activated if all wheel speeds are zero and the ABS-function is not active.
34	SNSR. RR-GAP	RIGHT REAR SENSOR	Detection for the air gap of the tone wheel. This detection will be activated if all wheel speeds are zero and the ABS-function is not active.
35	MOTOR PUMP	MOTOR PUMP	Faulty or seized up motor pump.

Fig. 46 ABS diagnostic trouble code identification (1 of 3)—1994-95 Elantra and Sonata

Diagnostic trouble code No.	SRI lamp flash pattern	Diagnosis item	Check Item
64	LR WHEEL SENSOR - CIRCUIT.OPEN	LEFT REAR SENSOR CIRCUIT	Sensor open circuit or short to 12 Volt detection for the left rear wheel.
65	RR WHEEL SENSOR - CIRCUIT OPEN	RIGHT REAR SENSOR CIRCUIT	Sensor open circuit or short to 12 Volt detection for the right rear wheel.
66	LF WHEEL SENSOR - SHORT GND	LEFT FRONT SENSOR CIRCUIT	Sensor short to GND detection for the left front wheel
67	RF WHEEL SENSOR - SHORT GND	RIGHT FRONT SENSOR CIRCUIT	Sensor short to GND detection for the right front wheel.
68	LR WHEEL SENSOR - SHORT GND	LEFT REAR SENSOR CIRCUIT	Sensor short to GND detection for the left rear wheel.
69	RR WHEEL SENSOR - SHORT GND	RIGHT REAR SENSOR CIRCUIT	Sensor short to GND detection for the right rear wheel.
71	LF TONE WHEEL TOOTH MISSING	LEFT FRONT TONE WHEEL	Detection for missing teeth on the tone wheel or speed jumps over-100g on the left front wheel.
72	RF TONE WHEEL TOOTH MISSING	RIGHT FRONT TONE WHEEL	Detection for missing teeth on the tone wheel or speed jumps over-100g on the right front wheel.
73	LR TONE WHEEL TOOTH MISSING	LEFT REAR TONE WHEEL	Detection for missing teeth on the tone wheel or speed jumps over-100g on the left rear wheel.
74	RR TONE WHEEL TOOTH MISSING	RIGHT REAR TONE WHEEL	Detection for missing teeth on the tone wheel or speed jumps over -100g on the right rear wheel.
77	ABS CONTROL MODULE	ABSCM ERROR	Check for ABSCM (ABS Control module) error.

Fig. 45 ABS diagnostic trouble code identification (4 of 4)—except 1994-95 Elantra and Sonata

Diagnostic trouble code No.	Scan Tool display	Diagnosis item	Description
67	SNSR. RF-SHRT	RIGHT FRONT SENSOR CIRCUIT	Sensor short to GND detection for the right front wheel.
68	SNSR. LR-SHRT	LEFT REAR SENSOR CIRCUIT	Sensor short to GND detection for the left rear wheel.
69	SNSR. RR-SHRT	RIGHT REAR SENSOR CIRCUIT	Sensor short to GND detection for the right rear wheel.
71	SNSR. LF-S. JMP	LEFT FRONT TONE WHEEL	Detection for missing teeth on the tone wheel or speed jumps over-100g on the left front wheel.
72	SNSR. RF-S.JMP	RIGHT FRONT TONE WHEEL	Detection for missing teeth on the tone wheel or speed jumps over-100g on the right front wheel.
73	SNSR. LR-S.JMP	LEFT REAR TONE WHEEL	Detection for missing teeth on the tone wheel or speed jumps over-100g on the left rear wheel.
74	SNSR. RR-S.JMP	RIGHT REAR TONE WHEEL	Detection for missing teeth on the tone wheel or speed jumps over -100g on the right rear wheel.
77	ABSCM-FAIL	ABSCM ERROR	Detection of a ABSCM (ABS Control module) error.

Fig. 48 ABS diagnostic trouble code identification (3 of 3)—1994–95 Elantra and Sonata

Diagnostic trouble code No.	Scan Tool display	Diagnosis item	Description
36	MP RLY-OPEN	MOTOR RELAY CIRCUIT	Detection for a open circuit or a short circuit to GND from the motor pump relay.
37	MP RLY-SHRT	MOTOR RELAY CIRCUIT	Detection for a short circuit to +12 Volt from the motor pump relay.
38	MP BATT-SHRT	PUMP MOTOR	Detection for a short circuit at the motor pump
39	MP GND-SHRT	PUMP MOTOR	Detection for a short circuit to GND at the motor pump
41	FAIL RLY-SHRT	FAIL SAFE RELAY	Fail safe relay contacts are short circuit.
42	FAIL RLY-OPEN	FAIL SAFE RELAY	Fail safe relay contacts are open circuit
43	FAIL COIL	FAIL SAFE RELAY COIL	The current from the fail safe relay is too high or too low
44	ABS SRI-GND	SERVICE REMINDER INDICATOR	Detection of a short circuit of the Service Reminder Indicator (Permanently on)
45	ABS SRI-DIODE	SERVICE REMINDER INDICATOR DIODE	Detection for a open circuit of the diode for the Service Reminder Indicator ABS.
54	ABS SRI-BATT	SERVICE REMINDER INDICATOR	Detection for a short circuit to +12V of the Service Reminder Indicator .
55	ABS SRI-OPEN	SERVICE REMINDER INDICATOR	Detection for a open circuit of the Service Reminder Indicator ABS.
56	BATT. VOLT-LO	BATTERY VOLTAGE	Battery voltage out of the function range (Under voltage) for the system.
57	BATT.VOLT-HI	BATTERY VOLTAGE	Battery voltage out of the function range (Over voltage) for the system.
62	SNSR. LF-OPEN	LEFT FRONT SENSOR CIRCUIT	Sensor open circuit or short to 12 Volt detection for the left front wheel
63	SNSR. RF-OPEN	RIGHT FRONT SENSOR CIRCUIT	Sensor open circuit or short to 12 Volt detection for the right front wheel.
64	SNSR. LR-OPEN	LEFT REAR SENSOR CIRCUIT	Sensor open circuit or short to 12 Volt detection for the left rear wheel.
65	SNSR. RR-OPEN	RIGHT REAR SENSOR CIRCUIT	Sensor open circuit or short to 12 Volt detection for the right rear wheel.
66	SNSR. LF-SHRT	LEFT FRONT SENSOR CIRCUIT	Sensor short to GND detection for the left front wheel

Fig. 47 ABS diagnostic trouble code identification (2 of 3)—1994–95 Elantra and Sonata

As a wheel approaches lock-up, the controller actuates the appropriate build/decay or isolation solenoid. Depending on the inputs from each respective wheel speed sensor, the ECM may cycle one of the 2 isolation valves; thus stopping the flow of fluid from the master cylinder to either the LF/RR or RF/LR brake circuit or the ECM may cycle any combination of the 4 build/decay solenoids; thus allowing the system to build brake pressure at the caliper or release (decay) pressure to the modulator sump. This reduces the tendency of the vehicle to skid sideways under braking.

The hydraulic unit or modulator contains the 6 solenoid valves, 4 shuttles, 2 sumps, release check valves, proportioning valves, accumulator and the pump/motor assembly which provides pressurized fluid for the anti-lock system when necessary.

Hydraulic units are not interchangeable between vehicles. The units are not serviceable; if any fault occurs within the hydraulic unit, the entire unit must be replaced.

The Electronic Control Unit (ECU) receives inputs from the 4 speed sensors, brake light switch and the diagnostic connector. The ECU outputs signals to the 6 solenoid valves, ABS warning light relay and pump motor relay if detecting an impending wheel lock-up.

Each wheel is equipped with a magnetic sensor which produces a small AC voltage linearly proportional to wheel speed (11 Hz/mph). The sensor is mounted a fixed distance from a toothed ring which rotates with the wheel. The sensors are replaceable but not interchangeable; each must be fitted to its correct location. The toothed rings are replaceable, although disassembly of the hub or axle shaft is required.

Both the amber ANTI-LOCK light and red BRAKE light are located on the instrument cluster. Each lamp warns the operator of a possible fault in the respective system. A fault in one system may cause the other lamp to illuminate depending on the nature and severity of the problem. The operation or behavior of the amber warning lamp is one of the prime diagnostic tools for the system.

At no time should the warning lamp be lit while the engine is running. Once the vehicle speed exceeds 3 mph, the system performs a self-check of the pump and solenoid function. Any failure in these circuits will cause the warning lamp to re-light, warning the operator of a problem.

Reading Codes

➡ **1994–95 Elantra and Sonata, diagnostic codes may only be read by using a Hyundai Multi-Use Tester (MUT), or equivalent scan tool.**

1. Ground terminal 15 of the Diagnostic Link Connector (DLC) using a suitable wire or paper clip.
2. Turn the ignition **ON**.
3. The ABS lamp on the instrument panel will be illuminated for 2 seconds.
4. After a 3 second pause, the lamp will start to flash stored trouble codes.
5. The first digit of the code is determined by counting the number of long (1.5 second) flashes. After a 2 second pause, the second digit of the code is determined by counting the number of short (0.5 second) flashes.
6. Additional codes will be flashed after a 3 second pause.
7. Once all codes have been flashed, unground the DLC.

CLEARING CODES

➡ **On 1994–95 Elantra and Sonata, diagnostic codes may only be cleared by using a Hyundai Multi-Use Tester (MUT), or equivalent scan tool.**

Diagnostic codes are retained in memory until the negative battery cable has been removed for 15 seconds or more.

If the negative battery cable is not removed, the diagnostic codes remain in memory until the ignition is turned on and the vehicle is driven at a speed greater than 13 mph twenty times or more.

Wheel Speed Sensor

TESTING

1. Raise and support the vehicle safely.
2. Disconnect the wheel speed sensor electrical harness.
3. Check for AC voltage between the sensor terminals while turning the wheels. If AC voltage is not detected, the sensor is faulty.
4. Use an ohmmeter to measure resistance between the pins of the sensor. Correct resistance should be 1,275–1,495 ohms for front sensors and 1,260–1,540 ohms for rear sensors.
5. If resistance is not within specification, the sensor is faulty.
6. With the ohmmeter still connected, manipulate and pull gently on the cable, trying to expose a hidden break in the line. Do not use excess force. Be suspicious of areas where the cable bends or turns during routing.
7. Lower the vehicle.

REMOVAL & INSTALLATION

◆ **See Figure 50**

1. Raise and safely support the vehicle.
2. Remove the wheel and tire.
3. Remove the inner fender or splash shield as required.
4. Beginning at the sensor end, carefully disconnect or release each clip and retainer along the sensor wire. Take careful note of the exact position of each clip; they must be reinstalled in the identical position.
5. Disconnect the sensor connector at the end of the harness.
6. Remove the bolt holding the speed sensor bracket to the knuckle and remove the assembly from the vehicle.

➡**The speed sensor has a pole piece projecting from it. This exposed tip must be protected from impact or scratches. Do not allow the pole piece to contact the toothed wheel during removal or installation.**

7. Remove the sensor from the bracket.

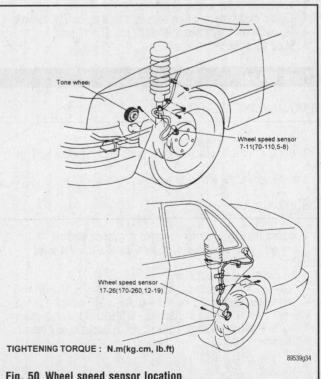

Tone wheel

Wheel speed sensor
7-11(70-110, 5-8)

Wheel speed sensor
17-26(170-260, 12-19)

TIGHTENING TORQUE : N.m(kg.cm, lb.ft)

89539g34

Fig. 50 Wheel speed sensor location

To install:

8. Assemble the sensor onto the bracket and tighten the bolt to 5–8 ft. lbs. (7–11 Nm) on front sensors and 12–19 ft. lbs. (17–25 Nm) on rear sensors.

9. Route the cable correctly and loosely install the clips and retainers. All clips must be in their original position and the sensor cable must not be twisted. Improper installation may cause cable damage and system failure.

➡**The wiring in the harness is easily damaged by twisting and flexing.**

10. Tighten the screws and bolts for the cable retaining clips.
11. Install the inner fender or splash shield, if removed.
12. Install the wheel and tire. Lower the vehicle to the ground.

Modulator

TESTING

1. Disconnect the modulator electrical harness.
2. Check resistance between terminals 1–5, 2–6, 3–7 and 4–8.
3. Resistance should be 3.10–3.34 ohms.
4. If resistance is not within specification, modulator may be faulty.

REMOVAL & INSTALLATION

1. Remove the air cleaner assembly.
2. Disconnect the ABS relay box, motor pump and modulator harnesses.
3. Disconnect the brake lines from the modulator.
4. Remove the relay box.
5. Remove the modulator.

➡**Never attempt to disassemble the modulator. There are no user serviceable parts in the modulator. When transporting or storing the modulator, keep it in an upright position with all ports sealed. The modulator should never be drained.**

6. Installation is the reverse of removal.
7. Tighten modulator mounting bolts to 12–19 ft. lbs. (17–26 Nm).
8. Tighten brake line fittings to 9–12 ft. lbs. (13–17 Nm).
9. Bleed the brake system.

Tone Wheel

REMOVAL & INSTALLATION

1. Remove the wheel hub.
2. Using a hydraulic press, carefully press the tone wheel from the hub.
3. Installation is the reverse of removal.

TESTING

1. Inspect the tone wheel for damaged or missing teeth.
2. Inspect the air gap between the tone wheel and wheel speed sensor.
3. Air gap should be as follows:
• 1994–95 Elantra and Sonata front—0.008–0.043 in. (0.2–1.1mm)
• 1994–95 Elantra and Sonata rear—0.008–0.047 in. (0.2–1.2mm)
• Except 1994–95 Elantra and Sonata—0.008–0.051 in. (0.2–1.3mm)
4. The tone wheel should be replaced if it is damaged or if the air gap is incorrect.

ABS Relay

TESTING

1. Remove the relay from its mount and disconnect the harness.
2. Use an ohmmeter to check continuity. There should be no continuity between terminals 1 and 5. Continuity should exist between terminals 2 and 4.
3. Apply 12 volts to pin 2 and ground pin 4. With power applied, continuity should be found across terminals 1 and 5.
4. If any test condition is not met, the relay must be replaced.

REMOVAL & INSTALLATION

1. Ensure that the ignition is **OFF**.
2. Loosen the screw and remove the ABS relay box cover.
3. Remove the relay from the box by pulling straight up.
To install:
4. Insert the relay firmly into the relay box.
5. Install the relay box cover and tighten the screw securely.
6. Check the system for proper operation.

Pump Motor Relay

TESTING

1. Remove the relay from its mount near the hydraulic unit.
2. Use an ohmmeter to check continuity. There should be no continuity between terminals 1 and 4. There should be continuity between terminals 2 and 3.
3. Apply 12 volts to terminal 2 and ground terminal 3. With power applied, there should be continuity between terminals 1 and 4.
4. If any test condition is not met, the relay must be replaced.

REMOVAL & INSTALLATION

1. Ensure that the ignition is **OFF**.
2. Loosen the screw and remove the ABS relay box cover.
3. Remove the relay from the box by pulling straight up.
To install:
4. Insert the relay firmly into the relay box.
5. Install the relay box cover and tighten the screw securely.
6. Check system for proper operation.

ABS Warning Lamp Relay

TESTING

1. Remove the relay from the relay box located in the engine compartment.
2. Use an ohmmeter to check continuity. There should be continuity between terminals 1 and 3. Continuity with approximately 0 ohms resistance should also exist between terminals 2 and 4.
3. Apply 12 volts to terminal 1 and ground terminal 3. With power applied, there should be no continuity between terminals 2 and 4.
4. If any test condition is not met, the relay must be replaced.

REMOVAL & INSTALLATION

1. Ensure that the ignition is **OFF**.
2. Loosen the screw and remove the ABS relay box cover.
3. Remove the relay from the box by pulling straight up.

To install:
4. Insert the relay firmly into the relay box.
5. Install the relay box cover and tighten the screw securely.
6. Check system for proper operation.

ABS Electronic Control Unit (ABS-ECU)

TESTING

There are no methods currently available to field test an ECU. Most field testing usually involves testing the components and circuits associated with the ECU in addition to all ECU power and ground circuits. If all components and circuits are functional, substituting a known good ECU is a common practice.

REMOVAL & INSTALLATION

1. Ensure that the ignition is **OFF** throughout the procedure.
2. Disconnect the multi-pin connector from the control unit.
3. Remove the 4 retaining bolts and remove the control unit from the left fenderwell.
To install:
4. Place the control unit in position and tighten the retaining bolts.
5. Connect the multi-pin connector and secure.
6. Turn ignition switch **ON** and verify operation of control unit.

Bleeding The ABS System

There are no special bleeding procedures for the ABS system.

BRAKE SPECIFICATIONS
All measurements in inches unless noted

Year	Model		Brake Disc Original Thickness	Brake Disc Minimum Thickness	Brake Disc Maximum Runout	Brake Drum Diameter Original Inside Diameter	Brake Drum Diameter Max. Wear Limit	Brake Drum Diameter Maximum Machine Diameter	Minimum Lining Thickness Front	Minimum Lining Thickness Rear
1994	Elantra		0.866	0.787	0.006	8.000	8.079	—	0.059	0.059
	Excel		0.750	0.669	0.006	7.087	7.165	—	0.039	0.039
	Scoupe		0.750	0.669	0.006	7.100	7.165	—	0.039	0.031
	Sonata	F	0.866	0.787	0.004	9.000	9.079	—	0.079	0.039
	Sonata	R ①	0.472	0.413	0.005	—	—	—	—	0.031
1995	Accent		0.750	0.669	0.002	7.090	7.165	—	0.039	0.039
	Elantra		0.866	0.787	0.002	8.000	8.079	—	0.059	0.059
	Scoupe		0.750	0.669	0.002	7.100	7.165	—	0.039	0.031
	Sonata	F	0.866	0.787	0.004	9.000	9.079	—	0.079	0.039
	Sonata	R ①	0.472	0.413	0.005	—	—	—	—	0.031
1996	Accent		0.750	0.669	0.002	7.090	7.165	—	0.039	0.039
	Elantra		0.866	0.787	0.002	8.000	8.079	—	0.059	0.059
	Sonata	F	0.866	0.787	0.004	9.000	9.079	—	0.079	0.039
	Sonata	R ①	0.472	0.413		—	—	—	—	0.031
1997	Accent		0.750	0.669	0.002	7.090	7.165	—	0.039	0.039
	Elantra		0.866	0.787	0.002	8.000	8.079	—	0.059	0.059
	Sonata	F	0.866	0.787	0.004	9.000	9.079	—	0.079	0.039
	Sonata	R ①	0.472	0.413	0.005	—	—	—	—	0.031
	Tiburon	F	0.866	0.787	0.002	8.000	8.079	—	0.079	0.059
	Tiburon	R ①	0.354	NA	NA	—	—	—	—	0.031
1998	Accent		0.750	0.669	0.002	7.090	7.165	—	0.039	0.039
	Elantra		0.866	0.787	0.002	8.000	8.079	—	0.059	0.059
	Sonata	F	0.866	0.787	0.004	9.000	9.079	—	0.079	0.039
	Sonata	R ①	0.472	0.413	0.005	—	—	—	—	0.031
	Tiburon	F	0.866	0.787	0.002	8.000	8.079	—	0.079	0.059
	Tiburon	R ①	0.354	NA	NA	—	—	—	—	0.031

① With rear disc brakes

89539c01

Troubleshooting the Brake System

Problem	Cause	Solution
Low brake pedal (excessive pedal travel required for braking action.)	• Excessive clearance between rear linings and drums caused by inoperative automatic adjusters	• Make 10 to 15 alternate forward and reverse brake stops to adjust brakes. If brake pedal does not come up, repair or replace adjuster parts as necessary.
	• Worn rear brakelining	• Inspect and replace lining if worn beyond minimum thickness specification
	• Bent, distorted brakeshoes, front or rear	• Replace brakeshoes in axle sets
	• Air in hydraulic system	• Remove air from system. Refer to Brake Bleeding.
Low brake pedal (pedal may go to floor with steady pressure applied.)	• Fluid leak in hydraulic system	• Fill master cylinder to fill line; have helper apply brakes and check calipers, wheel cylinders, differential valve tubes, hoses and fittings for leaks. Repair or replace as necessary.
	• Air in hydraulic system	• Remove air from system. Refer to Brake Bleeding.
	• Incorrect or non-recommended brake fluid (fluid evaporates at below normal temp).	• Flush hydraulic system with clean brake fluid. Refill with correct-type fluid.
	• Master cylinder piston seals worn, or master cylinder bore is scored, worn or corroded	• Repair or replace master cylinder
Low brake pedal (pedal goes to floor on first application—o.k. on subsequent applications.)	• Disc brake pads sticking on abutment surfaces of anchor plate. Caused by a build-up of dirt, rust, or corrosion on abutment surfaces	• Clean abutment surfaces
Fading brake pedal (pedal height decreases with steady pressure applied.)	• Fluid leak in hydraulic system	• Fill master cylinder reservoirs to fill mark, have helper apply brakes, check calipers, wheel cylinders, differential valve, tubes, hoses, and fittings for fluid leaks. Repair or replace parts as necessary.
	• Master cylinder piston seals worn, or master cylinder bore is scored, worn or corroded	• Repair or replace master cylinder
Decreasing brake pedal travel (pedal travel required for braking action decreases and may be accompanied by a hard pedal.)	• Caliper or wheel cylinder pistons sticking or seized	• Repair or replace the calipers, or wheel cylinders
	• Master cylinder compensator ports blocked (preventing fluid return to reservoirs) or pistons sticking or seized in master cylinder bore	• Repair or replace the master cylinder
	• Power brake unit binding internally	• Test unit according to the following procedure: (a) Shift transmission into neutral and start engine (b) Increase engine speed to 1500 rpm, close throttle and fully depress brake pedal (c) Slow release brake pedal and stop engine (d) Have helper remove vacuum check valve and hose from power unit. Observe for backward movement of brake pedal. (e) If the pedal moves backward, the power unit has an internal bind—replace power unit

Troubleshooting the Brake System (cont.)

Problem	Cause	Solution
Spongy brake pedal (pedal has abnormally soft, springy, spongy feel when depressed.)	· Air in hydraulic system · Brakeshoes bent or distorted · Brakelining not yet seated with drums and rotors · Rear drum brakes not properly adjusted	· Remove air from system. Refer to Brake Bleeding. · Replace brakeshoes · Burnish brakes · Adjust brakes
Hard brake pedal (excessive pedal pressure required to stop vehicle. May be accompanied by brake fade.)	· Loose or leaking power brake unit vacuum hose · Incorrect or poor quality brakelining · Bent, broken, distorted brakeshoes · Calipers binding or dragging on mounting pins. Rear brakeshoes dragging on support plate. · Caliper, wheel cylinder, or master cylinder pistons sticking or seized · Power brake unit vacuum check valve malfunction · Power brake unit has internal bind · Master cylinder compensator ports (at bottom of reservoirs) blocked by dirt, scale, rust, or have small burrs (blocked ports prevent fluid return to reservoirs). · Brake hoses, tubes, fittings clogged or restricted · Brake fluid contaminated with improper fluids (motor oil, transmission fluid, causing rubber components to swell and stick in bores · Low engine vacuum	· Tighten connections or replace leaking hose · Replace with lining in axle sets · Replace brakeshoes · Replace mounting pins and bushings. Clean rust or burrs from rear brake support plate ledges and lubricate ledges with molydisulfide grease. **NOTE:** If ledges are deeply grooved or scored, do not attempt to sand or grind them smooth—replace support plate. · Repair or replace parts as necessary · Test valve according to the following procedure: (a) Start engine, increase engine speed to 1500 rpm, close throttle and immediately stop engine (b) Wait at least 90 seconds then depress brake pedal (c) If brakes are not vacuum assisted for 2 or more applications, check valve is faulty · Test unit according to the following procedure: (a) With engine stopped, apply brakes several times to exhaust all vacuum in system (b) Shift transmission into neutral, depress brake pedal and start engine (c) If pedal height decreases with foot pressure and less pressure is required to hold pedal in applied position, power unit vacuum system is operating normally. Test power unit. If power unit exhibits a bind condition, replace the power unit. · Repair or replace master cylinder **CAUTION:** Do not attempt to clean blocked ports with wire, pencils, or similar implements. Use compressed air only. · Use compressed air to check or unclog parts. Replace any damaged parts. · Replace all rubber components, combination valve and hoses. Flush entire brake system with DOT 3 brake fluid or equivalent. · Adjust or repair engine

tcca9c02

Troubleshooting the Brake System (cont.)

Problem	Cause	Solution
Grabbing brakes (severe reaction to brake pedal pressure.)	• Brakelining(s) contaminated by grease or brake fluid	• Determine and correct cause of contamination and replace brakeshoes in axle sets
	• Parking brake cables incorrectly adjusted or seized	• Adjust cables. Replace seized cables.
	• Incorrect brakelining or lining loose on brakeshoes	• Replace brakeshoes in axle sets
	• Caliper anchor plate bolts loose	• Tighten bolts
	• Rear brakeshoes binding on support plate ledges	• Clean and lubricate ledges. Replace support plate(s) if ledges are deeply grooved. Do not attempt to smooth ledges by grinding.
	• Incorrect or missing power brake reaction disc	• Install correct disc
	• Rear brake support plates loose	• Tighten mounting bolts
Dragging brakes (slow or incomplete release of brakes)	• Brake pedal binding at pivot	• Loosen and lubricate
	• Power brake unit has internal bind	• Inspect for internal bind. Replace unit if internal bind exists.
	• Parking brake cables incorrrectly adjusted or seized	• Adjust cables. Replace seized cables.
	• Rear brakeshoe return springs weak or broken	• Replace return springs. Replace brakeshoe if necessary in axle sets.
	• Automatic adjusters malfunctioning	• Repair or replace adjuster parts as required
	• Caliper, wheel cylinder or master cylinder pistons sticking or seized	• Repair or replace parts as necessary
	• Master cylinder compensating ports blocked (fluid does not return to reservoirs).	• Use compressed air to clear ports. Do not use wire, pencils, or similar objects to open blocked ports.
Vehicle moves to one side when brakes are applied	• Incorrect front tire pressure	• Inflate to recommended cold (reduced load) inflation pressure
	• Worn or damaged wheel bearings	• Replace worn or damaged bearings
	• Brakelining on one side contaminated	• Determine and correct cause of contamination and replace brakelining in axle sets
	• Brakeshoes on one side bent, distorted, or lining loose on shoe	• Replace brakeshoes in axle sets
	• Support plate bent or loose on one side	• Tighten or replace support plate
	• Brakelining not yet seated with drums or rotors	• Burnish brakelining
	• Caliper anchor plate loose on one side	• Tighten anchor plate bolts
	• Caliper piston sticking or seized	• Repair or replace caliper
	• Brakelinings water soaked	• Drive vehicle with brakes lightly applied to dry linings
	• Loose suspension component attaching or mounting bolts	• Tighten suspension bolts. Replace worn suspension components.
	• Brake combination valve failure	• Replace combination valve
Chatter or shudder when brakes are applied (pedal pulsation and roughness may also occur.)	• Brakeshoes distorted, bent, contaminated, or worn	• Replace brakeshoes in axle sets
	• Caliper anchor plate or support plate loose	• Tighten mounting bolts
	• Excessive thickness variation of rotor(s)	• Refinish or replace rotors in axle sets

tcca9c03

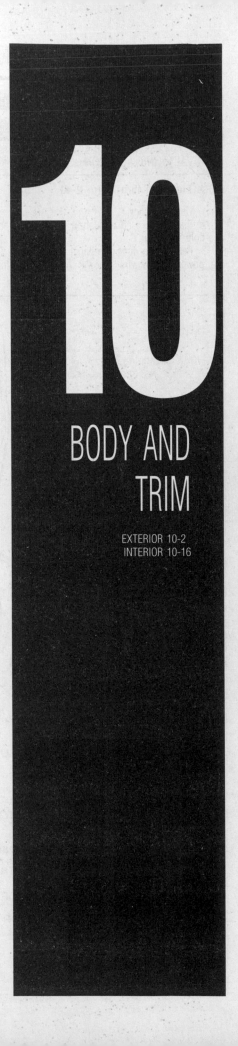

10

BODY AND
TRIM

EXTERIOR 10-2
INTERIOR 10-16

EXTERIOR

Doors

REMOVAL & INSTALLATION

◆ **See Figures 1 thru 12 (p. 2–8)**

1. Open the door.
2. Place some kind of support stand under the door or have someone hold it for you.
3. Remove the door trim panel and disconnect the door speaker wiring, power window wiring, power mirror and central locking system wir-

ing. If equipped with manual window regulators, insert a screwdriver behind the regulator handle to release the clip and remove the handle.
4. Remove the hinge-to-pillar bolts.
5. Disconnect the door limiter strap.
6. Remove the door.

To install:

7. Support the door and connect the door limiter strap.
8. Continue supporting the door and install the hinge-to-pillar bolts. Tighten the bolts to 26–30 ft. lbs. (36–42 Nm).
9. Connect the door accessory wiring and install the door trim panel.
10. Close and open the door several times to make sure it works prop-

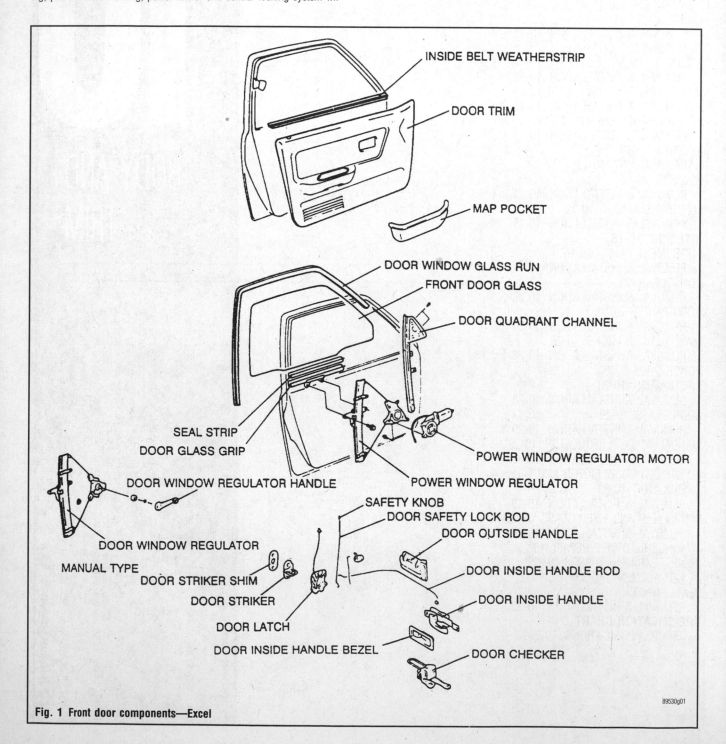

Fig. 1 Front door components—Excel

89530g01

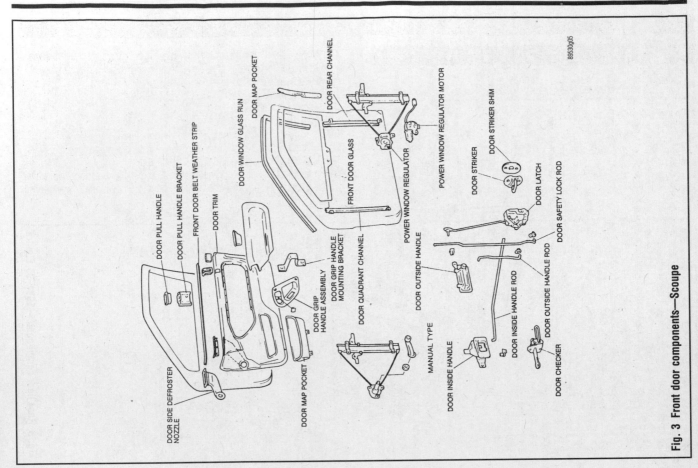

89530g05

Fig. 3 Front door components—Scoupe

Labels (Fig. 3):
DOOR MAP POCKET
DOOR REAR CHANNEL
DOOR WINDOW GLASS RUN
DOOR WINDOW REGULATOR MOTOR
DOOR STRIKER SHIM
DOOR STRIKER
FRONT DOOR GLASS
POWER WINDOW REGULATOR MOTOR
DOOR LATCH
DOOR SAFETY LOCK ROD
DOOR PULL HANDLE
DOOR PULL HANDLE BRACKET
FRONT DOOR BELT WEATHER STRIP
DOOR TRIM
DOOR GRIP HANDLE MOUNTING BRACKET
DOOR QUADRANT CHANNEL
POWER WINDOW REGULATOR
DOOR OUTSIDE HANDLE
DOOR OUTSIDE HANDLE ROD
DOOR GRIP HANDLE ASSEMBLY
DOOR INSIDE HANDLE ROD
DOOR OUTSIDE HANDLE ROD
DOOR SIDE DEFROSTER NOZZLE
DOOR MAP POCKET
MANUAL TYPE
DOOR INSIDE HANDLE
DOOR CHECKER

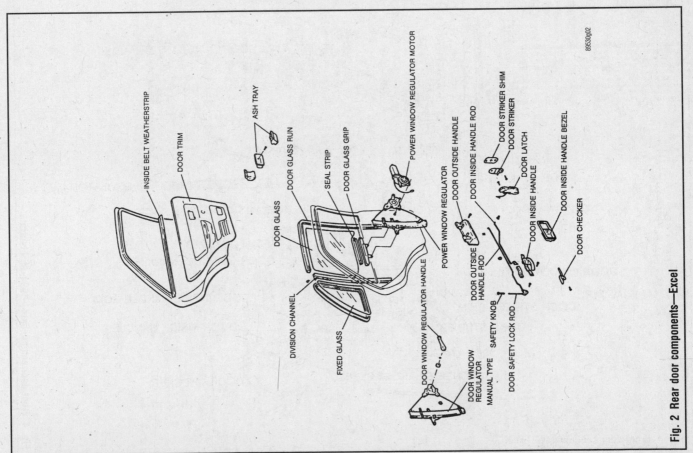

89530g02

Fig. 2 Rear door components—Excel

Labels (Fig. 2):
INSIDE BELT WEATHERSTRIP
DOOR TRIM
ASH TRAY
DOOR GLASS RUN
SEAL STRIP
DOOR GLASS GRIP
POWER WINDOW REGULATOR MOTOR
DOOR OUTSIDE HANDLE
DOOR INSIDE HANDLE ROD
DOOR STRIKER SHIM
DOOR STRIKER
DOOR LATCH
DOOR INSIDE HANDLE
DOOR INSIDE HANDLE BEZEL
DOOR GLASS
POWER WINDOW REGULATOR
DOOR OUTSIDE HANDLE ROD
DOOR CHECKER
DIVISION CHANNEL
FIXED GLASS
DOOR WINDOW REGULATOR HANDLE
DOOR WINDOW REGULATOR
MANUAL TYPE
SAFETY KNOB
DOOR SAFETY LOCK ROD

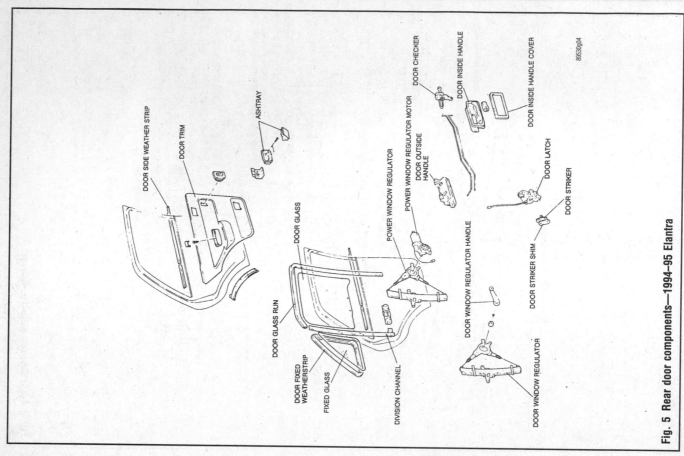

Fig. 5 Rear door components—1994–95 Elantra

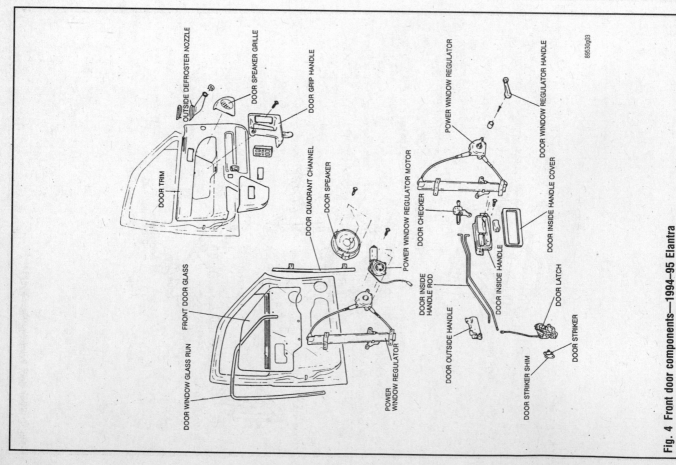

Fig. 4 Front door components—1994–95 Elantra

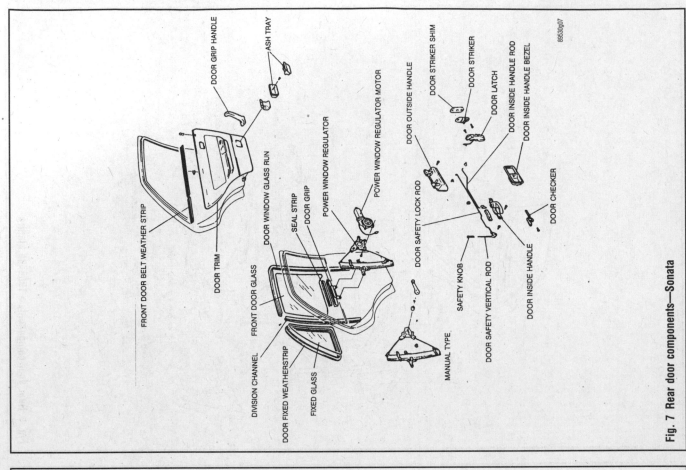

Fig. 7 Rear door components—Sonata

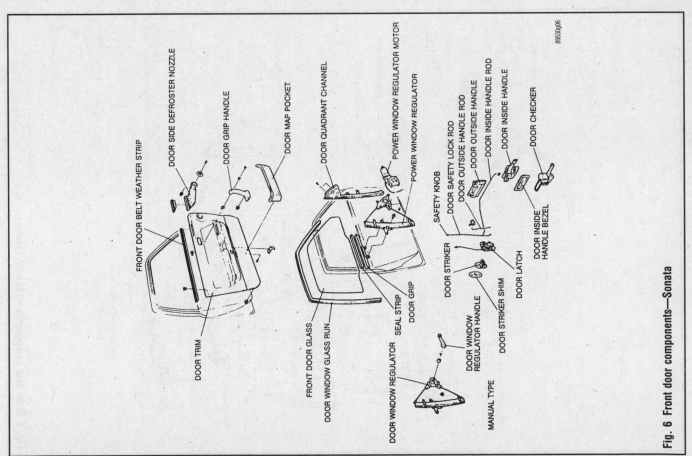

Fig. 6 Front door components—Sonata

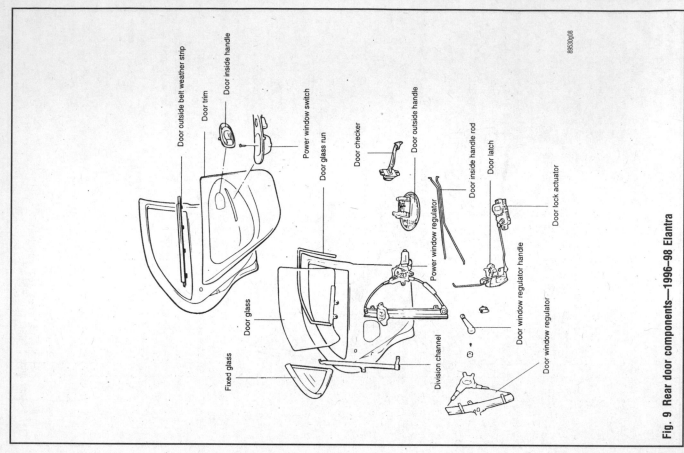

Fig. 9 Rear door components—1996–98 Elantra

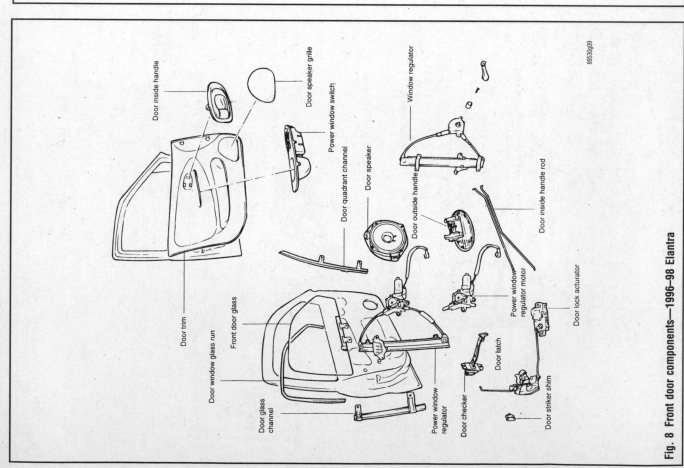

Fig. 8 Front door components—1996–98 Elantra

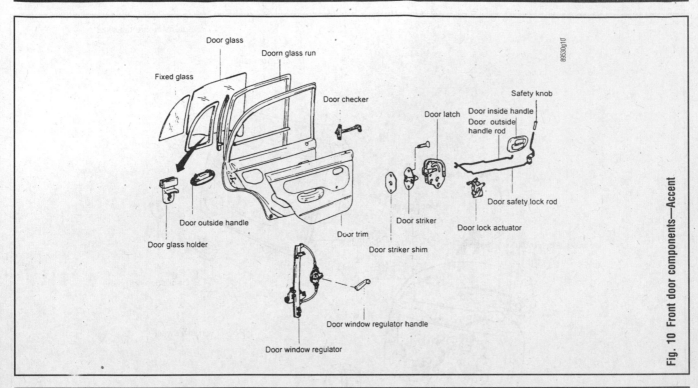

89530g10

Fig. 10 Front door components—Accent

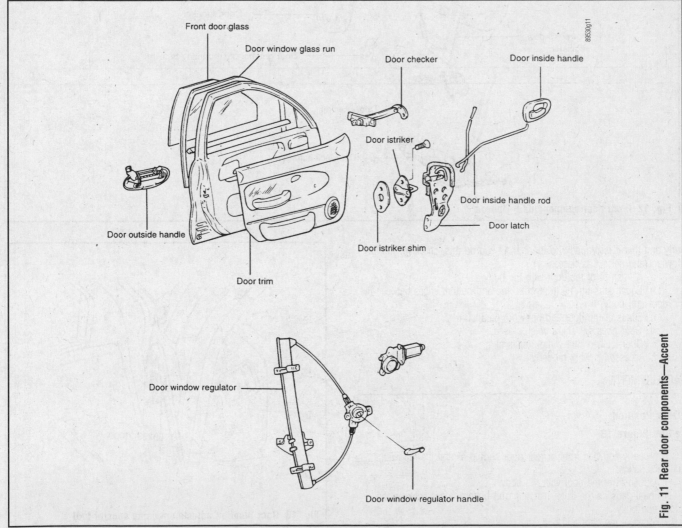

89530g11

Fig. 11 Rear door components—Accent

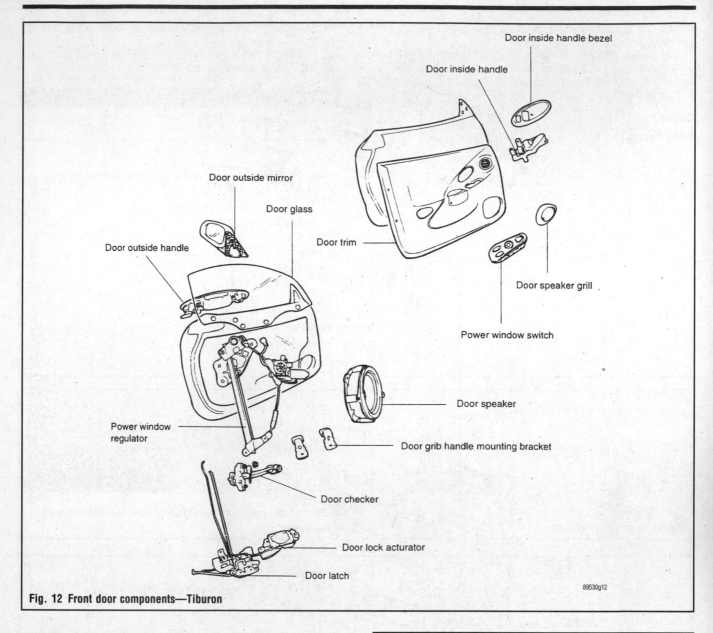

Fig. 12 Front door components—Tiburon

erly and that it is properly positioned. As you do this, check for the following (and correct as necessary):

    a. A flush fit of the door with the body.

    b. Equal gaps on the front, rear, top and bottom edges between the door and body.

    c. Edges of the door and body are parallel.

    d. Door does not shake when closed.

    e. Door latches shut without slamming.

    f. Accessories work properly.

ADJUSTMENT

Door Position

▶ **See Figure 13**

A properly adjusted front or rear door should exhibit the following characteristics:

• A flush fit of the door with the body

• Equal gaps on the front, rear, top and bottom edges between the door and body

• Edges of the door and body are parallel

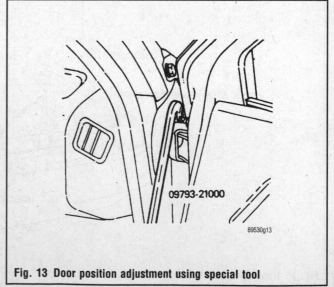

Fig. 13 Door position adjustment using special tool

If the door is not positioned as described above, a door position adjustment must be performed.

Door position adjustment is made by means of Special Tool 09793-21000, or equivalent, at the hinges. When using this tool, make sure that the painted surfaces in the immediate area are covered with masking tape to protect the paint.

Striker

♦ See Figure 14

If the door striker is adjusted properly, the door will not shake when closed and it will latch shut with minimal closing effort. If the door does not perform as described, then the striker must be adjusted. To adjust the door striker, perform the following:

1. Trace a thin pencil line around the striker plate for reference.
2. Loosen the striker screws.
3. Move the striker IN or OUT to make the latch tighter or looser.

4. Move the striker UP or DOWN to align the striker with the latch opening.
5. Tighten the latch screws and recheck. Hold the outside handle out and push the door against the body to make sure the striker fits flush.

Hood

REMOVAL & INSTALLATION

♦ See Figure 15

➡Cover the front body area with a blanket for protection when removing and installing the hood.

1. Open the hood and have an assistant support it.
2. Matchmark the hood-to-hinge position.
3. Remove the hinge-to-hood bolts and lift off the hood.

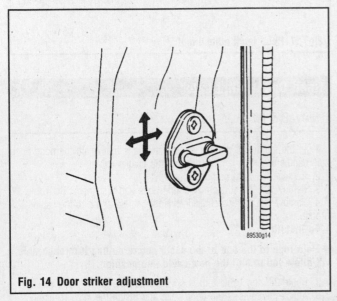

Fig. 14 Door striker adjustment

Always matchmark the hood-to-hinge position when removing the hood

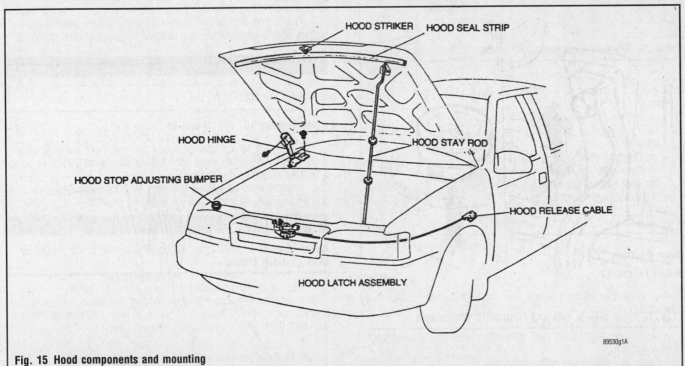

Fig. 15 Hood components and mounting

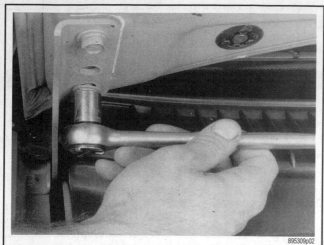

Loosen the hood attaching bolts while a helper supports the hood

To install:

4. Install the hood in position and align the marks made during removal.

5. Install the hinge bolts and tighten to 16–19 ft. lbs. (22–27 Nm).

6. Check the alignment of the hood, and adjust as needed.

ALIGNMENT

 See Figures 16 and 17

1. Adjust the hood side-to-side and fore-aft fit by loosening the hood-to-hinge bolts and repositioning the hood as necessary.

2. Hood lock centering adjustment is made by loosening the lock plate bolts and moving the plate as necessary.

3. Hood vertical fit is adjusted by raising or lowering the hood stops.

Fig. 16 Hood side-to-side and vertical lift adjustments

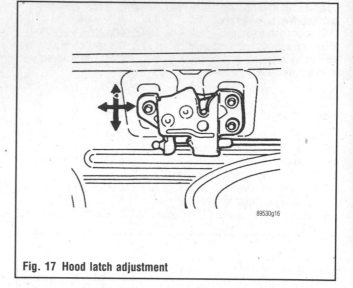

Fig. 17 Hood latch adjustment

Hood Opener and Latch

REMOVAL & INSTALLATION

1. In the interior of the car, remove the bolts that retain the hood latch handle assembly and disconnect the opener cable.

2. Remove the front bumper assembly.

3. Remove the hood latch mounting bolts and disconnect the cable.

4. Remove the driver's side inner fender shield and pull the cable through the wheelwell.

To install:

➡ Tie a rope to the end of the cable before pulling it through; this will allow you to pull the new cable into position.

5. Route the new cable into position. Install the inner fender shield.

6. Attach the cable at the hood latch and install the latch retaining bolts. Tighten the bolts to 5–6 ft. lbs. (7–9 Nm).

7. Connect the cable at the release assembly inside the vehicle and install the release assembly retaining bolts. Adjust the hood latch as needed.

Hatch

REMOVAL & INSTALLATION

➡ **See Figures 18, 19, 20 and 21**

1. Disconnect the defroster grid wires and rear wiper wiring. The connectors for the wiper are found behind the quarter panel trim.

2. Disconnect the rear washer hose.

3. Have an assistant support the hatch. With the hatch fully open, unbolt the hydraulic supports from the hatch and C-pillar.

❊❊ CAUTION

Never attempt to unbolt the supports with the hatch closed or even partially closed.

4. Remove the hinge-to-hatch bolts and lift off the hatch.

5. Installation is the reverse of the removal procedure. Tighten the hinge-to-hatch bolts to 20–25 ft. lbs. (28–35 Nm). Lubricate the hatch latch with white lithium or suitable chassis grease.

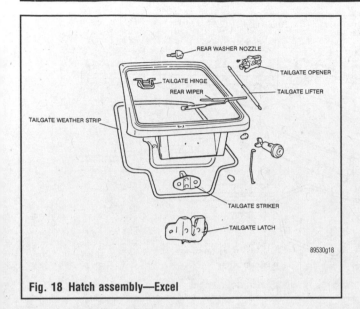

Fig. 18 Hatch assembly—Excel

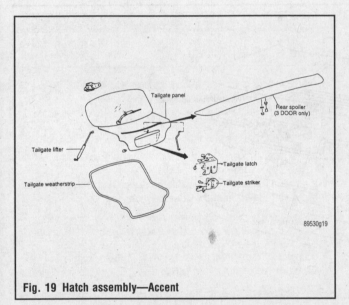

Fig. 19 Hatch assembly—Accent

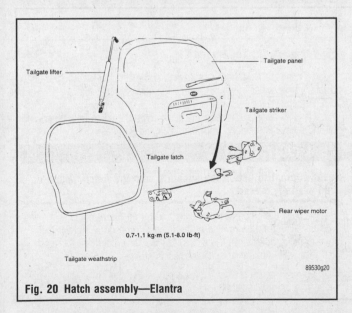

Fig. 20 Hatch assembly—Elantra

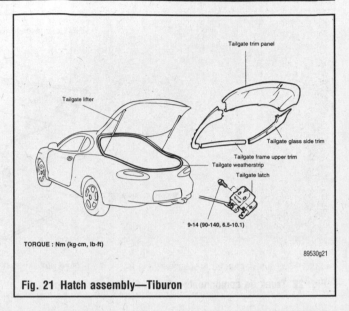

TORQUE : Nm (kg·cm, lb·ft)

Fig. 21 Hatch assembly—Tiburon

ALIGNMENT

1. Side-to-side and fore-aft positioning can be adjusted by loosening the hinge bolts and moving the hatch as necessary.
2. Striker adjustment is made by loosening the striker bolts and moving the striker as necessary.

Trunk Lid

REMOVAL & INSTALLATION

▶ **See Figures 22, 23 and 24**

1. Raise the trunk lid fully.
2. Matchmark the lid-to-hinge position.
3. Disconnect the main trunk wiring connectors.
4. Have someone hold the lid while you remove the nuts securing the lid to the hinges.

To install:

5. Install the trunk lid in position, aligning the matchmarks made during removal. Install the retaining bolts and tighten to 5–6 ft. lbs. (7–9 Nm). Lubricate the trunk lid latch with white lithium or suitable chassis grease.
6. Adjust the trunk lid as needed.

ALIGNMENT

1. Loosen the trunk lid hinge attaching bolts until they are just loose enough to move the trunk lid.
2. Move the trunk lid fore and aft to obtain a flush fit between the trunk lid and the rear fender.
3. To obtain a snug fit between the trunk lid and weatherstrip, loosen the trunk lid lock striker attaching bolts enough to move the lid, working the striker up and down and side-to-side as required.
4. After the adjustment is made, tighten the striker bolts securely.

Grille

REMOVAL & INSTALLATION

1. Open the hood.
2. Remove the grille attaching screws and clips.
3. Remove the grille from the vehicle.
4. Installation is the reverse of the removal procedure.
5. Tighten the grille attaching screws securely.

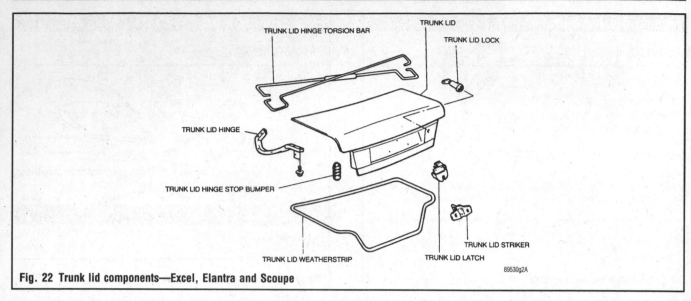

Fig. 22 Trunk lid components—Excel, Elantra and Scoupe

89530g2A

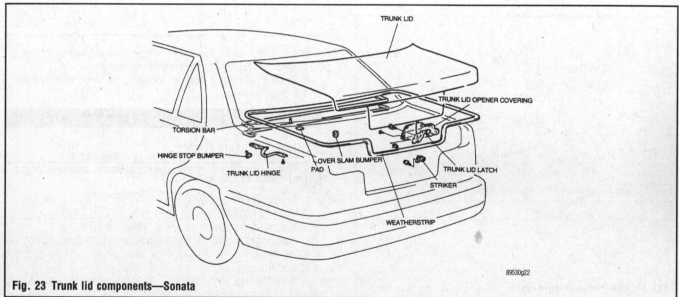

Fig. 23 Trunk lid components—Sonata

89530g22

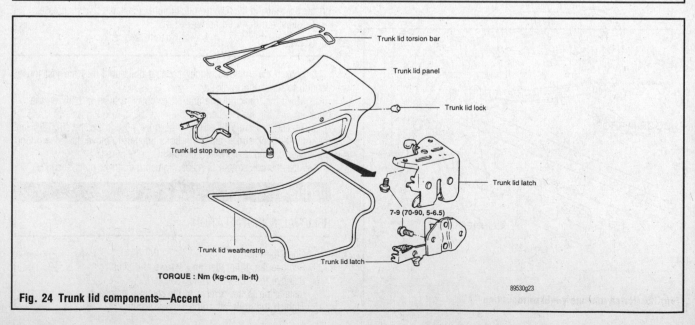

TORQUE : Nm (kg·cm, lb-ft)

Fig. 24 Trunk lid components—Accent

89530g23

Manual Outside Mirror

REMOVAL & INSTALLATION

♦ **See Figure 25**

1. Remove control knob handle.
2. Remove door corner finisher panel.
3. Remove mirror body attaching screws, and then remove mirror body.
4. Installation is in the reverse order of removal.

➡ **Apply sealer to the rear surface of door corner finisher panel during installation to prevent water leakage.**

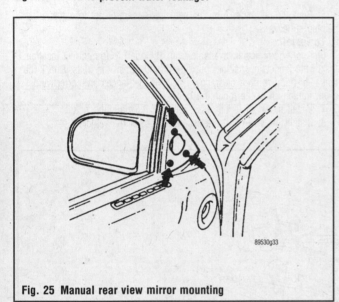

Fig. 25 Manual rear view mirror mounting

Power Outside Mirror

REMOVAL & INSTALLATION

♦ **See Figure 26**

1. Remove door corner finisher panel.
2. Remove mirror body attaching screws, and then remove mirror body.
3. Disconnect the electrical lead.
4. Installation is in the reverse order of removal.

➡ **Apply sealer to the rear surface of door corner finisher panel during installation to prevent water leakage.**

Antenna

REPLACEMENT

♦ **See Figure 27**

1. Open the trunk.
2. Remove the luggage trim after removing the retaining screws.
3. Remove the two nuts that attach the antenna assembly to the support pillar.
4. Disconnect the antenna wiring harness.
5. Remove the antenna support cable.
6. Remove the antenna assembly from the support pillar and lift it out of the trunk.
   To install:
7. Position the antenna assembly on the support pillar and secure it with the support cable.
8. Connect the wiring harness.
9. Install and tighten the two support pillar attaching nuts.
10. Place the key in the ignition and check that the antenna operates properly.
11. Install the side luggage trim and close the trunk.

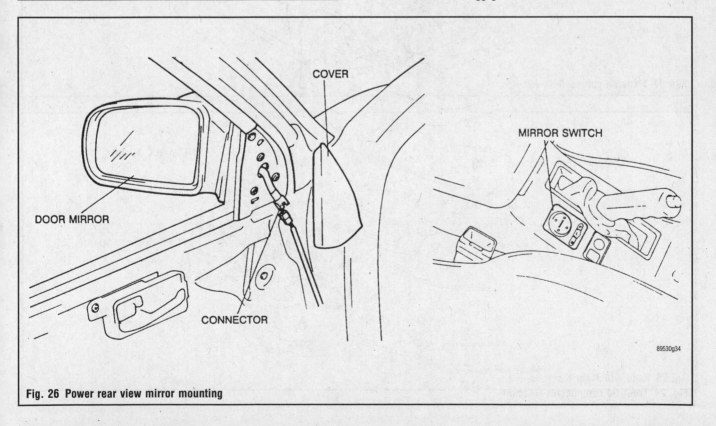

Fig. 26 Power rear view mirror mounting

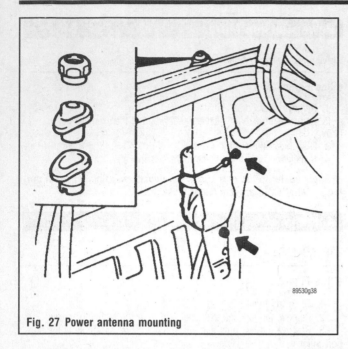

Fig. 27 Power antenna mounting

Fenders

REMOVAL & INSTALLATION

▶ **See Figure 28**

1. Raise and support the front of the vehicle so that it is just off of the ground.
2. Remove the tire and wheel assembly.
3. Unfasten its bolts, then remove the inner fender cover assembly.
4. Remove the fender mounting bolts.

➡ **The fender is joined to the body with sealer at some points. When removing the fender, a small putty knife will help to break the seal in these areas.**

5. Remove the fender from the vehicle. Be careful not to damage the painted surfaces.

To install:

6. Apply body sealer (available from Hyundai) to the correct location. Install the fender in position, but do not yet tighten the bolts. Check the fender-to-hood-to-door clearance. Once the clearances are correct and even, tighten all of the mounting bolts.
7. Install the inner fender assembly and its mounting bolts.
8. Install the wheel and tire assembly. Lower the vehicle.

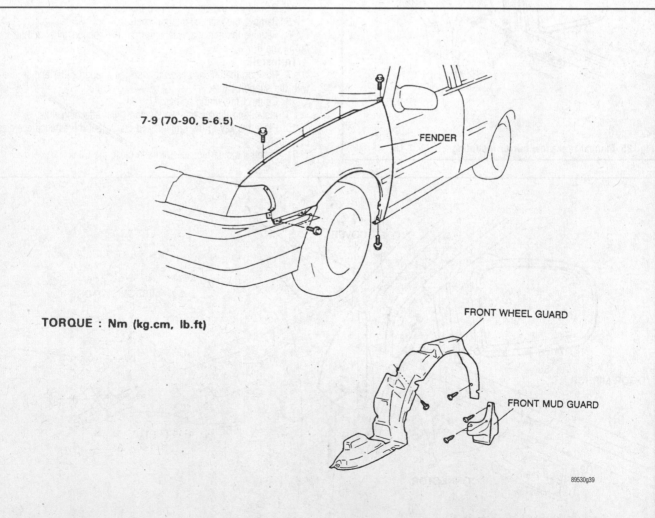

Fig. 28 Fender fastener locations

Electric Sunroof

REMOVAL & INSTALLATION

▶ See Figure 29

Sunroof Glass and Sunshade

1. Slide the sunshade all the way back. Pry the plug out of each mount bracket cover, remove the screw, then slide the cover off to the rear.
2. Close the glass fully. Remove the nuts from the front and rear mounts on both sides.
3. Remove the glass by lifting it up and pulling it towards the front of

the vehicle. Once the glass is removed, pull the sunshade out. When removing the sunshade, it is okay to bend the sunshade slightly to aid in the removal.
4. Installation is the reverse order of the removal procedure.

Sunroof Motor, Drain Tube and Frame

1. Remove the headliner from inside of the vehicle.
2. Remove the sunroof motor by removing 2 bolts and 3 nuts from the bottom of the motor mount plate. Disconnect the motor wire harness at the connector and remove the motor.
3. Slide back the drain tube clamps and remove the drain tubes. Remove the 11 mounting bolts from the sunroof frame and remove the frame from the vehicle.

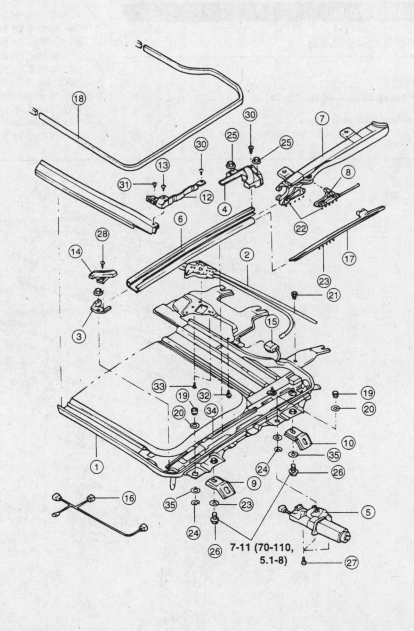

1. Frame Assembly
2. Drive Unit
3. Front Holder Rail
4. Rear Holder Rail
5. Sunroof Motor Assembly
6. Sunroof Guide Rail
7. Sunroof Rail Lifter
8. Sunroof Slider Rail
9. Set Bracket A
10. Set Bracket B
11. Deflector Assembly
12. Rail Deflector Link
13. Clip
14. Front Drip Rail
15. Relay
16. Harness Assembly
17. Timing Rear Rail
18. Seal Tape
19. Adjust Nut
20. Washer
21. Clip
22. Grease
23. Washer
24. Ring-E
25. Nut
26. Bolt
27. Screw
28. Screw
29. Screw
30. Screw
31. Screw
32. Screw
33. Screw
34. Sealer
35. Washer

TORQUE : Nm (kg·cm, lb·ft)

7-11 (70-110, 5.1-8)

89530g40

Fig. 29 Power sunroof assembly components

To install:

4. Insert the frame's rear pins into the body holes, then install the rest of the assembly in the reverse order of the removal procedure.

➡️**Before installing the sunroof motor, measure the effort required to close the sliding panel using a suitable spring scale. If the load is over 22 lbs., check the side clearance and the glass height adjustment. Be sure when using the spring scale to protect the leading edge of the sunroof with a shop rag.**

Sunroof Cable Replacement

With the sunroof out of the vehicle, remove the guide rail mounting nuts, lift off the guide rails and remove the cables with the rear mounts attached. Be sure to fill the groove in each grommet with a suitable sealant and apply a suitable grease to the inner cable.

Wind Deflector

A gap between the deflector seal and roof molding will cause wind noise when driving at high speed with the roof opened.

1. Open the sunroof and pry the rail covers off of both sides. Loosen the deflector mounting nuts. The wind deflector can be adjusted 2.0mm forward or backward.

2. Adjust the deflector forward or backward so that the edge of its seal touches the roof molding evenly.

3. The height of the deflector when opened cannot be adjusted. If it is damaged or deformed, replace it.

INTERIOR

Instrument Panel

REMOVAL & INSTALLATION

Except Sonata

◆ See Figures 30 thru 41 (p. 16–21)

1. Remove the steering wheel.
2. Remove the upper and lower steering column shrouds.
3. Remove the hood release handle mounting screws.
4. Remove the lower fascia panel.
5. Remove the side lower crash pad.
6. Remove the glove box.
7. Remove the main lower crash pad.
8. Pull the instrument cluster forward and disconnect all the electrical wiring, as well as the speedometer cable.
9. Remove the heater control assembly.
10. Remove the front speaker grille from the main crash pad.
11. Remove the front speaker.

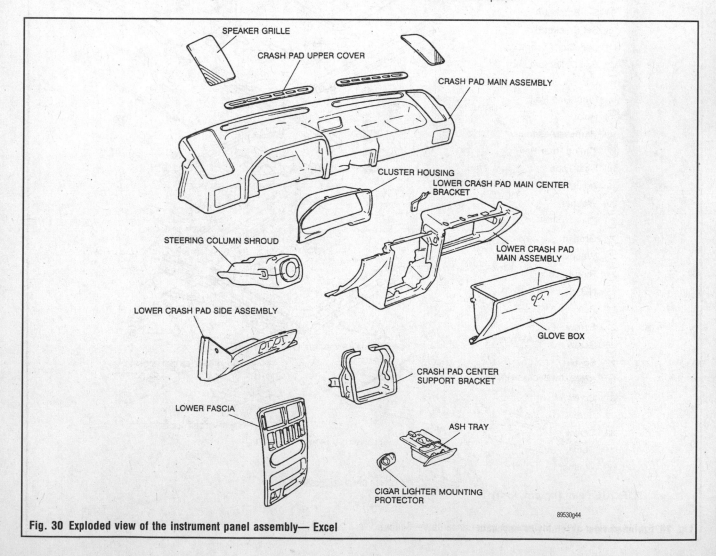

Fig. 30 Exploded view of the instrument panel assembly— Excel

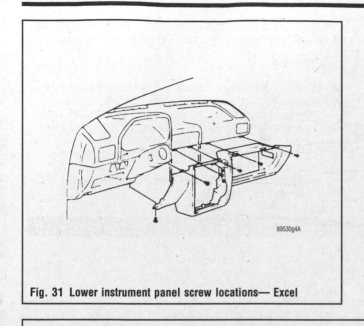

Fig. 31 Lower instrument panel screw locations— Excel

89530g4A

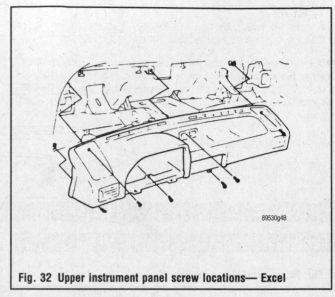

Fig. 32 Upper instrument panel screw locations— Excel

89530g4B

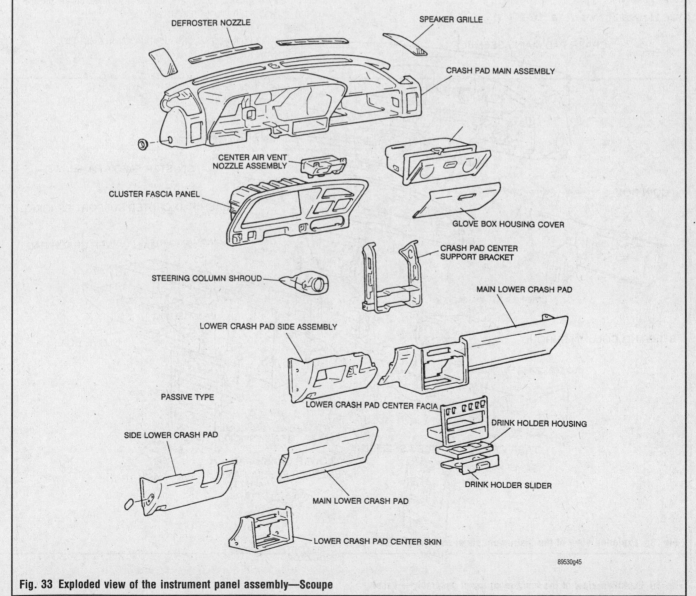

DEFROSTER NOZZLE

SPEAKER GRILLE

CRASH PAD MAIN ASSEMBLY

CENTER AIR VENT NOZZLE ASSEMBLY

CLUSTER FASCIA PANEL

GLOVE BOX HOUSING COVER

CRASH PAD CENTER SUPPORT BRACKET

STEERING COLUMN SHROUD

MAIN LOWER CRASH PAD

LOWER CRASH PAD SIDE ASSEMBLY

PASSIVE TYPE

LOWER CRASH PAD CENTER FACIA

DRINK HOLDER HOUSING

SIDE LOWER CRASH PAD

MAIN LOWER CRASH PAD

DRINK HOLDER SLIDER

LOWER CRASH PAD CENTER SKIN

89530g45

Fig. 33 Exploded view of the instrument panel assembly—Scoupe

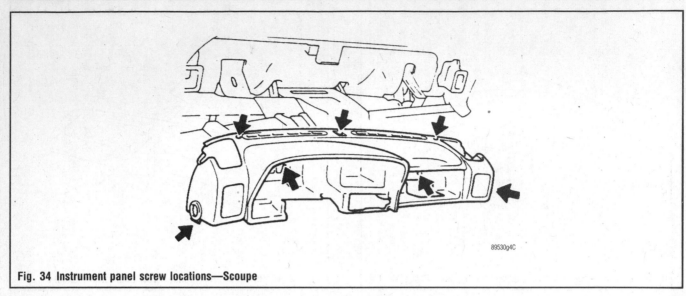

Fig. 34 Instrument panel screw locations—Scoupe

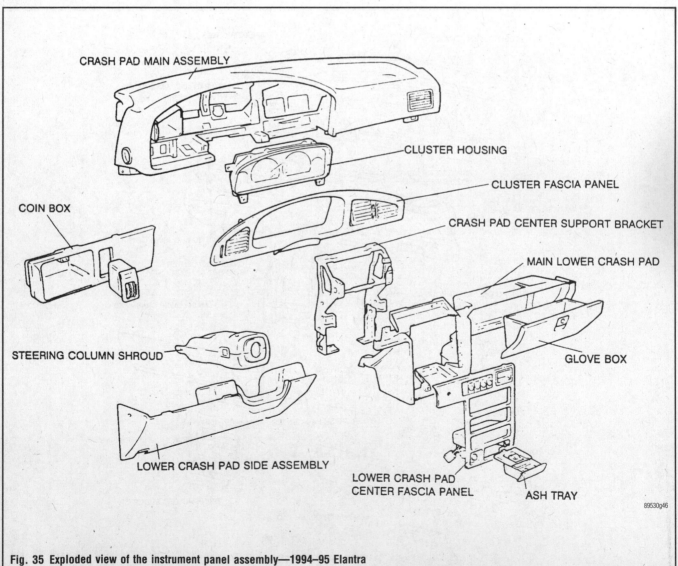

CRASH PAD MAIN ASSEMBLY

CLUSTER HOUSING

CLUSTER FASCIA PANEL

COIN BOX

CRASH PAD CENTER SUPPORT BRACKET

MAIN LOWER CRASH PAD

STEERING COLUMN SHROUD

GLOVE BOX

LOWER CRASH PAD SIDE ASSEMBLY

LOWER CRASH PAD
CENTER FASCIA PANEL

ASH TRAY

Fig. 35 Exploded view of the instrument panel assembly—1994–95 Elantra

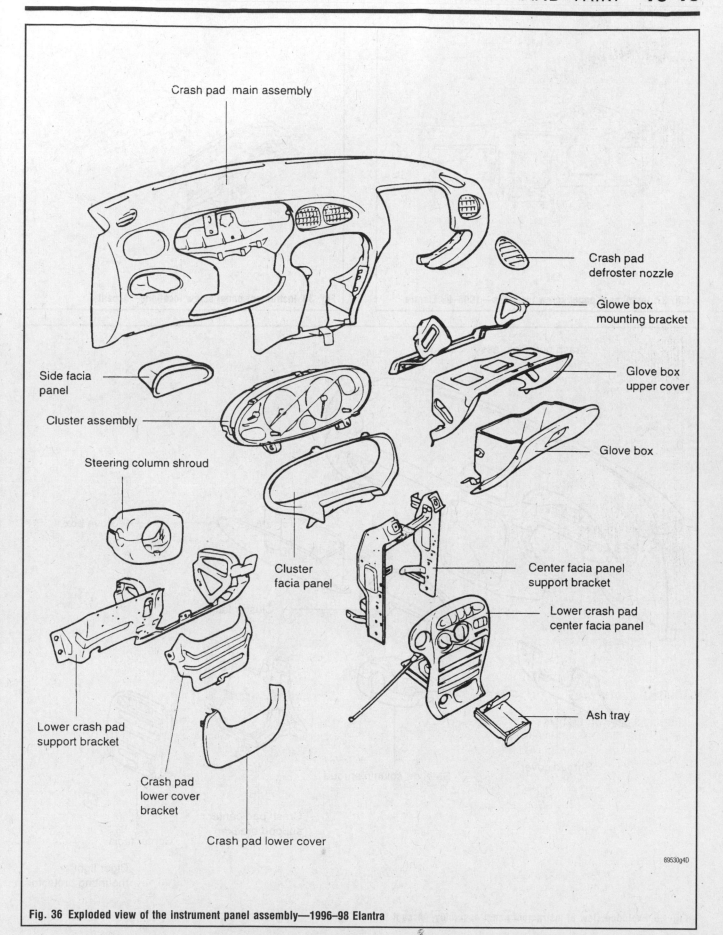

Crash pad main assembly

Crash pad defroster nozzle

Glowe box mounting bracket

Side facia panel

Glove box upper cover

Cluster assembly

Glove box

Steering column shroud

Cluster facia panel

Center facia panel support bracket

Lower crash pad center facia panel

Lower crash pad support bracket

Ash tray

Crash pad lower cover bracket

Crash pad lower cover

89530g4D

Fig. 36 Exploded view of the instrument panel assembly—1996–98 Elantra

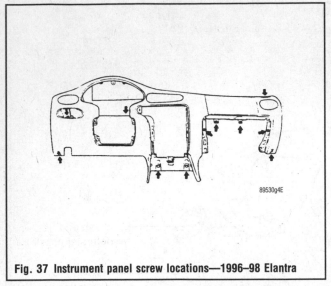

Fig. 37 Instrument panel screw locations—1996–98 Elantra

89530g4E

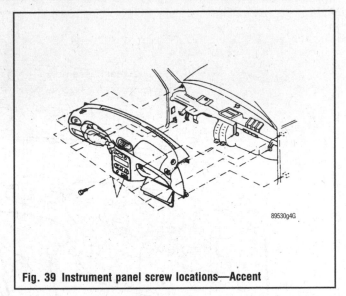

Fig. 39 Instrument panel screw locations—Accent

89530g4G

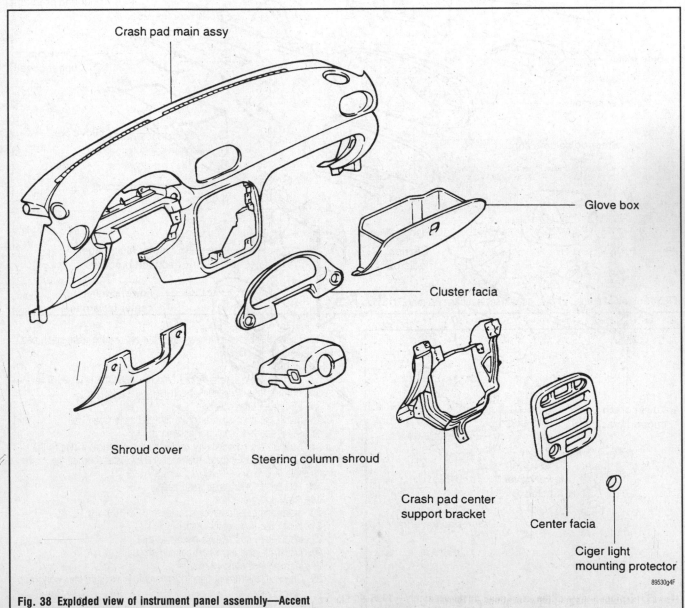

Crash pad main assy

Glove box

Cluster facia

Shroud cover

Steering column shroud

Crash pad center
support bracket

Center facia

Ciger light
mounting protector

89530g4F

Fig. 38 Exploded view of instrument panel assembly—Accent

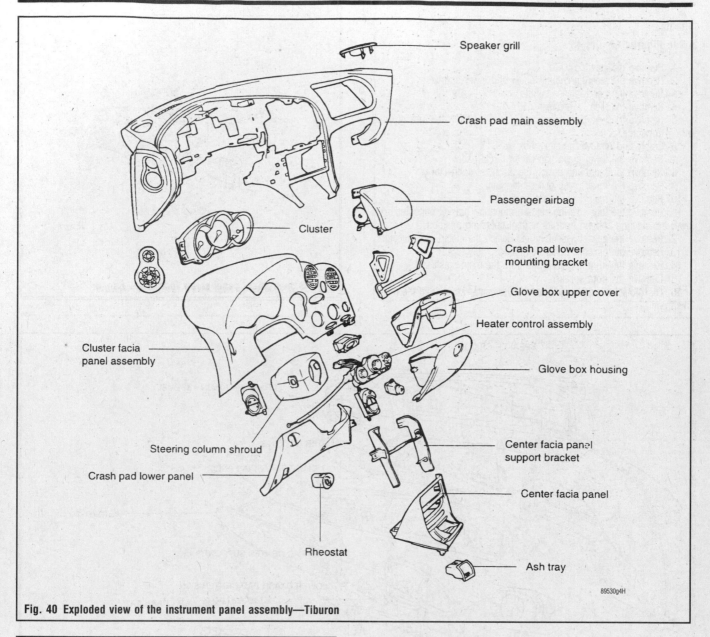

Speaker grill

Crash pad main assembly

Passenger airbag

Cluster

Crash pad lower
mounting bracket

Glove box upper cover

Heater control assembly

Cluster facia
panel assembly

Glove box housing

Steering column shroud

Center facia panel
support bracket

Crash pad lower panel

Center facia panel

Rheostat

Ash tray

89530g4H

Fig. 40 Exploded view of the instrument panel assembly—Tiburon

12. Remove the six retaining screws and remove the main crash pad from its mounting brackets.

To install:

13. Position the main crash pad onto the mounting brackets, then install and tighten the six retaining screws.

14. Install the front speaker.

15. Install the front speaker grille into the main crash pad.

16. Install the heater control assembly.

17. Connect the speedometer cable and the electrical wiring to the rear of the instrument cluster, then install the cluster (but not the main crash pad).

18. Install the lower main crash pad.

19. Install the glove box.

20. Install the side lower crash pad.

21. Install the lower fascia panel.

22. Install the hood release handle screws.

23. Install the steering wheel column shrouds.

24. Install the steering wheel.

25. Check all instrument panel functions to make sure they work properly.

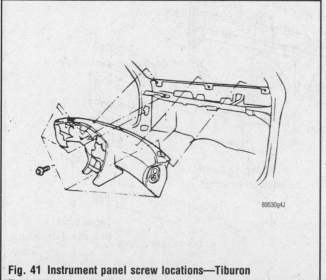

89530g4J

Fig. 41 Instrument panel screw locations—Tiburon

Sonata

▶ **See Figures 42 and 43**

1. Remove the steering wheel.
2. Remove the steering column upper and lower shrouds.
3. Remove the hood release handle.
4. Remove the side lower crash pad.
5. Remove the fuse box mounting screws and allow the fuse box and wiring to dangle.
6. Empty and remove the glove box.
7. Remove the lower crash pad center fascia panel.
8. Remove the radio and detach the electrical connector.
9. Remove the lower crash pad center skin.
10. Remove the main lower crash pad.
11. Remove the four steering column mounting bracket bolts and lower the steering column from its normal operating position.
12. Remove the cluster assembly and detach the electrical connectors.
13. Remove the air conditioner control assembly.
14. Remove the front speaker grille from the main crash pad.
15. Remove the front speaker.
16. Disconnect the defroster nozzle upper center cover from the main crash pad.

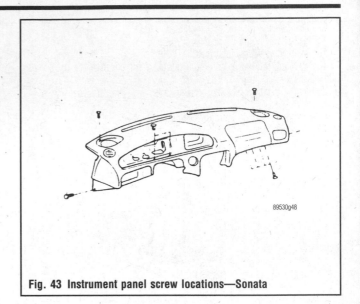

89530g48

Fig. 43 Instrument panel screw locations—Sonata

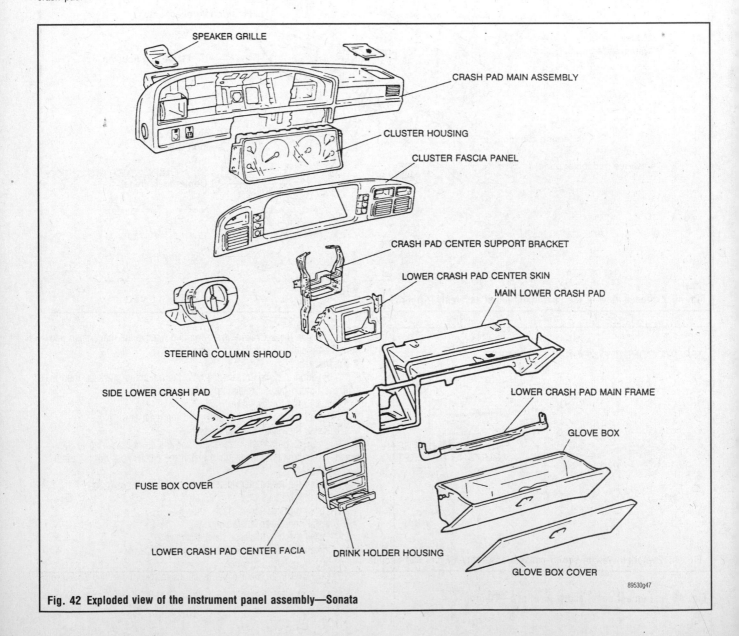

SPEAKER GRILLE

CRASH PAD MAIN ASSEMBLY

CLUSTER HOUSING

CLUSTER FASCIA PANEL

CRASH PAD CENTER SUPPORT BRACKET

LOWER CRASH PAD CENTER SKIN

MAIN LOWER CRASH PAD

STEERING COLUMN SHROUD

SIDE LOWER CRASH PAD

LOWER CRASH PAD MAIN FRAME

GLOVE BOX

FUSE BOX COVER

LOWER CRASH PAD CENTER FACIA

DRINK HOLDER HOUSING

GLOVE BOX COVER

89530g47

Fig. 42 Exploded view of the instrument panel assembly—Sonata

17. Remove the main crash pad.
To install:
18. Install the main crash pad.
19. Connect the defroster nozzle upper center cover to the main crash pad.
20. Install the front speaker and speaker grille into the main crash pad.
21. Install the air conditioner control assembly.
22. Connect the electrical connectors to the rear of the cluster assembly and install it.
23. Raise the steering wheel from the lowered position and install the four steering column mounting bracket bolts.
24. Install the main lower crash pad.
25. Connect the wiring to the radio and install.
26. Install the lower crash pad fascia panel.
27. Install the glove box.
28. Raise the fuse box and wiring into place and install the fuse box mounting screws.
29. Install the lower side crash pad.
30. Install the hood release handle.

31. Install the upper and lower steering column shrouds.
32. Install the steering wheel.

Console

REMOVAL & INSTALLATION

Except Sonata

◆ **See Figures 44, 45, 46, 47 and 48 (p. 23–25)**

1. As required, remove the rear console mounting screws and remove the rear console.
2. Unscrew the shifter knob from the shifter lever. Remove the shifter lever boot (manual transaxles) or the shift lever indicator plate (automatic transaxles).
3. Remove the front console retaining screws, disconnect the wiring and remove the console.
4. Installation is the reverse of the removal procedure.

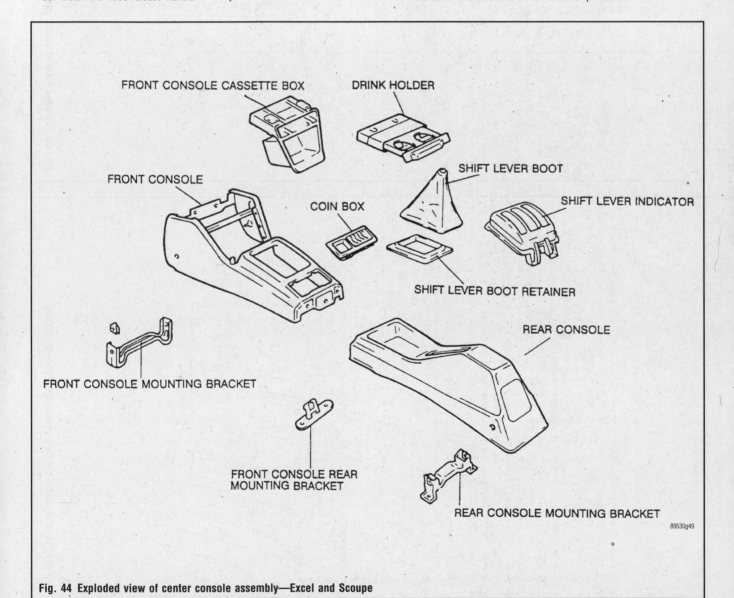

Fig. 44 Exploded view of center console assembly—Excel and Scoupe

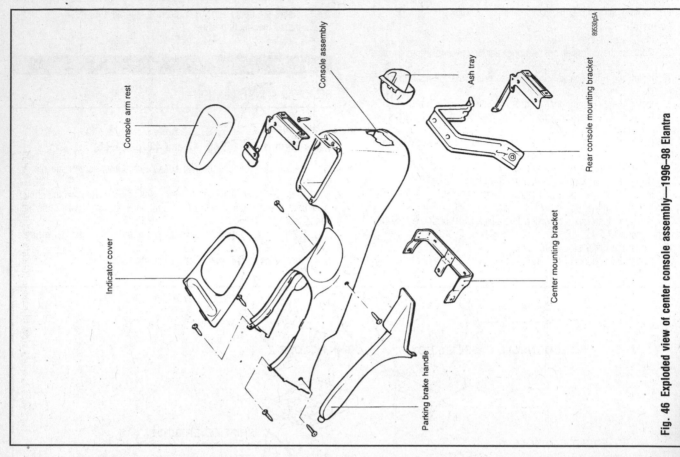

89530g5A

Console arm rest

Console assembly

Ash tray

Rear console mounting bracket

Indicator cover

Center mounting bracket

Parking brake handle

Fig. 46 Exploded view of center console assembly—1996–98 Elantra

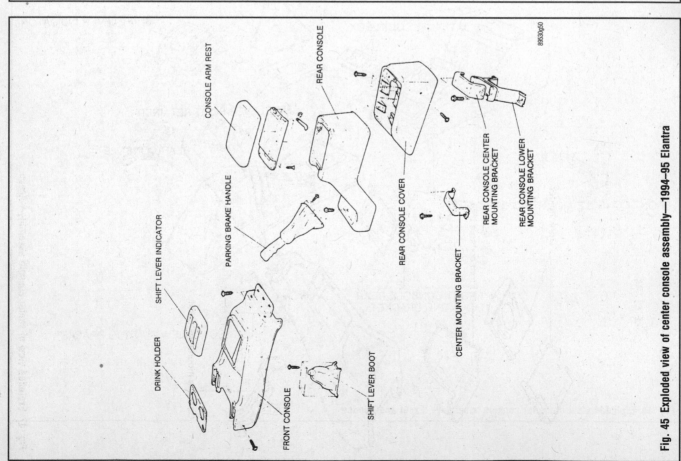

89530g50

CONSOLE ARM REST

REAR CONSOLE

REAR CONSOLE CENTER MOUNTING BRACKET

REAR CONSOLE LOWER MOUNTING BRACKET

SHIFT LEVER INDICATOR

PARKING BRAKE HANDLE

REAR CONSOLE COVER

CENTER MOUNTING BRACKET

DRINK HOLDER

SHIFT LEVER BOOT

FRONT CONSOLE

Fig. 45 Exploded view of center console assembly—1994–95 Elantra

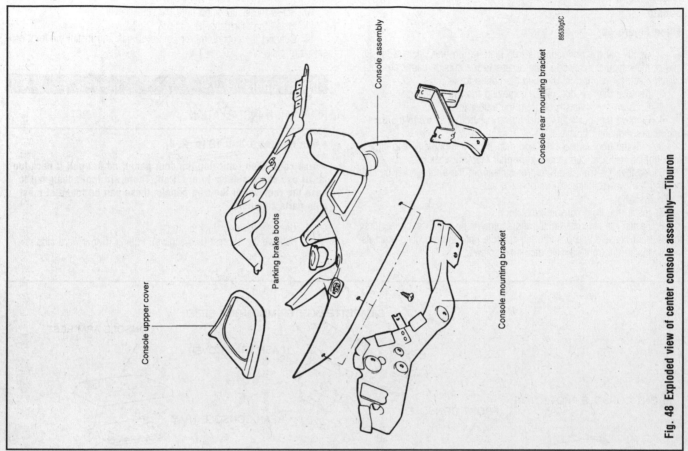

Console assembly

Console rear mounting bracket

Parking brake boots

Console uppper cover

Console mounting bracket

89530g5C

Fig. 48 Exploded view of center console assembly—Tiburon

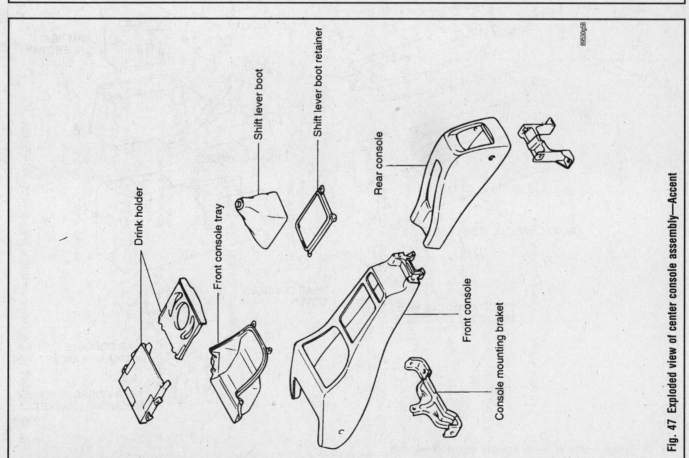

Shift lever boot

Shift lever boot retainer

Rear console

Drink holder

Front console tray

Front console

Console mounting braket

89530g5B

Fig. 47 Exploded view of center console assembly—Accent

Sonata

▶ **See Figure 49**

1. Gently pry the front console trim plate up on one side and loosen one of the retaining screws to gain access to the outside mirror control switch electrical connector. Unfasten the connector.

2. Remove the rear console by removing the two retaining screws.

3. Unscrew the shifter knob from the shifter lever.

4. Remove the four screws that attach the front console to the front and center mounting brackets.

5. Pull the front console out and detach the ashtray lamp and cigarette lighter electrical connectors from their respective sockets.

6. Remove the front console protectors from the front bracket by removing the two retaining screws on each side.

To install:

7. Install the front console protectors.

8. Fasten the cigarette lighter and ashtray lamp electrical connectors to the front console and position the console onto the mounting brackets.

9. Install the front console mounting screws.

10. Screw the shifter knob onto the shifter lever.

11. Install the rear console.

12. Connect the outside mirror control switch and install the front console trim plate.

Door Panels

REMOVAL & INSTALLATION

▶ **See Figures 1 thru 12 (p. 2–8)**

➥**Use care when removing the door panel; do not pull it back too far or use sharp objects to pry it off. There are tools designed to ease the removal of the trim panels; these can be found at most auto parts suppliers.**

1. Unscrew the door lock button.

2. Remove the armrest (two screws). Pulling it downward aids removal.

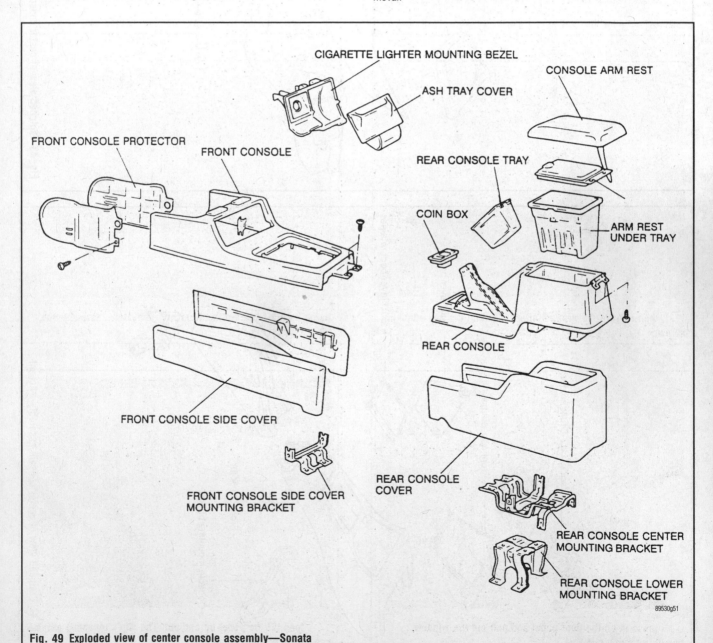

Fig. 49 Exploded view of center console assembly—Sonata

89530g51

Unscrew the door lock button . . .

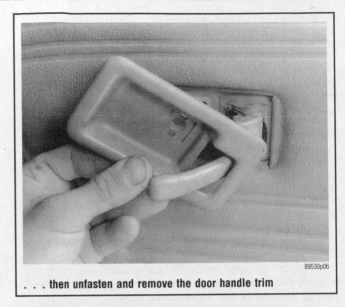

. . . then unfasten and remove the door handle trim

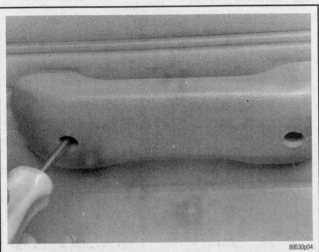

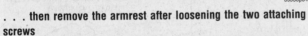

. . . then remove the armrest after loosening the two attaching screws

Using a door panel removal tool, or equivalent, carefully pop out the panel clips . . .

. . . press in on the door panel and pull out the window handle retaining clip . . .

. . . then lift the panel up and out. The clip's mounting points can be seen at the arrows

3. Press in on the door trim panel and, using needlenosed pliers or a soft cloth, pull out the window handle retaining clip. Slide the handle off the regulator stud.

4. Remove the door handle trim.

5. Remove the outside rear view mirror mounting cover, then remove the mounting screws and mirror. On cars with remotely controlled mirrors, remove the control knob.

6. Remove the door weatherstripping.

7. The trim panel is held to the door by means of snap clips. Slide a wooden spatula or equivalent behind the trim panel edge and move it along until you come to one of the clips. Pry the clip out of its hole in the door. Pry only at the clip, never somewhere in between clips. The clips are easily torn from the door panel. Repeat this procedure for each snap clip.

8. Disconnect the speaker wiring and electric window wiring, if so equipped.

To install:

9. Connect the electric window and speaker wiring to the door panel, if so equipped.

10. Position the panel onto the door frame. Carefully whack the snap clips into position with the heel of your hand. Take care that they are lined up right over the hole before inserting them.

11. Install the door weatherstripping.

12. Install the rear view mirror and remote control knob if so equipped.

13. Install the door handle trim and door handle.

14. Slide the regulator handle onto the stud and install the retaining clip. The window handle should be installed at a 45° angle up to the right, with the glass fully closed.

15. Install the armrest.

16. Install the door lock button.

REMOVAL & INSTALLATION

1. Remove the door panel and sealing screen.
2. Remove the lock cylinder from the rod by turning the resin clip.
3. Loosen the nuts attaching the outside door handle and remove the outside door handle.
4. Remove the screws retaining the inside door handle and door lock, and remove the door lock assembly from the hole in the inside of the door.
5. Remove the lock cylinder by removing the retaining clip.

To install:

6. Install the lock cylinder and clip to the door.
7. Install the door lock assembly and handles.
8. Install the door panel and all attaching parts.

Power Door Lock Actuators

REMOVAL & INSTALLATION

♦ **See Figure 50**

1. Disconnect the negative battery cable.
2. Remove the door panel.
3. Detach the actuator's electrical connector. Disconnect the required linkage rods.
4. Remove the actuator assembly retaining screws. Remove the actuator assembly from the vehicle.
5. Installation is the reverse of the removal procedure.

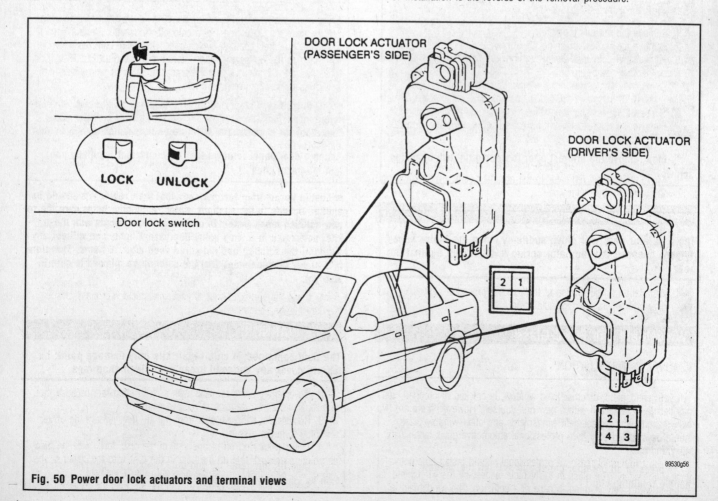

Fig. 50 Power door lock actuators and terminal views

Door Glass

REMOVAL & INSTALLATION

1. Lower the glass fully.
2. Remove the door trim panel and door trim seal.
3. Remove the bolts securing the glass channel to the regulator.
4. Remove the felt strip from the window frame.
5. Push the glass up and lift it from the door.
6. Installation is the reverse of removal.

Manual Window Regulator

REMOVAL & INSTALLATION

♦ **See Figures 1 thru 12 (p. 2–8)**

1. Remove the door trim panel.
2. Remove the door glass panel.
3. Unfasten the door regulator channel mounting bolts and remove the regulator, along with the retainer clip and spacers, through an access hole in the door panel. Note the positions of any anti-rattle pads. Make sure they go back in their original positions.
4. Installation is the reverse of the removal procedure.

Electric Window Motor and Regulator

REMOVAL & INSTALLATION

♦ **See Figures 3 thru 12 (p. 3–8)**

1. Remove the mirror trim plate.
2. Remove the screws attaching the armrest.
3. Remove the door trim panel by removing the attaching screws and the clips, then pull it upward.
4. Lower the door glass until the mounting bolts can be seen.
5. Disconnect the power window harnesses, then remove the armrest.
6. Support the glass and remove the glass-to-regulator attaching bolts.
7. Remove the regulator mounting bolts, then remove the regulator assembly through the lower hole in the door.
8. With the regulator removed from the door, before removing the motor from the regulator, mark the sector gear and regulator position.
9. Move the window regulator to the original position by connecting a 12 volt source to the motor.

❊❊ CAUTION

The regulator gear will move suddenly when the motor is removed, because the regulator spring is tensioned against the gear.

10. Installation is the reverse of the removal procedure. Lubricate the sector gear and rollers prior to installation.

Windshield and Fixed Glass

REMOVAL & INSTALLATION

If your windshield, or other fixed window, is cracked or chipped, you may decide to replace it with a new one yourself. However, there are two main reasons why replacement windshields and other window glass should be installed only by a professional automotive glass technician: safety and cost.

The most important reason a professional should install automotive glass is for safety. The glass in the vehicle, especially the windshield, is designed with safety in mind in case of a collision. The windshield is specially manufactured from two panes of specially-tempered glass with a thin layer of transparent plastic between them. This construction allows the glass to "give" in the event that a part of your body hits the windshield during the collision, and prevents the glass from shattering, which could cause lacerations, blinding and other harm to passengers of the vehicle. The other fixed windows are designed to be tempered so that if they break during a collision, they shatter in such a way that there are no sharp or pointed edges on the glass pieces. The professional automotive glass technician knows how to install the glass in a vehicle so that it will function optimally during a collision. Without the proper experience, knowledge and tools, installing a piece of automotive glass yourself could lead to additional harm if an accident should ever occur.

Cost is also a factor when deciding to install automotive glass yourself. Performing this could cost you much more than a professional may charge for the same job. Since the windshield is designed to break under stress, an often life saving characteristic, windshields tend to break VERY easily when an inexperienced person attempts to install one. Do-it-yourselfers buying two, three or even four windshields from a salvage yard because they have broken them during installation are common stories. Also, since the automotive glass is designed to prevent the outside elements from entering your vehicle, improper installation can lead to water and air leaks. Annoying whining noises at highway speeds from air leaks or inside body panel rusting from water leaks can add to your stress level and subtract from your wallet. After buying two or three windshields, installing them and ending up with a leak that produces a noise while driving and water damage during rainstorms, the cost of having a professional do it correctly the first time may be much more alluring.

We here at Chilton, therefore, advise that you have a professional automotive glass technician service any broken glass on your vehicle.

WINDSHIELD CHIP REPAIR

There is something, however, that you can do to prolong or even prevent the need for replacement of a chipped windshield. There are many companies, such as Loctite®, which offer windshield chip repair products, such as the Bullseye™ Windshield Repair Kit (Part No. 16067). These kits are not meant to correct cracks or holes in your windshield, only chips caused by gravel or stones.

➥**Check with your state and local authorities on the laws for state safety inspection. Some states or municipalities may not allow chip repair as a viable option for correcting stone damage to your windshield.**

To fix a stone chip in your windshield with the Loctite® Bullseye™ Windshield Repair Kit, perform the following:

➥**Loctite Corporation recommends that their repair kits should be applied outside in the sunlight, which, evidently, helps cure the repair solution much faster. In one of our experiments with these kits, performed in a shop using fluorescent lights and without any sunlight, the solution had not cured even after 18 hours. Therefore, it is highly recommended that the solution be allowed to cure in sunlight.**

1. Clean the damaged area of your windshield with glass cleaner, then dry the area completely.

❊❊ WARNING

The fluid contained in chip repair kits may damage paint; be sure to cover any exposed areas with clean shop rags.

2. Cover any painted surfaces with a clean shop rag, because the chip repair fluid may damage or remove paint.
3. Remove the adhesive disc from the kit, then remove the center hole plug from the disc.
4. Peel the backing off of one side of the disc, then, with the disc tab pointing upward, line up the hole in the disc with the center of the chip on the windshield. Press the disc onto the windshield.
5. Remove the plastic pedestal from the kit. Peel the paper off of the

Small chips on your windshield can be fixed with an aftermarket repair kit, such as the one from Loctite®

. . . then press it on the windshield so that the chip is centered in the hole

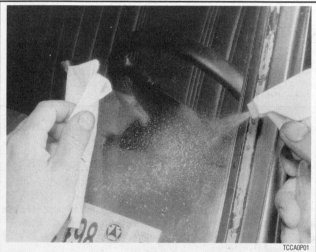

To repair a chip, clean the windshield with glass cleaner and dry it completely

Be sure that the tab points upward on the windshield

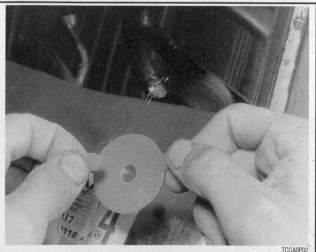

Remove the center from the adhesive disc and peel off the backing from one side of the disc . . .

other side of the disc, then align the pedestal with the disc, making sure that the tabs are also aligned. Press the pedestal firmly onto the disc.

6. Remove the fluid applicator (syringe) from the kit and remove the cap from its tip.

7. Thread the syringe into the pedestal tube.

➡ **During the next step, pull the plunger back until you feel it hit the stop on the inside of the syringe.**

8. While holding the syringe with one hand, gently pull back the syringe's plunger with the other hand, hold it there for 5–10 seconds, then abruptly release the plunger. Repeat this step 10 times.

9. Allow the entire assembly to sit, undisturbed, for 30 minutes.

10. From inside the vehicle, inspect the damaged area for any residual air bubbles. A flashlight may be necessary. If any air bubbles remain, repeat Steps 8 and 9.

11. Allow the repair kit to sit undisturbed until the solution has fully hardened or set. The light level where you are performing the repair largely dictates the length of time the repair solution needs to completely set. If the repair is performed in a bright, sunny area, it should set up in approximately 1 hour. If the repair is performed inside or on a cloudy day, allow 4–5 hours for it to fully set.

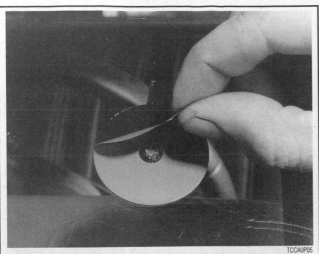

Peel the backing off the exposed side of the adhesive disc . . .

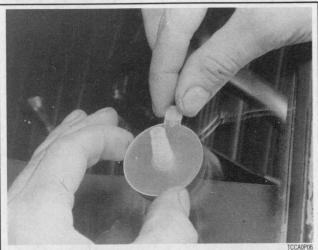

. . . then position the plastic pedestal on the adhesive disc, ensuring that the tabs are aligned

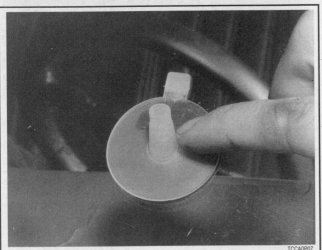

Press the pedestal firmly on the adhesive disc to create an adequate seal . . .

. . . then install the applicator syringe nipple in the pedestal's hole

➡ If the repair must be performed indoors and it does not set in a few hours, an ultraviolet lamp may help expedite the curing process. However, according to the manufacturer, this should not be necessary.

12. Remove the syringe from the pedestal.

13. Using a pair of pliers or a utility knife, if necessary, remove the pedestal and adhesive disc from the windshield.

14. Clean up any excess compound with glass cleaner.

➡ For other brands of windshield repair kits, follow the manufacturer's instructions enclosed with the kit.

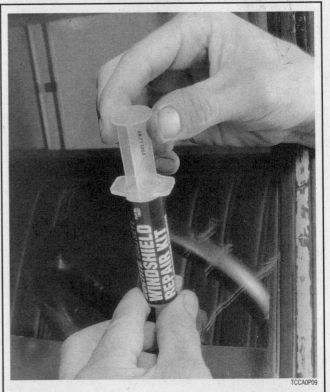

Hold the syringe with one hand while pulling the plunger back with the other hand

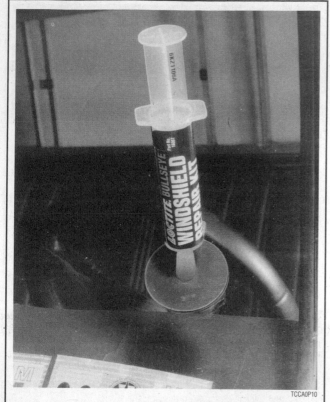

TCCA0P10

After applying the solution, allow the entire assembly to sit until it has set completely

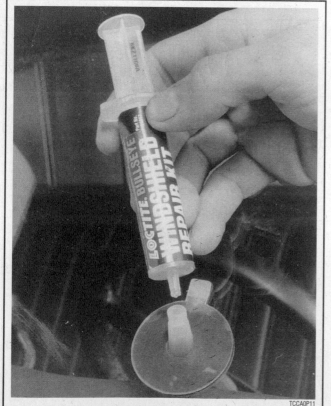

TCCA0P11

After the solution has set, remove the syringe from the pedestal . . .

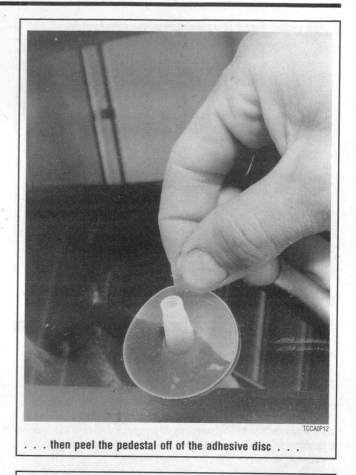

TCCA0P12

. . . then peel the pedestal off of the adhesive disc . . .

TCCA0P13

. . . and peel the adhesive disc off of the windshield

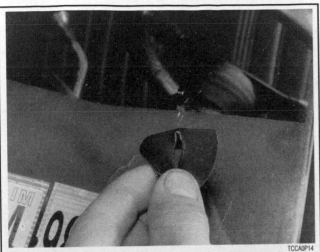

The chip will still be slightly visible, but it should be filled with the hardened solution

Inside Rear View Mirror

REPLACEMENT

◆ **See Figure 51**

➡ Breakaway mounts are used with the inside rear view mirrors. The breakaway mounts are designed to detach from the mirror bracket in the event of an air bag deployment during a collision. Excessive force, up-and-down, or side-to-side movement can cause the mirror to detach from the windshield glass.

1. Mark the mirror mounting bracket location on the outside surface of the windshield with a wax pencil.
2. Loosen the mirror assembly setscrew.
3. Remove the mirror assembly by sliding it upward and away from the mounting bracket.
4. If the bracket mouting pad remains on the windshield, apply low

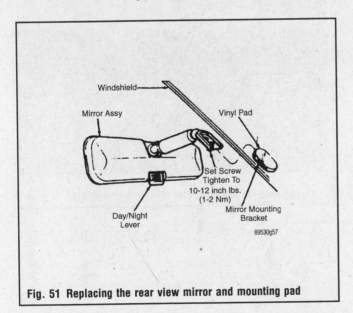

Fig. 51 Replacing the rear view mirror and mounting pad

heat from an electric heat gun until the glue softens. Peel the mounting pad off the windshield and discard.

To install:

5. Make sure the glass, bracket and adhesive kit are at least at a room temperature of 65–75°F (18–24°C).
6. Thoroughly clean the bonding surfaces of the glass and bracket to remove the old adhesive. Use a mild abrasive cleaner on the glass and fine sandpaper on the bracket to lightly roughen the surface. Wipe it clean with the alcohol-moistened cloth.
7. Crush the accelerator vial of the rear view mirror repair kit, and apply the accelerator to the bonding surface of the bracket and windshield. Follow the directions for drying time.
8. Apply two drops of adhesive to the mounting surface of the bracket. Quickly spread the adhesive evenly over the mounting surface of the bracket using the applicator.
9. Quickly position the mounting bracket on the windshield. The $\frac{3}{8}$in. (10mm) circular depression in the bracket must be facing you. Press the bracket firmly against the windshield and hold for the appropriate drying time stated in the directions.
10. Allow the bond to set. Remove any excess bonding material from the windshield with an alcohol dampened cloth.
11. Attach the mirror to the mounting bracket and tighten the setscrew to 10–20 inch lbs. (1–2 Nm).

Seats

REMOVAL & INSTALLATION

Front

◆ **See Figures 52, 53, 54, 55 and 56 (p. 34–36)**

1. Remove the seat adjuster cover screws and remove the cover.
2. Remove the seat track mounting bolts.
3. Fold the seat back forward and tilt the seat assembly back.
4. Disconnect the electrical leads and remove the seat from the vehicle. Remove components from the seat as needed.

To install:

5. Install the seat assembly into the vehicle. Connect the electrical leads and install the seat track mounting bolts. Tighten the bolts to 25–40 ft. lbs. (35–55 Nm) and the nuts to 17–26 ft. lbs. (24–36 Nm).
6. Install the adjuster cover. Test the operation of the seat on the track.

Rear

◆ **See Figures 57 thru 62 (p. 36–39)**

1. Remove the seat back mounting bolt from between the seat cushions.
2. Lift the lower part of the seat at the front to release it from the clips and pull it from the vehicle.
3. On late model Excels and Elantras, remove the 2 side seat back mounting bolts and pull the side seat backs up, then out of the vehicle.
4. Tilt the seat back forward and remove the clips that retain the carpet to the rear of the seat back.
5. On early model Excels, remove the 4 retaining bolts at the seat back hinges and remove the seat back.
6. On models with fold down rear seats, remove the rear seat pivot hinge clips and remove the seat backs one at a time.
7. Install the seat back components in reverse order. Tighten the seat back hinge bolts to 12–19 ft. lbs. (17–26 Nm). Install all of the plastic clips and make sure that they are completely seated.

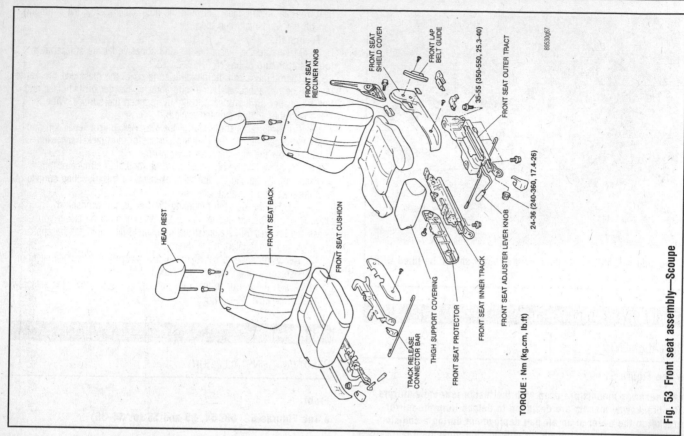

89530g67

TORQUE : Nm (kg.cm, lb.ft)

Fig. 53 Front seat assembly—Scoupe

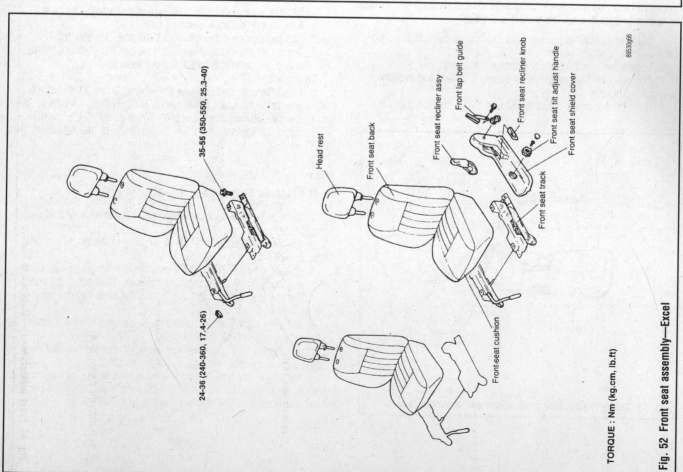

89530g66

TORQUE : Nm (kg.cm, lb.ft)

Fig. 52 Front seat assembly—Excel

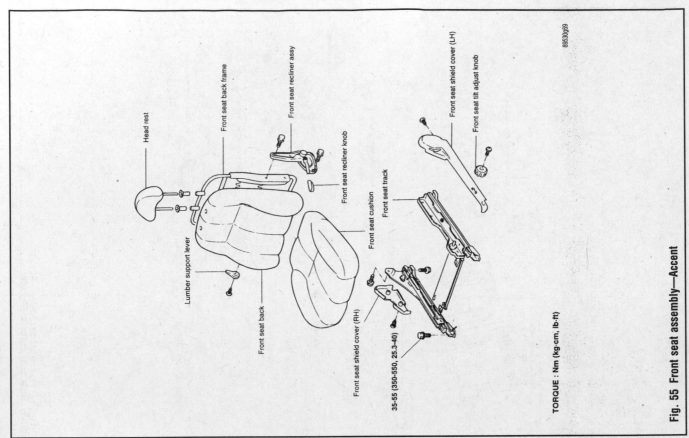

TORQUE : Nm (kg·cm, lb·ft)

Fig. 55 Front seat assembly—Accent

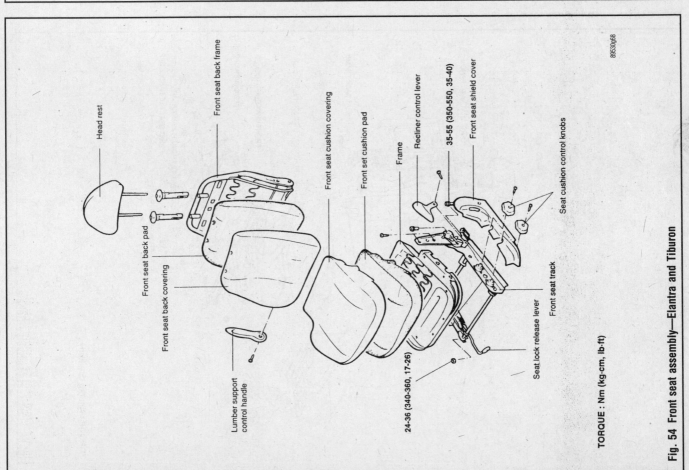

TORQUE : Nm (kg·cm, lb·ft)

Fig. 54 Front seat assembly—Elantra and Tiburon

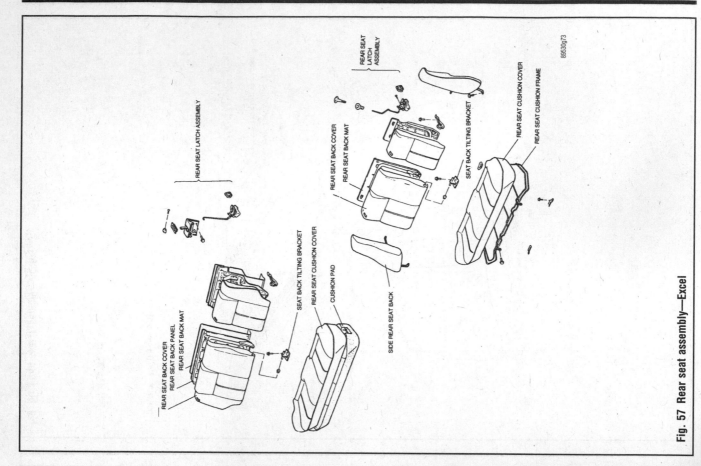

89530q73

REAR SEAT LATCH ASSEMBLY

REAR SEAT LATCH ASSEMBLY

REAR SEAT BACK COVER
REAR SEAT BACK MAT

SEAT BACK TILTING BRACKET

REAR SEAT CUSHION COVER

REAR SEAT CUSHION COVER
REAR SEAT CUSHION FRAME

SEAT BACK TILTING BRACKET

CUSHION PAD

SIDE REAR SEAT BACK

REAR SEAT BACK COVER
REAR SEAT BACK PANEL
REAR SEAT BACK MAT

Fig. 57 Rear seat assembly—Excel

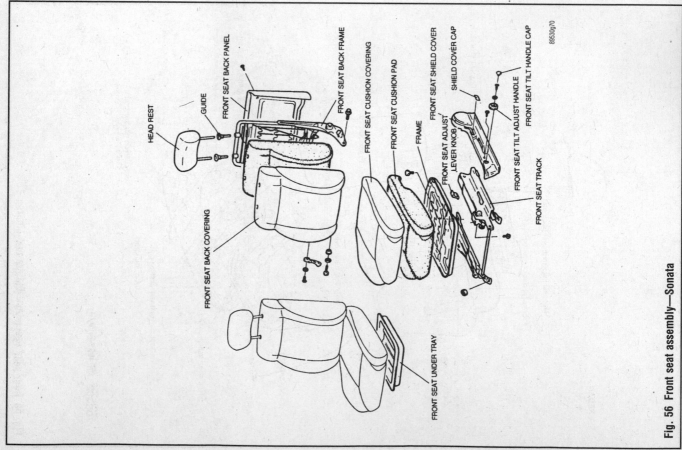

89530q70

HEAD REST

GUIDE

FRONT SEAT BACK PANEL

FRONT SEAT BACK FRAME

FRONT SEAT CUSHION COVERING

FRONT SEAT CUSHION PAD

FRONT SEAT SHIELD COVER

SHIELD COVER CAP

FRAME

FRONT SEAT ADJUST
LEVER KNOB

FRONT SEAT TILT ADJUST HANDLE

FRONT SEAT TILT HANDLE CAP

FRONT SEAT TRACK

FRONT SEAT BACK COVERING

FRONT SEAT UNDER TRAY

Fig. 56 Front seat assembly—Sonata

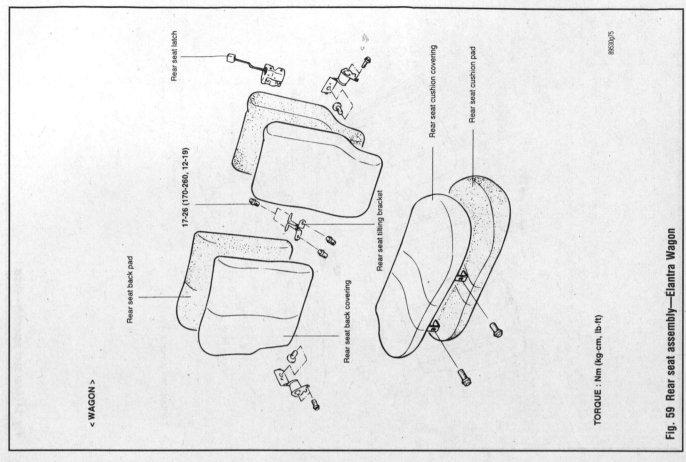

< WAGON >

Rear seat latch

Rear seat cushion covering

Rear seat cushion pad

17-26 (170-260, 12-19)

Rear seat tilting bracket

Rear seat back pad

Rear seat back covering

TORQUE : Nm (kg·cm, lb·ft)

89530g75

Fig. 59 Rear seat assembly—Elantra Wagon

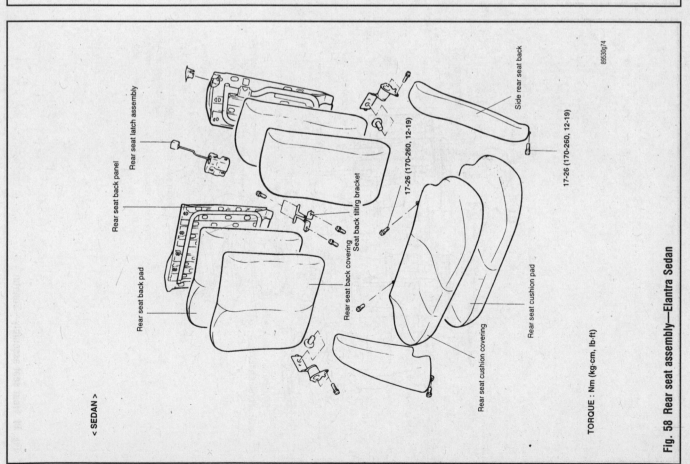

< SEDAN >

Rear seat latch assembly

Rear seat back panel

Rear seat back pad

Side rear seat back

17-26 (170-260, 12-19)

17-26 (170-260, 12-19)

Seat back tilting bracket

Rear seat back covering

Rear seat cushion pad

Rear seat cushion covering

TORQUE : Nm (kg·cm, lb·ft)

89530g74

Fig. 58 Rear seat assembly—Elantra Sedan

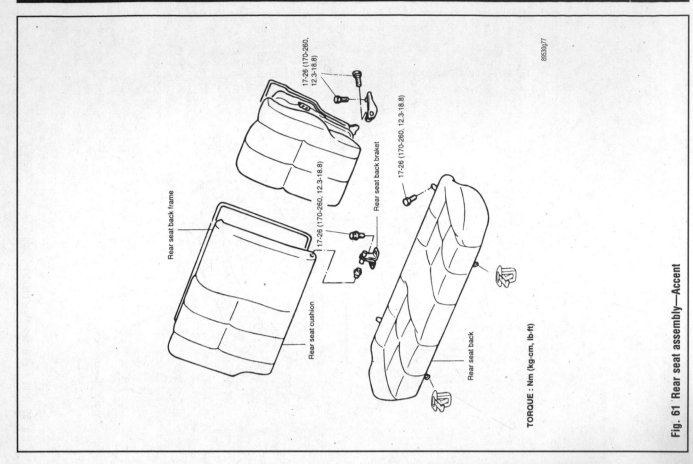

89530g77

Rear seat back frame

17-26 (170-260, 12.3-18.8)

17-26 (170-260, 12.3-18.8)

Rear seat back braket

17-26 (170-260, 12.3-18.8)

Rear seat cushion

Rear seat back

TORQUE : Nm (kg-cm, lb-ft)

Fig. 61 Rear seat assembly—Accent

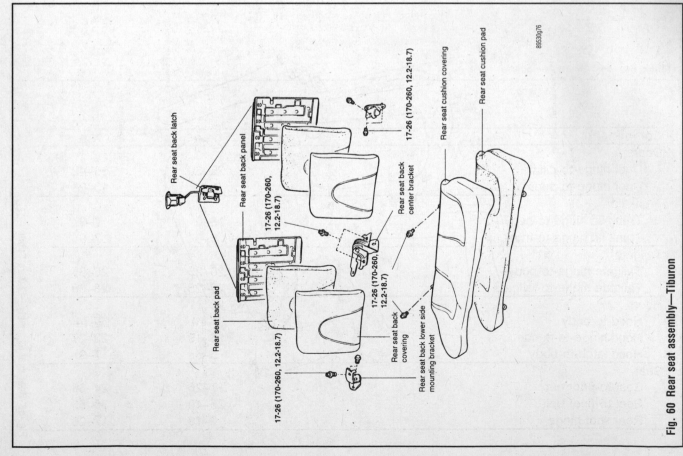

89530g76

Rear seat back latch

Rear seat back panel

17-26 (170-260, 12.2-18.7)

17-26 (170-260, 12.2-18.7)

Rear seat cushion covering

Rear seat cushion pad

Rear seat back center bracket

Rear seat back pad

17-26 (170-260, 12.2-18.7)

17-26 (170-260, 12.2-18.7)

Rear seat back covering

Rear seat back lower side mounting bracket

Fig. 60 Rear seat assembly—Tiburon

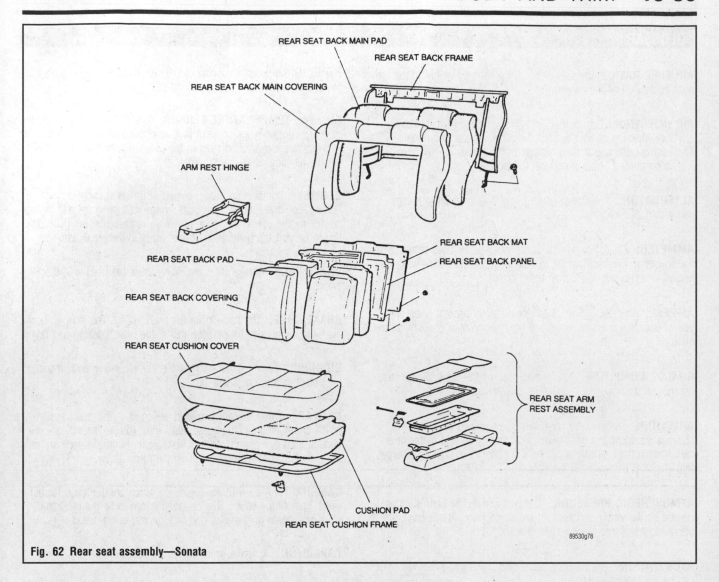

Fig. 62 Rear seat assembly—Sonata

TORQUE SPECIFICATIONS

Components	Ft. Lbs.	Nm
Doors		
Door hinge-to-pillar	26–30	36–42
Door hinge-to-door	9–19	13–26
Trunk lid		
Trunk lid hinge-to-body	5–6	7–9
Trunk lid hinge-to-trunk lid	5–6	7–9
Tailgate		
Tailgate hinge-to-body	20–25	28–35
Tailgate hinge-to-tailgate	20–25	28–35
Hood		
Hood-to-body	7–10	9–14
Hood hinge-to-hood	16–19	22–27
Hood latch-to-body	5–6	7–9
Seat		
Seat-to-floor nut	17–26	24–36
Seat-to-floor bolt	25–40	35–55
Rear seat hinge	12–19	17–26

GLOSSARY

AIR/FUEL RATIO: The ratio of air-to-gasoline by weight in the fuel mixture drawn into the engine.

AIR INJECTION: One method of reducing harmful exhaust emissions by injecting air into each of the exhaust ports of an engine. The fresh air entering the hot exhaust manifold causes any remaining fuel to be burned before it can exit the tailpipe.

ALTERNATOR: A device used for converting mechanical energy into electrical energy.

AMMETER: An instrument, calibrated in amperes, used to measure the flow of an electrical current in a circuit. Ammeters are always connected in series with the circuit being tested.

AMPERE: The rate of flow of electrical current present when one volt of electrical pressure is applied against one ohm of electrical resistance.

ANALOG COMPUTER: Any microprocessor that uses similar (analogous) electrical signals to make its calculations.

ARMATURE: A laminated, soft iron core wrapped by a wire that converts electrical energy to mechanical energy as in a motor or relay. When rotated in a magnetic field, it changes mechanical energy into electrical energy as in a generator.

ATMOSPHERIC PRESSURE: The pressure on the Earth's surface caused by the weight of the air in the atmosphere. At sea level, this pressure is 14.7 psi at 32°F (101 kPa at 0°C).

ATOMIZATION: The breaking down of a liquid into a fine mist that can be suspended in air.

AXIAL PLAY: Movement parallel to a shaft or bearing bore.

BACKFIRE: The sudden combustion of gases in the intake or exhaust system that results in a loud explosion.

BACKLASH: The clearance or play between two parts, such as meshed gears.

BACKPRESSURE: Restrictions in the exhaust system that slow the exit of exhaust gases from the combustion chamber.

BAKELITE: A heat resistant, plastic insulator material commonly used in printed circuit boards and transistorized components.

BALL BEARING: A bearing made up of hardened inner and outer races between which hardened steel balls roll.

BALLAST RESISTOR: A resistor in the primary ignition circuit that lowers voltage after the engine is started to reduce wear on ignition components.

BEARING: A friction reducing, supportive device usually located between a stationary part and a moving part.

BIMETAL TEMPERATURE SENSOR: Any sensor or switch made of two dissimilar types of metal that bend when heated or cooled due to the different expansion rates of the alloys. These types of sensors usually function as an on/off switch.

BLOWBY: Combustion gases, composed of water vapor and unburned fuel, that leak past the piston rings into the crankcase during normal engine operation. These gases are removed by the PCV system to prevent the buildup of harmful acids in the crankcase.

BRAKE PAD: A brake shoe and lining assembly used with disc brakes.

BRAKE SHOE: The backing for the brake lining. The term is, however, usually applied to the assembly of the brake backing and lining.

BUSHING: A liner, usually removable, for a bearing; an anti-friction liner used in place of a bearing.

CALIPER: A hydraulically activated device in a disc brake system, which is mounted straddling the brake rotor (disc). The caliper contains at least one piston and two brake pads. Hydraulic pressure on the piston(s) forces the pads against the rotor.

CAMSHAFT: A shaft in the engine on which are the lobes (cams) which operate the valves. The camshaft is driven by the crankshaft, via a belt, chain or gears, at one half the crankshaft speed.

CAPACITOR: A device which stores an electrical charge.

CARBON MONOXIDE (CO): A colorless, odorless gas given off as a normal byproduct of combustion. It is poisonous and extremely dangerous in confined areas, building up slowly to toxic levels without warning if adequate ventilation is not available.

CARBURETOR: A device, usually mounted on the intake manifold of an engine, which mixes the air and fuel in the proper proportion to allow even combustion.

CATALYTIC CONVERTER: A device installed in the exhaust system, like a muffler, that converts harmful byproducts of combustion into carbon dioxide and water vapor by means of a heat-producing chemical reaction.

CENTRIFUGAL ADVANCE: A mechanical method of advancing the spark timing by using flyweights in the distributor that react to centrifugal force generated by the distributor shaft rotation.

CHECK VALVE: Any one-way valve installed to permit the flow of air, fuel or vacuum in one direction only.

CHOKE: A device, usually a moveable valve, placed in the intake path of a carburetor to restrict the flow of air.

CIRCUIT: Any unbroken path through which an electrical current can flow. Also used to describe fuel flow in some instances.

CIRCUIT BREAKER: A switch which protects an electrical circuit from overload by opening the circuit when the current flow exceeds a predetermined level. Some circuit breakers must be reset manually, while most reset automatically.

COIL (IGNITION): A transformer in the ignition circuit which steps up the voltage provided to the spark plugs.

COMBINATION MANIFOLD: An assembly which includes both the intake and exhaust manifolds in one casting.

COMBINATION VALVE: A device used in some fuel systems that routes fuel vapors to a charcoal storage canister instead of venting them into the atmosphere. The valve relieves fuel tank pressure and allows fresh air into the tank as the fuel level drops to prevent a vapor lock situation.

COMPRESSION RATIO: The comparison of the total volume of the cylinder and combustion chamber with the piston at BDC and the piston at TDC.

CONDENSER: 1. An electrical device which acts to store an electrical charge, preventing voltage surges. 2. A radiator-like device in the air conditioning system in which refrigerant gas condenses into a liquid, giving off heat.

CONDUCTOR: Any material through which an electrical current can be transmitted easily.

CONTINUITY: Continuous or complete circuit. Can be checked with an ohmmeter.

COUNTERSHAFT: An intermediate shaft which is rotated by a mainshaft and transmits, in turn, that rotation to a working part.

CRANKCASE: The lower part of an engine in which the crankshaft and related parts operate.

CRANKSHAFT: The main driving shaft of an engine which receives reciprocating motion from the pistons and converts it to rotary motion.

CYLINDER: In an engine, the round hole in the engine block in which the piston(s) ride.

CYLINDER BLOCK: The main structural member of an engine in which is found the cylinders, crankshaft and other principal parts.

CYLINDER HEAD: The detachable portion of the engine, usually fastened to the top of the cylinder block and containing all or most of the combustion chambers. On overhead valve engines, it contains the valves and their operating parts. On overhead cam engines, it contains the camshaft as well.

DEAD CENTER: The extreme top or bottom of the piston stroke.

DETONATION: An unwanted explosion of the air/fuel mixture in the combustion chamber caused by excess heat and compression, advanced timing, or an overly lean mixture. Also referred to as "ping".

DIAPHRAGM: A thin, flexible wall separating two cavities, such as in a vacuum advance unit.

DIESELING: A condition in which hot spots in the combustion chamber cause the engine to run on after the key is turned off.

DIFFERENTIAL: A geared assembly which allows the transmission of motion between drive axles, giving one axle the ability to turn faster than the other.

DIODE: An electrical device that will allow current to flow in one direction only.

DISC BRAKE: A hydraulic braking assembly consisting of a brake disc, or rotor, mounted on an axle, and a caliper assembly containing, usually two brake pads which are activated by hydraulic pressure. The pads are forced against the sides of the disc, creating friction which slows the vehicle.

DISTRIBUTOR: A mechanically driven device on an engine which is responsible for electrically firing the spark plug at a predetermined point of the piston stroke.

DOWEL PIN: A pin, inserted in mating holes in two different parts allowing those parts to maintain a fixed relationship.

DRUM BRAKE: A braking system which consists of two brake shoes and one or two wheel cylinders, mounted on a fixed backing plate, and a brake drum, mounted on an axle, which revolves around the assembly.

DWELL: The rate, measured in degrees of shaft rotation, at which an electrical circuit cycles on and off.

ELECTRONIC CONTROL UNIT (ECU): Ignition module, module, amplifier or igniter. See Module for definition.

ELECTRONIC IGNITION: A system in which the timing and firing of the spark plugs is controlled by an electronic control unit, usually called a module. These systems have no points or condenser.

END-PLAY: The measured amount of axial movement in a shaft.

ENGINE: A device that converts heat into mechanical energy.

EXHAUST MANIFOLD: A set of cast passages or pipes which conduct exhaust gases from the engine.

FEELER GAUGE: A blade, usually metal, of precisely predetermined thickness, used to measure the clearance between two parts.

FIRING ORDER: The order in which combustion occurs in the cylinders of an engine. Also the order in which spark is distributed to the plugs by the distributor.

FLOODING: The presence of too much fuel in the intake manifold and combustion chamber which prevents the air/fuel mixture from firing, thereby causing a no-start situation.

FLYWHEEL: A disc shaped part bolted to the rear end of the crankshaft. Around the outer perimeter is affixed the ring gear. The starter drive engages the ring gear, turning the flywheel, which rotates the crankshaft, imparting the initial starting motion to the engine.

FOOT POUND (ft. lbs. or sometimes, ft.lb.): The amount of energy or work needed to raise an item weighing one pound, a distance of one foot.

FUSE: A protective device in a circuit which prevents circuit overload by breaking the circuit when a specific amperage is present. The device is constructed around a strip or wire of a lower amperage rating than the circuit it is designed to protect. When an amperage higher than that stamped on the fuse is present in the circuit, the strip or wire melts, opening the circuit.

GEAR RATIO: The ratio between the number of teeth on meshing gears.

GENERATOR: A device which converts mechanical energy into electrical energy.

HEAT RANGE: The measure of a spark plug's ability to dissipate heat from its firing end. The higher the heat range, the hotter the plug fires.

HUB: The center part of a wheel or gear.

HYDROCARBON (HC): Any chemical compound made up of hydrogen and carbon. A major pollutant formed by the engine as a byproduct of combustion.

HYDROMETER: An instrument used to measure the specific gravity of a solution.

INCH POUND (inch lbs.; sometimes in.lb. or in. lbs.): One twelfth of a foot pound.

INDUCTION: A means of transferring electrical energy in the form of a magnetic field. Principle used in the ignition coil to increase voltage.

INJECTOR: A device which receives metered fuel under relatively low pressure and is activated to inject the fuel into the engine under relatively high pressure at a predetermined time.

INPUT SHAFT: The shaft to which torque is applied, usually carrying the driving gear or gears.

INTAKE MANIFOLD: A casting of passages or pipes used to conduct air or a fuel/air mixture to the cylinders.

JOURNAL: The bearing surface within which a shaft operates.

KEY: A small block usually fitted in a notch between a shaft and a hub to prevent slippage of the two parts.

MANIFOLD: A casting of passages or set of pipes which connect the cylinders to an inlet or outlet source.

MANIFOLD VACUUM: Low pressure in an engine intake manifold formed just below the throttle plates. Manifold vacuum is highest at idle and drops under acceleration.

MASTER CYLINDER: The primary fluid pressurizing device in a hydraulic system. In automotive use, it is found in brake and hydraulic clutch systems and is pedal activated, either directly or, in a power brake system, through the power booster.

MODULE: Electronic control unit, amplifier or igniter of solid state or integrated design which controls the current flow in the ignition primary circuit based on input from the pick-up coil. When the module opens the primary circuit, high secondary voltage is induced in the coil.

NEEDLE BEARING: A bearing which consists of a number (usually a large number) of long, thin rollers.

OHM: (Ω) The unit used to measure the resistance of conductor-to-electrical flow. One ohm is the amount of resistance that limits current flow to one ampere in a circuit with one volt of pressure.

OHMMETER: An instrument used for measuring the resistance, in ohms, in an electrical circuit.

OUTPUT SHAFT: The shaft which transmits torque from a device, such as a transmission.

OVERDRIVE: A gear assembly which produces more shaft revolutions than that transmitted to it.

OVERHEAD CAMSHAFT (OHC): An engine configuration in which the camshaft is mounted on top of the cylinder head and operates the valve either directly or by means of rocker arms.

OVERHEAD VALVE (OHV): An engine configuration in which all of the valves are located in the cylinder head and the camshaft is located in the cylinder block. The camshaft operates the valves via lifters and pushrods.

OXIDES OF NITROGEN (NOx): Chemical compounds of nitrogen produced as a byproduct of combustion. They combine with hydrocarbons to produce smog.

OXYGEN SENSOR: Used with the feedback system to sense the presence of oxygen in the exhaust gas and signal the computer which can reference the voltage signal to an air/fuel ratio.

PINION: The smaller of two meshing gears.

PISTON RING: An open-ended ring which fits into a groove on the outer diameter of the piston. Its chief function is to form a seal between the piston and cylinder wall. Most automotive pistons have three rings: two for compression sealing; one for oil sealing.

PRELOAD: A predetermined load placed on a bearing during assembly or by adjustment.

PRIMARY CIRCUIT: The low voltage side of the ignition system which consists of the ignition switch, ballast resistor or resistance wire, bypass, coil, electronic control unit and pick-up coil as well as the connecting wires and harnesses.

PRESS FIT: The mating of two parts under pressure, due to the inner diameter of one being smaller than the outer diameter of the other, or vice versa; an interference fit.

RACE: The surface on the inner or outer ring of a bearing on which the balls, needles or rollers move.

REGULATOR: A device which maintains the amperage and/or voltage levels of a circuit at predetermined values.

RELAY: A switch which automatically opens and/or closes a circuit.

RESISTANCE: The opposition to the flow of current through a circuit or electrical device, and is measured in ohms. Resistance is equal to the voltage divided by the amperage.

RESISTOR: A device, usually made of wire, which offers a preset amount of resistance in an electrical circuit.

RING GEAR: The name given to a ring-shaped gear attached to a differential case, or affixed to a flywheel or as part of a planetary gear set.

ROLLER BEARING: A bearing made up of hardened inner and outer races between which hardened steel rollers move.

ROTOR: 1. The disc-shaped part of a disc brake assembly, upon which the brake pads bear; also called, brake disc. 2. The device mounted atop the distributor shaft, which passes current to the distributor cap tower contacts.

SECONDARY CIRCUIT: The high voltage side of the ignition system, usually above 20,000 volts. The secondary includes the ignition coil, coil wire, distributor cap and rotor, spark plug wires and spark plugs.

SENDING UNIT: A mechanical, electrical, hydraulic or electromagnetic device which transmits information to a gauge.

SENSOR: Any device designed to measure engine operating conditions or ambient pressures and temperatures. Usually electronic in nature and designed to send a voltage signal to an on-board computer, some sensors may operate as a simple on/off switch or they may provide a variable voltage signal (like a potentiometer) as conditions or measured parameters change.

SHIM: Spacers of precise, predetermined thickness used between parts to establish a proper working relationship.

SLAVE CYLINDER: In automotive use, a device in the hydraulic clutch system which is activated by hydraulic force, disengaging the clutch.

SOLENOID: A coil used to produce a magnetic field, the effect of which is to produce work.

SPARK PLUG: A device screwed into the combustion chamber of a spark ignition engine. The basic construction is a conductive core inside of a ceramic insulator, mounted in an outer conductive base. An electrical charge from the spark plug wire travels along the conductive core and jumps a preset air gap to a grounding point or points at the end of the conductive base. The resultant spark ignites the fuel/air mixture in the combustion chamber.

SPLINES: Ridges machined or cast onto the outer diameter of a shaft or inner diameter of a bore to enable parts to mate without rotation.

TACHOMETER: A device used to measure the rotary speed of an engine, shaft, gear, etc., usually in rotations per minute.

THERMOSTAT: A valve, located in the cooling system of an engine, which is closed when cold and opens gradually in response to engine heating, controlling the temperature of the coolant and rate of coolant flow.

TOP DEAD CENTER (TDC): The point at which the piston reaches the top of its travel on the compression stroke.

TORQUE: The twisting force applied to an object.

TORQUE CONVERTER: A turbine used to transmit power from a driving member to a driven member via hydraulic action, providing changes in drive ratio and torque. In automotive use, it links the driveplate at the rear of the engine to the automatic transmission.

TRANSDUCER: A device used to change a force into an electrical signal.

TRANSISTOR: A semi-conductor component which can be actuated by a small voltage to perform an electrical switching function.

TUNE-UP: A regular maintenance function, usually associated with the replacement and adjustment of parts and components in the electrical and fuel systems of a vehicle for the purpose of attaining optimum performance.

TURBOCHARGER: An exhaust driven pump which compresses intake air and forces it into the combustion chambers at higher than atmospheric pressures. The increased air pressure allows more fuel to be burned and results in increased horsepower being produced.

VACUUM ADVANCE: A device which advances the ignition timing in response to increased engine vacuum.

VACUUM GAUGE: An instrument used to measure the presence of vacuum in a chamber.

VALVE: A device which control the pressure, direction of flow or rate of flow of a liquid or gas.

VALVE CLEARANCE: The measured gap between the end of the valve stem and the rocker arm, cam lobe or follower that activates the valve.

VISCOSITY: The rating of a liquid's internal resistance to flow.

VOLTMETER: An instrument used for measuring electrical force in units called volts. Voltmeters are always connected parallel with the circuit being tested.

WHEEL CYLINDER: Found in the automotive drum brake assembly, it is a device, actuated by hydraulic pressure, which, through internal pistons, pushes the brake shoes outward against the drums.

MASTER

INDEX